ECONOMICS
Principles and Practices

GARY E. CLAYTON, Ph.D.

GLENCOE
McGraw-Hill

New York, New York   Columbus, Ohio   Woodland Hills, California   Peoria, Illinois

ABOUT THE AUTHOR

Gary E. Clayton teaches economics and finance at Northern Kentucky University in Highland Heights, Kentucky. Dr. Clayton received his Ph.D. in Economics from the University of Utah, has taught economics and finance at several universities, and has authored textbooks—including two at the college level—as well as a number of articles in various educational, professional, and technical journals. Dr. Clayton has also appeared on a number of radio and television programs, and is currently a guest commentator specializing in economic statistics for "Marketplace," which is broadcast on American Public Radio and originates at the University of Southern California.

Dr. Clayton has a long-standing interest in economic education. He has participated in and directed numerous economic education workshops. In 1976 he received the Outstanding Citizen Certificate of Recognition from the state of Arkansas for his work in economic education. He also received a third-place award in the college division of the International Paper Company competition, an award sponsored by the National Council on Economic Education. He has served as Vice President for the Kentucky Council on Economic Education and, in 1993, received the state's highest honor when he received a commission as an honorary Kentucky Colonel. During the summer months, he participates in various study-abroad programs that take college students to Europe.

Send all inquiries to:
Glencoe/McGraw-Hill
8787 Orion Place
Columbus, OH 43240

ISBN 0-02-823048-5

Printed in the United States of America.
  8 9 10 11 12   027/046   03

CONTENTS

CONTENTS

ADAM SMITH
ECONOMIST
page 18

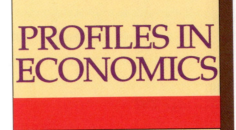

PROFILES IN ECONOMICS

ANITA RODDICK
ENTREPRENEUR
page 42

J. BRUCE LLEWELLYN
ENTREPRENEUR
page 68

NINFA LAURENZO
ENTREPRENEUR
page 91

H. ROSS PEROT
ENTREPRENEUR
page 116

GARY BECKER
ECONOMIST
page 139

CHARLES WANG
ENTREPRENEUR
page 162

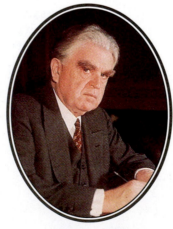

JOHN L. LEWIS
LABOR LEADER
page 188

ALICE RIVLIN
ECONOMIST
page 221

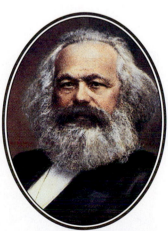

CONTENTS

CASE STUDIES: ISSUES IN FREE ENTERPRISE

WRITING ABOUT ECONOMICS

HELP WANTED

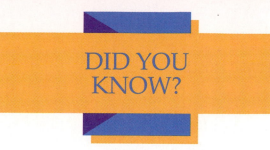

DID YOU KNOW?

CONTENTS

Skills

ECONOMIC SKILLS

CRITICAL THINKING SKILLS

Figure 13.8
The New York Stock Exchange

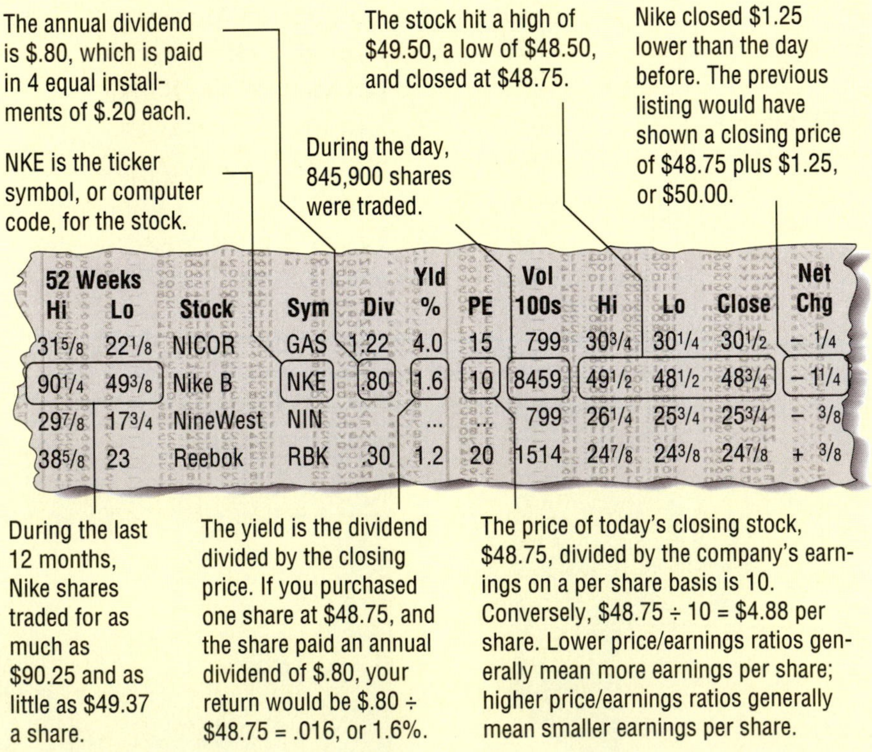

The annual dividend is $.80, which is paid in 4 equal installments of $.20 each.
NKE is the ticker symbol, or computer code, for the stock.
The stock hit a high of $49.50, a low of $48.50, and closed at $48.75.
During the day, 845,900 shares were traded.
Nike closed $1.25 lower than the day before. The previous listing would have shown a closing price of $48.75 plus $1.25, or $50.00.
During the last 12 months, Nike shares traded for as much as $90.25 and as little as $49.37 a share.
The yield is the dividend divided by the closing price. If you purchased one share at $48.75, and the share paid an annual dividend of $.80, your return would be $.80 ÷ $48.75 = .016, or 1.6%.
The price of today's closing stock, $48.75, divided by the company's earnings on a per share basis is 10. Conversely, $48.75 ÷ 10 = $4.88 per share. Lower price/earnings ratios generally mean more earnings per share; higher price/earnings ratios generally mean smaller earnings per share.

52 Weeks Hi	52 Weeks Lo	Stock	Sym	Div	Yld %	PE	Vol 100s	Hi	Lo	Close	Net Chg
31 5/8	22 1/8	NICOR	GAS	1.22	4.0	15	799	30 3/4	30 1/4	30 1/2	− 1/4
90 1/4	49 3/8	Nike B	NKE	.80	1.6	10	8459	49 1/2	48 1/2	48 3/4	− 1 1/4
29 7/8	17 3/4	NineWest	NIN		...	...	799	26 1/4	25 3/4	25 3/4	− 3/8
38 5/8	23	Reebok	RBK	.30	1.2	20	1514	24 7/8	24 3/8	24 7/8	+ 3/8

LIFE SKILLS

CONTENTS
Charts, Graphs, and Maps

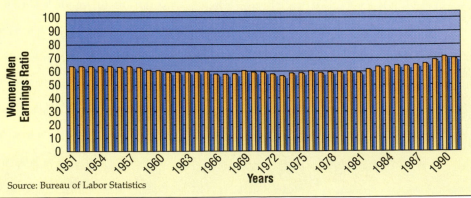

Figure 8.8
Median Female Income as a Percentage of Male Income

Over the years, the income earned by females has been only a fraction of that earned by males. The low point was in 1973 when female income was only 56.6% of male income. The high was in 1990 when the figure was 71.1%. **What explains the income gap between men and women?**

Source: Bureau of Labor Statistics

Figure 6.2
A Model of the Gadgets Market

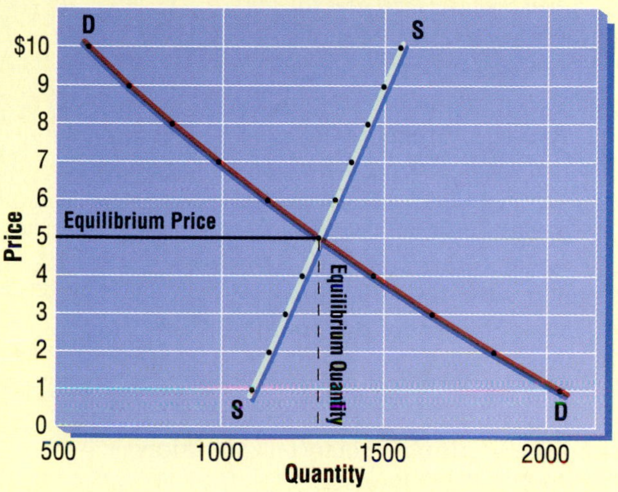

According to the model of the gadgets market, $5 is the equilibrium price that "clears" the market. At that price, 1,300 gadgets will be supplied and an equal number purchased. **What happens to the supply of gadgets if the price is lowered to $3?**

CONTENTS

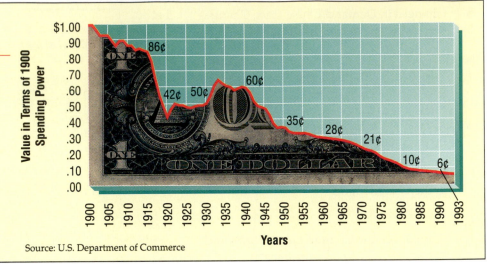

Figure 16.4
The Declining Value of the Dollar

When the price level goes up, the purchasing power of the dollar goes down. When the price level goes down, as it did during the Great Depression, the purchasing power of the dollar goes up. Today, the dollar buys less than 6 percent of the goods and services it purchased in 1900. **If inflation continues, what will happen to the purchasing power of the dollar?**

Source: U.S. Department of Commerce

Figure 19.3
Capitalism in Asia—The Asian Tigers

Because of the dynamic growth and economic progress made by South Korea, Hong Kong, Singapore, and Taiwan since the end of World War II, they are sometimes called the "Asian Tigers." Some observers have even suggested that the Guangdong Province of mainland China could be added to this list. **How have the Asian Tigers relied on capitalism to spur their economic growth?**

Basic Concepts in Economics

Economics: Principles and Practices incorporates the 22 Basic Concepts established in *A Framework for Teaching the Basic Concepts* published by the National Council on Economic Education.

FUNDAMENTAL ECONOMIC CONCEPTS

1. Scarcity

Scarcity is the condition that results from the imbalance between relatively unlimited wants and the relatively limited resources available for satisfying those wants.

2. Opportunity Costs and Trade-Offs

Opportunity cost is the forgone benefit of the next best alternative when scarce resources are used for one purpose rather than another. Trade-offs involve accepting or choosing less of one thing to get more of something else.

3. Productivity

Productivity is a measure of the amount of output (goods and services) produced per unit of input (productive resources) used.

4. Economic Systems

Economic systems are the ways in which people organize economic life to deal with the basic economic problems of scarcity and opportunity cost.

5. Economic Institutions and Incentives

Economic institutions include households and families and formal organizations such as corporations, government agencies, banks, labor unions, and cooperatives. Incentives are factors that motivate and influence human behavior.

6. Exchange, Money, and Interdependence

Exchange is a voluntary transaction between buyers and sellers in which producers trade their surpluses. Money serves as a medium of exchange. Interdependence means that decisions or events in one part of the world or in one sector of the economy affect decisions and events in other parts of the world or sectors of the economy.

MICROECONOMIC CONCEPTS

7. Markets and Prices

Markets are institutional arrangements that enable buyers and sellers to exchange goods and services. Prices are the amounts of money that people pay in exchange for a unit of a particular good or service.

8. Supply and Demand

Supply is defined as the different quantities of a resource, good, or service that will be offered for sale at various possible prices during a specific time period. Demand is defined as the different quantities of a resource, good, or service that will be purchased at various possible prices during a specific time period.

9. Competition and Market Structure

Competition is determined by the number of buyers and sellers in particular markets. Market structure refers to the extent to which competition prevails in particular markets.

10. Income Distribution

Income distribution may be classified into functional distribution—the division of an economy's total income into wages and salaries, rent, interest, and profit; or income distribution may be classified into personal distribution of income, classifying the different population groups by the number of them receiving different amounts of income.

11. Market Failures   **Market failures** occur when there are inadequate competition, lack of access to reliable information, resource immobility, externalities, and the need for public goods.

12. The Role of Government   The **role of government** includes establishing a framework of law and order in which a market economy functions. The government plays a direct and an indirect role in the economy as both a producer and a consumer of goods and services.

MACROECONOMIC CONCEPTS

13. Gross Domestic Product   **Gross Domestic Product** (GDP) is defined as the market value of the total output of all final goods and services produced within a country's boundaries during one year.

14. Aggregate Supply   **Aggregate supply** is the total amount of goods and services produced by the economy during a period of time at a given price level.

15. Aggregate Demand   **Aggregate demand** is the total amount of spending on goods and services in the economy during a period of time at a given price level.

16. Unemployment   **Unemployment** is defined as the number of people without jobs who are actively seeking work. This is also expressed as a rate when the number of unemployed is divided by the number of people in the labor force.

17. Inflation and Deflation   **Inflation** is a sustained increase in the average price level of the entire economy. **Deflation** is a sustained decrease in the average price level of an entire economy.

18. Monetary Policy   **Monetary policy** consists of actions that affect the amount of money and the cost of credit available in the economy.

19. Fiscal Policy   **Fiscal policy** consists of changes in taxes, in government expenditures on goods and services, and in transfer payments that are designed to affect the level of aggregate demand in the economy.

INTERNATIONAL ECONOMIC CONCEPTS

20. Absolute and Comparative Advantage and Barriers to Trade   **Absolute advantage and comparative advantage** are concepts that are used to explain why trade takes place. Comparative advantage is based on opportunity cost and refers to a country's ability to produce goods and services relatively more efficiently. **Barriers to trade** deny citizens the benefits of relatively more efficient production in other countries.

21. Exchange Rates and Balance of Payments   An **exchange rate** is the price of one nation's currency in terms of another nation's currency. The **balance of payments** of a country is a statistical accounting which records, for a given period, all payments one country makes to the rest of the world and all the receipts that it receives from the rest of the world.

22. International Aspects of Growth and Stability   **International aspects of growth and stability** are more important today than in the past because all nations are much more interdependent.

Adapted from the National Council on Economic Education's A Framework for Teaching the Basic Concepts. In the fall of 1991, the United States Department of Commerce replaced GNP with GDP as the nation's most inclusive measure of output.

FUNDAMENTAL ECONOMIC CONCEPTS

CHAPTER 1
What Is Economics?

CHAPTER 2
Economic Systems and Decision Making

CHAPTER 3
Business Organizations and Economic Institutions

Our nation cannot afford to have high school students who lack the basic skills to understand vital economic issues. . . . Without a solid education in economics at the pre-college level, many adults will never have the slightest chance of learning how the economy functions and their roles in the wealth-creating process.

—William B. Walstad, Professor of Economics,
December 28, 1988

Economics and You

In this unit, discover what part economics plays in the following situations:
- You must choose between buying gas for your car or taking your friend out for pizza.
- Your friend from Russia is stunned by all the shoes available at your local shoe store.
- The same product is less expensive at a department store than at a specialty shop.

A farmer harvests his crop by implementing the factors of production—land, labor, entrepreneurship, and capital.

As a consumer, you must make choices from many alternatives.

CHAPTER 1

What Is Economics?

SECTION 1
Scarcity and the Science of Economics

SECTION 2
Trade-Offs and Opportunity Costs

SECTION 3
Basic Economic Concepts

CHAPTER PREVIEW

People to Know
- Adam Smith
- Credit Manager

Applying Economic Concepts to Your Life

Trade-Offs Resources are scarce. Time is scarce. Sometimes it seems as if you have a million things to do, and you just don't know what to do first. You may have many alternatives to select from, and you have to make choices—but which choice is the right one? One choice may prevent another. Believe it or not, the study of economics will help you become a *better* decision maker because it helps you develop a "way of thinking" about *trade-offs* and decision making.

Journal Writing

For one week, keep track of all your economic decisions—the money you spend, the items you buy, the choices you make. Be aware of each decision and your reasons for making it.

Section Preview

Objectives

After studying this section, you will be able to:

1. **Explain** the nature of scarcity and show its relationship to economics.

2. **Describe** the factors of production.

3. **Examine** the three basic economic questions each society must decide.

4. **Define** economics and identify the four key elements within its scope.

Key Terms

scarcity, factors of production, land, capital, financial capital, labor, entrepreneur, economics

Applying Economic Concepts

Scarcity We never seem to have enough! If you were asked to make a list of items you would like to have—and if the list could be as long as you wanted—it might take several days to finish the task. If we asked others to do the same, we would probably end up with more items than we could ever hope to produce. This is the essence of *scarcity*—a condition caused by unlimited wants in a world of limited resources.

Many things in life seem to be "free" when, actually, they are not. For example, you may think you are being treated to a "free" lunch when your friend uses a "buy one, get one free" coupon at a restaurant. While you may not pay for it then and there, someone had to pay the farmer for raising the food, the truck driver for delivering the food, the chef for preparing the food, and the server for serving the food. Who is that "someone"? Although it may come as a surprise, that someone may be you!

TINSTAAFL

When a business offers someone a "free" lunch, the price of that lunch is usually buried somewhere in the price the firm charges for its products. The "free" lunch may be offered to make a sale. If the person later orders services or products from the business, the firm will recover some, if not all, of the cost of the lunch.

If the individual does not buy, then someone else will pay for the lunch by paying higher prices. The more a business gives away "free," the more it has to charge for the items it produces and sells. In the end, someone always pays for the supposedly "free" lunch. **1**

Unfortunately, most things in life are not free because someone has to pay for the production in the first place. Economic educators have a term, *TINSTAAFL*, which describes this concept. In short, this term means that *There Is No Such Thing As A Free Lunch*. This concept is one of the keys to understanding the fundamental economic problem.

The Fundamental Economic Problem

The fundamental economic problem facing all societies is that of **scarcity**—the condition that arises because society does not have enough resources to produce all the things people would like to have. The problem of scarcity is not, as some people might think, caused by a shortage of money. ✓

Suppose that everyone in a society suddenly became wealthier than they ever thought possible. Even if everyone became millionaires, they would still go without many of the things they want and need. Who would want to work? Most people would probably try to spend their money on houses, boats, cars, vacations, and other things. At first, store owners would be delighted to sell their merchandise. The supply of items

Figure 1.1
Scarcity

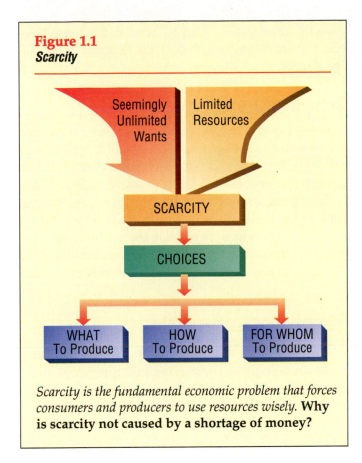

Seemingly Unlimited Wants

Limited Resources

SCARCITY

CHOICES

WHAT To Produce

HOW To Produce

FOR WHOM To Produce

Scarcity is the fundamental economic problem that forces consumers and producers to use resources wisely. **Why is scarcity not caused by a shortage of money?**

in the stores would not last long, however. With few people working, it would be almost impossible to order more inventory from factories. Shelves would soon be empty, and there would be nothing left to buy.

The huge increase in everyone's income would not solve the economic problem of scarcity. Most likely, it would have the opposite effect—the entire economy would come to a halt until people found that their money was practically, if not totally, worthless. Thus, the problem of scarcity is not caused by a shortage of money, but by a lack of resources needed to make all the things people want.

Factors Of Production

The reason people cannot satisfy all their wants and needs is the scarcity of productive resources. These resources, or **factors of production**, are land, capital, labor, and entrepreneurship. They provide the means for a society to produce and distribute its goods and services. **2**

Land

In economics, **land** refers to the "gifts of nature," or natural resources not created by human effort. "Land" includes deserts, fertile fields, forests, mineral deposits, cattle, whales, sunshine, and the climate necessary to grow crops.

Because only so many natural resources are available at any given time, economists tend to think of land as being fixed, or in limited supply. Not enough good farmland exists to feed all of the earth's population, nor enough sandy beaches for everyone to enjoy, nor enough minerals to meet our expanding energy needs indefinitely.

Capital

Another factor of production is **capital**—the tools, equipment, and factories used in the production of goods and services. Such items also are called capital goods to distinguish them from **financial capital**, the money used to buy the tools and equipment used in production.

Capital is unique in that it is the result of production. A bulldozer, for example, is a capital good used in construction. It was built in a factory, however, which makes it the result of earlier production. Like the bulldozer, the cash register in a neighborhood store is a capital good. It, too, is the result of earlier

QUICK CHECK

Checking Understanding

1. Why is there no such thing as a "free" lunch?
2. What are the four factors of production?

Applying Economic Concepts

 Scarcity During World War II, silk and nylon were used for making parachutes. As a result, women's stockings became scarce. Women dealt with this scarcity by painting their legs with makeup, simulating nylons, or by drawing seams up the backs of their legs.

DID YOU KNOW?

Shelling Out In colonial times, money was in short supply. Because of this, people often used shelled corn to pay for goods and services. The practice has not survived the centuries, but the slang expression *shell out*—meaning *pay for*—has.

production and is used for the record keeping associated with the sale of goods and services.

Labor

A third factor of production is **labor**—people with all their efforts, abilities, and skills. This category includes all people except for a unique group of individuals called entrepreneurs, which we single out because of their special role in the economy.

Unlike land, labor is a resource that may vary in size over time. Historically, factors such as population growth, immigration, famine, war, and disease have had a dramatic impact on both the quantity and quality of labor.

Entrepreneurs

Some workers have a special status because they are the innovators responsible for much of the change in our economy. These people are called entrepreneurs. An **entrepreneur** is a risk-taker in search of profits.

Entrepreneurs often are thought of as the driving force in the American economy because they exhibit a knack for starting a new business or bringing new products to market. Their initiative combines the resources of land, labor, and capital into new products. 1

Three Basic Questions

To provide for the needs of its people, a society must answer three basic economic questions. In so doing, it makes decisions about the ways its limited resources are going to be used.

Figure 1.2
The Factors of Production

THE FACTORS OF PRODUCTION

LAND

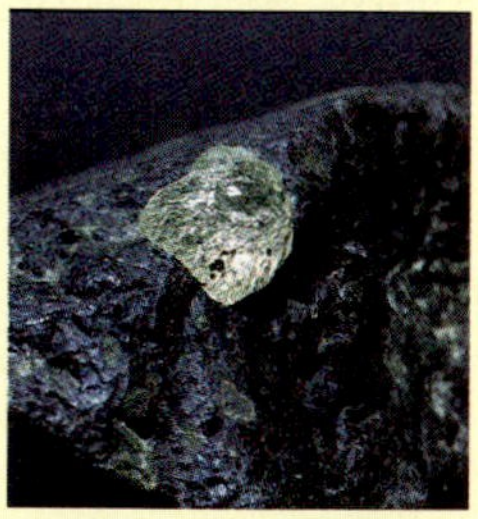

LAND *includes the "gifts of nature," or natural resources not created by human effort.*

CAPITAL

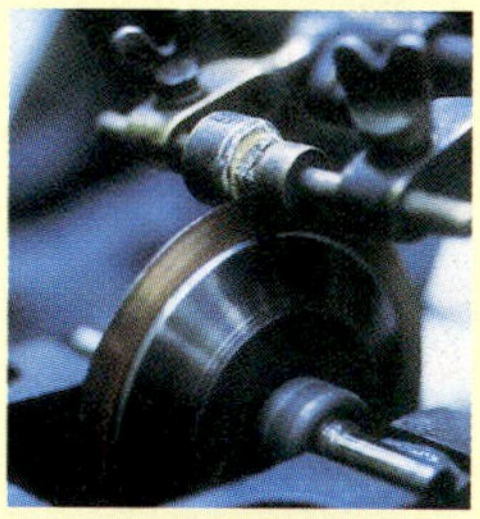

CAPITAL *includes the tools, equipment, and factories used in production. Capital is unique in that it is the result of production.*

LABOR

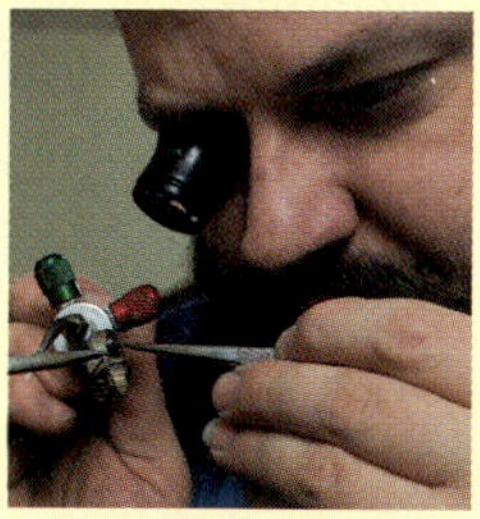

LABOR *includes people with all their efforts and abilities, excluding those individuals with unique entrepreneurial abilities.*

ENTREPRENEURS

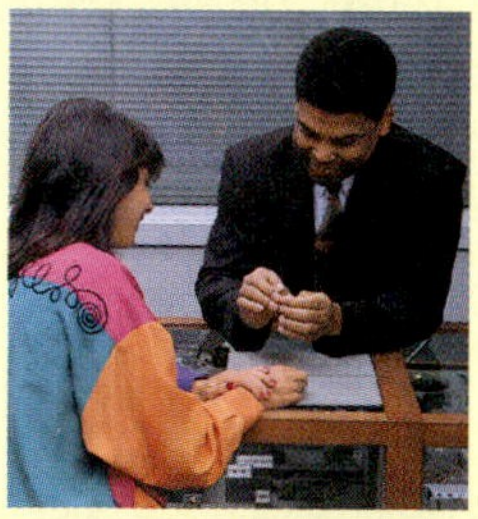

ENTREPRENEURS *include those unique risk-taking individuals who have the ability to start a new business or bring a product to market.*

The productive resources in a modern economy include LAND, CAPITAL, LABOR, and ENTREPRENEURIAL ABILITY. All four factors of production are necessary for production to take place. **What four factors of production are necessary to bring jewelry to consumers?**

What To Produce

The first question is that of WHAT to produce. Should a society devote most of its resources to producing military equipment or to other items such as food, clothing, or housing? Suppose the decision is to produce housing. Should its limited resources then be used for low-income, middle-income, or upper-income housing? How many of each will be needed? A society cannot have everything its people want, so it must decide WHAT to produce.

How To Produce

A second question is that of HOW to produce. Should factory owners use assembly-line methods that require little labor, or should they use less equipment and more workers? If an area has many unemployed people, the second method might be better. On the other hand, assembly-line methods in countries where capital is widely available usually have lower production costs. Lower costs make many manufactured items less expensive and, therefore, available to more people.

For Whom To Produce

The third question deals with FOR WHOM to produce. After a society decides WHAT and HOW to produce, the items produced must be allocated to someone. If the society decides to produce housing, should it be distributed to workers, professional people, or government employees? Perhaps another group is more deserving. Who decides? In the end, the result is the same. If not enough houses exist for everyone, a choice must be made as to who will receive the existing supply.

These three choices about WHAT, HOW, and FOR WHOM to produce are not easy for any society to make. Nevertheless, a society has few options. It must answer the three basic questions as long as there are not enough resources to satisfy the fundamental economic problem of scarcity. Different societies answer these questions in different ways. **2**

The Meaning and Scope of Economics

Economics is the study of human efforts to satisfy what appear to be unlimited and competing wants through the careful use of relatively scarce resources. It is also a social science because it deals with the behavior of people as they cope with the fundamental problem of scarcity.

Description

Economics deals with the *description* of economic activity. It is concerned with what is produced and who gets how much, as well as with topics such as unemployment, inflation, international trade, the interaction of business and labor, and the effects of government spending and taxes. Description, however, is not enough because description alone leaves many important "why" and "how" questions unanswered.

Analysis

In order to answer such questions, economics must focus on the *analysis* of economic activity as well. Why, for example, are prices of some items high while others are low? Why are incomes higher in some states than in others? How do taxes affect people's desire to work and save?

Checking Understanding

1. Why are entrepreneurs considered the "driving force" in the American economy?
2. Why must a society face the choices about WHAT, HOW, and FOR WHOM to produce?

Applying Economic Concepts

 Entrepreneurs Think of a local entrepreneur— maybe even yourself! What factors of production did the entrepreneur combine into a new product?

Explanation

Economics is also concerned with the *explanation* of economic activity. After economists understand how things work, it is useful and even necessary to communicate this knowledge to others. In this manner, the study of economics helps us better understand our world.

Prediction

Finally, economics is concerned with *prediction*, anticipating the likely consequences of different courses of action. Suppose a community wants to raise revenue to build a health-care facility. Should the funds be raised through voluntary contributions, payroll taxes, property taxes, or by some other means? Economists can help predict the consequences of different courses of action, but the final choice is still up to the people in the community.

In the end, the scope of economics is limited to four key elements—description, analysis, explanation, and prediction. Economists study what is, or tends to be, and how it came to be. Economists can be compared to nuclear physicists who can explain how to make a nuclear bomb and what damage the bomb can do. As scientists, however, they are not expected to judge whether or not the bomb should be used in war. People must make up their own minds about that.

Economists do not hand down economic rules for people to obey. Deciding what is to be done is the responsibility of all citizens in a democratic society. The study of economics will not lead to ethical judgments for economic problems, but it will help us to become more informed citizens and better decision makers.

SECTION 1
REVIEW

Reviewing Terms and Facts

1. **Define** scarcity, factors of production, land, capital, financial capital, labor, entrepreneur, economics.
2. **Describe** the fundamental economic problem.
3. **Describe** the factors of production.
4. **List** the three basic economic questions any society must answer.
5. **Identify** the four key elements that define the scope of economics.

Critical Thinking

6. **Analyzing Information** Give an example of a supposedly "free" item that you see every day. Explain why the item is not really free by stating who or what actually pays for it.

Applying Economic Concepts

7. **Scarcity** How does scarcity affect your life? Provide several examples of items you have had to do without because limited resources could not keep up with your wants.

Interpreting Line Graphs

"A picture is worth a thousand words." How many times have you heard that expression? Often it is true. A graph, like a picture, can present much information in a more concise way than words. Graphs are drawings that compare numerical values. Graphs often are used to compare changes over time or differences between places, groups of items, or other related events.

Explanation

The line graph is a common type of graph. The information being compared usually appears on the left side of the graph—the vertical axis—with time appearing along the bottom of the graph—the horizontal axis. Dots or other symbols are sometimes used to show numerical values, and they are frequently connected with a line to keep the information from getting mixed up with other values in the graph.

The steps involved in interpreting line graphs are:

a. Read the title of the graph. This should tell you what to expect or look for.
b. Familiarize yourself with the information on the horizontal axis.
c. Familiarize yourself with the information on the vertical axis.
d. Examine where the dots are placed on the graph.
e. Determine what the line(s) or curve(s) symbolizes. Sometimes the lines are even labeled to make the graph easier to read.
f. Compare the line(s) in the graph to the horizontal and vertical axes to determine the point being made.

Practice

Examine the line graph, then answer the questions that follow.

1. What does the line graph show?
2. What information is presented along the horizontal axis?
3. What information is presented along the vertical axis?
4. How did consumers spend most of their money in 1959?
5. In which category in 1959 did consumers spend the least?
6. What do all the expenditures add up to in 1959?
7. What kinds of changes took place over time?
8. Which category of consumer expenditures was the largest in 1991?

Additional Practice

For further practice interpreting line graphs, complete the Reinforcing Skills exercise in the Chapter 1 Review on page 29.

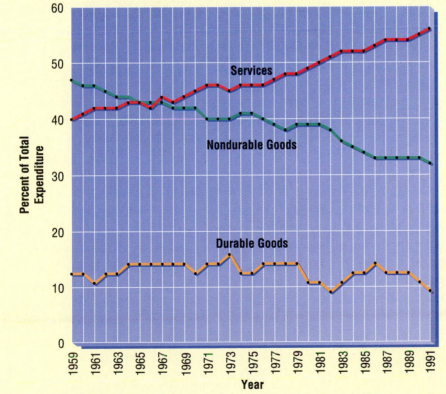

Figure 1.3
Consumer Expenditures by Category

Services

Nondurable Goods

Durable Goods

Percent of Total Expenditure

Year

Source: *Economic Report of the President,* 1993

Section Preview

Objectives

After studying this section, you will be able to:

1. **Understand** that trade-offs are present whenever choices are made.

2. **Discover** that trade-offs are costs in the form of opportunities given up when one course of action is chosen instead of another.

3. **Evaluate** the opportunity cost that an economy faces when resources are allocated to the production of one good instead of another.

Key Terms

trade-offs, opportunity cost, production possibilities frontier

Applying Economic Concepts

Trade-Offs What did you do last night—homework, watch TV, listen to CDs, visit a friend? Because you could not do all those things at once, you had to make a choice. Your decision to do one thing instead of another involved a *trade-off*. Trade-offs are alternatives, and they have costs that can be expressed as the next best option that you gave up in order to do something else. If you think about it, life is full of trade-offs.

The process of making a choice is not always easy. Still, individuals, businesses, government agencies, and any other groups that try to satisfy people's wants and needs must make decisions. To become a good decision maker, you need to know how to identify the problem, and then analyze all your alternatives in a way that carefully considers the costs and benefits of each possibility. **1**

Trade-Offs Among Alternatives

Because people cannot have everything they want, they face **trade-offs,** or alternative choices, when spending their income or time. While choices are not always easy to make, a decision-making grid such as that in **Figure 1.4** shows one way to approach such problems. This grid summarizes a decision made by Jesse, a newspaper carrier whose dilemma was to spend a gift of $50 in the best way possible.

Jesse discovered that several alternatives seemed appealing—a soccer ball, jeans, a portable cassette player, several CDs, and concert tickets. At the same time, he realized that each item had advantages and

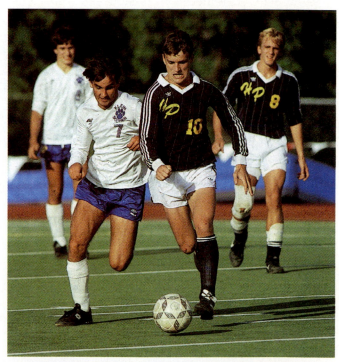

Opportunity Cost *These students have considered the opportunity costs of playing soccer instead of another activity.* **What may be an opportunity cost of playing organized sports?**

Figure 1.4
Jesse's Decision-Making Grid

ALTERNATIVES	CRITERIA				
	Costs $50 or Less	Durable	Will Parents Approve?	Future Expenses Unnecessary	Can Use Anytime
Several CDs	yes	yes	yes	yes	no
Concert Tickets	yes	no	no	no	no
Cassette Player	yes	yes	yes	no	yes
Soccer Ball	yes	yes	yes	yes	no
Jeans	yes	yes	yes	yes	yes

Adapted from Trade-Offs, © 1978 Agency For Instructional Technology (AIT)

A decision-making grid is a good way to list and then evaluate alternatives when a decision must be made.

What do economists mean when they talk about *costs*?

disadvantages. Some items were more durable than others, and some might require his parents' consent. Some even had additional costs while others did not—the cassette player required batteries and the concert tickets required the use of his parents' car.

To help with his decision, Jesse drew a grid that listed his alternatives and several criteria to judge them. Then he used pluses and minuses to evaluate each alternative. In the end, Jesse chose the jeans because they satisfied more of his criteria than any other alternative.

Using a decision-making grid is an effective way to analyze an economic problem. Among other things, it forces you to consider a number of relevant alternatives. For another, it requires you to identify the decision criteria used to evaluate the alternatives. Finally, it forces you to evaluate each alternative based on the criteria. ✓

Opportunity Cost

People often think of cost in terms of dollars. To an economist, however, cost often means more than the price tag placed on a good or service. Instead, economists think in terms of **opportunity cost**—the cost of the next best alternative use of money, time, or resources when one choice is made rather than another.

When Jesse decided on the jeans, his opportunity cost was the next best choice—the soccer ball or the cassette player—that he gave up. Suppose a person spends $5,000 on a used car. The opportunity cost of the purchase is the value of the stereo, apartment, vacation, or other items and activities that could have been bought with money spent on the car.

Even time has an opportunity cost. Suppose your friend had a chance to earn $50 for a morning's work but ended up oversleeping because the alarm never

QUICK CHECK

Checking Understanding

1. What do you need to know to become a good decision maker?

Applying Economic Concepts

✓ **Trade-Offs** In Figure 1.4, Jesse's criteria included expense, durability, parental consent, and so on. What criteria would you use to evaluate alternatives? Why?

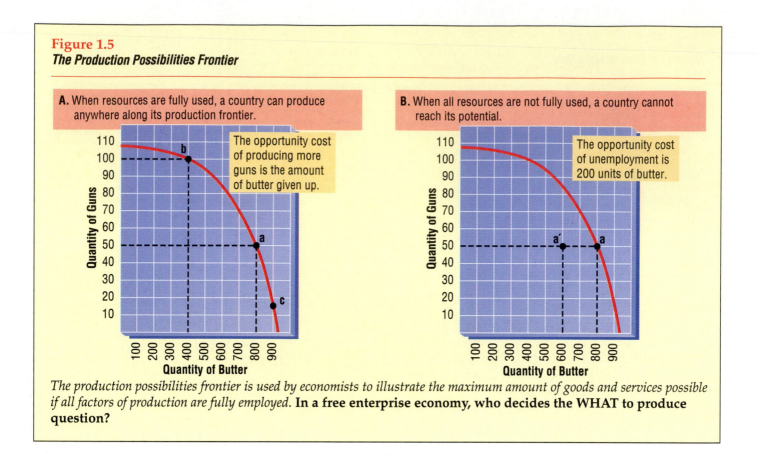

Figure 1.5
The Production Possibilities Frontier

A. When resources are fully used, a country can produce anywhere along its production frontier.

The opportunity cost of producing more guns is the amount of butter given up.

(Graph A: Quantity of Guns (vertical axis, 10–110) vs. Quantity of Butter (horizontal axis, 100–900). Point b at ~100 guns/400 butter, point a at 50 guns/800 butter, point c at ~15 guns/900 butter.)

B. When all resources are not fully used, a country cannot reach its potential.

The opportunity cost of unemployment is 200 units of butter.

(Graph B: Quantity of Guns (vertical axis, 10–110) vs. Quantity of Butter (horizontal axis, 100–900). Point a′ at 50 guns/600 butter, point a at 50 guns/800 butter.)

The production possibilities frontier is used by economists to illustrate the maximum amount of goods and services possible if all factors of production are fully employed. **In a free enterprise economy, who decides the WHAT to produce question?**

went off. In this case, the opportunity cost of the morning's rest was $50.

When economists talk about costs, they are talking in terms of alternatives that are given up. Thus, part of making economic decisions involves recognizing and evaluating alternatives as well as making choices from among the alternatives.

The Production Possibilities Frontier

A popular model economists use to illustrate the concept of opportunity cost is the **production possibilities frontier**. The frontier is a diagram representing various combinations of goods and/or services an economy can produce when all productive resources are fully employed. In the classic example, a mythical country called Alpha has a limited supply of resources and produces two kinds of goods— guns and butter. At current production levels, Alpha produces 50 units of guns and 800 units of butter annually. Point **a** in Graph **A** on **Figure 1.5** represents this level.

Now, suppose that Alpha decided it did not have enough guns to protect itself. It could then shift resources from the production of butter into the production of guns. This might make butter production drop to 400 units, and allow gun production to rise to 100 units. Point **b** in Graph **A** represents this new combination of output. The opportunity cost of producing the additional 50 units of guns is the 400 units of butter given up.

Points **a** and **b** represent only two possible mixes of output. If Alpha needed more butter, it could shift enough resources to produce at point **c** in Graph **A**. The production possibilities frontier, which appears as a smooth curve in **Figure 1.5**, is made up of a large number of combinations of output such as those represented by points **a**, **b**, and **c**.

It is also possible for Alpha to produce the mix of output shown at point **a′** in Graph **B**. In this case, all resources are not fully employed. Workers in the butter industry, for example, may be on strike, causing the output of butter to fall to 600 units. In this case, the opportunity cost of the strike would be the 200 units of butter not produced because of idle resources.

Production at **a'** could also be the result of other idle resources such as factories that have been built but are not being used. Workers may have chosen to enjoy four weeks of vacation a year rather than two. As long as some resources are not used, the country cannot produce on its frontier—which is another way of saying that it cannot reach its full production potential.

The production possibilities frontier is just one of the many tools used by economists to describe the economy. Realistically, economies are able to produce more than two goods or services, but the concept is easier to illustrate if only two products are examined. Even so, a simple model such as **Figure 1.5** is sometimes all that economists need to analyze an actual problem.

Trade-Offs *In the cartoon, the king faces a trade-off between crops and catapults.* **What is the opportunity cost of obtaining two more catapults?**

SECTION 2 REVIEW

Reviewing Terms and Facts

1. **Define** trade-offs, opportunity cost, production possibilities frontier.
2. **Describe** how the rows and columns in a decision-making grid are related to trade-offs and opportunity costs.
3. **Explain** how opportunity cost is involved when resources are shifted from the production of one good to another.

Critical Thinking

4. **Making Generalizations** Explain the advantages of using a decision-making grid to evaluate alternatives.

Applying Economic Concepts

5. **Trade-Offs** Identify several possible uses of your time that will be available to you after school today. What will you actually do, and what will be the opportunity cost of your decision?

PROFILES IN ECONOMICS

ADAM SMITH
(1723–1790)

Adam Smith was a Scottish economist and philosopher. His best-known work, *An Inquiry into the Nature and Causes of the Wealth of Nations*, was published in 1776. More commonly called *The Wealth of Nations*, the book offered a detailed description of life and trade in English society. It also scientifically described the basic principles of economics for the first time.

After graduating from Glasgow University in Scotland, Smith traveled to England and enrolled at Oxford University. His stay lasted six years.

Smith returned to Scotland to lecture at Edinburgh

Buyers and sellers meet at the Covent Garden Market.

University and Glasgow University, where he was immensely popular with his students. He also traveled extensively. While in Europe, Smith met and exchanged ideas with French writer Voltaire, Benjamin Franklin, and the French economist Quesnay. His travels helped him formulate the ideas put forth in *The Wealth of Nations*.

PRODUCTIVITY AND WEALTH
Smith observed that labor becomes more productive as each worker becomes more skilled at a single job. He said that new machinery and the division and specialization of labor would lead to an increase in production and greater wealth for

the nation. Smith also argued that wealth was the sum of the nation's goods produced by labor, regardless of who owned those goods.

INVISIBLE HAND
One of Smith's most important contributions dealt with competition in the marketplace. He argued that competition, together with the free market system, would act as an *invisible hand* that guided resources to their most productive use. He believed that under competitive conditions, individuals acting naturally in their own self-interest, and with a minimum of government intervention, would bring about the greatest good for society as a whole.

LAISSEZ-FAIRE
The Wealth of Nations was ridiculed by the aristocracy in Parliament. Businesspeople, however, were delighted to have a moral justification for their growing wealth and power. Eventually, the doctrine of *laissez-faire*, meaning no government intervention in economic affairs, became the watchword of the day in Great Britain.

Examining the Profile

1. **Making Generalizations** Summarize Smith's philosophies on productivity, wealth, the invisible hand, and the role of government in the economy.

2. **For Further Research** Research Smith's views and the effects of his economic philosophies on the American free enterprise system.

SECTION 3
Basic Economic Concepts

Section Preview

Objectives

After studying this section, you will be able to:

1. **Understand** the difference between needs and wants, and goods and services.
2. **Explain** the relationship among value, utility, and wealth.
3. **Describe** the importance of productivity.
4. **Understand** the importance of economics to the American free enterprise system.

Key Terms

need, want, free product, economic product, good, consumer good, capital good, durable good, nondurable good, service, consumer, consumption, conspicuous consumption, value, paradox of value, utility, wealth, production, productivity, specialization, division of labor, human capital, economic interdependence, market, factor market, product market, free enterprise economy

Applying Economic Concepts

Conspicuous Consumption Do you have an expensive item that you enjoy showing off? *Conspicuous consumption*, the use of an expensive good, service, or other extravagant purchase to impress others, is fairly common. More than likely, this economic term applies to someone you know.

Economics, like any other social science, has its own vocabulary. To understand economics, a review of some key terms is necessary. Fortunately, most economic terms are widely used, and many will already be familiar.

Needs and Wants

Sometimes we hear a term so often we do not even know that it is a basic economic concept. Two terms, *needs* and *wants*, are cases in point.

Needs and Wants   *Food represents a basic need related to survival, while a sports car and CD player are usually considered wants.* **Which of your needs might be considered wants by other societies?**

Need

A **need** is a basic requirement for survival. People have basic needs such as food, clothing, and shelter. People also have higher level needs, such as communication, love, acceptance, knowledge, hope, and accomplishment. These needs are part of the makeup of each person.

Want

A **want** is a means of expressing a need. Food, for example, is a basic need related to survival. To satisfy this need, a person may "want" a pizza, hamburger, taco, or other favorite food. Any number of foods will satisfy the basic need for nourishment. Given a person's budget, some choices might seem reasonable while others might not. The point is that the range of things represented by the term *want* is much broader than that represented by the term *need*. ✔

Goods, Services, and Consumers

Some things, such as sunshine or air, are known as **free products** because they are so plentiful. No one could possibly own them, and no price can be attached to them. Some are so important that life would be impossible without them. Even so, free products are not scarce enough to be a major concern in the study of economics.

Instead, economics is concerned with **economic products**—goods and services that are useful, relatively scarce, and transferable to others. Economic products are scarce in an economic sense. That is, one cannot get enough to satisfy individual wants and needs. Because of these characteristics, economic products command a price.

Goods

The terms *goods* and *services* are used to describe the many things people desire. A **good** is a tangible commodity like a book, car, or compact disc player. A **consumer good** is intended for final use by individuals. A manufactured good used to produce other goods and services is called a **capital good**. An example of a capital good would be a robot welder in a factory, an oven in a bakery, or a computer in a high school.

Any good that lasts three years or more when it is used on a regular basis is called a **durable good**. Durable goods would include both capital goods such as robot welders and consumer goods such as automobiles. A **nondurable good** is an item that lasts for less than three years when it is used on a regular basis. Examples of nondurable goods include food, writing paper, and most clothing items. **1**

Services

The other type of economic product is a **service**, or work that is performed for someone. Services include haircuts, home repairs, and forms of entertainment such as concerts. They also include the work that doctors, lawyers, and teachers perform.

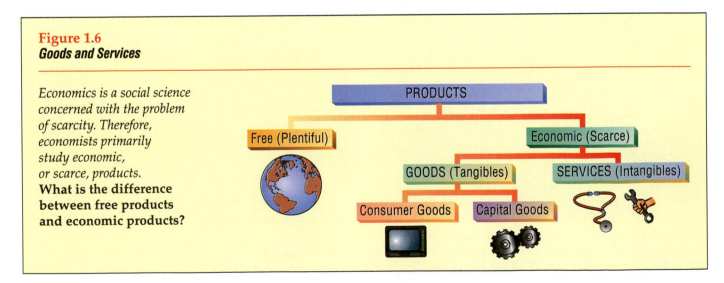

Figure 1.6
Goods and Services

Economics is a social science concerned with the problem of scarcity. Therefore, economists primarily study economic, or scarce, products. **What is the difference between free products and economic products?**

PRODUCTS

Free (Plentiful)

Economic (Scarce)

GOODS (Tangibles)

SERVICES (Intangibles)

Consumer Goods

Capital Goods

Wealth *Forests and farmland are natural resources and items of wealth.* **Why are natural resources considered part of the nation's wealth?**

The difference between a good and a service is that a service is something that cannot be touched or felt.

Consumers

People who use goods and services to satisfy wants and needs are **consumers**, and they play an important role in many economies. As consumers, people indulge in **consumption**—the process of using up goods and services in order to satisfy wants and needs.

Some consumers carry the process of consumption to extreme limits. **Conspicuous consumption**—the use of a good or service to impress others—is fairly common. A person may wear expensive jewelry or drive a flashy car. While that person obviously enjoys the use of these items, at least part of the enjoyment comes from showing off his or her expensive tastes to others.

Value, Utility, and Wealth

In economics, **value** refers to something that has a worth that can be expressed in dollars and cents. Someone may say, for example, that he or she has a valuable coin, antique doll, baseball card, or model train collection. In each case, value is determined by the price someone would pay for the item. Why, however, does something have value, and why are some things worth more than others? To answer these questions, it helps to review an early problem faced by economists.

Paradox of Value

Early economists observed that some things, such as water, were essential to life yet had little monetary value. Other things, such as diamonds, were not essential but had much higher value. The problem

Checking Understanding

1. What is the difference between a durable good and a nondurable good?

Applying Economic Concepts

☑ **Needs vs. Wants** Advertisers often present wants as needs to promote their products. Provide an example of an advertisement that influenced you to view a want as a need.

became known as the diamond-water paradox, or the **paradox of value**, and the solution to the problem helps us determine the nature of value.

At first, it seemed paradoxical that so many essentials had little value while other items had much higher value. Later, economists decided that part of the reason was due to scarcity. For example, water is so plentiful in many areas that it has little or no value. On the other hand, diamonds are so scarce that they have great value. In order for something to have value, then, it has to be somewhat scarce. Scarcity by itself, however, is not enough to create value.

Utility

For something to have value, it must also have **utility**, or the capacity to be useful to someone. Utility is not something that is fixed or measured, like weight or height. Instead, the utility of a good or service may vary from one person to the next. One person may get a great deal of enjoyment from a home computer; another may get very little. One person may enjoy a rock concert; another may not. A good or service does not have to have utility for everyone, only utility for some.

For something to have value, it must be scarce and have utility. This is the solution to the paradox of value. Diamonds are scarce and have utility—and therefore a value that can be stated in monetary terms. Water has utility, but is not scarce enough in most places to give it much value.

Wealth

Another concept is **wealth**—the sum of those economic products that are tangible, scarce, useful, and transferable from one person to another. Most economic goods are counted as wealth, but services are not. The reason for this is that it is difficult to measure the value of services accurately.

For example, it is difficult to measure the contribution people's abilities and talents make to a nation's wealth. If a country's material possessions were taken away, its people, through their skilled efforts, would probably restore these possessions. On the other hand, if a country's people were taken away, its wealth would deteriorate.

A country's total wealth is the stockpile of useful, scarce, transferable, and tangible things in existence at a given time. The nation's wealth includes all such items as natural resources, factories, stores, houses, motels, theaters, furniture, clothing, books, video games, and even footballs.

Productivity

When the factors of production—land, labor, entrepreneurship, and capital—are present, **production**, or the process of creating goods and services, can take place. Even the production of the service called education requires the factors of production. The chalkboards, desks, and audiovisual equipment used in schools are capital goods. Another requirement is labor, represented by the services of teachers, administrators, and other employees. Land, such as the iron ore, granite, and timber used to make the building and desks, as well as the lot where the school is located, also is needed. It is nearly impossible to provide the service of education without all the factors of production.

The efficient use of productive resources is called **productivity**. Productivity goes up whenever more output can be produced with the same amount of inputs. Productivity also goes up if the same output can be produced with fewer inputs.

Productivity is usually discussed in terms of labor, but it applies to all factors of production. For this reason, business owners try to buy the most efficient capital goods, and farmers try to use the most fertile land for their crops. In a world of relatively scarce resources, productivity is a key issue.

Specialization of Labor

Increases in productivity often occur when people specialize. In economics, **specialization** means that productive inputs do whatever task they are able to do best. For example, an excellent carpenter with average skills in other areas might want to build a house. Even if the carpenter could build the entire house without any help, it might be better to hire other workers who specialize in foundations, plumbing, and electrical wiring. The carpenter might even save money by first working for someone else, and then using the money to hire the specialized workers.

Specialization, also known as the **division of labor**, takes place when workers perform fewer tasks more frequently. A worker who performs several tasks many times every day is likely to become more proficient than a worker who performs hundreds of different tasks once a week.

Labor is not the only factor of production that can specialize. Complex industrial robots are often built to perform one or two simple assembly-line tasks. Regions, countries, and states even specialize. Idaho specializes in potatoes, Iowa specializes in corn, and Texas specializes in oil, cotton, and cattle. **1**

Human Capital

Finally, productivity tends to increase when firms invest in **human capital**, the sum of skills, abilities, health, and motivation of people. Investments by government and businesses in training, health care, and employee motivation tend to increase the amount of production that takes place with a given amount of labor. Employers are usually rewarded with higher quality products and increased profits. Workers often benefit from higher pay, better jobs, and more satisfaction with their work and leisure.

Economic Interdependence

The American economy has a remarkable degree of **economic interdependence**. This interdependence means that actions in one part of the country or the world have an economic impact on what happens elsewhere. Bad weather in one part of the world can affect sugar prices in the United States, and a change in sugar prices can affect the price of snack foods and

Figure 1.7

Relationship Between Income & Education

Education	Median Income for Males	Females
Less than 9th Grade	$10,319	$6,268
9th to 12th Grade (no diploma)	$14,736	$7,055
High School Graduate & Equivalency	$21,546	$10,818
Some College, no degree	$26,591	$13,963
Associate Degree	$29,358	$17,364
Bachelor Degree	$36,067	$20,967
Master's Degree	$43,125	$29,747
Professional Degree	$63,741	$34,063
Doctorate Degree	$51,845	$37,242

Source: U.S. Department of Commerce, Bureau of the Census

A formal education is one way to invest in human capital. **How does this type of investment pay off for both employers and employees?**

the demand for sugar substitutes. Because of this interdependence, we need to understand how all the parts fit together. ☑

The Circular Flow of Economic Activity

To the economist, a **market** is a location or other mechanism that allows buyers and sellers to deal readily in a certain economic product. Markets may

Checking Understanding

1. In what does your state or community specialize? Why?

Applying Economic Concepts

☑ **Economic Interdependence** How do you get to school or work each day? Chances are that you depend on someone else, perhaps someone you don't even know such as a bus driver or subway operator. Most activity involves similar economic interdependence.

be local, regional, national, or global. All markets are similar, however, in that their economic activity has a distinct circular flow.

How does this circular flow operate? Individuals earn their incomes in **factor markets**—the markets where productive resources are bought and sold. Here, entrepreneurs hire labor for wages and salaries, land is provided in return for rent, and money is loaned for interest or invested for a profit. When individuals receive their incomes, they spend it in **product markets**—markets where producers offer goods and services for sale. **1**

In a similar way, business firms receive payments in the product markets when they sell goods and services to individuals. This pays for the land, labor, and capital bought in the factor markets. These resources are then used to manufacture additional products that are sold in the product markets.

Figure 1.8 illustrates the circular flow of economic activity that links economic markets, money, resources, businesses, and consumers. In the diagram, money circulates on the outside to illustrate payments for goods, services, and factors of production, which flow in the opposite direction on the inside.

The Road Ahead

The study of economics does more than explain how people deal with scarcity. It provides insight as to how incomes are earned and spent, how jobs are created, and how the economy works on a daily basis. It also provides a more detailed understanding of a **free enterprise economy**—one in which consumers and privately owned businesses, rather than the government, jointly make the majority of the WHAT, HOW, and FOR WHOM decisions.

In addition, the study of economics will provide a working knowledge of property rights, competition, supply and demand, the price system, and the economic incentives that make the American economy function. Along the way, topics such as unemployment, the business cycle, inflation, and economic growth will be covered. The role of business, labor, and government in the American economy also will be examined. Finally, the relationship of the United States economy to the international economy will be explored.

The study of economics helps people become better decision makers. Economic issues often are

Economic Interdependence   *If poor weather or disease causes coffee production to decrease, coffee drinkers in the United States may switch to drinking tea.* **How might you be affected by war in an oil-producing country?**

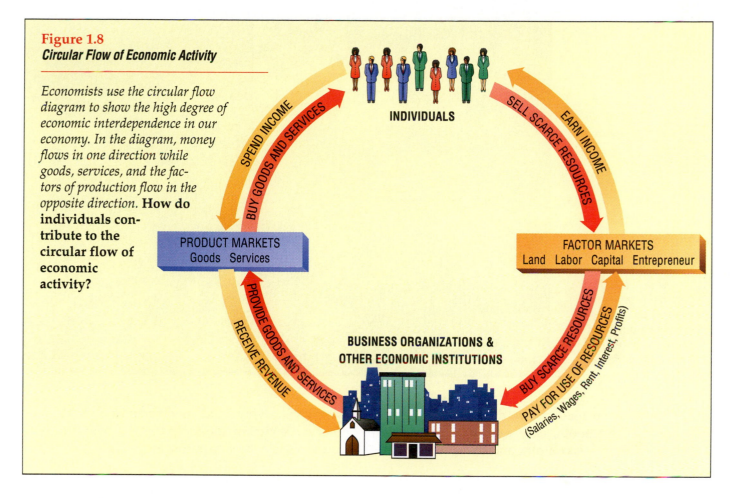

Figure 1.8
Circular Flow of Economic Activity

Economists use the circular flow diagram to show the high degree of economic interdependence in our economy. In the diagram, money flows in one direction while goods, services, and the factors of production flow in the opposite direction. **How do individuals contribute to the circular flow of economic activity?**

INDIVIDUALS

SPEND INCOME
BUY GOODS AND SERVICES

SELL SCARCE RESOURCES
EARN INCOME

PRODUCT MARKETS
Goods   Services

FACTOR MARKETS
Land Labor Capital Entrepreneur

PROVIDE GOODS AND SERVICES
RECEIVE REVENUE

BUY SCARCE RESOURCES
PAY FOR USE OF RESOURCES
(Salaries, Wages, Rent, Interest, Profits)

BUSINESS ORGANIZATIONS &
OTHER ECONOMIC INSTITUTIONS

debated during political campaigns, and voters need to understand the issues before deciding which candidate to support. A voter may have to decide between the candidate who favors higher taxes and more government spending and the candidate who favors lower taxes and less government spending. Other candidates may favor limiting imports, and even others may favor free trade.

The study of economics does not provide voters with clear-cut answers to all questions. It does help them have a better understanding of the issues involved, however. In doing so, the study of economics helps people make more informed choices in the voting booths.

Textbook economics can be divided into neat sections for study, but the real world is not so orderly. Most people live in dynamic societies in which things are constantly changing. Events take place daily, and economies almost always are in a state of flux. In addition, the people of the world differ. Not everyone has the same kind or degree of ambition, strength, greed, or luck. Opinions also differ, and some issues never seem to be settled.

QUICK CHECK

Checking Understanding

1. What is the difference between a factor market and a product market?

Applying Economic Concepts

☑ **Economic Interdependence**   In the global economy of the 1990s, United States consumers and businesses are directly affected by events around the world. Now, more than ever, understanding economics is vital to understanding how you will be affected by social and political forces.

Economics and Politics
Economic issues played a major role in the 1992 presidential campaign. **How does the study of economics help people make more informed choices in the voting booth?**

No matter what road people decide to take, they will not have a smooth, easy ride. In practice, the world of economics is complex and the road ahead is bumpy. Studying and understanding economics, however, is vital to understanding many of the political and social forces operating around us.

SECTION 3 REVIEW

Reviewing Terms and Facts

1. **Define** need, want, free product, economic product, good, consumer good, capital good, durable good, nondurable good, service, consumer, consumption, conspicuous consumption, value, paradox of value, utility, wealth, production, productivity, specialization, division of labor, human capital, economic interdependence, market, factor market, product market, free enterprise economy.

2. **Explain** the conditions that must be present for something to have value.

3. **Provide** three examples of items that could be considered as wealth.

4. **Explain** the importance of productivity.

Critical Thinking

5. **Determining Cause and Effect** How does education relate to the productivity of human capital?

Applying Economic Concepts

6. **Production** Using a product that is familiar to you, explain how each of the factors of production was used in its production.

What Is Economics?

Vocabulary

The following terms are defined in Chapter 1:

SECTION ONE
- scarcity *(p. 8)*
- factors of production *(p. 9)*
- land *(p. 9)*
- capital *(p. 9)*
- financial capital *(p. 9)*
- labor *(p. 10)*
- entrepreneur *(p. 10)*

- economics *(p. 11)*

SECTION TWO
- trade-offs *(p. 14)*
- opportunity cost *(p. 15)*
- production possibilities frontier *(p. 16)*

SECTION THREE
- need *(p. 20)*
- want *(p. 20)*
- free product *(p. 20)*
- economic product *(p. 20)*

- good *(p. 20)*
- consumer good *(p. 20)*
- capital good *(p. 20)*
- durable good *(p. 20)*
- nondurable good *(p. 20)*
- service *(p. 20)*
- consumer *(p. 21)*
- consumption *(p. 21)*
- conspicuous consumption *(p. 21)*
- value *(p. 21)*
- paradox of value *(p. 22)*
- utility *(p. 22)*

- wealth *(p. 22)*
- production *(p. 22)*
- productivity *(p. 22)*
- specialization *(p. 22)*
- division of labor *(p. 23)*
- human capital *(p. 23)*
- economic interdependence *(p. 23)*
- market *(p. 23)*
- factor market *(p. 24)*
- product market *(p. 24)*
- free enterprise economy *(p. 24)*

Section 1

Scarcity and the Science of Economics (pages 8–12)

Most things in life are not free. Economic educators use the term *TINSTAAFL—There is No Such Thing As A Free Lunch*—to describe this concept.

The fundamental economic problem is **scarcity**, the result of limited resources in a world of seemingly unlimited wants. These resources, or **factors of production**, are **land**, **capital**, **labor**, and **entrepreneurship**. They provide the means for a society to produce and distribute its goods and services. Because of scarcity, all societies must face the three basic questions of WHAT, HOW, and FOR WHOM to produce.

Reviewing the Main Idea

How does the term *TINSTAAFL* relate to scarcity?

Section 2

Trade-Offs and Opportunity Costs (pages 14–17)

Individuals face **trade-offs** among alternatives. The **opportunity cost** of an economic decision is the alternative given up when one course of action is chosen over another. Countries make trade-offs when they choose to produce some goods rather than others. Economists use the **production possibilities frontier** to illustrate opportunity cost.

Reviewing the Main Idea

How is cost measured? How can it be illustrated?

Section 3

Basic Economic Concepts (pages 19–26)

All people have basic **needs**, which come from the desire to survive, and higher-level needs such as success and love. A **want** is a way of expressing a need, but the concept of a want is much broader than a need.

The study of economics deals with those **goods** and **services** that are useful, relatively scarce, and transferable to others. **Wealth** has monetary **value** and includes natural resources, **consumer goods**, and **capital goods**.

Consumers help determine which goods and services will ultimately be produced. In order for **production** to take place, the factors of production must be used. **Productivity** relates to the efficient use of resources. Productivity tends to go up when workers specialize in the things they can do best and when investments in **human capital** are made.

The study of economics helps people make informed consumer and business decisions. It also helps people understand how a **free enterprise economy**—one in which consumers and privately owned businesses, rather than the government—jointly make the WHAT, HOW, and FOR WHOM decisions.

Reviewing the Main Idea

What are five key economic concepts?

Reviewing Key Terms

Write the key term that best completes the following sentences.

a. scarcity
b. human capital
c. utility
d. opportunity cost
e. factors of production
f. capital goods
g. value
h. consumer goods
i. consumers
j. services

1. Economic products designed to satisfy people's wants and needs are called _____.
2. The _____ of a CD player can be expressed in dollars and cents.
3. Haircuts, repairs to home appliances, and entertainment are examples of _____.
4. _____ arises because society does not have enough resources to produce all the things people would like to have.
5. The _____ of going to a football game instead of working would include the money not earned at your job.
6. _____ is the sum of the skills, abilities, health, and motivation of people.
7. _____ is another name for the capacity of a product to be useful.
8. The only factors of production that are themselves the result of earlier production are _____.
9. Land, labor, entrepreneurship, and capital are _____.
10. People who use goods and services to satisfy their wants and needs are called _____.

Reviewing the Facts

SECTION 1 *(pages 8–12)*

1. **Explain** why economists say there is no such thing as a "free" lunch.
2. **Identify** the cause of scarcity.
3. **List** the three basic economic questions each society must face.
4. **Explain** why economics is considered a social science.

SECTION 2 *(pages 14–17)*

5. **Explain** the meaning of a trade-off.
6. **Describe** the nature of an opportunity cost.
7. **Identify** the economic concept illustrated by the production possibilities frontier.

SECTION 3 *(pages 19–26)*

8. **Explain** the difference between a need and a want.
9. **Distinguish** between free products and economic products.
10. **Discuss** why services are excluded when the wealth of a nation is measured.
11. **Name** the factors of production used in production.
12. **Explain** why economists argue that productivity is important.
13. **Distinguish** between product markets and factor markets.
14. **Explain** why economic education is important.

Critical Thinking

1. **Drawing Conclusions** Think of circumstances that could change a free product to an economic one. What are they, and what characteristics must the new economic products have?
2. **Determining Cause and Effect** Suppose that Alpha, in **Figure 1.5** on page 16, decided to produce more butter and fewer guns. What would Alpha have to do to make the change? What would be the opportunity cost of producing more butter? What conditions would have to be met for the new mix of guns and butter to be on the production possibilities frontier?
3. **Analyzing Information** How will the study of economics help you become a better decision maker?
4. **Synthesizing Information** Examine the circular flow diagram in **Figure 1.8** on page 25 and explain how you fit into one or more parts of the overall process.

CHAPTER 1 REVIEW

Applying Economic Concepts

1. **Scarcity** What effect would a large increase in every citizen's income have on the economy of a nation?
2. **Trade-Offs and Opportunity Cost** If you decide to go to college after graduation from high school, what will be the opportunity cost of that decision? Use a specific example.

Reinforcing Skills

INTERPRETING LINE GRAPHS

Examine the line graph, then answer the questions below.

1. What is the subject of this line graph?
2. What information is shown along the horizontal axis?
3. What information is shown along the vertical axis?
4. Do the series shown in the graph reflect spending by all consumers? Explain.
5. Which category of consumer spending has increased the most over the years? By how much?
6. Which category of consumer spending has decreased the most over the years? By how much?

Individual Activity

Decision making is a part of everyday life. One area in which we must make decisions is in spending our income. Describe a decision that you may have to make about how to spend $50. Make a list of three to five alternatives from which you could choose. State the criteria you feel are most important in helping you judge the alternatives you have listed. Use the decision-making grid to evaluate each alternative in terms of your criteria. Make your decision.

Cooperative Learning Activity

Organize into groups of four or five. In your group, create an ideal economic society, listing the kinds of natural, human, and manufactured resources you would include in it. Then, compare the lists of all the groups, and write all the resources on the chalkboard. What prevents real life from having all these resources?

Writing About Economics

THE INFORMATIVE STYLE

In the **Journal Writing** activity on page 7, you were asked to keep track of all your "economic decisions"—the money you spent, the items you bought, the choices you made, and the reasons for making those choices—for one week. Using the informative style of writing discussed on page 554, explain how this awareness of your decisions helped you become a better decision maker.

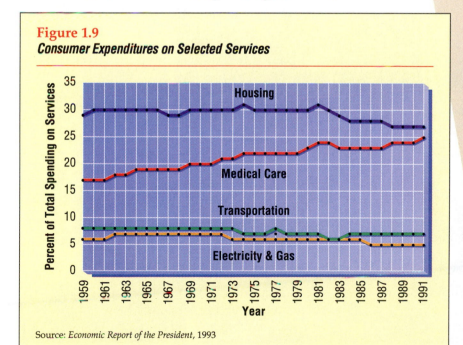

Figure 1.9
Consumer Expenditures on Selected Services

Source: *Economic Report of the President, 1993*

In a market economy, consumers have the opportunity to choose from a variety of goods and services.

CHAPTER 2

Economic Systems and Decision Making

CHAPTER PREVIEW

People to Know

- Anita Roddick
- Real Estate Agent

Applying Economic Concepts To Your Life

Consumer Sovereignty Have you ever asked, "Why doesn't someone invent a product that does this?" Or, "Whose idea was it to make that?" In effect, you're asking who decides the "WHAT to produce" question in our society. Government? Businesses? Another group? You're right if you said government and businesses, but another group bigger than both of those combined is the most influential. Consumers—including you—ultimately decide WHAT will be produced.

Journal Writing

For one week, be an inventor and write down ideas for products or services that you think should be produced. Keep in mind that your products should appeal to many consumers.

Economic Systems

Section Preview

Objectives

After studying this section, you will be able to:

1. **Describe** the characteristics of the traditional economy.
2. **Explain** the strengths and weaknesses of the command economy.
3. **Examine** the strengths and weaknesses of a market economy.

Key Terms

economic system, traditional economy, command economy, market economy

Applying Economic Concepts

Tradition Do your parents want you to follow in their footsteps? Enter the same profession? Take over the family business? Attend the same college they went to? *Tradition* plays a stabilizing role in our lives. Even the American free enterprise economy, characterized by freedom and competition, has some elements of tradition.

The survival of any society depends on its ability to provide food, clothing, and shelter for its people. Because these societies face scarcity, decisions concerning WHAT, HOW, and FOR WHOM to produce must be made.

All societies have something else in common. They have an **economic system,** or an organized way of providing for the wants and needs of their people. The way in which these provisions are made determines the type of economic system they have. Three major kinds of economic systems exist—traditional, command, and market.

Traditional Economy

Many of our actions spring from habit and custom. Why, for example, do so many people eat turkey on Thanksgiving? Why does the bride toss the bouquet at a wedding? Why do most people shake hands with strangers, or leave tips in restaurants? For the most part, these practices have been handed down from one generation to the next and have become tradition. ✓

In a society with a **traditional economy,** the allocation of scarce resources and nearly all other economic activity stems from ritual, habit, or custom. Habit and custom also dictate most social behavior. Individuals are not free to make decisions based on what they want or would like to have. Instead, their roles are defined by the customs of their ancestors. They know what goods and services will be produced, how to produce them, and how such goods and services will be distributed. 1

The Inuit society of northern Canada in the last century is an example of a traditional economy. For generations, parents taught their children how to survive in a harsh climate, make tools, fish, and hunt. Their children, in turn, taught these skills to the next generation.

The Inuit hunted, and it was traditional to share the spoils of the hunt with other families. If a walrus or bear was taken, hunters divided the kill evenly into as many portions as there were heads of families in the hunting party. The hunter most responsible for the kill had first choice, the second hunter to help with the kill chose next, and so on. Later, members of the hunting party shared their portions with other families, because the Inuit shared freely and generously with one another.

The hunter had the "honor" of the kill and the respect of the village—rather than a physical claim to the entire kill itself. Because of this tradition of sharing, and as long as skilled hunters lived in the community, a village could survive the long harsh winters. This custom was partially responsible for the Inuit's survival in northern Canada for thousands of years.

Traditional Economy *This Pueblo artist in New Mexico uses her ancestors' techniques for weaving.* **What drives economic activity in a traditional economy?**

Strengths

The main strength of a traditional economy is that everyone knows which role to play. Little uncertainty exists over WHAT to produce. If you are born into a family of hunters, you hunt. If you are born into a family of farmers, you farm. Likewise, little uncertainty exists over HOW to produce, because you do everything the same way your parents did. Finally, the FOR WHOM question is determined by the customs and traditions of the society. Life is generally stable, predictable, and continuous.

Weaknesses

The main drawback of the traditional economy is that it tends to discourage new ideas and new ways of doing things. The traditional society even punishes people for breaking rules or acting differently. The lack of progress leads to a lower standard of living than other types of economic societies have. **2**

Command Economy

Other societies have a **command economy**—one in which a central authority makes most of the WHAT, HOW, and FOR WHOM decisions. Economic decisions are made at the top, and people are expected to go along with choices their leaders make. Command economies can be found in North Korea, Cuba, and the People's Republic of China. Until recently, the communist bloc countries of Eastern Europe and the former Soviet Union also had command economies.

In the former Soviet Union, for example, the government made major economic choices. The State Planning Commission directed nearly all aspects of the Soviet economy. It determined needs, decided goals, and set production quotas for major industries.

If the State Planning Commission wanted to stress growth of heavy manufacturing, it shifted resources from consumer goods to that sector. If it wanted to strengthen national defense, it directed resources to the production of military equipment and supplies.

Checking Understanding

1. How are roles defined in a traditional economy?
2. What is the main weakness of a traditional economy?

Applying Economic Concepts

 Traditional Economy Elements of tradition carry over from one generation to the next in many American "household economies." Ask your parents what traditions they learned in regard to chores and money management.

Strengths

The main strength of a command system is that it can change direction drastically in a relatively short time. The former Soviet Union went from an agricultural society to a leading industrial nation in just a few decades. It did so by emphasizing heavy industry and industrial growth rather than the production of consumer goods.

During this period, the central planning agency shifted resources around on a massive scale. Consumer goods were virtually ignored, and when the country faced a shortage of male workers on construction projects, the government put women to work with picks, shovels, and wheelbarrows.

Weaknesses

Several important drawbacks limit the command economy. One is that the command system is not designed to meet the wants and needs of individuals. In the case of Soviet industrial development, an entire generation was forced to do without such consumer goods as cars, home appliances, and adequate housing. People often were told to sacrifice for the good of the state and the benefit of future generations.

A second weakness of the command economy is the lack of incentives for people to work hard. In most command economies, workers with different skills and responsibilities receive similar wages. In addition, people seldom lose their jobs, regardless of the quality of their work. As a result, some people work just hard enough to fill production quotas set by planners.

This pattern can have unexpected results. At one time in the former Soviet Union, central planners set production quotas for electrical motors to be measured in tons of output per year. Workers soon discovered that the easiest way to fill the quota was to add weight to the motor. As a result, Soviet workers made some of the heaviest electrical motors in the world. They also produced some of the heaviest chandeliers in the world for the same reason. Some were so heavy that they fell from ceilings.

A third weakness is that the command economy requires a large decision-making bureaucracy. Many clerks, planners, and others are needed to operate the system. Most decisions cannot be made until after consulting a number of people and processing a large amount of paperwork. These procedures slow decision making and raise the costs of production.

Yet a fourth weakness of a command economy is that it does not have the flexibility to deal with minor, day-to-day problems. Even when some change is needed, the sheer size of the bureaucracy discourages even the smallest adjustments. As a result, command economies tend to lurch from one crisis to the next—or collapse completely as in the case of the former Soviet Union.

Finally, people with new or unique ideas find it difficult to get ahead in a command economy. Opportunities for individual initiative are rare. Each person is expected to perform a job in a factory, in the bureaucracy, or on a farm according to the economic decisions made by central planners.

Market Economy

In a **market economy,** people and firms act in their own best interests to answer the WHAT, HOW, and FOR WHOM questions. In economic terms, a market is an arrangement that allows buyers and sellers to come together in order to exchange goods and services. A market could be in a specific location, such as a farmer's market or flea market. A list of phone numbers for lawn-mowing services posted on a local bulletin board also acts as a market. As long as a mechanism exists for buyers and sellers to get together, a market can exist.

In a market economy, people's decisions act as votes. When consumers buy a particular product, they are casting their dollar "votes" for that product. After the "votes" are counted, producers know what people want. Because producers are always looking for goods and services that consumers will buy, the consumer plays a key role in determining WHAT to produce.

Strengths

An ideal market economy has several advantages over traditional and command economies. First, a market economy can adjust to change over time. During the gasoline shortage of the 1970s, for example, consumers reduced their demand for large, gas-guzzling automobiles and increased their demand for smaller, fuel-efficient ones. Because automakers still wanted to sell cars, they moved resources from the production of large cars to small ones.

When gas prices leveled off in 1985 and then declined in 1986, the trend slowly began to reverse. Consumers wanted to buy large cars again, so automakers adjusted by making larger yet more fuel-efficient automobiles. Changes in a market economy, then, tend to be gradual. Unlike the traditional economy, change is neither prohibited nor discouraged. Unlike the command economy, change is neither delayed because of bureaucracy, nor suddenly forced on people by others.

A second major strength of the market economy is the freedom that exists for everyone involved. Producers may make whatever they think will sell. They also decide the HOW question by making their products in the most efficient manner. Consumers, on the

Figure 2.1
Comparing Economic Systems

	Traditional	Command	Market
STRENGTHS	*Sets forth certain economic roles for all members of the community	*Capable of dramatic change in a short time	*Is able to adjust to change gradually
			*Individual freedom for everyone
	*Stable, predictable, and continuous life	*Does not meet wants and needs of consumers	*Notable lack of government interference
			*Decentralized decision making
		*Lacks effective incentives to get people to work	*Incredible variety of goods and services
WEAKNESSES	*Discourages new ideas and new ways of doing things	*Requires large bureaucracy, which consumes resources	*High degree of consumer satisfaction
		*Has little flexibility to deal with small, day-to-day changes	
	*Stagnation and lack of progress		*Rewards only productive resources. Many people are too young, too old, or too sick to work.
		*New and different ideas discouraged, no room for individuality	*Must guard against market failures

Every society has an economic system, or an organized way of answering the WHAT, HOW and FOR WHOM questions. The type of system that is best for a society depends on the ability of that system to satisfy people's wants and needs, and to fulfill its economic goals. **What conditions must be met for a market economy to be effective?**

other hand, may spend their money on whatever goods and services they wish.

A third strength is the relatively small degree of government interference. Except for certain important concerns, such as national defense and environmental protection, the government tries to stay out of the way so that buyers and sellers can go about their business. As long as competition exists, the market economy tends to take care of itself.

A fourth advantage is that decision making in a market economy is decentralized. Literally billions—if not trillions—of individual economic decisions are made daily. Collectively, these decisions direct scarce resources into uses that consumers favor. Because individuals make these decisions, everyone has a voice in the way the economy runs.

A fifth strength of the market economy is the incredible variety of goods and services provided to consumers. Almost any product can and will be produced if a buyer for it exists. Recent products include everything from pocket cellular telephones to 24-hour cable television cartoon networks to pump basketball shoes. In short, if a product can be imagined, if it can be produced, and if consumers are willing to buy it, that product will be produced in a market economy.

A sixth strength is the high degree of consumer satisfaction. The wide range of products available in a market economy makes it possible for almost everyone to satisfy their tastes. In addition, a choice one group makes does not mean that another group cannot have what it wants. If 51 percent of the people want blue shirts, and 49 percent want white ones, people in both groups can still get what they want. Unlike an election, the minority does not have to live with choices the majority makes.

Weaknesses

The primary weakness of the market economy deals with the FOR WHOM question. In general, rewards in a market economy go to the most productive resources. This distribution system may be fine in the case of land or capital, but it can be a problem for the productive resource called labor. Some people may be too young, too old, or too sick to support themselves. These people would have difficulty surviving in a pure market economy without the government or private groups providing for their basic needs.

In addition, markets sometimes do not work as they should. Markets work best when three conditions are met. First, markets must be reasonably competitive, allowing producers to compete with one another to offer the best value for the price. Second, resources must be reasonably free to move from one activity to another. Workers, for example, need the freedom to change jobs if they do not like the ones they have. Likewise, producers need the freedom to produce the goods and services the best way they know how. Third, everyone should have access to adequate information so that alternatives can be known and wise choices made. If any of these conditions are not met, the market itself may fail.

SECTION 1 REVIEW

Reviewing Terms and Facts

1. **Define** economic system, traditional economy, command economy, market economy.
2. **Identify** the strengths and weaknesses of a traditional economy.
3. **List** the strengths and weaknesses of a command economy.
4. **Name** six strengths of a market economy.

Critical Thinking

5. **Making Comparisons** How are the WHAT, HOW, and FOR WHOM questions answered in the command and market economies?

Applying Economic Concepts

6. **Consumer Sovereignty** Give an example of a recent product that has succeeded and a product that has failed in our market economy because of consumers' influence.

CRITICAL THINKING SKILL

Formulating Questions

Imagine that your teacher asks you and three of your friends in class to do a group report on the traditional economy of the Inuit. After you say that you are not sure how to begin, the teacher suggests that you start by asking effective questions.

Explanation

Effective questions serve a specific purpose and provide desired information. If you ask questions without having a carefully planned strategy for doing so, much time can be wasted and confusion may result. Effective questions help you "get to the point" and allow you to better understand any given topic.

The three steps involved in formulating effective questions are:

a. Determine what information you need to know.
b. Decide what materials or people you should consult.
c. Consider what questions you should ask.

Practice

Note how the above steps are applied to asking effective questions about Inuit society.

An Inuit woman prepares fish the way her ancestors did.

a. What do you need to know?
  - the historical roles and significance of Inuit society members
  - the nature of Inuit activities in their present-day economy
b. Who or what should you consult for information?
  - your textbook
  - reference listings in the library
  - encyclopedias and other reference books
  - a person who is familiar with Arctic societies
  - magazines such as *National Geographic, American Heritage,* or *American History Illustrated*
c. What questions should you ask?
  - Who are the Inuit?
  - What specific tasks and roles do members of their society perform?
  - How do the Inuit learn their economic roles?
  - What elements limit change for the Inuit economy?
  - What problems and challenges do they encounter?
  - What effect, if any, has modern technology had on the traditional economy of the Inuit?

Now, suppose you want to learn about the command economy of the People's Republic of China. List at least five questions you should ask that relate to the topic and narrow its focus.

Additional Practice

For further practice in formulating effective questions, complete the Reinforcing Skills exercise in the Chapter 2 Review on page 51.

Section Preview

Objectives

After studying this section, you will be able to:

1. **Describe** the basic economic and social goals used to evaluate economic performance.
2. **Examine** the trade-offs among economic and social goals.

Key Terms

Social Security, inflation, fixed income

Applying Economic Concepts

Freedom and Equity Do you have enough *freedom* to do the things you want? Do your parents and friends treat you in an *equitable,* or fair, manner? More than likely, your answers to questions such as these have an effect on your happiness and satisfaction with life. People tend to ask the same types of questions about their economy. Does it allow them economic freedom? Is it equitable? The answers to these and other questions help us determine whether or not we are satisfied with our economic system.

Whether a particular economic system is best for a society depends on its ability to satisfy the needs of its people. These needs are, in part, defined by the economic and social goals the society sets for itself. Goals are important because they serve as benchmarks that help people determine if the system meets their needs. If a system meets most—but not all—of the needs, people may demand laws to change the system until their needs are met.

Economic and Social Goals
Federal legislation makes it illegal to discriminate against handicapped persons. **Why are economic goals important?**

Economic and Social Goals *In the Great Flood of 1993, thousands of people were displaced along the Mississippi River and its tributaries.* **What goal of the American economy was set to provide for those in need?**

Economic and Social Goals

In the United States, people share many broad social and economic goals. While it might be difficult to find them listed in any one place, they are repeated many times in the statements that friends, relatives, community leaders, and elected officials make. We can categorize those statements into seven major economic and social goals.

Economic Freedom

In the United States, people place a high value on the freedom to make their own economic decisions.

People like to choose their own occupation, employer, and uses for their money. Business owners like the freedom to choose where and how they produce. The belief in economic freedom, like political freedom, is one of the cornerstones of American society. **1**

Economic Efficiency

Americans recognize that resources are scarce and that factors of production must be used wisely. If resources are wasted, fewer goods and services can be produced and fewer wants and needs can be satisfied. Economic decision making must be efficient so that benefits gained are greater than costs incurred. ✔️

Checking Understanding

1. What are some of the economic choices people and producers in the United States are free to make?

Applying Economic Concepts

✔️ **Economic Efficiency** In 1813 Francis Lowell combined all the stages of textile production—spinning, weaving, bleaching, dyeing, and printing—under one roof. His efficient mill launched the nation's industrial revolution, changing manufacturing from the home to the factory.

Economic Equity

Americans have a strong sense of justice, impartiality, and fairness. Many people, for example, believe in equal pay for equal work. As a result, it is illegal to discriminate on the basis of age, sex, race, religion, or disability in employment. In addition, laws protect consumers against false advertising, unfair pricing, and dangerous products. Many private businesses even have retirement programs for their employees.

Economic Security

Americans desire protection from such adverse economic events as layoffs and illnesses. States have set up funds to help workers who lose their jobs. Many employers have insurance plans to cover the injuries and illnesses of their workers. On the national level, Congress has set up **Social Security**—a federal program of disability and retirement benefits that covers most working people.

Full Employment

When people work, they earn income for themselves while they produce goods and services for others. If people do not have jobs, however, they cannot support themselves or their families, nor can they produce output for others. As a result, people want their economic system to provide as many jobs as possible.

Price Stability

Another goal is to have stable prices. If **inflation**—a rise in the general level of prices—occurs, workers need more money to pay for food, clothing, and shelter. People on a **fixed income**—an income that does not increase even though prices go up—find that bills are harder to pay and that planning for the future is more difficult. Price stability makes budgeting easier and adds a degree of certainty to the future.

Economic Growth

The last major goal of most Americans is economic growth. Most people hope to have a better job, a newer car, better clothes, their own home, and a number of other things in the future. Growth is needed so that people can have more goods and services in the future. Because the population is likely to grow, economic growth is necessary to meet everyone's future needs.

Future Goals?

The seven goals listed above are ones on which most people seem to agree. As our society evolves, however, it is entirely possible that new goals may be added. Do people feel that a cleaner environment is important enough to be added to the list of goals? Should we add the preservation of an endangered species such as the spotted owl, humpback whale, or timber wolf to the list? In the end, Americans themselves must decide on the goals important to them.

Economic and Social Goals *Price stability is especially important to those people who have fixed incomes.* **What is a fixed income?**

Economic and Social Goals
A new pipeline in Alaska provides more oil for American consumers. At the same time, however, it disrupts the ecosystem of the Alaskan wilderness. **What other trade-offs can you cite?**

Trade-Offs Among Goals

People sometimes have different ideas about how to reach a goal. At other times, the goals themselves might conflict. Even economic policies have opportunity costs. A policy that keeps foreign-made shoes out of the United States could help the goal of full employment in the local shoe industry. This policy might work against individual freedom, however, if people ended up with fewer choices. A new shopping center built near the highway may stimulate economic growth. At the same time, it may threaten the stability and security of downtown merchants.

Even an increase in the minimum wage might involve a conflict of goals. On one hand, people might argue that an increase is the equitable, or "right," thing to do. Others might argue that increasing the minimum wage raises unemployment and restricts the freedom of employers to pay wages that they think are fair.

For the most part, people, businesses, and government usually are able to resolve conflicts of goals. Fortunately, the economic system of the United States is flexible enough to allow choices, accommodate compromises, and still satisfy the majority of Americans most of the time.

SECTION 2 REVIEW

Reviewing Terms and Facts

1. **Define** Social Security, inflation, fixed income.
2. **List** seven major goals of the United States economy.
3. **Explain** how an increase in the minimum wage might involve a conflict of goals.

Critical Thinking

4. **Analyzing Information** What characteristics does the United States economy have that allow it to resolve conflicts among goals?

Applying Economic Concepts

5. **Freedom and Equity** How do laws against false advertising promote economic equity?

ANITA RODDICK
(1942–)

A nita Roddick is a self-described former hippie, social activist, and wildly successful entrepreneur. In 1976 Anita and Gordon Roddick opened their first store—The Body Shop—in Brighton, England, with a $6,500 loan.

Born in the small English town of Littlehampton, Roddick worked in the family cafe. She graduated from the Maude Allen Secondary Modern School for Girls and nearly pursued a career as an actress. Instead, she studied English, history, and art at the University of Bath.

Roddick traveled extensively. Her sense of humor and adventurous spirit marked her as a maverick. Her company, The Body Shop, has proven to be a maverick, too.

Roddick's cosmetics are made from natural ingredients and renewable resources, which she discovered during her many travels. They are sold in inexpensive biodegradable or refillable containers. In addition, her products are never tested on animals.

women." The Body Shop, therefore, does not promote idealized notions of beauty. Anthropologists are hired to study how people in different cultures care for their skin and hair. Roddick then encourages local communities in developing countries to grow the natural ingredients used in her cosmetics.

Roddick is deeply involved with education and the campaign to preserve the rain forests. Her company trucks are painted with slogans such as IF YOU THINK EDUCATION IS EXPENSIVE, TRY IGNORANCE and THE INDIANS ARE THE CUSTODIANS OF THE RAIN FORESTS, THE RAIN FORESTS ARE THE LUNGS OF THE WORLD. IF THEY DIE, WE DIE.

FRANCHISING POLICY Roddick is a shrewd entrepreneur. When others clamored to open their own Body Shop stores, Roddick and her husband franchised the company. Store managers finance their own stores in return for the use of The Body Shop name and its products. By 1993, more than 900 stores had opened in more than 40 countries, with a new store being opened every 2½ days! Sales reached $231 million during the 1990-1991 operating year.

The Body Shop employs people in Nepal to create handmade paper from recycled materials.

COSMETICS Anita Roddick produces cosmetics. The Body Shop, however, is quite different from other cosmetics industries.

ENVIRONMENTALLY AWARE Roddick is sensitive to women's issues and global concerns. "I hate the beauty business," she declared in her autobiography. "It is a monster industry selling unattainable dreams. It lies. It cheats. It exploits

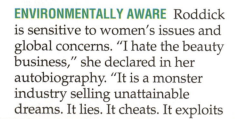

Examining the Profile

1. **Making Comparisons** What makes The Body Shop different from other cosmetics companies?

2. **For Further Research** Research and write about the effects of Roddick's TRADE NOT AID policies with developing nations.

Capitalism and Free Enterprise

Section Preview

Objectives

After studying this section, you will be able to:

1. **Explore** the characteristics of a free enterprise system.
2. **Describe** the role and importance of the entrepreneur.
3. **Examine** the role of the consumer as "sovereign" of the economy.
4. **Describe** the role that government plays in a free enterprise economy.

Key Terms

capitalism, voluntary exchange, private property, profit, profit motive, consumer sovereignty, mixed economy, modified private enterprise economy

Applying Economic Concepts

Voluntary Exchange Who benefits when you buy something—you or the seller? As long as the transaction involves a *voluntary exchange*, you may both benefit—or the exchange would not have happened in the first place. The market economy is very popular because of voluntary exchange—everybody benefits when a transaction takes place.

A market economy is sometimes described as being based on **capitalism,** a system in which private citizens own the factors of production. A market economy also is based on free enterprise, because businesses are allowed to compete for profit with a minimum of government interference. Both terms—*capitalism* and *free enterprise*—describe the United States economy.

the freedom to choose their occupation and their employer. To a lesser extent, they can choose to work where and when they want. They may work on the West Coast, East Coast, or in Alaska. They may work days, nights, indoors, outdoors, in offices, or in their homes.

Characteristics of a Free Enterprise Economy

A free enterprise economy has four important characteristics—economic freedom, voluntary exchange, private property, and the profit motive. These characteristics satisfy many of the economic goals that most Americans seem to share, and they encourage competition.

Economic Freedom

Economic freedom is a characteristic of capitalism often taken for granted. Individuals as well as businesses enjoy this freedom. People, for example, have

Economic Freedom *The freedom to own a business is a hallmark of free enterprise.* **What other characteristics does a free enterprise economy have?**

With economic freedom, people can choose to have their own business or to work for someone else. They can apply for jobs, and they have the right to accept or reject employment if offered. Economic freedom also means that people can leave jobs and move on to others that offer greater opportunity.

Businesses also enjoy economic freedom. They are free to hire the best workers, and they have the freedom to produce the goods and services they feel will be the most profitable. Businesses can make as many or as few goods and services as they want, and they can sell them wherever they please. They have the right to charge whatever price they feel is profitable, and they are free to risk success or failure.

Voluntary Exchange

A second characteristic of capitalism is **voluntary exchange**—the act of buyers and sellers freely and willingly engaging in market transactions. Moreover, transactions are made in such a way that both the buyer and the seller are better off after the exchange than before it occurred. Buyers, for example, can do many things with their money. They can deposit it in the bank, hide it under a mattress, or exchange it for goods or services. If they spend their money on a product, they must believe that the item being purchased is of greater value to them than the money they gave up. **1**

Figure 2.2
Characteristics of Free Enterprise and Capitalism

Economic Freedom
People may choose their jobs, employers, and how to spend their money.
Businesses may choose what products to sell and what to charge for them.

Voluntary Exchange
Buyers and sellers may engage freely and willingly in market transactions.

Private Property
People may control their possessions as they wish.

Profit Motive
People and organizations may improve their material well-being by making money.

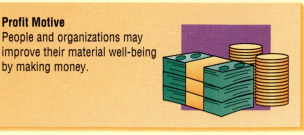

The terms free enterprise *and* capitalism *are often used to describe a market system in which the factors of production are owned by private citizens, and businesses are allowed to compete for profits with a minimum amount of government interference.* **What items are included under the category of private property?**

With voluntary exchange, sellers also have many opportunities to sell their products. If they exchange their goods and services for cash, they must feel that the money received is more valuable than the product being sold, or they would not sell in the first place. In the end, the transaction benefits both buyer and seller or it would not have taken place. Both the buyer and the seller got something they believed had more value than the money or products given up.

Private Property

Another major feature of capitalism and free enterprise is **private property,** the concept that people have the right and privilege to control their possessions as they wish. Private property includes both tangible items such as houses and cars and intangible items such as skills and talents. People are free to make decisions about their property and their own abilities. They have the right to use or abuse their property as long as they do not interfere with the rights of others. People can also sell or not sell their abilities or services as they see fit.

Private property gives people the incentive to work, save, and invest. When people are free to do as they wish with their property, they are not afraid to use, accumulate, or lend it. Private property also helps give people the incentive to get ahead. People know that if they succeed, they will be able to keep any rewards they might earn. **2**

Profit Motive

Under free enterprise and capitalism, people are free to risk their savings or any part of their wealth in a business venture. If the venture goes well for them, the people will earn rewards for their efforts. If things go poorly, they could lose part or even all of the

HELP WANTED

Real Estate Agent
▼

We want real estate agents to assist in renting, selling, and buying property for clients. In return, you will receive a percentage of the rent or sale price of the property. Your tasks will include obtaining listings—owner agreements to place properties for rent or sale—advertising the property, and showing the property to prospective renters and buyers. You must be familiar with fair-market values, zoning laws, local land-use laws, housing and building codes, insurance coverage, mortgage and interest rates, and credit and loan policies. You also may need to know about leasing practices, business trends, location needs, transportation, utilities, and labor supply. Agents often must work evenings and weekends because your schedule is determined by that of your clients.

▼

Education: High-school diploma and a real-estate license
Salary: Commission based on number of houses sold

investment. The very possibility of financial gain, however, leads many people to become entrepreneurs, or those who risk entering business in hopes of earning a profit.

What, however, is profit? Consider the earlier case of voluntary exchange. Remember that the buyer gives up money to obtain a product, and the seller gives up the product to obtain money. Unless both parties believe they will be better off afterward than

---

Checking Understanding

1. What is *voluntary exchange*?
2. What incentives does private property give people?

Applying Economic Concepts

☑ **Private Property** The right to inherit property is another feature of private ownership in a capitalist system. In the United States, people may arrange to leave their property to whomever they choose after they die.

Entrepreneurship *John Johnson started* Ebony *magazine in 1945. Today, his business has sales of $275 million annually.* **Why is Johnson considered an entrepreneur?**

before, neither will make the exchange. When exchange takes place, it does so only because both parties feel they will make a profit.

Profit, then, is the extent to which persons or organizations are better off at the end of a period than they were at the beginning. The **profit motive**—the driving force that encourages people and organizations to improve their material well-being—is largely responsible for the growth of a free enterprise system based on capitalism.

The Role of the Entrepreneur

The entrepreneur is one of the most important people in the economy. The entrepreneur organizes and manages land, labor, and capital in order to seek the reward called profit.

Entrepreneurs often start up new businesses. They are the ones who open new restaurants, automobile repair shops, video arcades, and computer stores. They include people who may have worked for others at one time, but have decided to quit and start their own businesses. Entrepreneurs want to be "their own boss" and are willing to risk everything to make their dreams come true. ✓

Many entrepreneurs fail. Of course, others survive and manage to stay in business with varying degrees of success. A few, and only a very few, manage to become fantastically wealthy and famous. Some of the better-known ones include Bill Gates, who founded Microsoft, John Johnson of Johnson Publishing Co., and Mary Kay Ash, who founded Mary Kay Cosmetics.

Despite the rate of failure among entrepreneurs, the dream of success is often too great to resist. The entrepreneur is both the spark plug and the catalyst of the free enterprise economy. When an entrepreneur is successful, everybody benefits. The entrepreneur is rewarded with profits, a growing business, and the satisfaction of a job well done. Workers are rewarded with more and better-paying jobs. Consumers are rewarded with new and better products. The government is rewarded with a higher level of economic activity and higher tax receipts. These receipts can be used to build roads, schools, and libraries for people not even connected with the original entrepreneur. 1

Nor does it stop there. Profits an entrepreneur generates attract an interest in the industry. When this happens, new firms rush in to "grab a share" of the profits. To remain competitive and stay in business, the original entrepreneur may have to improve the quality or cut prices, which means that customers can buy more for less. In the end, the entrepreneur's search for profits can lead to a chain of events that involves new products, greater competition, more production, higher quality, and lower prices for consumers.

The Role of the Consumer

In the United States, consumers often are thought of as having power in the economy because they determine which products are ultimately produced. For example, a company may try to sell a certain item to the public. If consumers like the product, it will sell, and the producer will be rewarded for his or her efforts. If consumers reject the product and refuse to

The Role of Government *Among other goods and services, local governments build and maintain city parks.* **How do state and local governments act as regulators?**

purchase it, the firm may go out of business. **Consumer sovereignty** describes the role of the consumer as sovereign, or ruler, of the market. More commonly, this is expressed in a different way by saying that "the customer is always right."

In recent years, producers have had outstanding successes with various products, including home video games, certain dolls, toy robots, and personal computers. Most consumers rejected other products, such as gasohol—gasoline with a 10 percent grain alcohol content—and diesel engines for cars.

Consumers' wants change constantly as modern communications and travel expose people to new ideas and products. Millions of consumers want home computers, even though they were barely known just 15 years ago. Americans use goods and services from every geographic area. Californians

soak their waffles in maple syrup made in Vermont, and New Englanders enjoy vegetables grown in Texas's Rio Grande Valley. Many Americans buy Japanese automobiles, Persian rugs, African purses, and European works of art.

Consumers, then, play an important role in the American free enterprise economy. They have a say in what is—and what is not—produced when they express their wants in the form of purchases in the marketplace.

The Role of Government

The economic system of the United States is highly complex. It is based primarily on free enterprise and capitalism, but it also includes elements of command

---

Checking Understanding

1. What aspects of the economy benefit when an entrepreneur succeeds?
2. How do American consumers express their wants?

Applying Economic Concepts

☑ **Entrepreneurship** Starting a business sometimes involves finding a new way to put together existing products and methods. Ray Kroc founded the McDonald's food chain, but he did not invent the hamburger or the drive-in restaurant.

and traditional economies. Even the role of the government in the United States economy reflects the desires, goals, and aspirations of its people. Government—national, state, and local—has become a protector, provider of goods and services, consumer, regulator, and promoter of national goals.

Protector

As protector, the United States government enforces laws such as those against false and misleading advertising, impure food and drugs, environmental hazards, and unsafe automobiles. It also enforces laws against abuses of individual freedoms. Employers, for example, cannot discriminate against workers because of their age, sex, race, or religion. In short, the government protects property rights, enforces contracts, and generally tries to make sure that everyone follows the "rules of the game" to ensure an efficient and fair economy.

Provider and Consumer

All levels of government provide goods and services for citizens. The national government supplies defense services, for example. State governments provide education and public welfare. Local governments often provide parks, libraries, and bus services. In the process, government consumes factors of production just like any other form of business.

Regulator

In its role as a regulator, the national government is charged with preserving competition in the marketplace. It also oversees interstate commerce, communications, and even entire industries such as banking and nuclear power. Many state governments regulate insurance rates and automobile registrations. Even local governments regulate business activity with their control over the granting of building and zoning permits.

Promoter of National Goals

Government reflects the will of a majority of its people. Many functions of government reflect people's desire to modify the economic system to achieve the economic goals of freedom, efficiency, equity, security, full employment, price stability, and economic growth. A government program such as Social Security, as well as laws dealing with the minimum wage and child labor, reveal how Americans have modified their free enterprise economy.

Because of these modifications, the United States is said to have a **mixed economy** or a **modified private enterprise economy**—one in which people carry on their economic affairs freely but are subject to some government intervention and regulation. This system most likely will undergo further change as the goals and objectives of the American people change.

SECTION 3 REVIEW

Reviewing Terms and Facts

1. **Define** capitalism, voluntary exchange, private property, profit, profit motive, consumer sovereignty, mixed economy, modified private enterprise economy.
2. **List** the four major characteristics of capitalism.
3. **Describe** the role of the profit motive in a free enterprise system.
4. **Explain** the importance of the consumer in a free enterprise economy.
5. **Identify** the four roles of the government in the American economy.

Critical Thinking

6. **Determining Cause and Effect** How have Americans' varying economic goals modified their free enterprise economy?

Applying Economic Concepts

7. **Voluntary Exchange** Cite at least three examples of voluntary exchanges you made this week. How are you better off by having made the exchanges? Did the person with whom you exchanged gain, too? How?

Vocabulary

The following terms are defined in Chapter 2:

SECTION ONE
- economic system (p. 32)
- traditional economy (p. 32)

- command economy (p. 33)
- market economy (p. 34)

SECTION TWO
- Social Security (p. 40)
- inflation (p. 40)
- fixed income (p. 40)

SECTION THREE
- capitalism (p. 43)
- voluntary exchange (p. 44)
- private property (p. 45)
- profit (p. 46)
- profit motive (p. 46)

- consumer sovereignty (p. 47)
- mixed economy (p. 48)
- modified private enterprise economy (p. 48)

Section 1
Economic Systems (pages 32–36)

Economic systems help societies provide for the wants and needs of their people. The three systems that have evolved over time are the traditional, command, and market economies.

In a **traditional economy,** the WHAT, HOW, and FOR WHOM questions are answered by traditions and customs handed down from generation to generation. Everyone has a specific role, but this can lead to an economy that remains stagnant.

In a **command economy**, a central authority decides the three basic questions. The individual has little or no role in economic planning. Command economies have one major strength, however—the ability to change production plans rapidly.

A **market economy** is characterized by freedom and decentralized decision making. Market economies have several strengths. Among these are the ability to adjust to change over time, personal freedom, a notable lack of government intervention, and the large variety of goods and services available to the consumer.

Reviewing the Main Idea
Why is economic decision making necessary?

Section 2
Evaluating Economic Performance (pages 38–41)

A society can use its goals to evaluate its economic system. In the United States, these goals include economic freedom, economic efficiency, economic equity, economic security, full employment, price stability, and economic growth.

While most Americans agree on these goals, it is not always possible to satisfy everyone at the same time. People's goals also are likely to change in the future as our economy evolves.

Reviewing the Main Idea
How is economic decision making different in traditional, command, and market economies?

Section 3
Capitalism and Free Enterprise (pages 43–48)

The economic system of the United States is based on **capitalism** and free enterprise. Characteristics of capitalism include four major features: economic freedom, **voluntary exchange, private property,** and the **profit motive.**

The driving force in the economy is the entrepreneur in search of profits. Consumers also play a major role in helping to determine WHAT to produce. The government's role is that of protector, provider and consumer of goods and services, regulator, and promoter of goals. The United States economy today is a **mixed economy** or **modified private enterprise economy** in which people conduct their economic affairs freely but with some government regulation.

Reviewing the Main Idea
What is the entrepreneur's role in the United States economy? The consumer's role? The government's role?

Reviewing Key Terms

Write the letter of the key term that best matches each definition below.

a. economic system   f. inflation
b. consumer sovereignty g. command economy
c. voluntary exchange   h. fixed income
d. private property   i. traditional economy
e. profit motive   j. capitalism

1. the idea that people rule the market
2. a society's organized way of providing for its people's wants and needs
3. the driving force that encourages people to improve their material well-being
4. a rise in the general level of prices
5. a system in which the factors of production are owned by private citizens
6. the right and privilege to control one's own possessions
7. an economic system in which habit and custom dictate most economic and social behavior
8. an economic system in which a central authority makes economic decisions
9. the situation in which the money one receives does not increase even though prices go up
10. the act of buyers and sellers freely conducting business in a market

Reviewing the Facts

SECTION 1 (pages 32–36)
1. **Describe** the main strength and weakness of a traditional economy.
2. **List** the five major weaknesses of the command economy.
3. **Explain** how consumers influence a market economy.
4. **Describe** how a market economy, a traditional economy, and a command economy adapt to change.

SECTION 2 (pages 38–41)
5. **Describe** the seven major economic goals upon which most Americans seem to agree.
6. **Identify** the objective of Social Security.
7. **Explain** how any two of the seven major economic goals might conflict.
8. **Explain** the importance of setting economic goals.

SECTION 3 (pages 43–48)
9. **State** how people and businesses benefit from economic freedom.
10. **Explain** the importance of the entrepreneur in a free enterprise economy.
11. **Provide** examples of how the government acts as protector, provider and consumer of goods and services, regulator, and promoter of national goals.

Critical Thinking

1. **Checking Consistency** Some people believe the profit motive conflicts with the goals of economic security and equity. Do you agree or disagree? Why or why not?
2. **Determining Cause and Effect** How can the movement of people and the communication of ideas affect the type of economic system a society has?

Applying Economic Concepts

1. **Tradition** Most people tip for service in restaurants, but not for service at clothing stores or gas stations. Explain how this illustrates economic behavior by tradition rather than by market or command.
2. **Freedom and Equity** Explain the role you as a consumer must play in obtaining economic equity for yourself.
3. **Economic Incentives** What incentive does owning private property give people?

Reinforcing Skills

FORMULATING QUESTIONS

You learned that asking effective questions is an important part of any research process. It helps you narrow the topic and determine what kinds of information to research.

The three steps involved in formulating effective questions are:
a. Determine what information you need to know.
b. Decide what materials or people you should consult.
c. Consider what questions you should ask.

News reporters, whose livelihood depends on asking effective questions, follow another simple formula. With every breaking story, they find out the five W's—who, what, where, when, and why? The five W's, however, are merely aids to asking effective questions. All five may not need to be answered. In some cases, who, what, and why are more important to answer than when and where.

In addition, be prepared to adjust your preliminary list of questions. After you start researching, the answers you get most likely will trigger new questions. Effective questions depend on a constant interplay between what you already know and what more you need to know.

Now, suppose you want to learn about the State Planning Committee of the former Soviet Union or the current command economy of North Korea. List at least five questions you should ask that relate to the topic and narrow its focus.

Individual Activity

Interview a local entrepreneur to learn what influenced that person to become an entrepreneur. What risks and challenges did he or she face in getting started? How did the entrepreneur learn about the business? How does one go about setting up a business in the area? What functions and/or regulations are performed by the local government? Do these regulations appear to be related to the seven goals stated in the chapter? After the interview, share your findings with the rest of the class.

Cooperative Learning Activity

Working in groups of three, select three nations that typify the three types of economic systems discussed in this chapter. Describe what has or has not been accomplished in the country because of the type of economic system that exists there. Include any other information that is relevant, such as the amount and pace of change that has occurred recently in the economy. As a group, prepare a chart—similar to Figure 2.1 on page 35—that briefly states your findings. Then have each member of your group take part in presenting the information in your chart to the rest of the class.

Writing About Economics

THE PERSUASIVE STYLE

In the **Journal Writing** activity on page 31, you were asked to write ideas for products and services you would like to produce. Using the persuasive style of writing discussed on page 554, write a paragraph persuading a consumer to buy one of your products.

This sole proprietor owns and operates a flower shop to make a profit.

CHAPTER 3

Business Organizations and Economic Institutions

SECTION 1
Business Organizations

SECTION 2
Business Growth and Expansion

SECTION 3
Other Organizations and Institutions

CHAPTER PREVIEW

People to Know

- J. Bruce Llewellyn
- Sales Clerk

Applying Economic Concepts to Your Life

Economic Institutions Do you work at a business? Belong to a church? Participate in a club? The United States has many different *economic institutions* that use, or represent, the factors of production needed to satisfy the needs and wants of consumers. Chances are these businesses and economic institutions play a significant role in your life.

Journal Writing

As you make purchases during the week, keep a record of all the businesses you visit. Classify each business according to its formal structure—sole proprietorship, partnership, corporation, or cooperative. In some cases, the firm's name may reveal the form of organization. In other cases you may have to ask the manager.

Business Organizations

Section Preview

Objectives

After studying this section, you will be able to:

1. **Describe** the characteristics of the sole proprietorship.
2. **Understand** the strengths and weaknesses of the partnership.
3. **Describe** the structure and features of the corporation.

Key Terms

economic institution, business organization, sole proprietorship, unlimited liability, inventory, fringe benefit, limited life, partnership, general partnership, limited partnership, articles of partnership, limited liability, corporation, incorporate, charter, stock, stockholder, shareholder, dividend, common stock, board of directors, preferred stock, proxy, bond, principal, interest, organizational chart, bankruptcy, unlimited life, revenue

Applying Economic Concepts

Stockholders More than likely, someone you know is a *stockholder*, or part owner, of a major corporation—perhaps IBM, General Motors, Disney, a local bank, or some other company. The United States has more than 3.5 million corporations, and it is not unusual for medium-sized corporations to issue several million shares of stock each. No wonder so many people are stockholders!

In the United States, many important decisions are made by **economic institutions**—persons and organizations that use or represent the factors of production. One of the major economic institutions is the **business organization**—a profit-seeking enterprise that serves as the main link between scarce resources and consumer satisfactions. Most farms, corner drugstores, hospitals, clothing and shoe stores, computer manufacturers, trucking companies, and law firms fall into this category. These businesses compete with one another for the chance to satisfy consumers' wants and needs.

Sole Proprietorships

The most common form of business organization in the United States today is the **sole proprietorship**—a business owned and run by one person. Although the most numerous of all business organizations, sole proprietorships generally are smallest in size. They collectively have only a fraction of the total sales of all business. Even so, they often are relatively the most profitable. As **Figure 3.3** on page 63 shows, sole proprietorships today earn almost one-fourth of all business profits. ✔

Sole Proprietorship *This baker has established a sole proprietorship so that he can be "his own boss."* **What are other reasons for establishing sole proprietorships?**

Forming a Sole Proprietorship

The sole proprietorship is the easiest form of business to start. No single way exists for setting up a sole proprietorship, and it involves almost no red tape except for occasional licenses and fees required by government agencies. Most sole proprietorships open for business as soon as they set up operations.

Someone could start a sole proprietorship simply by setting up a lemonade stand in his or her front yard. Someone else might decide to mow lawns, do gardening, open a grocery store, run a gas station, or open a restaurant. A sole proprietorship can be run out of a home or from an office space in a professional building. Sole proprietorships represent many different types of businesses.

Economic Strengths

The first strength of a sole proprietorship is the ease with which it may be started. If someone has an idea or an opportunity to make a profit, he or she has only to decide to go into business and then do it.

The second strength is the relative ease in managing a sole proprietorship. Decisions may be made quickly, without having to consult a co-owner, boss, or "higher-up." This gives the owner considerable flexibility, which is very important in some kinds of economic activity. If a problem comes up, the owner can make an immediate decision. **1**

A third strength is that the owner may enjoy the profits of good management without having to share them with other owners. The possibility of suffering a loss exists, but the lure of profits makes people willing to take risks.

Fourth, the sole proprietorship does not have to pay business income taxes because the business is not recognized as a separate legal entity. The owner still

Sole Proprietorships *Most sole proprietorships are small like this outdoor recreation shop.* **How does one set up a sole proprietorship?**

must pay individual income taxes on profits taken from the sole proprietorship, but the business itself is exempt from any tax on income. Aside from one or two minor reports, the owner does not even have to fill out any complicated tax forms beyond those normally required for wage and salary purposes at the end of the year.

Suppose, for example, Mr. Winters owns and operates a small hardware store in a local shopping center, as well as a small auto repair business in a garage next to his home. Because neither business depends on the other, and because the only thing they have in common is ownership, the two businesses appear as separate and distinct economic activities. For tax purposes,

Checking Understanding	**Applying Economic Concepts**
1. Who makes the decisions in a sole proprietorship?	**Market Structures** Sole proprietorships account for more than 70 percent of American businesses, yet only 6 percent of total sales.

Partnership *Partnerships represent about 9 percent of all business organizations in the United States.* **What may partnership agreements contain?**

however, everything is lumped together at the end of the year. When Mr. Winters files his personal income taxes, the profits from each business, along with wages and salaries earned from other sources, are combined. He does not pay taxes on each of the businesses separately.

A fifth strength of sole proprietorship is psychological. Many proprietors feel a certain amount of personal freedom by being their own boss. They also feel their satisfaction is worth more than a higher salary they might earn working for someone else. Some have a strong desire to see their name in print, have dreams of great wealth or community status, or want to make their mark in history.

A sixth strength is the ease of getting out of business if the owner decides to do so. The owner simply stops offering goods or services for sale. No complicated legal or tax considerations must be met.

Economic Weaknesses

One of the main weaknesses of a sole proprietorship is that the owner has **unlimited liability**. This means that the owner is personally and fully responsible for all losses and debts of the business. If the business fails, the owner's personal possessions may be taken away to satisfy business debts.

Consider, for example, the earlier case of Mr. Winters who owns and operates two businesses. If the

hardware business should fail, Mr. Winters's personal wealth, which includes the automobile repair shop, may be legally taken away to pay off debts arising from the hardware store.

A second weakness of a sole proprietorship is the difficulty in raising financial capital. Generally, a great deal of money is needed to set up a business, and even more is required to support its expansion. A problem may arise because the personal financial resources available to most sole proprietors are limited. Banks and other lenders usually do not want to lend money to new or very small businesses. The sole proprietor often raises financial capital by tapping savings or borrowing from family members.

A third weakness concerns size and efficiency. A business usually needs to be a certain size before it can operate efficiently. A retail store, for example, may need to hire a minimum number of employees just to be open during normal business hours. It may also need to carry a minimum **inventory**—a stock of finished goods and parts in reserve—to satisfy customers or to keep production flowing smoothly. The proprietor must have the financial capital to hire enough labor and inventory to operate efficiently.

A fourth weakness is that the proprietor often has limited managerial experience. The owner-manager of a small company may be an inventor who is highly qualified as an engineer but lacks the "business sense" or time to oversee the orderly growth of the company. This owner may have to hire others to do the types of work—sales, marketing, and accounting—that he or she cannot do.

A fifth weakness is the difficulty of attracting qualified employees. Because proprietorships tend to be small, employees often have to be skilled in several areas. In addition, many top high-school and college graduates are more likely to be attracted to positions with larger, well-established firms than small ones. This tendency is especially true when the larger firms offer **fringe benefits**, or employee benefits in addition to wages and salaries. Fringe benefits include paid vacations, sick leave, retirement, and health or medical insurance.

A sixth weakness of the sole proprietorship is **limited life**. This means that when the owner dies, quits, or sells the business, the firm itself legally ceases to exist. **1**

Partnerships

A **partnership** is a business jointly owned by two or more persons. It shares many of the same strengths and weaknesses of a sole proprietorship. Collectively, partnerships represent about 9 percent of all business organizations in the United States, but they have only a small fraction of total business sales and profits.

Types of Partnerships

The most common form of partnership is a **general partnership**, one in which all partners are responsible for the management and financial obligations of the business. In a **limited partnership**, at least one partner is not active in the daily running of the business, although he or she may have contributed funds to finance the operation. **2**

Partnership *Finding the right partner or partners is essential in a partnership.* **What is the difference between a general partnership and a limited partnership?**

Forming a Partnership

Like a proprietorship, a partnership is relatively easy to start. Because more than one owner is involved, formal legal papers called **articles of partnership** usually are drawn up to specify arrangements between partners. Although not always required, these papers state ahead of time how profits—or losses—are divided.

The partnership articles may specify that the profits be divided equally or by any other arrangement suitable to the partners. They also may state the way future partners can be taken into the business and the way the property of the business will be distributed if the partnership ends.

QUICK CHECK

Checking Understanding

1. What happens to a sole proprietorship when the owner dies?
2. What is the most common form of partnership?

Applying Economic Concepts

☑ **Market Structures** Partnerships are not limited to retail outlets. Many law firms, doctors, and dentists form partnerships as well.

Economic Strengths

Like the sole proprietorship, the first strength of the partnership is its ease of establishment. Even the costs of the partnership articles are minimal if they are spread over several partners.

Ease of management is the second strength. Generally, each partner brings different ideas and areas of expertise to the business. One partner might have a talent for marketing, another for production, another for bookkeeping and finance, and yet another for shipping and distribution. The partners usually agree ahead of time to consult with each other before making any major decisions.

Because the partnership is not a separate legal entity, a third strength is the lack of special taxes on a partnership. As in a proprietorship, the partners withdraw profits from the firm and then pay individual income taxes on them at the end of the year. The only minor difference is that each partner has to submit a special schedule to the Internal Revenue Service detailing the profits from a partnership. This schedule is for informational purposes only and does not give a partnership any special legal status.

Fourth, partnerships can usually attract financial capital more easily than proprietorships. They generally are a little bigger and, if established, have a better chance at getting a bank loan. If money cannot be borrowed, the existing partners can always take in new partners who bring financial capital with them as part of their price for joining the business. 1

A fifth strength of a partnership is the slightly larger size, which makes efficiency easier to reach. In some areas, such as medicine and law, a relatively small firm with three or four partners may be just the right size for the market. Other partnerships, such as accounting firms, may have literally hundreds of partners offering services throughout the United States.

A sixth strength is that many partnerships find it easier to attract top talent into their organizations. Because most partnerships today offer specialized services, top graduates seek out the more prestigious firms to apply their recently acquired skills in law, accounting, and other fields.

Figure 3.1
Stock Ownership

To own a share of stock is to own part of the company that sells the stock. A stockholder, then, owns part of a company's plant and equipment and has a voice in how the company is managed. The actual amount of a company that a stockholder owns varies with how many shares of stock are held. If a corporation offers a total number of 1,500,000 shares, for example, owning 15 shares means a stockholder owns a 1/100,000 part of that corporation. **How does common stock differ from preferred stock?**

Economic Weaknesses

The main weakness of a general partnership is that each partner is fully responsible for the acts of all other partners. If one partner causes the firm to suffer a huge loss, each partner is fully and personally responsible for the loss. This weakness is the same as the unlimited liability feature of a sole proprietorship. It is more complicated, however, because more owners are involved. As a result, most people are extremely careful when they choose a business partner. **2**

In the case of a limited partnership, the limited partner is not fully liable for the losses and debts of the business. This principle is known as **limited liability** and means that the investor's responsibility for the debts of the business is limited by the size of his or her investment in the firm. If the business fails, or if huge debts remain, the limited partner loses only the original investment, and the other partners must make up the rest.

A second weakness of the partnership is that it has limited life. As with sole proprietorships, when a partner dies, quits, or a new partner is added, the original firm legally ceases to exist. A business can, however, still exist in the eyes of the public even though it goes through a legal change. For example, the partnership of A, B, and C may be known as the Widget Company. If a change in ownership occurs, the new partnership may reach an agreement with the old one that allows it to use the same name.

A third weakness is the potential conflict between partners. Sometimes partners discover that they do not get along, and they either have to work together or leave the business. If the partnership is very large, it is fairly easy for these types of problems to develop, even though everyone thought they would get along well in the first place.

Corporations

Although many sole proprietorships and partnerships can be found in the United States, approximately 90 percent of all business is done by corporations. A **corporation** is a form of business organization recognized by law as a separate legal entity having all the rights of an individual. A corporation has the right to buy and sell property, enter into legal contracts, and sue and be sued.

Forming a Corporation

Unlike a sole proprietorship or partnership, a corporation is a very formal and legal arrangement. People who would like to **incorporate**, or form a corporation, must file for permission from the national government or the state where the business will have its headquarters. If approved, a **charter**—a government document that gives permission to create a corporation—is granted. The charter states the name of the company, address, purpose of business, and other features of the business.

The charter also specifies the number of shares of **stock**, or ownership parts of the firm. These shares are certificates of ownership and are sold to investors called **stockholders** or **shareholders**. The money is then used to set up the corporation. If the corporation is profitable, it may eventually issue a **dividend**—a check representing a portion of the corporate earnings or profits—to each stockholder.

Corporate Structure

After an investor purchases stock, he or she becomes an owner and has certain ownership rights. The extent of these rights, however, depends on the

---

Checking Understanding

1. Why are partnerships able to attract more capital than sole proprietorships?
2. What is the main weakness of a general partnership?

Applying Economic Concepts

☑ **Market Structures** The United States has more than 3.5 million corporations. This figure represents about 19 percent of American business organizations.

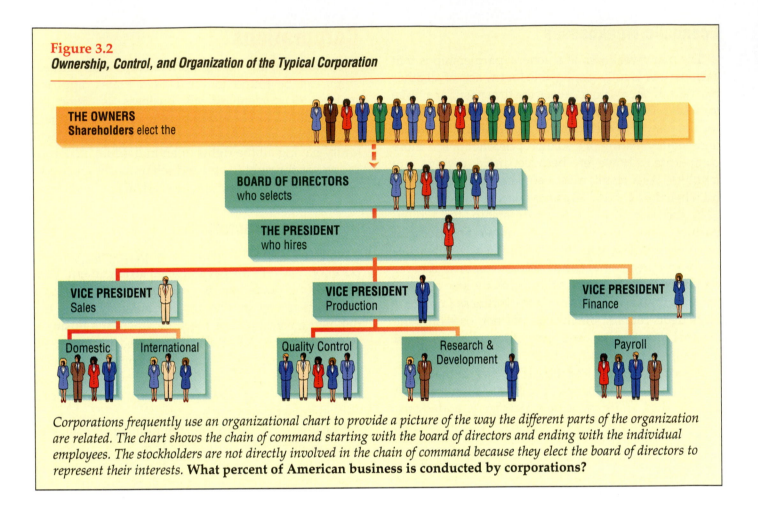

Figure 3.2
Ownership, Control, and Organization of the Typical Corporation

THE OWNERS
Shareholders elect the

BOARD OF DIRECTORS
who selects

THE PRESIDENT
who hires

VICE PRESIDENT
Sales

VICE PRESIDENT
Production

VICE PRESIDENT
Finance

Domestic

International

Quality Control

Research & Development

Payroll

Corporations frequently use an organizational chart to provide a picture of the way the different parts of the organization are related. The chart shows the chain of command starting with the board of directors and ending with the individual employees. The stockholders are not directly involved in the chain of command because they elect the board of directors to represent their interests. **What percent of American business is conducted by corporations?**

type of stock the investor purchases. The two types of stock available to the investor are common and preferred.

Common stock represents basic ownership of a corporation. The owner of common stock usually receives one vote for each share of stock owned. This vote is used to elect a **board of directors** whose duty is to direct the corporation's business by setting broad policies and goals. The board also hires a professional management team to run the business on a daily basis.

Preferred stock represents nonvoting ownership of the corporation. Owners of preferred stock receive dividends before common stockholders. If the corporation goes out of business, and if some property and funds remain after other debts have been paid, preferred stockholders get their investment back before common stockholders. They do not, however, have the right to elect representatives to the board of directors.

In theory, a stockholder who owns a majority of a corporation's common stock can elect board members and control the company. If the corporation is very small, the stockholder might even elect himself or herself—and other family members—to the board of directors.

In practice, this is not done very often, because most corporations are so large and the investment by the typical stockholder is so small. Most small stockholders either do not vote, or they turn their votes over to someone else. This is done with the use of a **proxy**, a ballot that gives a stockholder's representative the right to vote on corporate matters. **1**

Economic Strengths

The main strength of a corporation is the ease of raising financial capital. If the corporation needs more capital, it can sell stock to investors. The revenue can then be used to finance or expand operations.

Corporations *Owners of common stock elect a board of directors that, in turn, hires managers to run the business.* **How do common stockholders differ from preferred stockholders?**

In addition to selling stock, a corporation may decide to issue bonds. A **bond** is a written promise to repay the amount borrowed at a later date. **2** The amount borrowed is known as the **principal**. While the money is being borrowed, the corporation pays **interest**, the price paid for the use of another's money.

A second strength of a corporation is that the directors of the corporation can hire the best management available to run the firm. If the corporation is big enough, it can hire specialized talent in nearly all areas. Although some owners may know little or nothing about the business, the people who are running it do. Because the structure of a corporation is usually complex, a diagram called an **organizational chart** like Figure 3.2 is used to show how the different parts of a corporation are related.

A third strength of a corporation is that it provides limited liability for its owners. The corporation, not its owners, is fully responsible for its debts and obligations. Suppose, for example, a court finds that a cor-

poration owes a huge amount of money. The corporation might first try to work out some payment terms with the court. If that fails, it might try to satisfy its debt by selling off some assets of the corporation. If, however, the corporation cannot pay off the debt, it can declare **bankruptcy**, court-granted permission to not pay some or all of its debts, which forces it out of business. Under such circumstances, the investors (stockholders) would lose only their investment in the company, the amount limited to the money invested in stock. They would lose nothing else.

Because limited liability is so attractive, many firms incorporate just to take advantage of it. Suppose Mr. Winters who owns the hardware store and the auto repair business now decides to set up each business as a corporation. If the hardware business should fail, his personal wealth, which includes the automobile repair business, is safe. Mr. Winters may lose all the money invested in the hardware business, but that would be the extent of his loss.

Checking Understanding

1. How do most small stockholders vote on corporate business?
2. What is a corporate bond?

Applying Economic Concepts

Business Organizations In the early 1990s, two types of industries—wholesale/retail trade and service businesses—accounted for 48 percent of all the corporations in the United States.

A fourth strength of a corporation is **unlimited life**, meaning that the business continues to exist even when ownership changes. The corporate organization is recognized as a legal entity, or separate unit, so long as it continues to stay in business. Even if ownership changes, the name of the company stated in its charter stays the same, and the corporation continues to do business.

A fifth strength of the corporation is the ease of transferring ownership. If a person owns stock in a corporation but no longer wants to be an owner, he or she simply sells the stock to someone else, who then becomes an owner. It is much easier for the owner of a corporation to leave the business than for sole proprietors or partners to find buyers for their portions of ownership should they decide to leave.

Economic Weaknesses

One weakness of the corporate structure is the difficulty and expense of getting a charter. Depending on the state, attorney's fees and filing expenses can run from a few hundred to several thousand dollars. Because of this expense, many people prefer to set up sole proprietorships or partnerships.

Another weakness of the corporation is that the owners, or shareholders, have little say in how the business is run after they have voted for members of the board of directors. Many investors purchase stock because they hope to receive a dividend. Others buy stock hoping that it will increase in value over time so they can sell it for a profit. In most cases, however, the ability of the shareholder to influence corporate policy is limited to voting for the board of directors.

Because the corporation is recognized as a separate legal entity, it has to pay income taxes just like private individuals. The corporation is required to keep detailed records of **revenues**—earnings from sales, dividends, interest, or other operations—and expenses so that it can pay taxes on its profit.

Finally, corporations are subject to more government regulation than either sole proprietorships or partnerships. Corporations must register with the state in which they are chartered. If a corporation wants to sell its stock to the public, it must follow regulations set forth by the federal Securities and Exchange Commission (SEC). It may also have to provide certain financial information about sales and profits. Even an attempt to take over another business may require federal government approval.

SECTION 1 REVIEW

Reviewing Terms and Facts

1. **Define** economic institution, business organization, sole proprietorship, unlimited liability, inventory, fringe benefit, limited life, partnership, general partnership, limited partnership, articles of partnership, limited liability, corporation, incorporate, charter, stock, stockholder, shareholder, dividend, common stock, board of directors, preferred stock, proxy, bond, principal, interest, organizational chart, bankruptcy, unlimited life, revenue.

2. **Describe** the characteristics of the sole proprietorship.
3. **List** the strengths and weaknesses of the partnership.
4. **Explain** the strengths and weaknesses of the corporation.

Critical Thinking

5. **Predicting Consequences** When a corporation wants to introduce a potentially profitable but risky product, it frequently sets up a separate company that has its own corporate structure. Why do you think the corporation does this?

Applying Economic Concepts

6. **Economic Institutions** Find someone you know who owns shares of stock. Ask that person if their shares are common or preferred, and how often that person has a chance to vote for the management of that company. Research to find out the number of ownership shares issued by the corporation.

Reading a Circle Graph

Have you ever sat at a dinner table and watched someone dish out pieces of apple pie? When the pie is cut evenly, everybody gets the same size slice. If one slice is cut a little larger, however, someone else gets a smaller piece.

Explanation

A circle graph is like a sliced pie; often, it is even called a pie chart. Circle graphs show relationships among the parts of a whole and are used to show proportion rather than absolute amounts. By looking at a circle graph, you can see how the sections compare with each other in size. The size of these sections is determined by converting percentages to degrees, based on 360° in a circle.

To read a circle graph, follow these steps:
- Examine the graph to determine the subject of discussion.
- Identify the "slices" of the pie to see what each is supposed to represent. Sometimes each section is labeled directly on the graph; at other times you will have to refer to a key at the bottom of the graph.
- Look for numerical information included to help determine the relative size of the slices.
- Draw conclusions based on this information.

Practice

The "Numbers" circle graph in **Figure 3.3** may be analyzed in the following way:

- The whole—the uncut pie—represents the total number of business organizations in the United States.
- There is one section or "slice" for each form of business organization—sole proprietorship, partnership, and corporation.
- Numerical labels are given to indicate the exact percentages of each form of organization.
- Sole proprietorships are the most numerous; partnerships the least.

Examine the other two circle graphs in **Figure 3.3**, then answer the questions that follow.
1. Can you tell the total number of business organizations by looking at these graphs? Explain.
2. Is any single form of business organization responsible for more than one-half of the nation's sales? Explain.
3. Is it easy to conclude the answer to question 2 without looking at the percentages? Why or why not?
4. What percent of total sales do corporations have? How do you know?
5. Which form of business organization is relatively the most profitable (or has the largest percentage of profits for their sales)?

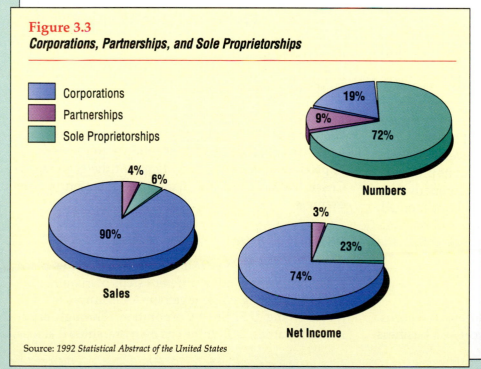

Figure 3.3
Corporations, Partnerships, and Sole Proprietorships

- Corporations
- Partnerships
- Sole Proprietorships

Numbers: 19%, 9%, 72%

Sales: 4%, 6%, 90%

Net Income: 3%, 23%, 74%

Source: *1992 Statistical Abstract of the United States*

Additional Practice

For further practice in reading circle graphs, complete the Reinforcing Skills exercise in the Chapter 3 Review on page 74.

Business Growth and Expansion

Section Preview

Objectives

After studying this section, you will be able to:

1. **Describe** two ways that businesses in the United States can expand and grow.
2. **Describe** the characteristics of the conglomerate.
3. **Explain** the nature of the multinational corporation and the way it differs from the conglomerate.

Key Terms

merger, horizontal merger, vertical merger, conglomerate, multinational

Applying Economic Concepts

Merger Have you ever noticed that the names of businesses, banks, and other financial institutions seem to keep changing? Sometimes firms change their names because they want to improve their image. More often, the names change because of a *merger*, when two or more businesses combine to form a single enterprise.

In the United States, many businesses expand by buying out or joining with another business. This process is called a **merger**, or combination of two or more business enterprises to form a single firm.

Business Combinations

When one corporation merges with another, one of the two usually gives up its separate legal identity. Sealtest, for example, merged with Southern Dairies when it bought Southern's common stock from investors. Southern then lost its corporate identity when its name was changed to Sealtest. ✅

Sometimes the firm that is bought out keeps its name for public relations purposes. When Kraft Foods later merged with Sealtest by buying Sealtest stock, the two became one legal entity. Because Sealtest was a brand name many people trusted, however, Kraft continued to use the Sealtest label on many of its products.

At other times, the name of the new company may reflect the identities of the companies that merged. When Chase National Bank and the Bank of Manhattan merged, the new organization was called the Chase Manhattan Bank of New York.

Reasons for Merging

Businesses tend to merge for different reasons. Sometimes the merger takes place because a business wants to be larger. When Kroger, a major Midwest retail food chain, merged with Dillon, another retail food chain, Kroger became one of the largest food retailers in the country.

Another reason for a merger is efficiency. When two firms merge, they no longer need two presidents, two treasurers, and two advertising agencies. The new firm can have more retail outlets, or manufacturing capabilities, without significantly increasing management costs. In addition, the new firm can standardize its products, buy more merchandise to get better discounts, and make more effective use of its advertising.

Horizontal Merger

Economists generally recognize two types of mergers. The first is a **horizontal merger**, which takes place when two or more firms that produce the same kind of product join forces. The merger of the two banks, Chase National and the Bank of Manhattan, is one example.

Vertical Merger

The second is a **vertical merger**, which takes place when firms involved in different steps of manufacturing or marketing come together. An example is USX, formerly the U.S. Steel Corporation. Through separate companies, USX mines its own ore, ships it across

Figure 3.4
Business Combinations

HORIZONTAL MERGER

NICKEL SAVINGS BANK + PEOPLE'S BUILDING & LOAN ASSOCIATION = NICKEL SAVINGS & LOAN ASSOCIATION

BOSTON ENTERPRISES = FAST DELIVERY, INC.

VERTICAL MERGER

HICKORY TREE FARMS + BOSTON ENTERPRISES

Horizontal mergers *involve businesses that make the same product or provide the same service. Sometimes, the name of the new company reflects the identity of the firms that merged.*

Vertical mergers *take place when firms taking part in different steps of manufacturing or marketing come together. Sometimes, one of the companies may lose its identity as a result of the merger.* **Why do companies merge?**

the Great Lakes, smelts it, and makes steel into many different products. Vertical mergers take place when companies believe that it is important to protect themselves against the loss of suppliers. 1

Conglomerates

A corporation may become so large through mergers and acquisitions that it becomes a conglomerate. A **conglomerate** is a firm that has at least four businesses, each making unrelated products, none of which is responsible for a majority of its sales.

Diversification is one of the main reasons for conglomerate mergers. Firms believe that if they do not "put all their eggs in one basket," their overall sales and profits will be protected. Isolated economic happenings, such as bad weather or the sudden change of consumer tastes, may affect some product lines at some point, but not all at one time. 2

During the 1970s and early 1980s, conglomerate mergers were popular in the United States. The cigarette and tobacco firm of R. J. Reynolds became a conglomerate, at one time owning the largest containerized shipping firm in the country (Sea-Land),

Checking Understanding

1. How do vertical mergers differ from horizontal mergers?
2. What is diversification?

Applying Economic Concepts

 Role of Government The federal government is concerned about mergers that allow a company to become a monopoly. The antitrust division of the Federal Trade Commission investigates suspicious mergers.

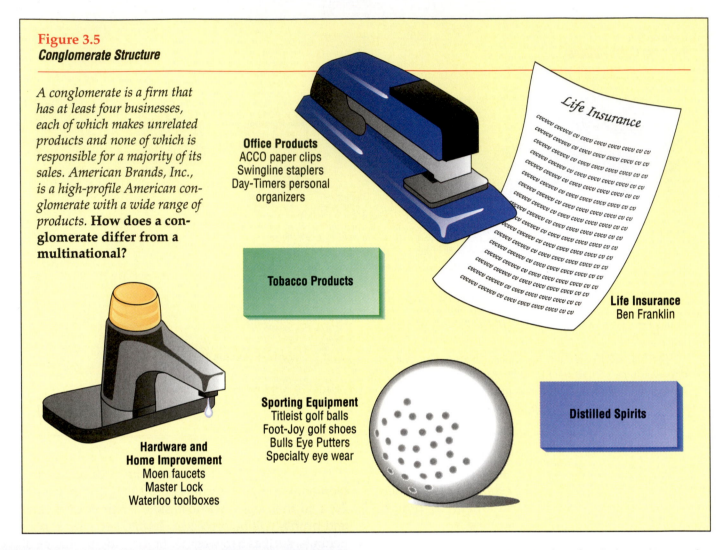

Figure 3.5
Conglomerate Structure

A conglomerate is a firm that has at least four businesses, each of which makes unrelated products and none of which is responsible for a majority of its sales. American Brands, Inc., is a high-profile American conglomerate with a wide range of products. **How does a conglomerate differ from a multinational?**

Office Products
ACCO paper clips
Swingline staplers
Day-Timers personal
organizers

Life Insurance
Ben Franklin

Tobacco Products

Hardware and Home Improvement
Moen faucets
Master Lock
Waterloo toolboxes

Sporting Equipment
Titleist golf balls
Foot-Joy golf shoes
Bulls Eye Putters
Specialty eye wear

Distilled Spirits

the nation's second largest fast-food chain (Kentucky Fried Chicken), the nation's largest fruit and vegetable processor (Del Monte), and the second largest producer of wine and distilled spirits (Heublein).

Since the late 1980s, interest in forming new conglomerates in the United States has declined. In Asia, however, conglomerates such as Samsung, Gold Star, and Daewoo are still dominant in Korea, as are Panasonic, Sony, and Mitsubishi in Japan.

Multinationals

Other large corporations have become multinational in scope. A **multinational** is a corporation that has manufacturing or service operations in a number of different countries. It is, in effect, a citizen of several countries at one time. As such, a multinational is subject to the laws of, and is likely to pay taxes in, each country where it has operations.

Multinationals are important because they have the ability to move resources, goods, services, and financial capital across national borders. A multinational with its headquarters in Canada, for example, is likely to sell bonds in France. The proceeds may then be used to expand a plant in Mexico that makes products for sale in the United States.

Multinationals may also be conglomerates if they make a number of unrelated products, but they are more likely to be called a multinational if they conduct their operations in several different countries.

Economic Strengths

Multinationals are usually welcomed for three reasons. First, multinationals help spread new technology worldwide. Second, they generate new jobs in areas where jobs are needed. Third, multinationals produce tax revenues for the host country. Many developing nations find the new technology, jobs, and revenue that multinationals provide helpful in improving their nations' economies.

Economic Weaknesses

Multinationals have several drawbacks. Because they are large and wealthy, they may influence the political life of a host nation. Multinationals also may

exploit the economy of the host nation by paying low wages to workers, by exporting scarce natural resources, or by adversely interfering with the development of local businesses. In addition, workers in major industrialized nations sometimes argue that when multinationals build a plant abroad, they take away jobs at home.

SECTION 2 REVIEW

Reviewing Terms and Facts

1. **Define** merger, horizontal merger, vertical merger, conglomerate, multinational.
2. **Describe** the two ways a business can merge.
3. **Explain** why corporations may become conglomerates.
4. **List** the strengths and weaknesses of multinationals.

Critical Thinking

5. **Evaluating Information** In a newspaper or magazine, find an article about a merger. What companies merged? What reasons, if any, were given for the merger? Was the merger horizontal or vertical? How can you tell?

Applying Economic Concepts

6. **Merger** Locate and report on an example of a merger in your community. Start by looking for a business that recently changed its name. Inquire to find out if it was a vertical or a horizontal merger. Ask about the previous names of the firms involved in the merger, and find out why they selected the current name for the merged enterprise.

PROFILES IN ECONOMICS

J. BRUCE LLEWELLYN

(1927–   )

J. Bruce Llewellyn—"The Boss" to those who know him—is an entrepreneur with a business record that matches his stature. Among other businesses, Llewellyn owns the Philadelphia Coca-Cola Bottling Co., the third largest African American-owned company in America.

The son of Jamaican immigrants, Llewellyn grew up working in his father's restaurant in White Plains, New York. He also sold Fuller Brushes and magazines on the side. He joined the army at age 16, then used his severance pay 4 years later to open a liquor

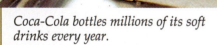

Coca-Cola bottles millions of its soft drinks every year.

store in Harlem and to finance his education. He received a degree in public administration from New York University, a Master's degree in Business Administration from Columbia University, and a law degree from the New York Law School.

FEDCO FOOD STORES

Llewellyn worked in the District Attorney's office in New York and was a partner in his own law firm. In 1969 he took a chance when a chain of 10 Fedco Food stores was put up for sale. Unable to come up with the $3 million price, he approached some banking friends and arranged one of the first leveraged buyouts attempted in the United States.

The chain was successful, and before long Llewellyn came to the attention of Washington, D.C. In 1978, President Jimmy Carter asked Llewellyn to be Secretary of the Army, but he turned it down

because the position did not involve business. He accepted Carter's second offer to join the Overseas Private Investment Corporation, however. This position gave him the opportunity to negotiate with foreign ministers and heads of state on large-scale investment projects.

COCA-COLA BOTTLING COMPANY

After he left Washington, Llewellyn teamed up with basketball star "Dr." Julius Erving and entertainer Bill Cosby to purchase one-third of the Coca-Cola Bottling Company of New York in 1983. Llewellyn then sold the profitable Fedco stores for $20 million and turned his interests to communications. He invested in radio and TV stations, eventually purchasing Queen City Broadcasting, a major TV station, in 1985. That same year, Llewellyn, Erving, and Cosby sold the New York Coca-Cola shares and purchased the entire Philadelphia Coca-Cola Bottling Company for $75 million. It, too, prospered under Llewellyn's leadership, with sales of about $266 million in 1992.

Friends and associates credit Llewellyn's success to his intelligence, his upbeat attitude, and his entrepreneurial knack of being able to organize business.

Examining the Profile

1. **Analyzing Information** How did Llewellyn diversify his holdings?

2. **For Further Research** Research and write about Llewellyn's leveraged buyout of Fedco Food stores.

Section Preview

Objectives

After studying this section, you will be able to:

1. **Describe** the purpose of various nonprofit organizations.
2. **Explain** the direct and indirect role of government in our economy.

Key Terms

nonprofit organization, cooperative, co-op, consumer cooperative, service cooperative, credit union, producer cooperative, labor union, collective bargaining, professional association, chamber of commerce, Better Business Bureau, public utility

Applying Economic Concepts

Nonprofit Organizations At one time or another, you have probably joined a church, club, or civic organization. Why did you join? To earn money? Probably not. Likewise, many of these organizations do not seek to earn profits, although they do share other characteristics of a business. They are *nonprofit organizations,* and they exist for reasons other than making money for their members.

Business organizations operate in hopes of earning a profit for their owners. Other economic organizations, including schools, churches, hospitals, and cooperative associations, operate on a "not-for-profit" basis. Still others, like labor unions and professional organizations, represent their members in matters of pay, working conditions, and the public perception of their members. Government is an economic institution as well.

Nonprofit Organizations

Many economic institutions, such as schools, medical care facilities, and churches, operate as **nonprofit organizations**. Similar to their profit-seeking counterparts, they work in a businesslike way to make the best use of scarce resources. The main difference is that nonprofit organizations do not seek financial gain for their members. They often provide goods and services to consumers while they pursue other rewards such as improving educational standards, seeing the sick become well, and helping those in need.

Many nonprofit organizations are legally incorporated to take advantage of the unlimited life feature. They are similar to profit-seeking businesses, but do not issue stock, pay dividends, or pay income taxes. Other examples include private welfare groups, adoption agencies, and youth or civic clubs. Their activities often produce revenues and expenses, but they keep the surplus to further the work of the institution.

Nonprofit organizations make use of the factors of production and serve many needs. Their efforts are difficult to analyze economically, however, because the value of their products is not easy to measure. Even so, the large number of these organizations shows that they are an important part of the productive process.

Cooperative Associations

Another example of a nonprofit economic organization is the **cooperative**, or **co-op**. A cooperative is a voluntary association of people formed to carry on some kind of economic activity that will benefit its members. Cooperatives fall into three major classes—consumer, service, and producer.

Consumer Cooperative

A **consumer cooperative** is a voluntary association that buys bulk amounts of goods, such as food and clothing, on behalf of its members. Its aim is to offer its members products at prices lower than those charged by regular businesses.

Figure 3.6
Cooperatives in the United States

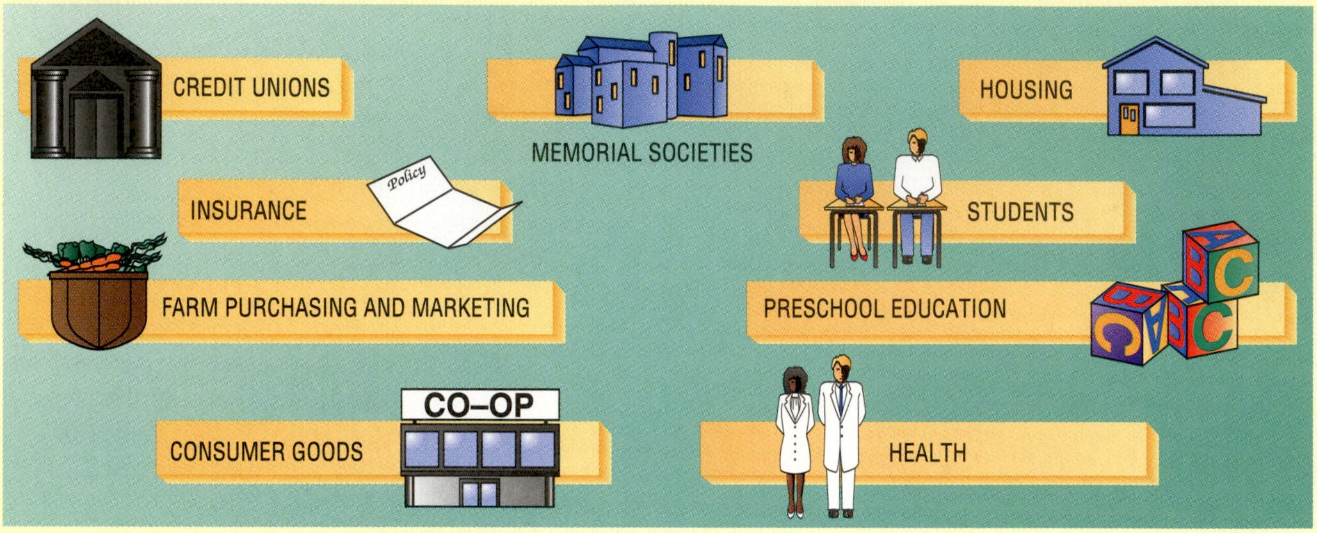

CREDIT UNIONS

MEMORIAL SOCIETIES

HOUSING

INSURANCE

STUDENTS

FARM PURCHASING AND MARKETING

PRESCHOOL EDUCATION

CONSUMER GOODS

CO-OP

HEALTH

Source: National Cooperative Business Association.

The cooperative, *or co-op, is a voluntary association of people formed to carry on some kind of economic activity that will benefit its members.* **How do the three kinds of cooperatives differ?**

Service Cooperative

A **service cooperative** deals with services rather than goods. Service co-ops offer members insurance, credit, and other similar services. One example of a service co-op is a **credit union** made up of employees from a particular company or government agency.

Credit unions receive their funds from members. In return, members earn interest on their deposits and may borrow money from the credit union. In most cases, they can borrow at better rates and more quickly than they could from for-profit banks or commercial loan companies. 1

Producer Cooperative

A **producer cooperative** helps members sell their products. In the United States, most cooperatives of this kind are made up of farmers. The co-op helps the farmers sell their crops directly to central markets or to companies that use the members' products. Some co-ops, such as the Ocean Spray cranberry co-op,

market their products directly to consumers. Any savings that the producer co-op makes in marketing costs go to its members.

Labor Unions

Another important economic institution is the **labor union**. A labor union, such as the United Auto Workers, is an organization formed to work for its members' interests in various employment matters. The union speaks for workers when disputes arise over pay, working hours, and other job-related matters. Labor union representatives also negotiate with management for benefits such as health care coverage, life insurance, and vacations. **Collective bargaining** refers to the negotiations between representatives of labor and management.

In the early days of organized labor in the United States, most unions were local. Later, some unions joined with others to become more powerful. In time, the labor movement reached most parts of the country, spread into Canada, and joined the international labor movement. Today most local unions are affiliated with a national or an international organization. Part of the local union dues that union members and workers pay goes to support the activities of the parent organization.

Professional and Business Organizations

Many workers belong to professional societies, trade associations, or academies. While these groups are similar to unions, they do not work in quite the same way.

Professional Associations

One such organization is a **professional association**—a group of people in a specialized occupation that works to improve the working conditions, skill levels, and public perceptions of the profession. Some professional associations require members of the profession to join; others have voluntary membership.

Many college professors belong to the American Association of University Professors. Lawyers belong to the American Bar Association, and some business leaders belong to the Financial Executives Institute or the American Management Association. Many social studies teachers belong to the National Education Association or the National Council for the Social Studies.

Business Associations

Often, businesses organize to promote their collective interest. Most cities and towns have a **chamber of commerce** that promotes the welfare of its members and the community. The typical chamber sponsors activities ranging from educational programs to neighborhood clean-up campaigns to lobbying for favorable business legislation.

Some business associations help protect the consumer. The **Better Business Bureau**, a nonprofit organization sponsored by local businesses to provide general information on companies, is one of these. It maintains records on consumer inquiries and complaints and sometimes offers various consumer education programs. **2**

Government

All levels of government play a dual role as links between consumers and resources. Sometimes government has a direct role, while at other times the role is more indirect.

Direct Role of Government

Many government agencies produce and distribute certain goods and services to consumers, giving government a direct role in linking consumers and resources. The federal government, for example, owns and operates the Tennessee Valley Authority (TVA). The TVA is a government corporation that uses the factors of production to produce electric power for a 7-state area in the South.

The federal government also uses many scarce resources to create a service that benefits all Americans—national defense. State and local governments use the factors of production to provide police and fire protection, rescue services, schools, and court systems. At the same time, all levels of government help develop and maintain roads, libraries, and parks. In

---

Checking Understanding	**Applying Economic Concepts**
1. Why do many people prefer to deal with credit unions rather than banks?	**Role of Government** The TVA was one of President Franklin Roosevelt's New Deal programs designed to combat the Great Depression. It built dams to generate power and bring electricity to the rural South.
2. What is the Better Business Bureau?	

these ways, government plays a direct part in the productive process.

Indirect Role of Government

The government plays an indirect role when it acts as an umpire to make sure the market economy operates as the rules say it should. One such case is the regulation of **public utilities**—investor- or municipal-owned companies that offer an important service to the public, such as water or electric service. Because most public utilities have no competitors, some government controls usually are needed. Government established regulatory control of the cable television industry in 1993 because it felt that some operators were charging too much. Without competition, utilities and other companies having exclusive rights in certain areas may not offer reasonable services at reasonable rates.

The government also plays an indirect role when it grants money to people in the form of Social Security, veterans benefits, financial aid to college students, and unemployment compensation. These payments give people a power they otherwise might not have—the power to "vote" in the market. When people cast votes in the form of dollars, they make their demands felt in the market. This power influences the production of goods and services that, in turn, affects the allocation of scarce resources.

The Role of Government *The federal government helps maintain the beauty of Yosemite National Park.* **What indirect roles does the government play?**

SECTION 3 REVIEW

Reviewing Terms and Facts

1. **Define** nonprofit organization, cooperative, co-op, consumer cooperative, service cooperative, credit union, producer cooperative, labor union, collective bargaining, professional association, chamber of commerce, Better Business Bureau, public utility.
2. **Identify** several nonprofit organizations in your community.
3. **Explain** the dual role of government as an economic institution.

Critical Thinking

4. **Evaluating Information** Make a list of 10 activities performed by your local government: for example, goods and services provided, regulations issued, laws enforced, and so on. Classify each as to its direct or indirect influences on the local economy.

Applying Economic Concepts

5. **Nonprofit Organizations** Name a nonprofit organization that you or one of your friends have joined. State the purpose of the organization, and then compare its activities to profit-making organizations. If your organization collects more than it spends, what does it do with the extra money?

Vocabulary

The following terms are defined in Chapter 3:

SECTION ONE
- economic institution (p. 54)
- business organization (p. 54)
- sole proprietorship (p. 54)
- unlimited liability (p. 56)
- inventory (p. 56)
- fringe benefit (p. 57)
- limited life (p. 57)
- partnership (p. 57)
- general partnership (p. 57)
- limited partnership (p. 57)
- articles of partnership (p. 57)
- limited liability (p. 59)
- corporation (p. 59)
- incorporate (p. 59)
- charter (p. 59)
- stock (p. 59)
- stockholder (p. 59)
- shareholder (p. 59)
- dividend (p. 59)
- common stock (p. 60)
- board of directors (p. 60)
- preferred stock (p. 60)
- proxy (p. 60)
- bond (p. 61)
- principal (p. 61)
- interest (p. 61)
- organizational chart (p. 61)
- bankruptcy (p. 61)
- unlimited life (p. 62)
- revenue (p. 62)

SECTION TWO
- merger (p. 64)
- horizontal merger (p. 64)
- vertical merger (p. 64)
- conglomerate (p. 65)
- multinational (p. 66)

SECTION THREE
- nonprofit organization (p. 69)
- cooperative (p. 69)
- co-op (p. 69)
- consumer cooperative (p. 69)
- service cooperative (p. 70)
- credit union (p. 70)
- producer cooperative (p. 70)
- labor union (p. 70)
- collective bargaining (p. 70)
- professional association (p. 71)
- chamber of commerce (p. 71)
- Better Business Bureau (p. 71)
- public utility (p. 72)

Section 1
Business Organizations (pages 54–62)

A **business organization** can be set up as a **sole proprietorship**, a **partnership**, or a **corporation**. Sole proprietorships are small, easy-to-manage enterprises one person owns. Partnerships are owned by two or more persons and are, for the most part, slightly larger in size than sole proprietorships. Individual investors called **stockholders** own corporations. Owners of **common stocks** vote to elect the **board of directors** who, in turn, selects a professional management team to carry out the corporation's policies.

Reviewing the Main Idea
What are three forms of business organizations?

Section 2
Business Growth and Expansion (pages 64–67)

Businesses may expand through combinations called **mergers**. Mergers take place because firms want to become bigger or more efficient. A **horizontal merger** occurs when two similar firms come together. A **vertical merger** is one that involves two or more firms at different stages of manufacturing a product.

Sometimes a series of mergers may result in a **conglomerate**, a very large firm that has at least four different businesses, none of which is responsible for a majority of sales. A **multinational** can be an ordinary corporation or a conglomerate, but it must have manufacturing or service operations in a number of different countries.

Reviewing the Main Idea
Why and how might a business expand?

Section 3
Other Organizations and Institutions (pages 69–72)

Nonprofit organizations operate like a business, but on a not-for-profit basis. Instead, they exist to further the benefit of a cause or the welfare of their members. Nonprofit organizations include churches, hospitals, schools, and **cooperatives**. They also include **labor unions**, **professional associations**, business associations, and government.

Reviewing the Main Idea
What are the features of nonprofit organizations?

Reviewing Key Terms

Classify each of the numbered terms below into the following categories (some terms may apply to more than one category):

Sole Proprietorships
Partnerships
Corporations
Nonprofit Organizations

1. bond
2. stock
3. organizational chart
4. incorporate
5. cooperative
6. dividend
7. unlimited life
8. charter
9. labor union
10. professional association
11. limited partner
12. general partnership
13. board of directors
14. credit union
15. proxy

Reviewing the Facts

SECTION 1 *(pages 54–62)*
1. **Explain** the strengths and weaknesses of a sole proprietorship.
2. **Identify** the strengths and weaknesses of a partnership.
3. **Explain** the structure and strengths of a corporation.

SECTION 2 *(pages 64–67)*
4. **Describe** the difference between a horizontal and a vertical merger.
5. **Explain** why a corporation would choose to become a conglomerate.
6. **Identify** the characteristics of a multinational corporation.

SECTION 3 *(pages 69–72)*
7. **Describe** the difference between a nonprofit institution and other forms of business organizations.
8. **List** three examples of cooperative associations.
9. **Describe** the purpose of a labor union.
10. **Identify** three types of business or professional organizations.
11. **Compare** the direct and the indirect roles of government.

Critical Thinking

1. **Making Comparisons** If you were planning to open your own business, which form of business organization would you prefer—sole proprietorship, partnership, or corporation? Give reasons for your answer.
2. **Evaluating Information** Do you think mergers are beneficial for the United States economy? Defend your response.

Applying Economic Concepts

1. **Economic Institutions** Cite a case in your community where a cooperative would fulfill a definite economic need. Explain why you think so, and then tell what kind of cooperative you would set up.
2. **The Role of Government** Which do you think is more appropriate—the direct or indirect role of government? Defend your position.

Reinforcing Skills

READING A CIRCLE GRAPH

Study the circle graph on page 75, then answer the following questions.
1. What does the whole of the circle graph represent?
2. How many industrial groups are represented in the graph?
3. Which industry has relatively more partnerships?

4. Can you tell exactly how many partnerships are in the Finance and Insurance industry? Explain.
5. Which industry has the fewest number of partnerships?

Individual Activity

List the strengths and weaknesses of each type of business organization discussed in Chapter 3. Then share the list with the owner of a business in your community. Ask the owner how his or her business is organized. Ask which items on the list were the most influential in deciding how to organize the business and if any additional items should be added to the list. Write a summary report stating whether you think that the form of business organization chosen was the best for the business.

Cooperative Learning Activity

Organize into small groups of three or four for the purpose of designing a new business. First, decide on a hypothetical product your firm would like to produce. Then consider how each of the following lettered items will affect the formal structure (proprietorship, partnership, or corporation) of the business.

(a) the risk of the product
(b) the amount of financial capital needed to open the business
(c) your willingness to share the profits with other owners
(d) the cost and amount of paperwork involved with the start-up of the business
(e) the amount of personal liability you are willing to assume for the actions of others

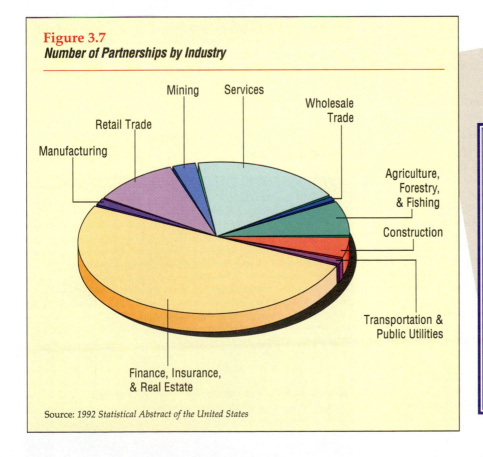

Figure 3.7
Number of Partnerships by Industry

Mining
Services
Wholesale Trade
Retail Trade
Manufacturing
Agriculture, Forestry, & Fishing
Construction
Transportation & Public Utilities
Finance, Insurance, & Real Estate

Source: 1992 Statistical Abstract of the United States

Writing About Economics

THE CLASSIFICATORY STYLE

In the **Journal Writing** activity on page 53, you were asked to keep a record of all the businesses you visited during the week, classifying each according to its formal business structure. Using the classificatory style of writing discussed on page 554, compare the products typically offered at the businesses you visited. Explain any patterns you noticed as to the type of products offered by the different forms of business structures.

SHOULD AIRLINES REMAIN DEREGULATED?

In the early 1970s, the commercial airline industry was one of the most closely regulated industries in the economy. For more than 40 years, the Civil Aeronautics Board (CAB) was charged with major supervisory responsibilities. Congress passed the Airline Deregulation Act of 1978, which phased out the CAB.

The intent of airline deregulation was to stimulate competition, increase productivity, and generate lower fares for consumers. Should airlines remain deregulated?

Pro

The nation's skies are full of fliers saving billions annually because of one of the federal government's rare successes, airline deregulation, begun 15 years ago.

The average fare (price charged per passenger mile) is a third less than in 1978. Fares have declined in 10 of the past 11 years.... In the first decade of deregulation, annual passenger traffic exploded from 250 million to 450 million....

Employment in the industry (average salary, $52,000) is up 75 percent since deregulation. The average number of accidents per year is down 53 percent.

Most secondary cities have more flights than in 1978, thanks partly to new regional airlines finding market niches....

Such airlines are prospering primarily because of low prices. Deregulation has proved that Americans have become aggressive shoppers for bargains.... The extinction of failed competitors is not a "problem"; it is freedom working through capitalism's process of creative destruction.

—GEORGE WILL, "NATION BENEFITS FROM AIRLINES' VIGOROUS COMPETITION," *THE COLUMBUS DISPATCH*, JULY 26, 1993.

▲ *Ticket agents reroute passengers whose flights were canceled.*

▼ *Air traffic controllers provide flight information for departing planes.*

Although many airlines have folded, new companies have provided competition. ◄

The ground crew hurries to ready the plane for departure. ▼

Con
Airline deregulation was supposed to bring more consumer choice, more price competition, and lower fares. At first, dozens of new airlines entered markets, forcing down prices. But the established carriers responded by selectively undercutting cheap fares, setting up "fortress hubs," and forcing the upstarts out of business. The airlines also used computerized reservation systems to complicate fare structures mercilessly.

I often fly between Boston and Washington. No matter how far in advance I book, the fare is $662.50 coach round-trip, and identical on all airlines. [I]f I were flying for a corporation that buys tickets in bulk, the fare would be about $300. . . .

Evidently, despite the mistaken theories of the deregulators, a highly capital-intensive industry with a standard product, such as airlines, cannot stand pure price-competition—for all the profits would soon be competed away. Airlines dwell not in an Adam Smith world but in a world . . . in which "efficiency" depends more on technical advances than on price wars.

. . . Discriminatory pricing should be prohibited. . . . The deregulators should admit that their experiment went down in flames.
—ROBERT KUTTNER, "FLYING IN THE FACE OF REASON: WHY THE SKIES NEED REREGULATING," BUSINESS WEEK, MAY 3, 1993.

Analyzing the Case Study

1. How was the airline industry affected by deregulation?
2. What evidence does George Will cite to explain that deregulation has positively affected the airline industry?
3. What evidence does Robert Kuttner cite to explain that deregulation has negatively affected the airline industry?
4. With which opinion do you agree? Why?

MICRO-ECONOMICS

The law of supply and demand is learned in infancy. The infant demands a clean diaper and is willing to supply peace and quiet in exchange. Mother demands peace and quiet and is willing to supply a clean diaper in exchange. The terms of trade are arranged. . . . One scream equals one diaper. The price of one diaper is one scream.

—Jude Wanniski, *The Way the World Works*, 1989

Economics and You

In this unit, discover what part economics plays in the following situations:
- Your favorite style of athletic shoes always seems to be sold out.
- The price of agricultural products decreases during the summer.
- The government regulates your local cable television company.

The forces of supply and demand are embodied in the buyers and sellers at the New York Stock Exchange.

People waiting in line to see a movie exemplify demand— the desire, ability, and willingness to pay.

CHAPTER 4

Demand

SECTION 1
What Is Demand?

SECTION 2
The Law of Demand

SECTION 3
Elasticity of Demand

CHAPTER PREVIEW

People to Know

- Ninfa Laurenzo
- Buyer

Applying Economic Concepts to Your Life

Demand Why is it unlikely that you will find many boat dealerships in a desert? Or many advertising agencies in a rural area? Before a business sets up shop, it researches the potential *demand* for its product. If consumers don't have the desire, ability, or willingness to buy the product, the business will not succeed.

Journal Writing

For one week, keep a journal of your expenditures. Separate the items into goods and services, being specific about the nature of the entries and the amount spent on each. If you buy gas for your car, for example, make a note of whether the gas is regular, premium, or some other type.

What Is Demand?

Section Preview

Objectives

After studying this section, you will be able to:

1. **Explain** the meaning and concept of demand.
2. **Explain** the purpose of a demand schedule.
3. **Illustrate** the concept of demand in the form of a graph.

Key Terms

demand, microeconomics, demand schedule, demand curve

Applying Economic Concepts

Demand In a market economy, your opinions count when you cast your dollar "votes" for the goods and services you like best. You express your *demand* for a product when you are willing and able to purchase it.

Most people think of demand as being the desire to have or to own a certain economic product. In this sense, anyone who would like to own a swimming pool could be said to "demand" one. In order for demand to be counted in the marketplace, however, wanting a product must coincide with the ability and willingness to pay for it. Only those people with **demand**—the desire, ability, and willingness to buy a product—can compete with others who have similar demands. **1**

Demand, like many other topics in this unit, is a microeconomic concept. **Microeconomics** is that part of economics that deals with behavior and decision making by small units, such as individuals and firms. Collectively, these micro concepts help explain how prices are determined and how individual economic decisions are made.

An Introduction to Demand

A knowledge of demand is essential to understand how a market economy works. Knowledge of demand is also important for sound business planning.

Suppose you are planning to start a television repair business. Before you begin, you need to know where the demand is. You should set up your shop in a neighborhood with many television sets and few repair shops. Less demand for your services would exist in areas having few television sets and many repair shops.

After you think you know where to locate the shop, how do you measure the demand for your services? You may visit other shops and gauge the reactions of consumers to different prices. You may poll consumers about prices and determine demand from this data. You could study data compiled over past years, which would show consumer reactions to higher and lower prices. ☑️

Location *The owner of a music store has set up shop near a stereo business.* **Why is this location a good one?**

Figure 4.1
The Demand for Compact Discs

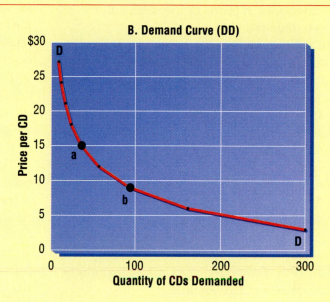

A. Demand Schedule

Price per CD	Number of CDs Demanded
$27	10
24	13
21	18
18	25
15	37
12	58
9	94
6	162
3	300

B. Demand Curve (DD)

The demand schedule is a listing that shows the amount demanded at each and every price. The demand curve shows the same information in the form of a graph. The graph shows that the demand curve is downward sloping, which means that more will be demanded at lower prices, and less at higher prices. **Why do you suppose that is true?**

All of these methods would give you a general idea as to the desire, willingness, and ability of people to pay. Gathering precise data on how consumers actually behave, however, is not easy. Even so, it is possible to treat the concept of demand in a more formal manner. Economists use schedules and diagrams to represent approximations of consumer behavior. Surveys, a valuable part of economic analysis, often strengthen predictions about people's behavior. 2

The Demand Schedule

If you asked people in different industries about the demand for their products, you would get many different answers. A person in the oil industry might say that the demand for oil is 46 million barrels per day. Someone in agriculture might say that the daily demand for wheat is 10 million bushels. Someone in the steel industry might say that the demand for steel is 2 million tons per day.

Checking Understanding

1. How do economists define demand?
2. What tools do economists use to measure demand?

Applying Economic Concepts

 Role of Government The Small Business Administration, an arm of the federal government, aids people who want to go into business. Part of this service includes conducting workshops where potential business owners learn how to gauge demand and set prices.

Although each person is in a different industry, they all have one thing in common. Each person has a general idea about current sales, and each sees demand as measured in terms of the sales volume in his or her own industry.

Economists, however, want to know more than the amount purchased at a certain price. They also want to know how much will be bought at higher and lower prices. The average price of crude oil may have been $17 per barrel last year, with 16 million barrels demanded at that price. How much oil would have been demanded if the price had been $21 or $12 per barrel? In economic analysis, demand means that the full range of possibilities has been considered.

Economists want to see the market as a whole. They want to know the amount people will demand at each and every possible price. The result, shown in **Figure 4.1**, is a **demand schedule**—a listing that shows the quantity demanded at all prices that might prevail in the market at a given time.

DID YOU KNOW?

The Demand for Jeans American consumers have the desire, ability, and willingness to pay for jeans. The total amount spent on jeans in 1992 amounted to $2,253,167,000.

Demand Illustrated

To see how an economist would analyze demand for an economic product, look at the demand schedule in panel A of **Figure 4.1**. The data in the schedule represent an estimate of the demand for compact discs in a certain store on a given day.

The schedule shows that if the price is $27 per disc, people would demand only 10 CDs. At a slightly lower price—$21—people would demand 18 CDs. As the price gets lower and lower, even more CDs would be demanded.

The demand for CDs also can be shown graphically. To do so, the information in the schedule simply is transferred to a graph. On the graph in **Figure 4.1**, point **a** shows that at a price of $15, people will buy 37 CDs. Point **b** shows the quantity demanded at $9, and so on. After all the price-quantity observations listed in the schedule have been transferred to the graph, the points are connected to form the curve that is labeled **DD**.

The curved line **DD** is the **demand curve** for CDs. The curve, like the schedule, tells the quantity that consumers will demand at each and every price. Both the demand schedule and the demand curve illustrate demand. The schedule presents the information in the form of a table. The curve, which is always downward-sloping, presents the information in the form of a graph.

SECTION 1 REVIEW

Reviewing Terms and Facts

1. **Define** demand, microeconomics, demand schedule, demand curve.
2. **Explain** how the common view of demand is different from the economist's view of demand.
3. **Describe** the relationship between the demand schedule and demand curve.

Critical Thinking

4. **Determining Cause and Effect** Explain how your dollars act as "votes" for the products you like best.

Applying Economic Concepts

5. **Demand** Record the names and approximate prices of the last two items you purchased. In general, would you have spent your money differently if the price of each item was twice as high? Would you have spent your money differently if each of the items cost half as much as it did? Explain your responses.

Determining Cause and Effect

As you read a mystery novel, you may try to figure out which events or actions caused the principal character to act in specific ways. When you read economics, you can make better sense of actions if you determine cause-and-effect relationships.

Explanation

A *cause* is any condition, person, or event that makes something happen. What happens as a result of a cause is known as an *effect*. The connection between what happens and what makes it happen is known as a cause-and-effect relationship.

A cause may have both immediate and long-term effects. An *immediate cause* leads directly to an event. If you are exposed to a virus, for example, you may catch a cold. Other indirect, underlying causes, however, may have contributed to the cold, such as lack of sleep or poor diet.

The following guidelines will aid you in identifying cases of cause-and-effect relationships in written material:

- Look for "clue words" that alert you to cause and effect, such as *because, led to, brought about, produced, as a result of, so that, thus, since, outcome, as a consequence, resulted in, gave rise to,* and *therefore.*
- Look for logical relationships between events, such as "She did this, and that happened."
- Cause and effect is usually expressed in more than one sentence or paragraph. Look for similar events in another time or place, and examine that event for similar causes and effects.

Practice

Several examples of cause-and-effect relationships as they relate to the Law of Demand are written below. Decide which action(s) is the cause and which is the effect. Remember that one cause may produce several effects, or one effect may result from several causes. Rewrite the sentences as one sentence, tying them together with a cause-and-effect clue word.

1. a. More cassette tapes are demanded.
   b. The price of cassette players goes down.

2. a. A substitute for gasoline is available.
   b. The price of gasoline goes down.

3. a. The price of bakery goods goes down.
   b. The price of sugar goes down.
   c. Customers buy more bakery goods.

High gasoline prices may cause more mass transit systems to be developed.

Additional Practice

For further practice in determining cause and effect, complete the Reinforcing Skills exercise in the Chapter 4 Review on page 101.

The Law of Demand

Section Preview

Objectives

After studying this section, you will be able to:

1. **Explain** the causes of a change in quantity demanded.
2. **Describe** the factors that could cause a change in the level of demand.
3. **Understand** the relationship between the demand curve and diminishing marginal utility.

Key Terms

Law of Demand, change in quantity demanded, income effect, substitution effect, change in demand, substitutes, complements, marginal utility, diminishing marginal utility

Applying Economic Concepts

Change in Demand More than likely, the number of CDs you buy is affected by your income. Would you buy more if you got a new job that paid twice as much? Would you buy fewer CDs if you lost your job or if your allowance stopped? A *change in demand* happens whenever you or others change the amount of a product you buy—even though the price of that product remains unchanged.

The exact prices and quantities illustrated in the demand schedule in **Figure 4.1** point out an important feature of demand in general. That is, relatively high prices are associated with relatively low quantities demanded. Similarly, low prices are associated with high quantities demanded. This relationship of demand and price is expressed by the **Law of Demand,** which states that the demand for an economic product varies inversely with its price. **1**

The correlation between demand and price does not happen by chance. Common sense and simple observation show that the Law of Demand works. For consumers, price is an obstacle to buying. When prices fall, consumers generally buy more. We all see the Law of Demand at work when consumers flock to stores on bargain days and during special sales when prices are temporarily reduced. ✓

Change in the Quantity Demanded

The table and graph in **Figure 4.1** show that 37 CDs are demanded at a price of $15 each. When the price falls to $9, however, 94 CDs are demanded. This movement *along* the demand curve shows a **change in quantity demanded**—or a change in the quantity

of the product purchased in response to a change in price. An examination of the income and substitution effects helps explain why this happens.

Law of Demand *If the price of bicycle gear drops, this shopper will be better able and more willing to buy a helmet.* **How does this situation reflect the Law of Demand?**

Figure 4.2
A Change in Demand for Compact Digital Discs

A. New Demand Schedule

Price per CD	Original Quantity of CDs Demanded	New Quantity of CDs Demanded
$27	10	14
24	13	18
21	18	25
18	25	36
15	37	52
12	58	81
9	94	132
6	162	227
3	300	420

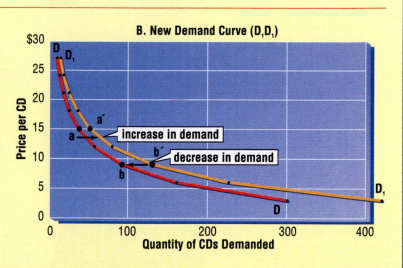

A change in demand means that people are willing to buy a different quantity at each and every price. An increase in demand occurs when the demand curve shifts to the right to D_1D_1. A decrease in demand occurs when the demand curve shifts to the left. **What might cause a change in demand for CDs?**

The Income Effect

When prices drop, consumers pay less for the product and, as a result, have some extra real income to spend. At a price of $15 per CD, consumers spent $555 to buy 37 CDs. If the price drops to $9, they will spend only $333 on the same quantity. The consumers are now $222 richer because of the drop in price, and they may spend more on CDs.

Part, but not all, of the increase from 37 to 94 units purchased is due to consumers feeling richer. This change in the amount purchased is known as the **income effect,** or the change in quantity demanded because of a change in the consumer's real income when the price of a commodity changes. 2

The Substitution Effect

A lower price also means that CDs will be relatively less expensive than other goods and services such as concerts, movies, and other forms of entertainment. As a result, consumers will have a tendency to purchase more CDs relative to these products. The **substitution effect** is the change in quantity demanded because of the change in the relative price of the product.

The rest of the increase from 37 to 94 CDs purchased that is not due to the income effect is a result of the substitution effect. Together, the income and substitution effects explain why consumers increase consumption of CDs to 94 when the price drops from $15 to $9.

QUICK CHECK

Checking Understanding

1. What is the relationship between price and quantity demanded?
2. How does the income effect change the quantity of a product demanded as the price of the product goes down?

Applying Economic Concepts

 Economic Systems The Law of Demand is a powerful force in our market economy. In a command economy, however, central planners choose what is produced and prices. Most command economies have failed, in part because they ignore consumer demand.

Consumer Tastes *Advertisers may spend millions of dollars annually to increase the popularity of their products.* **What happens to the demand curve for a product if consumers buy more of it at each and every price?**

Change in Demand

Sometimes we observe that people are willing to buy different amounts at the same prices. This is known as a **change in demand** and is different from a change in quantity demanded. When the *quantity demanded* changes, it does so because of a change in the price of the product, and movement occurs along the current demand curve. When there is a *change in demand*, the entire demand curve shifts—to the right to show an increase in demand or to the left to show a decrease in demand for the product. Therefore, a change in demand results in an entirely new curve.

A change in demand is illustrated in the schedule and graph in **Figure 4.2.** The schedule shows that people are willing to buy more at each and every price. At a price of $18, for example, consumers are now willing to buy 36 CDs instead of 25. At $15, they are willing to buy 52 CDs instead of 37. When this information is transferred to the graph, the demand curve appears to have shifted to the right to show an increase in demand.

Demand can change for several reasons. Changes in consumer incomes, consumer tastes, or the prices of related goods all can cause demand to change. When this happens, however, a new schedule must be constructed to reflect the new demand at all of the possible prevailing prices. **1**

Consumer Income

Changes in consumer income can cause a change in demand. As incomes rise, consumers are able to buy more products at each and every price. When this happens, the demand curve generally shifts to the right. If incomes decline, consumers buy less of a good at each and every price. The demand curve then shifts to the left, showing a decrease in demand. ✅

Consumer Tastes

Advertising, news reports, trends, and even seasons can affect consumer tastes. For example, when a product is advertised, its popularity increases and people tend to buy more of it. If consumers want more of an item, they buy more of it at each and every price. As a result, the demand curve shifts to the right. On the other hand, if people tire of a product, they buy less at each and every price, causing the demand curve to shift to the left.

Prices of Related Products

A change in the price of related products can cause a change in demand. Some products are known as **substitutes** because they can be used in place of other products. Butter and margarine are classic examples of substitutes, and a change in the price of one can affect the demand for the other.

An increase in the price of butter could cause the demand for margarine to increase. Likewise, an increase in the price of margarine would cause the demand for butter to increase. In general, the demand for a product tends to increase if the price of its substitute goes up. The demand for a product tends to decrease if the price of its substitute goes down. **2**

Other related goods are known as **complements,** because the use of one increases the use of the other. Film and cameras are two complementary goods. A decrease in the price of cameras means that more cameras will be sold, and that the demand for film will increase. In the same way, an increase in the price of cameras will cause a decrease in the demand for film. Thus, an increase in the price of one good usually leads to a decrease in the demand for its complement.

The Gillette Corporation makes razor handles and razor blades. To generate a high demand for their products, the price of razor handles is kept low. The profit earned on each razor handle is very small, but the razor blades are sold at very profitable prices. As a result, the company is able to use the profits on the blades to more than offset the profits lost on the handles. Given the complementary nature of the two products, it is unlikely that demand for Gillette blades would have been as high if the handles had been more expensive.

Diminishing Marginal Utility

By selecting from among alternative ways of spending their incomes, consumers try to get the most useful and most satisfactory combination of goods and services. In economics, remember, this usefulness or satisfaction from consumption is called utility.

How do people decide which economic products will provide them with the greatest utility? One answer is found in an analysis of what economists call **marginal utility**—the extra usefulness or satisfaction a person gets from acquiring one more unit of a product. Marginal utility is the amount of satisfaction added "at the margin."

For example, how much satisfaction would you get from a single glass of ice-cold lemonade after playing a hard game of tennis or basketball on a hot summer afternoon? Whatever amount you get is the marginal utility of that particular glass of lemonade. If you still are a little thirsty after drinking one glass of lemonade, you may decide to drink another. How much

QUICK CHECK

Checking Understanding

1. What is the difference between a change in demand and a change in quantity demanded?
2. Why are butter and margarine considered substitute goods?

Applying Economic Concepts

 Demand Economists classify a few goods as inferior goods. Demand for these goods varies inversely with income. People who are laid off may increase their demand for rice, potatoes, and bologna, even though their income goes down.

extra satisfaction will you get from the second glass? Once again, the extra satisfaction you get is the marginal utility of the second glass.

Consumers generally keep on buying a product until they reach a point where the last unit consumed gives enough, and only enough, satisfaction to justify the price. In the case of the lemonade, the marginal utility of the first glass probably is far greater than the initial amount you paid for the drink. Even the second glass may yield satisfaction greater than the price. In time, however, the marginal utility of still one more glass of lemonade will be less than its price. Sooner or later, the very thought of one more glass of lemonade may make you ill. When you reach the point that the marginal utility is less than the price, you will stop buying.

The lemonade example illustrates the principle of **diminishing marginal utility.** The principle states that the more units of a certain economic product a person acquires, the less eager that person is to buy still more. As people's wants for a particular product become more fully satisfied, they become less willing to spend their limited incomes to buy more of that product.

The principle of diminishing marginal utility can also be used to explain the downward-sloping nature of the demand curve. A shopper may decide to buy two sweaters at one price, for example, but would not

Diminishing Marginal Utility *These people cannot possibly eat another slice of pizza.* **How does this situation reflect the principle of diminishing marginal utility?**

buy three unless the price is even lower. The consumer gets the most utility from the first sweater, a little less from the second, and even less for the third. As a result of the diminishing marginal utility from each successive purchase, lower prices are necessary to encourage the shopper to buy more sweaters. In short, people will buy less at high prices and more when the price goes down.

SECTION 2 REVIEW

Reviewing Terms and Facts

1. **Define** Law of Demand, change in quantity demanded, income effect, substitution effect, change in demand, substitutes, complements, marginal utility, diminishing marginal utility.
2. **Describe** the difference between a change in quantity demanded and a change in demand.
3. **Explain** how the principle of diminishing marginal utility can be used to explain the shape of the demand curve.

Critical Thinking

4. **Drawing Conclusions** What happens to the price and the quantity of goods or services sold when a store runs a sale? How do these factors relate to the downward-sloping demand curve?

Applying Economic Concepts

5. **Change in Demand** Name a product that you recently bought because it went on sale. Identify

at least one substitute for that product, and a complement if possible. What happened to your demand for the substitute good when you purchased the sale item? What happened to your demand for the complementary item when you purchased the sale item? Distinguish between a change in quantity demanded and a change in demand.

Ninfa Laurenzo's story is a remarkable one. Widowed with 5 children in 1969, and faced with bankruptcy in 1973, she fought her way back to head a thriving, multimillion dollar corporation that operates 34 restaurants and employs more than 1,300 people. What happened between 1973 and 1993, and why was Laurenzo so successful?

In many ways, Ninfa Maria Laurenzo was similar to many other small business owners in America. She and her husband, Tommy Laurenzo, started a business making and wholesaling

Laurenzo and her son show off Ninfa's cuisine.

tortillas and pizza dough—a mix of products reflecting Laurenzo's Hispanic and her husband's Italian heritage—in Houston's barrio. Laurenzo was left with the small family business and five children after her husband's death.

NINFA'S, INC. As she struggled with the factory, debts mounted, and Laurenzo was soon hard-pressed to try something else. As a last resort, she mortgaged her house and, with a $5,000 loan from a friend, opened a small restaurant in a corner of the factory. The restaurant had 10 tables, and Laurenzo used the pots, pans, dishes, and silverware from her family kitchen. In July 1973, the restaurant opened to the public with $16 in the cash register and only her children to help.

One week later, a fire destroyed a portion of it, which had to be rebuilt. When it reopened, it offered a small but unique menu that combined the best of Mexican regional cuisine with some of the family's favorite Italian dishes. The food was well received, and the prices were right. Despite a modest expansion of the restaurant, the line of customers waiting for a table still stretched out into the street. A second restaurant was opened in 1976, followed by a third in 1977, and a fourth in 1978. Today, Ninfa's, Inc., includes 11 full-service restaurants known for their gourmet Mexican food.

EXPANSION Laurenzo, however, did not stop. In 1987 she opened the first of 10 Bambolino's Italian Kitchens. In 1989 Ninfa's, Inc., purchased Atchafalaya River Cafe, which offered a full range of authentic Cajun dishes, including barbecued alligator, gumbo, and an extensive seafood menu. Ninfa's, Inc., now owns a total of 34 restaurants in Houston, Dallas, and Lafayette, Louisiana.

Laurenzo's success was the result of a number of factors. Above all, she had an idea, a quality product, and the willingness to take enormous risks to make it work.

Examining the Profile

1. **Making Generalizations** How does Ninfa Laurenzo epitomize the entrepreneur's role in the American economy?

2. **For Further Research** Research to discover other entrepreneurial restauranteurs and how they made their niche in the American economy.

Elasticity of Demand

Section Preview

Objectives

After studying this section, you will be able to:

1. **Analyze** the elasticity of demand for a product.

2. **Explain** the three determinants of demand elasticity.

Key Terms

demand elasticity, elastic, inelastic, unit elastic

Applying Economic Concepts

Elasticity of Demand Why are you charged a premium price when a new movie first comes out? Why do prices tend to go down after the movie has been out for a few months? The answer is that the producer is maximizing the revenue collected from you and your friends. The *elasticity of demand* for a product helps to determine how the product will be priced—and how much you will pay for the product.

The Law of Demand shows that people buy more of an economic product at lower prices than at higher ones. It does not tell how much more, however. Likewise, if prices go up, sales will go down. How much will sales go down, however? If a business owner is thinking about raising prices, how much will be lost in sales?

Demand Elasticity

The answer to these questions is found in the concept of **demand elasticity**—a term used to indicate the extent to which changes in price cause changes in the quantity demanded.

Elastic Demand

The demand for most products is such that consumers do care about changes in price. Demand is **elastic** when a relatively small change in price causes a relatively large change in the quantity demanded. The demand for T-bone steaks, for example, generally is regarded as elastic. At a regular price of $5.59 per pound, only a certain number of people will buy it. If it is put on sale for $3.39 per pound, however, consumers may rush to buy this kind of steak.

Inelastic Demand

For other products, demand may be largely **inelastic,** which means that a given change in price causes a relatively smaller change in the quantity demanded. A higher or lower price for table salt probably will not bring about much change in the quantity bought because people can consume only so much salt. Even if the price was cut in half, the quantity demanded might not rise very much, if at all. Then, too, the portion of a person's annual budget that is spent on salt is so small that even if the price doubled, it would not make much difference to consumers.

Specific vs. General Market

When considering the elasticity of demand for a product, it is necessary to define the market being studied. The demand for gasoline at a particular gas station is likely to be very elastic. If the station raised prices by 10 percent, the amount of gasoline sold would drop significantly because some customers would buy it elsewhere. If the station lowered prices by 10 percent, the amount of gasoline sold would go up a great deal because people would go out of their way to buy "cheap" gasoline.

On the other hand, the demand for gasoline in general is likely to be inelastic. If all gas stations raised

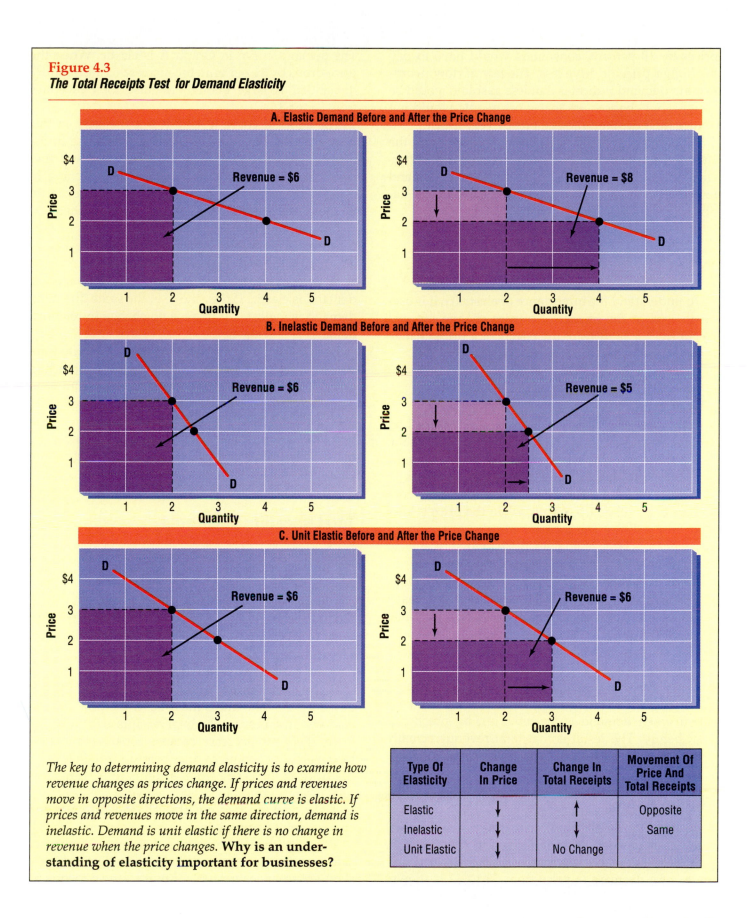

Figure 4.3
The Total Receipts Test for Demand Elasticity

A. Elastic Demand Before and After the Price Change

Revenue = $6

Revenue = $8

B. Inelastic Demand Before and After the Price Change

Revenue = $6

Revenue = $5

C. Unit Elastic Before and After the Price Change

Revenue = $6

Revenue = $6

The key to determining demand elasticity is to examine how revenue changes as prices change. If prices and revenues move in opposite directions, the demand curve is elastic. If prices and revenues move in the same direction, demand is inelastic. Demand is unit elastic if there is no change in revenue when the price changes. **Why is an understanding of elasticity important for businesses?**

Type Of Elasticity	Change In Price	Change In Total Receipts	Movement Of Price And Total Receipts
Elastic	↓	↑	Opposite
Inelastic	↓	↓	Same
Unit Elastic	↓	No Change	

prices by 10 percent, consumers would have to pay the higher price or drive less. The law of downward-sloping demand indicates that less gasoline would be bought, but chances are that most people would not reduce their demand for gasoline by very much.

Economists, then, are careful when discussing the elasticity of demand. It makes a great deal of difference, for example, whether the elasticity of demand for gasoline refers to the gasoline a particular gas station sells or to gasoline in general.

Total Receipts Test

To understand the importance of elasticity, it is useful to look at the impact of a price change on total receipts. This analysis of the effects of a price change is sometimes called the total receipts test.

How to Determine Total Receipts

Total receipts, or total revenue, are determined by multiplying the price of a product by the quantity sold. By observing changes in a company's total receipts when the price changes, we can test for elasticity.

If demand for a product is elastic, the amount consumers buy will go up sharply when the price is lowered only a little. The increase in sales at the lower price means a large enough increase in total receipts to surpass the total receipts earned at the original price.

If demand is inelastic, a lower price would mean a small increase in the quantity demanded. Increased sales would not be enough, however, for total receipts to rise.

The total receipts test also works the opposite way. If demand is elastic, higher prices will mean lower total receipts because the quantity demanded goes down sharply. The quantity demanded also goes down when demand is inelastic, but by much less than before. The result is that total revenue actually increases when prices are raised on inelastic goods.[1]

Three Results

The relationship between changing prices and total receipts or revenues is summarized in Figure 4.3. In each of the demand curves, the impact on total revenues of a decrease in price from $3 to $2 is shown.

The demand curve in Graph **A** is elastic. When the price drops by $1 per unit, the increase in the quantity demanded is large enough to raise total revenues from $6 to $8.

The demand curve in Graph **B** is inelastic. In this case, when the price drops by $1, the increase in the quantity demanded is not enough to prevent revenues from falling below $6. The demand curve in Graph **C** is called **unit elastic** because total revenues neither increase nor decrease when the price changes.

The three changes noted in the graphs are recorded in the table, which shows that the key to elasticity is the way that revenues and prices change. If revenues and prices move in opposite directions, demand is elastic. If they move in the same direction, demand is inelastic. If there is no change in revenue, demand is unit elastic.

Even though all the price changes illustrated are decreases, the results would be the same if prices had gone up instead of down. If the price rises from $2 to $3 in Graph **A,** for example, receipts fall from $8 to $6. Prices and revenues still move in opposite directions as shown in the table. The results of the summary table are also valid for the demand curves in Graphs **B** and **C**.

Total Receipts Illustrated

Observe the demand for sugar, as shown in the demand schedule and graph in Figure 4.4. Between 60 and 70 cents per pound, the demand for sugar is elastic. When the price falls from 70 cents to 60 cents, total receipts rise. When the price increases from 60 cents to 70 cents, total receipts go down. Prices and revenues thus move in opposite directions, so the demand curve is elastic in this region.

Between the prices of 40 to 50 cents per pound, however, the demand is inelastic. If the price is lowered within this span, the total receipts also would be lower. Receipts decrease because consumers are not responsive to changes in price below a certain level. If the price is increased from 40 cents to 50 cents, the total receipts would increase. Therefore, the key to the inelastic demand curve is that changes in price and changes in revenue are in the same direction.

Elasticity, then, is something that reveals how price changes affect revenues. Whether the demand for a product is elastic, inelastic, or unit elastic depends on

Figure 4.4
Elasticity of Demand for Granulated Sugar

A. Demand Schedule

Price per Pound	Number of Pounds Demanded	Total Receipts
$ .80	1,250	$1,000
.70	1,500	1,050
.60	2,000	1,200
.50	2,500	1,250
.40	3,000	1,200
.30	4,000	1,200
.20	5,000	1,000
.10	6,000	600

B. Demand Curve

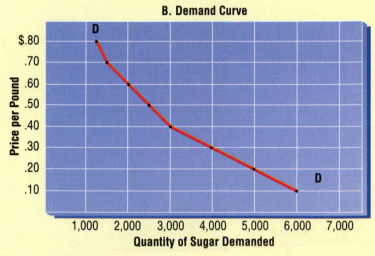

The elasticity of demand changes as prices change. At any price between $.80/lb and $.50/lb, demand is elastic because total receipts go up as prices go down. The revenue is unchanged between $.40 and $.30, which means that demand is unit elastic. When the price drops below $.30/lb, demand is inelastic because a drop in price causes a drop in revenue.
Which price will maximize total receipts?

the price range and the product being considered. The total receipts test will determine the proper classification of the product.

Elasticity and Pricing Policies

An understanding of elasticity helps businesses determine pricing policies that can be used to increase revenues. Physicians, for example, normally have an inelastic demand for their services. To raise their revenues, they simply raise their prices. On the other hand, the owner of a neighborhood gas station has an elastic demand for products. To increase revenues,

prices must be lowered. If the owner raised prices, customers would go to other stations, and the gas station's total revenues would fall.[2]

Analysis of demand elasticity has also helped telephone companies. The demand for local telephone services tends to be inelastic. As a result, the phone rates for local phone services have risen over the years. Demand for long-distance services, however, tends to be elastic. Phone companies tend to lower long-distance rates to increase the total revenue collected from consumers.

It may seem paradoxical, but the telephone industry has discovered that it can increase the amount of

Checking Understanding

1. How do economists use the total receipts test to determine whether the demand for a product is elastic or inelastic?
2. Why is it important for businesses to understand elasticity?

Applying Economic Concepts

Role of Government The federal government regulates the price of telephone services because telephone companies have monopolies in each market. Without regulation, the companies could charge whatever they pleased.

Demand Elasticity *The elasticity of demand for a product varies according to needs, substitutes, and amount of income for the purchase.* **Do you think the demand for a boat is elastic or inelastic? Why?**

revenue collected from consumers by lowering long-distance rates and raising local rates. Both pricing policies were predicted by examining the elasticity of demand for the services.

An understanding of demand elasticity also explains why the government taxes products with relatively inelastic demands. High taxes often are placed on utility services, tobacco, and alcoholic beverages because the demand for these products is relatively inelastic. People will pay almost any price, within limits, for these goods. A moderate tax on cigarettes, for example, has only a minor impact on the amount sold even though the price goes up. ✔️

Determinants of Demand Elasticity

We can estimate the elasticity of demand for a product by considering three factors: the urgency of need, the availability of adequate substitutes, and the amount of income required to buy the item.

Can the Purchase Be Delayed?

A consumer's need for a product is sometimes urgent and cannot be put off. One example is the case of insulin. If a diabetic needs insulin, an increase in its price is not likely to make him or her put off buying the drug. The demand for tobacco also tends to be inelastic because the product is addictive.[1]

In a less extreme case, such as the need for a tank of gasoline, the consumer might be able to wait a day or two. A limit still exists on the ability to go without, however. In such a case, the demand for the product is likely to be inelastic, so an increase in price causes only a small reduction in the amount bought.

A 50 percent drop in the price of insulin or gasoline probably would not cause a sustained increase in the amount bought. Sales may initially rise because of the lower price, but limits exist as to stockpiling these goods. A drop in the price of insulin probably would not cause the consumer to actually use more. A drop in the price of gasoline probably would have more of an impact on purchases in the long run than in the short run.

If the product were tomatoes or T-bone steaks instead of insulin or gasoline, people might react differently to price changes. If their prices increased, consumers could delay buying either of these items without suffering any great inconvenience. Consumers might buy much more if the price dropped significantly.

The ability to postpone the purchase of a product, then, is one of the determinants of elasticity. If the

Figure 4.5
Estimating the Elasticity of Demand

	ECONOMIC PRODUCTS							
Determinants of Elasticity Yes (elastic) No (inelastic)	Tomatoes	T-bone Steak	Table Salt	Gasoline from a Particular Station	Gasoline in General	Services of Medical Doctors	Insulin	Butter
Can Purchase Be Delayed?	yes	yes	no	yes	no	no	no	yes
Are There Adequate Substitutes?	yes	yes	no	yes	no	no	no	yes
Does Purchase Use A Large Portion Of Income?	no	no	no	yes	yes	yes	no	no
Type Of Elasticity	Elastic	Elastic	Inelastic	Elastic	Inelastic	Inelastic	Inelastic	Elastic

The elasticity of demand can usually be estimated by examining the answers to three key questions. All three answers do not have to be the same in order to determine elasticity, and in some cases the answer to a single question is so important that it alone might dominate the answers to the other two. **If you applied the three questions to a college education, what would be the elasticity of demand for higher education?**

purchase can be delayed, the demand for the product tends to be elastic. If it cannot be delayed, the demand tends to be inelastic.

Are Adequate Substitutes Available?

If adequate substitutes are available, consumers can switch back and forth between a product and its substitute to take advantage of the best price. If the price of steaks and butter goes up, buyers can switch to chicken and margarine. With enough substitutes, even small changes in the price of a product will cause people to switch. When this happens, the quantity sold at a single store may change a great deal, significantly impacting the store's total receipts.

If a product has many substitutes, the demand for it tends to be elastic. The fewer substitutes available for a product, the more inelastic the demand. **2**

Does the Purchase Use a Large Portion of Income?

The third determinant is the amount of income required to make the purchase. The demand for table

Checking Understanding
1. Why is the demand for insulin inelastic?
2. Why is the demand for a product with many substitutes elastic?

Applying Economic Concepts

 Taxation A key part of President Clinton's 1993 health-care reform plan was a hefty tax on cigarettes. The administration contended that because smokers had higher health-care costs, they should pay more to fund national insurance.

salt tends to be inelastic because a container usually costs less than a dollar and lasts several months. An increase in price is not likely to be noticed by the buyer or to affect the amount bought.

The purchase of a new car, however, is another matter. Because the average price of a new car is likely to be around $18,000, even a small increase can amount to several hundred extra dollars. People tend to be more sensitive to price increases or decreases on expensive items than on less expensive ones. When the products require a large portion of income, the demand tends to be elastic. When they require a small portion of income, the demand tends to be inelastic.

The three major determinants of demand elasticity are summarized in **Figure 4.5**. Some products, such as table salt, are easy to classify. Unless a salt-free diet is required for medical reasons, the consumption of salt is something that generally is not postponed. Salt is a product for which there are few adequate substitutes, and it requires only a small portion of income. Therefore, the demand for salt is inelastic.

Other cases are not as clear-cut. The demand for the services of doctors tends to be inelastic even though such services require a large portion of income. The lack of adequate substitutes and the reluctance to put off seeing a doctor when one is sick make the demand for such services inelastic. In the case of other products such as steak, tomatoes, and butter, the amount of

"Scalpel . . ."

Elasticity *If doctors' fees dropped significantly, there would be only a small change in quantity demanded.* **Why is this true?**

income required to purchase them probably is less important than the availability of substitutes and the ability to put off buying these products.

SECTION 3 REVIEW

Reviewing Terms and Facts

1. **Define** demand elasticity, elastic, inelastic, unit elastic.
2. **Explain** how total receipts are determined.
3. **List** the three determinants of demand elasticity.

Critical Thinking

4. **Making Generalizations** Determine your demand elasticity for air travel during holidays by answering these three questions: Can the purchase of a round-trip ticket be delayed? Are adequate substitutes available for air travel? Does the purchase consume a large portion of your income? Write a summary statement explaining your demand elasticity for air travel during holidays.

Applying Economic Concepts

5. **Demand Elasticity** Why are people willing to pay more for a movie when it first comes out, and why are movie theaters willing to lower the prices after the movie has been out for awhile? Analyze the three determinants of demand elasticity for new movies, as well as movies that have been out for several months, to see if theaters are maximizing their revenues in each case.

Vocabulary

The following terms are defined in Chapter 4:

SECTION ONE
- demand (p. 82)
- microeconomics (p. 82)

SECTION TWO
- demand schedule (p. 84)
- demand curve (p. 84)
- Law of Demand (p. 86)
- change in quantity demanded (p. 86)
- income effect (p. 87)
- substitution effect (p. 87)
- change in demand (p. 88)
- substitutes (p. 88)
- complements (p. 89)
- marginal utility (p. 89)
- diminishing marginal utility (p. 90)

SECTION THREE
- demand elasticity (p. 92)
- elastic (p. 92)
- inelastic (p. 92)
- unit elastic (p. 94)

Section 1

What Is Demand? (pages 82–84)

Demand is counted in the market when desire for a product is coupled with the ability and willingness to pay. This economic principle can be illustrated as a **demand schedule** that lists the quantity of a product people are willing to buy at various prices, and as a downward-sloping **demand curve** that graphically illustrates the same relationship.

Reviewing the Main Idea

Illustrate the concept of demand using both a schedule and a graph.

Section 2

The Law of Demand (pages 86–90)

The **Law of Demand** states that people will purchase more of a product at lower prices and less at higher prices. A **change in quantity demanded** means people buy a different quantity of a product if that product's price changes. This principle is shown graphically as a movement along the demand curve.

Whenever the price of a product changes, it generates both an **income effect** and a **substitution effect.** Both help explain why the demand curve is downward-sloping.

A **change in demand** means that people have changed their minds about the amount they would buy at each and every price. An increase in demand is illustrated by a shift of the entire demand curve to the right, a decrease by a shift to the left. Demand changes because of changes in consumer incomes, tastes, or the prices of related goods such as **substitutes** and **complements.**

Marginal utility tends to decrease with each successive purchase. The principle of **diminishing marginal utility** helps explain why the demand curve is downward-sloping. It states that consumers usually keep on buying a product until they reach a point at which the last unit consumed gives enough, and only enough, satisfaction to justify the price.

Reviewing the Main Ideas

What is the difference between a change in demand and a change in quantity demanded?

Section 3

Elasticity of Demand (pages 92–98)

Demand elasticity is a concept that relates changes in the quantity demanded to changes in price. If a change in price causes a relatively larger change in the quantity demanded, demand is **elastic.** If a change in price causes a relatively smaller change in the quantity demanded, demand is **inelastic.** Demand is **unit elastic** if a change in price does not affect the total revenues from the sale of the product.

A knowledge of demand elasticity is important because it tells businesses how a change in price will affect their total revenues. It also helps predict future price changes. Demand elasticity is influenced by the ability to postpone a purchase, the substitutes available, and the proportion of income required by the purchase.

Reviewing the Main Idea

How do the three determinants of demand elasticity help classify the elastic or inelastic nature of demand for a product?

Reviewing Key Terms

Match each word or phrase below with the correct illustration. Some will have more than one answer.

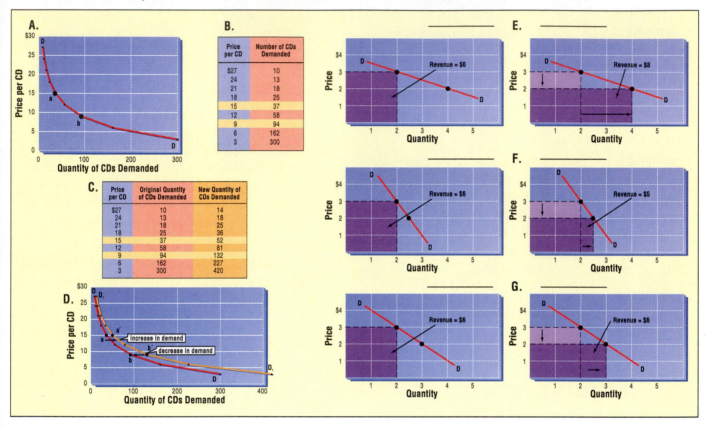

1. elastic demand
2. demand schedule
3. change in demand
4. unit elastic
5. demand curve
6. schedule showing change in quantity demanded
7. inelastic demand

Reviewing the Facts

SECTION 1 *(pages 82–84)*

1. **Explain** what demand means in economics.
2. **Describe** a demand schedule and a demand curve. How are they alike?
3. **Explain** why the demand curve is downward-sloping.

SECTION 2 *(pages 86–90)*

4. **Describe** the difference between a change in quantity demanded and a change in demand.
5. **Identify** the three factors that can cause a change in the level of demand.
6. **Explain** how the principle of diminishing marginal utility is related to the downward-sloping demand curve.

SECTION 3 *(pages 92–98)*

7. **Describe** the difference between elastic demand and inelastic demand.
8. **Explain** how the total receipts test can be used to determine demand elasticity.
9. **List** the three determinants of demand elasticity and describe their effects on the demand curve.

Critical Thinking

1. **Making Generalizations** Do you think the Law of Demand accurately reflects most people's behavior regarding certain purchases? Why or why not?
2. **Analyzing Information** List several examples of products that are so important that their use cannot be delayed or postponed. What type of demand elasticity are these products likely to have?

Applying Economic Concepts

1. **Demand** How do you think the demand for pizza would be affected by (1) an increase in everyone's pay; (2) an increase in the cost of gasoline; and (3) a decrease in the price of hamburgers? Explain your answers.
2. **Demand Elasticity** How would you, as a business owner, be likely to change the price of your product if you knew the demand elasticity of that product?

Reinforcing Skills

DETERMINING CAUSE AND EFFECT

For each statement below, write a sentence that is either a cause or an effect of the action in the statement.

1. *Cause:* The price of football tickets rises.
   Effect:
2. *Cause:*
   Effect: A record number of customers shopped at Sweater City today.
3. *Cause:* The price of gold drops.
   Effect/Cause:
   Effect:

Individual Activity

List five items you buy regularly. Use the determinants of demand elasticity in **Figure 4.5** on page 97 to classify each item and determine its overall elasticity. If the price of each item increased, what would happen to the total amount of money you would spend on each? What would happen to the amount spent if the price of each item decreased? Use the total receipts test to check your conclusions.

Cooperative Learning Activity

Working in teams of four, have each team interview four students in the school, asking the following questions: (a) What three purchases have you made recently? (b) Do any of these purchases represent a recent change in your buying habits? (c) Was the change caused by a change in income, a change in preference, or a change in the price of substitutes or complements?

After completing the interviews, each team should summarize the information it obtained. Categorize the purchases in which there was a change in demand according to the three reasons listed above. Each team should report its findings and discuss the conclusions drawn from this information.

Writing About Economics

THE CLASSIFICATORY STYLE

In the **Journal Writing** activity on page 81, you were asked to list your expenditures for one week, separating the items into goods and services. Using the classificatory style of writing discussed on page 554, describe the elasticity of the goods and services you purchased.

The higher the price of CDs, the more will be offered for sale.

CHAPTER 5

Supply

SECTION 1
What Is Supply?

SECTION 2
The Theory of Production

SECTION 3
Supply and the Role of Cost

CHAPTER PREVIEW

People to Know

- H. Ross Perot
- Market Researcher

Applying Economic Concepts to Your Life

Law of Supply How many hours do you spend studying every night? How many hours would you study if you were paid $1 an hour? $10 an hour? If you would study more for a higher price, you are following the *Law of Supply*, which states that the quantity supplied varies directly with its price.

Journal Writing

For one week, record every service or job you perform for someone else. Include any part-time jobs as well as errands, housekeeping chores, and baby-sitting, if pertinent. Organize the services and the amount of time spent on each into two columns: Paid Work and Unpaid Work.

Section Preview

Objectives

After studying this section, you will be able to:

1. **Understand** the meaning and concept of supply.
2. **Explain** the difference between the supply schedule and the supply curve.
3. **Explain** what is meant by a change in quantity supplied.
4. **Specify** the reasons for a change in supply.

Key Terms

supply, supply schedule, supply curve, Law of Supply, quantity supplied, change in quantity supplied, change in supply, subsidy, supply elasticity

Applying Economic Concepts

Supply If someone asks you to supply baby-sitting or yard work services after school, what is the first thing that comes to mind? If you are like most people, the answer is pay—and the higher the pay, the more work you are willing to supply. *Supply* is the amount of production—in this case, your efforts—provided over a wide range of prices.

When economists consider demand, they are interested in people's willingness and ability to purchase a product over a wide range of prices. In the case of supply, economists are concerned with people's ability and willingness to offer products for sale over a wide range of prices. 1

An Introduction to Supply

Economists are concerned with the market as a whole. They want to know how much of a certain product sellers will supply at each and every possible market price. **Supply**, then, may be defined as a schedule of quantities that would be offered for sale at all possible prices that could prevail in the market. The supply of television sets, for example, is the number of sets that manufacturers will likely produce if the prevailing market is $700, $500, $300, or any other price.

Everyone who offers an economic product for sale is a supplier. When you look for a job, you offer your services for sale. Your economic product is your labor, and you would probably be willing to supply more labor for a high wage than you would for a low one. ☑

All suppliers of economic products must make a similar decision. Each supplier must decide how much to offer for sale at various prices—a decision made according to what is best for the individual

Supply *Suppliers offer different models of electronic equipment at various prices.* **How does the price of a product affect the quantity offered for sale?**

seller. What is best depends, in turn, upon the cost of producing the goods or services. Still, it is reasonable to predict that the higher the price, the greater the quantity the seller will offer for sale.

Figure 5.1
The Supply of T-Shirts

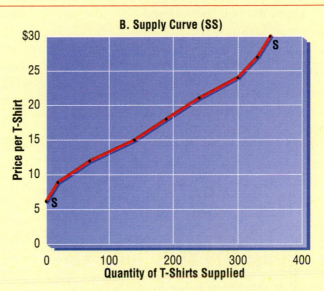

A. Supply Schedule

Price per T-Shirt	Quantity of T-Shirts Supplied
$30	350
27	330
24	300
21	240
18	190
15	140
12	70
9	20
6	0

The supply schedule is a listing that shows the quantity supplied at each and every price. The supply curve shows the same information in the form of a graph. The figure shows that the supply curve is upward sloping, which means that less will be supplied at lower prices, and more at higher prices. **How does the Law of Supply differ from the Law of Demand?**

Supply and the Supply Schedule

Suppose you are a Student Council officer whose job is to obtain T-shirts for every senior in your class. Because you will need so many shirts, you will want to get the best possible price. To do this, you could make inquiries, meet with manufacturers, and then ask for bids.

You would discover that when you offer a low price, some suppliers would not be interested in your business at all, and others would offer only small quantities. At a price of $9 a shirt, for example, suppliers might offer only 20 shirts. If you offered a higher price, such as $21 a shirt, they might be willing to supply 240 shirts.

After you gather all the data, you can construct a **supply schedule** like the one in panel **A** of **Figure 5.1**. The supply schedule tells the quantities offered at each and every possible market price.

Supply Curve

The data presented in the supply schedule also can be shown graphically. The **supply curve**, labeled **SS** in **Figure 5.1**, slopes upward and to the right to reflect the tendency of suppliers to offer greater quantities for sale at higher prices. **2**

The supply curve is the opposite of the demand curve. If you hold **Figure 5.1** in front of a mirror, you

Checking Understanding

1. How does supply differ from demand?
2. Why does the supply curve slope upward and to the right?

Applying Economic Concepts

 Role of Government In our modified market economy, the federal government guarantees most workers a minimum wage of $4.25 per hour. Workers who receive tips must earn an hourly wage of $2.13.

will see what looks like a demand curve. Just as the demand curve showed that greater amounts would be bought at lower prices, the supply curve shows that greater amounts will be offered for sale at higher prices.

Law of Supply

The tendency of suppliers to offer more for sale at high prices than at low prices forms the basis for the **Law of Supply**. The law states that the quantity supplied, or offered for sale, varies directly with its price. In other words, if prices are high, suppliers will offer greater quantities for sale. If prices are low, they will offer smaller quantities for sale. **1**

Change in Quantity Supplied

The amount that producers bring to market at any one price is called the **quantity supplied**. A **change in quantity supplied** is the change in amount offered for sale in response to a change in price.

In **Figure 5.1**, for example, 350 T-shirts are supplied when the price is $30. If the price decreases to $24, 300 T-shirts are supplied. If the price then changes to $21, 240 T-shirts are supplied. These changes illustrate a change in the quantity supplied, which is also represented as a movement *along* the supply curve.

In a competitive economy, producers generally react to changing prices in just this way. While the interaction of supply and demand usually determines the final price for the product, the producer has the freedom to adjust production. If the price falls, the producer may offer less for sale, or even leave the market altogether if the price goes too low. If prices rise, the producer may offer more units for sale to take advantage of the better prices.

Change in Supply

Sometimes producers offer different amounts of products for sale at all possible prices in the market. This is known as a **change in supply**.

The schedule and graph in **Figure 5.2** illustrate a change in supply. The schedule in panel **A** shows an increase in supply—with more T-shirts brought to market at each and every price. At the original price of $21

per shirt, 240 shirts were available. After the change in supply, 298 shirts were produced for the same price. The schedule shows a similar increase at every price, resulting in the supply curve shifting to S_1S_1.

For a decrease in supply to occur, less would be offered for sale at each and every price, and the supply curve would shift to the left. Changes in supply, whether increases or decreases, occur for the following reasons.

Cost of Inputs

A change in the cost of inputs could cause a change in supply. In the T-shirt illustration, supply may have increased because of a decline in the cost of such inputs as cotton or ink. If the price of the inputs goes down, producers can produce more T-shirts at each and every price.

An increase in the cost of inputs has the opposite effect. If cotton, ink, and labor costs rose, producers would not be willing to produce as many shirts at each and every price. Instead, they would offer fewer products for sale, and the supply curve would shift to the left.

Productivity

If management motivates its workers to do a better job or if workers are trained to work more efficiently, productivity increases. More T-shirts would be produced during every production period. The supply curve shifts to the right because more shirts are produced at every possible price in the market.

If workers are unmotivated, untrained, or unhappy, productivity decreases. The supply curve shifts to the left because fewer goods are brought to the market at every possible price.

Technology

New technology tends to shift the supply curve to the right. The introduction of a new machine, chemical, or industrial process can affect supply by lowering the cost of production. When production costs go down, the producer is usually willing to produce more goods and services at each and every price in the market. **2**

New technologies do not always work as expected, of course. Equipment might break down or parts

Figure 5.2
A Change in the Supply of T-Shirts

A. New Supply Schedule

Price per T-Shirt	Original Number of T-Shirts Supplied	New Number of T-Shirts Supplied
$30	350	430
27	330	406
24	300	370
21	240	298
18	190	238
15	140	178
12	70	94
9	20	34
6	0	0

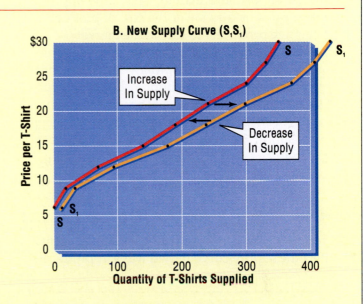

B. New Supply Curve (S,S₁)

A change in supply means that producers are willing to offer a different quantity for sale at each and every price. An increase in supply occurs when the supply curve shifts to the right. A decrease in supply occurs when the supply curve shifts to the left. **How does a change in supply differ from a change in quantity supplied?**

might be difficult to obtain, which would shift the supply curve to the left. These examples are exceptions, however. New technology almost always increases supply.

Number of Sellers

Another factor affecting changes in supply is the number of sellers in the market. Because the supply curve represents the different quantities that *all* producers offer at various prices, supply increases—or shifts to the right—when more suppliers enter the market.

If some suppliers leave the market, fewer goods are offered for sale at all possible prices. Supply decreases, and the supply curve shifts to the left.

Taxes and Subsidies

Taxes have the same impact as an increase in the cost of inputs. If the producer's inventory is taxed or fees paid to receive a license to produce, the cost of production goes up. This causes the supply curve to shift to the left. When production costs go down, supply increases and the supply curve shifts to the right.

Checking Understanding

1. Why are sellers likely to supply more goods when prices are high?
2. Why does new technology shift the supply curve to the right?

Applying Economic Concepts

☑ **Competition** When Dallas-based Southwest Airlines expanded its low-cost, no-frills service nationwide in the 1990s, other airlines scrambled to lower their prices to remain competitive. Consumers benefited from lower prices.

Subsidies—government payments to individuals, businesses, or other groups to encourage or protect a certain type of economic activity—have the opposite effect of taxes. Subsidies lower the cost of production and encourage producers to stay in the market.

Historically, farmers have received substantial subsidies to support their income. Many farmers would have gone out of business without a supporting subsidy. When the government grants a subsidy, production costs go down. Producers stay in the market, thus increasing supply. When subsidies are repealed, costs go up, producers leave the market, and the supply curve shifts to the left.

Expectations

Expectations, or the anticipation of future events, can affect the supply curve in two ways. If producers think the price of their product is likely to go up, they may withhold some of the supply, causing the market supply to decrease. The supply curve shifts to the left.

On the other hand, producers may expect lower prices for their output in the future. In this situation, they will try to produce and sell as much as possible right away. The supply curve shifts to the right.

Government Regulation

Government regulations also cause a change in supply. When the government mandates new auto safety features such as stronger bumpers, air bags, and emission controls, cars cost more to produce. Producers adjust to the higher cost imposed by the safety standards by producing fewer cars at each and every price in the market.

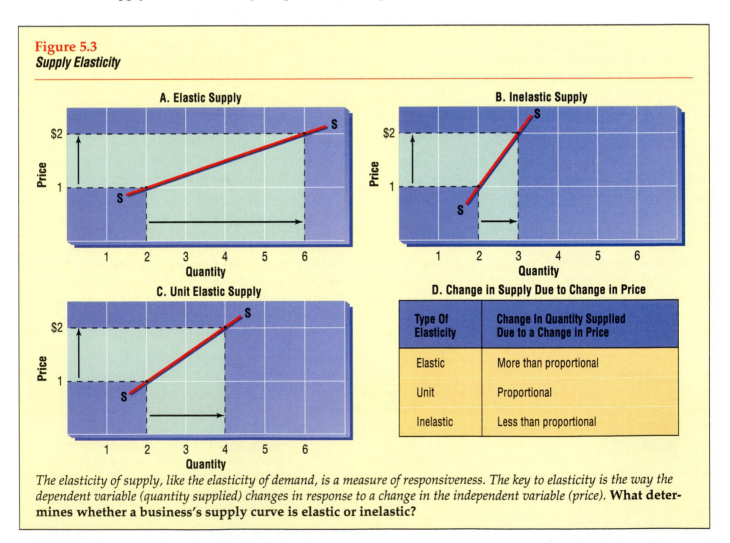

Figure 5.3
Supply Elasticity

A. Elastic Supply

B. Inelastic Supply

C. Unit Elastic Supply

D. Change in Supply Due to Change in Price

Type Of Elasticity	Change In Quantity Supplied Due to a Change in Price
Elastic	More than proportional
Unit	Proportional
Inelastic	Less than proportional

The elasticity of supply, like the elasticity of demand, is a measure of responsiveness. The key to elasticity is the way the dependent variable (quantity supplied) changes in response to a change in the independent variable (price). **What determines whether a business's supply curve is elastic or inelastic?**

In general, increased—or tighter—government regulations restrict supply. The regulations increase the cost of inputs or add new features to the product. Relaxed government regulations allow producers to lower the cost of production and to reduce features on products, which results in a shift of the supply curve to the right.

Elasticity of Supply

Just as demand has elasticity, there is elasticity of supply. **Supply elasticity** tells the way in which changes in the quantity supplied are affected by changes in price. If a small increase in price, for example, causes a relatively larger increase in output, the supply curve is said to be elastic. If the quantity supplied changes very little, supply is inelastic.

Supply Elasticities

Three kinds of supply elasticity are illustrated in **Figure 5.3**. The supply curve in Graph **A** is elastic, because the change in price causes a relatively large change in quantity supplied. Doubling the price from $1 to $2 causes the quantity brought to market to triple.

Graph **B** shows an inelastic supply curve, because the change in price causes a relatively smaller change in quantity supplied. When the price is doubled from $1 to $2, the quantity brought to market goes up only 50 percent, or from 2 to 3.

Graph **C** shows a unit elastic supply curve. In this case, a given change in price causes a proportional change in the quantity supplied. The price doubles from $1 to $2, which causes the quantity brought to market also to double.

Determinants of Supply Elasticity

The extent to which a business's supply curve is elastic or inelastic depends on the nature of its production. The supply curve of shale oil, for example, is likely to be inelastic in the short run. No matter what price is being offered, companies will find it difficult to increase output because of the huge amount of capital and technology needed before production can be increased very much.

The supply curve is likely to be elastic, however, for kites, candy, and other products that can be made quickly without huge amounts of capital and skilled labor. If consumers are willing to pay twice the price for any of these products, most producers will be able to gear up quickly to significantly increase production.

Comparing Demand and Supply Elasticity

Basically, little difference exists between supply elasticity and demand elasticity. If quantities are being purchased, the concept is demand elasticity. If quantities are being brought to market for sale, the concept is supply elasticity. Elasticity for both supply and demand is a measure of responsiveness to a change in price.

SECTION 1 REVIEW

Reviewing Terms and Facts

1. **Define** supply, supply schedule, supply curve, Law of Supply, quantity supplied, change in quantity supplied, change in supply, subsidy, supply elasticity.
2. **Describe** the difference between the supply schedule and the supply curve.
3. **Explain** the difference between a change in quantity supplied and a change in supply.
4. **List** the factors that can cause an increase or decrease in supply.

Critical Thinking

5. **Determining Cause and Effect** According to the Law of Supply, how does price affect the quantity offered for sale?

Applying Economic Concepts

6. **Supply** Provide an example of an economic good whose producer would increase the quantity supplied if price were to go up.

Analyzing Editorials

American newspapers have a long tradition of taking stands on economic issues. Editors make a sharp distinction between news stories, which make up most of the contents of the daily paper, and editorials, which are placed in a special section. Unlike a news story, whose purpose is to inform, the purpose of an editorial is to persuade the reader to accept a certain point of view.

Explanation

To analyze an editorial, follow these steps:
- Determine what topic is being discussed.
- Read the editorial carefully to find out what opinion the editors are expressing on that topic.
- Note the arguments and evidence they present to back up their opinion.
- Decide whether you think the editorial is persuasive. Ask: Do I have enough information to form an opinion on this issue?

Practice

Read the editorial below, which appeared in *The Wall Street Journal* on July 26, 1993. Then answer the questions that follow.

1. What is the topic under discussion?
2. What opinion does the writer express about post-industrial society?
3. What evidence and arguments does the writer present to back up his or her opinion?
4. Do you have enough information to make a decision about whether you agree with the writer's point of view? If not, what other information would you need?

Most of us in post-industrial society, unlike our not-so-distant ancestors, don't make useful things. . . . we deal in intangible merchandise, such as this little essay, or arguments laid down in a legal brief, or lectures to post-graduate students. . . .

The fundamental problem of the post-industrial age has to do with measuring the social value of these activities.

In a post-industrial society, where people have no direct sense of how much medical malpractice suits or paper shuffling bureaucracy costs, it also becomes very hard to measure whether the society as a whole is moving toward greater well-being or is retrogressing. In a lecture on BBC4 TV last March, business tycoon Sir James Goldsmith . . . observed that the size of the U.S. economy has quadrupled in the last 50 years and science and technology have achieved incredible innovations. "And yet, American society is deeply ill," he said.

"American cities that are wracked with crime, drug taking, alcoholism, suicide and family breakdown are, according to official figures, considered 'richer' than many of the cities that have survived elsewhere in the world and which are still rich in stability and contentment." In short, it is relatively easy to measure the total output of a society, but is not so easy to measure the quality of that output.

In the post-industrial age, it thus becomes more necessary to measure human progress subjectively, for example through opinion polls. We know that a very high proportion of the people of the industrial world today are unhappy with government, which may mean they are not especially happy with the quality of their lives.

—excerpts from "Global View" by George Melloan,
The Wall Street Journal, July 26, 1993.

Additional Practice

For further practice in analyzing editorials, complete the Reinforcing Skills exercise in the Chapter 5 Review on page 124.

The Theory of Production

Section Preview

Objectives

After studying this section, you will be able to:

1. **Explain** the theory of production.
2. **Understand** the importance of marginal product and its application to economics.
3. **Describe** the three stages of production and how they relate to the concept of diminishing returns.

Key Terms

theory of production, short run, long run, Law of Variable Proportions, production function, raw materials, total product, marginal product, stages of production, diminishing returns

Applying Economic Concepts

Diminishing Returns Have you ever worked too hard at something—where the outcome of your efforts was less than the work involved? Sometimes you reach a stage of *diminishing returns*, a stage where you still make progress but at a diminished rate.

Suppliers face a complex task. The production of an economic good or service requires a combination of land, labor, capital, and entrepreneurship. Some combinations are more efficient than others, and all combinations affect both output and the cost of production. The **theory of production** deals with the relationship between the factors of production and the output of goods and services. It looks at how output changes when inputs change.

The theory of production generally is based on the **short run**, a period of production that allows producers to change only the amount of variable inputs—usually assumed to be labor. This contrasts with the **long run**, a period of production long enough for all inputs, including capital, to vary.

Law of Variable Proportions

The **Law of Variable Proportions** states that in the short run, output will change as one input is varied while the others are held constant. Although the name of the law is probably new to you, the concept is not.

If you prepare chili, you know that one pinch of chili powder will make the chili taste better. Two pinches may make it taste better yet. If you keep adding chili powder, however, at some point the chili begins to taste terrible. Basically, preparing chili provides an example

of the Law of Variable Proportions at work. As the amount of the input—the chili powder—varies, so does the output—the quality of the chili.

In an economic sense, the Law of Variable Proportions deals with the relationship between the input of productive resources and the output of final products. The law helps answer the question, How is the output of the final product affected as more units of one variable input or resource are added to a fixed amount of other resources?

Al, do whatever you have to do to increase productivity. Threaten, cajole, fire at will. Have fun.

Productivity *The economist would not consider this advice to Al the best way to increase productivity.* **On what is the theory of production based?**

A farmer, for example, may have all the land, machines, workers, and other items needed to produce a crop. The farmer, however, may have some questions about the use of fertilizer. How will the crop yield be affected if different amounts of fertilizer are added to fixed amounts of the other inputs? In this case, the variable input is the fertilizer added per acre.

Perhaps a plant manager wants to know, given the existing machines and equipment, how the final output would be affected if one or several workers are hired. The Law of Variable Proportions will also help answer this question.

Of course, it is possible for all inputs to be varied at the same time. The farmer may want to know what will happen to output if not only the fertilizer but also the quantities of the other factors of production are varied. The plant manager may be interested in finding out what will happen if the company not only hires more workers, but also buys several new machines and other equipment. When more than one factor of production is varied, however, it becomes harder to tell what the effect on final output will be.

The Production Function

The Law of Variable Proportions can be illustrated by using a **production function**—a concept that relates changes in output to different amounts of a single input while other inputs are held constant. The production function can be illustrated with a schedule such as the one in panel **A** of Figure 5.4, or with a graph like the one in panel **B**. **1**

The first two columns in the production schedule list hypothetical figures on a business's output as the number of workers is varied from 0 to 10. With no workers, for example, there is no output. If the number of workers increases by one, output rises to 14. Add yet another worker and total output rises to 42.

This information is used to construct the production function that appears in the graph. The variable input is shown on the horizontal axis with total production on the vertical axis.

In this example, only the number of workers changes, and all other productive resources remain the same. No changes occur in the amount of machinery used, the level of technology, or quantities of **raw materials**—unprocessed natural products used in

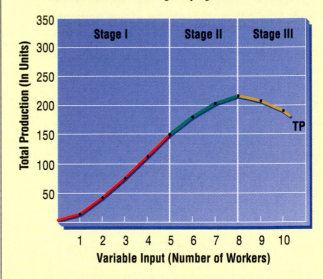

Figure 5.4
The Law of Variable Proportions

A. Production Schedule Using Varying Amounts of Labor

Number of Workers	Total Product (In Units)*	Marginal Product (In Units)*	
0	0	0	Stage I
1	14	14	
2	42	28	
3	75	33	
4	112	37	
5	150	38	
6	180	30	Stage II
7	203	23	
8	216	13	
9	207	−9	Stage III
10	190	−17	

*All figures refer to production/productivity per worker per day.

B. Production Function Using Varying Amounts of Labor

The Law of Variable Proportions shows how total output will change when all inputs except one are fixed. The law can be illustrated as a production schedule as in A, or as the production function shown in B. In this example, labor is the variable input, while all other variables are held constant. **How are the three stages of production related to the Law of Variable Proportions?**

Production Function
In most companies, managers hold regular production meetings at which they evaluate past performance and set future goals. **Why is the use of the production function important in business?**

production. Under these conditions, any change in output must be the result of the variation in the number of workers.

Total Product

The second column in the production schedule in **Figure 5.4** shows **total product**, or total output produced by the firm. The numbers seem to indicate that the plant barely operates when it has only a few workers. Perhaps the workers find it difficult to attend the machines, keep the supply of raw materials flowing smoothly, or remove and package the finished product. These same workers may also have to keep the plant clean and perform other maintenance. Some machines may stand idle much of the time.

As more workers are added, however, total product rises. More machinery can be operated, and plant output rises. Workers can specialize in certain jobs, so that each worker's special talents can be used to the fullest. One group of workers may run the machines while another takes care of maintenance. A third may handle the assembly work. By working in this way—as a coordinated whole—the firm can be very productive.

As even more workers are added, output rises but at a slower rate. Eventually, total product goes as high as it can. Adding the ninth and tenth workers causes total output to go down because these workers just get in the way of the others. Although the ideal number of workers cannot be determined until costs are considered, it is clear that the ninth and tenth workers will not be hired. **2**

Checking Understanding	**Applying Economic Concepts**
1. What does a production function show?	**Division of Labor** Henry Ford developed the assembly line in the early 1900s. He found that productivity increased dramatically if each worker repeated the same task—attaching the gas tank, for example—over and over. By 1922 the company earned $264,000 a day.
2. What point must eventually be reached if companies continue adding workers?	

Stages of Production
As workers are added to this assembly line, output increases—but only to a certain point. **What would happen if company officials doubled the number of workers in this factory?**

Marginal Product

The measure of output shown in the third column of the production schedule is one of the more important concepts in economics. The measure is known as **marginal product**, the extra output generated by adding one more unit of variable input. Another way to explain marginal product is to say that it is the change in total product caused by the addition of one more unit of variable input.

Note that the marginal productivity of the fifth worker is 38 units, which is more than that of any preceding worker. After the fifth worker is added, however, each worker adds less to the total output. The marginal product of the seventh worker is 23 units of output, and the marginal product of the eighth falls to 13. By the time we get to the ninth worker, marginal product is negative, which is why the ninth worker will not be hired.

Three Stages of Production

When it comes to determining the optimal number of variable units to be used in production, changes in marginal product are of special interest. **Figure 5.4** shows the three **stages of production**—increasing returns, diminishing returns, and negative returns—that are based on the way marginal product changes as variable inputs are added.

STAGE I: Increasing Returns

Hiring the first five workers illustrates the first stage of the Law of Variable Proportions. Each worker contributes more than the previous worker to total output. The first stage is defined as the stage where marginal product is increasing.

In this first stage, the individual workers may not be able to handle the equipment efficiently because of too much machinery and other resources per worker. Not enough workers are present to handle the job well. As the number of workers rises, however, the workers use the available resources better. The result of all this is increasing returns per worker.

As long as each new worker hired contributes more to total output than the worker before, total output rises at a faster rate. Because marginal output increases by larger amounts every time a new worker is added, Stage I is known as the stage of increasing returns.

Companies, however, would not knowingly produce in Stage I for very long. As a firm discovered that each new worker added more output than the last, the firm would be tempted to hire another worker. After all, if the fourth worker produced more than the third, and if the fifth worker added more output than the fourth, a sixth worker would be hired.

STAGE II: Diminishing Returns

In Stage II, the total production keeps growing but by smaller and smaller amounts. Any additional workers hired may stock shelves, package parts, and do other jobs that leave the machine operators free to spend more time at the machines. The increase in total production, however, is less than it was when the other workers were hired. Each worker, then, makes a diminishing but positive contribution to total output.

Stage II illustrates the principle of **diminishing returns**. As more units of a certain variable input are added to a constant amount of other resources, total output keeps rising, but only at a diminishing rate. In **Figure 5.4**, the addition of the seventh worker adds 23 new units of output, but the eighth worker adds only 13.

STAGE III: Negative Returns

Adding the ninth and tenth workers makes an even greater difference. Too many workers have been hired, and they are getting in each other's way. Marginal product is negative and total plant output decreases. Labor service, which could be used to advantage in some other job area, is wasted.

Most companies would not hire workers whose addition would cause total production to decrease. Therefore, the number of workers hired would be found only in Stage II. The exact number of workers hired depends on the cost of each worker. If the cost is low, eight workers might be hired. If the cost is high, fewer than eight but no less than six workers would be hired.

SECTION 2 REVIEW

Reviewing Terms and Facts

1. **Define** theory of production, short run, long run, Law of Variable Proportions, production function, raw materials, total product, marginal product, stages of production, diminishing returns.
2. **Explain** how marginal product is related to total product and how it is measured.

3. **Describe** how marginal product changes in each of the three stages of production.

Critical Thinking

4. **Demonstrating Reasoned Judgment** You need to hire workers for a project you are directing. You may add one worker at a time in a manner that will allow you to measure the added contribution of each worker. At what point will you stop hiring workers? Relate this process to the three stages of the production function.

Applying Economic Concepts

5. **Diminishing Returns** Provide an example of a time when you entered a period of diminishing returns or even negative returns. Explain why this might have occurred.

H. ROSS PEROT
(1930–)

Henry Ross Perot is an entrepreneur's entrepreneur. *Reader's Digest* called him the "world's first populist billionaire." In 1993 *Fortune* magazine estimated that he was one of the 50 richest people in the world, with a net worth of $3.3 billion. Ross Perot is perhaps the only person on earth to have amassed a multi-billion dollar fortune, rescued hostages in Iran, and run for President of the United States.

Perot was born in Texarkana, Texas. He showed an early aptitude for business, making money

In 1993 Perot petitioned Congress to cut spending and balance the budget.

selling greeting cards, saddles, and newspapers.

He achieved the rank of Eagle Scout and later enrolled at the United States Naval Academy.

After serving on a destroyer at the close of the Korean War, he joined IBM as a sales representative, but stayed with the company for only five years. In his final year, he filled his annual sales quota in just three weeks!

At age 32, Perot left IBM and set up Electronic Data Systems (EDS) with $1,000 in savings. EDS was an information-processing corporation with shares privately held by Perot and his employees.

In 1968 Perot reorganized EDS and took it public by selling some of his privately owned shares.

The price soon rose to $23/share. The 9 million shares Perot kept for himself were worth almost $200 million, prompting *Fortune* to describe Perot as "The Fastest Richest Texan Ever."

In 1970 Perot offered $100 million of his own fortune to ransom American prisoners of war held in North Vietnam. When two EDS employees were jailed in Iran by the Ayatollah Khomeini in 1979, Perot organized a commando raid that freed his employees. Later, a best-selling book and TV mini-series, *On the Wings of Eagles*, immortalized the event.

In 1984 General Motors bought EDS by exchanging 11 million shares of GM stock for Perot's shares in EDS, making Perot the largest single shareholder in General Motors. He became a member of the board of directors, but failed to convert the other board members to his entrepreneurial style. General Motors soon bought back Perot's shares for nearly $700 million, or about twice the market price.

Perot established Perot Systems in 1988, which competed directly with his former company, EDS. More recently, he tested his talents in the 1992 presidential election.

Examining the Profile

1. **Demonstrating Reasoned Judgment** With which aspect of Perot's entrepreneurship are you most impressed? Why?

2. **For Further Research** Research Perot's 1992 bid for the presidency, summarizing his campaign platform.

Supply and the Role of Cost

Section Preview

Objectives

After studying this section, you will be able to:

1. **Identify** the relationship between productivity and cost.
2. **Define** four key measures of cost.
3. **Identify** two key measures of revenue.

Key Terms

fixed cost, overhead, depreciation, variable cost, total cost, marginal cost, total revenue, marginal revenue, marginal analysis, break-even point, profit-maximizing quantity of output

Applying Economic Concepts

Marginal Cost Have you thought about what you will do after graduating from high school? Go to college? Get a job? Have you considered the cost of these options? Economists view options in terms of *marginal cost*—in this case, the additional cost of getting more education versus the cost of going directly into the job market.

An analysis of the Law of Variable Proportions tells us that a business should hire enough labor to produce in Stage II. Before we can specify the exact number of variable inputs, however, we must consider the relationship between productivity and costs.

Productivity and Cost

Different grades of coal, wood, steel, cotton, and glass, as well as most other raw materials, have different productivities. Businesses that use raw materials in manufacturing must decide which grade best suits their needs. Because efficiency is related to both cost and productivity, it is important that care be taken in selecting the proper materials.

Suppose an electric power company that uses coal can choose from among three different grades. Grade A coal sells for $40 per ton, grade B for $33, and grade C for $30. The cost and productivities of each is shown in the chart in **Figure 5.5**. Notice that grade A coal would be more productive than the other two, yielding 2,500 kilowatt-hours of electric power for each ton of coal used.

If we consider the cost effectiveness of the different grades of coal, the figure shows that grade A costs 1.6 cents per kilowatt-hour generated. Grade C also has a cost of 1.6 cents per kilowatt-hour, while grade B has a cost of 1.5 cents.

Both grade C, which is the cheapest and least productive, and grade A, which is the most expensive and most productive, cost more per final unit than grade B. Grade B is the most efficient from a cost point of view.

Figure 5.5
Productivity, Cost, and Efficiency of Various Grades of Coal

Grades of Coal	Price Per Ton	Kilowatt Hours of Electric Power per Ton of Coal Used (Estimated)	Production Cost per Kilowatt Hour of Electric Power
A	$40	2500	1.6¢
B	$33	2200	1.5¢
C	$30	1875	1.6¢

Different grades of coal have different productivities. The most efficient grade is not always the most, or the least, expensive. **Why is it necessary for businesses to consider productivity as well as cost?**

This example shows that both productivity and cost must be considered to make the best production decision. This also holds true for a manufacturer of razor blades that must consider the different grades of steel, as well as for a hotel that must consider the different grades of carpeting. In the end, efficient production is a function of the quality and cost of inputs used.

Measures of Cost

Because the cost of inputs influences efficient production decisions, a business must analyze costs before making its decisions. To make the decision-making process easier, cost is divided into several different categories.

Fixed Cost

The first kind of cost is **fixed cost**—the cost that a business incurs even if the plant is idle and output is zero. It makes no difference whether the business produces nothing, very little, or a large amount. Total fixed cost, or **overhead**, remains the same. ✓

Fixed costs include salaries paid to executives, interest charges on bonds, rent payments on leased properties, and local and state property taxes. Fixed costs also include **depreciation**—the gradual wear and tear on capital goods over time and through use. A machine, for example, will not last forever because its parts will wear out slowly and, after a time, break.

Fixed costs do not change when output changes. Consider the table in **Figure 5.6**, which is an extension of the production schedule in **Figure 5.4**. Regardless of the level of total output, the total fixed cost amounts to $70, as shown in the fourth column of the table. Because executive salaries, interest payments, taxes, and other overhead charges do not change with changes in output, fixed costs never vary.

Variable Cost

Another kind of cost is **variable cost**—a cost that does change when the business rate of operation or output changes. While fixed costs generally are associated with machines and other capital goods, variable costs generally are associated with labor and raw materials. Workers may be laid off or used again as output changes. Other examples of variable costs include the electric power to run the machines or freight charges on shipments of the final product.

In **Figure 5.6** the assumption has been made that the only variable cost is labor. If one worker costs $46 per day, the total variable cost for one worker is $46. Two workers, or two units of variable input, cost $92, and so on.

Fixed Costs *Whether this computer graphics firm is producing to its full capacity (left) or is idle (right), the firm still incurs fixed costs.* **What do fixed costs generally include?**

Figure 5.6
Marginal Product, Cost, and Revenues

STAGES OF PRODUCTION	PRODUCTION SCHEDULE			COSTS				REVENUES		Total Profits
	Number of Workers	Total Product	Marginal Product	Total Fixed Costs +	Total Variable Costs =	Total Costs	Marginal Costs	Total Revenue	Marginal Revenue	
STAGE I	0	0	0	70	0	70		0		–70
	1	14	14	70	46	116	3.29	28	2.00	–88
	2	42	28	70	92	162	1.64	84	2.00	–78
	3	75	33	70	138	208	1.39	150	2.00	–58
	4	112	37	70	184	254	1.24	224	2.00	–30
	5	150	38	70	230	300	1.21	300	2.00	0
STAGE II	6	180	30	70	276	346	1.53	360	2.00	14
	7	203	23	70	322	392	2.00	406	2.00	14
	8	216	13	70	368	438	3.54	432	2.00	–6
STAGE III	9	207	–9	70	414	484	—	414	2.00	–70
	10	190	–17	70	460	530	—	380	2.00	–150

The concepts of marginal product, marginal cost, and marginal revenue are central to economic analysis. Marginal product is used to define the three stages of production. Marginal cost and marginal revenue are used to determine the profit-maximizing quantity of output. **How do total costs differ from marginal costs?**

Total Cost

The **total cost** of production is the sum of the fixed and variable costs. Total cost takes in all the costs a business faces in the course of its operations. The business represented in **Figure 5.6**, for example, might employ six workers—costing $46 each for a total of $276—to produce 180 units of total output. If no other variable costs existed, and if fixed costs amounted to $70, the total cost of production would be $346. **1**

If the workers go on strike, the total cost of production would fall to $70 even though no output is produced. The total cost of production is equal to the fixed costs plus the variable costs, which, in this case, are zero if the workers are on strike.

Marginal Cost

The other measure of cost is **marginal cost**—the extra cost incurred when a business produces one additional unit of a product. Because fixed costs do not change from one level of production to another, marginal cost is the increase in variable costs that stems from using additional factors of production. **2**

Checking Understanding

1. How do businesses calculate total costs?
2. What are the four measures of cost that businesses must consider?

Applying Economic Concepts

 Investment In recent years many companies have relocated to the Sunbelt where wages and rents are lower than in the North. Even foreign firms have moved there. BMWs will be assembled in South Carolina; Mercedes Benz in Alabama.

For example, **Figure 5.6** shows that the addition of the first worker increased the total product by 14 units. Because total variable costs increased by $46, each of the additional 14 units cost $3.29. If another worker is added, 28 more units of output will be produced for an additional cost of $46. The marginal, or extra, cost of each unit of output is $46 divided by 28, or $1.64.

Practical Applications of Cost Principles

The combination, or mix, of inputs affects supply. If most of the costs of a certain business are fixed and only a few costs vary with output, total output could be increased with very little additional cost.

Gas Stations

Consider, for example, a self-serve gas station with several pumps and a single attendant who works in an enclosed booth on the lot. This operation is likely to have large fixed costs. These include overhead expenses such as the cost of the lot—which may be located at a busy corner—the pumps and tanks, and the taxes and licensing fees paid to state and local governments.

The variable costs, on the other hand, are likely to be quite small. These include the hourly wage paid to the employee, the cost of electricity for lights and pumps, and the cost of the gas sold. When all costs are included, however, the ratio of variable to fixed costs is small.

As a result, it does not cost much more for the owner to operate the station 24 hours a day, seven days a week. The extra cost of keeping the station open between the hours of midnight and 6:00 A.M. is minimal. The extra wages, the electricity, and other variable costs are minor and may well be covered from the profits of the extra sales. **1**

Another gas station may have a different mix of costs. Suppose a full-service station located nearby offers the services of a mechanic as well as several attendants who wait on customers.

If the station has been around long enough, management may even own the land. Taxes and occupation licenses may have to be paid, but fixed costs are likely to be less than those of the other gas station. The need for the attendants and the mechanic, however, means that the variable costs are higher in comparison to fixed costs. As a result, this station is likely to operate for fewer hours and during the busiest time of the day. Thus, the mix of inputs and the nature of their costs has an impact on the amount of service offered by the owner.

Movie Theaters

A movie theater operator is faced with a similar situation. After the decision is made to show a movie, it makes little difference in cost as to whether 10 or 1,000 people come to the theater per day. The operating expenses are about the same regardless of how many customers show up.

Because marginal costs are low, little extra expense is involved in showing a movie in the early afternoon. The owner is concerned about recovering the large fixed costs and is more likely to schedule a number of movies at different times and prices throughout the day. ✔

Measures of Revenue

Businesses use two key measures of revenue to decide what amount of output will produce the greatest profits. The first is total revenue, and the second is marginal revenue.

Total Revenue

The **total revenue** is the number of units sold multiplied by the average price per unit. If 42 units are sold at $2 each, the total revenue is $84.

The total revenue column in **Figure 5.6** shows this measurement. If each unit brings an average of $2, then 14 units of total product generates $28 of total revenue, 75 units generates $150, and so on.

Marginal Revenue

Marginal revenue is the extra revenue associated with the production and sale of one additional unit of output. It is the most useful measure of revenue both for businesses and economists.

The marginal revenues in **Figure 5.6** are determined by dividing the change in total revenue by the marginal product. When a business has no workers, it produces no output, and it receives no revenue. When it adds the first worker, total output jumps to 14 units, and $28 of total revenue is generated. Because the $28 is earned from the sale of 14 units of output, each unit must have added $2. Therefore, the marginal, or extra, revenue each unit of output brings in is $2.

Whenever an additional worker is added, the marginal revenue computation remains the same. If the business employs five workers, it produces 150 units of output and generates $300 of total revenue. If a sixth worker is added, output increases by 30 units, and total revenues increase to $360. To have increased total revenue by $60, each of the 30 additional units of output must have added $2.

If each unit of output sells for $2, the marginal revenue earned by the sale of one more unit is $2. For this reason, the marginal revenue appears to be constant at $2 for every level of output. While marginal revenue is constant in **Figure 5.6**, however, this will not

always be the case. Businesses often find that marginal revenues start high and then decrease as more and more units are produced and sold. **2**

Marginal Analysis

Economists use **marginal analysis**, a type of decision making that compares the extra benefits to the

---

QUICK CHECK

Checking Understanding

1. Why are the extra costs of operating a gas station 24 hours a day minimal?
2. How does marginal revenue differ from total revenue?

Applying Economic Concepts

☑ **Demand** Theater owners generally lower prices during the day, hoping that lower prices will increase demand during an otherwise lax period. Airlines follow the same principle by drastically cutting fares to Europe in the winter when demand is usually very low.

extra costs of an action. Marginal analysis is helpful in a number of situations, including break-even analysis and profit maximization.

Break-even Analysis

When the business represented in **Figure 5.6** employs its first worker, it generates total revenue of $28 and total costs of $116, giving it a total profit of $-88. The addition of the next worker increases total revenue to $84 and total costs to $162, which changes total profits to $-78. As more workers are added, total profits eventually become positive.

Eventually the business reaches the **break-even point**—the total output or total product the business needs to sell in order to cover its total costs. In **Figure 5.6**, the break-even point is 150 units of total product.

Profit Maximization

A business wants to do better than break even, however. It wants to make as much profit as it can. We already know that the business represented in **Figure 5.6** will break even when it hires the fifth worker. How many workers and what level of output will be needed to generate the maximum profits?

The business can make this decision by comparing marginal costs and marginal revenues. The business would probably hire the sixth worker, for example, because the extra output would only cost $1.53 to produce and would generate $2 in revenues. In general, as long as the marginal cost is less than the marginal revenue, the business will keep hiring workers.

Having made a profit on the sixth worker, most likely the business would go ahead and hire the seventh. This time, however, the cost of the additional output would equal the additional revenue earned when the product was sold. The addition of the seventh worker neither adds to, nor takes away from, total profits. The company would not hire the eighth worker because the seventh one did not make a positive contribution toward total profits.

When marginal cost is less than marginal revenue, new inputs should be hired and output should expand. The **profit-maximizing quantity of output** is reached when marginal cost and marginal revenue are equal. In **Figure 5.6**, profits are maximized when the seventh worker is hired. Other combinations may generate the same amount of profits, but no other combination will be more profitable. The difference between total revenue and total cost is maximum here.

SECTION 3
REVIEW

Reviewing Terms and Facts

1. **Define** fixed cost, overhead, depreciation, variable cost, total cost, marginal cost, total revenue, marginal revenue, marginal analysis, break-even point, profit-maximizing quantity of output.
2. **Explain** the relationship between productivity and cost.
3. **Identify** two key measures of revenue.
4. **Explain** the use of marginal analysis for break-even and profit-maximizing decisions.

Critical Thinking

5. **Analyzing Information** Many oil-processing plants operate 24 hours a day, using several shifts of workers to maintain operations. How do you think a plant's fixed and variable costs affect its decision to operate around the clock?
6. **Checking Consistency** In Figure 5.6, total profits are the same after the sixth worker is hired as after the seventh worker is hired. Why should the company hire the seventh worker?

Applying Economic Concepts

7. **Marginal Cost** What is the marginal cost of your decision to buy a new car when you graduate? How much more would a new car cost than a used one?

Vocabulary

The following terms are defined in Chapter 5:

SECTION ONE
- supply (p. 104)
- supply schedule (p. 105)
- supply curve (p. 105)
- Law of Supply (p. 106)
- quantity supplied (p. 106)
- change in quantity supplied (p. 106)

- change in supply (p. 106)
- subsidy (p. 108)
- supply elasticity (p. 109)

SECTION TWO
- theory of production (p. 111)
- short run (p. 111)
- long run (p. 111)
- Law of Variable Proportions (p. 111)
- production function (p. 112)

- raw materials (p. 112)
- total product (p. 113)
- marginal product (p. 114)
- stages of production (p. 114)
- diminishing returns (p. 115)

SECTION THREE
- fixed cost (p. 118)
- overhead (p. 118)
- depreciation (p. 118)
- variable cost (p. 118)

- total cost (p. 119)
- marginal cost (p. 119)
- total revenue (p. 121)
- marginal revenue (p. 121)
- marginal analysis (p. 121)
- break-even point (p. 122)
- profit-maximizing quantity of output (p. 122)

Section 1
What Is Supply? (pages 104–109)

Supply is the quantities of output that producers will bring to market at each and every price. Supply can be represented by a **supply schedule** or a **supply curve**. The **Law of Supply** states that the quantity of an economic product offered for sale varies directly with its price. If prices are high, suppliers will offer greater quantities for sale. If prices are low, they will offer smaller quantities for sale.

A **change in quantity supplied** is represented by movement along the supply curve. A **change in supply** is a change in the quantity that will be supplied at each and every price.

An increase in supply is represented graphically as a shift of the supply curve to the right. A decrease in supply appears as a shift of the supply curve to the left.

Reviewing the Main Idea
What is meant by supply?

Section 2
The Theory of Production (pages 111–115)

The **Law of Variable Proportions** states that the quantity of output will vary as increasing units of a single input are added. This law is represented graphically in a **production function**.

The two most important measures of output are **total product** and **marginal product**. Three **stages of production**—increasing returns, **diminishing returns**, and negative returns—show the way marginal product changes as variable inputs are added. Most production takes place in Stage II under conditions of diminishing returns.

Reviewing the Main Idea
What are the three stages of production?

Section 3
Supply and the Role of Cost (pages 117–122)

Several important measures of cost exist. The first is **total cost**, which consists of **fixed cost** and **variable cost**. **Marginal cost** is the increase in variable costs that stems from producing an additional unit of output.

The mix of variable and fixed costs a business faces will affect the way the business operates. When marginal costs are small, businesses tend to stay open longer. The opposite tends to happen when marginal costs are high.

Businesses use two key measures of revenue to decide what amount of output will produce the greatest profits. The two measures are **total revenue** and **marginal revenue**, which is the change in total revenue when one more unit of output is sold. A business maximizes its profits when the marginal cost is exactly equal to marginal revenue. Other quantities of output may yield the same profit, but none will yield more.

Reviewing the Main Idea
What are the four main measures of cost?

Reviewing Key Terms

Write the letter of the key term that best matches each definition below.

a. depreciation
b. diminishing returns
c. fixed cost
d. marginal analysis
e. marginal product
f. marginal revenue
g. production function
h. profit-maximizing quantity of output
i. total cost
j. variable cost

1. a production cost that does not change as total business output changes
2. a type of decision making that compares the additional costs with the additional benefits of an action
3. associated with Stage II of production
4. a production cost that changes when output changes
5. a graphical representation of the theory of production
6. the additional output produced when one additional unit of input is added
7. the change in total revenue
8. the gradual wearing out of capital goods
9. the sum of variable and fixed costs
10. when marginal revenue equals marginal cost

Reviewing the Facts

SECTION 1 (pages 104–109)
1. **Describe** what is meant by supply.
2. **Distinguish** between the supply schedule and the supply curve.
3. **Explain** what is meant by a change in quantity supplied.
4. **Identify** the factors that cause a change in supply.

SECTION 2 (pages 111–115)
5. **Describe** the Law of Variable Proportions.
6. **Explain** the difference between total product and marginal product.
7. **Identify** the three stages of production.

SECTION 3 (pages 117–122)
8. **Describe** the relationship between marginal cost and total cost.
9. **Identify** four measures of cost.
10. **Describe** one practical application of cost principles.

Critical Thinking

1. **Determining Cause and Effect** Explain why companies with very large fixed costs and small variable costs are most likely to operate or stay open for extended periods.
2. **Making Generalizations** Why might production functions tend to differ from one firm to another? Give several examples that support your answer.

Applying Economic Concepts

1. **Marginal Analysis** Give an example of a recent decision you made in which you used, perhaps without knowing it, the tools of marginal analysis.
2. **Diminishing Returns** Label the following actions according to their placement in the stages of production: (a) After many hours of studying, you are getting confused and forgetting some of the material you learned earlier. (b) You are studying for a test and learning rapidly. (c) After a few hours, you are still learning but not as fast as before.

Reinforcing Skills

ANALYZING EDITORIALS

Read the following editorial, which appeared in *The New York Times* on July 17, 1993. Then answer the questions that follow.

[Supplying aid] to Russia can be used to the advantage of the United States.

The availability of badly needed consumer goods— toothpaste, soap, detergent, hygiene products, over-the-

counter drugs—would represent tangible proof to the Russian people that they are on their way to becoming European citizens. It would also help to establish disiribution channels for consumer goods.

The best way to spend the aid is subsidizing United States manufacturers to build consumer-goods manufacturing plants in Russia. While not at first profitable, it would establish American companies in a market that in a few decades could be as large as the United States market. The plants would also serve as models for modern manufacturing facilities.

1. What topic is being discussed?
2. What opinion does the writer express?
3. What evidence and arguments does the writer present to back up his or her opinion?
4. Do you have enough information to make a decision about whether you agree with the writer's point of view? If not, what other information would you need?

Individual Activity

Calculate the marginal cost of going to college. First, list the expenses you would incur if you went to college, including tuition, room and board, books, and transportation. Then list any revenues you might receive in the form of scholarships, part-time jobs, and so forth. Combine the two to find out how much money you might have at the end of the year.

Next, list the expenses you would incur if you elected to go to work, including clothes, a car, rent, and so on. Offset these expenses with your income to find out how much money you would have at the end of the year. Finally, compare the two estimates. The difference is the marginal cost of your education.

Costs	$ Spent at Current Output Level	$ Spent with Output Down 50%	$ Spent with Output Doubled	Cost Classification
1.				
2.				
3.				

Cooperative Learning Activity

Working in pairs, use the following steps to learn more about costs. (1) Interview a local business owner or manager to learn more about that business's costs. (2) Select a time period to analyze, such as one week or one month. (3) Make a list of all inputs used during that period of time. (4) For each type of cost, make an estimate of the dollars spent, given the current rate of output or sales. Construct a matrix similar to the one below, and record this information in the first two columns. Ask how the dollar amount might change for each type of cost if output or sales were to fall by 50 percent, and record this in the third column. Do the same for a doubling of sales or output, and record this information in the fourth column. (5) Based on the estimates for three different levels of output, make a judgment as to whether each cost is more likely to be fixed or variable. Discuss your findings with the rest of the class.

Writing About Economics

THE PERSUASIVE STYLE

In the **Journal Writing** activity on page 103, you were asked to log all the services and jobs you supply for others for one week. Summarize the difference in the number of hours spent on paid work as opposed to unpaid work, describing any difference in attitude you may have toward unpaid work. Then, using the persuasive style of writing discussed on page 554, write a paragraph explaining why students should get paid for the hours they spend studying and going to school.

Prices for products in a market economy are determined by the interaction of supply and demand.

CHAPTER 6

Prices and Decision Making

CHAPTER PREVIEW

People to Know

- Gary Becker
- Budget Analyst

Applying Economic Concepts to Your Life

Price What factors do you consider when you make a decision to buy something? You probably consider color, style, usefulness, and, of course, *price*. Price may be one of the most important factors of all. Economists certainly think so, because they regard the price of an item as a signal to both buyers and sellers.

Journal Writing

Visit an area shopping mall and look for examples of surpluses and shortages, making a list of from 5 to 10 items for each concept. Almost any sale item can be an example of surplus. Rain checks or sellouts of an item signal a shortage.

Prices as Signals

Section Preview

Objectives

After studying this section, you will be able to:

1. **Explain** how prices act as signals to both producers and consumers.
2. **Describe** the advantages of using prices as a way to allocate economic products.
3. **Understand** the difficulty of using rationing and other non-price criteria to allocate scarce goods and services.

Key Terms

rationing, ration coupon

Applying Economic Concepts

Rationing Have you and your friends ever tried to share something—a candy bar, cake, or pizza—when there really wasn't enough to go around? If so, you already know about the difficulties of sharing something fairly. Sharing is a form of *rationing*, or allocation, and it is an important concept in economics.

Prices play an important role in our economy. They act as signals that convey information to the buyers and sellers in a market. A high price is a signal for producers to produce more and for buyers to buy less. A low price is a signal for producers to produce less and for buyers to buy more. **1**

Advantages of Prices

Prices serve as a link between producers and consumers. In doing so, they help decide the three basic WHAT, HOW, and FOR WHOM questions all societies face. Without prices, the economy would not run as smoothly, and allocation decisions would have to be made some other way, perhaps by some form of government bureaucracy. Prices perform the allocation function very well for several reasons.

Neutral

First, prices in a free market economy are neutral. They favor neither the producer nor the consumer. Instead, they are a result of competition between buyers and sellers. The more competitive the market, the more efficient the price adjustment process.

If the market is less competitive, prices tend to favor some groups more than others.

Flexible

Second, prices in a market economy are surprisingly flexible. Unforeseen events such as weather, strikes, natural disasters, and even wars affect the prices for many items. Buyers and sellers react to the new level of prices and adjust their consumption and production accordingly. Before long, the system functions smoothly again as it had before. The ability of the price system to absorb unexpected "shocks" is one of the strengths of a market economy. ☑

Price flexibility also allows the market economy to accommodate change. The development of the personal computer provides an example. At first, personal computers were relatively scarce and expensive. Their high prices attracted new producers. The resulting competition, along with advances in technology and production methods, soon drove prices lower. Consumers wanted more computers at lower prices, and more were manufactured to meet the demand. Thus, a major innovation—the computer—entered the economy with the help of the price system and without the involvement of government or one of its bureaucracies.

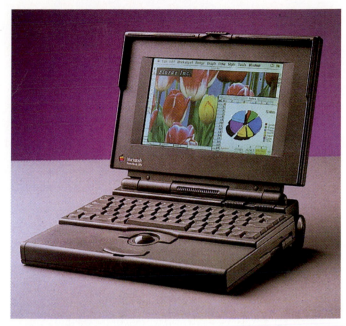

Price Flexibility *The computer on the left is an older model. The computer on the right is a newer model. If the prices for both computers were adjusted for inflation, the earlier model would cost more.* **Why do you think this is so?**

Freedom of Choice

Third, the price system provides for maximum freedom of choice for everyone. Because a market economy typically provides a variety of products at a wide range of prices, consumers have many choices available to them. If the price is too high, a lower-priced product can usually be found. Even if a suitable alternative cannot be found, no one forces the consumer to pay a certain price for a product in a competitive market economy. **2**

In command economies, such as those found in Cuba and North Korea, consumers face limited choices. Government planners, rather than prices, allocate both resources and products. The government usually decides if a product will be produced, and then limits the product's variety to keep production costs down. Items such as food, transportation, and housing often are offered to citizens at artificially low prices, but seldom are enough produced to satisfy everyone. Many people go without.

No Administrative Cost

Fourth, prices have no cost of administration. Competitive markets tend to find their own prices without outside help or interference. No bureaucrats need to be hired, no committees formed, no laws passed, or other decisions made. Even when prices adjust from one level to another, the change is usually so gradual that people hardly notice.

QUICK CHECK

Checking Understanding

1. What signal does a high price send to buyers and sellers?
2. How does the price system provide for freedom of choice?

Applying Economic Concepts

 Economic Systems One of the challenges that the former command economies of eastern Europe face is rapidly rising prices. Under communism the government set artificially low prices. When supply and demand were allowed to set prices, costs skyrocketed.

"They call it a sticker price because it shows how hard they're going to stick us."

Prices *This consumer has a negative view of prices.* **What are the positive aspects of prices in a market economy?**

Efficient

Finally, prices are efficient because they are easily understood by everyone. This allows people to make decisions quickly and efficiently, with a minimum of time and effort. Suppose that you want to buy a prod-uct that is in short supply. You can still go ahead with the purchase if you can afford its high price. On the other hand, the purchase can be postponed, a substitute can be found, or you can otherwise adjust your behavior.

Prices are even used to influence driving behavior. In some parts of Hong Kong, for example, traffic congestion is a major problem. To encourage drivers to change their driving habits, a system of variable tolls is used with higher tolls during rush hours and lower rates at other times.

Other nonprice allocation systems may require people to fill out application forms, wait in lines, obtain permits, or meet other criteria in order to obtain the scarce good or service. All of these methods allocate resources, but they usually take time and effort. Imagine the frustration you would feel if you stood in line for hours to purchase a product at an artificially low price—only to find that the good sold out just as you reached the head of the line. **1**

Allocations Without Prices

Think what life would be like without a price system. How would a car dealer allocate a limited sup-

Nonprice Allocation *In command economies such as that in the former Soviet Union, government planners set artificially low prices.* **How did this type of nonprice allocation affect the amount of goods produced?**

ply of sports cars? Would intelligence, or perhaps good looks, or even political connections, determine who could get a car? Most people probably view these criteria as unfair.

Still, without prices, some other system must be used to allocate scarce goods and services. One such method is **rationing**—a system under which a government agency decides everyone's fair share. Under such a system, people receive a **ration coupon,** similar to a ticket or a receipt, that entitles the holder to purchase a certain amount of the product. Rationing has been used before, especially during wartime, but many problems are associated with it.

The Problem of Fairness

The first problem with rationing is that almost everyone feels his or her share is too small. During the oil crisis of the early 1970s, for example, the government made plans for, but never implemented, a gas rationing program. One of the major problems with the program was determining how to allocate the gas rationing coupons. Some people argued that the only fair way to allocate gas was to give everyone exactly the same number of coupons. Drivers of newer and more fuel-efficient cars, however, got farther on a gallon of gas than someone who owned an older gas-guzzler. Those who used public transportation needed even fewer coupons.

Consumers debated about who needed gas the most. Driving distances also were debated. Those who lived in western states claimed that, because they drove longer distances than their eastern counterparts, westerners should receive more coupons. Some advocated rationing coupons according to the number of cars registered, so that every owner got "X" number of coupons per car. This plan discriminated against the large family with only one car, and

it seemed to favor young couples who owned two or even three cars.

Some people thought they were more important than others. Should politicians and government bureaucrats get a certain allocation before the remaining coupons are divided among the rest of the citizens? Any number of ways to allocate gas coupons existed, but fairness was still a difficult issue. **2**

QUICK CHECK

Checking Understanding

1. What nonprice systems help allocate resources in a market economy?
2. What are the major problems with rationing?

Applying Economic Concepts

✓ **Rationing** The United States used rationing during World War II. Families received ration coupons for goods such as meat and butter based on the number of people in the household. Coupons had to be presented at the time the purchase was made.

High Administrative Cost

A second problem with rationing is the cost. Someone has to pay for printing coupons and the salaries of the people who distribute them. In addition, no matter how much care is taken, some coupons will be stolen, sold, or counterfeited and used to consume the product allocated for someone else.

In the case of the gas shortage of the 1970s, millions of coupons were actually printed and stored in warehouses around the country. The plan called for the coupons to be distributed at local post offices. Committees set up in every community would hear and then rule on hardship cases. The plan would have been expensive to implement. In addition to the cost of printing, shipping, storing, and even guarding the coupons, additional postal and other administrative workers would have had to be hired to distribute the coupons and deal with complaints.

Diminished Incentives

A third problem is that rationing has a negative impact on people's incentive to work and produce. Even if the system was set up so that everyone received an equal share, why should one person work harder than another when each would share equally in the stock of goods and services? What would motivate either person to work at all?

People sometimes lose the incentive to use the rationed good in a careful manner. In the case of the gas rationing coupons, would people have used the

Rationing *During World War II, shoppers had to buy meat with ration coupons.* **How are prices determined in a rationing system?**

gas wisely after they had enough coupons? Some people would still drive rather than carpool or take a bus. Others would be tempted to use all the gas they got even if they did not need it.

Nonprice allocation mechanisms, such as rationing, raise a number of issues that do not need to be addressed under a price allocation system. As long as we have prices, goods can be allocated through a system that is neutral, efficient, flexible, inexpensive, and full of choices.

SECTION 1 REVIEW

Reviewing Terms and Facts

1. **Define** rationing, ration coupon.
2. **List** five advantages of using prices to allocate goods and services.
3. **Explain** the difficulties of allocating goods and services without a price system.

Critical Thinking

4. **Determining Cause and Effect** List five items you would like to buy. How does the price of each item affect your decision to allocate your scarce resources—your money and your time? Describe the way in which prices act as signals to help you make your decisions.

Applying Economic Concepts

5. **Rationing** From your own experience, describe a situation that required some form of rationing. What criteria were used to allocate the good or service, and what were some of the problems with each of the criteria?

Interpreting Political Cartoons

Do you turn to the comics section of the newspaper first? Most people enjoy reading comic strips, but newspapers have another type of cartoon known as the *political cartoon*—a drawing that gives visual commentary on current events.

Explanation

In political cartoons, artists use humor and satire to express opinions about political and economic issues. The purpose of most political cartoons is to inform and influence public opinion in an entertaining way. Because political cartoons reflect the opinions of individual artists, they usually appear on the editorial pages of newspapers.

To interpret the meaning of a political cartoon, study its pictures, words, and symbols to discover its main idea and point of view. Cartoonists often exaggerate drawings to make their points more forcefully. For example, a group of poor people may be represented by one very thin person. Cartoonists also use symbols. The figure of Uncle Sam, for example, is a symbol for the United States government.

Follow these steps to interpret political cartoons.
- Read the title and information in the cartoon to determine its general topic.
- Analyze the symbols in the cartoon.
- Identify the main idea and the cartoonist's point of view.

Practice

Study the cartoon and answer the questions below.
1. Who does the man sitting on the table represent?
2. Who does the second man represent?
3. What is the second man doing?
4. What is the main point of this cartoon?
5. What do you think the cartoonist's attitude is about this issue?
6. How did you form that conclusion?

HEALTH CARE in AMERICA

CHECK BOOK

DANZIGER
The Christian Science Monitor
Los Angeles Times Syndicate

Additional Practice

For further practice in interpreting political cartoons, complete the Reinforcing Skills exercise in the Chapter 6 Review on page 149.

Section Preview

Objectives

After studying this section, you will be able to:

1. **Understand** how prices are determined in competitive markets.
2. **Explain** the importance of an economic model.

Key Terms

economic model, market equilibrium, surplus, shortage, equilibrium price, loss leader

Applying Economic Concepts

Equilibrium Price Have you ever sold something to a friend? Perhaps you wanted to sell at one price and your friend wanted to buy at another. After some compromise, you probably agreed on a price, and the exchange took place. Your price was an *equilibrium price*, or one that clears the market.

In a market economy, everyone who participates in the market jointly determines prices. Prices are considered neutral and impartial.

The Adjustment Process

In economic markets, buyers and sellers have exactly the opposite hopes and intentions. Buyers want to find good buys at low prices. Sellers hope for high prices and profits. Neither side can get exactly what it wants, so some adjustment is necessary to reach a compromise. Even so, both sides benefit as long as the process is voluntary, or the transaction would not have occurred in the first place.

To understand how the adjustment takes place, suppose a new product called a *gadget* is introduced. The gadget, for illustrative purposes, is an innovative home security device. Because the product is new, producers cannot be sure what price to charge for it. They will have to experiment and see if the market forces of supply and demand will help resolve the issue.

An Economic Model

In order to demonstrate how a market works, we can use an **economic model**—a set of assumptions that can be listed in a table, illustrated with a graph, or even stated algebraically—to help analyze behavior and predict outcomes. Information about the market is shown in **Figure 6.1**, where the price and consumer demand

for gadgets appear in the first two columns and the quantity supplied appears in the third column. **1**

The demand schedule in columns 1 and 2 reflects the Law of Demand—as the price goes down, more gadgets are demanded. Likewise, the supply schedule in columns 1 and 3 reflects the Law of Supply—as the price goes up, the gadget-makers are willing to supply more. These schedules can also be illustrated graphically as in **Figure 6.2**, where supply and demand curves appear in the same diagram.

The demand curve in **Figure 6.2** represents the ability and willingness of consumers to purchase the product. The supply curve in **Figure 6.2** represents the ability and willingness of suppliers to offer various quantities of gadgets over a range of different prices. When we put the supply curve and the demand curve together, we have a visual representation of all the buyers and sellers in the market.

Market Equilibrium

In a competitive market, the adjustment process moves toward **market equilibrium**—a situation in which prices are relatively stable, and the quantity of goods or services supplied is equal to the quantity demanded. In terms of the economic model in **Figure 6.2**, equilibrium is reached when the price is $5, and the quantity supplied is 1,300 units. **2**

How does the market find the equilibrium price of $5 on its own, and why is the quantity supplied exactly equal to the quantity demanded at this price?

Figure 6.1
The Demand and Supply Schedules for Gadgets

Price (in dollars)	Quantity Demanded	Quantity Supplied	Shortage/Surplus	
$10	600	1550	950	**SURPLUS**
9	720	1500	780	
8	850	1450	600	
7	990	1400	410	
6	1140	1350	210	
5	1300	1300	0	**EQUILIBRIUM**
4	1470	1250	-220	**SHORTAGE**
3	1650	1200	-450	
2	1840	1150	-690	
1	2040	1100	-940	

The demand schedule for gadgets appears in the first two columns. The supply schedule appears in columns one and three. If you compare the quantities demanded and supplied at every price, you can see there is a surplus at every price at $6 and above, and a shortage at every price at $4 and below. $5 is the equilibrium price that balances the quantity demanded with the quantity supplied. **How is an equilibrium price reached?**

Why did the market not reach equilibrium at $7, or $6, or at some other price? In order to answer these questions, we have to examine the reactions of the buyers and sellers to various market prices.

Surplus

Because the market for gadgets is new, no one knows what the equilibrium price will be. If suppliers guess that the price will be $7 per gadget, they will want to produce 1,400 units for sale. As Graph **A** in **Figure 6.3** shows, consumers will buy only 990 of the 1,400 gadgets at a price of $7, leaving a surplus of 410.

A **surplus** is a situation in which the quantity supplied is greater than the quantity demanded at a given price. Suppliers may have built up inventories in their warehouses, only to find that they did not receive enough orders for the product. If the suppliers want to dispose of the surplus, they need to lower their price to attract more buyers. At a lower price, suppliers will also offer fewer gadgets for sale during the next trading period. The result is that a surplus causes the price to go down, the quantity demanded to rise, and the quantity supplied to be reduced. As long as the price is flexible, the surplus will only be temporary. ✓

QUICK CHECK

Checking Understanding

1. Why do economists use economic models? ✓
2. What is market equilibrium?

Applying Economic Concepts

✓ **Surplus** American farmers have been so productive that they have consistently harvested surpluses.

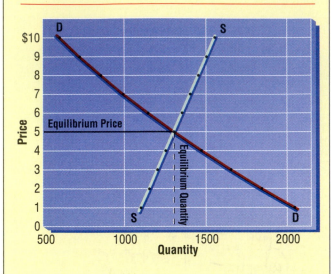

Figure 6.2
A Model of the Gadgets Market

According to the model of the gadgets market, $5 is the equilibrium price that "clears" the market. At that price, 1,300 gadgets will be supplied and an equal number purchased. **What happens to the supply of gadgets if the price is lowered to $3?**

Shortage

If $7 is too high, the producers might consider $4 on the second day. At that price, the quantity supplied changes to 1,250 gadgets. As Graph **B** in **Figure 6.3** shows, however, the $4 price is too low. At $4, the demand curve shows that consumers would buy 1,470 gadgets. Because only 1,250 are available, a shortage of 220 results.

A **shortage** is a situation in which the quantity demanded is greater than the quantity supplied at a given price. When a shortage in the market happens, producers have no more gadgets to sell even though additional buyers are willing to purchase the product at the existing price. Producers wish that they had charged higher prices for their products. The result is that a shortage causes the price and the quantity supplied to increase in the next trading period.

While our model does not show exactly how much the price will go up, we can assume that the next price will be less than $7, which we already know is too high. If the new price is $6, a surplus of 210, as seen in Graph **C** in **Figure 6.3**, will result. This surplus will cause the price to drop, but probably not below $4, which already proved to be too low.

Price Adjustment
Bookstores and other businesses often price certain goods below cost to attract customers. **What may result if the price for a given product is set too low?**

Figure 6.3
Dynamics of the Price Adjustment Process in the Gadgets Market

A. DAY 1: A price of $7 causes a surplus of 410.

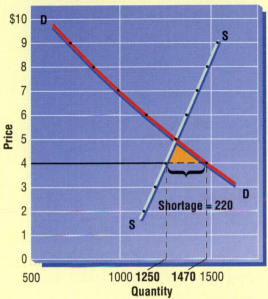

Surplus = 410

B. DAY 2: The previous surplus causes the price to drop. The new price is too low and a shortage develops.

Shortage = 220

C. DAY 3: The shortage in Day 2 causes the price to rise. The new price is too high.

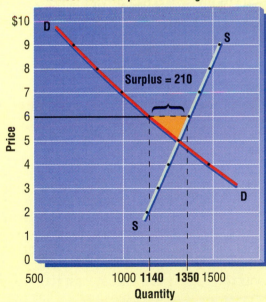

Surplus = 210

D. DAY 4: The surplus in Day 3 causes the price to drop, and equilibrium is reached.

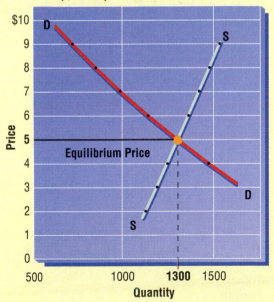

Equilibrium Price

In a competitive market, prices tend to gravitate toward equilibrium as a result of the constant pressures from temporary surpluses and shortages. **What is the difference between a surplus and a shortage?**

Equilibrium Price

When the price drops to $5, as shown in Graph **D** in **Figure 6.3**, the market finds its **equilibrium price.** The equilibrium price is the price that "clears the market" in that there is neither a surplus nor a shortage at the end of the trading period. While the model of the market cannot show exactly how long it will take to reach equilibrium, equilibrium will be reached.

Because of the pressure that temporary surpluses and/or shortages put on prices and quantities supplied, the market tends to seek its own equilibrium. Prices in the gadget market will eventually reach and then stay at $5, with production at 1,300 units, until something disturbs the market.

A Touch of Realism

The theory of competitive pricing represents a set of ideal conditions and outcomes. The theory serves as a model by which to measure the performance of other less competitive market structures.

Many markets do come close to the ideal. The prices of gasoline, foods, and many other items in your community will be relatively close from one store to the next. When the prices of these items do vary, it may be because the buyers are not well informed. A store may also be promoting a certain item as a **loss leader**—an item specially priced below cost to attract customers.

Although small price differences are found in a highly competitive market, large differences generally are not. Those that do exist do not last long. How long, for example, could a store sell its apples for $3.69 a bag if other stores were selling them for $1.99? At some point, customers would become sensitive to price and change their buying habits.

SECTION 2 REVIEW

Reviewing Terms and Facts

1. **Define** economic model, market equilibrium, surplus, shortage, equilibrium price, loss leader.
2. **Describe** how surpluses and shortages help the market find the equilibrium price.
3. **Explain** the importance of an economic model.

Critical Thinking

4. **Making Inferences** What do merchants usually do to move items that are overstocked? What does this tell you about the equilibrium price for the product?

Applying Economic Concepts

5. **Equilibrium Price** Choose one good or service—for example, unleaded gasoline, a gallon of milk, a local newspaper, a haircut. Visit at least four stores that carry the product, and note its price at each location. What do the individual prices tell you about the equilibrium price for the good or service?

PROFILES IN ECONOMICS

GARY BECKER
(1930–   )

Gary Stanley Becker is a professor of economics at the University of Chicago and a fellow of the Hoover Institution at Stanford. In 1992 he received the Nobel Prize in economics for his work applying economic analysis to social problems, including crime and punishment, racial and gender discrimination, the formation and breakup of families, drug and substance abuse, and the formation and importance of human capital.

ECONOMIC BASIS OF SOCIAL PROBLEMS Professor Becker views individual behavior as being based on the economic incentives of the marketplace

College graduates reflect an investment in human capital.

and rational self-interest. He believes that costs and benefits interact to help explain human behavior. Shortly after winning the Nobel Prize, he described his theory:

The number of children a couple has depends on the costs and benefits of child rearing. . . . [C]ouples tend to have fewer children when the wife works and has a better-paying job, when subsidies and tax deductions for dependents are smaller, when the cost of educating and training children rises, and so forth.

—Viewpoint,
Business Week, November 2, 1992

Professor Becker has extended economic analysis into areas normally studied by other social disciplines. He recognizes the contributions made by other social sciences in explaining human behavior, however. Becker argues, for example, that the sociologist helps explain human

behavior by identifying the broad social forces, such as peer group pressure, that cause some people to act as they do. When the sociologist's view is combined with the economic theory of costs, benefits, and personal welfare, an explanation for individual behavior becomes more powerful.

In the case of drug and substance abuse, Becker argues that, although addictive behavior has a psychological and a biological basis, the economist can help point out some of the economic circumstances that encouraged people to first become addicted. Economists can also help explain how a change in these economic circumstances—including housing, employment, and better career opportunities—might affect the addiction.

HUMAN CAPITAL Professor Becker helped popularize interest in the topic of human capital. He frequently uses the differences in earnings among high school dropouts, high school graduates, and college graduates to reinforce the point that education and training are rewarded in the marketplace.

Examining the Profile

1. **Identifying Cause and Effect** How can costs help explain why American families have grown smaller?

2. **For Further Research** Research the relationship between periods of economic growth and/or decline and the status of criminal activity during the same periods. Summarize your findings in a statistical table.

The Price System at Work

Section Preview

Objectives

After studying this section, you will be able to:

1. **Explain** how prices allocate resources between markets.
2. **Describe** the consequence of having a fixed price in a market.
3. **Apply** your knowledge of demand elasticity to predict the size of a price change.
4. **Understand** what is meant when markets talk.

Key Terms

rebate, price ceiling, minimum wage, price floor, target price, non-recourse loan, deficiency payment

Applying Economic Concepts

Shortage If you are planning to go to college, you should be aware some large universities actually turn students away because of a shortage of classroom space. This *shortage* is partially due to tuition. When tuition is too low, too many people have the ability and willingness to pay. Colleges and universities must then rely on nonprice criteria—state residency, class standing, and SAT or ACT scores—to allocate the existing spaces.

Prices are important because they help producers and consumers make decisions. The overall economy, however, is made up of many markets for many different products. In order to understand how the economy operates as a whole, the role of prices in this larger setting must be examined.

Prices as a System

A price in any given resource market helps sellers decide where to sell their resources and producers where to buy them. The same is basically true of all prices collectively. Prices serve as signals that allocate resources between markets.

Consider the way in which higher oil prices affected producers' and consumers' decisions in the 1970s. During this time, the price of oil went from $5 a barrel to as much as $40. Because the demand for oil is basically inelastic, people had to spend a greater part of their income on energy. Higher energy costs left them with less to spend elsewhere, a fact that affected other markets. ☑

The market for full-size automobiles was one of the first industries to feel the effects. Because most large cars did not get good gas mileage, people bought fewer big cars and more foreign-made, smaller automobiles. As the demand for big cars fell, producers ended up with unsold inventories of automobiles.

At first, automakers thought the increase in gas prices would be temporary, so they were reluctant to introduce smaller, more fuel-efficient models. As time went on, however, the surplus of unsold cars remained. To move their inventories, manufacturers began to offer a **rebate**—a partial refund of the original price of the product. The rebate was the

Prices *Farmers, like economists, try to predict changes in prices.* **What do prices tell buyers and sellers?**

same as a temporary price reduction, because consumers were offered $500, $600, and even $1,000 back on each new car they bought.

At the same time, automakers began reducing their production of large cars. Plants were closed, workers were laid off, and companies started to change to small car production. Many of the automobile workers who lost their jobs found new ones in other industries.

The result of higher prices in the international oil market was a shift of productive resources out of the large car market into other markets. Although the process was a painful one for those involved, it was a necessary one for a market economy. **1**

What Happens When Prices Are Fixed?

Up to now, we have assumed that the market was reasonably competitive and that prices, along with quantities offered for sale, were allowed to fluctuate. What happens when someone, usually the government, decides that prices should be fixed? How does this affect the signals that are sent, the decisions that are made in the marketplace, and the general allocation of resources?

Answers to these questions can be found by analyzing what happens in markets when prices are fixed too high or too low. The examples below will help us with the analysis.

Price Ceilings

Some cities, especially New York City, have experimented with rent controls to make housing more affordable. When rents are capped at artificially low rates, however, persistent "housing shortages" usually result.

Figure 6.4
Price Ceilings and Permanent Shortages

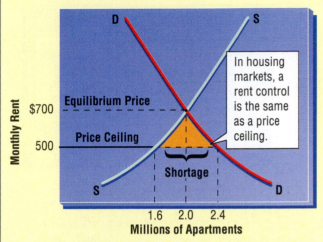

A shortage is created whenever a price ceiling is lower than the equilibrium price. In the figure, a ceiling price of $500 per month results in 2.4 million apartments demanded with only 1.6 million being supplied—leaving a shortage of .8 million, or 800,000 apartments. **Why are price ceilings established?**

The case of a **price ceiling,** the maximum legal price that can be charged, is shown in **Figure 6.4**. Without the ceiling, the market establishes monthly rents at $700. Two million apartments would be supplied and rented at that rate. If authorities thought $700 was too high, they could arbitrarily establish a price ceiling at $500 a month. Consumers, of course, would love the lower price and might demand 2.4 million apartments as a result. Landlords, on the other hand, would just as soon convert some apartments to other uses that offer higher returns. Therefore, only 1.6 million apartments would be offered at $500 per month. **2**

Checking Understanding

1. What was the result of higher prices in the international oil market?
2. How do price ceilings affect quantity supplied?

Applying Economic Concepts

☑ **Market and Prices** The cost of motor fuel—gasoline, ethanol, and diesel—more than tripled during the 1970s before dropping significantly in the mid-1980s.

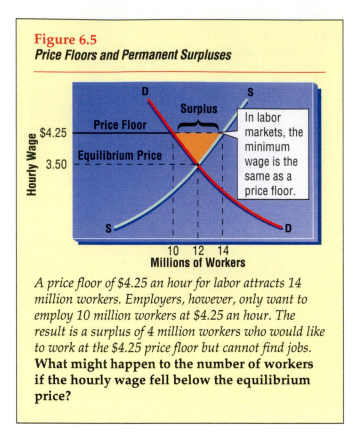

Surplus

Price Floor

Equilibrium Price

$4.25

3.50

In labor markets, the minimum wage is the same as a price floor.

Hourly Wage

D   S

S   D

10 12 14
Millions of Workers

A price floor of $4.25 an hour for labor attracts 14 million workers. Employers, however, only want to employ 10 million workers at $4.25 an hour. The result is a surplus of 4 million workers who would like to work at the $4.25 price floor but cannot find jobs.
What might happen to the number of workers if the hourly wage fell below the equilibrium price?

The result would be a shortage of 800,000 apartments, the difference between the 2.4 million demanded and the 1.6 million supplied. Are consumers better off? Perhaps not. More than likely, the better apartments were converted to condos or offices—leaving the poorer ones to be rented.

In addition, 800,000 people are now unhappy because they cannot get an apartment, although they are willing and able to pay for one. Prices no longer allocate apartments. Instead, landlords resort to long waiting lists or other nonprice criteria to assign apartments.

Rent controls freeze a landlord's total revenue and threaten his or her profits. As a result, the landlord tries to lower costs by providing the absolute minimum upkeep, thereby protecting profits. Landlords have no incentive whatsoever to add additional apartments if they feel rents are too low. ✔

The price ceiling, like any other price, affects the allocation of resources—but not in the way intended. The attempt to limit rents makes some people happy—the ones that get the apartments. Instead of providing affordable rental units to all, however,

apartments (scarce resources) are shifted out of the rental market and into the condo and business office markets. Some apartment buildings will even be torn down to make way for shopping centers, factories, or high-rise office buildings. **1**

Price Floors

Occasionally, prices are considered too low, and some people believe they should be kept higher. The **minimum wage,** the lowest legal wage that can be paid to most workers, is a case in point. The minimum wage is actually a **price floor,** or lowest legal price that can be paid for a good or service.

Figure 6.5 uses a minimum wage of $4.25 per hour. At this wage in the figure, 14 million people would want to offer their services. According to the demand curve for labor, however, only 10 million would be hired—leaving a surplus of 4 million workers.

The figure also shows that without the minimum wage, the actual demand and supply of labor would establish an equilibrium price of $3.50 per hour. At this wage, 12 million workers would offer their services and exactly the same number would be hired—which means that there would be no shortage in the labor market.

Many economists argue that the minimum wage actually increases the number of people who do not have jobs because employers hire fewer workers. In the case of **Figure 6.5**, the number of people who do not get jobs amounts to 2 million—the difference between the number that would work at the equilibrium price (12 million), and the number that actually work at the higher wage of $4.25 per hour. **2**

Is the current minimum wage higher or lower than the wage that would prevail in its absence? The answer to that question is not always clear, and it may vary from one market to another, as well as from one part of the country to another. Consider wages in your area. Do you think that your employer would pay you less if he or she were allowed to do so? Your response will provide a partial answer to the question.

Predicting Prices

Economists are concerned with both explanation and prediction. They use their models of the market to explain how the world around them works and to

Figure 6.6
Changes in Supply and the Elasticity of Demand

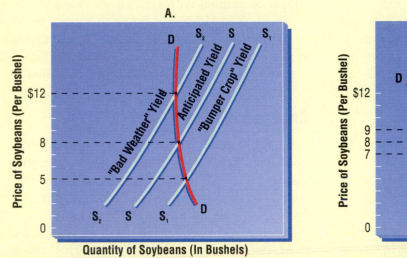

A.

Price of Soybeans (Per Bushel)

$12
8
5
0

"Bad Weather" Yield

Anticipated Yield

"Bumper Crop" Yield

S_2 S S_1 D

S_2 S S_1 D

Quantity of Soybeans (In Bushels)

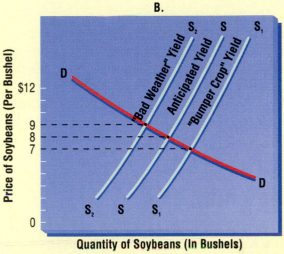

B.

Price of Soybeans (Per Bushel)

$12
9
8
7
0

D

"Bad Weather" Yield

Anticipated Yield

"Bumper Crop" Yield

S_2 S S_1

S_2 S S_1 D

Quantity of Soybeans (In Bushels)

Seasonal price changes in agriculture are often caused by changes in supply. The size of the price change also depends on the elasticity of demand for the product. The less elastic the demand, as in the diagram on the left, the larger the price change. The more elastic the demand, as in the diagram on the right, the smaller the price change. **What other factors may cause a change in prices?**

predict how certain events might affect the economy in the future. Even changes in prices can be explained and sometimes predicted. A change in price normally results from a change in supply, a change in demand, or changes in both. Demand elasticity also turns out to be important in predicting prices.

Changes in Supply

Consider the case of agriculture, in which wide swings in prices from one year to the next are fairly typical. A farmer may keep up with all the latest developments and have the best advice experts can offer. Even so, the farmer never is sure what price to expect for the crop. A soybean farmer may put in 500 acres of beans, expecting a price of $8 a bushel. The farmer knows, however, that the actual price may end up being anywhere from $5 to $12. The same is true for the cotton farmer who expects 80 cents a pound but may end up getting anywhere from 40 cents to $1.50.

One of the main reasons for the variation in agricultural prices is that weather influences farm output. After planting, all the farmer can do is wait. If it rains too much, the seeds will be washed away and the

QUICK CHECK

Checking Understanding

1. What was the unintended effect of rent controls?
2. How do many economists think the minimum wage affects unemployment?

Applying Economic Concepts

 Role of Government Many rent controls cap the amount a landlord can raise the rent for a current tenant only. When a new tenant takes the apartment, the forces of supply and demand set the rent. As a result, tenants with similar apartments might pay widely varying rents.

farmer must replant. If it rains too little, the seeds will not sprout. Even if the weather is perfect during the growing season, rain can still prevent the harvest from being gathered. The weather, then, can cause a change in supply.

The result, shown in Graph **A** in **Figure 6.6**, is that the supply curve is likely to shift, causing the price to go up or down. At the beginning of the season, the farmer may expect supply to look like curve SS. If a bumper, or record, crop is harvested, however, supply may look like S_1S_1. If bad weather strikes, supply may look like S_2S_2. Because the demand for food generally is inelastic, a small change in supply is enough to cause a large change in the price.

Demand Elasticity

What would have happened to prices if the demand for soybeans were highly elastic, as in Graph **B** of **Figure 6.6**? The results would be quite different. Because this demand curve is much more elastic, the

prices would only range from $7 to $9 a bushel instead of from $5 to $12 a bushel.

Economists consider demand elasticity whenever a change in supply occurs. When a given change in supply is coupled with an inelastic demand curve, as in Graph **A** in **Figure 6.6**, price changes a great deal. When the same change in supply is coupled with a very elastic demand curve, such as that in Graph **B** of **Figure 6.6**, the change in price is much smaller.

Changes in Demand

Changes in demand also may affect the price of a good or service. **Figure 6.7** shows how changes in demand for gold—coupled with a relatively fixed supply of gold—cause wide fluctuations in its price. Bad news, such as war, possible recessions, or other disasters, might cause people to suddenly increase their demand for gold to D_1D_1. This change in demand drives the price of gold to $600 an ounce.

Good news, such as peace agreements, economic growth, or a lower rate of inflation, might cause a decrease in demand to DD. The price of gold would then drop sharply to $400 an ounce. **1**

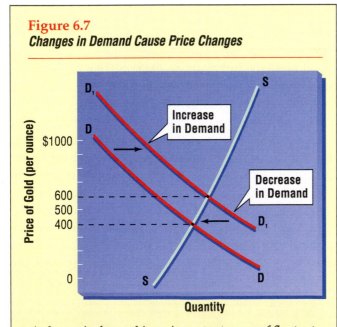

Figure 6.7
Changes in Demand Cause Price Changes

A change in demand is an important cause of fluctuating prices. An increase in demand increases the equilibrium price, and a decrease in demand lowers the price. Changes in consumer incomes, changes in tastes, and changes in the prices of related goods all can cause a change in demand. **What factors might increase the demand for gold?**

Agricultural Price Supports

In the 1930s, the federal government established the Commodity Credit Corporation (CCC), an agency in the Department of Agriculture. The CCC's job was to help stabilize agricultural prices. The stabilization took two basic forms—the first involving loan supports and the second involving deficiency payments. Both made use of **target prices,** which are essentially floor prices for farm products.

Loan Supports

Under the loan support program, a farmer could borrow money from the CCC at a target price. In return, the farmer pledged his or her crops as security. The loan was then used to plant, maintain, and harvest the crop. The farmer could either sell the crop in the market and use the proceeds to repay the CCC loan, or the farmer could keep the proceeds of the loan and let the CCC take possession of the crop. Because the loan was a **non-recourse loan**, the farmer,

Figure 6.8
Agricultural Price Supports

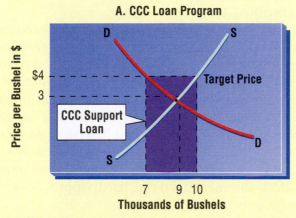

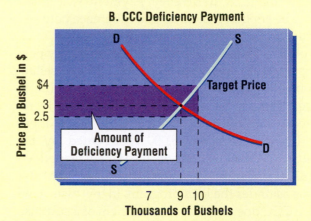

Under the CCC loan program in Graph A, the farmer pledges 10,000 bushels of wheat at the $4 target price to receive a $40,000 non-recourse loan. The farmer sells as much wheat as possible at or above the target price in the open market, and then defaults on the remainder of the loan, allowing the CCC to take control of 3,000 bushels of wheat. Under the deficiency payment program in Graph B, the farmer sells all 10,000 bushels on the market at $2.50 a bushel, and then receives a deficiency payment in the amount of $1.50 times 10,000, or $15,000 from the CCC. Either way, the farmer receives at least $40,000 for the wheat. **Which program avoids storage problems for the CCC?**

if unable to repay the money, faced no additional penalties other than forfeiting the crop. **2**

Graph **A** in **Figure 6.8** illustrates the CCC loan program. The target price at the beginning of the year was set at $4 a bushel for wheat. A farmer pledged 10,000 bushels of wheat to the CCC and received a $40,000 loan in return. When the crop was harvested, the farmer sold only 7,000 bushels in the market at $4/bushel, and repaid $28,000 of the CCC loan.

The farmer then forfeited the remaining 3,000 bushels of wheat to the CCC and kept the remainder of the loan, represented by the shaded area in the figure. In the end, the farmer received $4 a bushel for each of the 10,000 bushels produced—with 7,000 bushels sold

in the market and the remaining 3,000 picked up by the CCC. Without the loan program, the farmer would have produced 9,000 bushels and sold them at $3 each for a total revenue of $27,000.

Deficiency Payments

The problem with the CCC loan program was that the CCC soon faced enormous stockpiles of food. Surplus wheat was stored in rented warehouses or on open ground. Surplus milk was made into cheese and stored in underground caves. How could the CCC support farm prices, yet avoid the embarrassingly large surpluses?

Checking Understanding

1. How do world events affect the price of gold?
2. How does the loan support program work?

Applying Economic Concepts

☑ **Role of Government** Loans made by the Commodity Credit Corporation peaked in 1986, when the agency loaned $17,391,000. Since then, loans have decreased. In the early 1990s, they averaged less than $7 million per year.

The answer was to have farmers sell the crops on the open market for the best price they could get, and have the CCC make up the difference with a deficiency payment. A **deficiency payment** is a check sent to farmers that makes up the difference between the actual market price and the target price.

Graph **B** in **Figure 6.8** illustrates the deficiency payment program. The farmer made $25,000 selling 10,000 bushels at $2.50 each, which was $1.50 below the target price of $4.00 a bushel. The farmer, therefore, received deficiency payments of $1.50 times 10,000 bushels, or the $15,000 represented by the shaded area. When the deficiency payment was added to the $25,000 market sale, the farmer made $40,000—the same as under the loan program. In this case, however, the CCC does not have the problem of a surplus.

In exchange for the CCC price supports, farmers often have to promise to limit production. In some cases, such as peanut production, aerial photographs are taken to verify that the acreage is within the limits of the quota.

When Markets Talk

Markets are highly impersonal mechanisms that bring buyers and sellers together. Although markets do not talk in the usual sense of the word, they do communicate in that they speak collectively for all of the buyers and sellers who trade in the markets. Markets are said to talk when prices in them move up or down significantly.

Suppose the federal government announced that it would raise personal income taxes and corporate taxes to balance the federal budget. If investors thought this policy would not work or that other policies might be better, they might decide to sell some of their stocks and other investments for cash and gold, which could be used in case of an emergency. As the selling takes place, stock prices would fall, and gold prices would rise. It could be said that, in effect, the market voiced its disapproval of the new tax policy.

In a sense, then, the market did talk. Individual investors made decisions on the likely outcome of the new policy and sold stocks for cash or gold. Together, their actions were enough to influence stock prices and to send a signal to the government that investors did not favor the policy.

If investors' feelings were divided about the new policy, some would sell while others bought stocks. As a result, prices might not change, and the message would be that, as yet, the markets have not made up their minds.

SECTION 3
REVIEW

Reviewing Terms and Facts

1. **Define** rebate, price ceiling, minimum wage, price floor, target price, non-recourse loan, deficiency payment.
2. **Describe** two effects of having a fixed price other than the equilibrium price forced on a market.
3. **Explain** why price changes are more moderate when demand is highly elastic.
4. **Describe** how markets speak collectively for buyers and sellers.

Critical Thinking

5. **Determining Cause and Effect** The price of fresh fruit over the course of a year may go up or down by as much as 100 percent. Explain the causes for these changes in terms of changes in demand, changes in supply, and the elasticity of demand for fresh fruit.

Applying Economic Concepts

6. **Shortage** Identify a shortage of employees in your community—for example, not enough skilled doctors, teachers, or piano tuners. Use your knowledge of prices to explain how different wages or salaries could be used to remedy the shortage.

Vocabulary

The following terms are defined in Chapter 6:

SECTION ONE
- rationing *(p. 131)*
- ration coupon *(p. 131)*

SECTION TWO
- economic model *(p. 134)*
- market equilibrium *(p. 134)*

- surplus *(p. 135)*
- shortage *(p. 136)*
- equilibrium price *(p. 138)*
- loss leader *(p. 138)*

SECTION THREE
- rebate *(p. 140)*
- price ceiling *(p. 141)*

- minimum wage *(p. 142)*
- price floor *(p. 142)*
- target price *(p. 144)*
- non-recourse loan *(p. 144)*
- deficiency payment *(p. 146)*

Section 1

Prices as Signals (pages 128–132)

Prices serve as signals to both producers and consumers. High prices are signals to produce more and buy less. Low prices are signals to produce less and buy more.

Prices have several advantages, including neutrality, flexibility, freedom of choice, no administrative costs, and efficiency. Prices also have the advantage of being easily understood by everyone.

Other, nonprice-related allocation methods can be used, including **rationing.** These nonprice allocations, however, cause problems regarding fairness, high administrative costs, and diminished incentives to work and produce.

Reviewing the Main Idea

How do prices act as signals to both consumers and producers?

Section 2

How Prices Are Determined (pages 134–138)

In a competitive market, the forces of supply and demand establish prices. If the price is too high, a temporary **surplus** appears until the price goes down. If the price is too low, a temporary **shortage** appears until the price rises. Eventually the market reaches an **equilibrium price,** which causes neither a shortage nor a surplus.

The theory of competitive pricing represents a theoretical ideal that is seldom reached. Even so, absolutely pure competition is not needed for the theory to be practical.

Reviewing the Main Idea

How does the adjustment process work in a market as an equilibrium price is determined?

Section 3

The Price System at Work (pages 140–146)

A market economy is made up of many different markets, and different prices prevail in each. A change in one price affects more than the allocation of resources in that market. A price change affects the allocation of resources between markets.

Governments sometimes fix prices at levels above or below the equilibrium price. If the fixed price is a **price ceiling,** as with rent controls, a shortage usually appears for as long as the price is fixed. If the legal price is a **price floor,** as in the case of the **minimum wage,** a surplus usually results.

A change in supply or a change in demand can change prices. The elasticity of the demand curve affects the size of the price change. The more elastic the curve, the smaller the price change. The less elastic the demand curve, the larger the price change.

Agricultural price supports grew dramatically during the 1930s to support farm incomes. Loan support programs from the CCC allowed farmers to borrow against crops, then keep the loan and forfeit the crop if market prices were low. **Deficiency payments** are more commonly used, supplying the farmer with a check that makes up the difference between the **target price** and the actual price received for the product.

Reviewing the Main Idea

How do prices function collectively to allocate resources between markets?

Reviewing Key Terms

Write the key term that is an effect of the five causes stated below. Some causes may have more than one effect.

1. **Cause:** The government tries to keep prices down by legislating price ceilings. **Effect:** _____
2. **Cause:** The government wants to allocate scarce goods and services without the help of a price system. **Effect:** _____
3. **Cause:** A reasonably competitive market is experiencing alternating, yet consecutively smaller, surpluses and shortages. **Effect:** _____
4. **Cause:** People decide that farmers should receive a higher price for milk and cheese, so a price floor for these products is established. **Effect:** _____
5. **Cause:** A market is at equilibrium, but the product falls out of style before producers can reduce production. **Effect:** _____

a. rationing
b. economic model
c. surplus
d. shortage
e. equilibrium price
f. loss leader
g. price ceiling
h. price floor

Reviewing the Facts

SECTION 1 *(pages 128–132)*

1. **Describe** five advantages of using price as an allocating mechanism.
2. **List** three problems of allocating goods and services using nonprice-related methods.

SECTION 2 *(pages 134–138)*

3. **Cite** an example of an economic model used in this chapter.
4. **Explain** the role of shortages and surpluses in competitive markets.

SECTION 3 *(pages 140–146)*

5. **Explain** what is meant by a "system" of prices.
6. **Explain** why shortages and surpluses are not temporary when price controls are used.

7. **Describe** two causes of a price change in a market.
8. **Explain** what is meant by the statement that markets talk.

Critical Thinking

1. **Predicting Consequences** Suppose that your state wanted to make health care more affordable for everyone. To do this, state legislators put a series of price controls—price ceilings—in place that cut the cost of medical services in half. What would happen to the demand for medical services at the new, lower price? What would happen to the supply of medical services that doctors would be willing to provide at the new, lower price? Where do you think new doctors would prefer to set up practice? Explain the reasons for your answers.

2. **Making Generalizations** Some people argue that an equilibrium price is not a fair price. Explain why you agree or disagree with this argument.

Applying Economic Concepts

1. **Rationing** Suppose that a guest speaker visited your class and left 20 ballpoint pens as samples—not knowing that there were 30 students in the class. Devise a nonprice rationing system that would fairly allocate the scarce item to everyone in the class.

2. **Equilibrium Price** Many people feel that the minimum wage is too low. If it increased by $1 per hour, what would happen to the number of students who would want to work after school? What would happen to the number of workers that stores in your community would want to hire? Would the combination of these factors cause a shortage or a surplus of workers in your community? Provide an explanation for each of your answers.

Reinforcing Skills

INTERPRETING POLITICAL CARTOONS

Study the political cartoon below and then answer the following questions.

1. Who does the person represent?
2. What is happening to this person?
3. Describe the appearance of the person.
4. To what is the person connected?
5. What is the main point of this cartoon?
6. What do you think is the cartoonist's attitude about this issue?

Individual Activity

Construct an economic model by following these steps: (1) Select a product and list the kinds of inputs and their costs required in the product's manufacturing. (2) Construct a hypothetical supply curve for the product. (3) Determine the demand elasticity for the product: Does it have many substitutes? Can its purchase be postponed? Does it consume much income? (4) Construct a demand curve and combine it with the supply curve in a single graph. This is your economic model. (5) Now ask yourself the following questions: Is something likely to happen that would cause either of the curves to shift? If so, which one would shift? If either curve shifts, what happens to the price? (6) Finally, make reasonable predictions about the future price of your product.

Cooperative Learning Activity

Many groceries display the unit price—the cost per unit—of food items on their shelves. You can calculate unit price by dividing the price by the quantity. The unit price of a 15-ounce box of cereal that costs $3.75 is $0.25. When comparing unit price, the units of measure must be the same. Three pounds of coffee cannot be compared to 14 ounces of coffee, for example, until one or the other measure is converted.

Working in groups of five, compare the prices of at least two brands of one of these products: orange juice, coffee, chicken soup, frozen pizza, and flour. Calculate the unit price of each brand, and choose the brand that is the better buy for each food product. Share your findings with your group and then with the class as a whole.

Writing About Economics

THE INFORMATIVE STYLE

In the **Journal Writing** activity on page 127, you were asked to make a list of from 5 to 10 surpluses and shortages. Summarize your list and, using the informative style of writing discussed on page 554, explain why surpluses and shortages exist. Conclude by predicting how producers will respond to each example discussed.

Advertisers try to convince consumers that their product is better, hoping they will be willing and able to purchase more at a higher price.

CHAPTER 7

Competition, Market Structures, and the Role of Government

CHAPTER PREVIEW

People to Know
- Charles Wang
- Environmental Health Inspector

Applying Economic Concepts in Your Life

Market Structures Why are some products available at competitive prices? Why are other products priced higher? Factors such as demand and supply determine the price of a product. The nature of the business where you bought the product also plays a role in how much it costs. It pays to learn about competition and *market structures*.

Journal Writing

Choose a product offered by several producers that is advertised in newspapers or magazines. For one week, clip and save at least three different advertisements about your product. In your journal, evaluate each advertisement and summarize why you would or would not buy a particular brand.

Competition and Market Structures

Section Preview

Objectives

After studying this section, you will be able to:

1. **Explain** the characteristics of pure competition.
2. **Understand** the nature of monopolistic competition.
3. **Describe** the behavior and characteristics of the oligopolist.
4. **Identify** several types of monopolies.

Key Terms

laissez-faire, industry, market structure, pure competition, imperfect competition, monopolistic competition, product differentiation, nonprice competition, oligopoly, collusion, price-fixing, price war, independent pricing, price leadership, monopoly, natural monopoly, franchise, economies of scale, geographic monopoly, technological monopoly, patent, copyright, government monopoly

Applying Economic Concepts

Product Differentiation Name a popular brand of shoes or clothing that you simply must have. Can you name several competing brands that you consider to be poor substitutes? If so, *product differentiation* exists—and you will pay more because of it.

When Adam Smith published *An Inquiry into the Nature and Causes of the Wealth of Nations* in 1776, the average factory was small, and most business was competitive. **Laissez-faire,** the philosophy that government should not interfere with commerce, or trade, dominated Smith's writing. *Laissez-faire* is a French term that means "allow them to do." Under laissez-faire, the role of government is confined to protecting private property, enforcing contracts, settling disputes, and protecting businesses against foreign goods.

By the late 1800s, however, competition was weakening. In some markets, a series of mergers and acquisitions combined many small firms into a few very large businesses. As industries developed— **industry** meaning the supply side of the market, or all producers collectively—the nature of competitive markets changed.

Today, economists classify markets according to conditions that prevail in them. They ask questions such as: How many suppliers are there? How large is each supplier? Do the firms have any influence over price? How much competition exists between firms? What kind of economic product is involved? Are all firms in the market selling exactly the same product, or simply similar ones? Is it easy or difficult for new firms to enter the market?

The answers to these questions help determine **market structure,** or the nature and degree of competition among firms operating in the same industry. Markets are classified according to certain structural characteristics, and economists have names for these different market structures—pure competition, monopolistic competition, oligopoly, and monopoly. **1**

Pure Competition

An important type of market structure is **pure competition.** This market situation includes independent and well-informed buyers and sellers of exactly the same economic product. Five major conditions characterize purely competitive markets. ☑

Conditions for Pure Competition

The first condition is that a large number of buyers and sellers exist. No single buyer or seller is large enough or powerful enough to affect the price of the product.

The second condition is that buyers and sellers deal in identical products. Buyers do not prefer one seller's merchandise over another's. No difference in quality, no brand names, and no need to advertise exist. Think

Pure Competition *A farm market is a practical example of pure competition.* **What five major conditions characterize purely competitive markets?**

about the market for table salt. Because salt is always the same chemical— sodium chloride—no one brand of salt should be higher in price than any other.

The third condition is that each buyer and seller acts independently. As long as everyone acts independently, sellers compete against one another for the consumer's dollar. Buyers also compete against each other and against the seller to obtain the best price. The competition between buyers and sellers is one of the forces that keeps prices low.

The fourth condition is that buyers and sellers be reasonably well-informed about items for sale. If a store offered an item for sale at a low price, customers would know about it. Because all products are exactly the same, customers would have little reason to remain loyal to one seller. If sellers were reasonably well-informed of other sellers' prices, they would have to keep their own prices low to attract customers.

The fifth condition of a purely competitive market is that buyers and sellers be free to enter into, conduct, or get out of business. This freedom makes it difficult for a single producer in any industry to keep the market just to itself. Producers have to keep prices competitive, or new firms will enter the industry and take away some of their business.

Profit Maximization

Under pure competition, each individual firm is too small to influence price. Therefore, the firm views demand differently than the industry does. In a purely competitive market, supply and demand in the entire industry establishes the equilibrium price. After that price is set, each competitive firm selects a level of output that will maximize its profits at the market price. **2**

Checking Understanding

1. What are the four basic market structures?
2. How is price established in a purely competitive market?

Applying Economic Concepts

☑ **Competition** The concept of perfectly competitive markets can also be applied to labor. A perfectly competitive labor market exists when there are so many workers and employers that no firm or worker can affect wage rates.

The relationship between firm and industry is shown graphically in **Figure 7.1**. In Graph **A**, the market forces of supply and demand set the equilibrium price at $5. This price of $5, as shown in Graph **B**, now becomes a horizontal demand curve facing each competitive firm. Regardless of how many gadgets the firm makes or wants to make, it receives the market price of $5 each. Because it receives an additional $5 for every additional gadget it produces, the marginal revenue for the perfectly competitive firm is $5, the same as its price.

Just how many gadgets the company produces depends on its costs of production. Suppose the firm expands its production from zero to one gadget. The extra, or marginal, cost of producing the first gadget is $.93, shown in the table below Graph **B** of **Figure 7.1**. Producing the first gadget will be profitable for the firm, because the gadget can be sold for $5. What

happens when the firm produces the second gadget? This is also profitable because the marginal cost of the second unit is $2.90, and it can be sold for $5.

When the firm produces the third unit, however, marginal cost increases to $5. The firm does not lose any money on the sale, but with increasing marginal costs and fixed marginal revenues, it will not expand production beyond three gadgets. In the end, the purely competitive firm will increase production to the point where its marginal cost is equal to its marginal revenue. Then it will sell that output at the equilibrium price already determined by the market forces of supply and demand.

A Theoretical Situation

If all five conditions for pure competition are satisfied, no single buyer or seller would be able to affect

---

Figure 7.1
Pure Competition: Market Price and Profit Maximization

Price	Market Demand	Market Supply	Surplus/Shortage	Quantity Supplied	Marginal Revenue	Marginal Cost
10	600	1550	950			
9	720	1500	780	7	$5	
8	850	1450	600	6	5	
7	990	1400	410	5	5	$9.60
6	1140	1350	210	4	5	7.23
5	1300	1300	0	3	5	5.00
4	1470	1250	-220	2	5	2.90
3	1650	1200	-450	1	5	.93
2	1840	1150	-690	0	5	

When the market in A is purely competitive, the forces of supply and demand set the equilibrium price. The purely competitive firm treats this price as its demand curve, because it is the only price that matters. In other words, the firm in B will receive $5 for its output regardless of how much it produces. The $5 market price, therefore, becomes a constant marginal revenue amount. In order to maximize its profits, the firm will produce the quantity of output where its marginal cost is equal to its marginal revenue. This firm will maximize its profits when it produces 3 units for sale at the equilibrium price of $5 each. **Why is pure competition a theoretical situation?**

---

price. No preferred brands would exist because all products would be identical. No single seller would try to sell a product at a price higher than the prevailing market price because most or all customers would go to other sellers. No restrictions or barriers to keep either buyers or sellers from doing business would exist.

For these reasons, competition in its purest form is a theoretical situation. Few, if any, purely competitive markets exist, although local truck, or vegetable, farming comes close to satisfying all of the conditions. In this market, many sellers offer nearly identical products. The sellers do not band together to try to control prices, and both buyers and sellers have reasonable knowledge of the products and their prices. Finally, anyone who wants to enter the business by growing tomatoes, corn, or other products could do so with little difficulty. **1**

Why do economists study pure competition if it is largely theoretical? Pure competition is used as a benchmark to help evaluate other market structures. All market situations that lack one or more of the conditions of pure competition are given the general name of **imperfect competition.** Most firms and industries in the United States fall under this broad classification. Economists generally divide imperfect competition into three categories—monopolistic competition, oligopoly, and monopoly. **2**

Monopolistic Competition

Monopolistic competition is the market structure that has all the conditions of pure competition except for identical products. By making its product a little different, the monopolistic competitor tries to attract more customers and monopolize a small portion of the market.

Monopolistic Competition *Competitors in the same market generally can produce the same product for about the same cost.* **Why, then, do prices vary greatly for similar products?**

Product Differentiation

The characteristic that separates monopolistic competition from pure competition is called **product differentiation.** Although the product being sold is similar from one firm to another, it is not identical. The differences among the products may be real or perceived. The differentiation may even be extended to store location, store design, manner of payment, delivery, decorations, service, and so on. ✓

QUICK CHECK	*Checking Understanding*	*Applying Economic Concepts*
	1. What business comes closest to the purely competitive model? 2. What are the three categories of imperfect competition?	✓ **Advertising** The advertising industry tries to build product differentiation in consumers' minds. Ads often suggest that wearing certain clothes or fragrances will make the consumer more attractive and happier.

Many examples of differentiated products can be found. Some brands of athletic footwear have special shock-absorbing soles. Others have certain construction materials to reduce weight. Still others can be inflated to provide additional ankle support. In this case, the differences between the products are real. For different brands of aspirin, however, the difference may be largely imaginary. Federal law states that all aspirin must contain certain chemicals in certain proportions, yet many people believe that some highly advertised brands are better than others.

Nonprice Competition

When a product is differentiated, **nonprice competition** takes the place of price competition. Nonprice competition happens when advertising or other promotional campaigns try to convince buyers that the product is somehow better than another brand. Therefore, monopolistic competitors usually advertise or promote heavily to make their products seem different from everyone else's. The idea is to make the consumer think that the product is so special, or so exclusive, that nothing else really competes with it.

If the seller can differentiate a product in the mind of the buyer, the firm may be able to raise the price a little above its competitors' prices. This concept explains why producers of jeans such as Guess, Bugle Boy, Levi's, Calvin Klein, or Jordache spend so much on advertising and promotion. ☑

Profit Maximization

In monopolistic competition, similar products generally sell within a narrow price range without greatly affecting the seller's or competitor's total sales. The monopolistic aspect of this competition is the seller's ability to raise the price within this narrow range. The competitive aspect is that if sellers raise or lower the price enough, customers will forget minor differences and change brands.

The profit maximization behavior of the monopolistic competitor is no different from that of other firms. The firm produces the quantity of output where its marginal cost is equal to its marginal revenue, and then sells the product for whatever the market will bear. If the firm has successfully convinced consumers that its product is better, it can charge a higher price. If it did not convince consumers, it would not be able to

charge as much. For this reason, we seldom see a single price for athletic shoes, jeans, cosmetics, or other differentiated products.

The monopolistic competitor faces the same ease of market entry as the perfect competitor. With little to stop entry into the industry, the possibility of profits will draw new firms, each of which will produce a product only a little different from the ones already on the market. In time, both the number of firms in a particular industry and the supply of the product will become fairly stable with no great profits or losses. **1**

Oligopoly

A market situation in which a few very large sellers of a product dominate is known as **oligopoly.** The product of an oligopolist may be differentiated—as in the auto industry, or standardized—as in the steel

Nonprice Competition *If advertisers can make you believe their product is better than others, you might pay more for it.* **How has nonprice competition affected your buying habits?**

industry. The exact number of firms in the industry is not as important as the ability of any single firm to cause a change in output, sales, and prices in the industry as a whole. Because of these characteristics, oligopoly is further from pure competition than is monopolistic competition.

In the United States, many markets are already oligopolistic, and many more are becoming so. Pepsi and Coke dominate the soft drink market. McDonald's, Burger King, and Wendy's dominate the fast-food industry. A few large corporations dominate other industries such as the domestic airline industry, the domestic automobile industry, and long-distance telephone service.

Interdependent Behavior

Because so few firms are part of an oligopoly, whenever one firm does something, the other firms usually follow. If one airline announces discount fares, for example, all the other airlines generally match the lower prices in a matter of days, if not hours. Each oligopolist knows that the other firms in the industry have considerable power and influence. Therefore, firms tend to act together rather than let anyone upset the status quo.

Sometimes the interdependent behavior takes the form of **collusion,** a formal agreement to set prices or to otherwise behave in a cooperative manner. One form of collusion is **price-fixing**—agreeing to charge the same or similar prices for a product. In almost every case, these prices are higher than those determined under competition. The firms also might agree to divide the market so that each is guaranteed to sell a certain amount. Because collusion usually restrains trade, it is against the law. Even so, neither the threat of heavy fines nor jail sentences has kept some collusion from taking place.

Pricing Behavior

While an oligopolist can lower the price of its product at any time, the firm knows that other oligopolists are likely to follow suit very quickly. When one firm lowers prices, it could lead to a **price war,** or a series of price cuts by all producers that may lead to unusually low prices in the industry. For a short period, the prices might even be lower than the cost of production for many of the firms.

Raising prices is risky, too, unless the firm knows that rivals will follow. Otherwise, the higher-priced firm will lose sales to its lower-priced competition. Because of this potential to lose profits with price changes, oligopolists generally prefer to compete on a nonprice basis. **2**

Nonprice competition has the advantage of making it more difficult for rivals to react. If an oligopolist finds a new advertising gimmick or a way to change the product itself, the other firms are at a disadvantage for awhile. It takes them longer to catch up and to develop a better advertising campaign or a new physical attribute for their own products.

Some oligopolists follow a policy of **independent pricing.** The oligopolist sets its own price based on demand, the cost of inputs, and other factors. **Price leadership** takes place when one firm, sometimes the biggest and most powerful in the industry, takes the lead and initiates most of the price changes. The other firms follow because they fear a price war or because they believe they will be better off financially by doing so.

Profit Maximization

The oligopolist, like any other firm, maximizes its profits when it finds the quantity of output where its marginal cost is equal to its marginal revenue. Having

Checking Understanding

1. What draws new firms into a monopolistically competitive market?
2. Why are oligopolists usually reluctant to raise prices?

Applying Economic Concepts

 Cost of Advertising During the 1993 Super Bowl, about 50 commercials were aired. Advertisers paid as much as $850,000 for 30 seconds of national airtime—about $28,333 a second!

found this level of production, the oligopolistic company proceeds to charge whatever the market will bear.

The final price for the product is likely to be higher than it would be under monopolistic competition, and much higher than it would be under pure competition. Even when oligopolists do not collude formally, they still tend to act conservatively and seldom protest price hikes by their rivals.

Monopoly

The final category of economic markets is the exact opposite of pure competition. A pure **monopoly** is a market situation with only one seller of a particular economic product that has no close substitutes. The American economy has very few cases of pure monopolies.

Several factors prevent pure monopolies from occurring. First, the American people traditionally have disliked monopolies and have tried to outlaw them. Second, it is usually easy to find a reasonably close substitute for most products. Margarine can be used instead of butter, for example, and private automobiles can be substituted for bus, train, and airplane transportation. Third, new technologies often introduce products that compete with existing monopolies. The development of the fax machine, for example, allows businesses to send electronic letters that compete with the United States Postal Service.

Although no example of a pure monopoly exists, some—such as the local telephone company—are fairly close. Even the telephone company faces competition from other communication companies and the United States Postal Service, however. For all practical purposes, a monopoly situation does not have to be completely pure to qualify as a monopoly. When economists talk about monopolies, they really are talking about near monopolies—situations that are close to being pure.

Natural Monopoly

Sometimes the very nature of an industry dictates that society would be served best by a monopoly. A **natural monopoly**—a market situation where costs are minimized by having a single firm produce the product—is one example.

Two or more competing telephone companies serving the same area would be wasteful if they each needed their own telephone poles and lines. Imagine the confusion that would result if four or five competing transit company buses raced each other to the corner to pick up waiting passengers. Think what our city streets would be like if several competing water or gas

Geographic Monopoly
A lone store in an isolated area enjoys a geographic monopoly. **How does a geographic monopoly differ from a natural monopoly?**

companies all kept putting in or repairing water and gas lines.

To avoid such problems, government often gives a public utility company permission to act as a natural monopoly. This arrangement is known as a **franchise.** It gives a company the exclusive right to do business in a certain area without competition. By accepting such franchises, the companies also accept a certain amount of government regulation.

Another justification for the natural monopoly is lower cost. Suppose the cost of production goes down as a firm grows larger and larger. It would make sense for the firm to grow as much as possible to reduce its production costs. This growth results from **economies of scale,** a situation in which the larger the firm grows, the more efficiently it uses its personnel, plant, and equipment.

Geographic Monopoly

Sometimes a business has a monopoly simply because of its location. A drugstore operating in a town that is too small to support two or more such businesses becomes a **geographic monopoly** because no other business in the immediate area offers any competition. Likewise, the owner of the only gas station on a lonely interstate highway exit also has a type of geographic monopoly. Drivers on the interstate are usually not aware of other gas stations in the area.

A geographic monopoly may not always be able to maintain its status. If the only drugstore in a small town began to make a great deal of money, another may soon come along and compete. If the gas station along the interstate keeps its prices too high, other stations will open to take advantage of the profits.

Technological Monopoly

The special privileges given to those who invent a new product or process lead to another kind of monopoly called a **technological monopoly.** In this type of monopoly, a firm or individual has discovered a new manufacturing technique or has invented or created something entirely new.

Figure 7.2
Market Structures and Their Characteristics

	Number of Firms in Industry	Influence Over Price	Product Differentiation	Advertising	Entry Into Market	Examples
Pure Competition	Many	None	None	None	Easy	Perfect: None Near: Truck Farming
Monopolistic Competition	Many	Limited	Fair Amount	Fair Amount	Easy	Gas Stations Women's Clothing
Oligopoly	Few	Some	Fair Amount	Fair Amount	Difficult	Automobiles Aluminum
Pure Monopoly	One	Extensive	None	None	Almost Impossible	Perfect: None Near: Electricity

The term market structure *refers to the nature and degree of competition among firms operating in the same industry. Individual market structures—pure competition, monopolistic competition, oligopoly, and monopoly—are determined by the five characteristics listed in the columns above.* **In which market structure does nonprice competition play a major role?**

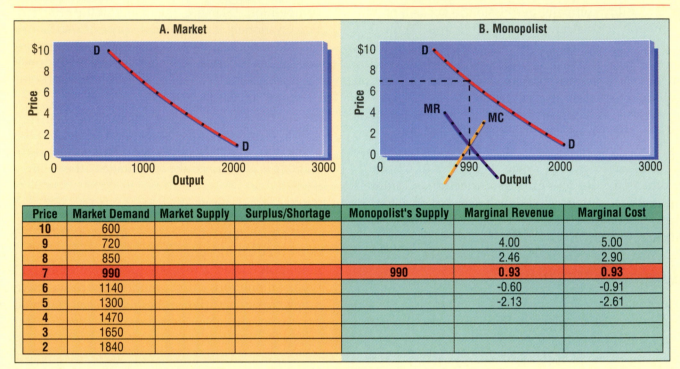

Figure 7.3
Monopoly: Market Price and Profit Maximization

Price	Market Demand	Market Supply	Surplus/Shortage	Monopolist's Supply	Marginal Revenue	Marginal Cost
10	600					
9	720				4.00	5.00
8	850				2.46	2.90
7	990			990	0.93	0.93
6	1140				-0.60	-0.91
5	1300				-2.13	-2.61
4	1470					
3	1650					
2	1840					

Because the monopolist is a "price maker," there is no supply curve for the market in A. Instead, the monopolist examines the market demand curve, and then decides how much to produce. In B, marginal revenue is computed from the market demand and then compared to marginal costs. The profit-maximizing quantity of output occurs at 990 gadgets, or where marginal costs are just equal to marginal revenue. After the monopolist determines that 990 gadgets will be produced, they will be priced for sale at $7 each. **What factors prevent pure monopolies from occurring?**

Article I, Section 8, of the Constitution of the United States gives Congress the power:

to promote the progress of science and useful arts, by securing for limited times to authors and inventors the exclusive right to their respective writings and discoveries.

The government fulfills this mandate by granting a **patent**—an exclusive right to manufacture, use, or sell any new and useful art, machine, manufacture, or composition of matter, or any new and useful improvement thereof. Inventions are covered for 17 years and designs can be patented for shorter periods, after which they become public property available for the benefit of all.

Art and literary works are protected in much the same way through a **copyright.** It gives authors or artists the exclusive right to publish, sell, or reproduce their work for their lifetime plus 50 years.

Government Monopoly

Still another kind of monopoly is a **government monopoly**—a business the government owns and operates. Government monopolies are found at the national, state, and local levels. In most cases, they involve products people need that private industry may not adequately provide.

At the local level, many towns and cities have monopolies that oversee water use. Some states control alcoholic beverages by requiring that they be sold only through state stores. At the national level, the government tightly controls the processing of weapons-grade uranium for military purposes.

Profit Maximization

Monopolies maximize profits the same way as other firms—they equate marginal cost with marginal revenue to find the profit-maximizing quantity of output. Suppose, for example, that the gadgets industry was dominated by a monopolist, instead of by many small producers as was the case in **Figure 7.1**. In addition, assume that the main difference between the monopolist and the pure competitor in **Figure 7.1** is size, with the monopolist being hundreds of times larger than the pure competitor.

The market for gadgets in Graph **A** in **Figure 7.3** shows only a demand curve and no supply curve. This situation occurs because the monopolist is the only supplier of gadgets. The monopolist is able to set a price and quantity of output most profitable to itself.

At a price of $10, the monopolist could sell 600 units for a total of $6,000. If the price dropped to $9, 720 gadgets could be sold for $6,480. Because an additional 120 units generated an additional $480 in total revenue, the extra, or marginal, revenue from the sale of each gadget must have been $480 divided by 120, or $4. The $4 is shown in the second column in Table **B** in **Figure 7.3**. The marginal revenue generated by expanding production to 850 units, 990 units, and so on, is computed the same way.

The marginal cost for the monopolist is shown in the third column in Table **B** of **Figure 7.3**. Marginal cost is initially low, but it steadily increases as production increases. By the time output reaches 990 units, the marginal cost is $.93, and goes even higher at higher levels of output.

When the monopolist equates marginal cost with marginal revenue, it finds that the profit-maximizing quantity of output is 990 units. These 990 gadgets will be sold for $7 each. Therefore the monopolist produces fewer gadgets than do the hundreds of pure competitors in **Figure 7.1**—990 gadgets instead of 1300—yet charges a higher price for each gadget.

SECTION 1 REVIEW

Reviewing Terms and Facts

1. **Define** laissez-faire, industry, market structure, pure competition, imperfect competition, monopolistic competition, product differentiation, nonprice competition, oligopoly, collusion, price-fixing, price war, independent pricing, price leadership, monopoly, natural monopoly, franchise, economies of scale, geographic monopoly, technological monopoly, patent, copyright, government monopoly.

2. **List** the five characteristics of pure competition.

3. **Describe** how the monopolistic competitor differs from the pure competitor.

4. **Explain** why the actions of one oligopolist affects others in the same industry.

5. **List** four types of monopolies.

Critical Thinking

6. **Synthesizing Information** Provide at least two examples of oligopolies in the United States today.

Applying Economic Concepts

7. **Product Differentiation** Make a list of as many clothing stores in your community as possible. Describe how each store tries to differentiate its products from the others.

PROFILES IN ECONOMICS

CHARLES WANG
(1944–   )

"There are CEOs who brag about never having touched a PC," says Charles Wang, head of Computer Associates (CA). "I say to them, 'Get your head out of the sand, kid.'" Wang's aggressive approach has helped him propel his company of 4 employees to one that earns $1.8 billion in computer software sales a year. Currently, Computer Associates is the largest independent supplier of software for giant IBM's mainframes.

HUMBLE BEGINNINGS Born in Shanghai, China, in 1944, Charles Wang and his family fled the communist regime in 1952 to settle in the United

Computer Associates was the first independent software company to top the billion-dollar mark.

States. Wang attended Queens College in New York and opened an American subsidiary of the Swiss-owned Computer Associates in New York City in 1976. Wang began operations with one product.

A SPECTACULAR SUCCESS Wang believed that the best way to help the fledgling company grow was to purchase existing software firms and market their products. He hoped this approach would spare his company the risk of developing its own products while allowing CA to get products to market sooner. Following this approach, Computer Associates purchased a number of firms throughout the 1980s. The firm was so successful that sales increased from $85 million in 1984 to $1 billion in 1989.

PROBLEMS ON THE HORIZON
Although sales were robust in 1989, the company did face certain challenges in the uneasy economic climate of the times.

Computer Associates posted a decline in both sales and income in 1990. Sales were flat in 1991.

Despite these setbacks, Wang remained optimistic about the future of his company. Rather than retreating, he launched a campaign to purchase still other software companies and did so in 1991 and 1992.

At the same time, Wang modified his vision of supplying software for the giant mainframe computers. Instead, he hoped to diversify into software for the popular personal computers. In 1992 mainframe software accounted for 80 percent of Computer Associates' sales. Wang predicted that in 2002, only 25 percent of sales would come from mainframes. The rest would come from personal computer software sales.

Examining the Profile

1. **Predicting Consequences** How might the story of Computer Associates and Charles Wang have been different if he had not decided to shift his company's emphasis away from mainframe software?

2. **For Further Research** Find out the current status of Computer Associates' sales. Write a summary of your findings.

Section Preview

Objectives

After studying this section, you will be able to:

1. **Discuss** the problems caused by inadequate competition.

2. **Understand** the importance of having adequate information.

3. **Describe** the nature of resource immobility.

4. **Explain** the nature of positive and negative externalities.

Key Terms

market failure, externality, negative externality, positive externality, public good

Applying Economic Concepts

Market Failure Have you ever felt that the perfect job is waiting for you—but you just can't seem to find it? If so, you're experiencing market failure. A *market failure* usually occurs when we don't have adequate information about the market. The result is that productive resources—including you—do not reach their maximum potential.

Those who favor a free enterprise system believe it brings about an efficient and automatic allocation of material and human resources for the benefit of the whole economy. Markets work best when four conditions are met: Adequate competition must exist in all markets. Buyers and sellers must be reasonably well-informed about conditions and opportunities in these markets. Resources must be free to move from one industry to another. Finally, prices must reasonably reflect the costs of production, including the rewards to entrepreneurs.

Sometimes, markets fail to perform as expected, and problems develop. A **market failure** occurs when any of the four conditions described above alter significantly. The most common market failures involve cases of inadequate competition, inadequate information, resource immobility, external economies, and public goods. These failures occur on both the demand and supply sides of the market.

Inadequate Competition

Over time, mergers and acquisitions have resulted in increasingly larger and fewer firms dominating various industries. The result, in extreme cases, is a monopoly.

Dangers of Monopolies

The greatest danger of a monopoly is that it denies consumers the benefit of competition. People cannot depend on the free market system to allocate resources efficiently, or to bring the greatest satisfaction. Instead, they must depend on the monopolist who is "above the market."

When a monopoly has gained control of an industry, it can use its position to prevent competition and restrict production. This situation brings about artificial shortages that cause higher prices.

Another danger of monopolies concerns resource allocation. Competition makes businesses become more efficient in using resources. Because monopolies are not under those pressures, however, they may waste and misallocate scarce resources.

Economic and Political Power

Inadequate competition may enable a business to influence politics by wielding its economic might. In the past, some large firms have used their huge capital resources to further the political careers of their owners, relatives, and friends.

A large corporation does not even have to be a monopoly for its economic power to translate to political power, although it certainly helps. A large

Maintaining Competition *Unlike consumer industries, there are a limited number of potential customers for military goods, such as these F16s manufactured by Lockheed in Fort Worth, Texas. Maintaining adequate competition is a difficult but worthwhile goal because competitive markets tend to police themselves and require less government intervention.* **How do large corporations sometimes wield political as well as economic power?**

corporation, for example, may want the state or local government to give it tax breaks or some other considerations. If the government refuses, the corporation may threaten to move its plant elsewhere, causing economic loss to the community. Because the community does not want to risk the loss, the corporation may get its way. ✅

Both Sides of the Market

If we consider the supply side of the market, it is clear that purely competitive or monopolistically competitive markets usually have enough firms to ensure competition. When it comes to oligopoly, however, we know that the temptation to collude is strong. No competition exists at all if a monopolist dominates the supply side of the market.

Inadequate competition may happen on the demand side of the market as well. In most cases, such as in the consumer goods and services markets,

numerous buyers can be found. How many consumers, though, will buy incredibly large office buildings, super computers, or M-1 tanks and high technology fighter jets?

Maintaining adequate competition is a difficult but worthwhile goal. If markets can be kept reasonably competitive, they tend to police themselves and require less government intervention. Accordingly, many government policies are geared to maintain or increase competition rather than to actually regulate a less competitive market. 1

Inadequate Information

If resources are to be allocated efficiently, everyone—consumers, businesspeople, and government officials—must have adequate information about market conditions. A secretary or an accountant may receive a competitive wage in the automobile industry,

Resource Immobility
Although closing military bases may save taxpayers' dollars, the federal employees who worked at the base may be unable to find other jobs in the community. **When is resource immobility not a problem?**

but are wages for the same skills higher in the insurance industry, or in the banking industry? A business may use its plant and equipment efficiently in the shoe industry, but would it be better off manufacturing tents and backpacking equipment? Even the treasurer of a small community needs to know if the town's surplus funds can earn a higher return if invested in Dallas, New York, Indianapolis, or Seattle. Information about conditions in many markets is needed before these questions can be answered.

Some information is easy to obtain, such as want ads or sale prices in the local newspaper. Other information is more difficult to obtain. An investor might write to several companies for information about their earnings and dividends. The investor might visit a local library to research various companies.

A free enterprise economy requires an incredible amount of information if resources are to be allocated efficiently. When adequate information is not available, it is difficult to employ resources to their fullest for the maximum benefit of society.

Resource Immobility

One of the more difficult problems in any economy is that of resource immobility. The efficient allocation of resources requires that land, labor,

Checking Understanding

1. Why is maintaining adequate competition a worthwhile goal?

Applying Economic Concepts

☑ **Market Failures** Large corporations often employ lobbyists at the state and national levels who try to persuade lawmakers to support legislation favorable to the company.

Externalities *Most economic activities generate externalities.* **Do you think the nearby airport expansion was a positive or a negative externality for the people living in this neighborhood? Why?**

entrepreneurs, and capital be free to move to markets where returns are the highest.

Sometimes this movement is not a problem. The secretary looking for a job in a large city usually has many choices. Aside from salary, concerns may center around the longer drive to work, finding a parking space, or walking a long distance from the bus stop. A store owner may quit selling shoes and decide to open a video rental or pizza parlor instead.

At other times, resources are simply not free or willing to move. What happens when a large auto assembly plant closes, leaving hundreds of workers without employment? Certainly some workers can find jobs in other industries, but not everyone can. Some workers may not be able to sell their homes. Other workers may not want to move away from friends and relatives to find new, higher-paying jobs in other cities.

Consider the problems caused when the national government closes military bases to save taxpayers' dollars. Thousands of workers are laid off in communities that have no immediate means of employing them. Resource mobility, assumed as an ideal in the competitive free enterprise economy, is much more difficult to accomplish in the real world. When resources are immobile or refuse to move, markets do not function as efficiently as they could.

Externalities

Many activities generate some kind of **externality,** or economic side effect that either benefits or harms a third party not directly involved in the activity.

Negative Externality

If an economic action harms a third party, the side effect is called an external cost, or **negative externality.** Suppose that a city undertakes a major expansion of the local airport to attract more businesses and jobs. People who live near the airport are likely to experience considerable inconvenience from construction, as well as from additional airport noise after the additional runways are built. These people may have had nothing to do with the airport expansion, but they suffer negative externalities from its construction.

Positive Externality

If the economic action benefits a third party, the beneficial side effect is called an external benefit, or **positive externality.** People living on the other side of town may benefit from the additional jobs generated by the airport expansion. A restaurant may sell more meals and hire more workers. Both the restaurant and the workers hired will gain from the positive externalities, or benefits, of the airport expansion.

Externalities as Market Failures

Externalities are classified as market failures because their costs and benefits are not reflected in the market prices paid by the buyers and sellers of the original product. Does the airline or the air traveler compensate the home owner for the diminished value of the home located near the new runway extension? Does the restaurant owner share the additional good fortune derived from the new business with the airline or the air traveler? In both cases

the answer is no. As a result, the prices that air travelers pay for air travel may not really reflect the external costs and benefits that the airport expansion generates.

Public Goods

Another form of market failure is the need for public goods. **Public goods** are those products, such as highways, flood control, national defense, and police and fire protection, that are collectively consumed by the population. The market, if left to itself, does not supply these items or only supplies them inadequately.

A market economy produces only those items that can be withheld if people refuse to pay for them. It would be difficult, for example, to get everyone to pay for a public good such as national defense. In addition, it would be difficult to withhold national defense from single individuals. The result is that the market economy does not produce national defense.

Although the market is very successful in satisfying individual wants and needs, it fails to satisfy them on a collective basis. If public goods are to be supplied, the government usually has to provide them.

Reviewing Terms and Facts

1. **Define** market failure, externality, negative externality, positive externality, public good.
2. **Explain** why markets need adequate competition and information.
3. **Explain** why resources are not always mobile and willing to move.
4. **Identify** two types of externalities.
5. **Explain** why the need for public goods is a form of market failure.

Critical Thinking

6. **Determining Cause and Effect** State one possible positive externality and one possible negative externality from the closing of a military base.

Applying Economic Concepts

7. **Market Failures** Cite at least two examples of situations in your community in which resources did not move from one market or industry to another because they were either unable or unwilling to move.

Making Generalizations

If you say, "We have a great football team," you are making a *generalization*, or general statement, about your team. If you go on to say that your team was last year's top-ranked team and has not lost a game this season, you have provided evidence to support your generalization. In many fields of study, it often is necessary to put together bits and pieces of information to arrive at a complete picture. Just as you put together pieces of a jigsaw puzzle, you can put together pieces of written information to arrive at a general statement.

Explanation

In some cases, authors will provide both the generalizations and the supporting statements. In other cases, only supporting statements are given, and you will need to make the generalizations on your own. When doing this, make sure that the supporting statements are directly related to the topic. Otherwise, your generalizations may be incorrect.

To make generalizations, follow these steps:
- Identify the subject matter.
- Gather facts and examples related to this subject.
- Identify similarities or patterns among these facts.

- Use these similarities or patterns to form some general ideas about the subject.
- Test your generalizations against other facts and examples.

Practice

Read the passage to the left about government regulation and market failures, then answer the questions that follow.
1. What is the generalization of the entire passage?
2. Write the statements that support the generalization you identified in question 1.
3. Write a generalization for each of the last three paragraphs.

While regulation based on a careful balancing of costs and benefits can sometimes improve market performance, policymakers often ignore the fact that the government is an imperfect regulator. There are three reasons to be cautious about government intervention as the solution to market failure.

First, regulators often lack accurate information about an industry and cannot always predict the effects of specific regulations. While the decision to regulate may be well-intentioned, the regulations themselves can have perverse and unintended consequences. For example, corporate average fuel economy standards have led manufacturers to produce lighter and therefore less crashworthy cars than they would have, resulting in an estimated several thousand additional highway deaths per year.

Second, the regulatory process tends to favor those groups or businesses that can most influence the process in their own interest, rather than in the interest of society as a whole. For example, Federal rules continue to restrict competition in various industries such as international ocean shipping and international aviation. Restraints on competition continue in part due to the fact that organized groups, such as those representing labor and firms in the industry, capture benefits from the rules . . . and therefore invest in maintaining those rules. . . .

Third, regulation does not always accommodate change well. While regulation may be imposed to achieve economic and social goals, it is administered as a legal process. It often takes years to accommodate new technologies or new ways of doing business. . . .
—*The Economic Report of the President, 1993*

Additional Practice

For further practice in making generalizations, complete the Reinforcing Skills exercise in the Chapter 7 Review on page 174.

Section Preview

Objectives

After studying this section, you will be able to:

1. **Discuss** the major antitrust legislation in the United States.
2. **Understand** the need for limited government regulation.
3. **Explain** the value of public disclosure.
4. **Discuss** the modifications to our free enterprise economy.

Key Terms

trust, price discrimination, cease and desist order, public disclosure

Applying Economic Concepts

Public Disclosure Do you have a credit card or a car loan? Did you notice that someone took the time to explain the size of monthly payments, the computation of the interest, and other important terms of the agreement? Disclosing this information is not merely an act of kindness on the part of the business. It is required by a federal *public disclosure* law so that you are a better-informed consumer.

Today, government has the power to maintain competition and to regulate certain monopolies that exist for the public welfare. In some cases, government has taken over certain economic activities and runs them as government-owned monopolies.

Antitrust Legislation

In the late 1800s, the United States passed laws to restrict monopolies, combinations, and **trusts**—legally formed combinations of corporations or companies.

Sherman Antitrust Act

In 1890 Congress passed the Sherman Antitrust Act "to protect trade and commerce against unlawful restraint and monopoly." The Sherman Act, described in **Figure 7.4**, was the country's first significant law against monopolies. It sought to do away with restraints and monopolies that hindered competition or made competition impossible.

By the early 1900s, a number of business organizations had been convicted under the Sherman Act. In 1911 the Supreme Court declared that the Standard Oil Company was practicing "unreasonable" restraint of trade and ordered that it be broken up into several smaller, independent companies.

Clayton Antitrust Act

The Sherman Act laid down broad foundations for maintaining competition. The act was not specific enough, however, to stop practices that restrained trade and competition. In 1914 Congress passed the Clayton Antitrust Act to give the government greater power against monopolies. Among other provisions, this act outlawed **price discrimination**—the practice of charging customers different prices for the same product—in cases where it might lead to monopoly or lessen competition.

Federal Trade Commission Act

The Federal Trade Commission Act was passed in the same year to enforce the Clayton Act. The act set up the Federal Trade Commission (FTC) and gave it the authority to issue cease and desist orders. A **cease and desist order** is an FTC ruling requiring a company to stop an unfair business practice, such as price-fixing, that reduces or limits competition among firms.

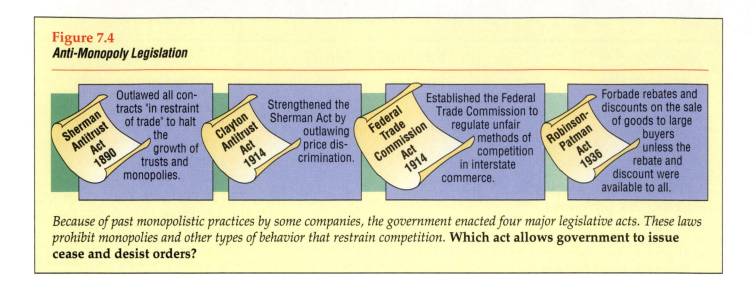

Figure 7.4
Anti-Monopoly Legislation

Sherman Antitrust Act 1890 — Outlawed all contracts "in restraint of trade" to halt the growth of trusts and monopolies.

Clayton Antitrust Act 1914 — Strengthened the Sherman Act by outlawing price discrimination.

Federal Trade Commission Act 1914 — Established the Federal Trade Commission to regulate unfair methods of competition in interstate commerce.

Robinson-Patman Act 1936 — Forbade rebates and discounts on the sale of goods to large buyers unless the rebate and discount were available to all.

Because of past monopolistic practices by some companies, the government enacted four major legislative acts. These laws prohibit monopolies and other types of behavior that restrain competition. **Which act allows government to issue cease and desist orders?**

Robinson-Patman Act

In 1936 Congress passed the Robinson-Patman Act in an effort to strengthen the Clayton Act, particularly the provisions that dealt with price discrimination. Under this act, companies could no longer offer special discount prices only to certain customers. The new law chiefly affected national organizations and chain stores, which were offering goods and services at lower prices than those paid by small independent businesses.

Government Regulation

Government maintains competition mainly by regulating some monopolists' prices and directing the quality of some services offered to the public. The goal is for the government to set the same prices that might exist if there were competition.

Local and state governments regulate many monopolies, such as cable television companies, electric utilities, and even telephone companies. A public commission or other government agency usually approves prices for their services. If the company wants to raise rates, it must argue its case before the commission. If the company wins, prices will go up. If they do not, prices will stay the same.

Agencies of the national government, such as those listed in **Figure 7.5**, regulate many businesses. Privately owned agencies, such as the Federal Reserve System, have certain regulatory powers such as the power to regulate the money supply, some daily bank operations, and even bank mergers.

Public Disclosure

One of the more potent weapons available to the government is **public disclosure,** or the requirement that businesses reveal information to the public. The Food and Drug Administration, for example, requires content labels on canned goods and other food products. The government also requires that corporations and certain firms disclose financial and operating information.

Any corporation that sells stock to the public and lists its stock on a stock exchange must file periodic reports with the Securities and Exchange Commission. The firms are also required to supply investors with annual reports on the money, securities, and property the investors own, as well as information on sales and profits.

Banks are required to file periodic reports to the Federal Reserve System and other federal agencies. This information is readily available to the firm's competitors as well as to its shareholders and is highly sought after by almost all firms in the industry.

The advantage of public disclosure is that it costs very little to administer and yet provides the market with enough information to prevent market failures. At the same time, businesses are not forced to give away their competitive trade secrets.

Figure 7.5
Federal Regulatory Agencies in the United States

Interstate Commerce Commission (ICC), 1887	Regulates rates and other aspects of commercial transportation by railroad, highway, and waterway.
Food and Drug Administration (FDA), 1906	Enforces laws to ensure purity, effectiveness, and truthful labeling of food, drugs, and cosmetics; inspects production and shipment of these products.
Federal Trade Commission (FTC), 1914	Administers antitrust laws forbidding unfair competition, price-fixing, and other deceptive practices.
Federal Communications Commission (FCC), 1934	Licenses and regulates radio and television stations and regulates interstate telephone, telegraph rates and services.
Securities and Exchange Commission (SEC), 1934	Regulates and supervises the sale of listed and unlisted securities and the brokers, dealers, and bankers who sell them.
National Labor Relations Board (NLRB), 1935	Administers federal labor-management relations laws; settles labor disputes; prevents unfair labor practices.
Federal Aviation Administration (FAA), 1958	Regulates air commerce; sets standards for pilot training, aircraft maintenance, and air traffic control; controls U.S. airspace.
Equal Employment Opportunity Commission (EEOC), 1964	Investigates and rules on charges of discrimination by employers and labor unions.
Environmental Protection Agency (EPA), 1970	Coordinates federal environmental programs to fight air and water pollution.
National Highway Traffic Safety Administration (NHTSA), 1970	Sets and enforces laws to promote motor vehicle safety and to protect drivers, passengers, and pedestrians; sets safety and fuel economy standards for new motor vehicles produced or sold in the U.S.
Occupational Safety and Health Administration (OSHA), 1970	Investigates accidents at the workplace; enforces regulations to protect employees at work.
Consumer Product Safety Commission (CPSC), 1972	Sets and enforces safety standards for consumer products.
Nuclear Regulatory Commission (NRC), 1974	Licenses and regulates civilian use of nuclear materials and facilities.
Federal Energy Regulatory Commission (FERC), 1977	Fixes rates and regulates the interstate transportation and sale of electricity, oil, and natural gas; issues permits and licenses for hydroelectric projects and gas pipelines; supervises mergers and stock issues of electric power and natural gas; sets rates for interstate transportation of oil by pipeline.

In order to promote competition and restrict unfair trade policies, the government has created a number of federal regulatory agencies to oversee the economy. Because of government's involvement in the economy, we now say that we have a modified free enterprise system. **With which of the agencies listed above are you familiar? Which affect you directly? Why?**

Modified Free Enterprise

Concern over monopolies is one reason for government intervention in the United States economy today. Historically, the freedom to pursue self-interest led some people and businesses to seek economic gain at the expense of others. Acting under the label of competition, some larger firms used their size and power to take advantage of smaller ones. In some markets, monopoly replaced competition.

Because of such conditions, laws to prevent "evil monopolies" and to protect the rights of workers were passed. Labor unions were supported to give workers more bargaining power. Food and drug laws were passed to protect people from false claims and harmful products. Some industries, such as public utilities, became subject to strict government regulation. All these actions led to a modification of free enterprise.

Restrictions on economic freedom are put there not to prevent the benefits of competition, but to bring about a more efficient use of resources. Government takes part in economic affairs for several reasons. One is to promote and encourage competition within the rules of fair play. Another is to prevent and do away with monopolies that do not allow the public to reap the benefits of competition. A third is to regulate industries in which a monopoly is clearly for the public good. As a result, today's modi-

fied private enterprise economy is a mixture of different market structures, different kinds of business organizations, and varying degrees of government regulation.

HELP WANTED

Environmental Health Inspector

▼

Your State Employment Service wants YOU—a responsible citizen—to become an inspector for the Environmental Health Department. Positions are available now for inspectors who enforce laws and regulations that protect the public. Your duties include ensuring that food and beverages served in public places meet government standards for cleanliness and safety; overseeing the treatment and disposal of waste; testing for pollutants; and initiating procedures to stop pollution. You are required to travel frequently, and your working conditions may be unfavorable. You will be trained in specific laws and inspection procedures.

▼

Education: College degree
Median salary: $30,300

SECTION 3 REVIEW

Reviewing Terms and Facts

1. **Define** trust, cease and desist order, price discrimination, public disclosure.
2. **Describe** four important antitrust laws.
3. **Provide** at least three examples of limited government regulation in the American economy.
4. **Provide** at least two examples of public disclosure.

5. **Explain** why the United States has a modified free enterprise economy.

Critical Thinking

6. **Synthesizing Information** Identify five examples of how government has intervened in the economy in your community.

Applying Economic Concepts

7. **Public Disclosure** Visit a bank in your community and ask for literature describing the computation of interest and conditions for withdrawal on various savings accounts. Why do you think the bank is so forthcoming on these issues?

Competition, Market Structures, and the Role of Government

Vocabulary

The following terms are defined in Chapter 7:

SECTION ONE
- laissez-faire (p. 152)
- industry (p. 152)
- market structure (p. 152)
- pure competition (p. 152)
- imperfect competition (p. 155)
- monopolistic competition (p. 155)

- product differentiation (p. 155)
- nonprice competition (p. 156)
- oligopoly (p. 156)
- collusion (p. 157)
- price-fixing (p. 157)
- price war (p. 157)
- independent pricing (p. 157)
- price leadership (p. 157)
- monopoly (p. 158)
- natural monopoly (p. 158)
- franchise (p. 159)

- economies of scale (p. 159)
- geographic monopoly (p. 159)
- technological monopoly (p. 159)
- patent (p. 160)
- copyright (p. 160)
- government monopoly (p. 160)

SECTION TWO
- market failure (p. 163)
- externality (p. 166)
- negative externality (p. 166)

- positive externality (p. 167)
- public good (p. 167)

SECTION THREE
- trust (p. 169)
- price discrimination (p. 169)
- cease and desist order (p. 169)
- public disclosure (p. 170)

Section 1

Competition and Market Structures (pages 152–161)

Pure competition is a **market structure** with many buyers and sellers, identical economic products, independent action by buyers and sellers, reasonably well-informed participants, and freedom for firms to enter or leave the market. **Monopolistic competition** has all the characteristics of pure competition except for **product differentiation. Oligopoly** is a market structure dominated by a few very large firms. The **monopolist** is a single producer that has the most control over supply and price. All firms, regardless of market structure, maximize profits by producing the quantity of output where marginal cost is equal to marginal revenue.

Reviewing the Main Idea
What are the four types of market structures?

Section 2

Market Failures (pages 163–167)

Market failures happen when sizable deviations occur from one or more of the conditions required for pure competition. Inadequate competition is one of the features of a failed market and can lead to oligopoly or monopolies. Inadequate information represents another market failure. Resource immobility, represented by factors of production that cannot or refuse to move to other markets, also poses an obstacle to efficient resource allocation.

Some activities cause market **externalities,** or economic side effects to third parties. Externalities are not reflected in the prices for the activities that caused the side effects in the first place, and thus represent a feature of market failure. **Public goods,** another form of market failure, are supplied by the government because the market cannot withhold supplies from those who refuse to pay.

Reviewing the Main Idea
What are the five main types of market failures?

Section 3

The Role of Government (pages 169–172)

Government takes part in economic affairs to promote and encourage competition. Its involvement by means of antitrust legislation, other forms of regulation, and **public disclosure** has modified the free enterprise economy. As a result, the modern economy is a mixture of different market structures, different forms of business organization, and some degree of government regulation.

Reviewing the Main Idea
How does the government promote competition?

Reviewing Key Terms

Use all the terms below in four paragraphs, with each paragraph about one of the major types of market structures.

collusion
copyright
geographic monopoly
imperfect competition
monopolistic competition
natural monopoly
oligopoly
price leadership
product differentiation
technological monopoly
price-fixing
franchise
government monopoly
independent pricing
monopoly
nonprice competition
patent
price war
pure competition

Reviewing the Facts

SECTION 1 *(pages 152–161)*

1. **Describe** the five characteristics of pure competition.
2. **Explain** the main characteristics of the monopolistic competitor.
3. **Contrast** the oligopolist and the pure competitor.
4. **Describe** the four types of monopolies.

SECTION 2 *(pages 163–167)*

5. **Explain** what happens when markets do not have enough competition.
6. **Provide** two examples of inadequate information in a market.
7. **Explain** what is meant by resource immobility.
8. **Explain** what is meant by positive and negative externalities.
9. **Account** for the reluctance of the private sector to produce public goods.

SECTION 3 *(pages 169–172)*

10. **Identify** four major antitrust laws.
11. **List** 10 major federal government regulatory agencies.
12. **Explain** how public disclosure is used as a tool to prevent market failures.
13. **Describe** a modified free enterprise economy.

Critical Thinking

1. **Making Generalizations** To what extent do you think government should be involved in the free enterprise economy? Defend your answer.
2. **Predicting Consequences** Do you think there would be any advantages to making monopolies or near monopolies break up into smaller, competing firms? If so, what are they? If not, why would there not be?

Applying Economic Concepts

1. **Market Failures** Explain how your newspaper, with its Help Wanted ads and weekly sale prices, helps prevent market failure.
2. **Market Structures** Identify a fast-food product that you consume regularly. Count the number of firms in your community that supply a similar product, and then determine the market structure for that product in your community.

Reinforcing Skills

MAKING GENERALIZATIONS

Making generalizations allows you to use specific details and examples to form a broader picture of situations and events. Read the excerpt below about telecommunications and the United States economy, then answer the questions that follow.

The U.S. telecommunications industry comprises thousands of businesses and over 1 million workers. Telephone services alone, including long distance, local, and cellular, are provided by over 2,000 companies employing over 700,000 people—about the same number as the entire

CHAPTER 7 REVIEW

U.S. automobile manufacturing industry. In 1991, reported local telephone revenues were $86 billion and long-distance revenues were $55 billion. . . . A second major segment of the telecommunications industry, the mass media, includes approximately 1,500 broadcast television stations, 11,000 radio stations, and 76 national cable television networks. In 1991, these industries earned about $36 billion in advertising revenues.

—The Economic Report of the President, 1993

1. What generalization can you make from this passage?
2. Write at least two statements that support the generalization you made in question 1.

nondurable good	large number of buyers and sellers	identical economic products	firms in industry act independently	everyone reasonably well-informed	firms free to enter/exit the market	probable market structure
1.						
2.						
3.						
4.						
5.						

Individual Activity

Draw a table like the one shown above. Then identify five nondurable goods that you recently purchased. In the table, list each item in the first five rows of the first column. Next, fill in columns 2-6 with a yes or no. From these responses, identify the probable market structure (column 7) for each of your five products.

Cooperative Learning Activity

Working in pairs, each pair will research one of the federal regulatory agencies outlined in **Figure 7.5**. Answer such questions as: What does the agency regulate? What led to the agency being formed? What changes did the agency create? How does the agency personally affect you? After your research is complete, present your research findings to the rest of the class.

Writing About Economics

THE EXPRESSIVE STYLE
In the **Journal Writing** activity on page 151, you were asked to evaluate at least three advertisements for a product. Using the expressive style of writing discussed on page 554, write a paragraph describing your product in such a way that consumers will want to buy it.

AGRICULTURAL PRICE SUPPORTS

The government helps farmers by offering agricultural price supports, or target prices, for some crops and dairy products. Farmers produce and sell a certain product at the going market price. If the market price is less than the target price for that product, farmers receive a "deficiency payment" from the government to make up the difference. Suppose the target price for a bushel of corn is $3.03. If the market price is $1.90 per bushel, the deficiency payment would be $1.13 per bushel.

Some people believe that agricultural price supports should be abolished. Others are firmly in favor of them. Should price supports be continued?

Pro

Since the origins of farm policy legislation in the 1930s, the federal government has attempted in numerous ways to increase the income of farm families. Assuring adequate income for farm families makes special moral sense now in light of comparable worth; that is, the remuneration of work according to its importance, difficulty, danger, and so on. . . .

For the sake both of farm families and rural communities, it is necessary to stabilize and raise net farm income to arrest the decline in the number of farm families. If rural communities are preserved, the farm bill also becomes an urban welfare bill by reducing migration into urban areas and by rendering less necessary the construction of new urban infrastructure and the expansion of urban services.

—ANDREW LARKIN, FROM "ETHICS, ECONOMICS, AND AGRICULTURAL POLICY: CONSIDERATIONS FOR THE 1990 FARM BILL," *JOURNAL OF ECONOMIC ISSUES*, JUNE 1990.

▲ *Many believe that farmers need price stability because of unstable weather and natural disasters.*

▼ *Farmers harvest a productive yield of soybeans.*

◀ *Grain silos store the harvest.*

▼ *Lack of price supports may result in many farmers leaving agriculture.*

FOR SALE
LAND BROKERS INC.

Con

Through subsidies, price supports, import barriers, and countless regulations, the Department of Agriculture continues to try to manage half of U.S. farming, with the predictable result of staggering waste and inefficiency. . . .

The problem at the root of farm programs is this: While a sound economy should produce an abundance of goods that can then be sold at a low price, our farm programs are designed to create a scarcity of goods that can then be sold at a high price. Having a "surplus" of corn does not mean that farmers produce too much corn, only that they produce more corn than can be sold at the government-inflated price. Farm productivity is good, so long as the market is permitted to function. If the government did not artificially inflate the price of corn and wheat, efficient U.S. farmers could plant fence row to fence row and dominate global markets. If high production then forced the price of corn and wheat very low—which wouldn't be the worst thing that could happen in a hungry world—then some farmers would switch to growing crops that people need more. And some farmers might even leave farming. . . .

—Dick Armey, from "Moscow on the Mississippi: America's Soviet-Style Farm Policy," *Policy Review*, 1990.

Analyzing the Case Study

1. What are price supports?
2. On what grounds does Larkin favor price supports?
3. On what grounds does Armey oppose price supports?
4. With which opinion do you agree? Why?

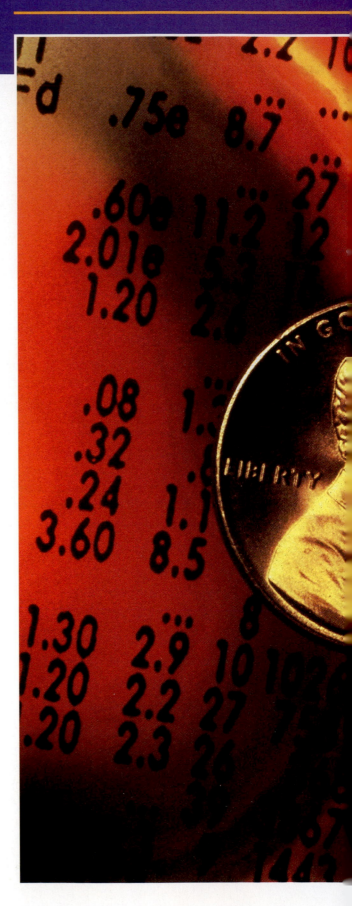

UNIT 3

MACRO-ECONOMICS: INSTITUTIONS

It's a billion here and a billion there; the first thing you know it adds up to real money.

—Everett Dirksen,
American politician, 1896–1969

 Economics and You

In this unit, discover what part economics plays in the following situations:
- Deductions are taken out of your paycheck.
- Your bank account is federally insured.
- Taxes pay for your high school education.
- Your savings account earns less than other investments.

Financial investments include buying stocks and bonds.

Union members march to gain public support for their position on labor.

CHAPTER 8

Employment, Labor, and Wages

SECTION 1
The Labor Movement

SECTION 2
Resolving Union and Management Differences

SECTION 3
Labor and Wages

SECTION 4
Employment Trends and Issues

CHAPTER PREVIEW

People to Know

- John L. Lewis
- Labor Relations Specialist

Applying Economic Concepts to Your Life

Opportunity Cost What kind of income do you want to earn after you graduate from high school? Will your current training and skills allow you to reach your income goal? The opportunity costs of your post-high school decisions may remain with you for a long time, so it is important to plan wisely.

Journal Writing

For one week, scan the Help Wanted section of your local newspaper. In your journal, summarize the job titles and job descriptions that you are interested in learning more about. Keep track of the salary ranges for those jobs that you summarize.

Section Preview

Objectives

After studying this section, you will be able to:

1. **Explain** why unions are still important today.
2. **Discuss** the development of the labor movement from the late 1700s to the 1930s.
3. **Relate** labor's successes during the Great Depression.
4. **State** the major labor developments since World War II.

Key Terms

macroeconomics, civilian labor force, craft or trade union, industrial union, strike, picket, boycott, lockout, company union, Great Depression, right-to-work law, jurisdictional dispute, independent union

Applying Economic Concepts

Civilian Labor Force Do you work, or are you actively looking for a job? If so, and if you are at least 16 years old, you probably belong to a group that economists call the *civilian labor force.*

This chapter and those that follow deal with **macroeconomics,** the part of economics that deals with the economy as a whole, and with the behavior and decision making by large units, such as labor unions and governments. One of these macro units is the **civilian labor force**—civilian men and women from 16 to 65 years old either working or actively looking for a job. The *civilian* classification excludes members of the armed forces, the prison population, and other institutionalized persons. 1

In 1992 the population of the United States was 255,414,000. Of this number, nearly half were members of the civilian labor force. As can be seen in **Figure 8.1**, this percentage has increased slowly since the end of World War II.

Unions and the Labor Force

Figure 8.1 also shows that a large majority of employed wage and salary workers have no connection with unions. According to the figure, 15.8 percent of employed wage and salary workers belong to unions, with an additional 2.1 percent of nonunion members being represented by unions.

Although the number of unionized workers may seem small, labor unions are important for a number of reasons. First, they have played a significant role in America's history, and they were responsible for much of the legislation that affects current pay levels and working conditions. Second, unions still have a substantial presence in a number of vital industries. Third, they represented nearly 18.6 million workers as recently as 1993.

Historically, unions tended to be concentrated in heavy manufacturing industries. More recently, unions have made major inroads in the service sector, especially among government workers. As **Figure 8.2** shows, 43.2 percent of all government workers were either unionized or represented by a union in 1993. ☑

Early Union Development

In 1778 printers in New York City joined together to demand higher pay. This protest was the first time anyone had tried to organize labor in America. Before long, unions of shoemakers, carpenters, and tailors sprang up, each hoping to negotiate agreements covering hours, pay, and working conditions. Only a small percentage of workers belonged to these unions. Of these, most were skilled and already had strong bargaining power.

Until about 1820, most of America's workforce was made up of farmers, small business owners, and

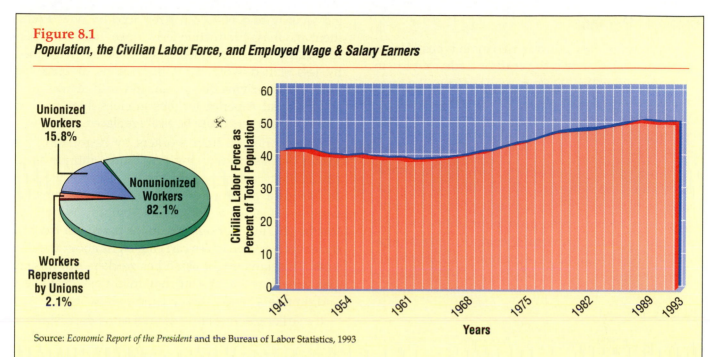

Figure 8.1
Population, the Civilian Labor Force, and Employed Wage & Salary Earners

Unionized Workers 15.8%

Nonunionized Workers 82.1%

Workers Represented by Unions 2.1%

Civilian Labor Force as Percent of Total Population

Years

Source: *Economic Report of the President* and the Bureau of Labor Statistics, 1993

In 1992 nearly half the population of the United States belonged to the civilian labor force. Of those in the labor force who were employed, fully 82.1 percent had no union affiliation, 15.8 percent were unionized, and another 2.1 percent were represented by unions even though the workers did not belong to a union. **Why do you think the labor force percentages have been increasing since World War II?**

people who were self-employed. Shortly after, however, immigrants began to enter the country in great numbers. Most were willing to work at any pay and under any conditions. They often posed a threat to existing wage and labor standards because they provided a supply of cheap, unskilled labor. **2**

At that time, public opinion was against union activity, and in some parts of the country, the law forbade labor unions. Labor organizers often were viewed as troublemakers, and many workers believed they could better negotiate with their employers on a one-to-one basis.

Civil War to the 1930s

During and after the Civil War, attitudes toward unions began to change. The Civil War led to higher prices, a greater demand for goods and services, and a growing shortage of workers. Industry expanded, and the farm population declined. Hourly workers in industrial jobs made up about one-fourth of the country's working population. Many of the cultural and linguistic differences between immigrants and American-born workers began to fade, and the labor force became more unified.

Checking Understanding

1. Who is included in the civilian labor force?
2. Why were immigrants viewed as a threat in the mid-1800s?

Applying Economic Concepts

☑ **Government Employees** In 1992 the number of employees working for federal, state, and local governments surpassed the number working in manufacturing jobs.

Types of Unions

By the end of the Civil War, two main types of labor unions existed. One was the **craft** or **trade union**—an association of skilled workers who perform the same kind of work. The Cigar Makers' Union, begun by union leader Samuel Gompers, is an example of this type of union. Other, more recent examples are shown in **Figure 8.3**.

The second type of union was the **industrial union**—an association of all workers in a given industry, regardless of the job each person performs. The growth of basic mass-production industries such as steel and textiles provided the opportunity to organize this kind of union. Because many of the workers in these industries were unskilled and could not join trade unions, they organized as industrial unions instead. 1

Union Activities

Although unions were making headway, American workers still faced many hardships. Workers had little job security and were often replaced by new equipment and mass-production techniques. Tasks once performed by those in skilled crafts could be performed by less skilled workers. With millions of unskilled immigrants arriving every year, and with many others leaving rural America for jobs in cities, high-paid or rebellious workers could be easily replaced.

Unions tried to help workers by negotiating for higher pay, better working conditions, and job security. If an agreement could not be reached, workers could **strike**, or refuse to work until certain demands were met. Unions also pressured employers by having the striking workers **picket**, or parade in front of the employer's business carrying signs about the dispute. The signs might ask other workers not to seek jobs with the company, or they might ask customers and suppliers to take their business elsewhere.

If a strike and picketing did not settle the dispute, a union could organize a **boycott**—a mass refusal to buy products from targeted employers or companies. If a boycott was effective, it hurt the company's business and reduced the employer's income.

Employer Resistance

Employers fought unions in a number of ways. Sometimes the owners called for a **lockout**, or a refusal to let the employees work until management demands were met. Violence often erupted when lockouts were used, and troops were sometimes brought in to keep peace.

At other times, management responded to a strike, or the threat of a strike, by hiring all new workers. Some owners even set up **company unions**—unions organized, supported, or run by employers—to head off efforts by others to organize workers.

Attitude of the Courts

Historically, the courts had an unfavorable attitude toward unions. Under English common law, unions were considered to be conspiracies against business and were prosecuted as such in the United States. This attitude lasted well into the 1800s. Even the Sherman Antitrust Act of 1890—aimed mainly at curbing monopolies—was used to keep labor in line.

In 1902 the United Hatters Union called a strike against a Danbury, Connecticut, hat manufacturer that

Figure 8.2
Union Membership and Representation by Industry

Industry	Percent of Employed Workers That Are:	
	Members of Unions	Represented by Unions
Government workers	36.7	43.2
Communications & Public Utilities	33.2	36.3
Transportation	29.0	30.3
Construction	20.0	21.1
Manufacturing	19.7	21.0
Mining	15.1	16.1
Wholesale Trade	6.8	7.5
Retail Trade	6.5	7.2
Services (general)	5.8	7.1
Agricultural Wage & Salary workers	2.4	2.8

Source: Bureau of Labor Statistics *News*, February 8, 1993

Labor unions have the most influence in the service industries, which include government, communications, public utilities, and transportation. Agriculture has the least amount of unionization, with manufacturing and mining in the middle. **Why is it still important to study labor unions?**

Figure 8.3
Trade (Craft) and Industrial Unions

TRADE (CRAFT) UNIONS

Printers' Union
Plumbers' Union
Machinists' Union
Electricians' Union
Carpenters' Union

Trade union members are workers who perform a particular kind of work.

INDUSTRIAL UNIONS

Members of an industrial union include all the workers in a particular industry, no matter what kind of work they perform. **What led to the growth of industrial unions?**

had turned down a union demand. The union applied pressure on stores not to stock hats made by the Danbury firm. The hat manufacturer took the union to court under the Sherman Antitrust Act. The Supreme Court ruled that the union was in restraint of trade, thereby dealing a severe blow to organized labor.

The Danbury Hatters case, and several others that followed it, encouraged organized labor to push for relief from the Sherman Antitrust Act. Relief came in 1914 when Congress passed the Clayton Antitrust Act. The Clayton Act stated that a person's labor was not a "commodity or article of commerce." It further stated that labor unions should not be looked upon as "illegal combinations or conspiracies in restraint of trade under the antitrust laws."

The courts, however, tended to disregard the Clayton Act. In 1921 the Supreme Court ruled that the Machinists' Union in New York violated the Sherman Antitrust Act. The union had tried to stop the sale and installation of newspaper printing presses made by a nonunion company in Michigan.

Labor During the Great Depression

The **Great Depression**—the greatest period of economic decline and stagnation in the history of the United States—began with the collapse of the stock market in October 1929, and reached bottom in 1933. It then took until 1939 for the economy to recover to the same level as it had been in 1929. ☑

Unemployment and Wages

Joblessness often stayed above 15 percent throughout the 1930s. During the depths of the Depression, one in four workers was without a job. Of those who did work, most received very little wages. In 1929 the average manufacturing wage had climbed to 55 cents per hour. By 1933, wages had plummeted to 5 cents per hour. **2**

The Great Depression brought misery to millions, but it also brought a change in attitude toward the

QUICK CHECK

Checking Understanding

1. How does an industrial union differ from a trade union?
2. What percentage of workers were unemployed during the Great Depression?

Applying Economic Concepts

 Stock Market During the last week of October 1929, $30 billion in stock value—about the same amount of money the United States spent in World War I—evaporated along with people's dreams of prosperity.

labor movement. Common problems united factory workers. As a result, union organizers renewed efforts to organize workers.

Prounion Legislation

Federal legislation began to help labor during the Depression. The Norris-LaGuardia Act of 1932 prevented federal courts from issuing rulings against unions that were engaged in peaceful strikes, picketing, or boycotts. Companies, therefore, had to negotiate directly with their unions, rather than take the unions to court.

The National Labor Relations Act (NLRA), or Wagner Act, of 1935 gave workers the right to join unions and to bargain collectively through their own chosen representatives. In addition, certain employer activities were defined as unfair labor practices. These practices included interfering with efforts to organize a union and discriminating against employees who engaged in union activities.

The NLRA also set up the National Labor Relations Board (NLRB). The Board was responsible for investigating workers' complaints concerning unfair labor practices. It also had the power to oversee union elections and to certify the results. If a fair election resulted in a union becoming the employees' bargaining agent, employers were required to recognize and negotiate with it.

Finally, in 1938 the Fair Labor Standards Act was passed. It applied to businesses that took part in or affected interstate commerce. The act set a minimum wage to begin in 1939 and called for time-and-a-half pay for overtime, which is now defined as over 40 hours per week. It also forbade labor by children under 16 years old and the holding of hazardous jobs by anyone under 18 years old.

Labor Since World War II

Organized labor was viewed favorably in the 1930s. By the end of World War II, however, public opinion had shifted again. Some people felt that Communists had infiltrated the unions. Others were upset by the loss of production because of strikes. In 1946 alone, more than 116 million workdays were lost because of work stoppages. People began to feel that management, not labor, was the victim.

Antiunion Legislation *Workers urge President Truman to veto the Taft-Hartley Act, which he did. Congress passed the act over Truman's veto.* **What did the act do?**

Antiunion Legislation

Antiunion feelings led to the Labor-Management Relations Act, or Taft-Hartley Act, of 1947. The act put limits on what unions could do in labor-management disputes. Among other things, it gave employers the right to sue unions for breaking contracts and prohibited unions from making union membership a condition for hiring. The act also made it illegal for unions to give money to political campaigns and ordered them to give 60 days' notice before going on strike.

The Taft-Hartley Act had two other provisions that worked against labor. The first was a controversial 80-day "cooling off" period that federal courts could use to delay a strike in the case of a national emergency.

The second was a tough antiunion provision contained in Section 14(b), which allowed individual states to pass right-to-work laws. A **right-to-work law** is a state law making it illegal to require a worker to join a union. If a state has such a law, workers cannot be forced to join a union even after they are hired. If a state does not have a right-to-work law, workers can be forced to join the union after they are hired.

In addition, the government tried to stop the criminal influences that had begun to emerge in the labor movement. The Labor-Management Reporting and Disclosure Act, or Landrum-Griffin Act, of 1959 tried to protect individual union members from unfair actions of unions and union officials. The act required unions to file regular financial reports with the government, and it limited the amount of money officials could borrow from the union. The act also required the election of union officials by secret ballot, and that they be held accountable for union funds.

AFL-CIO

The American Federation of Labor (AFL) began in 1886 as an organization of craft unions. It later added several industrial unions. The trade and industrial unions, however, did not always agree about the future of the union movement. In 1935 eight industrial unions in the AFL formed the Committee for Industrial Organization. Headed by John L. Lewis, president of the United Mine Workers of America, its goal was to bring about greater unionization in industry.

The AFL and Lewis, however, did not get along. In 1937 the AFL expelled the unions that made up the Committee for Industrial Organization. Those unions then formed the Congress of Industrial Organizations (CIO). The CIO quickly set up unions in industries that had not been unionized before, such as steel and automobiles. By the 1940s, the CIO had nearly 7 million members.

As the CIO grew stronger, it began to challenge the dominance of the AFL. Before long, the two were in a struggle for control of the labor movement. Each was trying to form unions in areas already organized by the other. In 1955, after almost 20 years of disagreement, the AFL and the CIO finally settled most of their differences and joined to form the American Federation of Labor and Congress of Industrial Organizations (AFL-CIO).

The merger settled many, but not all, of the basic differences between trade and industrial unions. Even today, the two may have a **jurisdictional dispute,** or a disagreement over which union should perform a certain job. Metal workers from an industrial union and pipe fitters from a trade union may not agree on who should install metal pipe.

Independent Unions

Although the AFL-CIO is a major force, other unions are also important in the labor movement. Many are **independent unions**—unions that do not belong to the AFL-CIO, such as the Brotherhood of Locomotive Engineers.

SECTION 1
REVIEW

Reviewing Terms and Facts

1. **Define** macroeconomics, civilian labor force, craft or trade union, industrial union, strike, picket, boycott, lockout, company union, Great Depression, right-to-work law, jurisdictional dispute, independent union.
2. **Explain** why unions are important today.
3. **Describe** several reasons for the rise of unions prior to 1930.

4. **State** why unions became successful during the Great Depression.
5. **Describe** the development of the AFL-CIO.

Critical Thinking

6. **Making Generalizations** How did the five major legislative acts passed between 1932 and 1959 reflect the rise and decline of the labor movement?

Applying Economic Concepts

7. **Civilian Labor Force** How would your participation in the civilian labor force be affected if you joined the armed services?

PROFILES IN ECONOMICS

JOHN L. LEWIS
(1880–1969)

For more than 40 years, John L. Lewis was a central figure in the American labor movement. His strong leadership and dynamic style made him a powerful, as well as controversial, labor organizer. As president of the United Mine Workers of America (UMW), Lewis left a lasting influence on twentieth century American labor history.

BEGINNINGS Lewis, the son of Welsh immigrants, had a limited education. He grew up in small midwestern towns, where his father worked as a miner. As a young man, Lewis also worked in the

Lewis addresses textile workers in Lawrence, Massachusetts.

mines, earning a living by his physical strength and ingenuity. He later told a convention of miners, "I have always found that if I

could not make a living in one place, I could in another. . . ."

Lewis became active in his local union and moved rapidly through the ranks. Within a decade, John L. Lewis had become president of the nation's largest labor union. Beginning in 1920, Lewis led the UMW for 4 decades when the labor movement was a dominant force in American life.

LABOR LEADER Lewis challenged the organizing principle of the American Federation of Labor (AFL), which separated unions on the basis of a single craft or trade. Although he respected AFL

leader Samuel Gompers, Lewis believed that unions should be made up of all unskilled workers in a mass-production industry. As a result of this conflict, Lewis split with the AFL and formed the Congress of Industrial Organizations (CIO).

Through strikes and negotiations, Lewis succeeded in raising wages and protecting union workers from unfair labor practices and unsafe conditions. His concern for the safety and well-being of miners was a hallmark of his leadership. The UMW's health and retirement fund resulted from Lewis's confrontations with government officials.

CONTRIBUTIONS AND CONTROVERSY As a person and as a labor leader, John L. Lewis sparked great controversy. He represented millions of poorly paid workers, while he lived in luxury. He upheld democratic ideals, while he ruled his own union with an iron hand. He helped establish a pattern of collective bargaining by defying the federal government.

Examining the Profile

1. **Making Comparisons** How did John L. Lewis's ideas about unions differ from those of the AFL?

2. **For Further Research** Find out how a clash between John L. Lewis and President Harry Truman led to government seizure of mines in 1946. Write a newspaper article about the event.

Resolving Union and Management Differences

Section Preview

Objectives

After studying this section, you will be able to:

1. **Explain** the differences between four kinds of union arrangements.
2. **Describe** several ways to resolve labor and management differences when collective bargaining fails.

Key Terms

closed shop, union shop, modified union shop, agency shop, grievance procedure, mediation, voluntary arbitration, compulsory arbitration, fact-finding, injunction, seizure

Applying Economic Concepts

Union Arrangements Does the company that you or your parents work for have a union? If so, are you or your parents required to join? Four different types of *union arrangements* exist, and one will apply to your situation.

Over the years, many differences have arisen between labor and management. Some, such as the 1981 air traffic controllers' strike or the 1984 professional football strike, make headlines. Others do not. In either case, labor and management generally manage to settle their differences without resorting to extreme measures. About .02 percent of annual working time is lost because of labor disputes.

Kinds of Union Arrangements

The labor movement has tried to organize workers in ways designed to help them deal more effectively with management. The ways in which workers are organized and settlements are reached have an important impact on the entire economy. Four general kinds of union arrangements have been identified.

Members of the Amalgamated Clothing Workers union march to promote the closed shop in the early 1920s. **How did the passage of the Taft-Hartley Act affect closed shops?**

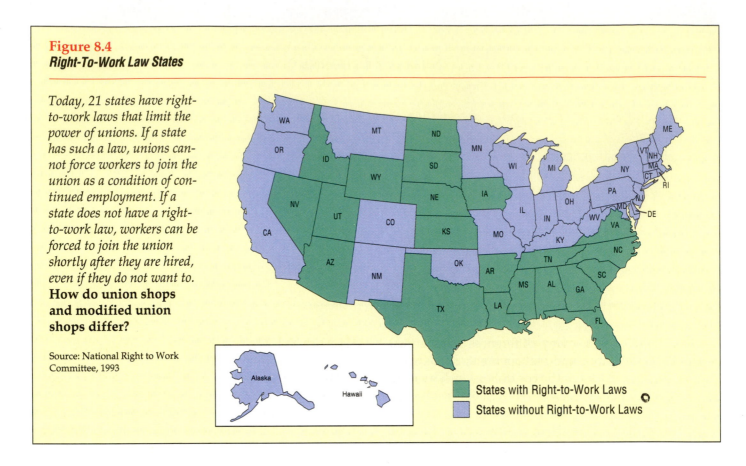

Figure 8.4
Right-To-Work Law States

Today, 21 states have right-to-work laws that limit the power of unions. If a state has such a law, unions cannot force workers to join the union as a condition of continued employment. If a state does not have a right-to-work law, workers can be forced to join the union shortly after they are hired, even if they do not want to. **How do union shops and modified union shops differ?**

Source: National Right to Work Committee, 1993

States with Right-to-Work Laws
States without Right-to-Work Laws

Closed Shops

The most restrictive arrangement is the **closed shop**—an arrangement in which the employer agrees to hire only union members. In effect, the union can determine who is hired by giving or denying a person union membership.

Although this kind of union arrangement was common in the 1930s and early 1940s, the Taft-Hartley Act of 1947 made the closed shop illegal for companies involved in interstate commerce. Because most firms in the United States today are directly or indirectly engaged in interstate commerce, few, if any, closed shops exist.

Union Shops

The second kind of arrangement is the **union shop.** Workers do not have to belong to the union to be hired, but they must join one soon after and remain a member for as long as they keep their jobs. No union shops, however, can require membership sooner than

30 days after employment. The only exception is the construction industry, in which the period is 7 days.

Today, 21 states have taken advantage of Section 14(b) and have passed right-to-work laws that prohibit mandatory union membership. These states are shown in **Figure 8.4**.

Modified Union Shops

The third kind of arrangement is a **modified union shop.** Under this arrangement, workers do not have to belong to a union to be hired and cannot be made to join one to keep their jobs. If workers voluntarily join the union, however, they must remain members for as long as they hold their jobs.

Agency Shops

The final arrangement is the **agency shop.** Under this kind of union arrangement, workers need not be union members to be hired or to keep their jobs. They must pay dues to the union, however, to help pay the costs of collective bargaining. Nonunion workers are subject to the contract negotiated by the union, whether or not they agree with it. Agency shops are primarily responsible for the 2.1 percent of employed wage and salary workers represented by unions in **Figure 8.1**.

Collective Bargaining

When labor and management take part in collective bargaining, a meeting occurs between representatives of both groups. A group of elected union officials represents workers, and company officials in charge of labor relations represent management. Collective bargaining requires compromise from both parties, and the discussions may go on for months. **1**

If the negotiations are successful, both parties agree on basic issues such as pay, working conditions, and fringe benefits. Because it is so difficult to anticipate future problems, however, a **grievance procedure**—a provision for resolving issues that may come up later—may also be included in the final contract.

Normally, union and management are able to reach an agreement. If the disputing parties cannot agree on certain points, other methods are available to resolve the differences.

Mediation

One way to resolve differences is through **mediation**—the process of bringing in a third person or persons to help settle a dispute. The mediator's primary goal is to find a solution that both parties will accept. A mediator must be absolutely neutral so that one party does not benefit at the expense of the other. If the mediator has the confidence and trust of both parties, he or she will be able to learn what concessions each side is willing to make.

In the end, the mediator recommends a compromise to both sides. Neither side has to accept a mediator's decision, although it often helps break the deadlock.

Arbitration

Another way differences can be cleared up is through **voluntary arbitration.** Both sides agree to place their differences before a third party whose decision will be accepted as final and binding. The arbitration is voluntary in that both sides agree to its use. It is different from mediation in that both sides agree in advance to abide by the decision of the third-party arbitrator. **2**

In some cases, such as the 1967 railroad strike, labor and management are forced to turn an unsettled dispute over to a third party for a binding decision. This is called **compulsory arbitration** and is seldom used in the United States.

Professional baseball has its own form of salary arbitration. When a player goes to arbitration, his agent and his team's owner submit salary recommendations. The arbitrator examines both in light of the player's performance and the salaries paid to other league players, and then selects one of the two recommendations.

Fact-Finding

A third way to resolve a dispute that collective bargaining cannot settle is through **fact-finding.** Labor and management agree to have an independent third party investigate the issues and recommend possible settlements. This process can be especially useful in situations where each side has deliberately distorted the issues to win public support, or when one side simply does not believe the claims made by the other side. Neither labor nor management has to accept the recommendations the fact-finding committee makes.

Checking Understanding

1. What is collective bargaining?
2. How does voluntary arbitration differ from mediation?

Applying Economic Concepts

✓ **Fact-Finding** Although labor and management may disregard the recommendations of a fact-finding committee, public opinion may sway the parties to accept the recommendations after they have been publicized.

Injunction and Seizure

A fourth way to settle labor-management disputes is through injunction or seizure. When vital industries are threatened, the government may resort to an **injunction**—a court order not to act. If issued against a union, it directs the union not to strike. If issued against a company, it directs the company not to lock out its workers. In 1978, after coal miners had been off the job for more than three months, President Jimmy Carter obtained an injunction that ordered the coal miners to return to work.

Under extreme circumstances, the government also may resort to **seizure**—a temporary takeover of operations. The purpose of seizure is to allow the government to negotiate with the union. This occurred in 1946 when the government seized the bituminous coal industry. While operating the mines, officials worked out a settlement with the miners' union.

Presidential Influence

As a last resort, the President of the United States may enter a labor-management dispute by publicly appealing to both parties to resolve their differences. This can be effective if the appeal has public support. In most cases, however, presidential influence occurs only in industries that affect the national interest, such as steel, airlines, or railroads.

The President also can fire federal workers. In 1981 President Ronald Reagan fired striking air traffic con-

trollers because they were federal employees who had gone on strike despite having taken an oath not to do so. Because they were fired, they were prohibited from accepting other federal jobs, a restriction removed by President Bill Clinton in 1993.

HELP WANTED

Labor Relations Specialist

▼

Are you a people person? Are you patient, fair-minded, and persuasive? Can you function under pressure? Our firm needs someone like you to formulate labor policy, oversee industrial labor relations, negotiate collective bargaining agreements, and coordinate grievance procedures to handle complaints resulting from contract disputes. You must be knowledgeable about wages and salaries, benefits, pensions, and union and management practices. Courses in labor law, collective bargaining, labor economics, labor history, and industrial psychology are a must.

▼

Education: Degree in labor relations
Median salary: $30,000

SECTION 2 REVIEW

Reviewing Terms and Facts

1. **Define** closed shop, union shop, modified union shop, agency shop, grievance procedure, mediation, voluntary arbitration, compulsory arbitration, fact-finding, injunction, seizure.
2. **List** four kinds of union arrangements.
3. **Describe** five ways to resolve union and management differences when collective bargaining fails.

Critical Thinking

4. **Making Comparisons** If you represented a company during a collective bargaining session, and if negotiations were deadlocked, what course of action would you recommend? Why?

Applying Economic Concepts

5. **Union Arrangements** Contact a firm that has a union in your community. Ask if all workers in the company are required to join, or if only some are. Based on your information, determine if the union arrangement is a closed shop, a union shop, a modified union shop, or an agency shop.

CRITICAL THINKING SKILL

Analyzing Information

On the day of an earthquake, you see a television interview of an excited eyewitness to the event. Two weeks later, you see a televised interview with a scientist who studies earthquakes but who was not an eyewitness to this particular earthquake. One account is probably more accurate than the other.

Explanation

In studying economics, you will encounter many different kinds of information. Analyzing information helps you see how each kind of information can contribute to your understanding of economics.

Most information falls into two broad categories—primary and secondary sources. Primary sources are documents created at the time the event occurred. Letters, journals, newspaper articles, and photographs are examples of primary sources. Secondary sources are documents created after an event occurred. Secondary sources often pull together information from many sources and provide an overview of events.

Information also takes the following forms: written evidence, visual evidence, and artifacts. Written evidence includes books, periodicals, letters, diaries, and government records and documents. Visual evidence includes charts and graphs, paintings, cartoons, photographs, and films. Artifacts are objects that humans made and used, such as tools, buildings, and toys.

Follow these steps to help you analyze information:
- identify the kind of information
- identify who created it and when
- examine the information and try to answer the "five W" questions: Who is it about? What is it about? When did it happen? Where did it happen? Why did it happen?
- summarize the key ideas

Practice

Read the passages highlighted below. Use the listed steps to help you analyze the information, then answer the questions below.

1. Is the first paragraph a primary or secondary source? How can you tell?
2. Is the second paragraph a primary or secondary source? How can you tell?
3. What events are described in the paragraphs?
4. Who was affected by these events?
5. When did these events take place?
6. Where did these events take place?
7. What are the key ideas?

Throughout the Depression, families who could not pay their rent or make their mortgage payments were evicted from their homes. Some moved in with relatives if they could. The less fortunate ended up in makeshift communities dubbed "Hoovervilles" on the outskirts of cities. One woman later described a Hooverville:

Here were all these people living in old, rusted-out car bodies. I mean that was their home. There were people living in shacks made of orange crates. One family with a whole lot of kids were living in a piano box. This wasn't just a little section, this was maybe ten-miles wide and ten-miles long. People living in whatever they could junk together.

—Peggy Terry, in *Hard Times*, by Studs Terkel

Additional Practice

For further practice in analyzing information, complete the Reinforcing Skills exercise in the Chapter 8 Review on page 207.

Section Preview

Objectives

After studying this section, you will be able to:

1. **Identify** four main categories of labor.

2. **Explain** the importance of non-competing labor grades.

3. **Describe** two different approaches to wage determination.

Key Terms

unskilled labor, semiskilled labor, skilled labor, professional labor, noncompeting labor grades, wage rate, traditional theory of wage determination, equilibrium wage rate, theory of negotiated wages, seniority, labor mobility

Applying Economic Concepts

Semiskilled Labor Have you ever mowed a lawn? Used a drill? Operated a washing machine? If so, your mechanical abilities might classify you as *semiskilled labor*. Semiskilled workers rarely earn a high salary, however, so you may want to think about how you can change your classification.

Many different occupations exist in the United States, and wages usually differ from one occupation to the next. To understand why wages differ, it helps to place workers into broad groups so that we can study the characteristics of each.

Categories of Labor

The four major categories of labor are based on the general level of skills needed to do a particular kind of job. These categories are unskilled, semiskilled, skilled, and professional or managerial.

Workers who lack the training to operate specialized machines and equipment make up the category of **unskilled labor.** Most of these people work mainly with their hands at such jobs as food serving, digging ditches, picking fruit, and mopping floors.

Workers with mechanical abilities are in the **semiskilled labor** category. They may operate electric floor polishers, dishwashers, and other machines that call for a minimal amount of training. 1

Workers who are able to operate complex equipment and who can do their tasks with little supervision belong to the category of **skilled labor.** Examples are carpenters, typists, tool and die makers, computer technicians, chefs, and computer programmers.

Workers with higher-level skills, such as doctors, teachers, lawyers, and executives of large companies, comprise the category of **professional labor.**

Noncompeting Labor Grades

Workers in one labor category generally do not compete with those in another category. Semiskilled workers do not compete with skilled laborers, and skilled laborers do not compete directly with professional workers. Economists, therefore, say that labor can be grouped into **noncompeting labor grades.**

For the most part, members of one group find it difficult to qualify for occupations open to a higher group. Several reasons explain why the workers in one group tend to stay in that group—cost, opportunity, and initiative.

Cost of Education and Training

Cost is one of the more difficult barriers to advancement. Some individuals have the ability and initiative to obtain additional technical skills, but they may not have the money to pay for the training. Many students have the aptitude to become college professors, but they lack the resources needed for four to six years of post-college study.

Lack of Opportunity

A lack of opportunity poses another barrier, even when people have the ability and the money to finance the additional education. Some people may live in areas where additional training and education are not available. Others may have the resources and grades to get into a specialized program such as medical school, but still may not be able to enter because the nearby schools have limited openings.

Lack of Initiative

Although they know that more skills are needed to get a better job, other individuals lack the initiative to get ahead. These people may never acquire additional training or education because they are not willing to put forth the extra effort.

Wage Determination

Most occupations have a **wage rate**—a standard amount of pay given for work performed. Differences in wage rates can be explained in two ways. The first uses the traditional tools of supply and demand. The second recognizes the influence of unions in the bargaining process.

Traditional Theory of Wages

The theory that uses the tools of supply and demand to explain differences in wage rates is called the **traditional theory of wage determination.** Professional managers and athletes, for example, are generally more scarce than ditchdiggers or fruit pickers and are more valuable to their employers.

The concepts of supply and demand can be used to illustrate the traditional approach. In **Figure 8.5,** Graph **A** shows what happens when a relatively large supply of ditchdiggers is coupled with a relatively low level of demand. In Graph **B**, a relatively small supply of professional athletes is paired with a relatively high level of demand. The intersection of supply and demand determines the **equilibrium wage**

rate—the wage rate that leaves neither a surplus nor a shortage in the labor market.

In most cases, the higher the level of skills or grade of labor, the higher the average annual wage rate, although wide salary variations exist within each group. Semiskilled workers will generally receive more than unskilled workers and skilled workers will receive more than semiskilled or unskilled workers. Professional workers generally earn more than any of the others. This relationship is readily evident

Categories of Labor *Each worker above has different skills and, as a result, receives different wages.* **Into which category of labor does each worker fall?**

QUICK CHECK	*Checking Understanding*	*Applying Economic Concepts*
	1. How does the category of semiskilled labor differ from unskilled labor?	☑ **Barriers to Advancement** In 1993 four years at a top private university cost about $100,000. Four years at an in-state public university averaged about $45,000.

in **Figure 8.6**. The occupations are arranged in descending order, with those having the highest level of skills and training at the top.

Several exceptions to the traditional theory exist. Some unproductive workers may receive high wages because of family ties or political influence. Other highly skilled workers receive low wages because of discrimination based on their race, gender, or location.

In addition, workers and employers do not always know what the market wage rate is or should be. A worker may accept a job that pays $4.35 an hour because he or she does not know that the firm next door is paying $4.75 for the same job. An employer may offer to hire someone for $275 a week without knowing that the same service can be obtained for $200. If the forces of supply and demand operate freely, however, wages and the market for labor will operate as the theory suggests.

Theory of Negotiated Wages

At times, the relative strength of organized labor and the collective bargaining process, rather than the forces of supply and demand, determine wages. Economists use the **theory of negotiated wages** to explain wage rates in these cases.

Unions, for example, may get higher wages for their members, but not always because labor is in short supply relative to the demand. Instead, strong union representatives may outnegotiate relatively weaker management representatives regardless of market conditions. **Figure 8.6** helps validate the the-ory of negotiated wages. The table shows that when workers are either unionized or represented by unions, median weekly salaries are significantly higher than for nonunion workers. This situation applies to all occupations except for the "managerial and professional specialty" category, whose members are seldom unionized.

Another factor that becomes important when unions and collective bargaining enter the picture is **seniority**—the length of time a person has been on the job. Because of their seniority, some workers receive higher wages than others who perform similar tasks. In many cases, senior workers are laid off last when the company cuts back on production.

Regional Wage Differences

Regardless of how wage rates are determined, they can still be different for the same job from one part of the country to another. Supply and demand, labor mobility, cost of living, and attractiveness of location all can make a difference in wage rates.

Labor Mobility

Skilled workers are scarce in some parts of the country and abundant in others. The extent of scarcity causes differences in wage rates. These differences, however, can be narrowed by **labor mobility**—the ability and willingness of workers to relocate in markets where wages are higher.

Figure 8.5
The Traditional Theory of Wage Determination

The market forces of supply and demand explain the equilibrium wage rate for the traditional theory of wage determination. When the supply of workers is large and the demand low, as in Graph A, annual salaries are low. When supply is limited and demand is high, as in Graph B, annual salaries are much higher.
How does the traditional theory of wage determination differ from the theory of negotiated wages?

A. Ditchdiggers

Price (Annual Salary)

Quantity

– – – $8,000

B. Professional Athletes

Price (Annual Salary)

Quantity

– $1,000,000

Figure 8.6
Median Weekly Earnings by Occupation and Union Affiliation

According to the Bureau of Labor Statistics, weekly earnings are significantly higher for the highly skilled occupations. The table also shows that workers who are represented by unions have substantially higher earnings than their nonunion counterparts. Because managerial and professional specialty workers are seldom unionized, the earnings are the same in both columns. **What can you infer about union negotiations from this figure?**

Occupation	Represented by Unions	Nonunion Workers
Managerial and Professional Specialty Includes executive, administrative, managerial, professional specialty	$655	$655
Precision Production, Craft, and Repair	616	438
Technical, Sales, and Administrative Support	494	394
Operators, fabricators, and laborers Includes machine operators, assemblers, inspectors, transportation and material moving occupations, handlers, equipment cleaners, helpers and laborers	491	314
Farming, Forestry, and Fishing	391	257

Source: Bureau of Labor Statistics *News*, February 8, 1993

Not all workers are equally mobile. Some are reluctant to move away from relatives and friends. Some may want to move, but they find that the cost is too high. Others do not want the inconvenience of buying a new house or renting a new apartment. As a result, the demand for certain skills remains high in some areas and low in others, and wages tend to vary.

Cost of Living

Another factor that affects wages is the cost of living. In Hawaii and many southern states, fresh fruits and vegetables are readily available. In addition, little money is spent on heavy clothing or on heating a home. In Alaska, however, food must be shipped in from thousands of miles away, people must have warm clothing, and every home must be well heated. The cost of living is obviously higher in Alaska than in most southern states. Wages, then, tend to be higher in Alaska than in most southern states.

Location

Location can also make a difference in wages. Some locations are thought to be so attractive that lower wages can be offered there. A person who likes to hunt and fish may be willing to work for less pay in Colorado or Montana than in New York City.

SECTION 3 REVIEW

Reviewing Terms and Facts

1. **Define** unskilled labor, semiskilled labor, skilled labor, professional labor, noncompeting labor grades, wage rate, traditional theory of wage determination, equilibrium wage rate, theory of negotiated wages, seniority, labor mobility.
2. **List** the four grades or categories of noncompeting labor.

3. **Explain** the two theories of wage determination.
4. **Describe** how climate and location can affect wages in different parts of the country.

Critical Thinking

5. **Evaluating Information** Randomly select three Help Wanted ads from your local paper. Read the skills required for each, and then classify each according to the four noncompeting labor groups.

Applying Economic Concepts

6. **Semiskilled Labor** If you were a semiskilled worker, what could you do to move into a higher category of noncompeting labor?

Employment Trends and Issues

Section Preview

Objectives

After studying this section, you will be able to:

1. **Explain** why union membership is declining.
2. **Describe** reasons for the discrepancy in pay between men and women.
3. **Understand** the minimum wage as it is measured in current and constant dollars.

Key Terms

giveback, two-tier wage system, glass ceiling, comparable worth, set-aside contract, current dollars, real or constant dollars, base year

Applying Economic Concepts

Minimum Wage Have you ever held a job at which you earned exactly $4.25 per hour? Do you know others who received the same wage? Is this an incredible coincidence, or is everyone equally skilled at their jobs? More than likely, everyone is receiving the federal *minimum wage* that was raised to $4.25 in 1991.

Several trends and issues have been observed in today's labor movement. These include the decline of union membership, the discrepancy in pay between men and women, and the minimum wage.

Decline of Union Influence

A significant trend in today's economy is the decline in both union membership and influence. As **Figure 8.7** shows, 35.5 percent of nonagricultural workers were members of unions in 1945. This number fell to 21.9 percent by 1980, and then dropped to under 15.8 percent by 1993.

Reasons for Decline

Several reasons are given for the decline in union membership and influence. The first is that many employers made a determined effort to keep unions out of their businesses. Some were active in their opposition and even hired consultants to map out legal strategies to fight unions. Other employers

---

Figure 8.7
Union Membership

Union membership grew rapidly after 1933 and peaked at 35.5 percent in 1945. Since then, it has declined gradually until accounting for 15.8 percent of the employed wage and salary workers in 1993. **What is perhaps the most important reason for the decline of unions?**

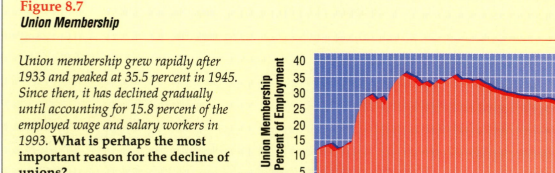

Source: Bureau of Labor Statistics

made workers part of the management team, adding employees to the board of directors or setting up profit-sharing plans to reward employees.

A second reason for union decline is that new additions to the labor force—especially women and teenagers—traditionally had little loyalty to organized labor. Because many of these workers represent second incomes to families, they have a tendency to accept lower wages. **1**

The third and perhaps most important reason for the decline is that unions are the victims of their own success. Unions raised their wages substantially above the wages paid to nonunion workers. As a result, many union-made products, especially in the automobile and steel industries, became so expensive that sales were lost to less expensive foreign competitors and nonunion producers. The loss in sales forced companies to cut back on production, which caused some workers to lose their jobs, and unions to lose some of their members.

Renegotiating Union Wages

Because unions have generally kept their wages above those of their nonunion counterparts, union wages have been under pressure. In some cases, unions agreed to lower their wages because foreign competition threatened industries. In other cases, industries were not profitable and, therefore, could not afford expensive union contracts.

One way employers have been able to reduce union wages is by asking for givebacks from union workers. A **giveback** is a wage, fringe benefit, or work rule given up when labor contracts are renegotiated. **2** When Chrysler faced stiff competition from domestic producers and foreign imports in 1981, workers agreed to give up more than $1 billion in wages and fringe benefits to keep the company open. In 1986 the United Steel Workers took a pay cut and agreed to a 10-year freeze on pension plan increases to help the LTV Corporation.

Some companies have been able to get rid of labor contracts by claiming bankruptcy. If a company can show the court that wages and fringe benefits contributed significantly to its problems, federal bankruptcy courts usually allow a company to terminate its union contract and establish lower wage scales. LTV threatened to use this tactic against the United Steel Workers in 1992, despite the union givebacks in 1986.

Another way of reducing union salary scales is with a **two-tier wage system.** This system keeps the high wage for current workers, but has a much lower wage for newly hired workers. In 1984 the United States Postal Service cut its starting pay for new employees by 25 percent.

Two-tiered systems can have an immediate impact on labor costs. The United States Postal Service hires about 40,000 new workers annually, so the savings were substantial. Even so, some employees in a two-tier wage system are concerned that new workers will be resentful toward older ones, especially as the new, lower-paid workers become a larger part of the workforce.

Lower Pay for Women

Overall, women face a considerable gap between their income and that received by men. As **Figure 8.8** shows, female income has been only a fraction of male income over a 40-year period. At least two causes explain this inequality, and several potential solutions exist. ☑

Checking Understanding	**Applying Economic Concepts**
1. Why do women and teenagers traditionally have little loyalty to labor unions? **2.** What is a giveback?	☑ **Cultural Influences** Child development experts claim sex stereotyping influences job choices. Girls are praised for being polite and compliant, behaviors that work against them in the labor force. Boys are encouraged to be assertive, which helps them succeed in demanding careers.

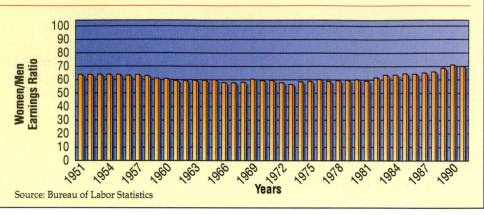

Figure 8.8
Median Female Income as a Percentage of Male Income

Over the years, the income earned by females has been only a fraction of that earned by males. The low point was in 1973 when female income was only 56.6% of male income. The high was in 1990 when the figure was 71.1%. **What explains the income gap between men and women?**

Source: Bureau of Labor Statistics

Gender and Occupation

One reason for the income inequality is that men and women are not evenly distributed among the various occupations. Men have tended to gravitate toward higher-paid occupations, and women have been crowded into a few, lower-paid occupations. The average pay men and women receive will not be equal if the pay is different for the two occupations.

Figure 8.9 shows that, historically, more men enter construction and engineering trades than do women. Likewise, women enter the private household service and office worker occupations in relatively greater numbers than men. As long as construction and engineering wages are higher than private household and office worker wages, men—on average—will earn more than women.

Many women's careers are also interrupted by childbearing, which affects their seniority. Even so, these reasons do not explain why the pay for men and women within the same occupation is often different.

Discrimination

Discrimination is often a major cause of income discrepancy between men and women. Women and minorities feel that their difficulties in getting raises and promotions are like encountering a **glass ceiling,** an invisible barrier that hinders their advancement up the white male-dominated corporate ladder.

Congress passed two major laws to prevent discrimination. The first was the Equal Pay Act of 1963, which prohibits wage and salary discrimination for jobs that require equivalent skills and responsibilities. This act applies only to men and women who work at the same job in the same business establishment.

The second law was the Civil Rights Act of 1964. Title VII of this act prohibits discrimination in all areas of employment on the basis of sex, race, color, religion, and national origin. The law applies to employers with 15 or more workers, and it specifically excludes religious associations and their educational institutions.

The Civil Rights Act of 1964 also set up the Equal Employment Opportunity Commission (EEOC). The EEOC investigates charges of discrimination, issues guidelines and regulations, conducts hearings, and collects statistics. If a pattern of discrimination is discovered, the government can bring suit against a company and force it to remedy the discrimination.

Comparable Worth

One of the corrective measures used to close the income gap between men and women takes the form of **comparable worth.** This principle means that people should receive equal pay for work that is different from, but just as demanding as, other types of work. It has been applied mainly to salary discrimination cases between men and women, although it can be applied to race and age as well. As such, comparable worth goes beyond the concept of equal pay for equal work.

In the state of Washington, a federal judge ruled that work performed by social service workers—most of whom were female—was just as demanding as some traditionally male occupations. The judge ordered the state to raise wages and give workers several years' back pay. In Illinois, job evaluators determined that the work done by highway workers was roughly equivalent to that done by nurses. In Minnesota, the work of delivery drivers was determined roughly comparable to that of pharmacy assistants.

Comparable worth decisions are not easy to make. Many factors, such as education requirements, occupational hazards, and degree of physical difficulty, must be considered. Some people believe that fair and unbiased comparisons of occupations are almost impossible and violate free-market principles. These people also argue that comparable worth is not needed as long as people are free to enter any profession they desire. Others argue that comparable worth is necessary to remove sex discrimination in the marketplace.

Comparable worth is widely used in the United States, Europe, and Canada. Today, more than half the states have examined the concept of comparable worth. Several, including California, Iowa, Minnesota, and Washington, have had comparable worth laws for state employees since 1984.

Set-Aside Contracts

Another corrective measure is the government **set-aside contract,** or a guaranteed contract reserved exclusively for a targeted group. The federal government, for

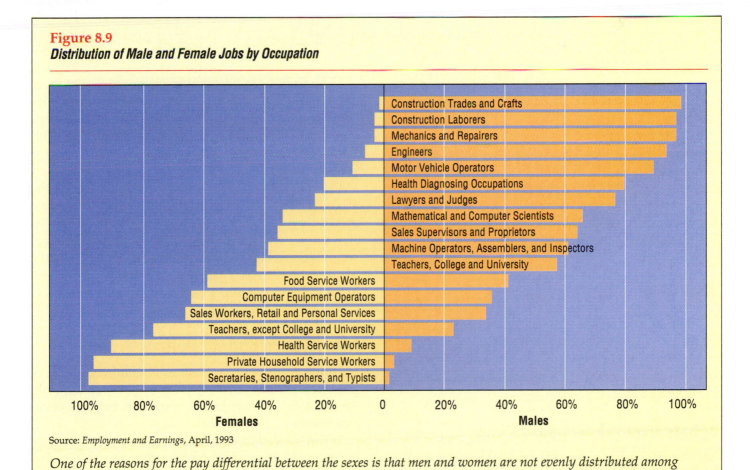

Figure 8.9
Distribution of Male and Female Jobs by Occupation

Construction Trades and Crafts
Construction Laborers
Mechanics and Repairers
Engineers
Motor Vehicle Operators
Health Diagnosing Occupations
Lawyers and Judges
Mathematical and Computer Scientists
Sales Supervisors and Proprietors
Machine Operators, Assemblers, and Inspectors
Teachers, College and University
Food Service Workers
Computer Equipment Operators
Sales Workers, Retail and Personal Services
Teachers, except College and University
Health Service Workers
Private Household Service Workers
Secretaries, Stenographers, and Typists

100%   80%   60%   40%   20%   0   20%   40%   60%   80%   100%
Females   **Males**

Source: *Employment and Earnings*, April, 1993

One of the reasons for the pay differential between the sexes is that men and women are not evenly distributed among occupations. If men tend to cluster in higher-paid occupations, and if women tend to cluster in lower-paid occupations, the average pay for men and women will differ. **What corrective measures may close the income gap between men and women?**

Comparable Worth *Comparable worth tries to close the income gap between men and women by requiring equal pay for equally demanding types of work.*
Why are comparable worth decisions difficult?

example, requires a certain percentage of defense contracts be reserved exclusively for minority-owned businesses.

In 1988 the state of California passed a law requiring that 5 percent of the state's bond contracts be set aside exclusively for women lawyers, bankers, and other females who help place the bonds in the hands of investors. Laws such as this are enacted to ensure that the state does not give all of its business to males in a male-dominated profession.

The Minimum Wage

The minimum wage—the lowest wage that can be paid by law to workers in a certain job—was first set in 1939 at $.25 per hour. As Graph **A** in **Figure 8.10** shows, the minimum wage increased over time until it reached $4.25 in 1991.

Debate Over the Minimum Wage

The minimum wage has always been controversial. The original intent of the law was to prevent the outright exploitation of workers and to provide some degree of equity and security to those who lacked the skills needed to earn a decent income.

Supporters of the minimum wage argue that these objectives—equity and security—are consistent with America's economic goals. Besides, they say, the wage is not very high in the first place. Others agree with the principle of the minimum wage but think the wage is too high.

Opponents of the minimum wage object to it on the grounds of economic freedom—also one of America's economic goals. They argue that employers should be free to pay whatever wage they want, or whatever wage the market will bear. This group feels that the wage discriminates against young people and is one of the reasons that many teenagers cannot find jobs.

Measured in Current Dollars

Graph **A** in **Figure 8.10** shows the minimum wage in **current dollars,** or in dollars that are not adjusted for inflation. The minimum wage is recorded exactly as it was from 1939 to 1993.

When viewed in this manner, it seems as if the minimum wage increased dramatically over time. The graph, however, does not take inflation into account. Because prices tend to increase over time, the purchasing power of the minimum wage is constantly being eroded.

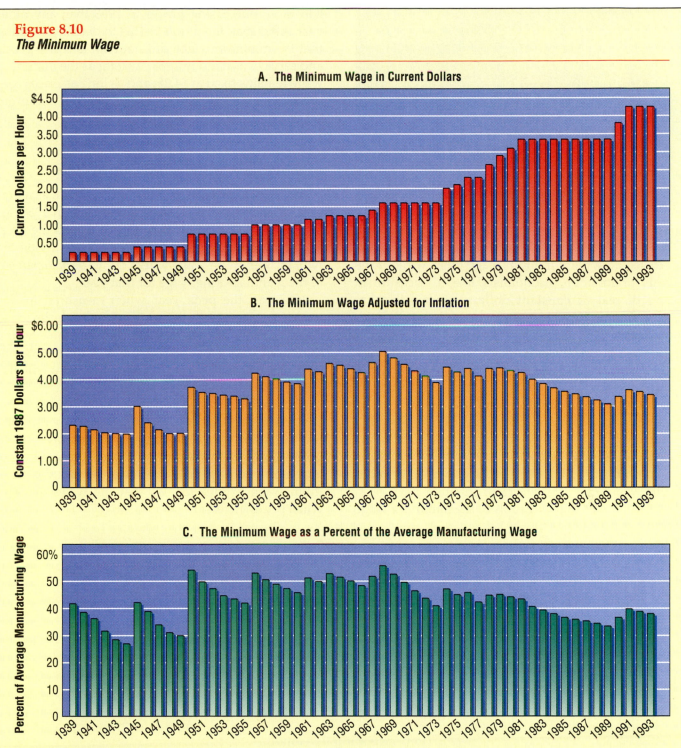

Figure 8.10
The Minimum Wage

A. The Minimum Wage in Current Dollars

B. The Minimum Wage Adjusted for Inflation

C. The Minimum Wage as a Percent of the Average Manufacturing Wage

Sources: *Statistical Abstract of the United States, Economic Report of the President,* 1993

When the minimum wage is expressed in current dollars, as in Graph A, it appears to have increased dramatically since it was established in 1939. When the minimum wage is adjusted for inflation, as in Graph B, or is viewed as a percentage of the average manufacturing wage, as in Graph C, the minimum wage has lost some ground since 1968. **What arguments do supporters and opponents of the minimum wage use to defend their positions?**

Adjusted for Inflation

To see how the minimum wage looks without the effects of inflation, economists like to measure in terms of **real** or **constant dollars**—dollars that are adjusted in a way that removes the distortion inflation causes.

To measure in constant dollars, a **base year**—a year that serves as the basis of comparison for all other years—is selected. Next, goods and services for all years are valued in terms of the base year prices. By holding prices constant, inflation is removed so that other changes are observed more clearly from one period to the next.

Graph **B** shows the purchasing power of the minimum wage after the effects of inflation have been removed. According to Graph **B**, the minimum wage had more purchasing power in 1968 than any other year. After that, the graph begins to decline, meaning that the minimum wage did not buy as many goods and services as it did in 1968. As long as the minimum wage remains fixed at $4.25, and as long as prices continue to rise, the purchasing power of the minimum wage will continue to decline.

Compared to Manufacturing Wages

In Graph **C**, the minimum wage is shown as a percent of the average manufacturing wage. In 1968, for example, the minimum wage was $1.60 and the average manufacturing wage was $2.88. If we divide the two, the minimum wage works out to be 55.6 percent of the manufacturing wage for that year.

1968 was the peak year when measured in this manner. After 1968 the ratio slowly declined to approximately 38 percent by 1993. As long as the minimum wage stays at $4.25, and as long as manufacturing wages continue to go up, this ratio will also continue to decline.

The minimum wage will certainly be raised again. What is not certain is when this will happen. When the minimum wage becomes unacceptably low to voters and their elected officials, Congress will increase it. Some people even want to link the minimum wage to inflation, so that the wage will rise when prices increase.

SECTION 4 REVIEW

Reviewing Terms and Facts

1. **Define** giveback, two-tier wage system, glass ceiling, comparable worth, set-aside contract, current dollars, real or constant dollars, base year.
2. **List** three reasons for the decline of unions.
3. **Describe** two reasons for the income gap between men and women.

4. **Explain** why it is necessary to consider inflation when examining the minimum wage.

Critical Thinking

5. **Demonstrating Reasoned Judgment** In your opinion, how have cultural stereotypes influenced the income gap between men and women?

Applying Economic Concepts

6. **Minimum Wage** A number of arguments exist both for and against the minimum wage. With which side do you agree? Why?

Vocabulary

The following terms are defined in Chapter 8:

SECTION ONE
- macroeconomics (p. 182)
- civilian labor force (p. 182)
- craft or trade union (p. 184)
- industrial union (p. 184)
- strike (p. 184)
- picket (p. 184)
- boycott (p. 184)
- lockout (p. 184)
- company union (p. 184)

- Great Depression (p. 185)
- right-to-work law (p. 186)
- jurisdictional dispute (p. 187)
- independent union (p. 187)

SECTION TWO
- closed shop (p. 190)
- union shop (p. 190)
- modified union shop (p. 190)
- agency shop (p. 190)
- grievance procedure (p. 191)
- mediation (p. 191)
- voluntary arbitration (p. 191)

- compulsory arbitration (p. 191)
- fact-finding (p. 191)
- injunction (p. 192)
- seizure (p. 192)

SECTION THREE
- unskilled labor (p. 194)
- semiskilled labor (p. 194)
- skilled labor (p. 194)
- professional labor (p. 194)
- noncompeting labor grades (p. 194)
- wage rate (p. 195)
- traditional theory of wage determination (p. 195)

- equilibrium wage rate (p. 195)
- theory of negotiated wages (p. 196)
- seniority (p. 196)
- labor mobility (p. 196)

SECTION FOUR
- giveback (p. 199)
- two-tier wage system (p. 199)
- glass ceiling (p. 200)
- comparable worth (p. 200)
- set-aside contract (p. 201)
- current dollars (p. 202)
- real or constant dollars (p. 204)
- base year (p. 204)

Section 1 The Labor Movement (pages 182–187)

Early union growth was slow because the nation was largely made up of farmers and small business owners. **Craft** or **trade unions** were the first to appear, followed by **industrial unions.**

Public attitudes toward labor changed significantly after the **Great Depression.** During the 1930s, the Norris-LaGuardia Act, the Wagner Act, and the Fair Labor Standards Act turned the tide in labor's favor. After World War II, the passage of the Taft-Hartley Act limited union activity.

Reviewing the Main Idea
What acts affected labor after the Depression?

Section 2 Resolving Union and Management Differences (pages 189–192)

There are four kinds of union arrangements: the **closed shop**, the **union shop,** the **modified union shop**, and the **agency shop.** Several methods are available to settle labor-management disputes if collective bargaining fails: **mediation, arbitration, fact-finding**, an **injunction,** and **seizure.**

Reviewing the Main Idea
How can labor-management disputes be resolved?

Section 3 Labor and Wages (pages 194–197)

Economists divide labor into four **noncompeting labor grades—unskilled, semiskilled, skilled,** and **professional labor.** The **traditional theory of wage determination** uses the market forces of supply and demand to explain wage rates. The **theory of negotiated wages** argues that the relative strength of unions is also a factor when determining wages.

Reviewing the Main Idea
How do the theories of wage determination differ?

Section 4 Employment Trends and Issues (pages 198–204)

Unions have declined for three reasons: employers have taken aggressive steps to avoid unions, new additions to the labor force have little loyalty to organized labor, and unions have priced themselves out of the market in some industries.

Women face a considerable gap between their income and that received by men. **Comparable worth** and **set-aside contracts** are corrective measures to close the gap.

Reviewing the Main Idea
What are two employment issues?

CHAPTER 8 REVIEW

Reviewing Key Terms

Define each of the terms below and then classify them as prounion, antiunion, or neither.

1. boycott
2. closed shop
3. company union
4. compulsory arbitration
5. fact-finding
6. giveback
7. grievance procedure
8. lockout
9. modified union shop
10. seizure
11. jurisdictional dispute
12. picket
13. right-to-work law
14. agency shop
15. strike
16. two-tier wage system
17. voluntary arbitration
18. mediation

Reviewing the Facts

SECTION 1 *(pages 182–187)*

1. **Describe** current union influence in terms of membership and workers represented by unions.
2. **Compare** the two types of unions in the post-Civil War period.
3. **Describe** the advances made by unions during the Great Depression.
4. **Outline** the progress of unions since World War II ended.

SECTION 2 *(pages 189–192)*

5. **Describe** the four types of union arrangements.
6. **Explain** five approaches to resolving a deadlock that may occur between a union and a company's management.

SECTION 3 *(pages 194–197)*

7. **Explain** the differences between the four major categories of noncompeting labor.
8. **Explain** why it is so difficult for workers to move from one category of labor to another.
9. **Compare** the two theories of wage determination.
10. **Discuss** the reasons for regional wage differences.

SECTION 4 *(pages 198–204)*

11. **Explain** why unions have lost members as well as influence in recent years.
12. **Describe** two corrective measures being taken to close the income gap between men and women workers.
13. **Identify** three ways to examine the minimum wage.

Critical Thinking

1. **Making Generalizations** Unions generally argue that the best interests of workers can be served when employees are members of a union. Do you agree or disagree with this argument? Defend your answer.
2. **Analyzing Information** Some people believe that in today's economy, the theory of negotiated wages is more useful than the traditional theory of wage determination. Explain why you agree or disagree.

Applying Economic Concepts

1. **Civilian Labor Force** As you go to and from school, be aware of the various occupations around you. List at least 20 occupations, then classify them according to the four major categories of labor.
2. **Minimum Wage** Poll at least 10 people of various ages, asking for their opinions on the following statement: There should be no minimum wage. Compile the responses and present your findings to the class.

Reinforcing Skills

ANALYZING INFORMATION

Read the passage, then answer the questions that follow.

It ought to be the employer's ambition, as leader, to pay better wages than any similar line of business, and it ought to be the workers' ambition to make this possible. Of course, there are workers in all factories who seem to believe that if they do their best, it will be only for the employer's benefit—and not at all for their own. It is a pity that such a feeling should exist. But it does exist and perhaps it has some justification. If an employer encourages workers to do their best, and the workers learn after a while that their best does not bring any reward, then they naturally drop back into "getting by." But if they see the profit of hard work in their pay envelope—proof that harder work means higher pay—they also begin to learn that they are a part of the business, and that its success depends on them and their success depends on it.

—Adapted from *My Life and Work* by Henry Ford and Samuel Crowther, 1922.

1. Is this a primary or secondary source? How can you tell?
2. Who is the author?
3. When was it written?
4. What is the passage about?
5. What emotions does the author express about the situation?
6. What are the key ideas?

Individual Activity

Randomly select 10 Help Wanted ads from your local newspaper and rank the ads in order of salary, putting the lowest-paid jobs first and the highest-paid jobs last. Examine the level of skills, training, and/or education required for each. Then explain how the wages and salaries are related to the level of skills, training, and education.

Cooperative Learning Activity

Organize into four groups, with each group being responsible for one of the following topics: union decline, renegotiated union agreements, the minimum wage, and pay discrepancies between men and women. Each group should prepare a three-minute radio or television newscast on their topic to be delivered to the remainder of the class. Each news report should briefly explain the controversies surrounding the issue and update the class with any current information on the topic. You will need to research the issue, using current magazine and newspaper sources as well as current statistical references.

Writing About Economics

THE PERSUASIVE STYLE

In the **Journal Writing** activity on page 181, you were asked to scan the Help Wanted section of your local newspaper, summarizing job titles and descriptions that you would like to learn more about. With this information, and using the persuasive writing style discussed on page 554, prepare a "Jobs Outlook" brochure to convince a peer that higher-paid jobs go to those with more training and skills.

Workers at the Internal Revenue Service process income tax returns.

CHAPTER 9

Sources of Government Revenue

CHAPTER PREVIEW

People to Know

- Alice Rivlin
- Accountant

Applying Economic Concepts to Your Life

Payroll Withholding Have you ever questioned why your paycheck has so many deductions? If so, you're not alone! The deductions can be confusing—especially with the *payroll withholding* for federal, state, county, city, and Social Security taxes. If 10 to 30 percent of your income is being withheld, you might want to find out more about it.

Journal Writing

For one week, keep a journal of all taxes you hear about on television or read about in the newspaper. Classify your journal entries into three categories: Federal, State, and Local Taxes.

SECTION 1
The Economics of Taxation

Section Preview

Objectives

After studying this section, you will be able to:

1. **Explain** the economic impact of taxes.
2. **List** three criteria for effective taxes.
3. **Understand** the two primary principles of taxation.
4. **Understand** how taxes are classified.

Key Terms

sin tax, tax loophole, benefit principle of taxation, ability-to-pay principle of taxation, proportional tax, average tax rate, progressive tax, marginal tax rate, regressive tax

Applying Economic Concepts

Equity Taxes usually are not a pleasant topic. If you are like most people, however, you are willing to pay your fair share. Fairness, or *equity*, one of the main economic goals discussed in Chapter 2, is important to most Americans—especially when it comes to paying taxes.

An enormous amount of money is required to run the federal, state, and local governments of the United States. In mid-1993, all three levels of government collected approximately $2.0 trillion—or $7,629 for every man, woman, and child in the United States.

To keep up with the tremendous demand for government services, total revenue collections by all levels of government have grown dramatically over the years. **Figure 9.1** shows that total collections, even when adjusted for inflation and population growth, increased nearly five times in 50 years. The figure also shows that the federal government collects the largest portion of revenues, although its share is declining.

The single most important way governments raise revenue is through taxes on income, sales, and property. Governments also collect revenue in the form of college tuitions, Social Security contributions, unemployment insurance contributions, and even driver's license fees. These revenues have an enormous impact on the economy.

Economic Impact of Taxes

Although taxes and other revenue-raising measures are necessary to support the operations of government, they reduce the income of individuals and businesses. Lower income affects the allocation of productive resources, consumer buying and saving habits, and the productivity and growth of the economy.

Resource Allocation

When a tax is placed on a good or service at the factory, the cost of production rises, which shifts the supply curve to the left. The decrease in supply, if demand remains unchanged, raises the price of the product.

People react to the higher price in the manner predicted by the downward-sloping demand curve—they buy less of the product. When sales fall, some manufacturers cut back on production and some workers may lose their jobs. The productive resources—land, capital, labor, and entrepreneurship—are allocated to another industry, or go unused.

Behavior Adjustment

Sometimes taxes are used specifically to change people's behavior. The so-called **sin tax** is a relatively high tax designed to raise revenue as well as reduce consumption of a socially undesirable product, such as liquor or tobacco. Canada used a sin tax in the 1980s when it quadrupled the tobacco tax, pushing the price of a pack of cigarettes to more than $4.00. The government raised considerable revenue from this source during that period. It also reduced per capita cigarette consumption by about one-third.

Figure 9.1
Revenue Collections by All Levels of Government

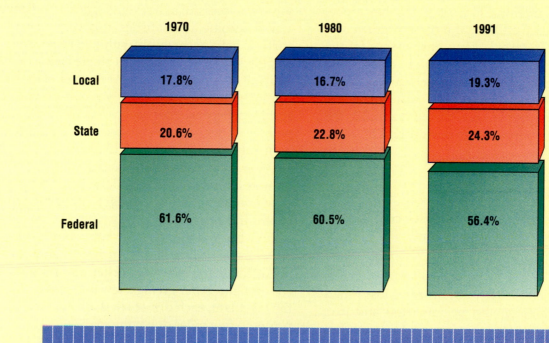

	1970	1980	1991
Local	17.8%	16.7%	19.3%
State	20.6%	22.8%	24.3%
Federal	61.6%	60.5%	56.4%

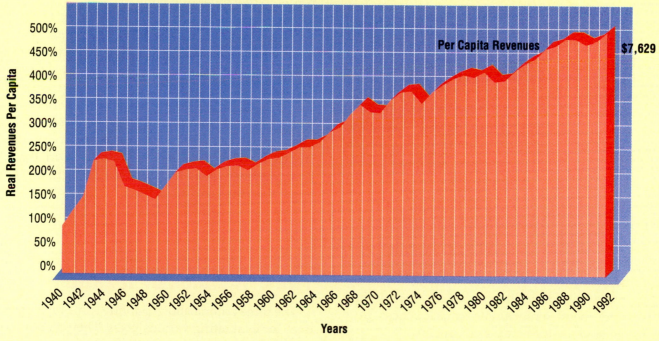

Per Capita Revenues $7,629

Real Revenues Per Capita

Years

Source: *Government Finances* and *The Economic Report of the President*, 1993

The composition of revenues collected by all levels of government is changing. The federal government's share, shown in the top of the figure, has declined while state and local government shares have increased. The lower part of the figure shows revenues for all levels of government after being adjusted for inflation and population growth. **In what forms do governments collect revenue?**

Productivity and Growth

Taxes can also hinder productivity and economic growth. If people think that income taxes are too high, they may lose the incentive to work. Why, they argue, should a person earn additional income if much of it will be paid out in taxes? Many businesses feel the same way. If business taxes get too high, there is less incentive to expand production, which in turn slows economic growth. High taxes may also affect the amount of money people save, further reducing the funds available for businesses to borrow and invest. **1**

Criteria for Taxes

To be effective, taxes must meet three criteria: they must be equitable, simple, and efficient.

Equity

The first criterion is equity or fairness. Most Americans feel that taxes should be impartial and just. Problems arise, however, when we try to define *fair*. Some people feel that a tax is fair only if everyone pays the same amount. Others feel it is fair only if wealthier people pay more than those with lower incomes. Still others feel that the only fair tax is a tax on someone else. ✅

We often hear complaints about **tax loopholes**—exceptions or oversights in the tax law that allow some people and businesses to avoid paying certain taxes. Loopholes are a fairness issue, and most people oppose them on the grounds of equity.

Simplicity

A second criterion is simplicity. Tax laws should be written so that both the taxpayer and the tax collector can understand them. This task is not always easy, but people seem more willing to pay taxes when they understand them. Unfortunate consequences may arise if tax laws are too complex or unclear.

Before 1993, for example, most Americans did not know that they were required to make Social Security payments on behalf of their household and domestic workers if they paid the workers more than $50 during a 3-month period. The failure to file these taxes embarrassed several cabinet-level nominees during the early months of President Clinton's administration.

Efficiency

A third criterion of an effective tax is efficiency. A tax should be relatively easy to administer and reasonably successful as a revenue-generating device.

The income tax satisfies this requirement fairly well. An employer simply withholds a portion of each employee's pay, then sends a single check to the government on a regular basis. At the end of the year, the employer notifies each employee of the amount of tax withheld. Because most payroll records are now computerized, neither the employer nor the employee is unduly burdened by this withholding system.

Other taxes, especially those collected in toll booths on state highways, are considerably less efficient. The state invests millions of dollars in heavily reinforced booths that span the highway. The cost to commuters is the wear and tear on their automobiles—including occasional collisions—as drivers simultaneously brake for the booth and jockey for position in the shortest line. After giving a few quarters and dimes to the attendant, each driver takes off again to repeat the process a few miles down the road.

Efficiency also means that the tax should raise enough revenue to be worthwhile. If it does not, or if it harms the economy in other ways, the tax has little value. One interesting case is the luxury tax Congress placed on small private aircraft in 1991. According to IRS records, only $53,000 in revenues were collected that year from this tax. At the same time, the tax raised the price of the aircraft, causing lower sales and layoffs in the private aircraft industry. In the end, unemployment benefits paid out were many times larger than the taxes brought in.

Two Principles of Taxation

The three criteria above provide some broad guidelines for evaluating various taxes. They do not, however, indicate how to select the persons or groups on whom the taxes will be imposed, or say how much each will pay. Because everyone is a potential taxpayer, "who pays what" is very important.

In general, taxes are based on two principles that have evolved over the years. These principles are the benefit principle and the ability-to-pay principle.

Taxation *The daycare worker in the left photograph and the professional city planner in the right photograph both have to pay taxes.* **According to the ability-to-pay principle, how is the amount each person has to pay determined?**

Benefit Principle

The **benefit principle of taxation** is based on two ideas. First, those who benefit from government services should be the ones to pay for them. Second, people should pay taxes in proportion to the amount of services or benefits they receive. **2**

Gasoline taxes are based on the benefit principle. Motorists who buy gasoline benefit from gas taxes because the taxes are used to build streets and highways. Those who drive more than others—and hence use streets and highways more than others—generally pay more taxes because the tax is included in the price of the gasoline.

The benefit principle has two limitations. The first is that many government services provide the greatest benefit to those who can least afford to pay for them. People who receive welfare payments or live in subsidized housing, for example, usually have the lowest incomes. Even if they could pay something, they would not be able to pay in proportion to the benefits received.

The second limitation is that the benefits often are hard to measure. Are people who pay for gasoline the only ones who benefit from the roads built with gasoline taxes? What about the property owners whose property increases in value because of the improved access? What about the hotel and restaurant owners

QUICK CHECK

Checking Understanding

1. How can taxes hinder productivity and economic growth?
2. What is the benefit principle of taxation?

Applying Economic Concepts

 Taxation A key component of President Clinton's health-care reform proposal of 1993 was a hefty hike in tobacco taxes. The rationale was that tobacco caused so many health problems that users should pay a higher portion of health-care costs.

Figure 9.2
Three Types of Taxes

Type of Tax	Income of $10,000	Income of $100,000	Summary
Proportional	*City Occupational Tax* $97.50, or .975% of income	*City Occupational Tax* $975.00, or .975% of income	As income goes up, the percent of income paid in taxes *stays the same.*
Progressive	*Federal Income Tax* $1,000 paid in taxes, or 10% of total income	*Federal Income Tax* $25,000 paid in taxes, or 25% of total income	As income goes up, the percent of income paid in taxes *goes up.*
Regressive	*State Sales Tax* $5,000 of food and clothing, taxed at 4% for a total tax of $200—or 2% of income	*State Sales Tax* $20,000 of food and clothing, taxed at 4% for a total tax of $800—or .8% of income	As income goes up, the percent of income paid in taxes *goes down.*

Proportional, progressive, and regressive are the three main types of taxes. The key to each is to see what happens to the percent of total income that goes to pay the tax when income goes up. **What impact on the economy do taxes have?**

who profit from tourists arriving by car or bus? These people may buy very little gasoline, but they still benefit from facilities that the gasoline tax helps provide.

Ability-to-Pay Principle

The second approach to taxation is the **ability-to-pay principle of taxation**, which is based on the concept that people should be taxed according to their ability to pay, regardless of the benefits they receive. The ability-to-pay principle is based on two factors. First, it recognizes that societies are not always able to measure the benefits derived from government spending. Second, it assumes that persons with higher incomes suffer less discomfort paying taxes than persons with lower incomes.

For example, a family of four with an annual taxable income of $10,000 needs every cent to pay for necessities. If the tax rate was 14 percent, this family would have to pay $1,400—a huge amount for them. On the other hand, a couple with no children and a taxable income of $80,000 could afford to pay a higher tax rate.

DID YOU KNOW?

Taxes and Revolution The issue of taxes has toppled governments. Rallying under the cry "No taxation without representation!" the American colonists fought for their independence from Great Britain. The lopsided tax structure of French society in the late 1700s—with 97 percent of the population supporting the lavish lifestyles of the aristocracy—was a major cause of the French Revolution.

Types of Taxes

Three general types of taxes exist in the United States today—proportional, progressive, and regressive. Each is classified according to the way in which the tax burden changes as income changes.

Proportional Tax

A **proportional tax** imposes the same percentage rate of taxation on everyone, regardless of income. If the income tax rate was 20 percent of all taxable income, a person with $10,000 in taxable income would pay $2,000 in taxes. A person with $20,000 in taxable income would pay $4,000.

If the percentage tax rate is constant, the **average tax rate**—total taxes paid divided by the total income—is constant, regardless of income. If a person's income goes up, the *percentage* of total income paid in taxes does not change.

Progressive Tax

A **progressive tax** is one that imposes a higher percentage rate of taxation on persons with high incomes than on those with low incomes. Progressive taxes use a **marginal tax rate**, the tax rate that applies to the next dollar of taxable income, that increases as the amount of taxable income increases. Therefore, the *percentage* of income paid in taxes increases as income goes up.

Suppose the tax system requires a person to pay $1,000 on $10,000 of taxable income, $4,000 on $20,000 of taxable income, or $20,000 on $60,000 of taxable income. The tax is progressive over this range because the percent of income paid in taxes—10, 20, and 30 percent respectively—rises as income rises.

Regressive Tax

A **regressive tax** is one that imposes a higher *percentage* rate of taxation on low incomes than on high incomes. For example, a person with an annual income of $10,000 may spend $5,000 on food and clothing, while another person with an annual income of $100,000 may spend $20,000 on the same essentials. If the state sales tax was 4 percent, the person with the lower income would pay a higher percentage of total income in taxes.

SECTION 1 REVIEW

Reviewing Terms and Facts

1. **Define** sin tax, tax loophole, benefit principle of taxation, ability-to-pay principle of taxation, proportional tax, average tax rate, progressive tax, marginal tax rate, regressive tax.
2. **Describe** how taxes affect the allocation of resources and productivity.
3. **List** three criteria used to evaluate taxes.
4. **Summarize** the two main principles of taxation.
5. **Explain** the three types of taxes.

Critical Thinking

6. **Analyzing Information** Think of the last tax that you paid. Using the criteria for progressive, proportional, and regressive taxes, determine which type of tax you think it is and explain why.

Applying Economic Concepts

7. **Equity** Which of the two principles of taxation—the benefit principle or the ability-to-pay principle—do you feel is the most equitable? Explain your answer.

The Federal Tax System

Section Preview

Objectives

After studying this section, you will be able to:

1. **Explain** the progressive nature of the individual income tax.
2. **Explain** the nature of FICA taxes.
3. **Describe** the importance of the corporate tax structure.
4. **Identify** other major sources of federal revenue.

Key Terms

individual income tax, payroll withholding system, Internal Revenue Service, tax return, indexing, FICA, medicare, corporate income tax, excise tax, luxury good, estate tax, gift tax, customs duty, user fee

Applying Economic Concepts

User Fees You dislike paying taxes, and politicians dislike talking about them—so they sometimes call taxes by a different name, *user fees*. When ranchers pay the government to graze their animals on federal land, or you pay a charge to enter a national park, remember that these are user fees. It sounds better that way.

The federal government collects taxes from a number of sources. As shown in **Figure 9.3**, the most important revenue services are individual income taxes, Social Security taxes, and corporate income taxes.

Individual Income Taxes

In 1913 the Sixteenth Amendment to the United States Constitution was ratified. The amendment states that:

The Congress shall have power to lay and collect taxes on incomes, from whatever source derived, without apportionment among the several States, and without regard to any census or enumeration.

Since the amendment was ratified, the federal government has relied heavily on the **individual income tax**—the tax on people's earnings—to finance its operations. In 1992 the federal government collected 43.6 percent of its total revenue from this source.

Payroll Deductions

In most cases, the individual income tax is paid over time through a **payroll withholding system**. Under this procedure, an employer uses federal tax tables to estimate the amount of taxes a worker would pay on a given paycheck, and then sends it directly to the government. The agency that receives the tax payment is the **Internal Revenue Service** (IRS), the branch of the Treasury Department in charge of collecting taxes.

After the close of the tax year on December 31, and before April 15 of the following year, the employee files a **tax return**—an annual report to the IRS summarizing total income, deductions, and the taxes withheld by employers. Any difference between the amount already paid and the amount actually owed, as determined by official tax tables like those shown in **Figure 9.4**, is settled when the return is filed. Most differences are usually caused by deductions and expenses that lower the amount of taxes owed, as well as by additional income received that was not subject to tax withholding. **1**

People who are self-employed do not have money withheld from their paychecks. Instead, they are required to send quarterly estimates of their taxes to the Internal Revenue Service. Self-employed individuals also must make a final settlement for the previous year sometime before April 15.

A Progressive Income Tax

The individual income tax is a progressive tax. According to the 1993 individual tax tables shown in **Figure 9.4**, single individuals paid a flat 15 percent on all income up to $22,100. After that, the marginal tax

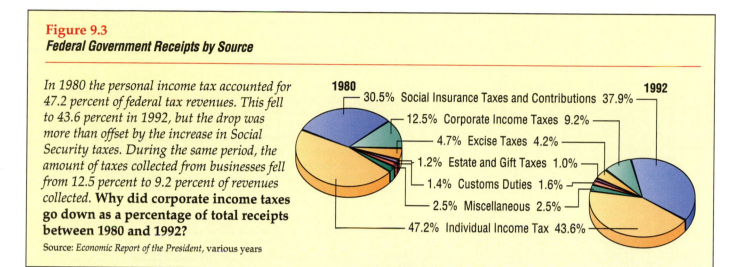

Figure 9.3
Federal Government Receipts by Source

In 1980 the personal income tax accounted for 47.2 percent of federal tax revenues. This fell to 43.6 percent in 1992, but the drop was more than offset by the increase in Social Security taxes. During the same period, the amount of taxes collected from businesses fell from 12.5 percent to 9.2 percent of revenues collected. **Why did corporate income taxes go down as a percentage of total receipts between 1980 and 1992?**

Source: *Economic Report of the President*, various years

1980

1992

30.5% Social Insurance Taxes and Contributions 37.9%
12.5% Corporate Income Taxes 9.2%
4.7% Excise Taxes 4.2%
1.2% Estate and Gift Taxes 1.0%
1.4% Customs Duties 1.6%
2.5% Miscellaneous 2.5%
47.2% Individual Income Tax 43.6%

rate jumps to 28 percent, 31 percent, 36 percent, and 39.6 percent, depending on the amount of taxable income. The tax schedule is similar for married individuals, with rates scaled so that couples earning higher incomes pay a larger percentage of their income in taxes. ☑

When a tax is progressive, the average tax rate—the total tax paid divided by income—goes up when income goes up. Graph **A** of **Figure 9.5** illustrates this point. The single individual with $10,000 of taxable income pays an average of 15 cents for every dollar earned. If the individual has $35,000 of taxable income, the marginal tax rate is higher (at 28 percent), which raises the average tax on every dollar to 19.4 cents. Likewise, the individual with $145,000 of taxable income pays an average of 28.9 cents on every dollar.

Indexing

Suppose a worker receives a small raise, just enough to offset the rate of inflation. Although that

worker is no better off, the raise may still push the worker into a higher tax bracket. Because of this possibility, the individual income tax has a provision for **indexing**—an upward revision of the tax brackets to keep workers from paying higher taxes just because of inflation. 2

A single individual with no dependents may have exactly $22,100 of taxable income in 1993. If the person receives a 5 percent raise the following year to offset inflation, the $1,105 raise would be taxed at the next marginal tax bracket of 28 percent. The result is that the individual gets pushed into a higher tax bracket simply because of inflation. If the bracket is indexed, or adjusted upward by 5 percent, the 28 percent marginal rate for 1994 would not apply until $23,205 is earned.

Indexing first took effect in 1985 and has been very popular with taxpayers, although some government officials argued against it. They opposed indexing because it reduced the amount of tax revenue the federal government could collect—revenue that could

QUICK CHECK

Checking Understanding

1. What is the deadline for filing federal income tax returns?
2. What is the purpose of indexing?

Applying Economic Concepts

 Comparative Economic Systems The United States has one of the lowest top tax rates of industrialized nations. The Netherlands' tax rate is 70 percent compared to France's 57 percent, Germany's 53 percent, Japan's 50 percent, and Sweden's 42 percent.

Figure 9.4
Individual Income Tax Rates for 1993

A. Single Individuals[1]

If taxable income is:	The tax is:
Not over $22,100	15% of taxable income
Over $22,100, but not over $53,500	$3,315, plus 28% of the amount up to $53,500
Over $53,500, but not over $115,000	$12,107, plus 31% of the amount up to $115,000
Over $115,000, but not over $250,000	$31,172, plus 36% of the amount up to $250,000
Over $250,000	$79,772, plus 39.6% of all income over $250,000

B. Married Filing Joint Returns[1]

If taxable income is:	The tax is:
Not over $36,900	15% of taxable income
Over $36,900, but not over $89,150	$5,535, plus 28% of the amount up to $89,150
Over $89,150, but not over $140,000	$20,165, plus 31% of the amount up to $140,000
Over $140,000, but not over $250,000	$35,929, plus 36% of the amount up to $250,000
Over $250,000	$75,529, plus 39.6% of all income over $250,000

[1]Prior to the Omnibus Budget Reconciliation Act of 1993, the highest marginal tax bracket for both single and married filing jointly was 31%.

According to the individual income tax tables above, a single individual with $20,000 of taxable income would pay $20,000 × .15, or $3,000 in taxes. If that same individual made $30,000, taxes would amount to $5,527, or ($7,900 × .28) + $3,315. Since 1985, individual tax brackets have been indexed, or adjusted upward to offset the impact of inflation. As a result, the brackets for 1994 and thereafter will be higher than those shown in this figure. **What type of tax is the individual income tax?**

FICA Taxes

The second most important federal tax is **FICA**. FICA stands for Federal Insurance Contributions Act and is levied on both employers and employees for Social Security and medicare. **Medicare** is a federal health-care program available to all senior citizens, regardless of income. The two components of FICA are taxed differently.

Social Security Taxes

In 1993 the Social Security component of FICA was 6.2 percent of wages and salaries up to $57,600. After that amount, Social Security taxes are not collected, regardless of income. A person whose income is $57,600 pays a Social Security tax of $3,571.20, the same amount a person who earns $1,000,000 pays.

be used to provide additional services or to reduce the deficit.

Because the Social Security tax is capped, it is proportional up to $57,600, and regressive thereafter. For example, a single individual in 1993 with $35,000 of taxable income would pay an average of 6.2 cents of Social Security taxes on every dollar earned. If that same individual made $129,000, the average tax per dollar would drop to 2.8 cents.

Medicare

Until 1993 the medicare component of FICA was set at a flat 1.45 percent of the first $135,000 of wages and salaries, with nothing additional paid thereafter. This cap was removed January 1, 1994, which makes the tax proportional at all levels of income.

When medicare and Social Security are considered together, as in Graph **B** of **Figure 9.5**, we can see the overall regressive nature of the FICA tax. For single individuals in 1993, the tax was level at 7.65 percent up to $57,600, and then declined. A single individual earning $35,000 in 1993 paid an average FICA tax of 7.65 cents per dollar. If that same individual made

$129,000, the average FICA tax paid dropped to 4.25 cents per dollar.

Corporate Income Taxes

The third largest category of taxes the federal government collects is the **corporate income tax**—the tax a corporation pays on its profits. The corporation is taxed separately from individuals because the corporation is recognized as a separate legal entity.

Four marginal tax brackets, which are slightly progressive, are placed on corporations. The first is at 15 percent on all income under $50,000. The second is at 25 percent on income from $50,000 to $75,000. The third tax bracket is at 34 percent on all income between $75,000 and $10 million. All taxable income over $10 million is taxed at 35 percent.

Other Federal Taxes

In addition to income, FICA, and corporate taxes, the federal government receives revenue in the form of excise taxes, estate and gift taxes, and customs duties.

Excise Taxes

An **excise tax** is a tax on the manufacture or sale of certain items, such as gasoline and liquor. Federal excise taxes also are found on telephone services, tires, legal betting, and coal. Because low-income families spend larger portions of their incomes on these goods than do high-income families, excise taxes tend to be regressive.

In 1991 Congress expanded the excise tax to include certain luxury goods. An economic product is called a

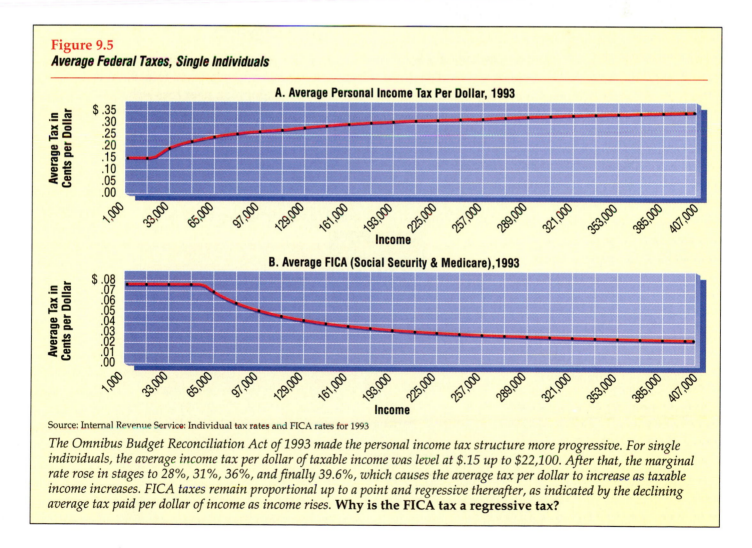

Figure 9.5
Average Federal Taxes, Single Individuals

Source: Internal Revenue Service: Individual tax rates and FICA rates for 1993

The Omnibus Budget Reconciliation Act of 1993 made the personal income tax structure more progressive. For single individuals, the average income tax per dollar of taxable income was level at $.15 up to $22,100. After that, the marginal rate rose in stages to 28%, 31%, 36%, and finally 39.6%, which causes the average tax per dollar to increase as taxable income increases. FICA taxes remain proportional up to a point and regressive thereafter, as indicated by the declining average tax paid per dollar of income as income rises. **Why is the FICA tax a regressive tax?**

Customs Duties *Government officials inspect goods entering the United States.* **What is a customs duty?**

Estate and Gift Taxes

The **estate tax** is the tax the government levies on the transfer of property when a person dies. Estate taxes can range from 18 to 55 percent of the value of the estate. Estates worth less than $600,000 are exempt.

The **gift tax** is a tax on donations of money or wealth and is paid by the person who makes the gift. The gift tax is used to make sure that wealthy people do not try to avoid taxes by giving away their estates before their deaths.

Customs Duties

A **customs duty** is a charge levied on goods brought in from other countries. Many types of goods are covered, ranging from automobiles to silver ore. The duties are relatively low, and they produce little federal revenue.

Miscellaneous Fees

About 2.5 percent of federal revenue is collected through various miscellaneous fees. Because taxes are generally so unpopular, **user fees**—charges levied for the use of a good or service—have been suggested with increasing frequency. President Ronald Reagan was one of the first Presidents to aggressively push for user fees instead of taxes. He proposed many user fees in his 1987 budget, including those paid by visitors to national parks as a means of providing additional funds for upkeep and maintenance.

luxury good (or service) if the demand for the good rises faster than income when income grows. The luxury tax amounted to 10 percent of the price of a passenger vehicle in excess of $30,000. Thus, a car costing $40,000 would be subject to a luxury tax of $1,000, or ($40,000–$30,000) × 10 percent. Originally, the 10 percent also applied to boats, aircraft, jewelry, and furs, but these categories were dropped by an act of Congress in 1993. The act retained the luxury tax on cars, but indexed it annually to keep pace with inflation.

SECTION 2
REVIEW

Reviewing Terms and Facts

1. **Define** individual income tax, payroll withholding system, Internal Revenue Service, tax return, indexing, FICA, medicare, corporate income tax, excise tax, luxury good, estate tax, gift tax, customs duty, user fee.
2. **Describe** the three largest components of federal revenues.
3. **Identify** the main marginal tax brackets in the corporate income tax structure.
4. **Describe** four other sources of government revenue.

Critical Thinking

5. **Demonstrating Reasoned Judgment** Defend or support the regressive nature of the current FICA tax.

Applying Economic Concepts

6. **User Fees** User fees have been compared to taxes based on the benefit principle of taxation. What are the pros and cons of having user fees as a way to charge admission to national parks?

PROFILES IN ECONOMICS

Alice Rivlin, Deputy Budget Director at the Office of Management and Budget (OMB), is one of the most highly respected economists serving in government today. A former director of the Congressional Budget Office (CBO), she is a seasoned pro with a wealth of experience in the area of public finance at the uppermost levels of government.

EDUCATION Dr. Rivlin received her Bachelor's degree from Bryn Mawr College in 1952 and her Ph.D. from Radcliffe College in 1958. She joined the prestigious Brookings Institution in 1957, but left to become of the Brookings Institution during this time. In 1992 Rivlin took a professorship at George Mason University.

She has written extensively and is known for straightforward and searing views put forth in her many writings. Her most important books include *The Role of the Federal Government in Financing Higher Education* (1961), *Systematic Thinking for Social Action* (1971), *Economic Choices* (1987), *Caring for the Disabled Elderly: Who Will Pay?* (1988), and *Reviving the American Dream* (1992).

Rivlin notes that the skills needed to succeed in college are the same skills that make workers more productive in the workplace.

Director of the Congressional Budget Office between 1975 and 1983. She also served as a director

BELIEFS Not afraid to be different, Rivlin often questions the status quo in provocative ways. She objects, for example, to the belief that education alone is the reason that some workers, on average, earn more than others. In a paper published in the *American Economic Review*, she argued that:

> . . . the only reason that education is correlated with income is that the combination of ability, motivation, and personal habits that it takes to succeed in education happens to be the same combination that it takes to be a productive worker.
>
> —"Income Distribution— Can Economists Help?" May, 1975

Dr. Rivlin's academic career at George Mason University was cut short when President Bill Clinton tapped her for the job at OMB in early 1993. His selection was widely applauded by economists and politicians of all persuasions. Rivlin is a blunt and outspoken opponent of budget deficits and argues that spending cannot be brought under control until Congress is willing to reform the pension system, subsidies, and other types of transfer payments.

Examining the Profile

1. **Analyzing Information** What relationship does Rivlin see between education and income?

2. **For Further Research** Research the work that Rivlin did for President Clinton in the mid-1990s.

State and Local Tax Systems

Section Preview

Objectives

After studying this section, you will be able to:

1. **Explain** how state governments collect taxes and other revenues.
2. **Differentiate** between state and local revenue systems.
3. **Interpret** paycheck deductions.

Key Terms

intergovernmental revenue, sales tax, property tax, real property, tangible personal property, intangible personal property, tax assessor, payroll withholding statement

Applying Economic Concepts

Sales Tax When you purchase an item in most states, you will pay an additional 3 to 6 cents in the form of a *sales tax*. The state sales tax is the tax paid most often, and it is the largest source of revenue for state governments.

State and local governments, like the federal government, raise revenue in many ways. They receive funds from sales taxes, utility revenues, college and university tuitions, license taxes, property taxes, insurance taxes, and taxes on tickets to theaters, sporting events, and other activities. They also receive **intergovernmental revenues**—funds collected by one level of government that are distributed to another level of government for expenditures.

State and local governments also use many of the same devices as the federal government to raise revenue. Most state and local governments impose income taxes, estate taxes, and gift taxes. Most impose taxes similar to the excise taxes on gasoline and cigarettes. As shown in **Figure 9.1**, state and local governments accounted for 43.6 percent of all government revenues.

State Government Revenue Sources

State governments collect their revenues from several sources. **Figure 9.6** shows the relative proportions of each source, the largest of which are examined below.

Sales Taxes

A **sales tax** is a general tax levied on consumer purchases of nearly all products. It is added to the final price the consumer pays, and merchants collect the tax at the time of sale. The taxes are then turned over to the proper state government agency on a weekly or monthly basis. Most states allow merchants to keep a small portion of what they collect to compensate for their time and bookkeeping costs.

The sales tax is the largest source of revenue for states, accounting for approximately 23 percent of total revenues collected. Only five states—Alaska, Delaware, Montana, New Hampshire, and Oregon—do not have a general sales tax. Sales tax rates vary widely for each of the other states, as **Figure 9.7** shows.

The sales tax is a very effective way for states and cities to raise revenue. The tax is difficult to avoid and, because it affects large numbers of consumers, it raises huge sums of money. The sales tax also is relatively easy to administer because the merchant collects it at the point of sale.

A sales tax, however, is a regressive tax because the percentage of income paid in sales tax goes down as income goes up. To counter this regressive feature, many states do not tax such necessities as food and drugs.

Intergovernmental Revenues

The funds that states receive from the federal government are the second largest source of state government revenues. These funds help finance state expenditures on welfare, education, highways, health, and hospitals.

Individual Income Taxes

On average, the third largest source of state revenues is the individual income tax. Overall, individual income tax revenues are about five times as large as the income tax collected from corporations.

Employee Retirement Contributions

Many states levy taxes, fees, or other assessments on their employees to cover the cost of state retirement funds and pension plans. According to **Figure 9.6**, employee retirement contributions by these workers were the fourth largest source of state revenue.

Other Revenues

The remaining revenues that state governments collect are interest earnings on surplus funds; tuition and other fees collected from state-owned colleges, universities, and technical schools; corporate income taxes; and hospital fees.

Local Government Revenue Sources

The major sources of local government revenue are also shown in **Figure 9.6**. The main categories are discussed below.

Intergovernmental Revenues

Local governments receive the majority of their revenues in the form of intergovernmental transfers from state governments. These funds are generally

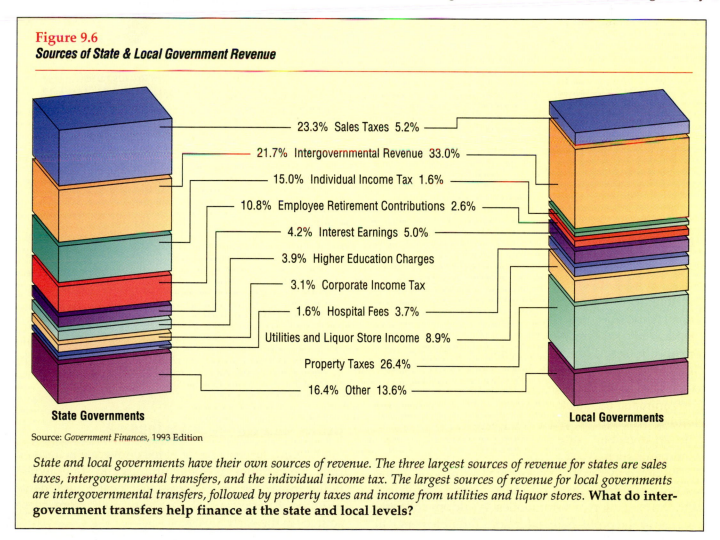

Figure 9.6
Sources of State & Local Government Revenue

23.3% Sales Taxes 5.2%
21.7% Intergovernmental Revenue 33.0%
15.0% Individual Income Tax 1.6%
10.8% Employee Retirement Contributions 2.6%
4.2% Interest Earnings 5.0%
3.9% Higher Education Charges
3.1% Corporate Income Tax
1.6% Hospital Fees 3.7%
Utilities and Liquor Store Income 8.9%
Property Taxes 26.4%
16.4% Other 13.6%

State Governments

Local Governments

Source: *Government Finances*, 1993 Edition

State and local governments have their own sources of revenue. The three largest sources of revenue for states are sales taxes, intergovernmental transfers, and the individual income tax. The largest sources of revenue for local governments are intergovernmental transfers, followed by property taxes and income from utilities and liquor stores. **What do intergovernment transfers help finance at the state and local levels?**

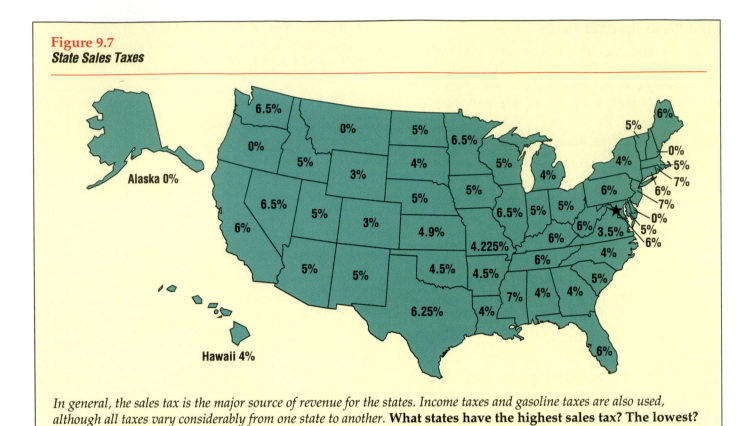

Figure 9.7
State Sales Taxes

In general, the sales tax is the major source of revenue for the states. Income taxes and gasoline taxes are also used, although all taxes vary considerably from one state to another. **What states have the highest sales tax? The lowest?**

intended for education and public welfare. A much smaller amount comes directly from the federal government, mostly for urban renewal. **1**

Property Taxes

The second largest source of revenue for local governments is the **property tax**—a tax on real property and tangible and intangible personal property. **Real property** includes real estate, buildings, and anything permanently attached, such as elevators and central air conditioners. **Tangible personal property** includes all tangible items of wealth not permanently attached to land or buildings, such as furniture, automobiles, farm animals, the stock of goods in retail stores, and clothing. **Intangible personal property** is property with an invisible value and is represented by paper documents such as a stock, bond, patent, or check.

The property tax that raises the most revenue is the tax on real estate. Taxes on other personal property, with the exception of automobiles, is seldom collected because of the problem of valuation. Tangible personal

property, for example, is not always brought to the attention of the **tax assessor**—the person who places value on property for tax purposes. As a result, many items that could be taxed never are.

In addition, some property would be difficult or expensive to evaluate fairly. How would tax assessors know the reasonable value of everyone's wedding silver, furniture, baseball card collections, computers, clothing, and other tangible property items? How many thousands of assessors would be needed to assess all these items in the first place? Therefore, those communities that do tax tangible and intangible property use very low rates and receive very little in revenues for their efforts. ✓

Utility and Liquor Store Income

The third largest source of local revenue is derived from the earnings of public utilities and state-owned liquor stores. **Figure 9.6** shows that local governments acquired 8.9 percent of their revenues from these sources in the early 1990s.

Figure 9.8
Biweekly Paycheck and Withholding Statement

The withholding statement attached to your paycheck summarizes many of the federal, state, and local taxes. Federal and state income tax withholdings are almost always shown, as is the FICA (Social Security and medicare) tax. Others withheld may include city income taxes and a number of voluntary deductions, such as health insurance payments and savings plans. **What percentage of this man's pay has been deducted from his paycheck?**

SMITH, SMITH, AND SMITH
ATTORNEYS AT LAW

$\frac{21-2}{000}$ Number 2,195,903

Date JUNE 25 19 93

Pay to the Order of: SAM YAMAGUCHI $ 584.59

Five Hundred Eighty-Four Dollars and 59/100 Dollars

THE CENTRAL BANK

Memo _____

NON NEGOTIABLE

⑆0314 ⑈0665⑆ 1 4785927

Treasurer

**PLEASE DETACH AND RETAIN THIS PORTION
AS YOUR RECORD OF EARNINGS AND DEDUCTIONS**

DATE	PAY END	VO.NO.	EMP. NO.	HRS.	MISC.	CR.UN.	INS.	GROSS
6/07/93	6/21/93		1376	80	3.20			800 | 00

107 | 00	40 | 01	4 | 00	61 | 20					584 | 59
FEDERAL	STATE	CITY	FICA	RET.	BONDS	OTHER		NET

Sales Taxes

Many towns and cities have their own sales taxes. Merchants collect these taxes right along with the state sales tax, at the point of sale. According to **Figure 9.6**, sales taxes were the fourth most important source of local government revenues. **2**

Other Sources

Local governments also collect a portion of funds in the form of hospital fees and personal income taxes. In general, the revenue sources available to local governments are much more limited than those available to the state and federal levels of government.

Examining Your Paycheck

Many of the taxes you pay to federal, state, and local governments are deducted directly from your paycheck. By examining the sample paycheck and **payroll withholding statement** in **Figure 9.8**, we can identify many of the revenue sources discussed in this chapter.

The worker to whom the check belongs makes $10 an hour and receives a check every two weeks. If the

QUICK CHECK

Checking Understanding

1. What is intergovernmental revenue?
2. How are state and local sales taxes collected?

Applying Economic Concepts

 Taxation Property taxes became extremely unpopular as real estate values rose in the 1970s and taxes skyrocketed. Taxpayers in several states, such as Massachusetts and California, voted to limit the amounts that could be levied.

length of the workweek is 40 hours, the worker's gross pay amounts to $800. The worker is single, has no deductions, and lives and works in Kentucky.

According to withholding tables the federal government supplied for 1993, biweekly workers making at least $800, but less than $820, have $107 withheld from their paychecks. Similar tables the state of Kentucky prepared specify that $40.01 is withheld for state income taxes. Because these are both estimates, and because even minor differences between the amounts withheld and the amount actually owed at the end of the year can grow, the worker will file state and federal tax returns between January 1 and April 15 of 1994 to settle the differences.

A half-percent city income tax amounts to $4 and is also deducted from the paycheck. Because the amount is relatively small, cities seldom require workers to file separate year-end tax forms such as those filed for federal and state income taxes.

The federal FICA tax amounts to 7.65 percent (6.20 percent for Social Security and 1.45 percent for medicare) of $800, or $61.20. The FICA is deducted from the gross pay, along with $3.20 in miscellaneous deductions, which leaves the worker with a net pay of $584.59.

If the worker has insurance payments or retirement contributions, purchases savings bonds, or puts money into a credit union, even more deductions will appear on the paycheck although they are not taxes. About the only major taxes that do not appear on the

Property Tax *This historical area of Boston, Massachusetts, has high property taxes.* **How do tangible and intangible personal property differ?**

paycheck are state sales taxes, local property taxes, and federal excise taxes—which are already built into the price of the products by the time they are bought.

SECTION 3 REVIEW

Reviewing Terms and Facts

1. **Define** intergovernmental revenue, sales tax, property tax, real property, tangible personal property, intangible personal property, tax assessor, payroll withholding statement.
2. **Explain** the four major sources of state tax revenues.
3. **Describe** the three major sources of local government revenues.
4. **List** the major types of state, local, and federal taxes reflected on a payroll withholding statement.

Critical Thinking

5. **Analyzing Information** State and local governments receive revenue from various sources. Which source do you think best satisfies the tax criteria listed in the chapter? Defend your answer.

Applying Economic Concepts

6. **Sales Taxes** Why do you think sales taxes are applied to food and beverages purchased at restaurants but not to food and beverages bought at grocery stores?

Distinguishing Fact From Opinion

Imagine that it is a presidential election year and your economics teacher has asked you to watch a televised debate between the two principal candidates. After watching the debate, you are asked to decide for whom to vote and to give a list of reasons for your decision. To decide, you must be able to distinguish between the facts and the opinions the candidates used during the debate.

Explanation

A fact is a statement or piece of information that can be proved or verified by evidence. An opinion presents a personal viewpoint that cannot be proved true or false. If you can distinguish fact from opinion, you will be better able to make judgments based on a combination of factual information and your own personal values and beliefs.

Use the following steps to help distinguish between fact and opinion in written material and visual media presentations.

- Look for words and phrases that indicate opinion, such as *I think, I believe, probably, seems to me, may, might, could, ought, in my judgment,* or *in my view.*
- Examine the material for expressions of approval and disapproval, such as *good, bad, poor,* and *satisfactory.*
- Be aware of such superlatives as *greatest, worst, finest,* and *best.*
- Look for words that have negative meanings, such as *squander, contemptible,* and *disgrace.*
- Note the use of generalizations that include words such as *none, every,* and *always.*
- Identify facts by looking for statements that can be checked for accuracy, such as names, dates, numbers, and specific actions. Facts often answer the *who, what, when,* and *where* questions.
- Determine whether the information is fact or opinion.

Practice

Use the steps to identify the following statements as either facts or opinions. Give reasons for your choices.

1. Taxes, especially federal taxes, waste consumers' incomes.
2. Taxes, including both taxes on income and sales taxes, reduce consumers' incomes.
3. The individual income tax went into effect in 1913 after Congress proposed and the states ratified the Sixteenth Amendment.
4. All major corporations use loopholes to avoid paying taxes.
5. All levels of government—federal, state, and local—collected about $2.1 trillion in taxes in the early 1990s.
6. The federal government squanders most of the tax money it collects.
7. Taxes should be equitable, simple, and efficient for all taxpayers.
8. The benefit principle of taxation is more fair than the ability-to-pay principle.
9. Lower-income families find it more difficult to pay for the benefits they receive directly from the government.
10. The Omnibus Budget Reconciliation Act of 1993 shifted some of the tax burden to the wealthy to help reduce the deficit.

Additional Practice

For further practice in distinguishing fact from opinion, complete the Reinforcing Skills exercise in the Chapter 9 Review on page 235.

Current Tax Issues

Section Preview

Objectives

After studying this section, you will be able to:

1. **Explain** what is meant by the incidence of a tax.

2. **Debate** the advantages and disadvantages of the value added tax.

3. **Describe** the major tax reforms since 1980.

Key Terms

incidence of a tax, value added tax (VAT), accelerated depreciation, investment tax credit, surcharge, alternative minimum tax

Applying Economic Concepts

Value Added Tax Have you ever not purchased an item because you lacked the extra cash to pay the sales tax? A sales tax is highly visible, in some places adding 7 percent or more to the cost of the product. You are less likely to react directly to a *value added tax*, however, because you may not even know it is there.

Most people feel that they already pay enough taxes. Federal, state, and local governments, however, never seem to have enough revenue to satisfy everyone's needs. For these and other reasons, three tax issues usually are of interest: the incidence of a tax, the value added tax, and tax reform.

Incidence of a Tax

Suppose a city wants to tax a local utility company to raise revenue. Who actually bears the burden of the tax? If the utility is able to raise its rates, consumers will likely bear most of the burden in the form of higher utility bills. If the company's rates are regulated, and if the company's profits are not large enough to absorb the tax increase, shareholders may receive smaller dividends—placing the burden of the tax on the owners. Another alternative is that the company may postpone a pay raise—shifting the burden of the tax to its employees.

This example illustrates the **incidence of a tax**—or the final burden of the tax. This issue is important because the incidence of a tax often can be shifted from one group to another. Although the incidence is usually different in each case, some outcomes can be predicted with the help of supply and demand analysis.

In general, the more elastic the demand for the product, the less likely the burden of the tax can be

shifted from the producer to the consumer. This example is illustrated with the supply and demand curves in **Figure 9.9**. Before the tax is passed, each market is in equilibrium with five units being sold at $4 each. If the government passes a tax of $1, the cost of production rises, causing producers to supply less output at each and every price. This causes the supply curve to shift from SS to S_1S_1. After the supply curve has shifted, the market must find a new equilibrium price and quantity.

Because consumers purchase fewer goods and services at higher prices, less should be demanded. Just how much less depends on the elasticity of demand for the product. If the demand is very inelastic, as in Graph **A**, the producer will be able to shift most of the tax, or about 90 cents, to the consumer. If the demand is very elastic, as in Graph **B**, the producer will be able to shift only some of the tax, or 50 cents, to the consumer. In both cases, the producer will have to absorb the rest of the tax.

The demand for products such as alcohol, tobacco, medicine, and low-cost housing tends to be inelastic. Because of this inelastic demand, much of the tax placed on the producer, seller, or supplier can be shifted directly to the consumer. If consumer demand is elastic, as in the case of new automobiles, luxurious yachts, upscale homes, and other items that consume a large portion of income, less of the tax is shifted to the consumer. In this case, more of the tax is absorbed by the producer.

The Value Added Tax

One of the more controversial taxes is the **value added tax** (VAT), a tax placed on the value that manufacturers add at each stage of production. It is similar to a national sales tax, and it has the potential to raise enormous amounts of revenues for the federal government. As such, it is a tax on consumption instead of income.

The Concept of Value Added

The production of almost any good or service involves numerous steps. Consider a hypothetical example concerning wooden baseball bats. First, loggers cut the trees and sell the timber to lumber mills. Second, the mills process the logs into smaller units for sale to bat manufacturers. The manufacturers then shape the wood into baseball bats.

After the bats are painted or varnished, they are sold to a wholesaler. The wholesaler sells them to retailers, and retailers sell them to consumers. The whole process is illustrated in **Figure 9.10**. The first column of numbers shows the value added at each stage of production. Without the VAT, the consumer ends up paying $10 for each bat.

Adding the VAT

If a 10 percent VAT is added at each stage of production, the cumulative value of the bat is 10 percent higher, and the consumer pays $11 instead of $10.

The VAT is very similar to a national sales tax, except that the 10 percent is levied on producers at every step of the production process, rather than simply added at the end. The size of the tax at each stage of production is small, hardly noticeable in some instances, but it still increases the price of the product by 10 percent.

Advantages of a VAT

As a way of raising revenue, the VAT has several advantages. First, it is hard to avoid because the tax collector simply levies it on the total amount of sales less the cost of inputs.

Second, the incidence of the tax is widely spread, which makes it harder for a single firm to shift the burden of the tax to one group or another. Third, the tax is not visible to the final consumer because it has been built into the price before the purchase is made. Because the consumer does not know the actual amount of tax paid, he or she is less likely to become angry about it. Fourth, the VAT is easy to collect because businesses would simply make their VAT payments to the government along with their regular tax payments. Finally, even a relatively small VAT can raise a tremendous amount of revenue, especially when it is applied to a broad range of products.

Disadvantages of a VAT

The main disadvantage of the VAT is that it tends to be invisible to consumers. In the example of the

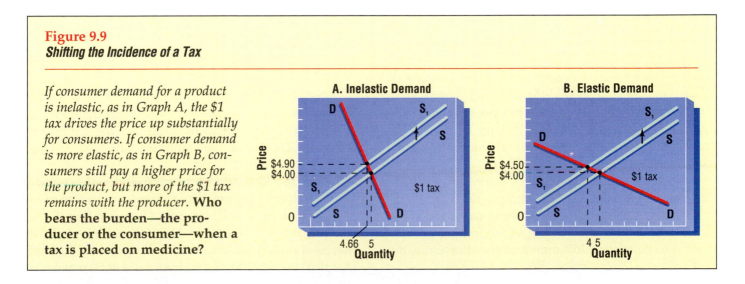

Figure 9.9
Shifting the Incidence of a Tax

If consumer demand for a product is inelastic, as in Graph A, the $1 tax drives the price up substantially for consumers. If consumer demand is more elastic, as in Graph B, consumers still pay a higher price for the product, but more of the $1 tax remains with the producer. **Who bears the burden—the producer or the consumer—when a tax is placed on medicine?**

A. Inelastic Demand

B. Elastic Demand

Figure 9.10
The Value Added Tax

		No Taxes		With a 10% Value Added Tax	
		Value Added	Cumulative Value	Value Added with a 10% VAT	Cumulative Value with VAT
Step 1	Loggers fell trees and sell the timber to the mills for processing.	$1	$1	$1 + .10 = $1.10	$1.10
Step 2	The mills cut the timber into blanks that will be used to make bats.	$1	$2	$1 + .10 = $1.10	$2.20
Step 3	Bat manufacturers shape, paint, or varnish the bats and sell them to wholesalers.	$5	$7	$5 + .50 = $5.50	$7.70
Step 4	The wholesalers sell the bats to retail outlets where consumers can buy them.	$1	$8	$1 + .10 = $1.10	$8.80
Step 5	The retailers put the bats on the shelves and wait for the consumers.	$2	$10	$2 + .20 = $2.20	$11.00
Step 6	**The consumer buys the bat for:**		**$10.00**		**$11.00**

The VAT tax is like a national sales tax added to each stage of production. As a result, it is built into the final price of a product and is less visible to consumers. It is widely used in Europe and is popular because even very low rates can raise very large amounts of revenue. **What are the advantages of a VAT?**

baseball bat, consumers may be vaguely aware that bat prices went from $10 to $11, but they might attribute this to a shortage of good wood, higher wages because of new union contracts, or some other increased cost of production. In short, consumers cannot be as vigilant about higher taxes when they cannot see them.

Another difficulty with the VAT is that it would compete with state sales taxes. Because the VAT is a federal tax, adding a VAT is like adding a federal sales tax to already-existing state taxes. If some of these bats were sold in Florida, would that state want to forgo its sales tax simply because a federal VAT was in place? Or would it want to impose its own state sales tax of 6 percent, raising the $11 price to $11.66?

The United States currently does not have a VAT, although it is widely used in Europe. Even so, a VAT will always be tempting because it can raise enormous sums of money. As long as the federal government is looking for additional sources of revenue, the VAT will be a likely choice. ✅

Tax Reform in the 1980s and 1990s

Tax reform has received much attention in recent years. The desire to lessen the tax burden on both individuals and businesses drove tax reforms in 1981 and 1986. In 1993 the need for additional government revenue drove tax reform.

Tax Reform in 1981

When President Reagan was elected in 1980, he believed that high taxes were the main deterrent to growth and prosperity. Accordingly, the Economic Recovery Tax Act of 1981 substantially reduced personal and business taxes. **1**

Before the Recovery Act, the individual tax code had 16 marginal tax brackets ranging from a low of 14 percent to a high of 70 percent. Compare this to the five brackets in **Figure 9.4**. The 1981 act lowered the marginal rates in all brackets, and capped the highest marginal tax wealthy individuals paid at 50 percent.

Businesses also got relief. One section of the act provided for **accelerated depreciation**, which allows companies to speed up the depreciation of their plants and equipment by taking larger depreciation charges right away. Because these charges are treated like a cost that is deducted from a firm's income before taxes are paid, accelerated depreciation saved corporations billions of dollars in taxes.

Another section of the act introduced the **investment tax credit** (ITC), which allowed a company to purchase tools and equipment and then receive a tax credit based on the amount spent. A company might purchase a $50,000 machine that qualified for a 10 percent, or $5,000, ITC credit. If the firm owed $12,000 in taxes, the credit reduced this amount to $7,000. ITCs were very popular because they gave businesses a way to directly reduce their tax bills.

Tax Reform in 1986

By the mid-1980s, people started feeling that the tax code favored the rich and powerful. In 1983 more than 3,000 millionaires paid no income taxes. In addition, tens of thousands of others had substantial incomes yet were not required to pay taxes.

Not only the wealthy legally avoided paying taxes. Many corporations did the same. Boeing, ITT, General Dynamics, Transamerica, First Executive Corporation, and Greyhound were profitable from 1981 to 1984. Instead of paying corporate income taxes, however, these companies applied tax losses in earlier years to current profits—and then collected tax refunds during each of those four years.

By the mid-1980s, most businesses were paying fewer taxes than in the past. In 1970, taxes on corporate business profits amounted to 16.9 percent of total federal revenues. By 1980, this figure had dropped to 12.5 percent and then to 8.4 percent in 1985.

In 1986 Congress passed the most sweeping tax reform act since income taxes were enacted in 1913. First, it ended the traditionally progressive individual income tax structure by reducing the 16 marginal tax brackets to two brackets (essentially the 15 percent and 28 percent brackets in **Figure 9.4**). The law also added a 5 percent **surcharge**—or additional tax above and beyond the base rate. Later, the surcharge was changed so that it became a third marginal bracket at 31 percent.

The law also made it difficult for the very rich to avoid taxes altogether. The **alternative minimum tax**, the personal income rate that applies whenever the amount of taxes paid falls below some designated level, was strengthened. Under this provision, people had to pay a minimum tax of 20 percent, regardless of other circumstances or loopholes in the tax code.

Finally, the reform act shifted about $120 billion of taxes from individuals to corporations over a 5-year period by removing a number of tax breaks for business. These included the removal of the ITC and a revision of the accelerated depreciation schedules.

Tax Reform in 1993

As the United States entered the 1990s, the impact of 10 years of tax cuts was beginning to show. Government spending was growing faster than revenues, and the government had to make up the difference by borrowing.

The Omnibus Budget Reconciliation Act of 1993 was driven more by the need for the government to balance its budget than to overhaul the tax brackets. It combined future spending cuts with tax hikes and affected government revenue in several ways. 2

The law added the two top marginal tax brackets of 36 and 39.6 percent shown in **Figure 9.4**. These two brackets affect the richest 1.2 percent of taxpayers. The law also removed the $135,000 cap on medicare

Checking Understanding

1. Why were taxes lowered in 1981?
2. Why did government leaders think more taxes were needed in 1993?

Applying Economic Concepts

 Taxation Many economists who favor a VAT point out that it taxes consumption rather than income. They believe the VAT would encourage Americans to save—and thus avoid the tax. More saving would free money for capital investment.

Taxation *Some people think any tax is too high, but this viewpoint is not very realistic.* **Who was affected most by tax reform in 1993?**

taxes. Before the act was passed, those individuals with more than $135,000 paid no additional medicare taxes, making it very regressive. The medicare tax is now proportional.

The alternative minimum tax, which targets the wealthiest 250,000 taxpayers, was also strengthened, making tax avoidance even more difficult for the very wealthy. Another provision prevented single individuals with taxable incomes in excess of $100,000, and couples with incomes in excess of $160,000, from claiming some deductions that would lower their taxes. Together, these two changes were expected to generate more than $110 billion in additional revenue over a 5-year period.

Some additional taxes were levied on the wealthiest 13 percent of Americans who receive Social Security payments. Estate taxes were increased on properties valued at more than $2.5 million, and the top marginal corporate tax bracket was raised from 34 to 35 percent.

Finally, the federal excise tax on gasoline was raised by 4.3 cents per gallon to its current level of 18.4 cents.

The act also included some tax cuts. Credits worth approximately $21 billion were given to lower-income working families with children, and about $4.6 billion in credits for low-income housing were granted. Businesses even received some tax cuts to offset the higher corporate tax rates, and approximately $5 billion of credits for research and experimentation were approved. Luxury taxes on yachts, planes, furs, and jewels were repealed.

The tax provisions of the Omnibus Budget Reconciliation Act were loosely modeled on the ability-to-pay principle of taxation. The bill shifted some of the tax burden to the wealthy. Except for the increase in the gasoline tax and the way some Social Security receipts were taxed, the law had almost no direct impact on single individuals earning less than $115,000 or couples earning less than $140,000.

SECTION 4 REVIEW

Reviewing Terms and Facts

1. **Define** incidence of a tax, value added tax, accelerated depreciation, investment tax credit, surcharge, alternative minimum tax.
2. **Provide** an example of how the incidence of a tax can be shifted.
3. **Explain** the main difference between the VAT and a national sales tax.

4. **Describe** the three major tax reform bills since 1980.

Critical Thinking

5. **Identifying Alternatives** Explain how you would recommend changes in the federal tax code if it were to be revised again in the near future.

Applying Economic Concepts

6. **Value Added Tax** Most people do not object to excise taxes—but mostly because they know little about them. How does this assertion apply to characteristics of the VAT?

Vocabulary

The following terms are defined in Chapter 9:

SECTION ONE
- sin tax (p. 210)
- tax loophole (p. 212)
- benefit principle of taxation (p. 213)
- ability-to-pay principle of taxation (p. 214)
- proportional tax (p. 215)
- average tax rate (p. 215)
- progressive tax (p. 215)
- marginal tax rate (p. 215)
- regressive tax (p. 215)

SECTION TWO
- individual income tax (p. 216)
- payroll withholding system (p. 216)
- Internal Revenue Service (IRS) (p. 216)
- tax return (p. 216)
- indexing (p. 217)
- FICA (p. 218)
- medicare (p. 218)
- corporate income tax (p. 219)
- excise tax (p. 219)
- luxury good (p. 220)
- estate tax (p. 220)
- gift tax (p. 220)
- customs duty (p. 220)
- user fee (p. 220)

SECTION THREE
- intergovernmental revenue (p. 222)
- sales tax (p. 222)
- property tax (p. 224)
- real property (p. 224)
- tangible personal property (p. 224)
- intangible personal property (p. 224)
- tax assessor (p. 224)
- payroll withholding statement (p. 225)

SECTION FOUR
- incidence of a tax (p. 228)
- value added tax (p. 229)
- accelerated depreciation (p. 231)
- investment tax credit (p. 231)
- surcharge (p. 231)
- alternative minimum tax (p. 231)

Section 1
The Economics of Taxation (pages 210–215)

Governments raise billions of dollars through taxes, license fees, tuition fees, and customs duties. Economists use three criteria—equity, simplicity, and efficiency—to judge the effectiveness of a tax. The **benefit principle** and the **ability-to-pay principle** help decide the group or groups that should bear the burden of the tax. Taxes can be placed into three groups—**proportional**, **progressive**, and **regressive**.

Reviewing the Main Idea
What are the three criteria for taxes and the two principles of taxation?

Section 2
The Federal Tax System (pages 216–220)

The main source of revenue for the federal government is the **individual income tax**, a progressive tax administered through a **payroll withholding system**. The second largest component of federal revenues is the **FICA** tax, collected to cover Social Security and **medicare**. The **corporate income tax** is the third largest source of federal revenue.

Reviewing the Main Idea
What are the main sources of revenue for the federal government?

Section 3
State and Local Tax Systems (pages 222–226)

State governments receive most of their revenues in the form of **sales taxes**, **intergovernmental revenues**, individual income taxes, and employee retirement contributions. Local governments receive revenues from **property taxes**, utilities, liquor stores, sales taxes, and the state and federal governments.

Reviewing the Main Idea
What are the main sources of revenue for both state and local governments?

Section 4
Current Tax Issues (pages 228–232)

Three major tax revision laws have gone into effect since 1980. The Economic Recovery Tax Act of 1981 provided for a substantial reduction in individual and corporate tax rates. The 1986 tax reform law closed some loopholes opened in 1981 and made the individual tax code more proportional. The Omnibus Budget Reconciliation Act of 1993 added marginal tax brackets to the individual tax code, thereby restoring the progressive nature of the tax.

Reviewing the Main Idea
How has tax reform been addressed since 1980?

Reviewing Key Terms

Write the letter of the key term that best matches each definition below.

a. ability-to-pay principle	**g.** individual income tax
b. corporate income tax	**h.** progressive tax
c. estate tax	**i.** proportional tax
d. excise tax	**j.** regressive tax
e. FICA	**k.** sales tax
f. indexing	**l.** sin tax
	m. VAT

1. annual adjustment of tax brackets to keep pace with inflation
2. average tax per dollar decreases as taxable income increases
3. average tax per dollar increases as taxable income increases
4. average tax per dollar unchanged as taxable income rises
5. designed to discourage consumption of socially undesirable goods or services
6. tax on the manufacture or sale of certain items
7. largest source of revenue for the federal government
8. largest source of revenue for state governments
9. national sales tax on value added at each stage of production
10. Social Security and medicare taxes
11. tax on the transfer of property when a person dies
12. tax paid by those who can most afford to pay
13. third largest source of income for the federal government

Reviewing the Facts

SECTION 1 *(pages 210–215)*
1. **Describe** how taxes can be used to affect people's behavior.
2. **Explain** the three criteria used to evaluate taxes.
3. **Name** the two principles of taxation.
4. **Compare** the three types of taxes.

SECTION 2 *(pages 216–220)*
5. **Describe** the main features of the individual income tax.
6. **Identify** the two components of FICA.
7. **Describe** the corporate income tax.
8. **Distinguish** between excise taxes, estate and gift taxes, and customs duties.

SECTION 3 *(pages 222–226)*
9. **Identify** the main sources of revenue for state governments.
10. **List** the main sources of revenue for local governments.
11. **Identify** the main types of taxes that are normally withheld from a worker's paycheck.

SECTION 4 *(pages 228–232)*
12. **Illustrate**, using supply and demand curves, how the incidence of a tax can be shifted.
13. **List** the advantages and disadvantages of a VAT.
14. **Identify** the three major tax reform bills enacted since 1980.

Critical Thinking

1. **Evaluating Information** Explain how the federal income tax does or does not satisfy each of the three criteria for taxes. Give examples to support your explanations.
2. **Synthesizing Information** If you were an elected official who wanted to increase tax revenues, which of the following would you prefer to use—individual income, sales, property, corporate income, user fees, or a VAT? Provide reasons for your decision.

Applying Economic Concepts

1. **User Fees** The following quote appeared in President George Bush's *1990 Budget of the United States*:

   A fee on recreational boaters who use the navigable waters of the United States is proposed. This largely high-income group receives substantial benefit from Coast Guard activities. Commercial boaters would be assessed similar fees and major shipping companies would share licensing and inspection costs.

In your own words, prepare a rationale for a user fee that you think should be enacted.

2. **Sales Taxes** Some people object to state and local governments imposing sales and property taxes. What would you say to these people in defense of the two taxes?

Reinforcing Skills

DISTINGUISHING FACT FROM OPINION

Read the following account of the effects of President Clinton's 1993 tax package. Then write three statements of fact and three statements of opinion that are found in this passage.

President Clinton's income-tax increase will squeeze only the wealthiest taxpayers. But the unlucky few will find it hard to escape the higher taxes. That won't stop them from trying. Wealthy taxpayers—those with $250,000 or more in taxable income—will be taxed at a top rate of 39.6%, up from 31% in 1992. So they are frantically looking for ways to shelter income.

"I've never seen people so frightened," said a financial adviser. "They want whatever will help them avoid taxes." Most of the once-loved loopholes that sheltered earned income are gone, erased by the 1986 tax-reform law.

So what's a high-salary executive to do? Anything that will defer salary or bonuses into the future when he or she might be in a lower tax bracket at retirement or tax rates might be lower.

—Janet L. Fix, *USA TODAY*, August 16, 1993

	Ability-to-Pay Principle	Benefit Principle
Regressive		
Proportional		
Progressive		

Individual Activity

Make a list of five taxes, charges, or user fees that you pay in your community. Draw a matrix like the one below and classify each of your five taxes in the appropriate places.

Cooperative Learning Activity

Working in groups of three, prepare three questions to be included on a survey about tax issues. Each question should be worded so that it can be answered by *yes*, *no*, or *no comment*. Evaluate the questions as a class, then poll community members about the issues. Discuss the responses you received.

Writing About Economics

THE CLASSIFICATORY STYLE

In the **Journal Writing** activity on page 209, you were asked to classify taxes you read or heard about into three categories: Federal, State, and Local Taxes. Using the classificatory style of writing discussed on page 554, evaluate each of your taxes according to the three criteria of taxation: equity, simplicity, and efficiency.

The construction of interstate highways is a joint federal-state government expenditure.

CHAPTER 10

Government Spending

SECTION 1
The Economics of Government Spending

SECTION 2
Federal Government Expenditures

SECTION 3
State and Local Government Expenditures

SECTION 4
Federal Deficits and the National Debt

CHAPTER PREVIEW

People to Know
- Debra J. Fields
- Law Enforcement Officer

Applying Economic Concepts to Your Life

Budget Deficit If you borrow money so that you can spend more than you earn, you run a deficit. When the government spends more than it collects, we say that a *budget deficit* has occurred.

Journal Writing

For one week, write in your journal all government expenditures that you hear about on television or read about in the newspaper. Classify your journal entries into three categories: Federal, State, and Local Government Expenditures.

The Economics of Government Spending

Section Preview

Objectives

After studying this section, you will be able to:

1. **Explain** why and how government expenditures have grown since the 1940s.

2. **Describe** two kinds of government expenditures.

3. **Describe** how government spending impacts the economy.

Key Terms

per capita, public sector, private sector, transfer payment, grant-in-aid, distribution of income

Applying Economic Concepts

Transfer Payments If someone you know has been unemployed, this person may have received a *transfer payment*—a payment for which the government receives neither goods nor services in return. In this case, the transfer payment is an unemployment check. Transfer payments are one of the tools used to promote the goal of economic security.

If all levels of government and all tasks assigned to them are considered, it becomes clear that governments spend huge sums on goods, services, transfer payments, and other programs.

Government Spending in Perspective

In mid-1993, total expenditures by federal, state, and local governments collectively amounted to $2,187,800,000,000, or more than $2.18 trillion—a number almost beyond comprehension! On a **per capita**, or per person, basis, this equaled a combined government expenditure of $8,488 for every man, woman, and child in the United States. Because American taxpayers fund these expenditures, the growth of government spending concerns everyone.

Historical Growth

Spending in the public sector did not begin to rise significantly until the 1940s. This increase occurred for two major reasons. The first was the huge amount of spending required because of World War II. The second was the change in public opinion that gave government a larger role in everyday economic affairs. **1** ✓

As the United States emerged from the Great Depression, government was called upon to regulate banks, public utilities, and many other activities. It also became involved with its citizens' economic welfare. Minimum wage laws, Social Security, welfare programs, education, highways, and transportation all began to receive greater attention.

Figure 10.1 shows the historical growth of government expenditures for all three levels of government. The spending has been adjusted for inflation by using constant dollars, and it is shown on a per capita basis to compensate for the growth in population during that period.

How Much Is Too Much?

Over time, many Americans accepted these increased government expenditures as the inevitable consequence of social and cultural change. Still, some people question how many goods and services government should provide—and, therefore, how many expenditures it should assume. Some people want more roads, schools, and welfare programs, while others want fewer. People also disagree on which services the federal government should provide and which state and local governments should provide.

Many people agree, however, that government is getting too expensive. The $8,488 all levels of government spent exceeded the $7,629 per capita revenues collected by all levels of government. As a result, government collectively spent $859 more per capita than it collected!

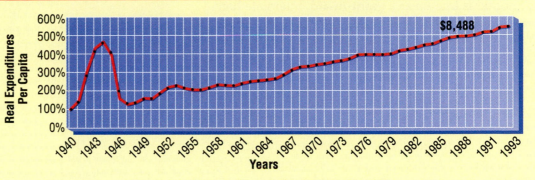

Figure 10.1
Real Per Capita Expenditures by All Levels of Government

In mid-1993, the number of dollars spent per person, even after adjusting for inflation, was 545 percent higher than in 1940. **How does the public sector differ from the private sector?**

$8,488

Real Expenditures Per Capita

Years

Source: *Government Finances*, 1993 Edition, and *Economic Report of the President*, 1993

Two Kinds of Government Spending

Federal, state, and local governments make up the **public sector** of the economy. For the most part, the public sector buys its goods and services from private individuals and businesses, which make up the **private sector** of the economy.

In general, government makes two broad kinds of expenditures. The first is for the purchase of goods and services. The second is in the form of payments to support the incomes of disadvantaged Americans and other designated groups. **2**

Public sector spending is very much like that of individuals and businesses. Even the problems each sector faces are similar. In both cases, resources are scarce and must be used efficiently.

Goods and Services

The government buys many goods, such as tanks for the army, missiles for the air force, and ships for the navy, and space shuttles. The government also needs buildings for offices, land for parks and agricultural testing grounds, and capital goods for schools, laboratories, and other production facilities. In addition, it buys paper clips and paper, computers, desks, filing cabinets, chairs, soap, and gasoline.

Government also hires people to work in its agencies and staff the military. Payments for these services include the wages and salaries paid to all government employees, including the President, governors, public school teachers, and mayors.

Many of the goods and services government provides are public goods—items consumed collectively rather than by single individuals. Public goods include such items as highways, national defense, schools, and police and fire protection.

Transfer Payments

The second kind of government expenditure is a **transfer payment**—a payment for which the government receives neither goods nor services in return. Transfer payments to individuals include Social Security, welfare, unemployment compensation, and aid to

Checking Understanding

1. Why did government spending rise dramatically in the 1940s?
2. What two broad kinds of expenditures does government make?

Applying Economic Concepts

 Government Spending World War II cost the United States 10 times more than World War I. From 1941 to 1945, the government's operating budget was $321 billion, nearly twice as much as its total spending in the previous 150 years.

people with handicapping conditions. People receive these payments solely because they need assistance.

A transfer payment one level of government makes to another is known as a **grant-in-aid**. Interstate highway construction programs are an example. The federal government grants money to cover the major part of the cost, while the states through which the highways will be built pay the rest. The construction of new public schools also can be financed through grants-in-aid.

Transfer payments also include subsidies—payments made to individuals or entire industries to encourage or protect a certain economic activity. Farmers, for example, often are paid subsidies to stabilize their incomes. In the past, airlines also received subsidies.

Impact of Government Spending

The issue of government spending is complex. The size of the public sector gives it the potential to impact people's daily lives in many ways. Several important effects of government spending are examined below.

Allocation of Resources

Government spending decisions directly affect the allocation of resources. If the government decides to spend its revenues on missile systems in rural areas rather than on social welfare programs in urban areas, economic activity is stimulated in rural areas as resources are shifted there.

The allocation of resources can be affected indirectly, too. In agriculture, the decision to support the prices of milk, grains, tobacco, or peanuts keeps the factors of production working in those industries.

Without government support, some land would become idle, some workers would have to find new jobs, and some capital would have to be used for other purposes.

Distribution of Income

Government spending also impacts the economy by affecting the **distribution of income**, or the way in which income is allocated to families, individuals, or other designated groups in the economy. The incomes

Resource Allocation
The opportunity cost of the government's funding of road construction is the schools, parks, and other facilities that do not receive the funds. **How does government spending affect the distribution of income?**

FRANK AND ERNEST ©by Bob Thaves

YOUR TAX DOLLARS AND A WHOLE LOT OF BORROWED MONEY AT WORK

THAVES 9-14

Grants-in-Aid *Although public education is primarily a local government expenditure, grants-in-aid often help finance the construction of new public schools.* **What is a grant-in-aid?**

of poor people, for example, can be directly affected by increasing or decreasing transfer payments.

Incomes are also indirectly affected when the government decides where to make expenditures. The decision to buy fighter planes from one factory rather than from another impacts the communities near both factories. Many businesses not linked to either company will feel the effects when workers are laid off or get new jobs and alter their spending habits.

The military base closings scheduled for the late 1990s have serious implications for income distribution. Communities around the military installations face devastating short-term reductions in incomes.

Competition With the Private Sector

When the government produces goods and services, it often competes with producers in the private sector. When the government provides national defense or a system of justice, it faces no competition. This is not always the case, however.

In regard to health care, the government runs a system of hospitals for military veterans. Taxpayer dollars fund these facilities, which compete with private-sector hospitals that offer similar services. Many county and city health departments offer free inoculations and other services to their citizens. These also compete with private physicians and health clinics.

SECTION 1 REVIEW

Reviewing Terms and Facts

1. **Define** per capita, public sector, private sector, transfer payment, grant-in-aid, distribution of income.
2. **Describe** the per capita growth in government spending since 1940.
3. **List** two kinds of government spending.
4. **Identify** three ways that government spending may impact the economy.

Critical Thinking

5. **Checking Consistency** The text states that most people agree that government is getting too expensive. Interview five people to see if they agree with this statement.

Applying Economic Concepts

6. **Transfer Payments** Do you think that transfer payments, such as unemployment compensation, are a successful or unsuccessful way to accomplish the goal of economic security? Defend your answer.

PROFILES IN ECONOMICS

DEBRA J. FIELDS
(1957–   )

In 1977, 20-year-old Debra Fields borrowed $50,000 to open her first store in Palo Alto, California. She rang up $50 in sales on opening day. Today, Mrs. Fields, Inc., is a $150 million empire, and Debbi Fields is probably the world's best-known chocolate chip cookie baker.

SUCCEEDING AND FAILING Mrs. Fields, Inc., grew rapidly at first. By 1987 Debbi and her husband, Randy, were running 543 owned-and-operated stores in 6 countries, including Japan and Australia. That year, cookie sales amounted to $104 million. The company went public on London's unlisted securities market, and the stock skyrocketed.

Mrs. Fields exhibits her "hands-on" approach to management.

The following year, however, Fields's cookie empire began to crumble. Too many new stores had been opened in the wrong locations—either too close to existing stores or in places where cookie sales did not match the stores' high rents. The rapid expansion made it difficult for Fields to continue her hands-on style of management.

Increased competition, fewer customers, and a downturn in the economy added to the problems. In 1988 Mrs. Fields, Inc., closed 97 stores, and stock collapsed to new lows. The net loss for that year was $19 million.

REBUILDING Fields's strategies for rebuilding her business included several steps. She hired professional executives to take over the managerial duties. She expanded her product line by developing Mrs. Fields Bakeries. In addition to cookies, these cafes offered a variety of lunch items, including muffins, breads, sandwiches, and soups. By 1990 profits were on the way up.

In March 1993, however, Mrs. Fields, Inc., was forced to give its lenders nearly 80 percent of the company in exchange for writing off a $94 million debt. Debbi Fields gave up her roles as president and CEO, but she remained the company's largest individual shareholder. Perhaps the biggest change in Mrs. Fields, Inc., was the licensing of franchise stores.

In spite of the ups and downs and major restructuring, Fields insisted, "Cookies are my life. I would not give this up for any amount of money. It's just that we started so young and made a few real estate mistakes along the way. But we've learned from them. We will get bigger and better from here."

Examining the Profile

1. **Understanding Cause and Effect** Why did Mrs. Fields, Inc., experience major financial setbacks in the late 1980s?

2. **For Further Research** Find out more about franchise agreements. Make a list of businesses that operate as franchises.

Section Preview

Objectives

After studying this section, you will be able to:

1. **Explain** how the federal budget is established.
2. **Describe** the major components of the federal budget.

Key Terms

federal budget, fiscal year, federal budget deficit, appropriations bill, medicaid

Applying Economic Concepts

Social Security Remember those FICA taxes deducted from your paycheck? The government does not save your FICA taxes until you retire. As soon as this money is collected from you, the government spends it as *Social Security* payments to others—that's why they are called transfer payments.

Before the federal government can spend anything, Congress must establish the **federal budget**—an annual plan outlining proposed revenues and expenditures for the coming year. The federal budget is prepared for a **fiscal year**—a 12-month financial planning period that may or may not coincide with the calendar year.

Establishing the Federal Budget

The federal budget is developed and approved in two main phases. First, the President prepares and submits a budget to Congress. Second, Congress approves the budget.

Executive Formulation

The federal budget sets forth the President's financial plan and indicates the government's priorities. The budget is prepared for a multiyear period, but the primary focus is the upcoming fiscal year.

The government's fiscal year starts on October 1 of every calendar year and expires on September 30 of the following year. Normally, the budget is required to be transmitted to Congress on or before the first Monday following January 3, although it usually takes a little longer when a new President takes office.

President Clinton, for example, was inaugurated on January 20, 1993. He sent his budget to Congress on April 8, 1993, for the fiscal year beginning on October 1, 1993, and ending on September 30, 1994. Because most of the budget expenditures actually take place in 1994, it is called the 1994 budget.

As the budget is prepared, the President confers with various government agencies, other Executive Office units, and the Office of Management and Budget (OMB). The OMB is the division of the executive branch primarily responsible for assembling the budget under presidential guidelines.

President Clinton's first budget, shown in **Figure 10.2**, projected $1,251.3 billion of revenues and $1,515.3 billion of expenditures. Because expenditures were larger than revenues, the budget projected a **federal budget deficit** of $264.0 billion for fiscal year 1994. Whether the numbers in a budget turn out to be accurate depends on a number of factors, including the health of the economy and, more importantly, the will of Congress.

Congressional Action

Congress has the power to approve, modify, or disapprove the President's proposed budget. First, the budget goes to the House of Representatives, which must set initial budget targets by May 15. Between this date and September 15, when the budget targets are to be finalized, the House assigns appropriations bills to various House appropriations subcommittees. An **appropriations bill** is a law that sets federal money aside for a specific purpose.

Figure 10.2
The 1994 Federal Budget

The 1994 federal budget projected expenditures of $1,515.3 billion and revenues of $1,251.3 billion—leaving a federal budget deficit of $264.0 billion.

How is the federal budget prepared?

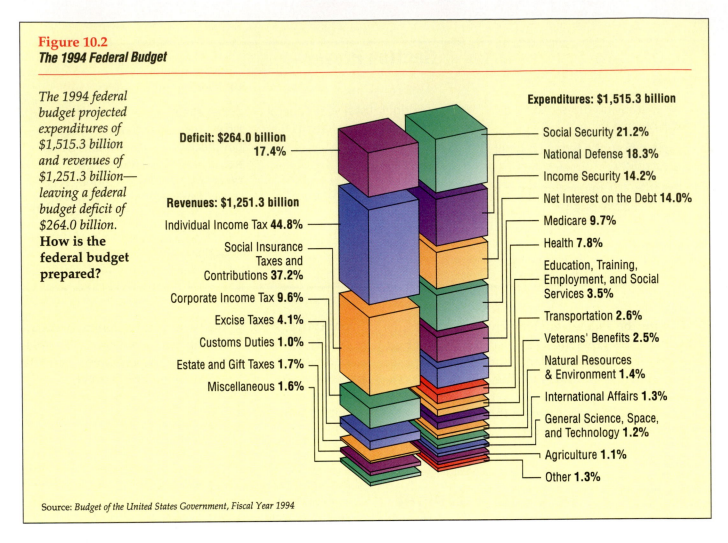

Deficit: $264.0 billion 17.4%

Revenues: $1,251.3 billion
Individual Income Tax **44.8%**
Social Insurance Taxes and Contributions **37.2%**
Corporate Income Tax **9.6%**
Excise Taxes **4.1%**
Customs Duties **1.0%**
Estate and Gift Taxes **1.7%**
Miscellaneous **1.6%**

Expenditures: $1,515.3 billion
Social Security **21.2%**
National Defense **18.3%**
Income Security **14.2%**
Net Interest on the Debt **14.0%**
Medicare **9.7%**
Health **7.8%**
Education, Training, Employment, and Social Services **3.5%**
Transportation **2.6%**
Veterans' Benefits **2.5%**
Natural Resources & Environment **1.4%**
International Affairs **1.3%**
General Science, Space, and Technology **1.2%**
Agriculture **1.1%**
Other **1.3%**

Source: *Budget of the United States Government, Fiscal Year 1994*

House subcommittees hold hearings on each bill and debate the measure. If the bill is approved, it is sent to the full House Appropriations Committee. If it passes there, the bill is sent to the entire House for all representatives to vote on it. After the House approves the final bill, it goes to the Senate. The Senate may approve the bill as sent by the House, or it may draft its own version. If any differences exist between the House and the Senate versions, a joint House-Senate conference committee tries to work out a compromise bill.

During this process, the House and the Senate often seek advice from several government bureaus and offices, including the Congressional Budget Office (CBO). The CBO is a congressional agency that evaluates the impact of legislation and projects future revenues and/or expenditures that will result from the legislation.

After the House and Senate both approve the compromise bill, it is sent to the President for signature. Because Congress literally took apart, rewrote, and put back together the President's budget, the final version may or may not resemble the original proposal. If the budget was altered too much, the President can veto the bill and force Congress to come up with a budget closer to the President's original version.

Major Spending Categories

The thousands of individual expenditures in the federal budget can be grouped into the broad categories shown in both **Figure 10.2** and **Figure 10.3**. The most important categories, historically accounting for more than 95 percent of all federal government expenditures, are described on page 246.

Figure 10.3
Federal Government Expenditures, 1980-1992

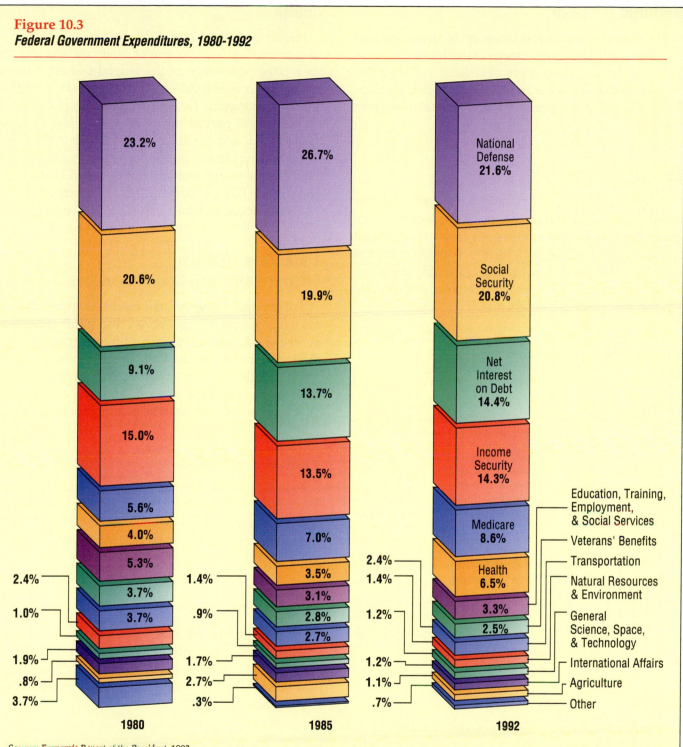

Source: *Economic Report of the President*, 1993

The major categories of federal government expenditures show some change from 1980 to 1992. National defense expenditures are down, while net interest payments on the debt, medicare, and health expenditures are up. Comparing actual expenditures in 1992 with the most recent budget proposal of the President reveals how the administration would like to shift future spending priorities. **What are the three largest federal spending categories?**

National Defense

Historically, the largest category of spending was national defense. This category includes military spending by the Department of Defense and defense-related atomic energy activities, such as the development of nuclear weapons and the disposal of nuclear wastes.

Social Security

A growing category, payments to aged and disabled Americans through the Social Security program, made up the second largest category of federal spending. Retired persons receive benefits from the Old-Age and Survivors Insurance (OASI) program. Others unable to work receive payments from disability insurance (DI) programs.

Interest on the Federal Debt

When the federal government spends more that it collects in taxes and other revenues, it borrows money to make up the difference. Interest on the federal debt made up the third largest category of federal spending in 1985 and 1992. The amount of interest paid varies with changes in interest rates and the amount of money borrowed.

Income Security

This category includes expenditures for retirement benefits to railroad workers, disabled coal miners, civil service retirement and disability programs, and retirement benefits for the military. Subsidized housing, child nutrition, and food programs for low-income families also fall under this category.

Medicare

Medicare, a health-care program available to all senior citizens regardless of income, began in 1966. The program provides an insurance plan that covers major hospital costs. It also offers optional insurance that provides additional coverage for doctor and laboratory fees, outpatient services, and certain equipment costs.

Health

Health-care services for low-income people, disease prevention, and consumer safety usually account for a large percentage of the federal budget. Federal spending for **medicaid**—a joint federal-state medical insurance program for low-income persons—makes up the largest part of health spending. The Occupational Safety and Health Administration (OSHA)—a federal agency that monitors occupational safety and health in the workplace—is also included in this category. So is AIDS and breast cancer research, as well as substance abuse and mental health service programs.

Education, Training, Employment, and Social Services

This budget category includes block grants for elementary, secondary, vocational, and adult education, as well as education for those with handicapping conditions. Other services, such as guaranteed student loans, youth summer employment programs, day-care, foster care, legal services, and care of neglected or homeless children, are also part of this category.

Veterans' Benefits

Federal spending for veterans amounted to a small percentage of the total budget. Among other goods and services, veterans receive education and training, guaranteed home loans, pensions, and hospital and medical care from these funds.

Transportation

This category includes federal expenditures on highways, highway safety, mass transit, railroads, airports, and air traffic regulation. It also includes ocean shipping and other marine safety and transportation expenditures.

Natural Resources and Environment

Money in this category is spent on water resources, conservation, and land management. Pollution control and federal land acquisition for recreational parks are also included.

General Science, Space, and Technology

This category includes expenditures for National Science Foundation programs and other general science programs for the Department of Energy and the Department of Defense. Space flight and space flight research are also supported with federal funds.

Agriculture

The majority of dollars allotted for agriculture are paid to farmers in the form of price supports, crop insurance, and guaranteed loans. Because most expenditures are directly related to the prices that farmers receive for their crops, the size of this category varies considerably from one year to another.

The government also supports the Farmers Home Administration (FmHA), a type of federal bank that makes loans to those with limited financial resources who live in rural areas. Agriculture extension, 4-H youth, and animal and plant health programs consume the remaining dollars in this category.

Other Spending

Other miscellaneous expenditures account for the remainder of the federal budget. This category includes commerce, energy, community and regional development, general government, and the administration of justice.

Federal Expenditures *The space shuttle* Challenger *conducts tests for the National Aeronautics and Space Administration.* **What percentage of 1992 federal expenditures went to General Science, Space, and Technology?**

SECTION 2 REVIEW

Reviewing Terms and Facts

1. **Define** federal budget, fiscal year, federal budget deficit, appropriations bill, medicaid.
2. **Describe** the two stages required to establish the federal budget.
3. **List** the largest components of federal government spending.

Critical Thinking

4. **Determining Cause and Effect** In recent decades, people have been living longer and families have been having fewer children. How will the combination of these two factors affect transfer payments, such as Social Security, in the future?

Applying Economic Concepts

5. **Social Security** Contact your local Social Security office to find out about a person's eligibility to receive Social Security payments. Ask about the age, eligibility requirements, the size of the Social Security payments, and other requirements that may apply.

Reading Statistical Tables

How many RBIs did your favorite shortstop drive in? How many touchdowns did your favorite wide receiver score? If you are a baseball or football fan, you probably love to keep records of statistics. Such information can be presented in a table.

Explanation

Economists also research and gather many facts and statistics. These facts can be placed in a table. Tabular data can help you analyze information because tables summarize a large amount of information in a small space. Tabular information is presented in rows and columns, which make it easy to read. Follow the steps below to learn how to read statistical tables.

- Read the title of the table to learn what content is being presented.
- Read any headings, or boxed heads, which may group information into subcategories.
- Read the information in the left-hand column, which often is organized alphabetically, chronologically, or geographically.
- The vertical columns to the right of the left-hand column are the body of the table. Compare the data presented in these columns.

Practice

Analyze the table on this page. Then use the steps outlined above to answer the following questions.
1. What is the title of the table?
2. What subheads are found in the table?
3. What information is being compared?
4. In which years was national defense the highest percentage of expenditures?
5. Which expenditures increased from 1980 to 1992?
6. Which expenditures decreased from 1980 to 1992?

Figure 10.4
Federal Government Expenditures, 1980-1992

Major Categories	1980	1985	1992	Major Categories	1980	1985	1992
National Defense	23.2%	26.7%	21.6%	Veterans' Benefits	3.7%	2.8%	2.5%
Social Security	20.6%	19.9%	20.8%	Transportation	3.7%	2.7%	2.4%
Net Interest on Debt	9.1%	13.7%	14.4%	Natural Resources & Environment	2.4%	1.4%	1.4%
Income Security	15.0%	13.5%	14.3%	General Science, Space, & Technology	1.0%	0.9%	1.2%
Medicare	5.6%	7.0%	8.6%	International Affairs	1.9%	1.7%	1.2%
Health	4.0%	3.5%	6.5%	Agriculture	0.8%	2.7%	1.1%
Education, Training, Employment & Social Services	5.3%	3.1%	3.3%	Other	3.7%	0.4%	0.7%
					100%	100%	100%

Additional Practice

For further practice in reading statistical tables, complete the Reinforcing Skills exercise in the Chapter 10 Review on page 263.

State and Local Government Expenditures

Section Preview

Objectives

After studying this section, you will be able to:

1. **Explain** how state and local governments approve spending.
2. **Identify** the major categories of state government expenditures.
3. **Identify** the major categories of local government expenditures.

Key Terms

balanced budget amendment

Applying Economic Concepts

Human Capital Local governments spend about 30 percent of their direct expenditures on elementary and secondary education—or about $765 for every man, woman, and child in the average state. These expenditures are an investment in *human capital*, which will result in more productive citizens. You are getting something in return for paying taxes!

The federal government is not the only level of government that has expenditures. State and local levels of government also have expenditures. Like the federal government, these governments must approve spending before revenue dollars can be released.

Approving Spending

At the state level, there are almost as many ways to approve spending as there are states. In most states, however, the process is loosely modeled after that of the federal government.

Some states have enacted a **balanced budget amendment** to their state constitution, which requires them to hold spending in line with revenues. Under these conditions, states are forced to cut spending when state revenues drop. A reduction in revenues may occur if sales taxes or state income taxes fall because of a decline in the general level of economic activity.

At the local level, the approval for spending often rests with the mayor, the city council, the county judge, or some other elected representative or body. Generally, the amount of revenues collected from property taxes and other local sources limits the spending of local agencies. If state and local governments are unable to raise the revenue they need, they face the problem of not having enough financial resources to hire teachers, police officers, or other local and state workers.

State Government Expenditures

The major types of state government expenditures are shown in Figure 10.5. Six of the most important categories, accounting for approximately 72 percent of all state spending, are public welfare, higher education, insurance trust funds, highways, hospitals, and interest on state debt.

Public Welfare

The largest category of expenditures for state governments usually is public welfare. These payments take the form of cash assistance, payments for medical care, expenditures to maintain welfare institutions, and other miscellaneous welfare expenditures.

Higher Education

Generally, the second largest category is higher education, a traditional responsibility of state governments with their networks of state colleges and universities. Local governments spend less in this area, usually to support community colleges and universities.

Figure 10.5
Direct Expenditures by State and Local Governments

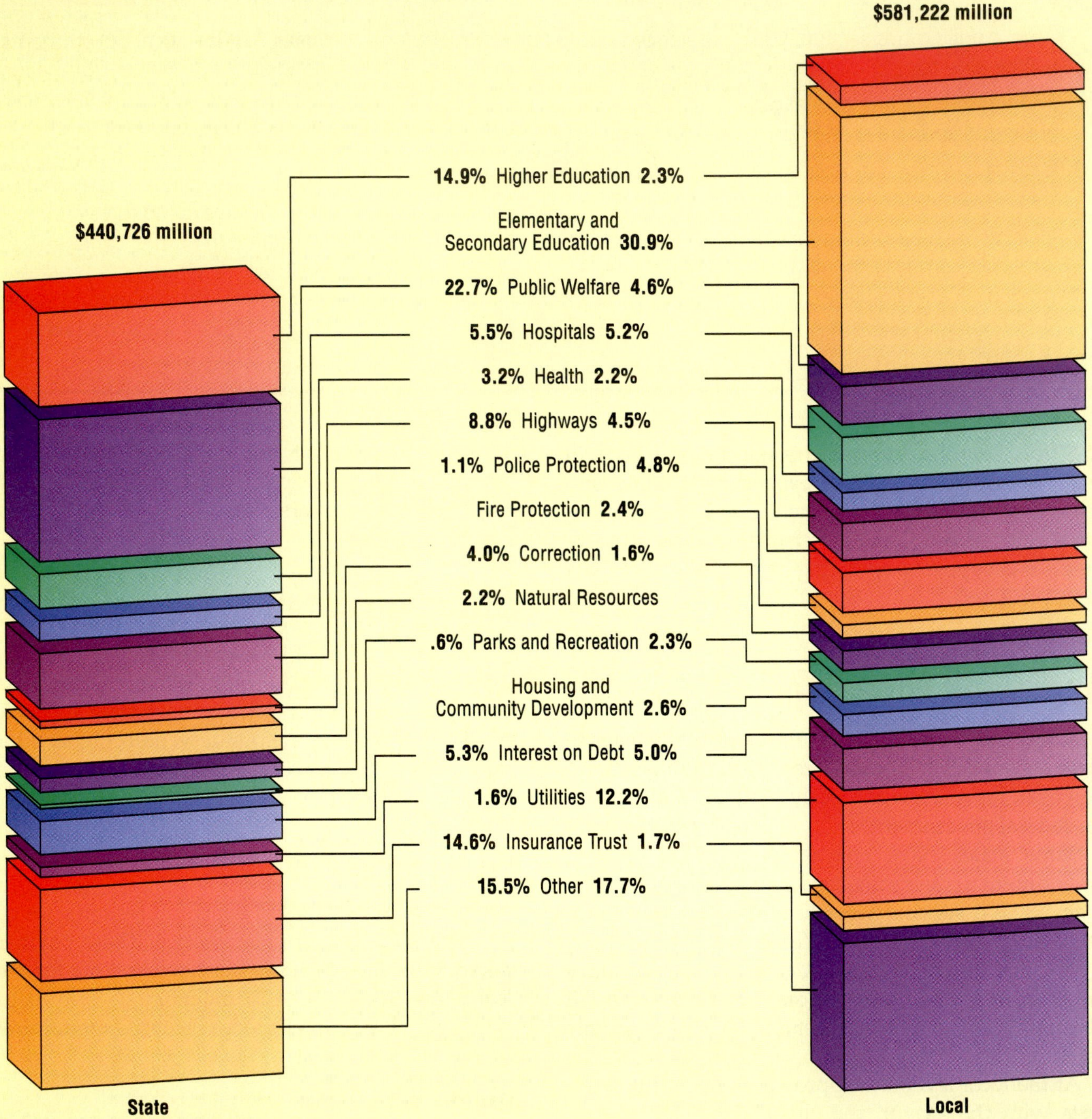

$581,222 million

$440,726 million

14.9%	Higher Education	2.3%
	Elementary and Secondary Education	30.9%
22.7%	Public Welfare	4.6%
5.5%	Hospitals	5.2%
3.2%	Health	2.2%
8.8%	Highways	4.5%
1.1%	Police Protection	4.8%
	Fire Protection	2.4%
4.0%	Correction	1.6%
2.2%	Natural Resources	
.6%	Parks and Recreation	2.3%
	Housing and Community Development	2.6%
5.3%	Interest on Debt	5.0%
1.6%	Utilities	12.2%
14.6%	Insurance Trust	1.7%
15.5%	Other	17.7%

State

Local

Source: *Government Finances, 1993 Edition*

State governments collect more revenue than do local governments. Because of intergovernmental transfers, however, local governments actually make more direct expenditures. **What are the three largest spending categories for state governments? For local governments?**

Insurance Trust Funds

Many states have their own retirement funds and insurance funds for state employees. These funds are invested until such time as people retire, become unemployed, or are injured on the job.

Highways

Highway construction and road improvement expenditures are a large category of state expenditures. The federal government builds and maintains much of the interstate highway system, but states maintain state roads and other highways that generally link smaller communities with larger ones.

Hospitals

Because most hospitals do not charge enough in fees to fully recover their costs, they often turn to state and local governments for help. As a result, hospital expenditures are a significant expense for both state and local governments.

Interest on Debt

Interest on state debt, generally in the form of bonds, is the sixth largest category of state government expenditure. In recent years, states have issued bonds to cover everything from general revenue to highways to university dormitories. The size of this component can increase significantly if interest rates rise.

Other Spending

The remaining 28 percent of direct state government expenditures consist of a variety of expenditures. The most important are in the areas of corrections, health, natural resources, and utilities.

Local Government Expenditures

Local governments include counties, municipalities, townships, school districts, and other special districts. The largest categories of spending by local governments make up approximately 67 percent of their total expenditures. These categories include elementary and secondary education, utilities, hospitals, interest on debt, police protection, public welfare, and highways.

Elementary and Secondary Education

Local governments have primary responsibility for elementary and secondary education. Expenditures in this category include teachers' and administrators' salaries, textbooks, and construction and maintenance of school buildings. 1

Public Utilities

Many public utilities, such as water and electricity, serve local needs. For most local governments, spending on utilities amounts to the second most important expenditure. Because fewer utilities serve people on a statewide basis, state governments spend a much smaller percentage of their budgets on public utilities.

Hospitals

Hospitals receive a large amount from local governments. Many hospitals are city- or municipal-owned, which makes them a large budget item for local governments.

Interest on Debt

State and local governments, like the federal government, sometimes borrow money to cover operating costs or capital spending. Interest payments in this

	Checking Understanding	**Applying Economic Concepts**
	1. Which level of government has the major responsibility for primary and secondary education?	☑ **The Role of Government** In recent decades, the number of school districts has declined. Better transportation has allowed many school districts to consolidate, thus saving money. The United States has about 14,700 school districts. It had 108,579 in 1942.

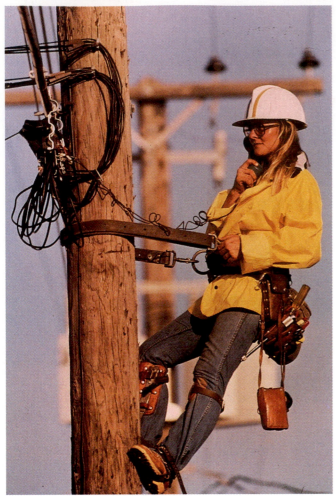

Local Government Expenditures *Spending on utilities, such as electricity, is a local government expenditure.* **What is the largest expenditure of local governments?**

category were nearly the same for both local and state governments. Like the federal government, interest expenses vary as interest rates go up and down.

Police Protection

Most localities have a full-time, paid police force to protect their community. As a result, police protection is a significant cost for local governments. Because there are far fewer state than local police forces, state spending for police protection is much lower.

Public Welfare

Local governments, like state governments, face public welfare expenditures. Unlike state governments, however, local governments spend much less on this category.

Highways

Local governments spend almost as much on highways, roads, and street repairs as they do on police protection. This expenditure includes the repair of potholes, street signs, and other street-related items.

Other Expenditures

The remaining local government expenditures, approximately 33 percent of the total, are spread over a wide range of categories. Among the most important are housing and community development, fire protection, and parks and recreation.

SECTION 3 REVIEW

Reviewing Terms and Facts

1. **Define** balanced budget amendment.
2. **Describe** how state governments handle the spending approval process.
3. **List** the six major categories of state spending.
4. **Identify** the major categories of local government spending.

Critical Thinking

5. **Making Generalizations** If you were to argue for reduced spending at the state and local levels, which categories shown in **Figure 10.5** would you pick? Explain the reasons for your choice(s).

Applying Economic Concepts

6. **Human Capital** How does the market reward those who have invested in human capital? Cite specific examples from your community.

Federal Deficits and the National Debt

Section Preview

Objectives

After studying this section, you will be able to:

1. **Explain** how the federal deficit is related to the federal debt.

2. **Relate** the impact of the federal debt on the economy.

3. **Describe** recent attempts to control the federal deficit.

Key Terms

deficit spending, federal debt, trust fund, Gross Domestic Product, crowding-out effect, balanced budget, entitlement

Applying Economic Concepts

Deficit Spending According to the 1994 *Budget of the United States Government*, approximately 14 cents of every federal dollar was spent on interest payments on the federal debt. When the government must borrow money to spend it, *deficit spending* occurs. American taxpayers—including you—must pay the interest on that borrowed money.

The amount of **deficit spending**—spending more than is collected in revenues—in recent years by the federal government has been staggering. Sometimes the government plans deficit spending. At other times, a deficit occurs because factors in the economy have reduced the amount of revenues or increased the amount of expenditures.

unemployment compensation, would go down. In a very strong economy, the deficit may be cut by 50 percent or more.

In contrast, if the economy turns out to be weaker than expected, tax collections could go down. People might lose their jobs, and unemployment compensation might rise. In that case, the deficit might be 50 percent larger than the one planned.

From the Deficit to the Debt

Figure 10.2 showed that the government projected a $264.0 billion federal deficit for 1994. This projection is based on a number of assumptions about the economy for the coming year. If the economy turns out to be stronger than expected, federal government revenues would go up and expenditures, such as

A History of Deficits

Recent history shows that deficits tend to appear more often than surpluses in the American economy. **Figure 10.6** shows the history of federal budget deficits and surpluses since 1940. The numbers in the figure have been converted to constant dollars so that inflation does not distort the deficits.

Federal Debt *In 1993 the federal debt reached $4.4 trillion.* **How does the federal debt impact the economy?**

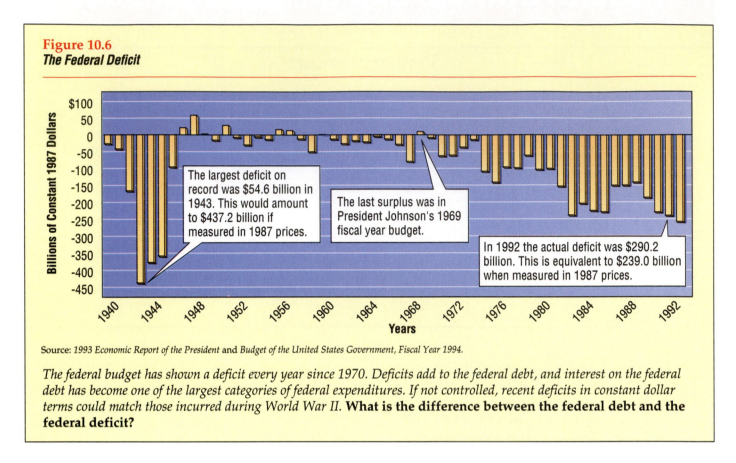

Figure 10.6
The Federal Deficit

The largest deficit on record was $54.6 billion in 1943. This would amount to $437.2 billion if measured in 1987 prices.

The last surplus was in President Johnson's 1969 fiscal year budget.

In 1992 the actual deficit was $290.2 billion. This is equivalent to $239.0 billion when measured in 1987 prices.

Source: *1993 Economic Report of the President* and *Budget of the United States Government, Fiscal Year 1994.*

The federal budget has shown a deficit every year since 1970. Deficits add to the federal debt, and interest on the federal debt has become one of the largest categories of federal expenditures. If not controlled, recent deficits in constant dollar terms could match those incurred during World War II. **What is the difference between the federal debt and the federal deficit?**

According to the figure, the largest deficits on record, in relative terms, were during World War II. The government quickly recovered, however, and by 1947 the budget was in surplus. The federal government then ran a series of modest deficits, along with an occasional surplus, through most of the 1950s and 1960s. The deficits began to grow larger under Presidents Nixon and Ford in the early 1970s.

Deficits fell somewhat during the Carter administration, but then started to increase after the passage of the 1981 Economic Recovery Tax Act during President Reagan's administration. The act dramatically lowered taxes on individuals and businesses, but did little to lower spending, so large deficits continued.

Deficits Add to the Debt

When the federal government runs a deficit, it must finance the shortage of revenue by borrowing from others. It generally does this by having the Department of the Treasury sell bonds and other forms of government debt to the public. If we add up all federal bonds and other debt obligations, we have a measure of the **federal debt**—the total amount borrowed from investors to finance deficit spending by the federal government.

This debt grows whenever the government sells more bonds to finance deficit spending in any given year. For example, the amount of debt the public held at the end of 1991 amounted to $2,687.9 billion. After adding the deficit for 1992 to this figure, plus some other government borrowing, the amount of public debt at the end of 1992 totaled $2,998.6 billion.

The debt will continue to grow as long as the government spends more than it collects in revenues. Therefore, a zero budget deficit in any given year does not mean that the debt will go away. A zero deficit only means that the debt will not get any larger.

How Big Is the Debt?

The national debt has grown almost continuously since 1900. That year the debt was $1.3 billion. By 1929 it had reached $16.9 billion, and by 1940 it was $50.7 billion. The debt increased to $290.5 billion by 1960,

Figure 10.7
Three Views of the Federal Debt

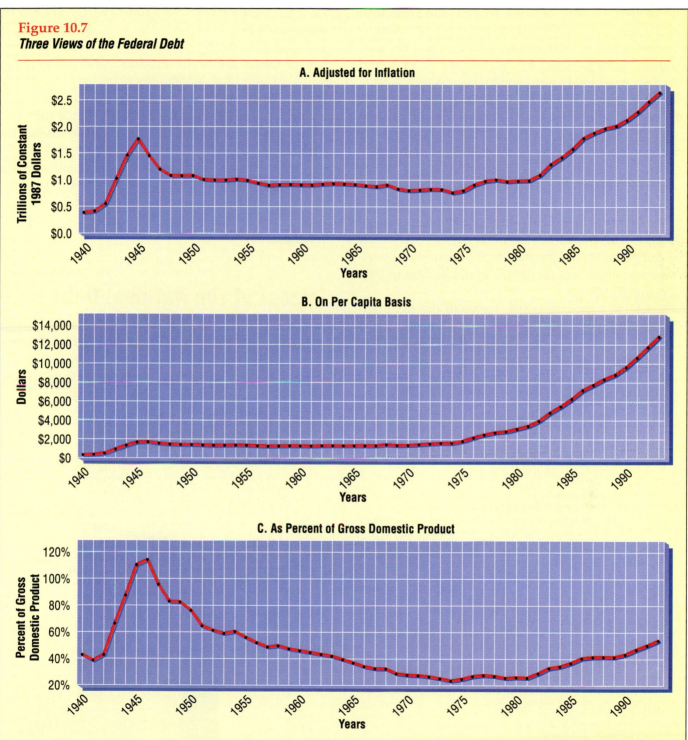

A. Adjusted for Inflation

B. On Per Capita Basis

C. As Percent of Gross Domestic Product

Source: 1993 Economic Report of the President and Budget of the United States Government, Fiscal Year 1994

The gross federal debt held by the public is huge. Graph A shows that from 1980 to 1993, the federal debt nearly tripled, even when constant dollars were used to remove the effects of inflation. When measured on a per capita basis, as in Graph B, expenditures more than quadrupled to reach $12,850 for every man, woman, and child in the United States. Finally, as shown in Graph C, the federal debt went from 26.2 percent of the Gross Domestic Product to 54.0 percent. **In what ways does the federal debt impact the American economy?**

and to $908.5 billion by 1980. By 1993 the gross total federal debt exceeded $4,410 billion—or $4.4 trillion.

Some of this debt, however, is money that the government owes to itself. In 1992 almost $1 trillion of this debt was held in government trust funds. A **trust fund** is a special account used to fund specific types of expenditures, such as Social Security and medicare. When the government collects the FICA tax, it puts the revenues in these trust accounts. The money is then invested in government securities until it is paid out.

Because trust fund balances represent money the government owes to itself, most economists tend to disregard this portion of the debt. Instead, they view the public portion of the debt as the economically relevant part of the federal debt. The public debt in 1993 exceeded $3 trillion.

Figure 10.7 presents three views of the total federal debt that the public held. Graph **A,** which is adjusted for inflation, shows that the debt did not increase dramatically until the 1980s. Graph **B,** computed on a per capita basis, also shows a dramatic increase in the 1980s. According to this view, the debt

on a per capita basis was approximately $12,850 by the end of 1993.

Graph **C** in the figure shows the debt as a percentage of **Gross Domestic Product** (GDP)—the dollar value of all final goods, services, and structures (houses and commercial buildings) produced within a country during any one year. By 1993 the debt had exceeded 54 percent of GDP, a level not seen since the early 1950s. 1

During the 1970s, many people thought that the debt was not a major problem. By the 1990s, however, many people became alarmed at the sudden increase in the size of the annual deficit and the growth of the federal debt.

Impact of the National Debt

The size of the federal debt has led some people to believe that the United States will go bankrupt if the debt ever gets too large. This, however, cannot happen because public debt is different from private debt.

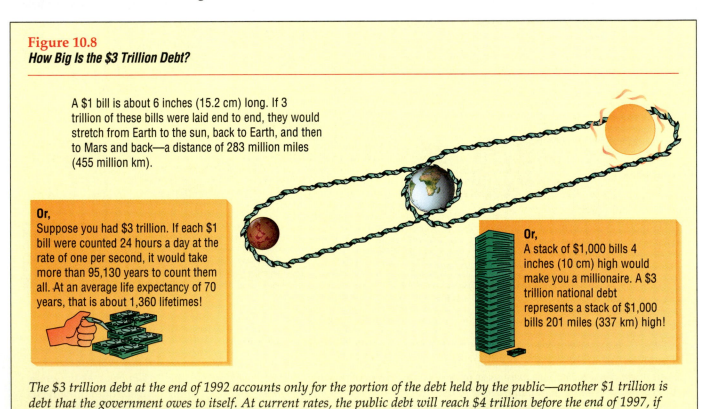

Figure 10.8
How Big Is the $3 Trillion Debt?

A $1 bill is about 6 inches (15.2 cm) long. If 3 trillion of these bills were laid end to end, they would stretch from Earth to the sun, back to Earth, and then to Mars and back—a distance of 283 million miles (455 million km).

Or,
Suppose you had $3 trillion. If each $1 bill were counted 24 hours a day at the rate of one per second, it would take more than 95,130 years to count them all. At an average life expectancy of 70 years, that is about 1,360 lifetimes!

Or,
A stack of $1,000 bills 4 inches (10 cm) high would make you a millionaire. A $3 trillion national debt represents a stack of $1,000 bills 201 miles (337 km) high!

The $3 trillion debt at the end of 1992 accounts only for the portion of the debt held by the public—another $1 trillion is debt that the government owes to itself. At current rates, the public debt will reach $4 trillion before the end of 1997, if not earlier.

Public vs. Private Debt

The key difference between public and private debt is that we owe most of the federal debt to ourselves, whereas private debt is owed to others. This difference is important for two reasons.

The first reason relates to the repayment of the debt. When private citizens borrow money, they usually make plans to repay the debt at some time in the future. When the federal government borrows, it gives little thought to eventual repayment. The government has no real reason to ever pay off the federal debt. When it is time to pay off old bonds, the government simply issues new ones—and then uses the proceeds to pay off the old bonds.

The second reason relates to the loss of purchasing power. When private individuals repay a debt, they give up purchasing power because the money is gone and cannot be used to buy more goods and services. When the federal government repays a debt, there is no loss of purchasing power because the taxes and revenue collected from some groups are simply transferred to others.

The exception is that foreign investors historically have owned 15 to 20 percent of the public debt. When payments are made to investors outside the United States, some purchasing power is temporarily diverted from the American economy.

The Distribution of Income

The federal debt can have a significant impact on the distribution of income within the economy. If the government borrows money from the wealthy, and if the burden of taxes falls on the middle class and the poor, taxes would be transferred to the rich in the form of interest payments on the debt.

If the government borrows money from the middle class, and if the burden of taxes falls on the rich, those taxes would be used to make interest payments to the middle class. The federal tax structure, as much as the size of the debt itself, determines the distribution effects.

A Transfer of Purchasing Power

Another important impact of the federal debt is that it causes a transfer of purchasing power from the private sector to the public sector. In general, the larger the public debt, the larger the interest payments and, therefore, the more taxes needed to pay them. When people have to pay more taxes to the government, they have less money to spend on their own needs.

If the federal government decides to significantly increase spending in areas such as national defense or health care, private individuals will have less to spend on cars, consumer goods, and vacations. If the government decides to fund this spending by borrowing, the transfer of purchasing power will continue for years as the interest payments are spread into the future.

Individual Incentives

A third impact of the federal debt is that the taxes needed to pay the interest can cut down the incentives to work, save, and invest. Individuals and businesses might feel less inclined to work harder and earn extra income if higher taxes will be placed on them. 2

Many people also feel that the government spends taxpayers' money in a careless manner. A community, for example, may secure a federal grant and use the

---

Checking Understanding

1. What does GDP include?
2. How can the federal debt affect worker incentive?

Applying Economic Concepts

 Federal Spending When Congress appropriates money for local federal projects, it is often called *pork-barrel legislation.* Although such projects may bring jobs and money into a state, taxpayers often view pork-barrel projects as a waste of their money.

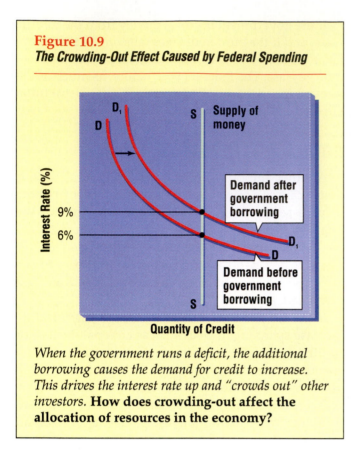

Figure 10.9
The Crowding-Out Effect Caused by Federal Spending

When the government runs a deficit, the additional borrowing causes the demand for credit to increase. This drives the interest rate up and "crowds out" other investors. **How does crowding-out affect the allocation of resources in the economy?**

funds to purchase expensive equipment that taxpayers in the community would never have approved. If people feel that their taxes are being squandered, they are less likely to save and invest.

Higher Interest Rates

When the government sells bonds to finance the deficit, it competes with the private sector for scarce resources. An example of this competition is the **crowding-out effect**—the higher-than-normal interest rates that heavy government borrowing causes. Private borrowers are forced to pay the higher rates or leave the market. This effect is illustrated in **Figure 10.9 1**

In the graph, the demand curve for credit in the money market is represented by DD and the supply of money by SS. If the government runs a deficit and tries to raise funds by selling bonds, it will cause the demand curve to shift to D_1D_1. The increased demand for money causes the interest rate to go up. This increase forces other borrowers to pay higher rates or to stay out of the market.

Dealing With the Deficit

Concern over the size of the federal deficit and the debt has led to a number of attempts to control it. Several of the more important attempts are described below.

Gramm-Rudman-Hollings

One of the first significant attempts to control the federal deficit took place when Congress tried to mandate a **balanced budget**, a budget with neither a surplus nor a deficit, by 1991. The legislation was formally called the Balanced Budget and Emergency Deficit Control Act of 1985, or Gramm-Rudman-Hollings (GRH) after its sponsors. At the time, both critics and supporters called the act one of the most important pieces of legislation passed since the Great Depression.

The key to GRH was a set of federal deficit targets for Congress and the President to meet over a six-year period. The federal deficit was to decrease each year until it reached zero in 1991. If Congress and the President could not agree on a budget that met the target in any given year, the automatic reductions would take over and reduce spending, splitting reductions equally between defense and nondefense expenditures. Legislators liked the law because it reduced spending without forcing Congress to vote against popular programs.

Figure 10.10
Major Features of the 1993 Omnibus Budget Reconciliation Act

SOCIAL SECURITY
Fewer than 13 percent of Social Security recipients—generally those with incomes that average over $50,000—would have to pay tax on a greater share of their benefits. No single retiree with income under $34,000, counting half his or her Social Security pension, or couple under $44,000 would be affected.

MEDICARE TAX
Effective Jan. 1, 1994, the $135,000 limit on the amount of annual wages and self-employment income subject to the Medicare tax would be eliminated.

CORPORATIONS
Higher taxes on corporations; a further cut in the deduction for business meals and entertainment, and a $1 million limit on the amount of an executive's salary that may be deducted.

ENERGY
Taxes on gasoline, now 14.1 cents a gallon, and diesel, now 20.1 cents, would rise by 4.3 cents on Oct. 1. The gas-tax increase, costing the typical household $30 to $50 a year, or a dime a day, as Clinton put it. This is the only part of the bill with an impact across the broad middle class.

INTEREST
Debt service costs will be lower.

GOVERNMENT PROGRAMS
A nearly $56 billion cut in the growth of reimbursements to doctors and hospitals for treating the elderly and disabled under medicare. Projected reductions in spending for the military and restraints on a variety of other federal spending programs.

ENTITLEMENTS
Increases in spending will be lowered.

Pie chart values: $24, $25, $29, $48, $65, $102, $115, $88 — in billions of dollars

INDIVIDUAL TAXES
A major income-tax increase on top earners costing those with incomes over $200,000 an extra $23,521 a year. The current top rate of 31 percent would rise, retroactive to Jan. 1, to 36 percent. A new 10 percent surtax would hit taxable income above $250,000, producing a new top rate of 39.6 percent.

Source: *USA Today*

Most of the provisions in the 1993 Omnibus Budget Reconciliation Act take effect over a five-year period. If the bill actually saves $500 billion over this period, it will only slow the rate of growth of the deficit, not eliminate the deficit. **What are entitlements?**

Despite the high hopes for GRH, the legislation was a shambles six years later. Instead of having reduced the deficit to zero in 1991, the country had its largest deficit ever of $269.5 billion.

GRH failed for two reasons. First, Congress discovered that it could get around the law by passing spending bills that took effect two or three years later. Because GRH only set the deficit estimate for one year at a time, these bills did not conflict with GRH.

Second, the economy started to decline in July 1990. This decline triggered a safety valve in the law that suspended automatic cuts when the economy was weak. The combination of spending bills that circumvented GRH, the suspension of automatic budget cuts, and the lower federal revenues caused by the declining economy all added to the enormous budget deficit. As a result, the much-anticipated arrival of the balanced budget never materialized. 2

QUICK CHECK

Checking Understanding
1. What is the crowding-out effect?
2. Why did the Gramm-Rudman-Hollings Act fail?

Applying Economic Concepts
 Federal Budget George Washington was able to put all the figures for the national government's first budget on one large piece of paper. Today the federal budget consists of more than 1,000 pages of small type.

Budget Enforcement Act of 1990

In 1990 Congress passed the Omnibus Budget Reconciliation Act, otherwise known as the Budget Enforcement Act (BEA). The main features of the act combined spending caps with a "pay-as-you-go" provision designed to limit discretionary spending.

Under this provision, reductions somewhere in the budget—or a tax increase—had to offset any new program that required additional spending. In addition, the BEA required that five-year revenue estimates be prepared for each new legislative act. If offsetting cost reductions could not be found, then mandatory, across-the-board spending cuts would be made to offset the extra costs.

BEA is much more difficult to circumvent than GRH, but several provisions limit it, also. First, it applies only to discretionary spending, not programs like Social Security and medicare that increase automatically. Second, it includes a safety provision that allows for suspension of the act if the economy enters a low-growth phase, or if the President declares an emergency. Because the act is new, however, it will be several years before its impact can be fully evaluated.

Omnibus Budget Reconciliation Act of 1993

President Clinton's Omnibus Reconciliation Act of 1993 was an attempt to trim approximately $500 billion from the deficit over a five-year period. By 1993 the federal deficit had reached such enormous proportions that the act was intended to reduce only the rate of growth of the deficit, not the deficit itself.

The package, whose major provisions are illustrated in **Figure 10.10**, was a mixture of tax increases and spending reductions. The program made the personal income tax even more progressive, and targeted the richest 1.2 percent of Americans for a tax increase.

Growth of Entitlements

Some of the fastest-growing programs in the federal budget are **entitlements**, broad social programs designed to provide minimum health, nutritional, and income levels for eligible individuals. Entitlements include Social Security, medicaid, medicare, agricultural price supports, federal employee retirement and health benefits, some unemployment compensation, and aid to the poor. These programs are called entitlements because individuals are entitled to draw on these programs if they meet the eligibility requirements.

The problem for deficit reduction is that entitlements represent some of the largest and fastest-growing programs in the federal budget. They are so large that meaningful deficit reduction cannot be accomplished unless these programs are altered. Because these programs support millions of Americans, however, deficit reduction in the future is likely to be as difficult as it has been in the past.

SECTION 4
REVIEW

Reviewing Terms and Facts

1. **Define** deficit spending, federal debt, trust fund, Gross Domestic Product, crowding-out effect, balanced budget, entitlement.
2. **Describe** how the federal deficit affects the debt.
3. **List** five ways the national debt can affect the economy.

4. **Identify** three recent attempts to bring the federal deficit under control.

Critical Thinking

5. **Making Generalizations** Make a list of five ways that you or your family directly benefit from federal government expenditures.

Applying Economic Concepts

6. **Deficit Spending** Identify those benefits that are directly related to entitlement programs. If you were given the task of reducing entitlement programs, which would you choose to reduce or alter? Provide reasons for your choices.

Government Spending

Vocabulary

The following terms are defined in Chapter 10:

SECTION ONE
- per capita (p. 238)
- public sector (p. 239)
- private sector (p. 239)
- transfer payment (p. 239)

- grant-in-aid (p. 240)
- distribution of income (p. 240)

SECTION TWO
- federal budget (p. 243)
- fiscal year (p. 243)
- federal budget deficit (p. 243)
- appropriations bill (p. 243)

- medicaid (p. 246)

SECTION THREE
- balanced budget amendment (p. 249)

SECTION FOUR
- deficit spending (p. 253)
- federal debt (p. 254)
- trust fund (p. 256)

- Gross Domestic Product (p. 256)
- crowding-out effect (p. 258)
- balanced budget (p. 258)
- entitlement (p. 260)

Section 1

The Economics of Government Spending (pages 238–241)

By mid-1993, expenditures by all levels of government exceeded $2.18 trillion, or $8,488 on a **per capita** basis. Most of the growth took place after the 1930s, but today many people question whether government spending has grown too much. Government expenditures pay for goods and services, some of which are **public goods**, and for **transfer payments** such as **grants-in-aid**, for which the government does not receive anything in return.

Reviewing the Main Idea

How has the growth of government spending affected the overall economy?

Section 2

Federal Government Expenditures (pages 243–247)

The President is responsible for developing the **federal budget** for the **fiscal year**, which begins every October 1. The three largest components of the federal budget, accounting for more than one-half of all federal expenditures, are national defense, Social Security, and interest on the **federal debt**. Income security, medicare, and health are the next largest categories.

Reviewing the Main Idea

What are the main categories of federal government expenditures from most to least important?

Section 3

State and Local Government Expenditures (pages 249–252)

State budgets go through an approval process that varies from state to state. The largest state expenditures include public welfare, higher education, and insurance contributions. Other programs include highways, hospitals, and interest on state debt.

The largest single category of spending for local governments is elementary and secondary education. Public utilities, hospitals, interest on debt, police protection, public welfare, and various other expenditures follow education.

Reviewing the Main Idea

What are the main categories of state expenditures from most to least important?

Section 4

Federal Deficits and the National Debt (pages 253–260)

The federal debt affects the economy in several ways. Taxes needed to pay the interest on the debt affect the distribution of income and also transfer purchasing power from the private sector to the government sector. Individual incentives to work, save, and invest may also be affected. Finally, higher interest rates can occur as the government competes for funds with the private sector.

Reviewing the Main Idea

How do taxes affect the allocation of resources?

CHAPTER 10 REVIEW

Reviewing Key Terms

Write a sentence about each pair of terms below. The sentences should show how the terms are related.

1. public sector, private sector
2. transfer payment, grant-in-aid
3. distribution of income, deficit spending
4. federal budget, fiscal year
5. appropriations bill, balanced budget amendment
6. deficit spending, federal debt
7. deficit spending, crowding-out effect
8. entitlement, balanced budget

Reviewing the Facts

SECTION 1 *(pages 238–241)*
1. **Describe** the magnitude of government spending since 1940.
2. **Identify** two kinds of government spending.
3. **Explain** three ways that government spending can impact the economy.

SECTION 2 *(pages 243–247)*
4. **Identify** the two stages of approval required to establish the federal budget.
5. **Identify** the 10 most important budget categories in the federal budget.

SECTION 3 *(pages 249–252)*
6. **Explain** how states model their budget approval process.
7. **Describe** the major categories of state and local spending.

SECTION 4 *(pages 253–260)*
8. **Discuss** the relationship of the federal deficit to the federal debt.
9. **Identify** how the debt can affect the economy.
10. **List** three legislative attempts to deal with the problem of federal budget deficits.
11. **Cite** at least six examples of entitlement programs.
12. **Explain** why entitlements are so named.

Critical Thinking

1. **Analyzing Information** Examine the major types of federal expenditures in Figure 10.2 on page 244. Classify each as to whether they are entitlement or non-entitlement programs.
2. **Making Comparisons** Compare the federal expenditures for the four years included in Figures 10.2 and 10.3. Identify at least three major differences in the expenditures. How do changes in spending reflect the priorities of the administration that develops the budget?

Applying Economic Concepts

1. **Human Capital** Which of the categories in Figures 10.2 and 10.3 reflect an investment in human capital?
2. **Deficit Spending** If you were a presidential adviser, what spending cuts would you suggest to balance the budget? Explain your reasoning.
3. **Budget Deficits** The federal government has made several attempts to deal with the problem of federal budget deficits. Identify the three important pieces of legislation discussed in the chapter, and outline their main features and weaknesses in a chart similar to the one below.

A. _____
   1. Features:

   2. Weaknesses:

B. _____
   1. Features:

   2. Weaknesses:

C. _____
   1. Features:

   2. Weaknesses:

Reinforcing Skills

READING STATISTICAL TABLES

Use the table below to answer the following questions.

1. What is the title of the table?
2. What subheads are found in the table?
3. What information is being compared?
4. Which company raised its prices the most? The least?

Individual Activity

Examine the list of spending categories in **Figure 10.5** on page 250, and note that each category represents one group of services provided at the state and local levels of government. Make a list of those services you or your family have directly used.

Then examine **Figure 10.2**, which categorizes federal expenditures. Make a list of federal services that you or your family have directly used or from which you have benefited.

Review the amount of revenue each level of government receives in the form of taxes you and your family pay. This information was shown graphically in **Figure 9.1** on page 211. Finally, in a paragraph, summarize which level of government services you use the most and which level of government receives the most revenue for their services.

Cooperative Learning Activity

Organize into groups of five. Using the list of federal government spending categories in this chapter, identify at least six categories that should be targeted for reduced spending. All members of the group should come to a consensus on which categories to cut. Provide reasons for your choices, then compare your results to the other groups in the class.

Figure 10.11
Price Per Pound of Ready-To-Eat Cereals

	1988	Oct. 1992*	Increase
Nabisco†	$2.22	$3.13	40.99%
Post	2.27	2.92	28.63
General Mills	2.67	3.43	28.46
Ralston Purina	2.54	3.20	25.98
Quaker	2.27	2.82	24.23
Private Labels, Generic	1.44	1.78	23.61
Kellogg's	2.40	2.84	18.33

*Latest figures available. †In January 1993, Nabisco's cold cereals were acquired by Kraft General Foods, which makes Post cereals.

Source: Prudential Securities

Writing About Economics

THE CLASSIFICATORY STYLE

In the **Journal Writing** activity on page 237, you were asked to classify expenditures you read or heard about into three categories: Federal, State, and Local Government Expenditures. Using the classificatory style of writing discussed on page 554, evaluate each of your entries as either goods and services expenditures or transfer payments.

*To successfully per-
form the functions of
money, coins and
currencies must be
portable, durable,
divisible, and stable
in value.*

CHAPTER 11

Money and Banking

CHAPTER PREVIEW

People to Know
- Oprah Winfrey
- Bank Teller

Applying Economic Concepts to Your Life

Money Why do you accept money in exchange for a good or service? Why are so many different kinds of money used around the world? *Money* is harder to define than you might think. We usually think of money in terms of what it can do for us, rather than in terms of its nationality, shape, or color.

Journal Writing

For one week, write in your journal the advertising claims you read or hear about from the financial institutions in your area.

SECTION 1
The Evolution of Money

Section Preview

Objectives

After studying this section, you will be able to:

1. **Explain** the three functions of money.
2. **Identify** four major types of money used in early societies.
3. **Trace** the origins of the United States dollar.
4. **Describe** the four characteristics of money.

Key Terms

barter economy, money, medium of exchange, measure of value, store of value, commodity money, fiat money, wampum, specie, bullion, monetary unit

Applying Economic Concepts

Barter Did you trade items when you were younger? Did you ever have trouble finding someone who would agree with your terms of the exchange? Trade, or *barter,* is one way to do business, but it is often tedious and time-consuming. That is why most societies use some form of money in their transactions.

Money is something that most people take for granted. Think what the world would be like without it, however. If we lived in a **barter economy,** a moneyless economy that relies on trade, life would be quite different. Without money, the exchange of goods and services would be greatly hindered, because the products some people have to offer are not always acceptable or easy to divide for payment. Money makes life easier for everybody in ways we may not have thought about.

What Is Money?

Basically, money is what money does. **Money** can be any substance that functions as a medium of exchange, a measure of value, and a store of value.

Medium of Exchange

As a **medium of exchange,** money is something generally accepted as payment for goods and services. In a barter society, trade may occur without a medium of exchange. In colonial times, for example, a merchant might have accepted a chicken in exchange for cloth, or a doctor might have exchanged medical services for potatoes. As societies become more complex, however, trading goods for other goods or services becomes difficult.

Measure of Value

As a **measure of value,** money expresses worth in terms that most individuals understand. To say that a bicycle is worth a television set or 50 bags of onions would be confusing. If a price tag in terms of dollars is put on the bicycle, however, most people can assess its value. They see the dollar price of one object in relation to the dollar price of others. Because one single measurement of value exists, consumers can trade with each other using the common denominator of money.

Store of Value

Money also serves as a **store of value.** Goods or services can be converted into money, which is easily stored until some future time. Money enables a period of time to pass between earning and spending an income.

Money in Early Societies

Money has evolved to make life easier for people. This evolution took place in societies that had virtually no contact with one another and that developed at different times. The result is money that comes in an incredible variety of forms, shapes, and sizes.

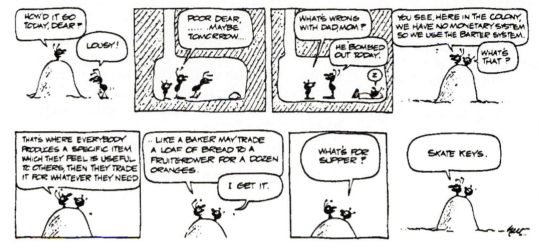

Barter Economy *As the cartoon shows, a barter economy can cause problems for those wanting to exchange goods for products they may use.* **How does money function as a medium of exchange?**

One of the earliest forms of money was the brightly colored cowrie shells found in parts of the South Pacific and Africa. In New Guinea, dog teeth served as a form of currency, while fishhooks often were used in the Marshall Islands. At Santa Cruz in the South Seas, the feathers of hundreds of honey-eating birds were attached to short sticks to make feather-stick money. Tea leaves compressed into "bricks" comprised money in ancient China, and compressed cheese was used in early Russian trade. The East African Masai used a currency made of miniature iron spears fastened together to form a necklace.

Today, some of this money would be classified as **commodity money**—money that has an alternative use as a commodity. The compressed tea leaves could be made into tea when not needed for trade. Other items became **fiat money**—money by government decree. Other early moneys included the tiny coins used in Asia Minor in the seventh century B.C. These coins had little use as a commodity, but served as money largely because the government said they were money. 1

The use of money became accepted because it served everyone's best interests to do so. In this sense, money was then—and is now—a social convention, much like the general acceptance of laws and government.

Money in Colonial America

The money early settlers in America used was similar to the money found in earlier societies. Some of it was commodity money, and some was fiat money.

Commodity Money

Many products—gunpowder, musket balls, corn, and hemp—served as commodity money. Perhaps the most famous colonial money was tobacco. In 1618 the governor of colonial Virginia gave it a monetary value of three English shillings, or 36 English pennies, per pound. 2

Wampum

Other colonies established fiat monies. In 1645 Connecticut set a monetary value for **wampum**—a

Checking Understanding

1. How does commodity money differ from fiat money?
2. What products in colonial America served as commodity money?

Applying Economic Concepts

 Barter Barter still has its uses. In some countries with very high tax rates, people sometimes prefer to be paid in goods and services rather than money. The reason? Income in the form of goods and services is less likely to come to the attention of the tax collector.

form of currency the Narraganset Native Americans made out of white conch and black mussel shells. Because the Narraganset and the settlers used wampum in trade, 6 white or 3 black shells were made equal to 1 English penny. In 1648 the General Court of Massachusetts passed a law ordering the wampum to be "suitably strung" in lengths of 1, 3, and 12 pennies.

Paper Currency

As time went on, other forms of money were used. In some cases, state laws allowed individuals to print their own paper currency. Backed by gold and silver deposits in banks, it served as currency for the immediate area.

Some states passed tax-anticipation notes that could be redeemed with interest at the end of the year. The governments printed the notes, which were used to pay salaries, buy supplies, and meet other expenditures until taxes were received and the notes redeemed. The taxes, however, were collected in coins whenever possible.

Paper money was issued to finance the Revolutionary War. In 1775 the Continental Congress authorized the printing of Continental Currency, or Continental dollars—a form of fiat paper currency with no gold or silver backing. By the end of the war, nearly $250 million had been printed and spent to pay soldiers and to buy materials. **1**

Money *Stone money is still used on the Yap Islands.*
Would this form of money be considered commodity money or fiat money?

Specie

Specie is money in the form of coins, usually made from silver or gold. In the American colonies, some coins were English shillings used to pay government officials. Other coins included Spanish *pesos*, Austrian *talers*, and various European coins that immigrants brought to the colonies.

Coins were the most desirable form of money because most contained silver. Coins, however, were in short supply. By 1776, only $12 million in specie circulated in the colonies. Nearly $500 million in paper currency was in circulation, about one-half of which private individuals and states issued. **2**

Origins of the Dollar

When George Washington became President, one of his first challenges was to set up a new money supply. Benjamin Franklin and Secretary of the Treasury Alexander Hamilton were asked to design the new money, which they based on the Spanish peso.

Pesos

By the late 1700s, the most plentiful coin in circulation was the Spanish peso, which had come to America through piracy and trade. Long before the American Revolution had begun, the Spanish were mining silver in Mexico. They melted the silver into **bullion**—ingots or bars of precious metals—or minted it into coins for shipment to Spain. When the Spanish treasure ships stopped in the West Indies for fresh provisions, they often became victims of Caribbean pirates who spent their stolen treasure in America's southern colonies. ✔

The colonies engaged in a profitable trade known as the triangular trade, which exported rum and imported enslaved Africans. As shown in **Figure 11.1**, molasses from the West Indies was shipped to New England, where much of it was made into rum. The rum was shipped across the Atlantic Ocean to Africa, where it was exchanged for enslaved Africans, who were packed into ships and taken across the Atlantic to the West Indies. There, they would be sold for molasses and for pesos. Part of the income was used to buy more molasses, which, along with pesos, was taken to New England to begin the triangle again.

Figure 11.1
The Triangular Trade

The triangular trade with Africa and the West Indies brought molasses, enslaved Africans, and Spanish pesos to the colonies. Pesos were also called dollars by the colonists because of their resemblance to the Austrian taler. Eventually, the dollar became the basic monetary unit of the United States. **What characteristics must money have to be a successful medium of exchange?**

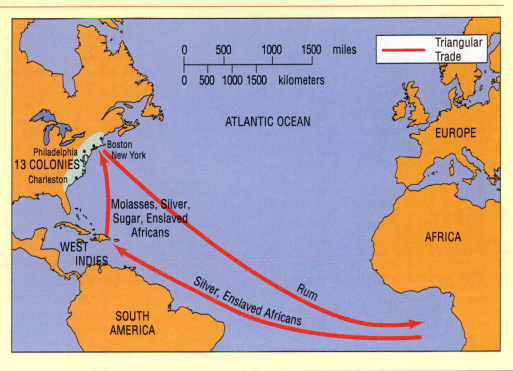

Talers

Pesos were known as pieces of eight, because they were divided into eight sub-parts known as *bits*. Because the pesos resembled the Austrian taler, they were nicknamed talers, which sounded like *dollars*. This term became so popular that Franklin and Hamilton decided to make the dollar the basic **monetary unit,** or standard unit of currency in a country's money system.

Rather than divide the dollar into eighths as the Spanish had done with the peso, Franklin and Hamilton decided to divide it into tenths, which was easier to understand. Even today, some of the terminology associated with the Spanish peso remains. Many people call a 25-cent coin—one quarter of a dollar—"two bits."

Characteristics of Money

The study of early money is useful because it helps determine the characteristics that give money its value. To be a successful medium of exchange, money must be portable, durable, divisible, and stable in value.

Checking Understanding

1. What was used to finance the Revolutionary War?
2. Why were coins a more desirable form of money than paper?

Applying Economic Concepts

 Inflation The silver mined by the Spanish in the 1500s and 1600s led to massive inflation in Spain after the silver was shipped there. The oversupply of money caused prices to go up and the value of money to fall.

Portability

Money must be portable, or easily transferred from one person to another. Most money of early societies was very portable—including dog teeth, feather-stick money, and compressed blocks of tea and cheese.

Durability

If money was not reasonably durable, it would not last when handled. Most colonial money was quite durable. Wampum did not require special care when being handled, and it lasted a long time. The fiat paper money of the colonial period had a type of durability in that it could be easily replaced by issuing new bills when old ones became worn.

Divisibility

Money should be easily divisible into smaller units, so that people use only as much as needed for any transaction. Most early money was highly divisible. In the case of the Masai's iron spear currency, the necklace was untied and some of the spears removed. The blocks of tea or cheese were cut with a knife. Bundles of tobacco leaves were broken apart.

Stability in Value

Finally, if something is to serve as money, it must be stable in value. It must be available, but in limited supply. The dog teeth of New Guinea, for example, were extracted from packs of wild dogs. Because the islanders hunted the dogs for their teeth, the wild dog population never grew too large. Stones used as money on the Yap Islands were carried in open canoes from other islands 400 miles away. Because navigation was uncertain and the weather unpredictable, only 1 canoe in 20 made the round-trip. This ratio kept the supply of stone money from growing too fast.

Commodity money was the least stable in value. In Virginia, people just started to grow their own money. So much tobacco was grown that its worth fell from 36 pennies a pound to 1 penny a pound. Eventually wampum also lost some of its value. Many settlers brought industrial dyes from Europe and used them to turn the white wampum into black, which doubled its value.

SECTION 1 REVIEW

Reviewing Terms and Facts

1. **Define** barter economy, money, medium of exchange, measure of value, store of value, commodity money, fiat money, wampum, specie, bullion, monetary unit.
2. **Describe** three functions of money.
3. **Name** five types of early money.
4. **Explain** how the dollar was adopted as the basic monetary unit.
5. **Identify** the four characteristics of money.

Critical Thinking

6. **Determining Cause and Effect** We sometimes hear rumors about changing our currency or specie to a different color, shape, or size. Explain how these changes would or would not affect the role money played.

Applying Economic Concepts

7. **Money** Write a brief critique of the following statement: "Money was invented to make our lives easier. As such, it is our servant, not our master. Those who treat money as the master rather than the servant do not really understand money."

Determining Relevance

Suppose you go to a store and see athletic shoes you want to buy.
"How much are they?" you ask.
"Prices have been slashed," the sales clerk replies.
"But how much?" you repeat.
"These shoes are a great deal!"
You try again.
"You've told me they're discounted, and that I can get a great deal. But how much are they?"
"They're $59.95—plus tax."
Finally, you have the information you need.

Explanation

As you see in the example above, two kinds of information—relevant information and irrelevant information—exist. Relevant information relates to a particular topic, issue, or main idea. It defines, explains, illustrates, or describes a cause or consequence of a main idea. Irrelevant information does not relate to the topic.

When you are studying economics or doing research, you must learn to determine the relevance of each piece of information. The following steps help you determine relevant information:

- Read or listen carefully, and determine the topic or main idea.
- State the topic as a question.
- Decide which pieces of information help to answer the topic question. Does the information define, explain, illustrate, or describe a cause or consequence of the main idea? If so, the information is relevant.

Practice

Use the steps to determine the relevance of the information in the highlighted paragraph, the topic of which is the effect of a money economy on Europe. Read the excerpt, then answer the questions that follow.

1. Rewrite the topic sentence as a question.
2. Which sentences are relevant to the question?
3. For each relevant sentence, write whether the information defines, explains, illustrates, or describes a cause or consequence of the main idea.

(a) The rise of a money economy had far-reaching consequences for Europe. (b) Initially, it led to the growth of banking. (c) Because traders came from many countries, they carried different currencies with different values. (d) Important sea and river routes connected western Europe with the Mediterranean, eastern Europe, and Scandinavia. (e) Moneychangers determined the value of the various currencies and exchanged one currency for another. (f) They also developed procedures for transferring funds from one place to another, received deposits, and arranged loans, thus becoming the first bankers in Europe. (g) The word bank comes from the banca, or bench, that the moneychangers set up at fairs. (h) The most famous fair was at Champagne in eastern France, located in almost the exact center of western Europe.

Additional Practice

For further practice in determining relevance, complete the Reinforcing Skills exercise in the Chapter 11 Review on page 291.

SECTION 2
Early Banking and Monetary Standards

Section Preview

Objectives

After studying this section, you will be able to:

1. **Explain** the history of privately issued bank notes.
2. **List** five major types of currencies introduced after the Civil War.
3. **State** two advantages and two disadvantages of a gold standard.
4. **Understand** why the United States has an inconvertible money standard.

Key Terms

monetary standard, state bank, wildcat bank, legal tender, greenback, United States note, National Banking System, national bank, National Bank note, national currency, gold certificate, silver certificate, Treasury coin note, gold standard, inconvertible fiat money standard

Applying Economic Concepts

Legal Tender The currency in your possession states "This note is legal tender for all debts, public and private." This statement is the government's way of establishing paper currency as a uniform money supply, sometimes called *legal tender*. Having a uniform money supply frees you from bartering so you have time for other activities.

Money does more than make it easy to buy and sell goods and services. It also frees time and other resources so that people—and the economy—are productive. In order for a complex economy like that of the United States to run smoothly, it needs a reliable money supply. A **monetary standard**—the mechanism designed to keep the money supply portable, durable, divisible, and stable in value—helps keep the money supply reliable. The United States has had several monetary standards.

Privately Issued Bank Notes

During the Revolutionary War, nearly $250 million worth of Continental Currency was printed. After the Revolution, Continental Currency was worthless, and people did not trust the government to issue anything except coin. Accordingly, Article 1, Section 8, of the United States Constitution states:

The Congress shall have the power

To coin money, regulate the value thereof, and of foreign coin, and fix the standard of weights and measures;

To provide for the punishment of counterfeiting the securities and current coin of the United States; . . .

To make all laws which shall be necessary and proper for carrying into execution the foregoing powers, and all other powers vested by this Constitution in the government of the United States, or in any department or officer thereof.

Article 1, Section 10, further states:

No State shall . . . coin money; emit bills of credit; make anything but gold and silver coin a tender in payment of debts. . . .

The Constitution, then, gave the federal government the power to mint coins. Section 8 was also widely interpreted to mean that the government could not print paper currency.

Growth of State Banking

By the late 1780s, only four banks existed in the United States. Each bank was allowed to issue its own money during the colonial period, and the new Constitution did not prohibit this practice. As a result, banks began to grow. By 1811 the country had about 100 banks, all but one of which was a **state bank**—a bank that receives its charter to operate from a state government.

The exception was the Bank of the United States which, like the state banks, was privately owned and operated. The Bank of the United States, however, was much larger than any of the state banks and had a federal rather than a state charter. The Bank acted much like the current Department of the Treasury in that it collected fees and made payments on behalf of the federal government.

State banks issued their own currency by printing their notes at local printing shops. People who wanted loans borrowed these notes and paid them back with interest. Because the federal government did not print paper currency until the Civil War, most of the money supply was paper currency that privately owned, state-chartered banks issued.

Abuses in Banking

Most banks printed only the amount of currency they could back with their gold and silver reserves so that people could redeem their notes for gold or silver. Others, however, printed large amounts of currency, and then spent it in distant cities. These banks, often located in remote areas, hoped it would take a long time for the notes to return to them for redemption. Banks that over-printed their currencies were called **wildcat banks** because people claimed a person had to be a wildcat to get to them.

Problems With Currency

Even when banks were honest, two problems with currency arose. First, each bank issued a different currency. Hundreds of different kinds of notes could be in circulation in any given city. Second, because a bank could print more money whenever it wanted, the temptation to issue too many notes always existed.

By the Civil War, the United States had more than 1,600 banks issuing more than 10,000 kinds of paper currency. Each bank was supposed to have backing in the form of gold or silver, but this was seldom the case. As a result, when people tried to buy something, their notes were often checked against the latest listing of good and bad bank notes.

Figure 11.2
The Metallic Content of United States Coins

	OLD PENNY	NEW PENNY	NICKEL	DIME	QUARTER	HALF DOLLAR	SUSAN B. ANTHONY DOLLAR
	95% copper 5% zinc	97.5% zinc 2.5% nickel	75% copper 25% nickel	91.7% copper 8.3% nickel	91.7% copper 8.3% nickel	91.7% copper 8.3% nickel	87.5% copper 12.5% nickel
Value*	4/10 of one cent	2/10 of one cent	One cent	4/10 of one cent	One cent	Two cents	One cent

*value varies with the price of metal

Source: Bureau of the Mint

The metallic content of coins is selected for both function and value. Metallic alloys that are durable and do not tarnish easily are used whenever possible. The metallic content of coins must also have very low value so that people do not melt them down for their specie content. **What types of currencies did the United States use between 1861 and 1900?**

Greenbacks *This turn-of-the-century greenback was officially backed by gold after 1900.* **What is legal tender?**

The Greenback Standard

Numerous currencies were in use in the United States between 1861 and 1900. One currency, however, dominated during these four decades and became the main monetary standard of the time.

Greenbacks

When the Civil War erupted, both the North and the South needed to raise enormous sums to finance the war. Congress tried to borrow money by selling bonds, but bond sales did not raise as much money as the government needed, so Congress decided to print money.

In 1861 Congress authorized the printing of $60 million of notes called demand notes. Each note, like the state bank notes in existence at the time, was signed by hand—a practice that required many clerks. Although these notes had no gold or silver backing, they were declared **legal tender**—a fiat currency that must be accepted in payment for debts. Because both sides of the notes were printed with green ink to distinguish them from the state notes already in circulation, the new notes were soon dubbed **greenbacks.**

Greenbacks were used mostly in the North, but more money was soon needed. In 1862 Congress passed the Legal Tender Act, which gave the national government the right to print $150 million of **United States notes,** a new currency that had no gold or silver backing. Almost one-half of the currency in circulation in 1863 was United States notes, also called greenbacks.

National Currency

As the war dragged on, and as the amount of greenbacks grew, people feared that the currency might become worthless. They avoided the greenback, and the government was forced to find another way to finance the war.

The answer was to create a **National Banking System** (NBS), which was to consist of financially sound and rigorously inspected private banks. These banks received their charters from the national government and were known as **national banks.** The government hoped the high standards for member banks would give people confidence in the system and its currency. Each bank would issue **National Bank notes** or **national currency,** which were to be uniform in appearance and backed by United States government bonds.

This backing made the currency seem more secure to the public. It also generated a demand for the bonds that the government sold at the outbreak of the Civil War. If a group wanted to set up a national bank, it had to first purchase government bonds as part of the requirement to get the national charter. The bonds were then put on deposit with the United States Treasury as backing against the currency. ☑

Initially, few state-chartered banks joined the system. It was easier for them to have money printed at a local printer than to buy bonds, secure a charter, and then exchange the bonds for national currency. In 1865 the federal government tried to force state banks into the National Banking System by placing a 10 percent tax on all privately issued bank notes. Because state-chartered banks could not afford the tax, they withdrew their notes from circulation, leaving only the greenbacks and national currency in circulation. 1

Gold Certificates

The removal of more than 10,000 different sizes and denominations of state bank notes simplified the currency system for everyone. Before long, however, new types of federal currency appeared.

In 1863 the government issued **gold certificates**— paper currency backed by gold on deposit with the United States Treasury. At first, these yellowbacks, so-called because of the bright yellow ink used on both sides of the bill, were printed in large denominations for banks to use in settling differences with each other at the end of the business day. By 1882, however, the government began printing gold certificates in $20 denominations for the public's general use.

Silver Certificates

In 1886 the federal government issued another kind of paper currency called a silver certificate. **Silver certificates** were modeled after the gold certificates and were backed by silver coins placed on deposit with the Treasury.

Silver certificates were printed as part of a program to support silver prices for miners in the West. The Bland-Allison Act, passed in 1878, required the federal government to buy large amounts of silver and then mint the ore into silver dollars.

Silver dollars were bulky and inconvenient to use, however, so the Bland-Allison Act was amended in 1886 to provide for the printing of silver certificates. Under the amendment, the government agreed to buy silver and hold it in reserve against the silver certificates—thereby pleasing the silver miners while giving the public an alternative to the generally unwanted silver dollars.

Treasury Coin Notes

In 1890 the federal government printed the fifth, and last, type of paper currency issued before the banking system was overhauled in 1913. The currency came in the form of **Treasury coin notes**— paper currency redeemable in both gold and silver. The law was repealed in 1893, and further issues of Treasury coin notes were ended. Because so many were issued in such a short period, however, Treasury coin notes remained in circulation until the 1930s.

The Gold Standard

In 1900 Congress passed the Gold Standard Act, which defined the dollar as being worth 1/20.67 ounce of gold. Congress thus put the country on a **gold standard**—a monetary standard under which the basic unit of currency is equivalent to, and can be exchanged for, a set amount of gold.

Going on the Gold Standard

The Gold Standard Act did not affect the type of currency people used. People continued to use gold certificates, silver certificates, United States notes, National Bank notes, and Treasury coin notes. The only difference was that they could exchange these notes for gold at the Treasury whenever they wanted.

Advantages of a Gold Standard

In general, a gold standard has two major advantages. First, people feel more secure about their money because they know they can always convert it into gold. Second, it prevents the government from printing too much paper currency. The theory is that as long as the government has promised to redeem its

Checking Understanding

1. Why did the National Banking System place a 10-percent tax on privately issued bank notes?

Applying Economic Concepts

 Greenback Party The Greenback Party was formed in 1874 to promote the printing of money not backed by gold. Made up mostly of farmers, the Greenbackers believed the issuance of more currency would enable them to pay off their debts.

Modern Money *Checking accounts have made modern money very portable.* **How does modern money rate in terms of durability, divisibility, and stability in value?**

paper currency in gold, it will print only that amount of money that can be backed by gold. The currency will remain relatively scarce and, therefore, will be more likely to keep its value.

When the United States went on the gold standard, it did not have enough gold to back all paper currency in circulation. This is usually the case for any country that goes on a gold standard, because a country only needs to have the appearance that its currency can be redeemed for gold. It is unlikely that all notes will be redeemed at one time.

Disadvantages of a Gold Standard

One disadvantage of a gold standard is that a growing economy needs a growing money supply, which requires a growing gold stock to back it. If new gold supplies cannot be found, the growth of the money supply eventually begins to slow and perhaps stop, restricting economic growth. Another disadvantage is that people may decide to convert their currency into gold, thereby draining the government of its gold reserves.

Abandoning the Gold Standard

The gold standard remained in force until the Depression years of the 1930s. By that time, banks began to fail, and many people could not find jobs. Because people felt safer holding gold rather than paper currency, they began to cash in their dollars for gold. Foreign governments with large holdings of dollars began to do the same thing.

In 1933 the federal government feared that it could not continue to back the money supply with gold, so it decided to go off the gold standard. On August 28, 1933, President Franklin D. Roosevelt declared a national emergency and decreed that anyone holding more than $100 worth of gold or gold certificates file a disclosure form with the United States Treasury.

Several months later, the Gold Reserve Act of 1934 was passed. It required citizens, banks, and businesses to turn their gold and gold certificates over to the United States government. Those who did were compensated with Federal Reserve notes and other forms of federal currency. Those who did not had their gold and gold certificate holdings confiscated.

The Inconvertible Fiat Money Standard

Since 1934 the United States has been on the **inconvertible fiat money standard.** Under this standard, the money supply is *inconvertible* because it cannot be converted into gold or silver by United States citizens. It is a *fiat* money standard because government decree declared dollars legal money. Since 1975, however, American citizens have been allowed to own gold.

A Managed Money Supply

The money supply of the United States, much like those of other major industrialized countries, is a managed money supply. The government or its designated agent tries to control the quantity, composition, and even the quality of the money supply.

This task is somewhat easier now that a single currency has replaced the early forms of currency. National currency and Treasury coin notes were withdrawn from circulation in the 1930s, and gold certificates were confiscated in 1934. The last issue of United States notes (greenbacks) took place in 1968, and some were still in circulation in the early 1970s. Silver certificates also circulated in the early 1970s, but the government stopped redeeming them for silver dollars in 1968.

Modern money consists largely of checking accounts, coins, and a single currency issued by the Federal Reserve System. How well the money functions depends in part on how well it satisfies the four characteristics of money examined earlier.

Characteristics of Modern Money

Although money has changed in shape, kind, and size over the years, modern money still shares many of the same characteristics of early money. As a medium of exchange, modern money satisfies the four characteristics of money.

Modern money is portable. When people carry checkbooks, they really are carrying very large sums of money, because checks can be written in almost any amount.

Modern money is also durable. Metallic coins last a long time under normal use, and they generally do not go out of circulation unless they are lost. Paper currency also is reasonably durable, with a $1 bill lasting about one year in circulation. Checks and checking accounts never wear out.

Modern money rates high on divisibility. The penny, which is the smallest denomination of coin, is small enough for almost any purchase. In addition, checks can be written for the exact amount.

Modern money has an uneven track record when it comes to stability in value, however. The high rates of inflation in the mid-1970s tell us that money was not as scarce as it could have been. The money supply, which often grew at a rate of 10 to 12 percent a year during that period, was considered a major cause of inflation.

SECTION 2 REVIEW

Reviewing Terms and Facts

1. **Define** monetary standard, state bank, wildcat bank, legal tender, greenback, United States note, National Banking System, national bank, National Bank note, national currency, gold certificate, silver certificate, Treasury coin note, gold standard, inconvertible fiat money standard.
2. **Explain** how privately issued bank notes became part of the money supply.

3. **List** the five major currencies in use after the Civil War.
4. **Explain** why the United States went off the gold standard.
5. **Identify** the characteristics of an inconvertible fiat money standard.

Critical Thinking

6. **Making Comparisons** Some experts have proposed a return to the gold standard. Explain why you think this may or may not be a good idea.

Applying Economic Concepts

7. **Legal Tender** Suppose that Federal Reserve notes did not exist to serve as "legal tender." What else could be done to establish a suitable money supply?

PROFILES IN ECONOMICS

OPRAH WINFREY

(1954–)

Millionaire Oprah Winfrey is one of the richest and most powerful women in America. She is the first African American woman to host a nationally syndicated weekday talk show. She also owns Harpo Productions, Inc., a Chicago-based movie production company. In addition, Winfrey has part ownership of three network-affiliated stations.

RISE TO THE TOP Winfrey credits her father's influence for making her a high achiever. Her own ambition and hard work, however, account for her enormous success. At the age of 17, Winfrey became a part-time radio newscaster on Nashville's WVOL. Two years later, while she was attending

Winfrey hosts her talk show.

Tennessee State University, she was hired as a reporter and anchor on WTVF-TV.

In 1976 Winfrey moved to Baltimore, where she found her niche in television as cohost of a Baltimore morning show called "People Are Talking." Winfrey's successful experience in Baltimore paved the way for her to become the undisputed "Queen of Talk" in Chicago.

In 1984 Winfrey took over the ailing "AM Chicago" on WLS-TV. She turned it into a smash hit, driving the successful "Phil Donahue Show" to another city and another time slot. In 1986 the "Oprah Winfrey Show" became nationally syndicated. Within months, it was the third highest rated show in syndication. It became the number one talk show, reaching between 9 and 10 million people daily in more than 190 cities and 12 foreign countries.

EXPANDING HORIZONS Winfrey became the first African American woman to own her own television and film production complex. Harpo Productions, Inc., (*Harpo* is *Oprah* spelled backwards) reaped about $50 million during the 1988-1989 season, when it assumed ownership and production of the "Oprah Winfrey Show."

By 1991, Oprah Winfrey's $80 million income placed her third on *Forbes* magazine's list of the richest entertainers in the business.

MAKING A DIFFERENCE Oprah Winfrey has used her wealth and influence to make a difference in the lives of others. "I'm starting a minority training program . . . specifically to bring more people of color into the film and television industry as producers," she explained. She also set up a "Little Sisters" program in Chicago's Cabrini Green housing project.

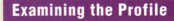

Examining the Profile

1. **Drawing Conclusions** Why is Oprah Winfrey considered one of the most powerful women in America?

2. **For Further Research** Find out about the many awards Oprah Winfrey has won. Make a time line of her career, showing major achievements.

Section Preview

Objectives

After studying this section, you will be able to:

1. **Explain** the development of the National Banking System.
2. **Relate** the effects of Depression-era bank failures on deposit insurance creation.
3. **Identify** three other forms of depository institutions.

Key Terms

dual banking system, Federal Reserve System, central bank, Federal Reserve note, run on the bank, bank holiday, commercial bank, demand deposit account, thrift institution, mutual savings bank, savings bank, Negotiable Order of Withdrawal, savings and loan association, share draft

Applying Economic Concepts

Demand Deposit Accounts You probably think that checking accounts are pretty useful. A number of post-Civil War bankers thought so, too. They developed *demand deposit accounts* as a way to avoid federal regulation of their activities, not to make life easier for their customers.

Banks fulfill two distinct needs in a community. They provide a safe place for people to deposit their money, and they lend excess funds to individuals and businesses temporarily in need of cash. In effect, banks act as economic institutions that bring savers and borrowers together.

The National Banking System

In 1863 the federal government tried to bring the state banks under control by passing the National Banking Act. It set up a system of nationally chartered and inspected banks known as the National Banking System. State banks were invited to become national banks by surrendering their state charters for federal ones.

National Bank Requirements

Those banks that joined the system had to fulfill certain requirements. One was to use *National* or *N.A.*, which stood for National Association, in their titles. The first bank in a community to join the system was generally called the First National Bank; the second, the Second National Bank; and so on. After a number of national banks existed in the community, new members used such titles as the People's National Bank of Commerce, Citizens' National Bank, and the Farmer's and Merchant's Trade Bank, N.A.

A second requirement was to pass stiff inspections by the Comptroller of the Currency, a Treasury Department official appointed by the President to supervise national banks. Because the inspections were rigorous, people knew that national banks, as a group, were relatively safe places to keep their deposits.

A third requirement was for banks to purchase government bonds, which were then used to back the national currency. This final requirement created a new demand for the war bonds that the government was trying to sell during the Civil War.

Dual Banking

Not all banks wanted to join the National Banking System. Some banks managed to remain independent even after the 10 percent tax was placed on privately issued bank notes. They decided to make loans by issuing checking accounts instead of currency.

Use of checking accounts was a relatively new idea. After several years of experimentation, however, many people discovered that checking accounts could be used effectively in place of currency. As a result, the number of state-chartered banks began to grow again after 1880. As shown in **Figure 11.3**, the number of state banks exceeded national banks by 1887.

By then the country had a well-established **dual banking system**—a system that allows banks to obtain charters from either the state or the federal government. Dual banking is a feature of banking

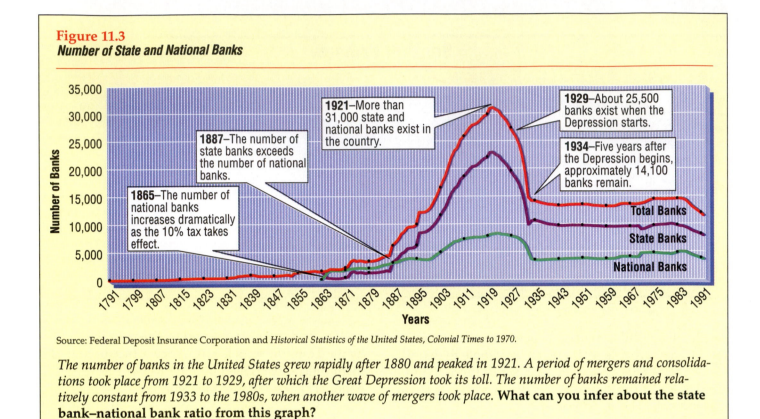

Figure 11.3
Number of State and National Banks

Source: Federal Deposit Insurance Corporation and Historical Statistics of the United States, Colonial Times to 1970.

The number of banks in the United States grew rapidly after 1880 and peaked in 1921. A period of mergers and consolidations took place from 1921 to 1929, after which the Great Depression took its toll. The number of banks remained relatively constant from 1933 to the 1980s, when another wave of mergers took place. **What can you infer about the state bank–national bank ratio from this graph?**

today, but a choice of charters was never the intent of the National Banking legislation when it was first enacted. Nor was it the intent of Congress when the 10 percent banknote tax was passed. Federal authorities just never thought that checking accounts would become so important.

Need for Further Reform

By 1910 banking reform again was needed. One major reason was that the National Banking System was not designed to deal with the unusually large number of checks being written. Checks written in one bank and deposited in another often took weeks to clear, even when the banks were in the same city.

Another reason for reform was that currency backed by government bonds was difficult to maintain. When the government started to run federal budget surpluses in the 1890s, it decided to reduce the public debt by buying back some of the bonds. Therefore, fewer bonds were available as reserves against the national bank notes.

A final problem was that banks had no place to go for help in times of need. When people needed to borrow money, they could go to a bank. When a national bank needed to borrow funds, however, it could only go to its competitors.

The Federal Reserve System

Reform came in 1913, when Congress created the **Federal Reserve System,** or Fed, to serve as the nation's first true **central bank**—a bank that can lend to other banks in times of need. All national banks were required to join the Fed, and all state-chartered banks were eligible to do so.

The member banks own the Federal Reserve System, although the President of the United States appoints its managers with the approval of Congress. The Fed also has its own currency, called **Federal Reserve notes,** that eventually replaced all other types of federal currency. Federal Reserve notes were backed by gold when first issued in 1914, but became inconvertible fiat money after 1934.

Banking During the Great Depression

Although the National Banking System and the Federal Reserve System were operational, many banks were only marginally sound during the 1920s. Part of the reason was the overabundance of banks, a result of the heated expansion that took place between 1880 and 1921. Although some consolidation occurred between 1921 and 1929, the banking industry was overextended when the Great Depression began in 1929.

Bank Failures

The number of bank failures during the 1930s was staggering! At the start of the Depression, about 25,500 banks existed—none of which had any deposit insurance for their customers. As a result, concern about the safety of the deposits often caused a **run on the bank**—a rush by depositors to withdraw their funds from a bank before it failed.

Panic was so widespread that on March 5, 1933, President Roosevelt announced a **bank holiday**—a brief period during which every bank in the country was required to close. Several days later, after Congress passed legislation that strengthened banking, most banks were allowed to reopen. By 1934 more than 10,000 banks had closed or merged with stronger partners. ✓

Federal Deposit Insurance

When banks failed during the Depression, people lost almost everything they had deposited. The Banking Act of 1933, sometimes known as the Glass-Steagall Act, was passed to strengthen the banking industry. Among other changes, the act created the Federal Deposit Insurance Corporation (FDIC) to insure customer deposits in the event of a bank failure. The initial coverage was only $2,500 per account, but it has since been increased to a maximum of $100,000. **1**

The insurance did little for those who lost their savings, but it has provided a sense of security in banking ever since. After the FDIC was created, people worried less about the safety of their deposits, reducing the number of runs on a bank.

Other Depository Institutions

Banks chartered by states or the National Banking System were generally known as **commercial banks** and were distinguished by two primary characteristics. First, they catered to the interests of business and commerce. Second, until the mid-1970s, they were the only financial institutions that issued **demand deposit accounts** (DDAs)—accounts whose funds could be removed by simply writing a check without prior approval from the depository institution. **2**

Other financial institutions accepted the deposits of small investors and, until the mid-1970s, generally did not have demand deposit accounts. These institutions included savings banks as well as savings and loan associations. Historically, they were called **thrift institutions,** or thrifts, because they generally paid higher rates of interest on savings accounts.

Savings Banks

One of the oldest savings institutions in the United States is the **mutual savings bank** (MSB), a depositor-owned financial organization operated only for the benefit of its depositors. Because they had no stockholders, boards of trustees made up of

---

QUICK CHECK

Checking Understanding

1. What is the purpose of the Federal Deposit Insurance Corporation?
2. What is a demand deposit account?

Applying Economic Concepts

 Bank Failures From March 5 to March 9, Secretary of the Treasury William Woodin and his advisers worked around the clock to hammer out legislation that would end the banking crisis.

businesspeople who served without pay managed MSBs. Later, many MSBs decided to sell stock to raise additional financial capital. These institutions became **savings banks** (SBs) because depositors do not mutually own them.

Mutual savings banks got their start in the early 1800s. At that time, commercial banks catered primarily to the needs of business and were not interested in the accounts of small wage earners. Savings banks emerged to fill that need. They were popular with consumers and began to spread west following the industrial growth of the large cities.

By the mid-1800s, commercial banks began to notice the savings accounts of factory workers and other wage earners. Commercial banks, along with the savings and loan associations of the period, began to compete more heavily with the savings banks. As a result, savings banks did not spread beyond their foothold in the industrial northeast and those states shown in **Figure 11.4**.

Even so, savings banks are a powerful influence in the economy. In 1972 the Consumer's Savings Bank of Worcester, Massachusetts, introduced a **Negotiable Order of Withdrawal (NOW) account,** a type of checking account that pays interest. Because commercial banks had a virtual monopoly on checking accounts at the time, they strongly opposed NOW accounts.

Despite the opposition, the savings banks had political power at the state level, and NOW accounts were allowed to remain in New England. At the national level, however, commercial bankers pushed for federal legislation that temporarily prevented NOW accounts from spreading outside New England. NOW accounts were not available to depository institutions nationwide until 1980.

Savings and Loan Associations

Another type of financial institution was the **savings and loan association** (S&L)—a financial institution that invested the majority of its funds in home mortgages. S&Ls began as cooperative clubs for home-builders in the 1800s. The association's members promised to deposit a certain sum regularly into the association. Members then took turns borrowing money to build a home. By doing this, people had an arrangement that

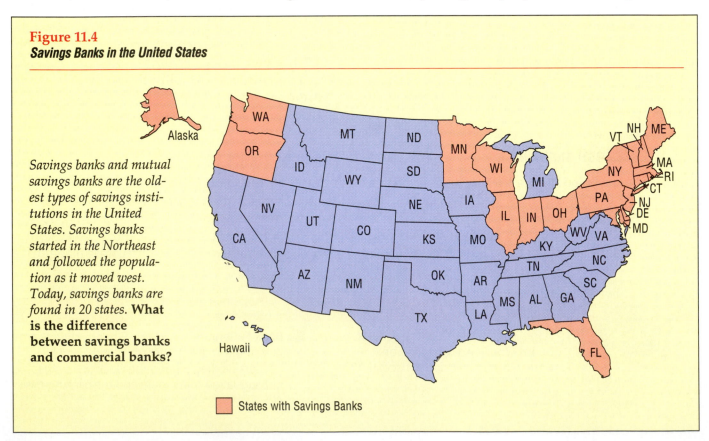

Figure 11.4
Savings Banks in the United States

Savings banks and mutual savings banks are the oldest types of savings institutions in the United States. Savings banks started in the Northeast and followed the population as it moved west. Today, savings banks are found in 20 states. **What is the difference between savings banks and commercial banks?**

☐ States with Savings Banks

individual savings and loan associations. The Board was modeled after components of the Federal Reserve System, which regulated commercial banks. The Federal Savings and Loan Insurance Corporation (FSLIC), a federal government agency much like the FDIC that serves commercial bankers, insured savings and loan deposits.

Credit Unions

A fourth type of depository institution is the credit union. Credit unions are owned and operated by and for their members. Costs are generally low because a sponsor, which may be the members' union or place of employment, often provides management, help, and office facilities.

Because most credit unions are organized around an employer, contributions generally are deducted directly from a worker's paycheck. In recent years, some credit unions followed the commercial and mutual savings banks by offering checking deposits. Known as **share drafts,** they look like any other check or NOW account and provide members with a way to earn interest on deposits that are also available on demand.

Credit union assets are the loans they make to members. Although these assets generally are relatively small, credit unions outnumber commercial banks, S&Ls, or mutual savings banks.

supplied funds for home-building in areas where other sources of financing were not available.

Later, in the 1930s, the Federal Home Loan Bank Board was created to supervise and regulate the

---

SECTION 3
REVIEW

Reviewing Terms and Facts

1. **Define** dual banking system, Federal Reserve System, central bank, Federal Reserve note, run on the bank, bank holiday, commercial bank, demand deposit account, thrift institution, mutual savings bank, savings bank, Negotiable Order of Withdrawal, savings and loan association, share draft.
2. **Explain** why the National Banking System was created.
3. **Explain** why deposit insurance developed in the 1930s.
4. **Identify** three depository institutions.

Critical Thinking

5. **Identifying Alternatives** The FDIC insures deposits up to $100,000. What would you do if you had $400,000 you wanted to deposit and insure?

Applying Economic Concepts

6. **Demand Deposit Accounts** When Adam Smith wrote *An Inquiry into the Nature and Causes of the Wealth of Nations,* he argued that a competitive economy functioned best when everyone pursued their own best interests. Explain how the self-interest of state-chartered banks in 1865 led to the development of demand deposit accounts.

Crisis, Reform, and Evolution in the 1980s

Section Preview

Objectives

After studying this section, you will be able to:

1. **Explain** the forces leading to deregulation of financial institutions in the 1980s.
2. **Relate** the history of the savings and loan crisis.

Key Terms

deregulation, Regulation Q

Applying Economic Concepts

Deregulation Has your school ever relaxed the dress code for a day? Do you know someone who took advantage of the *deregulation,* or the relaxation of rules, by wearing something inappropriate? The government deregulated the savings and loan industry in the 1980s. Some of those institutions did exactly the same thing—they acted inappropriately.

Because of the massive banking failures during the Great Depression, financial institutions were closely regulated from 1933 through the 1970s. The regulations even applied to maximum rates of interest that could be paid on various accounts, as well as to restrictions on how and to whom the institutions could lend their funds. **1**

By the late 1970s, almost all financial institutions—commercial banks, savings banks, and savings and loan associations—were begging for relief from federal regulations. When President Ronald Reagan was elected in 1980, the political climate changed, allowing **deregulation,** the removal or relaxation of government restrictions on business. ☑

A Decade of Deregulation

Commercial bankers and the savings and loan associations were the two main groups demanding deregulation. As a result of their lobbying, Congress relaxed restrictions on their activities. A closer look at the historical differences between the various types of financial institutions explains the desire for deregulation.

A Level Playing Field

Before 1980, Congress allowed savings banks and savings and loan associations to pay more interest on

Banking Practices *Most banks offer some form of electronic banking, including services for handicapped people.* **Why did financial institutions want deregulation?**

savings accounts than commercial banks paid. Commercial bankers, who felt at a competitive disadvantage, wanted legislation allowing them to pay the same interest rates as savings banks and S&Ls. The S&Ls were upset, however, because commercial banks and the New England savings banks could issue checking accounts, while they could not.

The savings and loans favored legislation that would allow them to have demand deposit accounts.

The Ohio S&L Crisis *Prior to 1985, all state-chartered savings institutions in Ohio were insured by a single, privately owned insurance company. The collapse of Home State Savings in March of that year triggered runs by depositors, which forced the governor to close every state-chartered thrift in the state.* **How did inadequate insurance contribute to the crisis in Ohio?**

They also wanted to make short-term, high-interest-rate loans on automobiles and other personal items that commercial banks made. At the same time, commercial banks wanted to make long-term, very stable, home-ownership loans dominated by the S&Ls. Because federal regulations governed their loans, none of the institutions could change the types of loans they were making without further legislation.

By the end of the 1970s, each type of financial institution seemed convinced that the others had an unfair advantage. By 1979 everyone was calling for a "level playing field" that would treat all financial institutions the same.

Deregulation Legislation

Sweeping deregulation took place in 1980 with the passage of the Depository Institutions Deregulation and Monetary Control Act (DIDMCA). The law had several provisions that reduced the differences between competing institutions.

First, **Regulation Q,** the federal requirement that set maximum interest rates on savings accounts, was to be phased out. This action eliminated the advantage that savings banks and S&Ls had over commercial banks when it came to paying higher interest rates on savings accounts. **2**

Second, NOW accounts could be offered on a nationwide basis by any type of financial institution. This provision eliminated the historical advantage that commercial banks had with their check issuing powers, and it eliminated the more recent advantage gained by the New England savings banks with their NOW accounts in 1972.

Third, all depository institutions could borrow from the Federal Reserve System in times of need, a privilege previously reserved for commercial banks. In return, all depository institutions were to set aside

Checking Understanding

1. Why were financial institutions closely regulated until the 1970s?
2. What was Regulation Q?

Applying Economic Concepts

 Deregulation In President Reagan's view, business and industry were hamstrung by government red tape. He believed this kept companies less profitable than they might otherwise be and accounted for some of the weaknesses in the American economy.

a certain percent of their customer's deposits in the form of a reserve. The primary purpose of this provision was to give the Fed more control over state-chartered financial institutions.

The Garn-St. Germain Act of 1982 accelerated deregulation by allowing S&Ls and savings banks to enter activities traditionally reserved for commercial banks. These activities included issuing credit cards, non-residential real estate loans, and commercial loans. By the mid-1980s, however, the effects of deregulation would precipitate a crisis in the savings and loan industry.

The Savings and Loan Crisis

The S&L crisis unfolded slowly during the 1980s. In 1980 the United States had 4,600 S&Ls. By mid-1988 bankruptcies and mergers reduced the number to about 3,000. By the mid-1990s fewer than 2,000 institutions survived. These failures and mergers can be traced to four major problem areas.

Deregulation

One of the causes of the savings and loan crisis was deregulation itself. S&L executives hoped to compete in new markets, but they often found themselves on unfamiliar ground. In addition, many S&Ls faced increased competition from commercial banks after the interest rate ceilings were removed.

High Interest Rates

Another major problem the S&L industry faced was the losses brought on by high interest rates in the mid-1970s and early 1980s. The institutions had made a number of long-term loans to homeowners and builders at low rates, often less than 10 percent, in the 1970s. By 1980, however, some interest rates had increased to more than 15 percent. S&Ls were in an unprofitable situation because they paid depositors more than 10 percent interest on short-term deposits but received less than 10 percent on money loaned out several years before. **1**

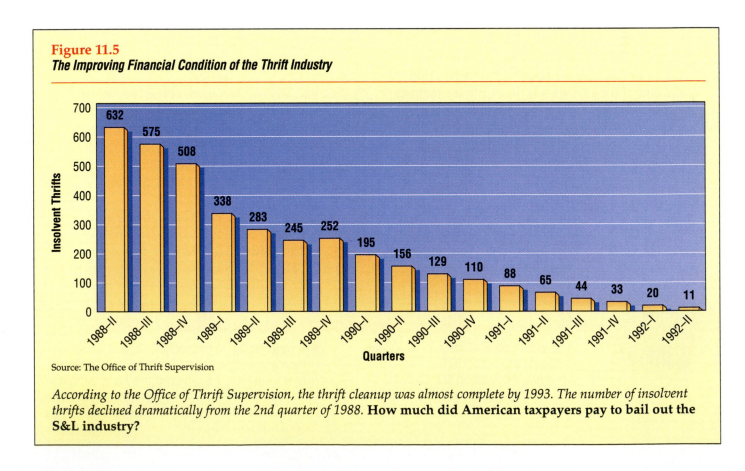

Figure 11.5
The Improving Financial Condition of the Thrift Industry

Source: The Office of Thrift Supervision

According to the Office of Thrift Supervision, the thrift cleanup was almost complete by 1993. The number of insolvent thrifts declined dramatically from the 2nd quarter of 1988. **How much did American taxpayers pay to bail out the S&L industry?**

Financial Reform *The FDIC insures banks like the one shown here. After the S&L crisis, the FDIC assumed insurance responsibilities for the thrift industry.* **What agency supervises S&Ls today?**

Inadequate Capital

Most financial institutions have capital reserves that can be used as a cushion to absorb losses when loans fail. Congress, however, gave the savings and loan industry permission to operate with low capital reserves—reserves that were approximately one-half the amount of those commercial banks kept. Bad loans made in the early 1980s hit the S&L industry especially hard, forcing many out of business.

Fraud

One of the consequences of deregulation was a reduced number of inspectors that verified compliance with all of the rules and regulations. As a result, a few institutions were able to engage in fraud on a scale seldom seen before.

Although the number of fraudulent institutions was small, they handled relatively large amounts of money. When they failed, a tremendous drain was put on the reserves of the FSLIC, the federal agency that insured S&Ls.

Reforming the Thrift Industry

The Financial Institutions Reform, Recovery, and Enforcement Act (FIRREA) was passed in 1989. This act effectively abolished the independence of the savings and loan industry and is regarded by many as

---

QUICK CHECK

Checking Understanding

1. How did high interest rates affect the S&L industry?

Applying Economic Concepts

☑ **Fraud** Officers in institutions such as Lincoln Savings and Loan in California made large loans to businesses that had little chance of succeeding. Often, the bankers knew—or even chose from their own circle of friends—the business's top executives.

the most significant financial legislation passed since the Depression.

Abolishing the FHLBB

Congress abolished the Federal Home Loan Bank Board, the supervisory body in charge of the S&L industry. Its functions were distributed to a new agency, the Office of Thrift Supervision (OTS).

The OTS is a part of the United States Treasury and has more than 2,000 employees and a budget of $200 million. Therefore, the executive branch of government, rather than an independent agency, now supervises the S&L industry.

Changing Federal Deposit Insurance

After 1989 the FSLIC's insurance responsibilities were transferred to the Federal Deposit Insurance Corporation. Rather than combine the insurance funds of the banks and the S&Ls, two separate funds were set up. The first was the Savings Association Insurance Fund (SAIF) for savings banks and savings and loan associations. The second was the Bank Insurance Fund (BIF), which insured commercial banks.

Disposing of Failed Thrifts

All deposits with savings and loans, including those that failed, were insured to a maximum of $100,000. Before FIRREA, the FSLIC would try to sell or merge the failed institution with a stable S&L in the area. If that was not possible, the FSLIC would try to recover as much money as it could from the failed institution and use the proceeds, along with FSLIC reserves, to pay depositors.

After FIRREA, a temporary agency called the Resolution Trust Corporation (RTC) was set up to dispose of failed thrifts. Because failed thrifts numbered in the hundreds, and because billions of dollars had to be paid out to depositors under the terms of the deposit insurance, Congress had to appropriate billions for the bailout.

As shown in Figure 11.5, the number of insolvent thrifts declined substantially between 1988 and 1992. The exact cost of the bailout may not be known for years, because it includes items such as future borrowing costs and legal fees that will extend well into the next century. Most experts estimate that the cost will eventually range from $300 to $500 billion—or about $1,500 for every man, woman, and child in the United States.

Allowing Sound Institutions to Continue

Many S&Ls were profitable during the crisis. These institutions were allowed to continue operations. In addition, many kept the words *savings and loan association* in the title. Others, however, chose to change their names to distance themselves from the crisis that tarnished so many reputations. Perhaps the most visible outward change is that notices posted at the entrance of S&Ls now say that the FDIC rather than the FSLIC insures the institutions.

SECTION 4
REVIEW

Reviewing Terms and Facts

1. **Define** deregulation, Regulation Q.
2. **Describe** the forces that led to deregulation.
3. **Explain** four causes of the savings and loan industry crisis.

Critical Thinking

4. **Identifying Central Issues** Which of the four causes of the S&L crisis do you think played the central role? Explain your answer.

Applying Economic Concepts

5. **Deregulation** List at least two other major industries in the United States economy that have been deregulated. How has deregulation affected these industries?

Vocabulary

The following terms are defined in Chapter 11:

SECTION ONE

- barter economy (p. 266)
- money (p. 266)
- medium of exchange (p. 266)
- measure of value (p. 266)
- store of value (p. 266)
- commodity money (p. 267)
- fiat money (p. 267)
- wampum (p. 267)
- specie (p. 268)
- bullion (p. 268)
- monetary unit (p. 269)

SECTION TWO

- monetary standard (p. 272)
- state bank (p. 272)
- wildcat bank (p. 273)
- legal tender (p. 274)
- greenback (p. 274)
- United States note (p. 274)
- National Banking System (p. 274)
- national bank (p. 274)
- National Bank note (p. 274)
- national currency (p. 274)
- gold certificate (p. 275)
- silver certificate (p. 275)
- Treasury coin note (p. 275)
- gold standard (p. 275)
- inconvertible fiat money standard (p. 276)

SECTION THREE

- dual banking system (p. 279)
- Federal Reserve System (p. 280)
- central bank (p. 280)
- Federal Reserve note (p. 280)
- run on the bank (p. 281)
- bank holiday (p. 281)
- commercial bank (p. 281)
- demand deposit account (p. 281)
- thrift institution (p. 281)
- mutual savings bank (p. 281)
- savings bank (p. 282)
- Negotiable Order of Withdrawal (p. 282)
- savings and loan association (p. 282)
- share draft (p. 283)

SECTION FOUR

- deregulation (p. 284)
- Regulation Q (p. 285)

Section 1 The Evolution of Money (pages 266–270)

Money is any substance that serves as a medium of exchange, a measure of value, and a store of value. All successful monies have 4 characteristics: portability, durability, divisibility, and stability in value.

Reviewing the Main Idea
What are characteristics and functions of money?

Section 2 Early Banking and Monetary Standards (pages 272–277)

A country uses a **monetary standard** to maintain the value of its currency. From the Revolution to the Civil War, privately owned state-chartered banks issued paper currency. In 1861 the national government sold bonds and printed **greenbacks** to finance the Civil War. Later, other federal currencies became popular, including **gold certificates, silver certificates, Treasury coin notes,** and **national currency.**

The **gold standard** was adopted in 1900. In 1934, however, the country went on an **inconvertible fiat money standard**, which meant that **Federal Reserve notes** and greenbacks could not be converted to gold.

Reviewing the Main Idea
Why does a country use a monetary standard?

Section 3 The Development of Modern Banking (pages 279–283)

The establishment of the National Banking System in 1863 brought uniformity to the banking system. The Comptroller of the Currency inspected member banks. The country also had a **dual banking system** because many state-chartered banks did not join the NBS. In addition to **commercial banks,** other depository institutions included **mutual savings banks, credit unions,** and **savings and loan associations.**

Reviewing the Main Idea
Where could money be deposited after 1863?

Section 4 Crisis, Reform, and Evolution in the 1980s (pages 284–288)

Deregulation, high interest rates, inadequate financial reserves, and fraud in the 1980s hurt the savings and loan associations. Congress abolished the separate status of the industry in 1989. Supervisory authority was transferred to the Office of Thrift Supervision.

Reviewing the Main Idea
How did deregulation affect financial institutions?

Reviewing Key Terms

Place each of the vocabulary terms in its correct historical period(s).

Historical Periods:
 a. Colonial: 1607–1776
 b. Pre-Civil War: 1789–1861
 c. Civil War-Pre-Depression: 1861–1929
 d. Depression: 1929–1939
 e. World War II-FIRREA: 1940–1989
 f. 1989–today

1. United States note _____
2. commercial bank _____
3. Continental dollar _____
4. deregulation _____
5. dual banking system _____
6. Federal Reserve System _____
7. gold certificate _____
8. gold standard _____
9. greenback _____
10. inconvertible fiat money standard _____
11. legal tender _____
12. mutual savings bank _____
13. national bank _____
14. wildcat bank _____
15. Negotiable Order of Withdrawal _____
16. run on the bank _____
17. savings and loan association _____
18. silver certificate _____
19. specie _____
20. state bank _____
21. Treasury coin note _____

Reviewing the Facts

SECTION 1 *(pages 266–270)*
 1. **List** the three functions of money.
 2. **Describe** five types of early money.

 3. **Discuss** the major forms of money used in the colonial period of United States history—1607–1776.
 4. **Explain** the relationship between the Spanish peso, the Austrian taler, and the United States dollar.
 5. **List** the four characteristics that give money its value.

SECTION 2 *(pages 272–277)*
 6. **Describe** the paper currencies used from the period of the American Revolution to the time of the Civil War.
 7. **Explain** the importance of the greenback during the Civil War.
 8. **Describe** two advantages and two disadvantages of a gold standard.
 9. **Evaluate** modern money as a medium of exchange.

SECTION 3 *(pages 279–283)*
 10. **List** three requirements for joining the National Banking System.
 11. **Describe** the main difference between the Federal Reserve System and the National Banking System.
 12. **Explain** why many banks failed during the Great Depression.
 13. **List** three other depository institutions in addition to commercial banks.

SECTION 4 *(pages 284–288)*
 14. **Identify** the financial institutions clamoring for deregulation in the 1970s.
 15. **Explain** why many savings and loan institutions were not strong enough to absorb the shocks of high interest rates and deregulation.
 16. **Describe** the status of the savings and loan industry today.

Critical Thinking

1. **Drawing Conclusions** Do you think the savings and loan crisis and the subsequent provisions of FIRREA characterized a revolution or an evolution of the banking system? Explain your answer.

2. **Expressing Problems Clearly** Design a chart you would use to test the stability of a depository institution.

Applying Economic Concepts

1. **Money** Ask your friends, parents, and neighbors if they have any examples of old currency. If so, make a note of (a) the name of the currency (gold certificate, silver certificate, United States note, etc.); (b) the date on the currency; (c) any mention of backing (silver certificates backed by silver dollars).

2. **Barter** Assume that you live in a bartering society. Organize a list of 10 items that you use frequently, and then identify alternate goods of comparable worth that you would be willing to trade for them.

Reinforcing Skills

DETERMINING RELEVANCE

A student preparing a report about money wants to illustrate her speech with photographs of commodity money. She shows you photographs of the following items. Which of the photographs would be relevant to her topic? Explain your answers.

1. a Phoenician coin
2. compressed tea leaves
3. wampum
4. folded tobacco
5. a tetradrachm
6. shelled corn

Individual Activity

Assume that the country is returning to privately issued bank notes such as those used before the Civil War. Design the currency you would like to see in circulation.

Cooperative Learning Activity

Working in groups of four, have each member survey one of the following financial institutions: a commercial bank, a savings and loan association, a savings bank (if one exists in your community), and a credit union. List the services that each offers. Compare your lists as a group, and then discuss the differences with the entire class.

Writing About Economics

THE INFORMATIVE STYLE

In the **Journal Writing** activity on page 265, you were asked to write the advertising claims you read or hear about from the financial institutions in your area. Group the advertising claims into four categories: commercial banks, savings banks, savings and loan institutions, and credit unions. Using the informative style of writing discussed on page 554, compare the ads of each group to differentiate the services provided and the costs charged by each type of institution.

The Federal Reserve Bank for the 12th Federal District is located in San Francisco, California.

CHAPTER 12

The Federal Reserve System and Monetary Policy

SECTION 1
The Federal Reserve System

SECTION 2
Monetary Policy

SECTION 3
Monetary Policy, Banking, and the Economy

CHAPTER PREVIEW

People to Know
- Milton Friedman
- Actuary

Applying Economic Concepts to Your Life

Stability in Value One feature of money that you rely on is that it is worth about the same amount from one year to the next. Money must have *stability in value* to function as it should—and many factors ensure that money has this feature.

Journal Writing

For one week, analyze the currency that comes into your possession. In your journal, keep track of the features that appear on the front and back of each bill, noting the similarities and differences between the various currencies.

The Federal Reserve System

Section Preview

Objectives

After studying this section, you will be able to:

1. **Identify** the primary regulatory agencies for each type of depository institution.
2. **Describe** the structure of the Federal Reserve System.
3. **Explain** the major regulatory responsibilities of the Fed.

Key Terms

member bank, bank holding company, truth-in-lending laws, Regulation Z, currency, coins, margin requirement

Applying Economic Concepts

Truth-in-Lending Laws Have you or your parents ever bought anything on credit? Have you ever had the salesperson explain the terms of the loan, and then ask you to sign forms saying that everything has been explained to you? All of this was done because of *truth-in-lending laws* that were designed to protect you, the consumer.

On December 23, 1913, Congress passed legislation creating the Federal Reserve System, or the Fed, as America's central bank. Today the Fed consists of the 12 districts shown in **Figure 12.1**, with its headquarters in Washington, D.C. The Fed serves as a clearinghouse for checks and has the power to control the money supply. In one way or another, its activities affect nearly all financial institutions in the United States.

The Fed and Other Regulatory Agencies

The differences between commercial banks, savings banks, savings institutions (savings and loans), and credit unions has narrowed considerably since 1980. Almost all institutions accept deposits, make loans, and offer checking accounts as well as other services. The differences between the types of financial institutions are so minor that people generally select a financial institution merely on the basis of convenience.

Despite the growing similarities, 5 principal regulatory bodies supervise the approximately 27,000 depository institutions in the United States. These agencies, along with the institutions they regulate, are shown in **Figure 12.2**.

The interesting aspect of the figure is the relatively small number of depository institutions, amounting to 3.5 percent of the total, that have the Federal

Reserve System as their primary regulator. These institutions are the 957 state-chartered banks that have chosen to become members of the Fed.

The Comptroller of the Currency supervises national banks, or banks with national charters, even though these banks also belong to the Fed. Banking agencies in the 50 states and the FDIC supervise state-chartered commercial banks that are not Fed members. Despite the small number of institutions the Fed directly regulates and inspects, however, its influence on the American economy is enormous.

Structure of the Fed

In 1993 the United States had more than 11,000 commercial banks. Almost 40 percent of these banks were **member banks**—banks that belonged to the Federal Reserve System.

Private Ownership

One of the unique features of the Fed is that member banks actually own it. As **Figure 12.3** illustrates, each member bank must contribute a small amount of financial capital upon joining. In return, each receives stock in the Federal Reserve System. Just like any other corporation, the Fed pays dividends to the commercial banks that own the stock. Because of the stock ownership feature, private commercial banks, not the federal government, own the Fed.

The private ownership has another privilege. The member banks also elect directors for each of the 12 district banks, and these directors in turn elect the district presidents. As a result, the banks in each district determine the makeup of the boards and the selection of the presidents of the 12 district banks.

Board of Governors

The President of the United States appoints the 7–member Federal Reserve Board of Governors to 14–year terms. Working out of Washington, D.C., the Board of Governors directs and controls the activities of the Fed. The Senate must confirm each appointment, and the appointments are staggered so that 1 vacancy must be filled every 2 years. One of the Board members serves as chairperson.

The Board is primarily a regulatory and supervisory agency. It sets general policies for Federal Reserve and member banks to follow, regulates certain operations of state-chartered member commercial banks, and conducts some aspects of monetary policy. It also makes a report each year to Congress and puts out a monthly bulletin that reports on national and international monetary matters.

Federal Open Market Committee

The Federal Open Market Committee (FOMC) makes decisions about the growth of the money supply and the level of interest rates. It includes the 7 members of the Board of Governors and 5 district Reserve bank presidents who serve 1-year rotating terms.

The committee meets about 8 times a year in Washington, D.C., to review the country's economy and make decisions about the cost and availability of credit. Most decisions are made in secret and are not revealed for several weeks.

Federal Advisory Council

The 12 district banks provide feedback to the Federal Reserve Board on matters concerning the overall health of the economy. This advice is offered through the Federal Advisory Council (FAC). It is made up of 12 members, each of whom is appointed by the

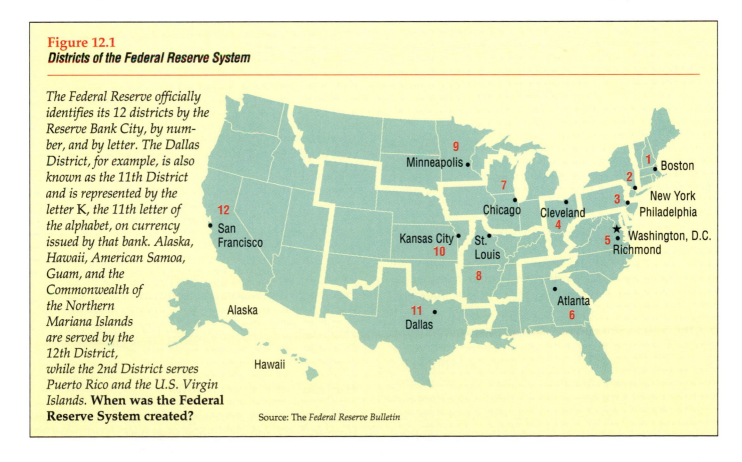

Figure 12.1
Districts of the Federal Reserve System

The Federal Reserve officially identifies its 12 districts by the Reserve Bank City, by number, and by letter. The Dallas District, for example, is also known as the 11th District and is represented by the letter K, the 11th letter of the alphabet, on currency issued by that bank. Alaska, Hawaii, American Samoa, Guam, and the Commonwealth of the Northern Mariana Islands are served by the 12th District, while the 2nd District serves Puerto Rico and the U.S. Virgin Islands. **When was the Federal Reserve System created?**

Source: The *Federal Reserve Bulletin*

Figure 12.2
Primary Regulators of Depository Institutions

The Fed regulates only 3.5% of all institutions, or about 8.4% of all commercial banks. **What financial institutions are regulated by the FDIC?**

Source: FDIC *Statistics on Banking, 1992* and the National Credit Union Association (NCUA)

	Type of Charter or Insurance Fund	Number of Institutions	Percent of Institutions	Primary Regulator
Commercial Banks	National Charter, Fed Member	3,594	13.3%	**Comptroller of the Currency**
	State Charter, Fed Member	957	3.5%	**Federal Reserve System**
	State Charter, Nonmember	6,914	25.6%	**Federal Deposit Insurance Corporation**
Savings Banks	Bank Insurance Fund (BIF) and Savings Assn Insurance Fund (SAIF)	532	2.0%	**Federal Deposit Insurance Corporation, Office of Thrift Supervision**
Savings Institutions	BIF	414	1.5%	**Federal Deposit Insurance Corporation**
	SAIF	1,977	7.3%	**Office of Thrift Supervision**
Credit Unions	State or Federal Charters	12,594	46.8%	**National Credit Union Association**
Total Depository Institutions		26,982		

member banks in the region. The FAC has little impact on the daily operations of the Fed, and meets with the Board only 4 times a year.

Responsibilities of the Fed

Many people think that the Fed is responsible for the on-site examinations and inspections that help ensure the soundness of the nation's banks. This task is but a minor part of the Fed's responsibilities because fewer than 10 percent of the commercial banks in the United States have the Fed as their primary regulator. **1**

The regulatory role of the Fed is much broader than inspections and examinations. It includes many regulatory functions and policy issues that concern safety and soundness in banking.

State Member Bank Supervision

All depository institutions—including commercial banks, savings banks, savings institutions, and credit unions—must maintain reserves against their customers' deposits. The Fed is responsible for monitoring the reserves of its state-chartered member banks, while other federal agencies monitor the reserves of nonmember banks and other depository institutions.

Originally, reserves were a matter of prudent banking practice, but today reserves fulfill two key roles. First, the banks use them to clear checks. Second, the Fed uses them to control the size of the money supply.

Holding Companies

The Fed also has broad legislative authority over **bank holding companies**—a form of corporation that owns one or more banks. Holding companies, unlike banks, do not accept deposits or make loans. They are simply corporate structures that own other banks. As a result, when people buy stock in a bank today, they generally purchase the stock of the holding company, which in turn owns one or more individual banks.

This arrangement may seem unusual, but the reasons for it are historical. Because of the bank failures during the Great Depression, many restrictions were put on banks. Bankers, in turn, tried to get around the restrictions by setting up holding companies that would not be subject to banking laws because they were not banks in the traditional sense. Later, Congress gave the Fed the power to regulate the activities of the holding companies so that they could not evade restrictions.

Today about 6,500 holding companies control approximately 8,500 commercial banks. In many cases, the holding company structure has resulted in even more regulation and supervision. For example, the FDIC may inspect and regulate 3 nonmember state banks that a single holding company owns, while the Fed regulates the holding company itself.

International Operations

Foreign banks have a large presence in the economy. By mid-1993, foreign banks operated more than 500

Figure 12.3
Structure of the Federal Reserve System

The Fed has a fairly simple organizational structure. The system is supervised by a 7-member Board of Governors appointed by the President and confirmed by the Senate. The Board also dominates the FOMC, which has primary responsibility for monetary policy. The member banks contribute a small amount of funds to the Fed and receive stock ownership shares in return. The member banks also provide advice to the Board through the Federal Advisory Council, which has one representative for every district bank. **What functions does the Board of Governors perform?**

FEDERAL OPEN MARKET COMMITTEE
Composition: 7 members of the Board of Governors, 5 presidents of district banks
Function: decides monetary policies

BOARD OF GOVERNORS
Composition: 7 members appointed by the President to 14-year terms
Function: supervises and regulates the Fed

FEDERAL ADVISORY COUNCIL
Composition: 1 representative from each of the 12 banks
Function: advises Board of Governors about the economy

12 DISTRICT BANKS

contributes funds   receives stock

MEMBER BANKS
Approximately 3,600 national and 950 state banks

---

branches and agencies in the United States. In addition, foreign banks owned shares of many large United States banks. In all, foreign banks control about 25 percent of all banking assets in the United States.

The Fed has broad authority to supervise and regulate these foreign banks. Branches and agencies of these banks are examined annually, and the Fed even has the power to terminate the domestic operations of foreign banks. **2**

In addition, the Fed authorizes and supervises the international operations of United States member banks and holding companies. Currently, member banks operate about 800 branches in foreign countries.

Mergers

A merger of two or more banks requires the approval of the appropriate federal banking authority. If the surviving bank is a state member bank, the Fed must approve the merger.

Banking authorities also approve other mergers. If two national banks merge, the Comptroller of the Currency must approve the merger. If two nonmember state banks merge, the appropriate federal agency for approval is the FDIC.

Figure 11.3 on page 280 shows the effect of mergers since 1980. The numerous mergers during this period substantially reduced the number of banks.

QUICK CHECK

Checking Understanding
1. Why are on-site inspections a minor role for the Fed?
2. Who regulates foreign banks that do business in the United States?

Applying Economic Concepts
✓ **Money Supply** About $1,038 worth of currency is in circulation for each of the more than 250 million Americans, yet the Fed can account for only about $260 per person. Officials think people in other countries hold the rest—about $196 billion.

Figure 12.4
Clearing a Check

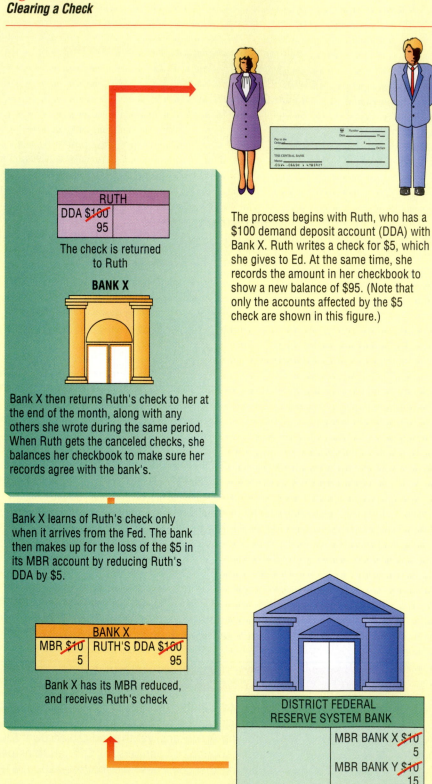

RUTH
DDA $~~100~~
95

The check is returned
to Ruth

BANK X

The process begins with Ruth, who has a $100 demand deposit account (DDA) with Bank X. Ruth writes a check for $5, which she gives to Ed. At the same time, she records the amount in her checkbook to show a new balance of $95. (Note that only the accounts affected by the $5 check are shown in this figure.)

ED
DDA $~~100~~
105

Ed deposits
check

BANK Y

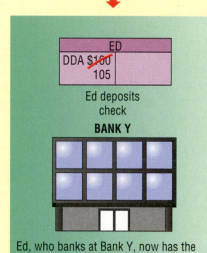

Bank X then returns Ruth's check to her at the end of the month, along with any others she wrote during the same period. When Ruth gets the canceled checks, she balances her checkbook to make sure her records agree with the bank's.

Ed, who banks at Bank Y, now has the check. If he decides to cash it, he will have $5 in currency in addition to his DDA of $100. If he decides to make a deposit, his DDA will rise to $105. Either way, Bank Y ends up with the check written by Ruth.

Bank X learns of Ruth's check only when it arrives from the Fed. The bank then makes up for the loss of the $5 in its MBR account by reducing Ruth's DDA by $5.

Because the check is drawn on Bank X, Bank Y gets payment for it by sending the check to the district Federal Reserve Bank. The Fed then processes the check by transferring $5 from Bank X's MBR account to Bank Y's MBR account. The Fed then sends Ruth's check to Bank X.

BANK X	
MBR $~~10~~ 5	RUTH'S DDA $~~100~~ 95

Bank X has its MBR reduced,
and receives Ruth's check

BANK Y	
MBR $~~10~~ 15	ED'S DDA $~~100~~ 105

Bank Y sends check to the Fed
district bank for payment

DISTRICT FEDERAL RESERVE SYSTEM BANK	
	MBR BANK X $~~10~~ 5
	MBR BANK Y $~~10~~ 15

Check Clearing

One major service the Fed performs is clearing checks, a process that makes extensive use of the reserves in the banking system. In general, reserves in the system are shifted from one bank to another, depending on the way checks are written on the member banks.

Figure 12.4 illustrates the check-clearing process. The person in the example writes a $5 check. As the check is processed through the banking system, funds are moved from one member bank's account to another until the check returns to the issuer. The money is then removed from the issuer's checking account.

The Fed clears millions of checks at any given time. To accomplish this task, it uses the latest high-speed, check-sorting equipment available. In some cases banks gather information from a check when it is deposited, and then transfer the information to computer files. These files are sent to the Fed, which uses the information to adjust member banks' accounts. In this way, the member bank's balance can be adjusted without the check having to go through the entire system.

Consumer Legislation

The Fed is responsible for some consumer legislation, primarily **truth-in-lending laws** that require sellers to make complete and accurate disclosures to people who buy on credit. Under a provision called **Regulation Z**, truth-in-lending disclosures are extended to millions of individuals by corporations, retail stores, automobile dealers, banks, and lending institutions.

If you buy furniture or a car on credit, you will discover that the seller must explain several items before

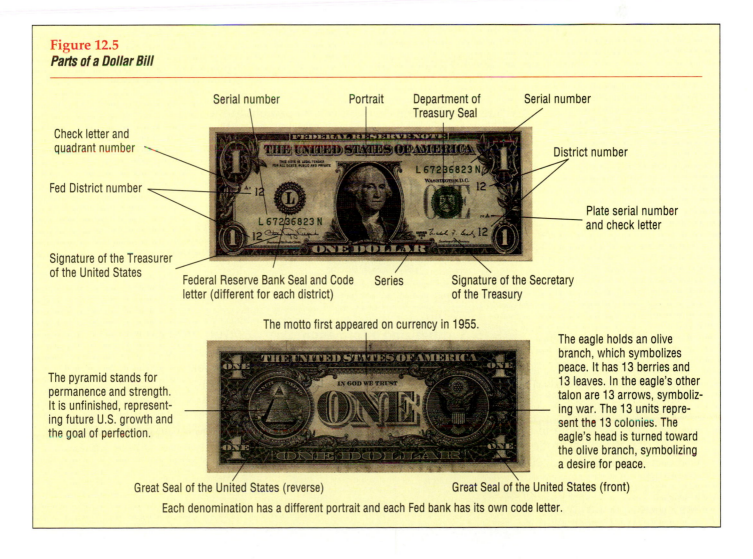

Figure 12.5
Parts of a Dollar Bill

Serial number — Portrait — Department of Treasury Seal — Serial number

Check letter and quadrant number

Fed District number

Signature of the Treasurer of the United States

Federal Reserve Bank Seal and Code letter (different for each district)

Series

Signature of the Secretary of the Treasury

District number

Plate serial number and check letter

The motto first appeared on currency in 1955.

The pyramid stands for permanence and strength. It is unfinished, representing future U.S. growth and the goal of perfection.

The eagle holds an olive branch, which symbolizes peace. It has 13 berries and 13 leaves. In the eagle's other talon are 13 arrows, symbolizing war. The 13 units represent the 13 colonies. The eagle's head is turned toward the olive branch, symbolizing a desire for peace.

Great Seal of the United States (reverse)

Great Seal of the United States (front)

Each denomination has a different portrait and each Fed bank has its own code letter.

you make the purchase. These items include the size of the down payment, the number and size of the monthly payments, and the total amount of interest over the life of the loan. In general terms, Congress mandates that appropriate disclosures be made. The Fed then decides on the specific type of information that would be of the most value to consumers.

Currency

Today's **currency,** the paper component of the money supply, is made up of Federal Reserve notes—fiat paper money issued by Federal Reserve banks and printed at the Bureau of Engraving and Printing. This currency, issued in amounts of $1, $2, $5, $10, $20, $50, and $100, is distributed to the Fed district banks for storage. These banks send it to member banks on request.

When tellers in banks come across currency that is mutilated or cannot be used for other reasons, they ship it to the Fed to be replaced. The Fed then destroys the old currency so that it cannot be put back into circulation. **Figure 12.5** illustrates some of the features of Federal Reserve notes.

The Bureau of the Mint produces **coins,** metallic forms of money, such as pennies, nickels, and dimes. After the coins are minted, they are shipped to the Fed district banks for storage until member banks need them.

Margin Requirements

Before the Great Depression, people speculated wildly on stocks. Easy credit in the form of **margin requirements,** minimum deposits left with a stockbroker to be used as down payments to buy other securities, made much of the speculation possible. For example, with a margin requirement as low as 10 percent, a person had to deposit only $100 with a stockbroker to purchase $1,000 worth of stocks. The stockbroker would supply the remaining $900.

If the stock rose to $1,300, it could be sold and the investor would net $400 after repaying the $900. If, however, the stock dropped to $900, the broker would sell the stock to protect his or her own loan if the investor could not come up with additional margin. Because credit was so easy to get and the margins were so easy to forfeit with even small drops in stock prices, many investors lost everything they had when stock prices crashed in 1929.

Today margin requirements are set at 50 percent for most stocks and bonds, meaning an investor has to put up at least half the money needed to buy eligible stocks and bonds. This requirement has been as high as 80 percent in the past, and is at the discretion of the Fed. The Fed also monitors stock market activity and publishes a list of stocks that are eligible for margin loans.

**SECTION 1
REVIEW**

Reviewing Terms and Facts

1. **Define** member bank, bank holding company, truth-in-lending law, Regulation Z, currency, coins, margin requirement.
2. **Describe** the structure of the Fed.
3. **Identify** the percentage of the nation's depository institutions and banks that the Fed directly regulates.
4. **List** eight areas in which the Fed has legal responsibility.

Critical Thinking

5. **Synthesizing Information** One of the responsibilities of the Fed is to approve or disapprove of mergers between state member banks. Explain how the mergers of two such banks would be classified according to the discussion of mergers in Chapter 3.

Applying Economic Concepts

6. **Truth-in-Lending Laws** Visit any local store that sells goods on credit—appliances, cars, or furniture, for example. Ask the owner or manager about the type of information that the store is required to disclose when the sale is made. Obtain copies of the disclosure forms and share them with your classmates.

PROFILES IN ECONOMICS

(1912–   )

Milton Friedman is an influential and conservative American economist closely associated with the school of thought known as monetarism. Dr. Friedman was affiliated with the National Bureau of Economic Research, taught at the University of Chicago from 1946 to 1977, and wrote a popular column for *Newsweek*. He currently works with the Hoover Institute at Stanford University.

COMPETITIVE CAPITALISM Dr. Friedman's writings have covered an extraordinary variety of topics, many of which were put forth in his early classic, *Capitalism and Freedom*, written in 1962. The major theme of the book was

Friedman believes the freedom to fail in a free enterprise economy is important—failures release resources for use elsewhere.

"the role of competitive capitalism . . . as a system of economic freedom and a necessary condition for

political freedom." This text put forth proposals such as opposition to agricultural subsidies and price controls, the creation of a volunteer army, a system of vouchers for public schools, and opposition to the minimum wage. Although his ideas were radical departures from prevailing thought at the time, the power of his arguments was such that many of his opinions came to fruition.

MONETARISM The general public is probably most familiar with Friedman through his short editorials that appeared in *Newsweek*

from 1968 to 1982. Within the academic community, Friedman has impeccable credentials in the area of monetary history. His writings are the definitive works on the growth of the money supply and its relationship to inflation and real changes in the economy.

Friedman has been most influential with his unwavering support of monetarism—the theory that the quantity of money does matter because of its impact on the overall state of the economy. The key to his argument is that changes in the rate of growth of the money supply have varying and unpredictable lags, which makes fine-tuning the economy virtually impossible. Friedman claims that the Federal Reserve System should let the money supply grow at a constant rate to avoid destabilizing the economy.

Friedman's arguments had an enormous impact on the economics profession. His views attracted a number of adherents and, before long, the school of monetarism grew. For his stabilization policy, Friedman was awarded the Nobel Prize in economics in 1976.

Examining the Profile

1. **Identifying Central Issues** What is the core of Friedman's stabilization policy?

2. **For Further Research** Research and report on Friedman's free market positions in his highly acclaimed book, *Free To Choose: A Personal Statement,* coauthored with Rose Friedman.

CHAPTER 12: *The Federal Reserve System and Monetary Policy* **301**

Section Preview

Objectives

After studying this section, you will be able to:
1. **Describe** how banks use fractional reserves in their operations.
2. **Apply** fractional reserves to the process of monetary expansion.
3. **Understand** the tools used to conduct monetary policy.

Key Terms

monetary policy, fractional reserve system, reserve requirement, legal reserves, member bank reserves, liabilities, assets, balance sheet, net worth, excess reserves, liquidity, certificate of deposit, savings account, time deposit, easy money policy, tight money policy, open market operations, trading desk, discount rate, discount window, collateral, moral suasion, selective credit controls

Applying Economic Concepts

Legal Reserves When you cash a check at a bank, you may have noticed the stacks of currency in the teller's drawer. These funds are kept on hand for check-cashing consumers like yourself, but the bank also keeps them for another reason. Coins and currency are part of the bank's *legal reserves,* or funds kept on hand because of legal requirements imposed on the banking system.

One of the Federal Reserve System's most important responsibilities is that of monetary policy. **Monetary policy** involves controlling the expansion and/or contraction of the money supply to influence the cost and availability of credit, thereby influencing economic activity.

Implementing monetary policy is a complex and highly structured process. In order to understand it better, it helps to understand the fractional reserve system upon which our banking system is based.

Fractional Bank Reserves

In the United States, banks operate under a **fractional reserve system,** which requires banks and other depository institutions to keep only a fraction of their deposits in the form of reserves. The formula used to compute the amount of reserves an institution must have is called the **reserve requirement.** The Fed, for example, may require depository institutions to keep 3 percent of their deposits as reserves. The Fed can change the reserve requirement as it sees fit.

The coins, currency, and deposits used to fulfill this requirement are the **legal reserves.** These normally take the form of currency that institutions hold in their vaults, plus deposits with the Federal Reserve district banks or other locations approved by the regulatory agencies.

The portion of the legal reserves the member banks keep at the Fed district banks is called **member bank reserves** (MBRs). Nonmember banks can hold their reserves at a Fed member bank, or they can obtain permission from their primary regulators to keep their reserves in another location.

How Banks Operate

To understand how a bank operates, it helps to examine the bank's liabilities and assets. Its **liabilities** are the debts and obligations to others. Its **assets** are the properties, possessions, and claims on others. Liabilities and assets generally are put together in the form of a **balance sheet**—a condensed statement showing all assets and liabilities at a given time. The balance sheet also reflects **net worth**—the excess of assets over liabilities, which is a measure of the value of a business.

Organizing a Bank

First, suppose someone obtains a charter to organize the hypothetical State Bank of Highland Heights.

The bank will have a corporate structure, and the organizers will supply $20 so that the bank can obtain buildings and furniture before it opens for business. In return for this investment, the owners receive stock, which shows as net worth. Panel **A** in **Figure 12.6** shows how the balance sheet of a hypothetical commercial bank might look as soon as it is organized.

The balance sheet shows the assets on the left and the liabilities and net worth on the right. To see why net worth is placed on the right side of the balance sheet, rearrange the definition of net worth from

Assets – Liabilities = Net Worth
to
Assets = Liabilities + Net Worth.

The balance sheet in the figure is sometimes called a *T-account* because of its appearance, and it merely separates the assets from the liabilities and net worth the same way as the equal sign does in the above equation. The T-account also works like the equal sign in that the entries on the left must always equal the entries on the right.

Accepting Deposits

Suppose that now a customer walks in and opens a checking account with $100 in currency. This transaction, shown in Panel **B** of **Figure 12.6**, is reflected on the balance sheet in two ways. First, to indicate that the money is owed to the depositor, the $100 checking account (or demand deposit) is carried as a liability. Second, to indicate that the cash is the property of the bank, it also appears as an asset on the balance sheet.

Actually, the $100 appears in two places on the asset side. $90 appears as cash, and $10 appears as required reserves—the amount that banks set aside according to law as a protection for depositors. The size of the reserve is determined by the reserve requirement, which is 10 percent in this example. If the requirement was 15 percent, $15 would be set aside.

Making Loans

Now that the bank has some cash in hand, it can make loans. In particular, it is free to loan out its **excess reserves,** the cash and currency not needed to

---

Figure 12.6
Balance Sheet Entries for a Hypothetical Commercial Bank

A. When a bank is organized as a corporation, the owners contribute cash used to buy buildings and furniture. In return, the owners receive stock.

Assets		Liabilities + NW	
Required Reserves:		Demand Deposits:	
Cash:	$20	Net Worth	
Loans:		Equity:	$20
Bonds:			
Buildings and Furniture:			
	$20		**$20**

B. When a customer opens an account, some of the deposit is set aside as a reserve, while the excess can be loaned out. Note that Net Worth (NW) remains unchanged.

Assets		Liabilities + NW	
Required Reserves:	$10	Demand Deposits:	$100
Cash:	$90	Net Worth	
Loans:		Equity:	$20
Bonds:			
Buildings and Furniture:	$20		
	$120		**$120**

C. When another person wants to borrow money, the bank can lend all cash in excess of its required reserves. The bank actually swaps one asset (cash) for another (the loan or account receivable).

Assets		Liabilities + NW	
Required Reserves:	$10	Demand Deposits:	$100
Cash:		Net Worth	
Securities:		Equity:	$20
Loans:	$90		
Bonds:			
Buildings and Furniture:	$20		
	$120		**$120**

The T-accounts for the hypothetical bank trace the receipt of deposits through the loan-generating process. When the bank finally reaches maturity, it will have a number of assets in the form of loans, reserves, cash, and even government securities. Demand deposits for each of the bank's depositors, along with CDs, savings accounts, and net worth, will appear on the opposite side of the ledger. **If the reserve requirement was 20%, how much could the bank lend?**

fulfill the reserve requirement. The excess reserves amount to $90 at this stage of the process.

If another person enters the bank and borrows the amount equal to the excess reserves, the $90 is moved from the cash line to the loans, or accounts receivable, line in the balance sheet. These changes appear in Panel **C.** Note that there is no change in total assets, only in their mix—a change from a non-interest-earning asset (cash) to an interest-earning one (a consumer loan).

If the bank charged 12 percent interest, it would earn $90 × .12, or $10.80 annually. This income, along with income earned on other loans, would then be used to pay its officers and employees, utility bills, taxes, other business expenses, and stock dividends.

Reaching Maturity

In time, the bank would grow and prosper, diversifying its assets and liabilities in the process. Most of a bank's deposits eventually return to the community in the form of loans, and some of those loans will return to the bank in the form of new deposits. **1**

The bank might even use some of its excess reserves to buy federal, state, or local bonds and other securities. The bonds and securities are helpful for two reasons. They earn interest and, therefore, are more attractive than cash. They also have a high degree of **liquidity**—they can be converted into cash in a very short time. Liquidity adds to the bank's ability to serve its customers. When the demand for loans increases, the bank can sell its bonds and loan the cash to customers.

The bank also might try to attract additional funds by introducing different kinds of products. One product is a **certificate of deposit,** a receipt showing that an investor has made an interest-bearing loan to a bank. Most banks also offer **savings accounts** and **time deposits,** interest-bearing deposits that cannot be withdrawn by check. The two accounts are similar, except that prior notice must be given to withdraw time deposits, while no prior notice is needed to withdraw savings. ☑

Unless costs are extremely high, the bank should be able to make a profit if it can maintain a 2-3 percent "spread" between the rate it charges on its loans, and the rate it pays for funds it borrows in the form of CDs, savings accounts, and time deposits. If a bank pays 6 percent interest on money it receives, for example, it must loan money at a minimum of 8 or 9 percent to make enough income to pay expenses.

Fractional Reserves and Monetary Expansion

The fractional reserve system allows the money supply to grow to several times the size of the reserves the banking system keeps. **Figure 12.7** shows how this can happen, but this time uses a reserve requirement of 20 percent.

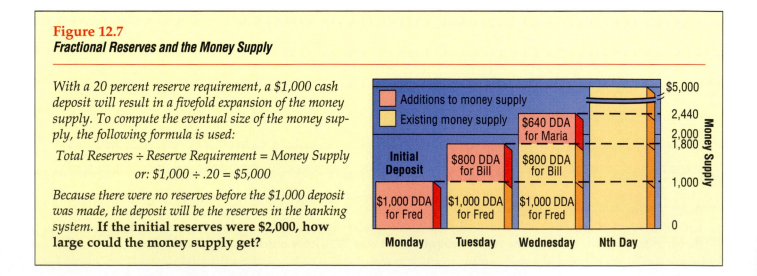

Figure 12.7
Fractional Reserves and the Money Supply

With a 20 percent reserve requirement, a $1,000 cash deposit will result in a fivefold expansion of the money supply. To compute the eventual size of the money supply, the following formula is used:

Total Reserves ÷ Reserve Requirement = Money Supply
or: $1,000 ÷ .20 = $5,000

Because there were no reserves before the $1,000 deposit was made, the deposit will be the reserves in the banking system. **If the initial reserves were $2,000, how large could the money supply get?**

Loans and Monetary Growth

In the figure, a depositor named Fred opens a demand deposit account (DDA) on Monday by depositing $1,000 cash in a national bank. By law, $200 of Fred's deposit must be set aside as a reserve in the form of vault cash or in an MBR with the Fed. The remaining $800 of excess reserves represents the bank's lending power. **2**

On Tuesday, the bank lends its excess reserves of $800 to Bill. Bill can take the loan either in cash or in the form of a DDA with the bank. If he decides to take the DDA, the money never leaves the bank. Instead, it is treated as a new deposit, and 20 percent, or $160, is set aside as a reserve. The remaining $640 are excess reserves that can be lent to someone else.

On Wednesday, Maria enters the bank and borrows $640. She, too, can take the loan in cash or a DDA. If she elects to do the latter, the bank has a new $640 deposit, 20 percent of which must be set aside as a required reserve, leaving $512 of excess reserves.

By Wednesday, Fred has a $1,000 DDA, Bill has an $800 DDA, and Maria has either $640 in cash or a $640 DDA. This amounts to $2,440 in the hands of the non-bank public by the end of the business day—a process that began on Monday with the deposit of $1,000. As long as the bank continues to have excess reserves, the lending process can continue.

Reserves and the Money Supply

Because each new loan is smaller than the one before, the money supply will stop growing at some point. A mathematical relationship exists between the dollar amount of reserves, the reserve requirement, and the size of the money supply. For example, if the dollar amount of reserves equals 20 percent of the money supply, we could write:

$$\text{Total Reserves} = .20 \times \text{Money Supply}$$
$$\text{or,}$$
$$\text{Total Reserves} \div .20 = \text{Money Supply}$$
$$\text{Therefore, } \$1,000 \div .20 = \$5,000$$

This formula shows that $1,000 of total reserves, given a 20 percent reserve requirement, will result in a money supply of $5,000. This amount is the final outcome of the example above when Fred makes his initial deposit.

If Maria takes the loan in cash, however, the monetary expansion process temporarily stops. Before long, though, she will spend the money and it will show up in another bank, enabling the expansion process to resume. Because most bank loans are in the form of DDAs or other accounts rather than cash, the interruption to the expansion process is not that significant.

After the money supply has reached its full size, further changes in the amount of reserves can still affect it. Using the symbol Δ, meaning *change in*, we see that:

$$\Delta \text{Reserves} = .20 \times \Delta \text{Money Supply}$$
$$\text{or,}$$
$$\Delta \text{Reserves} \div .20 = \Delta \text{Money Supply}$$

Someone, for example, might withdraw $5 from the bank and keep it permanently in a wallet. The money supply would then change by:

$$\Delta \text{Reserves} \div .20 = \Delta \text{Money Supply}$$
$$\text{or,}$$
$$-\$5 \div .20 = -\$25.$$

In other words, the money supply would shrink by $25, from $5,000 to $4,975.

Tools of Monetary Policy

The Fed has three major and two minor tools it can use to conduct monetary policy. Each tool affects the

---

Checking Understanding

1. How are bank deposits funneled back into the community?
2. What would the bank's lending power be if Fred deposited $1,500 rather than $1,000?

Applying Economic Concepts

 Deposit Insurance The FDIC currently covers losses up to $100,000. If you have several accounts under one name—$90,000 in a CD, $50,000 in a savings account, and $35,000 in a checking account—the maximum you can collect is $100,000.

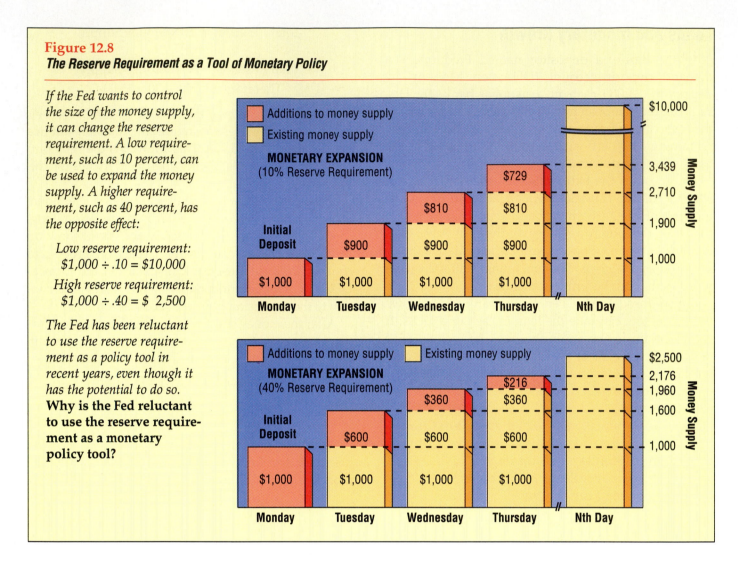

Figure 12.8
The Reserve Requirement as a Tool of Monetary Policy

If the Fed wants to control the size of the money supply, it can change the reserve requirement. A low requirement, such as 10 percent, can be used to expand the money supply. A higher requirement, such as 40 percent, has the opposite effect:

Low reserve requirement:
$1,000 ÷ .10 = $10,000

High reserve requirement:
$1,000 ÷ .40 = $ 2,500

The Fed has been reluctant to use the reserve requirement as a policy tool in recent years, even though it has the potential to do so.
Why is the Fed reluctant to use the reserve requirement as a monetary policy tool?

amount of excess reserves in the system, which in turn affects the monetary expansion process described above. The outcome of monetary policy is to influence the cost and availability of credit. The direction of change depends on the objectives of the Federal Reserve System.

Under an **easy money policy,** the Fed allows the money supply to grow and interest rates to fall, which normally stimulates the economy. When interest rates are low, people tend to buy on credit. This encourages sales at stores and production at factories. Businesses also tend to borrow and then invest in new plants and equipment when money is cheap. Under a **tight money policy,** the Fed restricts the growth of the money supply, which drives interest rates up. When interest rates are high, consumers and businesses borrow and spend less, which slows economic growth.

Reserve Requirement

The first tool of monetary policy is the reserve requirement. Within limits that Congress sets, the Fed can change this requirement for all checking, time, or savings accounts in the country.

This tool gives the Fed considerable control over the money supply. Suppose the Fed lowers the reserve requirement in the previous example from 20 to 10 percent. More money could be loaned to Bill, Maria, and others, and the money supply could reach $10,000. If the Fed raises the reserve requirement to 40 percent, however, less money would be loaned, and the money supply would be smaller. The effect of different reserve requirements is shown in **Figure 12.8**.

Historically, the Fed has been reluctant to use the reserve requirement as a policy tool, in part because other monetary policy tools work better. Even so, the reserve requirement can be a very powerful tool should the Fed decide to use it. **Figure 12.9** summarizes the impact of a change in the reserve requirement on the money supply in the manner just described, along with the impact of the other monetary tools described below.

Open Market Operations

The second and most popular tool of monetary policy is **open market operations**—the buying and selling of government securities in financial markets. Open market operations affect the amount of excess reserves in the banking system and, therefore, the ability of banks to support new loans.

Suppose the Fed decides to increase the money supply. To do so, it buys government securities from a dealer who specializes in large-volume transactions of those securities. The Fed pays for the securities by writing a check. The dealer then deposits the check with his or her bank. The bank forwards the check to the Fed for payment. At this point, the Fed "pays" the check by increasing the bank's MBR with the Fed. The result is that whenever the Fed writes a check, more reserves are pumped into the banking system. Because only some reserves are needed to back existing deposits, the excess reserves can be loaned out, thus increasing the money supply.

If the Fed wants to contract the money supply and drive up interest rates, it can sell billions of dollars of government securities back to dealers. Dealers pay for the purchase of securities with checks drawn on their own banks. The Fed then processes the checks by reducing the MBRs of dealers' banks. With fewer reserves in the banking system, fewer loans are made and the money supply contracts.

The Federal Open Market Committee, which reviews and recommends changes in monetary policy, conducts open market operations. Normally the FOMC tries to decide if the current level of interest rates and monetary growth is too high, too low, or just right. After the committee votes to set targets, officials at the trading desk take over. The **trading desk** is the physical location at the Fed's New York district bank where the buying and selling actually takes place. The officials at the desk buy and sell bonds daily to maintain the targets set by the FOMC. The desk is permanently located in New York to be close to the nation's financial markets.

Discount Rate

As a central bank, the Fed makes loans to other depository institutions. The **discount rate**—the interest the Fed charges on loans to financial institutions—is the third major tool of monetary policy.

A bank might obtain a loan from the Fed for two reasons. First, it could have an unexpected drop in its member bank reserves, which would shrink its excess reserves. In this case, the bank would go to the Fed and arrange a short-term loan to cover the shortfall. Second, a bank could be faced with seasonal demands for loans. A bank in an agricultural area, for example,

Figure 12.9
Summary of Monetary Policy Tools

Tool	Fed Action	Effect on Excess Reserves	Money Supply
Reserve Requirement	Lower Raise	Frees excess reserves because fewer are needed to back existing deposits in the system. More reserves are required to back existing deposits, excess reserves contract.	Expands Contracts
Open Market Operations	Buy bonds Sell bonds	Checks written by the Fed add to excess reserves in the system. Checks written by buyers are subtracted from reserves, excess reserves in the system contract.	Expands Contracts
Discount Rate	Lower Raise	Additional reserves can be obtained at lower cost, excess reserves expand. Additional reserves through borrowing now more expensive, excess reserves not added.	Expands Contracts

The key to monetary policy is to see how the excess reserves in the system are affected. **What happens to the money supply when the Fed increases excess reserves? Decreases excess reserves?**

might face a heavy demand for loans during the planting season. In that case, it would need additional MBRs to support the loans made in the spring.

The **discount window** is a teller's window at the Fed that depository institutions use to borrow member bank reserves. Before a bank actually borrows money, however, the terms of the loan are arranged in advance. Next, the depository institution delivers collateral to the window. **Collateral** is the property or other security used to guarantee payment of a loan. Then, when everything is complete, the loan is granted and appears as an increase in the institution's MBR account.

Changes in the discount rate affect the cost of borrowed MBRs. If the Fed wants an easy money policy, it may lower the rate and/or allow more borrowing than before. When this happens, it is sometimes said that the Fed is "opening" the window. The reverse is true if the Fed wants to follow a tight money policy. Then, it discourages borrowing by raising the rate or by making it more difficult to borrow. When this happens, the Fed is "closing" the window.

Most institutions can borrow from the Fed, including member and nonmember banks, savings institutions, and even credit unions. The Fed, however, views access to the window as a privilege rather than a right. As a result, the Fed may limit the number of times a borrower can go to the window.

Other Tools

The Fed may also use two other methods to control the money supply. These are moral suasion and selective credit controls.

Moral suasion is the use of persuasion such as announcements, press releases, articles in newspapers and magazines, and testimony before Congress. Moral suasion works because bankers often try to anticipate changes in monetary policy.

Suppose that the chairperson of the Fed is called before Congress to give his or her view on the state of the economy. Assume also that the chair states that interest rates are somewhat low, and that it would not hurt the economy if they should rise. Bankers might well expect a tighter money policy in the next few weeks. As a result, they might be less willing to loan their excess reserves, and they might even raise their interest rates by a small amount. In the end, the money supply might contract just slightly, even if the Fed did no more than offer its views.

A second method is **selective credit controls**— rules pertaining to loans for specific commodities or purposes. These controls took the form of minimum down payments on cars and other consumer goods during World War II and the Korean War. Selective credit controls during those periods were imposed to free factories to produce war materials. Selective credit controls are seldom used today.

SECTION 2 REVIEW

Reviewing Terms and Facts

1. **Define** monetary policy, fractional reserve system, reserve requirement, legal reserves, member bank reserves, liabilities, assets, balance sheet, net worth, excess reserves, liquidity, certificate of deposit, savings account, time deposit, easy money policy, tight money policy, open market operations, trading desk, discount rate, discount window, collateral, moral suasion, selective credit controls.

2. **Explain** how the availability of excess reserves determines whether a bank can make new loans.

3. **Describe** the three major tools of monetary policy.

Critical Thinking

4. **Drawing Conclusions** At times, someone with a good credit rating may not be able to get a loan. When this happens, the potential customer may be told to "come back next week" to try again. What does this tell you about the bank's reserves? How should the customer react to a situation like this?

Applying Economic Concepts

5. **Legal Reserves** Your local national bank is required to keep its reserves in the form of vault cash and member deposits with the Fed. Why do you suppose that other assets, such as common stocks or real estate, are not suitable reserves?

Monetary Policy, Banking, and the Economy

Section Preview

Objectives

After studying this section, you will be able to:

1. **Explain** how monetary policy affects interest rates in the short run.

2. **Relate** monetary expansion to inflation in the long run.

3. **Identify** the two major definitions of money.

4. **Describe** various steps taken to protect the safety of the banking system.

Key Terms

prime rate, quantity theory of money, monetizing the debt, M1, M2, problem bank list, creditor, agricultural bank, energy bank

Applying Economic Concepts

Money Where do you keep your money? On your person? In a savings or checking account? In the form of traveler's checks or NOW accounts? You, and millions of others, make *money* difficult to define. There are too many ways to hold your money—just ask the Fed!

The impact of monetary policy on the economy is complex. In the short run, monetary policy affects interest rates and the availability of credit. In the long run, it affects inflation. In addition, no one can be sure how long it will take for the effects of monetary policy to impact the economy.

Short-Run Impact

In the short run, an increase or a decrease in the supply of money affects the interest rate, or the price of credit. When the Fed expands the money supply, the cost of credit goes down. When the Fed contracts the money supply, the cost of credit goes up.

This short-run relationship between money and interest rates is shown in **Figure 12.10**. The demand curve for money has the usual shape, which shows that more money will be demanded when the price of money is low. The supply curve, however, does not have its usual shape. Instead, it is vertical, indicating that the supply of money is fixed at any given time.

Before the market is disturbed, the interest rate, as shown in Graph **A,** is at 12 percent. If the Fed expands the money supply to S_1S_1, the interest rate falls to 10 percent. A contraction of the money supply, as shown in Graph **B,** increases the rate from 12 to 14 percent.

Although the Fed tries to do what is best for the economy, people do not always agree with its decisions. In 1981, for example, the Fed was criticized for allowing interest rates to get too high. That year, the **prime rate**—the best or lowest interest rate commercial bankers charge their customers—reached 21.5 percent. Critics felt that the economy would have been better off if the Fed had expanded the money supply, thus lowering interest rates. Supporters, however, felt these policies reduced inflation.

Long-Run Impact

In the long run, changes in the supply of money affect the general level of prices. This relationship, formally known as the **quantity theory of money,** has been demonstrated repeatedly in history.

Historical Precedents

When the Spanish brought gold and silver back to Spain from the Americas, the increase in the money supply started inflation that lasted for 100 years. When the Continental Congress issued $250 million of currency during the Revolutionary War, the economy suffered severe inflation. A similar thing happened

Figure 12.10
Short-Run Impact of Monetary Policy

In the short run, the impact of monetary policy is on interest rates, or the price of credit. When the money supply expands, the price of credit goes down. When the money supply is contracted, the price of credit goes up. **Why is the supply of money, SS, shown as a vertical line?**

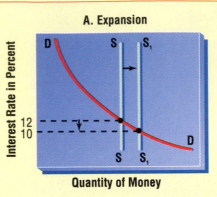

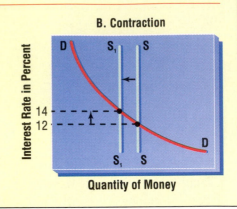

during the Civil War, when nearly $500 million of greenbacks were printed.

Monetizing the Debt

When the federal government financed the Vietnam War with deficit spending in the 1960s, the crowding-out effect threatened. To keep interest rates from going up, the Fed decided to **monetize the debt**—create enough extra money to offset the deficit spending.

The process of monetizing the debt is illustrated in **Figure 12.11**. DD and SS represent the initial demand and supply of money. Suppose, however, that the government borrows $25 billion, shifting the demand curve for money to D_1D_1. If the Fed does not take any action, the interest rate would rise from 10 to 12 percent and crowd out some investors. If the Fed wants to keep the interest rate from rising, it could increase the money supply to S_1S_1 and push interest rates back down to their original level.

In the short run, then, the Fed can increase the money supply just enough to keep the interest rate from rising. This procedure is effective if done infrequently. Repeated short-run attempts to keep rates low, however, result in a long-term expansion of the money supply, making inflation even worse.

Taming Inflation

Much of the federal debt was monetized from the late 1960s until the late 1970s. During this period, the money supply grew at rates of 12 percent or more for

several years in a row. As inflation got worse, the price of most goods and services—including interest rates—also went up. Attempts by the Fed to keep interest rates low by increasing the supply of money worked at first, but eventually inflation was aggravated. ☑

By 1980 the Fed realized that it had to choose between interest rates and inflation. It chose to control inflation. When this happened, the prime rate in 1981 reached 21.5 percent. Most people did not like the high interest rates at the time, but today they recognize that the tight money policies were necessary to bring down inflation.

Timing and Burden of Monetary Policy

When the Fed conducts monetary policy, it has two other issues to consider. The first involves timing, the second its burden.

Sometimes a tight money policy might show results in six months. At other times, the impact might not be felt for two years. The same happens when the Fed follows an easy money policy. Such variations in timing make it difficult to use monetary policy to fine-tune the economy. **1**

A second problem is that monetary policy has an uneven impact on the economy. If the Fed follows a tight money policy to control inflation, interest rates may increase. Higher rates hurt home-building and automobile sales, because the cost of borrowing goes up. If the Fed follows a loose monetary policy, interest

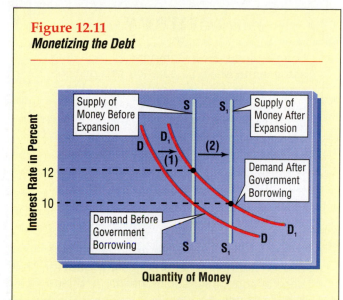

Figure 12.11
Monetizing the Debt

(chart)

Supply of Money Before Expansion

Supply of Money After Expansion

Demand After Government Borrowing

Demand Before Government Borrowing

Interest Rate in Percent

12

10

Quantity of Money

S S₁ D₁ D (2) (1) S S₁ D D₁

When (1) the government borrows to cover a deficit in the federal budget, interest rates tend to rise because of the increased demand for credit, raising the possibility of crowding out. If (2) the Fed expands the money supply just enough to offset the borrowing, interest rates may remain unchanged. **What are the long-run effects of monetizing the debt?**

rates may go down. Home-building and automobile sales will then benefit more than other industries.

The Politics of Interest Rates

Because of the way it can control the interest rate, the Fed often comes under a great deal of political pressure. A President, for example, can gain some say over monetary policy by appointing certain people to the Federal Reserve Board of Governors. After these appointments are made, however, the governors can conduct monetary policy as they wish.

Some Presidents have tried to increase control by criticizing the Fed. Others have threatened to introduce legislation to make the Fed less independent.

No such laws have been passed recently, although the threats do get the Fed's attention. Even so, the Fed often is reluctant to accommodate demands for lower interest rates because of the fear of inflation. Unlike many politicians, who often insist on lower interest rates during an election year, the Fed is more concerned about the health of the economy in the long run.

People tend to use the interest rate as a measure of the overall health of the economy. In particular, they think the economy is healthy when interest rates are low. This makes it difficult for elected officials when the Fed allows interest rates to rise.

Defining Money

With so many financial institutions offering various ways to deposit or hold one's money, the Fed has had to develop some new definitions of money to keep track of it.

Figure 12.12 on page 314 lists a number of components of the money supply, or ways that people have chosen to keep money. The Fed groups these together according to function and gives them names. The first is **M1**, which represents the transactional components of the money supply, or the components of the money supply that most closely match money's role as a medium of exchange. This definition of money includes traveler's checks, coins, currency, demand deposits, and other checkable deposits such as NOW accounts and credit union share drafts.

M2 is a measure of money that includes those components most closely conforming to money's role as a store of value. M2 includes M1, small denomination time deposits, savings deposits, and several other ways to hold money. **2**

QUICK CHECK

Checking Understanding

1. Why is it difficult to use monetary policy to fine-tune the economy?
2. What are the two measurements of the money supply?

Applying Economic Concepts

 Inflation Inflation peaked in 1980. Since then it has been significantly lower, with rates in the early 1990s hovering near 4 percent.

Bank Failures and Safety in Banking

The savings and loan crisis raises questions about the health of the banking system. Banks are more numerous and have far more assets than did the savings and loans.

Bank Failures

Figure 12.13 on page 317 shows that bank failures were a serious problem in the 1980s. Bank failures are a problem for four reasons. First, owners lose whatever investment they might have in a bank. This loss is a personal hardship for them just as the failure of any other business hurts its owners.

Second, publicity surrounding a bank failure strains the credibility of the banking system as a whole. Some depositors might try to withdraw funds or cancel dealings they have with sound banks.

Third, depositors of a failed bank may lose money, too. The extent of damage, however, depends on whether the bank is insured and, if so, how fast the FDIC comes to the rescue. Because the FDIC inspects banks on a regular basis, it generally knows when a bank is in trouble.

Fourth, the FDIC has to recover those losses by charging higher interest rates for deposit insurance on all banks. This raises the cost of banking to depositors.

If a bank is in jeopardy, the FDIC adds the bank's name to a confidential **problem bank list,** which is closely watched. If the problems get worse, the FDIC takes control of the bank. It can then either sell the problem bank to a stronger one, or it can liquidate the bank and pay off the depositors.

HELP WANTED

Actuary
▼

Longlife Insurance Company is recruiting actuaries to design insurance and pension plans. As an actuary, you must be able to gather and analyze statistics on death, sickness, injury, disability, unemployment, retirement, and property loss. This information is then used to establish how much the insured loss will be. You must calculate premium rates, ensuring that the price of the insurance is high enough to cover any claims and expenses Longlife Insurance Company might have to pay. You must be knowledgeable in subjects that can affect insurance practices, including general economic, social, health, and legislation trends.

▼

Education: Bachelor's Degree in Mathematics or Statistics; passage of actuarial examinations
Starting Salary: $28,500

Disposing of Failed Banks

When the FDIC takes over a bank, the shareholders know nothing of the FDIC's actions. The sale of one bank to another takes only a few weeks or days, and services are seldom interrupted. People usually find out about the sale when the bank opens for business under a new name. The FDIC uses such secrecy to prevent panic withdrawals and to prevent shareholders from selling their worthless stock to unsuspecting investors.

When the FDIC cannot find a buyer for a failed bank, it may declare the bank insolvent and close its doors. Within a few days, the FDIC begins to pay off depositors directly. This is generally a speedy process, but in some cases depositors do not recover their money for several months.

Depositors, of course, are only covered up to the $100,000 insurance limit. If an account has more than this, the depositor may go to court as a **creditor**—a person or institution to whom money is owed. There, a

---

DID YOU KNOW?

Counterfeit Money United States currency has features that impede counterfeiting it. The paper is specially made for the government printing office and has tiny blue and red silk fibers mixed in the cotton/linen pulp. In addition, the intricate border design is difficult to copy without resulting in broken lines.

suit is filed to recover the rest of the deposit. If the bank happens to be uninsured, depositors and others who have valuables stored in safe deposit boxes are simply out of luck. The chance is slim that a depositor will go to court and recover much, if anything, from the owners of an uninsured, failed bank.

Reasons for Failure

Banks fail for many reasons, but poor management is the main one. Some banks, for example, make loans without adequate collateral. Others fail to keep expenses in line with revenues. Even others are victims of a weak economy.

Many **agricultural banks**—banks with more than 25 percent of their loans in agriculture—have been hit hard recently because of falling land values and low prices for farm products. **Energy banks**—banks with more than 25 percent of their loans in gas, oil, and other energy areas—were also hit hard when oil prices declined sharply in 1985 and 1986. Many of these banks failed because too many of their loans were concentrated in a weak industry.

In the late 1980s, speculation in real estate was a major problem. Many borrowers used real estate for collateral, and then went out of business. When the banks took control of the property, they discovered that the property had lost its value and could be sold only for a loss. This situation was especially troublesome in the Northeast and the Southwest.

Finally, natural disasters may have an impact on banks. Many of the small commercial banks along the Mississippi River had a difficult time surviving the record floods of 1993, especially because some borrowers could not repay their loans.

New Capital Requirements

During the 1980s, banking authorities took steps to increase the amount of financial capital their owners must put in the bank. This capital is used as a cushion to absorb loan losses and, because it is the property of the bank's owners, the expectation is that the owners will be more careful when they make future loans.

Finally, the FDIC and other federal regulatory agencies are working to better coordinate and improve the quality of their standards and inspections. It has been a difficult and expensive period for the banking industry, but it did emerge from the 1980s intact, unlike the savings and loan industry.

SECTION 3 REVIEW

Reviewing Terms and Facts

1. **Define** prime rate, quantity theory of money, monetizing the debt, M1, M2, problem bank list, creditor, agricultural bank, energy bank.
2. **Describe** the short-run impact of monetary policy.
3. **Explain** the long-run impact of monetary policy.
4. **Identify** the problems associated with the timing and burden of monetary policy.
5. **Describe** the recent history of bank failures.

Critical Thinking

6. **Making Generalizations** Historically, expansions in the money supply have set off inflation. Something similar might have happened to you. Identify a period in your life when you had a little more money than usual. How did you spend the extra cash? Were prices as important to you then as they were at other times when you did not have as much to spend? Why do prices tend to increase faster when more money is available?

Applying Economic Concepts

7. **Money** Our money supply, as well as the different forms or ways to hold it, has changed considerably over the years. Describe one or two ways you think United States money might change even more in the future.

Reading a Bar Graph

Y ou just timed yourself running the 100-yard dash. Now you would like to compare your time to that of the other sprinters on your team. Organizing your times in a bar graph would allow you to visually compare all your times at once.

Explanation

Like line graphs, bar graphs are used to compare facts involving numbers. Bars, or columns, of different lengths are used to represent quantities or totals. Some bar graphs show changes over time, but most are used to compare quantities during the same time period. A bar graph might compare the number of students attending 5 different schools during the same year. A bar graph might also compare the 100-yard dash times of 5 students.

Bar graphs have horizontal and vertical axes that describe the information presented in the graph. Sometimes more than one set of facts are compared on a bar graph. The steps involved in reading a bar graph are:

- Read the title to learn the subject of the graph.
- Look at the horizontal and vertical axes to find out what information the graph presents.
- If the bars are color-coded, read the key indicating what the colors represent.
- Compare the lengths of the bars on the graphs.
- Use the information you have learned from the graph to draw conclusions about the subject.

Practice

Study the bar graph, then answer the questions below.
1. What is the subject of the graph?
2. What information is found along the horizontal axis?
3. What is being compared along the vertical axis?
4. What does the color red represent?
5. What do the striped bars represent?
6. Which component makes up the largest part of the money supply? The smallest part?
7. Which components make up M1?
8. Which components are included in M2?
9. What aspect of **Figure 12.12** surprised you the most? Why?

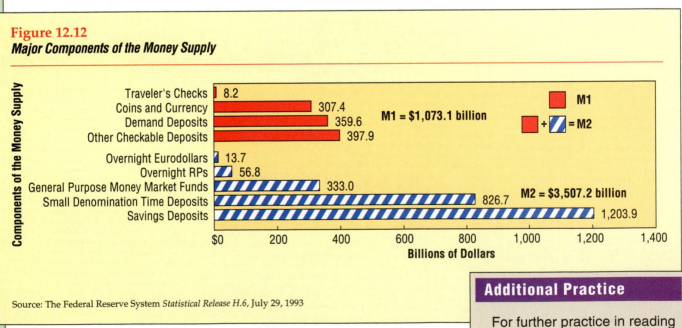

Figure 12.12
Major Components of the Money Supply

M1 = $1,073.1 billion

M2 = $3,507.2 billion

Traveler's Checks: 8.2
Coins and Currency: 307.4
Demand Deposits: 359.6
Other Checkable Deposits: 397.9
Overnight Eurodollars: 13.7
Overnight RPs: 56.8
General Purpose Money Market Funds: 333.0
Small Denomination Time Deposits: 826.7
Savings Deposits: 1,203.9

Components of the Money Supply

Billions of Dollars

$0 200 400 600 800 1,000 1,200 1,400

Source: The Federal Reserve System *Statistical Release H.6,* July 29, 1993

Additional Practice

For further practice in reading a bar graph, complete the Reinforcing Skills exercise in the Chapter 12 Review on page 317.

Vocabulary

The following terms are defined in Chapter 12:

SECTION ONE
- member bank (p. 294)
- bank holding company (p. 296)
- truth-in-lending laws (p. 299)
- Regulation Z (p. 299)
- currency (p. 300)
- coins (p. 300)
- margin requirement (p. 300)

SECTION TWO
- monetary policy (p. 302)
- fractional reserve system (p. 302)
- reserve requirement (p. 302)
- legal reserves (p. 302)
- member bank reserves (p. 302)
- liabilities (p. 302)
- assets (p. 302)
- balance sheet (p. 302)
- net worth (p. 302)
- excess reserves (p. 303)
- liquidity (p. 304)
- certificate of deposit (p. 304)
- savings account (p. 304)
- time deposit (p. 304)
- easy money policy (p. 306)
- tight money policy (p. 306)
- open market operations (p. 307)
- trading desk (p. 307)
- discount rate (p. 307)
- discount window (p. 308)
- collateral (p. 308)
- moral suasion (p. 308)
- selective credit controls (p. 308)

SECTION THREE
- prime rate (p. 309)
- quantity theory of money (p. 309)
- monetizing the debt (p. 310)
- M1 (p. 311)
- M2 (p. 311)
- problem bank list (p. 312)
- creditor (p. 312)
- agricultural bank (p. 313)
- energy bank (p. 313)

Section 1 The Federal Reserve System (pages 294–300)

The Fed is the nation's central bank whose stock is owned by its member banks. Its structure consists of a 7-member **Board of Governors**; a **Federal Open Market Committee** consisting of the 7 Board members and 5 district presidents; and a **Federal Advisory Council** with 12 members.

In addition to supervising state member banks, the Fed has broad authority over **bank holding companies,** the international operations of all commercial banks, some mergers, check clearing, consumer legislation dealing with **truth-in-lending laws,** the maintenance of the nation's currency, and **margin requirements.**

Reviewing the Main Idea
How is the Fed organized?

Section 2 Monetary Policy (pages 302–308)

Monetary policy and modern commercial banking operate on a **fractional reserve system.** The **legal reserves** a bank keeps determine the amount of loans it can make. The **net worth** of a bank is equal to the difference between its **assets** and its **liabilities.** When a bank receives a deposit, it sets some of the deposit aside as a reserve against the deposit. If any **excess reserves** exist, the bank can make new loans.

Monetary policy affects the size of the money supply, and hence the level of interest rates, by making use of the fractional reserve system. The first tool of monetary policy is the change in the **reserve requirement,** which is seldom used. The second and most popular tool is **open market operations.** A change in the **discount rate** is the third major tool. Two lesser tools include **moral suasion** and **selective credit controls** such as **margin requirements.**

Reviewing the Main Idea
How do open market operations allow the Fed to conduct monetary policy?

Section 3 Monetary Policy, Banking, and the Economy (pages 309–313)

In the short run, changes in the money supply interact with the demand for money to impact interest rates. The long-run impact of monetary policy is on inflation.

Because people keep their money in so many different ways and in so many different accounts, the Fed has devised two additional definitions of money. The first is **M1,** which represents the transactional component of money. The second is **M2,** which represents money's role as a store of value.

Reviewing the Main Idea
What are the short-term and long-term effects of changes in the money supply?

Reviewing Key Terms

Write the key term that best completes the following sentences.

balance sheet
holding company
certificate of deposit
discount window
easy money policy
excess reserves
legal reserves
M1

M2
monetary policy
monetizing the debt
moral suasion
open market operations
FOMC
selective credit controls
Board of Governors

1. The main governing body of the Fed is the _____.
2. A(n) _____ would expand the money supply and tend to lower interest rates.
3. _____ are the funds that banks use to satisfy the reserve requirement.
4. If a bank has _____, it is able to make additional loans to customers.
5. The most popular and effective tool of monetary policy is that of _____.
6. When the Fed increases the money supply to off-set the effects of government borrowing, it is _____.
7. The transactional component of the money supply is _____.
8. One of the most important responsibilities of the Fed is _____.
9. The part of the Fed that buys and sells government bonds as part of monetary policy is the _____.
10. A depository institution would go to the _____ if it wanted to borrow reserves from the Fed.

Reviewing the Facts

SECTION 1 *(pages 294–300)*
1. **Name** the five federal regulatory agencies that supervise the nation's depository institutions.
2. **Identify** the membership of the Board of Governors, the FOMC, and the FAC.
3. **Identify** the most important regulatory responsibilities of the Fed.

SECTION 2 *(pages 302–308)*
4. **Explain** how banks operate under a fractional reserve system of banking.
5. **Identify** the conditions that enable a bank to make new loans.
6. **Explain** how the total reserves and the reserve requirement can be used to compute the size of the money supply.
7. **Describe** the three major tools of monetary policy.

SECTION 3 *(pages 309–313)*
8. **Identify** the major short-run impact of monetary policy.
9. **Explain** how the long-run impact of monetary policy differs from its short-run impact.
10. **Explain** why the level of interest rates is politically sensitive.
11. **Describe** the steps taken to increase the safety of the commercial banking system.

Critical Thinking

1. **Making Comparisons** If you were on the Federal Reserve Board of Governors and could use only one method to control the money supply, which policy tool would you choose? Why?
2. **Drawing Conclusions** Defend or refute the following statement: The independence of the Federal Reserve System is essential to the health of the economy.

Applying Economic Concepts

1. **Money** Survey your parents to find out how they keep their money (CDs, traveler's checks, savings accounts, time deposits, banks, etc.). How many categories mentioned in this chapter do they use?
2. **Stability in Value** If you were to apply for a loan, how would the lending institution view you as a credit risk? Determine your net worth as a potential borrower by listing your assets and liabilities in a T-account, similar to the one shown in **Figure 12.6**. Refer to pages 302 and 303 for the definition of *net worth*.

Reinforcing Skills

READING A BAR GRAPH

Use the bar graph below to answer the following questions.

1. What is the subject of this bar graph?
2. What time span is covered?
3. What do the numbers along the vertical axis represent?
4. Which year saw the highest number of bank failures?
5. What does the trend seem to be since then?
6. Why was the number of bank failures high in the 1930s?

Individual Activity

Interview a person who works in a financial institution. A manager of a commercial bank may be interviewed about the bank's primary regulatory agencies, the cost of deposit insurance, and/or the origins of the bank's charter. A loan officer may be interviewed to explain how loans are made and what requirements must be met. A stockbroker may explain the use of margin requirements. After your interviews are completed, share your findings with the class.

Cooperative Learning Activity

Working in groups of four, draw the boundaries of the Federal Reserve districts on a map of the United States. Each group member should then survey three friends, asking them to list the Federal Reserve number that appears on their currency. Tabulate the number of times each district is named. As a group, compare your findings and write your group's district totals in their proper section on the map. Then compare your group's findings with the rest of the class, placing the new totals on a classroom map of Federal Reserve districts. From which district did most currency originate? Why?

Writing About Economics

THE EXPRESSIVE STYLE

In the **Journal Writing** activity on page 293 you were asked to analyze the currency that comes into your possession for one week, logging the various features that appear on the front and back of each bill. Assume that a foreign visitor wants to understand how United States currency works. Using the expressive writing style discussed on page 554, describe the specific features and their purpose.

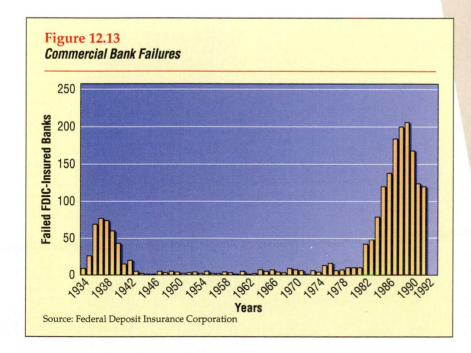

Figure 12.13
Commercial Bank Failures

Failed FDIC-Insured Banks

Years

Source: Federal Deposit Insurance Corporation

Wall Street is synonymous with money, investors, and the New York Stock Exchange.

CHAPTER 13

Financial Investments, Markets, and Equities

SECTION 1
Savings and the Financial System

SECTION 2
Investing in Financial Assets

SECTION 3
Investing in Equities, Futures, and Options

CHAPTER PREVIEW

People to Know
- Edward T. Lewis
- Stockbroker

Applying Economic Concepts to Your Life

Savings and Growth Do you have a car loan? Do your parents have a mortgage? Whose money enabled you to buy the car and home? It does not matter from whom you borrowed the money. What is important is that someone saved, which allowed you and your parents to borrow and, thus, experience economic growth.

Journal Writing

Scan the stock market listings in the business section of your local newspaper. Assume that you have $50,000 to invest in a stock portfolio, and select one or more stocks in which to invest. Read the economic skill—How to Read Stock Market Reports—on page 333. Then, in your journal, track the progress of your stock(s) for one week or more.

Savings and the Financial System

Section Preview

Objectives

After studying this section, you will be able to:

1. **Explain** why saving is important for capital formation.
2. **Explain** how the financial system works to transfer funds from savers to borrowers.
3. **Understand** the role of the major nondepository financial institutions in the financial system.

Key Terms

saving, savings, financial system, financial asset, financial intermediary, nonbank financial institution, finance company, bill consolidation loan, premium, mutual fund, pension, pension fund, real estate investment trust

Applying Economic Concepts

Financial Assets Do you have a checking account, savings account, or government savings bond? If so, you are a participant in the financial system. You have one or more *financial assets* that represent the transfer of funds from a saver to a borrower.

An economic system must be able to produce capital if it is to satisfy the wants and needs of its people. To produce capital, people must be willing to save, which releases resources for use elsewhere. To the economist, **saving** means the absence of spending, while **savings** refers to the dollars that become available in the absence of consumption. Both are vital to the American economy.

For investment to take place, someone in the economy must save. An individual can save as well as invest, as noted in the first example. Another person may save while someone else invests, as described in the second example. When people save, they are abstaining from consumption, which frees resources for others to borrow and use. These resources also make investments possible. **1**

Saving and Capital Formation

When people save, they make funds available to others. When businesses borrow these savings, new goods and services are created, new plants and equipment are produced, and new jobs become available. Saving makes economic growth possible. ☑

Suppose an entrepreneur wants to set up a business. He or she might save some income until he or she is ready to begin, keeping this money in a wallet or in a bank to earn interest. When enough funds have been saved to invest, the entrepreneur sets up shop.

Another entrepreneur might borrow funds from a bank to start a business immediately. If other people have been saving some of their income, the bank should have funds to lend. If people have been spending all of their income, however, the bank may not be able to make the loan even if it wanted to.

Financial Assets and the Financial System

For people to use the savings of others, the economy must have a **financial system**—a way to transfer savers' dollars to investors.

Financial Assets

When people save, they usually do so in a number of ways. They may put money in a savings account, a commercial bank, or a thrift. They may purchase a certificate of deposit at a depository institution or purchase a government or corporate bond. In each case, the savers obtain receipts for the funds they save.

For a savings account, a savings book or monthly computer statement is the saver's receipt. The receipt for a certificate of deposit (CD) often takes the form of

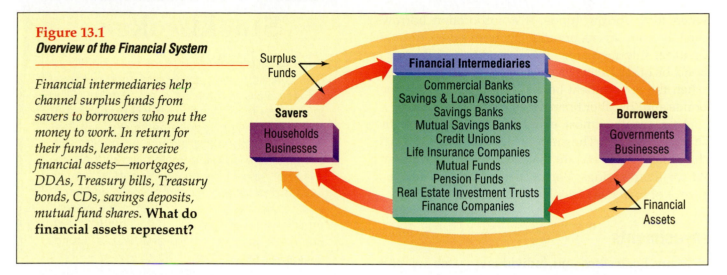

Figure 13.1
Overview of the Financial System

Financial intermediaries help channel surplus funds from savers to borrowers who put the money to work. In return for their funds, lenders receive financial assets—mortgages, DDAs, Treasury bills, Treasury bonds, CDs, savings deposits, mutual fund shares. **What do financial assets represent?**

a passbook, computer printout, or other document. Some government and most corporate bonds are printed on high-quality paper and are designed to convey a sense of value and worth.

Economists have another name for these receipts. They are **financial assets**, or claims on the property and the income of the borrower. These receipts are assets because they are property that has value. They represent claims on the borrower because they specify the amount loaned and the terms at which the loan was made. If the borrower defaults, the lender can use the financial asset as proof in court that funds were borrowed and that repayment is expected.

When funds are lent from one individual or business to another, a financial asset is generated. These assets are a critical part of our financial system.

The Financial System

Two of the main components of the financial system have already been described. The first component was the funds that the saver transferred to the borrower. The second was the financial assets or receipts that

certify the loans were made. The other three components of the financial system, illustrated in **Figure 13.1**, are the savers, borrowers, and institutions that bring the surplus funds and financial assets together. **2**

Any sector of the economy can supply savings, but the most important sectors are households and businesses. State and local governments provide some savings, but the government sector overall is a net borrower of funds. In **Figure 13.1** the savers provide some funds directly to the borrowers, as when households or businesses purchase bonds directly from the government or from the business sector. Other surplus funds, usually in much smaller amounts, are placed with a group of financial institutions that pool the funds and lend them to others.

These institutions are known as **financial intermediaries** and include the depository institutions, life insurance companies, pension funds, and other groups that channel savings from savers to borrowers. These institutions are especially helpful to the many small savers who have only limited savings to deposit.

The last major component of the financial system consists of the borrowers who generate financial assets

Checking Understanding

1. What is necessary before investment can take place?
2. What are the components of the financial system?

Applying Economic Concepts

 Saving Americans save a much smaller percentage of their income than the Japanese do. As a result, the Japanese have a larger pool of financial capital that can be used to fuel economic growth.

when they borrow funds. If a corporation borrows directly from savers, or indirectly from savers through financial intermediaries, the corporation will issue a bond or other financial asset to the lender. Likewise, when the government borrows, it issues government bonds and/or other financial assets to the lender.

As a result, almost everyone participates in the financial system. The smooth flow of funds through the system helps ensure that savers will have an outlet for their savings. Borrowers, in turn, will have a source of financial capital.

Investments

Many businesses and individuals watch for profitable investment opportunities. Among other things, they are looking for financial assets—corporate bonds, government bonds, certificates of deposit, and even savings accounts—in which they can invest.

Nonbank Financial Intermediaries

Savings banks, credit unions, commercial banks, and savings associations obtain funds when their customers or members make regular deposits. Another important group of financial intermediaries includes **nonbank financial institutions**. This group obtains funds in a different manner, and includes finance companies, life insurance companies, pension funds, and real estate investment trusts.

Finance Companies

One nonbank institution is a **finance company**, which makes loans directly to consumers and specializes in buying installment contracts from merchants who sell goods on credit. Without the help of finance companies, many small merchants would find it difficult to do business. Many merchants, for example, cannot afford to wait years for their customers to pay off high-cost items on the installment plan. Instead, the merchant sells the customer's installment contract to a finance company for a lump sum. Utilizing a finance company enables the merchant to advertise instant credit or easy terms without actually carrying the loan full term, absorbing losses for an unpaid

account, or taking customers to court for nonpayment of the loan.

Some finance companies make loans directly to consumers. These companies generally check a consumer's credit rating and will make a loan only if the individual qualifies. Because they make loans to some people considered "high risks," and because they pay more for the funds they borrow, finance companies charge more than commercial banks for loans.

One popular loan many consumer finance companies offer is a **bill consolidation loan**—a loan consumers use to pay off all other bills. The consumer then agrees to repay the finance company over a period of one or more years.

Life Insurance Companies

One of the major financial institutions that does not get its funds through deposits is the life insurance company. Although its primary function is to provide financial protection for survivors of the insured, it also collects a great deal of cash.

The head of a family, for example, may want to leave money for a spouse and children in case of death. To do this, he or she may buy a life insurance policy. The price paid for this policy is known as a **premium**, and it must be paid at specified times for the length of the protection.

Because insurance companies collect cash on a regular basis, they often lend surplus funds to others. They may make loans to banks in the form of large certificates of deposit. They also may negotiate other arrangements with smaller consumer finance companies.

Mutual Funds

A **mutual fund** is a company that sells stock in itself to individual investors and then invests the money it receives in stocks and bonds issued by other corporations. Mutual fund stockholders receive dividends earned from the mutual fund's investments. Stockholders can also sell their mutual fund shares for a profit, just like other stocks.

Mutual funds allow people to play the market without risking all they have in one or a few companies. The large size of the mutual fund makes it possible to hire a staff of experts to analyze the securities market before buying and selling securities.

The large size of most funds also allows them to buy many different stocks and bonds and build up a more diversified portfolio than most individual investors could. If the value of one investment fell sharply, the impact on the overall fund would be almost insignificant.

Pension Funds

Another nonbank or nondepository financial institution is the pension fund. A **pension** is a regular allowance intended to provide income security to someone who has worked a certain number of years, reached a certain age, or suffered a certain kind of injury. A **pension fund** is a fund set up to collect income and disburse payments to those persons eligible for retirement, old-age, or disability benefits.

In the case of private pension funds, employers regularly withhold a percentage of workers' salaries to deposit in the fund. During the 30-to-40-year lag between the time the savings are deposited and the time the workers generally use them, the money is usually invested in corporate stocks and bonds. Government pension funds are similar to private ones in that the government makes regular contributions to the fund that will pay benefits later.

Real Estate Investment Trusts

Still another nonbank financial institution is the **real estate investment trust** (REIT)—a company organized chiefly to make loans to construction companies that build homes. Although REITs are not widely known as financial institutions, they help provide billions annually for home construction.

REITs borrow most of their funds from banks and get their income from the rents and mortgage payments of the people who use their money. This income is then used to pay interest on the money borrowed.

Reviewing Terms and Facts

1. **Define** saving, savings, financial system, financial asset, financial intermediary, nonbank financial institution, finance company, bill consolidation loan, premium, mutual fund, pension, pension fund, real estate investment trust.

2. **Explain** why saving is required for capital formation.
3. **List** four financial assets.
4. **Name** five nonbank financial intermediaries.

Critical Thinking

5. **Making Generalizations** Why might a person choose to borrow money from a finance com-

pany that charges higher interest rates than commercial banks do?

Applying Economic Concepts

6. **Financial Assets** An I.O.U. that you draft and give to a friend in payment of a debt is an example of a financial asset. Explain why this is so.

PROFILES IN ECONOMICS

EDWARD T. LEWIS

(1940–)

As chairman and CEO of Essence Communications, Inc. (ECI), Edward T. Lewis heads one of the largest African American businesses in the United States. His struggle to make *Essence* magazine a success shows determination and entrepreneurial skill.

A NEW IDEA In the late 1960s, Shearson, Hammill & Company (now Shearson-Lehman, American Express) sponsored a conference to encourage initiative in African American capitalism. Edward Lewis, a financial analyst for the First National City Bank, was among those invited to attend. Lewis became interested in one of the ideas discussed at the

conference: a slick new magazine to appeal especially to African American women. He and three other young men began planning

Essence magazine currently has a monthly circulation of 950,000 and a readership of 5.1 million.

their new publication in the evenings after their regular jobs.

After two years, the group had raised $130,000. That was enough to launch the first issue of *Essence* in May 1970. The stylish magazine, which featured full-page color photos of African American models and cutting-edge articles, was exciting and different. After Lewis became publisher of *Essence,* the magazine became a success.

NEW VENTURES Recognizing the need to develop into a broad-based communications company, Lewis and his partner, Clarence O. Smith, began to diversify ECI. Beginning in 1984, ECI branched out into direct-mail marketing, licensing, art reproduction, book publishing, and television production.

Essence-By-Mail is a mail-order catalog featuring moderately priced merchandise. Essence Licensing markets eyewear, sewing patterns, and hosiery for women of color. Utilizing the *Essence* magazine format, Essence Television Productions, Inc., produced the award-winning "Essence," a weekly syndicated news show that aired from 1984 to 1988. Currently, Essence Television Productions, Inc., produces the "Essence Awards Show," the nation's most prestigious tribute to African American women.

ECI is also a major investor in Amistad Press, a minority book publishing company. Essence Art Reproductions markets reproductions of fine art created by African American artists. In addition, in 1992 ECI acquired a monthly, nonethnic business magazine, *Income Opportunities.*

Examining the Profile

1. **Analyzing Information** Why do you think publishing a fashion magazine for African American women was an innovative idea in the late 1960s?

2. **For Further Research** Examine several issues of *Essence* magazine. Based on the kinds of articles it publishes, write an analysis of the magazine's editorial policy.

Investing in Financial Assets

Section Preview

Objectives

After studying this section, you will be able to:

1. **Identify** four important investment considerations.
2. **Describe** the four characteristics of bonds.
3. **Describe** the characteristics of major financial assets.
4. **Understand** four views of markets for financial assets.

Key Terms

risk, coupon, maturity, par value, current yield, jumbo CD, junk bond, municipal bond, tax-exempt, savings bond, money market mutual fund, Treasury note, Treasury bond, Treasury bill, Individual Retirement Account, capital market, money market, primary market, secondary market

Applying Economic Concepts

Risk-Return Relationship How can you get the highest return for your money? Someone almost always has an idea for making a fast buck, but these ideas are often risky. Even so, this summarizes the *risk-return relationship* of investing—riskier projects must offer higher returns to be attractive, while less risky investments offer lower returns.

Before people invest in financial assets, they need certain information. Such information includes a basic understanding of investment considerations, the nature of bonds as financial assets, specific characteristics of other financial assets, and the markets for financial assets.

Basic Investment Considerations

When investors buy financial assets, they should keep several factors in mind. The first concerns the relationship between risk and return. The second has to do with the investor's personal investment goals. The third deals with the consistency of investing, and the last deals with avoiding some types of investments.

The Relationship Between Risk and Return

One of the most important relationships in the market is the relationship between risk and return. **Risk**, in an economic sense, is a situation in which the outcome is not certain, but the probabilities can be estimated.

Investors realize that financial assets are risky. Assets may go up or down in price, or the agency that issued the asset may even fail to redeem it, leaving the lender with a loss. As a result, investors demand a higher return to compensate for higher risk.

This relationship between risk and return is illustrated in **Figure 13.2**, which shows that riskier assets must offer higher returns to attract investors. As a result, the first consideration for any investor is the level of risk he or she can tolerate. If the investor is not comfortable with the riskiest assets, he or she should consider others.

Investment Objectives

Another factor an investor considers is the reason for investing. If the goal is to accumulate wealth for retirement, the investor might want to purchase assets that simply appreciate rather than generate income. If the purpose is to accumulate reserves to fund a vacation or to cover living expenses during periods of unemployment, a strategy that focuses on the accumulation of assets that are highly liquid, or easily sold, might be better. Some investors may prefer to accumulate assets that generate a steady stream of income like bonds. Others may already be in a high marginal tax bracket and may prefer to avoid assets that generate taxable income.

The source of income used for investment may help determine which assets are purchased. If the investor receives a steady salary and almost no other income, a payroll deduction plan that puts money in a special retirement fund or purchases government bonds might be best. If the investor receives periodic

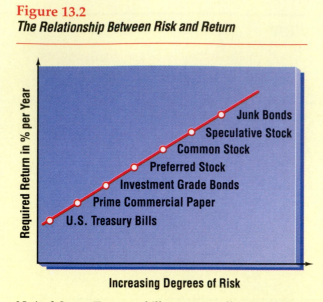

Figure 13.2
The Relationship Between Risk and Return

Junk Bonds
Speculative Stock
Common Stock
Preferred Stock
Investment Grade Bonds
Prime Commercial Paper
U.S. Treasury Bills

Required Return in % per Year

Increasing Degrees of Risk

United States Treasury bills are generally regarded as the safest of all possible investments, and they carry the lowest return. Junk bonds are regarded as the riskiest, which accounts for their high returns. **Why do investors generally require higher returns for some investments?**

bonuses, royalty payments, or other payments on a variable basis, the investor might consider corporate bonds or some other large-denomination financial asset. ☑️

In the end, each investor must consider his or her own circumstances and personal investment goals. Investors have a large number of financial assets, equities, and other investments from which to choose. The investor's knowledge of his or her own needs helps narrow the selection.

Consistency

Successful investors generally invest consistently over long periods of time. In most cases, the amount invested is not as important as investing on a regular basis.

Figure 13.3 shows how a very small deposit of $10 per month would grow over a 5-to-30-year period at various interest rates. The balance in the account accumulates fairly quickly, even at modest interest rates. Because $10 is a small amount, imagine how the account would grow if the deposit was for $25, $50, or

even $100 a month! Many investment advisers tell people to save something every month, even if it is not very much.

Avoiding Complexity

Most investors advise others to stick with what they know. Thousands of different investments are available, and many are fairly complicated. Although a person does not have to understand them all to be a good investor, knowing a few fundamentals is important.

One rule that many investors follow is this: if an investment seems too complicated, let it go. Similarly, an investment that promises fantastic returns or seems too good to be true probably is. A few investors do get lucky, but most investors build wealth because they invest regularly, and they try to avoid the investments that seem too far out of the ordinary. **1**

Bonds as Financial Assets

When an agency needs to borrow funds for long periods, it often issues bonds. Bonds are long-term obligations that pay a stated rate of interest for a specified number of years.

Bond Components

A bond has three main components: the **coupon**, or the stated interest on the debt; the **maturity**, or the life of the bond; and the principal, the amount that will be repaid to the lender at maturity. The principal is usually assigned a dollar value that is called the **par value** of the bond. As a result, the terms *par value* and *principal* are often used interchangeably.

Suppose, for example, a corporation sells a 6 percent, 20-year, $1,000 par value bond that pays interest semiannually. The coupon payment to the holder would be $30 semiannually (.06 times $1,000 divided by 2). When the bond reaches maturity, the company would retire the debt by paying the holder the par value of $1,000.

Bond Prices

The investor views the bond as a financial asset that will pay $30 twice a year for 20 years, plus a final

Figure 13.3
The Power of Compound Interest

This table shows what the balance in an account would look like if monthly deposits of $10 were compounded monthly. **What investment strategy is the key to future financial wealth?**

Annual Interest (in %)	Value at End of Year					
	5	10	15	20	25	30
0	$600	$1,200	$1,800	$2,000	$2,500	$3,600
2	$630	$1,327	$2,097	$2,948	$3,888	$4,927
4	$663	$1,472	$2,461	$3,668	$5,141	$6,940
6	$698	$1,639	$2,908	$4,620	$6,930	$10,045
8	$735	$1,829	$3,460	$5,890	$9,510	$14,904
10	$774	$2,048	$4,145	$7,594	$13,268	$22,605
12	$817	$2,300	$4,996	$9,893	$18,788	$34,950

par value payment of $1,000. Investors can offer $950, $1,000, $1,100, or any other amount for this future payment stream. Investors consider changes in future interest rates, the risk that the company will default, and other factors before they decide what to offer. Supply and demand will then establish the final price.

Bond Yields

In order to compare bonds, investors usually compute the bond's **current yield**, which is the annual interest divided by the purchase price. If an investor paid $950 for the bond described above, the current yield would be $60 divided by $950, or 6.32 percent. If the investor paid $1,100 for the bond, the current yield would be $60 divided by $1,100, or 5.45 percent. Although it may appear as if the issuer fixes the return on a bond when the bond is first issued, the interest received and the price paid determine the actual yield on the bond.

Because the creditworthiness of corporations and governments differ, all 6 percent, 20-year, $1,000 bonds

will not cost the same. Bonds are not insured, and there are no guarantees that the issuer will be around in 20 years to redeem the bond. Therefore, investors will pay more for bonds issued by an agency with an impeccable credit rating. Investors will pay less for a similar bond if it is issued by a corporation with a low credit rating.

Bond Ratings

Fortunately, investors have a way to check the quality of bonds. Two major corporations, Standard & Poor's and Moody's, publish bond ratings. They rate bonds on a number of factors, including the basic financial health of the issuer, the ability to make the future coupon and par value payments, and the issuer's past credit history.

The bond ratings, shown in **Figure 13.4**, use letters scaled from AAA, which represents the highest investment grade, to D, which generally stands for default. If a bond is in default, the issuer has not kept up with the interest or the par value payments. These

QUICK CHECK

Checking Understanding

1. What rules do many investors follow in regard to investment goals?

Applying Economic Concepts

☑ **Investment Objectives** Your investment objectives will probably change as you grow older. People in their 20s and 30s usually are not concerned about retirement, so they invest to accumulate wealth for other reasons, such as vacations or their children's college education.

Figure 13.4
Bond Classifications

Standard & Poor's Corporation and Moody's publish similar bond ratings. Junk bonds, those with ratings of BB or Ba and lower, are generally the riskiest types of bonds. **How do bond ratings affect the price of bonds?**

Source: Standard & Poor's Corporation, Moody's

Standard & Poor's		Moody's	
Highest Investment Grade	AAA	Aaa	Best Quality
High Grade	AA	Aa	High Quality
Upper Medium Grade	A	A	Upper Medium Grade
Medium Grade	BBB	Baa	Medium Grade
Lower Medium Grade	BB	Ba	Possesses Speculative Elements
Speculative	B	B	Generally not Desirable
Vulnerable to Default	CCC	Caa	Poor, Possibly in Default
Subordinated to Other Debt Rated CCC	CC	Ca	Highly Speculative, often in Default
Subordinated to CC Debt	C	C	Income Bonds not paying Income
Bond in Default	D	D	Interest and Principal Payments in Default

ratings are widely publicized, and investors merely have to ask to find out the rating of any bond they plan to purchase.

Bonds with high ratings sell at higher prices than do bonds with lower ratings. A 6 percent, 20-year, $1,000 par value bond with an AAA grade rating may sell for $1,100 and have a current yield of 5.45 percent. Another 6 percent, 20-year, $1,000 par value bond issued by a different company may have a BBB rating, and may therefore only sell for $950 because of the higher risk. The second bond, however, has a higher current yield of 6.32 percent. This point is the essence of the risk-return relationship—riskier investments require higher returns to compensate for the risk.

Financial Assets and Their Characteristics

The modern investor has a wide range of financial assets from which to choose. They vary in cost, maturity, and safety.

Certificates of Deposit

Certificates of deposit are one of the most common forms of investments available. Many people think of them as just another type of account with a depository institution, but they are really loans investors make to financial institutions. Because banks and others count on the use of these funds for a certain time period, they usually impose penalties when people try to cash in their CDs early.

Certificates of deposit are attractive to small investors because they cost as little as $100. Investors can also select the length of maturity, giving them an opportunity to tailor the expiration date to future expenditures such as college tuition, a vacation, or some other expense.

Finally, CDs issued by commercial banks, savings banks, and savings associations are included in the $100,000 FDIC insurance limit. The National Credit Union Association insures most CDs issued by credit unions. **Jumbo CDs**, or CDs in denominations of more than $100,000, are covered only to the $100,000 limit.

Corporate Bonds

Corporate bonds are perhaps the second most important source of corporate funds, the first being the sale of stock. Some individual corporate bonds have par values as low as $1,000, but par values of $10,000 are more common. The actual prices of the bonds are usually different from the par values because supply and demand for the bonds determines the price. **Figure 13.5** shows how to read a listing for corporate bonds.

Investors usually decide on the highest level of risk they are willing to accept, and then try to find a bond that has the best current yield. Exceptionally risky bonds, those that carry a Standard & Poor's rating of BB or lower, or a Moody's rating of Ba or lower, are also called **junk bond**s. These bonds carry a high rate of return as compensation for the possibility of default.

Investors usually purchase corporate bonds as long-term investments, but they can also be liquidated, or sold, quickly if the investor needs cash for other purposes. The Internal Revenue Service considers the interest, or coupon, payments on corporate bonds as taxable income, a fact investors must consider when they invest in bonds.

Municipal Bonds

Municipal bonds, or "munis," are bonds issued by state and local government units. States issue bonds to finance highways, state buildings, and some public works. Cities issue bonds to finance baseball and football stadiums or to finance libraries, parks, and other civic improvements.

Municipal bonds are attractive to investors for several reasons. First, they are generally regarded as safe because state and local governments do not go out of business. Because governments have the power to tax, it is generally presumed that they will be able to pay interest and principal in the future.

Most important, however, is that municipal bonds are generally **tax-exempt**—meaning that the federal government does not tax the interest paid to investors. In some cases, the states issuing the bonds also exempt the interest payments from state taxes, which makes them very attractive to investors. The tax-exempt feature also allows the governmental units to pay a lower rate of interest on the bonds, thereby lowering their cost of borrowing.

Government Savings Bonds

The federal government generates financial assets when it sells savings bonds. **Savings bonds** are low-denomination, nontransferable bonds issued by the United States government, usually through payroll-savings plans.

These bonds are usually available in denominations ranging from $50 to $10,000, and they are purchased at a discount from their redemption amount. For example, a new $50 savings bond may be obtained today for $25, but it could take up to 18 years before it could be redeemed for the full $50, depending on the interest rate. The government pays interest on these bonds,

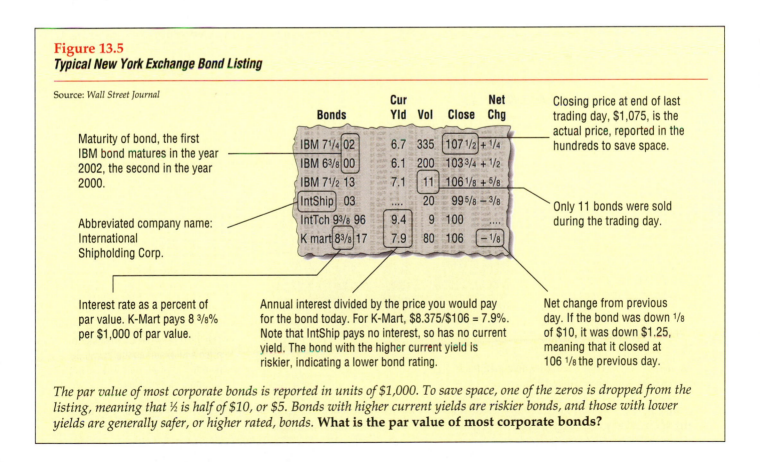

Figure 13.5
Typical New York Exchange Bond Listing

Source: *Wall Street Journal*

Maturity of bond, the first IBM bond matures in the year 2002, the second in the year 2000.

Abbreviated company name: International Shipholding Corp.

Bonds	Cur Yld	Vol	Close	Net Chg
IBM 7¼ 02	6.7	335	107½	+ ¼
IBM 6⅜ 00	6.1	200	103¾	+ ½
IBM 7½ 13	7.1	11	106⅛	+ ⅝
IntShip 03	....	20	99⅝	− ⅜
IntTch 9⅜ 96	9.4	9	100	....
K mart 8⅜ 17	7.9	80	106	− ⅛

Closing price at end of last trading day, $1,075, is the actual price, reported in the hundreds to save space.

Only 11 bonds were sold during the trading day.

Interest rate as a percent of par value. K-Mart pays 8 ⅜% per $1,000 of par value.

Annual interest divided by the price you would pay for the bond today. For K-Mart, $8.375/$106 = 7.9%. Note that IntShip pays no interest, so has no current yield. The bond with the higher current yield is riskier, indicating a lower bond rating.

Net change from previous day. If the bond was down ⅛ of $10, it was down $1.25, meaning that it closed at 106 ⅛ the previous day.

The par value of most corporate bonds is reported in units of $1,000. To save space, one of the zeros is dropped from the listing, meaning that ½ is half of $10, or $5. Bonds with higher current yields are riskier bonds, and those with lower yields are generally safer, or higher rated, bonds. **What is the par value of most corporate bonds?**

but it builds the interest into the redemption price rather than sending checks to millions of investors on a regular basis.

Savings bonds are attractive because they are easy to obtain and there is virtually no risk of default. They cannot be sold to someone else if the investor needs cash, but they can be redeemed early, with some loss of interest, if the investor must raise cash for other purposes. Most investors tend to hold long-term savings bonds, treating them as a form of automatic savings.

International Bonds

The United States government is not the only government to sell bonds. A number of countries issue bonds, although they are generally available only in large denominations usually starting at $1 million. **1**

Pension funds, insurance companies, and even large corporations with large cash reserves purchase these bonds. The risk of international bonds is harder to determine than other types of bonds, so investors have to choose carefully.

International bonds also have one other feature that makes them unique—they often make coupon and principal payments in another currency. The investor does not know if that currency will be stronger or weaker than the dollar when the payments are received in the future.

Money Market Mutual Funds

A special type of mutual fund is a **money market mutual fund**, a business that collects funds from small investors and then makes loans, usually in the form of large CDs, to other borrowers. ✔

Investors like the money market funds because they receive higher interest than they would receive from dealing directly with the banks. The drawback to the arrangement is that FDIC insurance covers neither the jumbo CDs nor the contributions to the funds. The money market mutual funds are slightly riskier than regular CDs, and so pay a higher return.

Treasury Notes and Bonds

When the federal government borrows funds for periods longer than 1 year, it issues Treasury notes and bonds. **Treasury notes** are United States government obligations with maturities of 2 to 10 years, while **Treasury bonds** have maturities ranging from

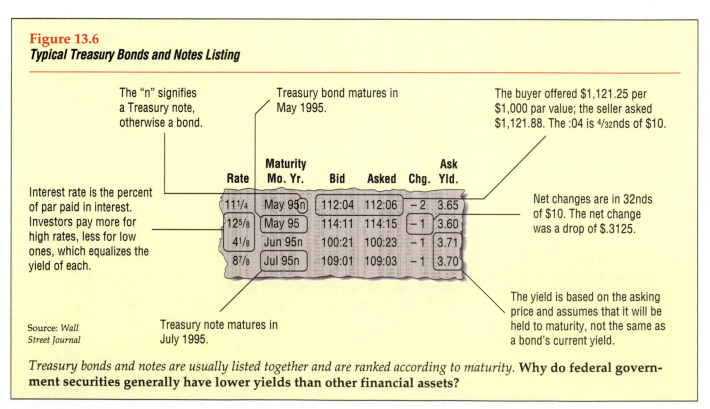

Figure 13.6
Typical Treasury Bonds and Notes Listing

The "n" signifies a Treasury note, otherwise a bond.

Treasury bond matures in May 1995.

The buyer offered $1,121.25 per $1,000 par value; the seller asked $1,121.88. The :04 is 4/32nds of $10.

Interest rate is the percent of par paid in interest. Investors pay more for high rates, less for low ones, which equalizes the yield of each.

Rate	Maturity Mo. Yr.	Bid	Asked	Chg.	Ask Yld.
11$\frac{1}{4}$	May 95n	112:04	112:06	− 2	3.65
12$\frac{5}{8}$	May 95	114:11	114:15	− 1	3.60
4$\frac{1}{8}$	Jun 95n	100:21	100:23	− 1	3.71
8$\frac{7}{8}$	Jul 95n	109:01	109:03	− 1	3.70

Net changes are in 32nds of $10. The net change was a drop of $.3125.

The yield is based on the asking price and assumes that it will be held to maturity, not the same as a bond's current yield.

Source: *Wall Street Journal*

Treasury note matures in July 1995.

Treasury bonds and notes are usually listed together and are ranked according to maturity. **Why do federal government securities generally have lower yields than other financial assets?**

Figure 13.7
Financial Assets and Their Markets

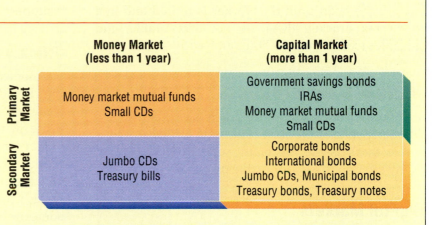

Markets are frequently described by the characteristics of the financial assets being traded. If the length of maturity is important, the market is sometimes called a money or capital market. If the ability to sell the asset to someone other than the original issuer is important, the market may be described as being a primary or secondary market. **Why do some financial assets, like CDs, appear in more than one market?**

	Money Market (less than 1 year)	Capital Market (more than 1 year)
Primary Market	Money market mutual funds Small CDs	Government savings bonds IRAs Money market mutual funds Small CDs
Secondary Market	Jumbo CDs Treasury bills	Corporate bonds International bonds Jumbo CDs, Municipal bonds Treasury bonds, Treasury notes

more than 10 to as many as 30 years. The only collateral that secures both is the faith and credit of the United States government. **Figure 13.6** shows how to read a listing for Treasury notes and bonds.

Treasury notes and bonds come in denominations of $5,000 for maturities of 2 to 3 years, and denominations of $1,000 for maturities longer than 4 years. The government also maintains computerized records of its debt holders, so that it can make periodic interest payments to those individuals. **2**

Although these financial assets have no collateral or backing, they are popular with investors because they are generally regarded as the safest of all financial assets. Because of the trade-off between risk and return, however, these assets also have the lowest returns of all financial assets.

Treasury Bills

Federal government borrowing generates other financial assets known as Treasury bills. A **Treasury bill**, also known as a T-bill, is a short-term obligation with a maturity of 13, 26, or 52 weeks in a minimum denomination of $10,000.

The bills do not pay interest directly, but instead are sold on a discount basis, much like government savings bonds. For example, an investor may pay the auction price of $9,300 for a 52-week bill that matures at $10,000. The $700 difference between the amount paid and the amount received is the lender's return. The lender is receiving $700 on a $9,300 investment, for a return of $700 divided by $9,300, or 7.5 percent.

Individual Retirement Accounts

Individual Retirement Accounts (IRAs) are long-term, tax-sheltered time deposits that an employee can set up as part of a retirement plan. If the worker's spouse also works, up to $2,000 per year can be deposited. Up to $2,250 can be deposited if the spouse is not working.

The worker deducts the deposit from his or her taxable income at the end of the year, thereby sheltering the $2,000 from income taxes. Taxes on the interest

Checking Understanding

1. Why are few Americans able to buy international bonds?
2. In what denominations are Treasury notes and bonds sold?

Applying Economic Concepts

 Money Market Mutual Funds Money market mutual funds were introduced in the 1970s when Regulation Q limited the interest that depository institutions could pay. The funds purchased jumbo CDs that were exempt from Regulation Q's limits.

and the principal will eventually have to be paid, but it gives the worker an incentive to save today, postponing the taxes until the worker is retired and in a lower tax bracket. IRAs are not transferable, and penalties exist if they are liquidated early.

Markets for Financial Assets

Investors often refer to markets according to the characteristics of the financial assets traded in them. These markets are not really separate entities, and many overlap to a considerable degree.

Capital Markets

When investors speak of the **capital market**, they mean a market where money is loaned for periods of more than one year. Long-term CDs and corporate and government bonds that have more than a year to mature all belong to this category. Capital market instruments are shown in the right-hand column of **Figure 13.7.**

Money Markets

When investors speak of the **money market**, they mean a market where money is loaned for periods of less than one year. The financial assets that belong to the money market are shown in the left-hand column of **Figure 13.7.** Note that a person who owns a CD with a maturity of one year or less takes part in the money market. If the CD has a maturity of more than one year, the person takes part in the capital market as a supplier of funds.

Primary Markets

Another way to view financial markets is to focus on the liquidity of a newly created financial asset. If the original issuer is the only one that would redeem it, the financial asset is said to be in the **primary market**.

Government savings bonds and IRAs are in this market because they are both nontransferable. Small CDs are in the primary market because investors tend to cash them in early, rather than try to sell them to someone else, if they need cash.

Secondary Markets

Suppose that a financial asset can be sold to someone other than the original issuer. It then becomes part of the **secondary market**, the market in which existing securities can be resold to new owners. Issuers of financial assets value secondary markets because the investor will not redeem the asset until it reaches maturity.

The major significance of the secondary market is the liquidity it provides to investors. If a strong secondary market exists for a financial asset, the investor knows that the asset can be liquidated fairly quickly and without penalty other than the fees paid to handle the transaction.

SECTION 2
REVIEW

Reviewing Terms and Facts

1. **Define** risk, coupon, maturity, par value, current yield, jumbo CD, junk bond, municipal bond, tax-exempt, savings bond, money market mutual fund, Treasury note, Treasury bond, Treasury bill, Individual Retirement Account, capital market, money market, primary market, secondary market.

2. **Describe** what is meant by the risk-return relationship.
3. **Identify** the four main characteristics of bonds.
4. **List** nine popular financial assets.
5. **Identify** four markets of financial assets.

Critical Thinking

6. **Evaluating Information** Of the four basic investment con-siderations described, which do you think is the most important? Explain your answer.

Applying Economic Concepts

7. **Risk-Return Relationship** If you had money to invest, in which financial asset(s) would you invest? Why?

How to Read Stock Market Reports

Open up the financial page of almost any newspaper, and you will see hundreds of rows of what almost appears to be a foreign language. Numbers, codes, prices, and percentages all seem to run together. What you are looking at is the stock market report.

Explanation

Stock prices are listed alphabetically each business day in the financial section of most newspapers. As each trading day begins, stocks usually open at the same price they closed at the day before. The price of a share of stock generally goes up and down throughout the day as the conditions of supply and demand change. At the end of the business day, each stock has a closing price. As a result, three prices generally are available each day for a share of stock—the high, the low, and the closing price. In many cases, the listing also gives such information as the yearly high and low prices, the annual dividend payment and yield, the number of shares sold on that day, and the net change in the price of the stock.

Practice

Figure 13.8 shows examples of stocks traded on the New York Stock Exchange. Read the descriptions of the information presented in the columns, then answer the questions that follow.

1. What was the highest price paid for Reebok during the 52-week period?
2. What was the closing price for Reebok on this particular day?
3. Of the stocks shown, which showed the greatest loss on this particular day?
4. Which stock made the biggest gain on this particular day?
5. Which stock paid the highest dividend?
6. Which stock had the lowest PE ratio?
7. Which stock had the highest PE ratio?
8. How many shares of Reebok were traded on this particular day?
9. If you had purchased 100 shares of Reebok at the year's lowest price, how would you be doing on this particular day?

Figure 13.8
The New York Stock Exchange

The annual dividend is $.80, which is paid in 4 equal installments of $.20 each.

NKE is the ticker symbol, or computer code, for the stock.

The stock hit a high of $49.50, a low of $48.50, and closed at $48.75.

During the day, 845,900 shares were traded.

Nike closed $1.25 lower than the day before. The previous listing would have shown a closing price of $48.75 plus $1.25, or $50.00.

| 52 Weeks | | Stock | Sym | Div | Yld % | PE | Vol 100s | Hi | Lo | Close | Net Chg |
Hi	Lo										
31 5/8	22 1/8	NICOR	GAS	1.22	4.0	15	799	30 3/4	30 1/4	30 1/2	− 1/4
90 1/4	49 3/8	Nike B	NKE	.80	1.6	10	8459	49 1/2	48 1/2	48 3/4	− 1 1/4
29 7/8	17 3/4	NineWest	NIN		...		799	26 1/4	25 3/4	25 3/4	− 3/8
38 5/8	23	Reebok	RBK	.30	1.2	20	1514	24 7/8	24 3/8	24 7/8	+ 3/8

During the last 12 months, Nike shares traded for as much as $90.25 and as little as $49.37 a share.

The yield is the dividend divided by the closing price. If you purchased one share at $48.75, and the share paid an annual dividend of $.80, your return would be $.80 ÷ $48.75 = .016, or 1.6%.

The price of today's closing stock, $48.75, divided by the company's earnings on a per share basis is 10. Conversely, $48.75 ÷ 10 = $4.88 per share. Lower price/earnings ratios generally mean more earnings per share; higher price/earnings ratios generally mean smaller earnings per share.

Additional Practice

For further practice in reading stock market reports, complete the Reinforcing Skills exercise in the Chapter 13 Review on page 341.

Investing in Equities, Futures, and Options

Section Preview

Objectives

After studying this section, you will be able to:

1. **Recognize** the characteristics of the major stock exchanges.

2. **Explain** how stock market performance is measured.

3. **Understand** how financial assets and equities can be traded in the future.

Key Terms

equities, Efficient Market Hypothesis, portfolio diversification, stockbroker, securities exchange, seat, Over-The-Counter market, DJIA, S&P 500, spot market, futures, futures market, option, call option, put option, options market

Applying Economic Concepts

Futures Markets Have you ever negotiated to receive your allowance early, or asked to be paid right away for a service to be completed later? This is the nature of a *futures market*. A contract is issued and payment is rendered for some future activity. Now you can tell your parents that you are not procrastinating; you are getting ready for a future in the world of finance!

I n addition to financial assets, investors may buy **equities**, or stocks that represent ownership shares in corporations.

When a market has identical products, large numbers of buyers and sellers, and reasonably good information, prices tend to be about the same from one supplier to the next. This concept explains why the majority of commercial banks, savings banks, and savings institutions pay about the same interest for certificates of deposit with a given maturity.

Market Efficiency

The markets for equities are similar in several respects. Large numbers of buyers and sellers exist, and information about the stocks and the companies that issue them is reasonably good. About the only difference is that some stocks cost more than others.

A number of factors influence the price of a share of stock. A large, profitable company may have a relatively small number of shares outstanding, which generally makes its shares worth more than those of a smaller and less profitable company. Expectations about the future also affect stock prices. For example, two companies may be equal in all respects, but one may have far better growth prospects.

The **Efficient Market Hypothesis** (EMH) is often used to help explain the pricing of equities. The hypothesis argues that stocks are always priced about right, and that bargains are hard to find. A leading expert on the topic explains how this might happen:

Essentially, the EMH states that there are some 100,000 or so full-time, highly trained, professional analysts and traders operating in the market and following some 3,000 major stocks. If each analyst followed only 30 stocks, there would still be 1,000 analysts following each stock. Further, these analysts work for organizations such as Merrill Lynch and Prudential Insurance, which have billions of dollars available with which to take advantage of bargains. As new information about a stock becomes available, these 1,000 analysts all receive and evaluate it at approximately the same time, so the price of the stock adjusts almost immediately to reflect new developments.

—from Eugene F. Brigham's *Fundamentals of Financial Management*

The implication for the investor is that it is almost impossible to "beat the market." If all stocks are priced about right, it does not matter which ones you purchase. The investor may get lucky and pick a stock about to go up, or the investor may get unlucky and pick a stock about to go down. As a result, the best strategy for an investor is **portfolio diversification**, or holding a number of stocks, so that increases in some could offset unexpected declines in others.

If an investor wants to obtain securities, the investor enlists the assistance of a **stockbroker**—a person who buys or sells securities. The broker arranges to have the stocks purchased at a stock exchange, or supplies the securities from an inventory, or buys them from some other broker.

Organized Stock Exchanges

A number of organized **securities exchanges**—places where buyers and sellers meet to trade securities—exist. An organized exchange gets its name from the way it conducts business. Members pay a fee to join, and trades can only take place on the floor of the exchange. One exchange, shown in **Figure 13.9**, dwarfs all others.

The New York Stock Exchange

The oldest, largest, and most prestigious of the organized stock exchanges in the United States is the New York Stock Exchange (NYSE), located on Wall Street in New York City. This exchange, like most other organized exchanges, has certain rules for both its members and the corporations listed on the exchange.

The NYSE has about 1,400 **seats**, or memberships that allow access to the trading floor. Large brokerage companies, such as Merrill Lynch, may own as many as 20 seats at any given time. The members may

pay from $500,000 to $1,000,000 for each seat. Members have the right to elect their own directors and vote on the rules and regulations that govern the exchange.

The NYSE lists about 2,400 stocks from approximately 1,900 companies. The companies must meet stringent requirements related to profitability and size, which virtually guarantee that the companies will be among the largest, most profitable, publicly held companies in the country. **Figure 13.8** on page 333 shows how prices are listed on the NYSE.

The American Stock Exchange

Another prestigious national exchange is the American Stock Exchange (AMEX), which is also located in New York City. It has approximately 660 seats and nearly 1,000 listed stocks.

For many years, the AMEX was the second largest organized exchange in the country behind the NYSE. Its growth then slowed, and some of the regional exchanges overtook the AMEX. Today the American is the fourth largest exchange in the country. Overall, the companies represented on the AMEX tend to be smaller and more speculative than those listed on the NYSE.

Regional Stock Exchanges

The regional exchanges include the Chicago, Pacific, Philadelphia, Boston, and Memphis exchanges, along with some smaller exchanges in other cities. Many of these exchanges originally listed corporations that were either too small or too new to be

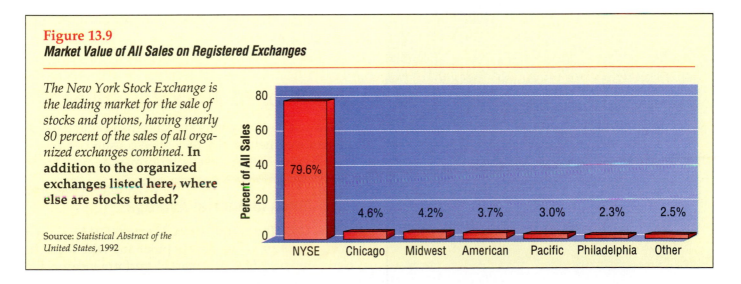

Figure 13.9
Market Value of All Sales on Registered Exchanges

The New York Stock Exchange is the leading market for the sale of stocks and options, having nearly 80 percent of the sales of all organized exchanges combined. **In addition to the organized exchanges listed here, where else are stocks traded?**

Source: *Statistical Abstract of the United States, 1992*

Percent of All Sales

NYSE 79.6% | Chicago 4.6% | Midwest 4.2% | American 3.7% | Pacific 3.0% | Philadelphia 2.3% | Other 2.5%

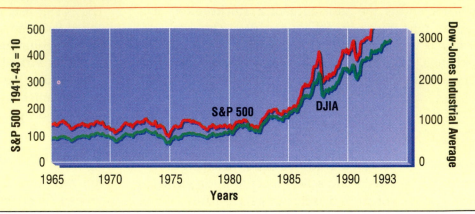

Figure 13.10
Tracking Stock Prices, the DJIA, and Standard & Poor's 500

The Dow-Jones Industrial Average and Standard & Poor's 500 are two indices used to track stock prices. The DJIA gets slightly more publicity, but the S&P 500 is also popular because it is more comprehensive. **Which index covers just the NYSE, and which index covers the NYSE, the AMEX, and OTC markets?**

listed on the NYSE or the AMEX. Today, however, many stocks are dual listed and can be found on the NYSE or AMEX as well as on a regional exchange. The regionals also meet the needs of the smaller and middle-sized corporations in their region. **1**

Global Stock Exchanges

Stock exchanges can be found throughout the world. Exchanges operate in such cities as Sydney, Tokyo, Hong Kong, Singapore, Johannesburg, and Frankfurt. Developments in computer technology and electronic trading have linked these markets so that most major stocks can be traded around the clock, somewhere in the world.

DID YOU KNOW?

Penny Stocks Low-priced stocks, generally selling for between 1 cent and $5 a share may sound like an appealing investment. Buyers, beware! Investing in these so-called penny stocks can be risky business. Many investors have been caught in scams that promised huge profits. Dishonest practices have swindled penny-stock investors out of billions of dollars. Some legitimate stocks do sell for low prices, however. Investors can protect themselves from fraud by consulting a reliable broker.

The Over-The-Counter Market

Despite the importance of the organized exchanges, the great majority of stocks in the United States are not traded on exchanges. Instead, they are traded on the **Over-The-Counter market** (OTC)—an electronic marketplace for securities that are not listed or traded on an organized exchange.

Securities traded on this exchange are listed in a sophisticated computer network called the National Market System (NMS). The members of the OTC market belong to the National Association of Securities Dealers (NASD). NASDAQ, the National Association of Securities Dealers Automated Quotation, is the listing that provides information on stocks that this group trades. The main difference between a NASDAQ listing and the NYSE is that very few of the OTC stocks pay dividends, mostly because they are new and growing companies.

Measures of Stock Performance

Because most investors are concerned about the performance of their stocks, they often consult two popular indicators of the market's performance.

Dow-Jones Industrial Average

The **Dow-Jones Industrial Average (DJIA)**, shown in **Figure 13.10**, is the most popular and widely publicized measure of stock market performance on the

Figure 13.11
Typical Mutual Fund Quotations

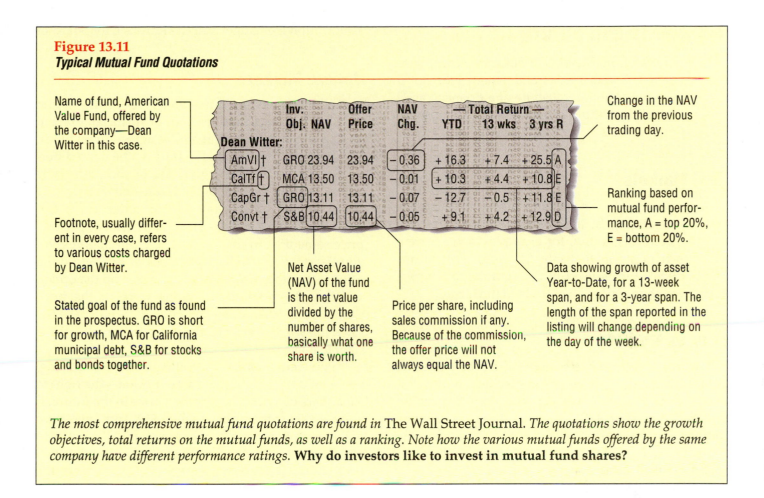

Name of fund, American Value Fund, offered by the company—Dean Witter in this case.

Footnote, usually different in every case, refers to various costs charged by Dean Witter.

Stated goal of the fund as found in the prospectus. GRO is short for growth, MCA for California municipal debt, S&B for stocks and bonds together.

Net Asset Value (NAV) of the fund is the net value divided by the number of shares, basically what one share is worth.

Price per share, including sales commission if any. Because of the commission, the offer price will not always equal the NAV.

Change in the NAV from the previous trading day.

Ranking based on mutual fund performance, A = top 20%, E = bottom 20%.

Data showing growth of asset Year-to-Date, for a 13-week span, and for a 3-year span. The length of the span reported in the listing will change depending on the day of the week.

The most comprehensive mutual fund quotations are found in The Wall Street Journal. *The quotations show the growth objectives, total returns on the mutual funds, as well as a ranking. Note how the various mutual funds offered by the same company have different performance ratings.* **Why do investors like to invest in mutual fund shares?**

NYSE. In 1884 the Dow-Jones corporation published the average closing price of 11 active stocks. Eventually, the list grew to cover the closing prices of 30 representative stocks listed on the NYSE.

The DJIA is constructed so that a "point" change equates to a 45-cent change in the total price of all 30 stocks. If the Dow-Jones drops 4 points, for example, the sum of the closing prices for the day of the 30 selected stocks is $1.80 less than the closing prices were the day before.

Standard & Poor's 500

Another popular measure is the **Standard & Poor's 500 (S&P 500),** a stock performance index that uses the price changes of 500 representative stocks as an indicator of overall market performance. Because the sum of 500 stock prices would be rather large, it is reduced to an index number. Unlike the Dow-Jones, the Standard & Poor's 500 reports on stocks listed on the NYSE, AMEX, and OTC markets. **2**

Checking Understanding

1. What are the two major stock exchanges?
2. What is the Standard & Poor's 500?

Applying Economic Concepts

Market Failures The greatest drop in the Dow-Jones Industrial Average was on October 19, 1987—Black Monday. By the end of trading, stocks had lost 508.32 points—a drop of 22.6 percent.

Trading in the Future

In **Figure 13.7**, markets were defined according to the life of the financial asset and whether or not it could be resold. Another attribute of a financial asset is time, which leads to a discussion of spot, futures, and options markets.

Spot Markets

A **spot market** is a market in which a transaction is made immediately at the prevailing price. The spot price of gold in London, for example, is the current price as it exists in that city. The term *spot* means "immediate" and is used to distinguish this market from two other markets that trade in the future.

Futures Markets

Futures are contracts to buy or sell at a specific date in the future, at a price specified today. For example, two parties may agree to buy a specified amount of gold at $450 an ounce three, six, or nine months in the future. The buyer would pay the money today, and the seller would deliver the commodity in the future.

Futures markets are the markets in which futures are bought and sold. Many of these markets are affiliated with the grain and livestock exchanges that originated in the Midwest. The markets include the New York Mercantile Exchange, the Chicago Board of Trade, the Chicago Mercantile Exchange, the New York Cotton Exchange, and the Kansas City Board of Trade.

Options Markets

Options are contracts that give investors the option to buy or sell commodities and/or financial assets at some point in the future at a price agreed upon today. Options are closely related to futures, the main difference being that options give one of the parties the opportunity to back out of the future delivery.

For example, you may pay $5 today for a **call option**—the right to *buy* a share of stock at a specified price some time in the future. If the call option gives you the right to purchase the stock at $70, and if the price of the stock drops to $30, you tear up the option and buy the stock at the going price. If the price should go to $100, however, you could purchase the stock for $70. Either way, the $5 option gives you the right to make the choice in the future.

If you were interested in selling instead of buying, you would have purchased a **put option**—the right to *sell* a share of stock at a specified price in the future. If you pay $3 for the right to sell at $50, and if the price of the stock drops to $40, you can require the buyer to pay the contract price for the stock. You would then net $47 from the sale, the $50 contract price minus the $3 paid for the option. If the price went to $80 instead, you would be better off to tear up the option and sell the stock for $80.

Options markets are the markets in which options are traded. Most of the exchanges that offer futures also sell options.

SECTION 3 REVIEW

Reviewing Terms and Facts

1. **Define** equities, Efficient Market Hypothesis, portfolio diversification, stockbroker, securities exchange, seat, Over-The-Counter market, DJIA, S&P 500, spot market, futures, futures market, options, call option, put option, options markets.

2. **Name** the major organized stock exchanges in the United States.

3. **Discuss** two measures of stock market performance.

4. **Identify** the difference between futures and options contracts.

Critical Thinking

5. **Making Generalizations** Does the Efficient Market Hypothesis support or refute your conceptions of playing the stock market? Explain.

Applying Economic Concepts

6. **Futures Markets** Would you ever invest in a futures contract? Why or why not?

Vocabulary

The following terms are defined in Chapter 13:

SECTION ONE
- saving *(p. 320)*
- savings *(p. 320)*
- financial system *(p. 320)*
- financial asset *(p. 321)*
- financial intermediary *(p. 321)*
- nonbank financial institution *(p. 322)*
- finance company *(p. 322)*
- bill consolidation loan *(p. 322)*

- premium *(p. 323)*
- mutual fund *(p. 323)*
- pension *(p. 323)*
- pension fund *(p. 323)*
- real estate investment trust *(p. 323)*

SECTION TWO
- risk *(p. 325)*
- coupon *(p. 326)*
- maturity *(p. 326)*
- par value *(p. 326)*
- current yield *(p. 327)*
- jumbo CD *(p. 328)*
- junk bond *(p. 328)*
- municipal bond *(p. 329)*
- tax-exempt *(p. 329)*

- savings bond *(p. 329)*
- money market mutual funds *(p. 330)*
- Treasury note *(p. 330)*
- Treasury bond *(p. 330)*
- Treasury bill *(p. 331)*
- Individual Retirement Account *(p. 331)*
- capital market *(p. 332)*
- money market *(p. 332)*
- primary market *(p. 332)*
- secondary market *(p. 332)*

SECTION THREE
- equities *(p. 334)*
- Efficient Market Hypothesis *(p. 334)*

- portfolio diversification *(p. 334)*
- stockbroker *(p. 335)*
- securities exchange *(p. 335)*
- seat *(p. 335)*
- Over-The-Counter market *(p. 336)*
- DJIA *(p. 336)*
- S&P 500 *(p. 337)*
- spot market *(p. 338)*
- futures *(p. 338)*
- futures market *(p. 338)*
- options *(p. 338)*
- call option *(p. 338)*
- put option *(p. 338)*
- options markets *(p. 338)*

SECTION 1

Savings and the Financial System (pages 320–323)

Saving is a process that makes **savings** available for others to invest. The economy has a **financial system** that transfers savings to investors. The **financial assets** generated in the process are issued by businesses, governments, and **financial intermediaries** that facilitate the transfer of funds from savers to investors. Financial intermediaries include **finance companies,** life insurance companies, **mutual funds, pension funds,** and **real estate investment trusts.**

Reviewing the Main Idea

What financial intermediaries exist to transfer funds from savers to investors?

SECTION 2

Investing in Financial Assets (pages 325–332)

A large number of financial assets are available to investors. Bonds issued by corporations, state and local governments, the United States government, and other governments make up a large component of financial assets. Certificates of deposit, **money market mutual funds,** and **individual retirement accounts** are other financial assets issued by a variety of private agencies.

Reviewing the Main Idea

What financial assets are available to investors?

SECTION 3

Investing in Equities, Futures, and Options (pages 334–338)

Equities, or stocks, are different from financial assets in that equities represent ownership of a corporation, rather than a loan to it. Many securities are traded on organized **securities exchanges** where members meet to buy and sell stocks.

Investors follow the **DJIA** to track the performance of stocks on the NYSE. **Standard & Poor's 500** index samples 500 representative stocks listed on various exchanges, including the **OTC market.**

Historically, farmers and purchasers of agricultural products developed a way of extending contracts over time. Today, **futures** contracts are widely used. If an investor wants the option to back out of a future delivery specified in a contract written today, he or she may be more interested in an **option** contract.

Reviewing the Main Idea

How are equities different from financial assets, and where are equities traded?

Reviewing Key Terms

For each of the investments below, write a brief paragraph that describes at least three of the term's principal characteristics.

1. Treasury bond
2. Treasury bill
3. equities
4. Treasury note
5. futures
6. Individual Retirement Account
7. jumbo CD
8. junk bond
9. money market mutual fund
10. municipal bond
11. options

Reviewing the Facts

SECTION 1 *(pages 320–323)*

1. **Explain** the relationship between savings and capital formation.
2. **Describe** how financial assets are created in the free enterprise system.
3. **Describe** five nonbank financial intermediaries in the American economy.

SECTION 2 *(pages 325–332)*

4. **Name** four considerations important to investors.
5. **Explain** how current yields are computed.
6. **Compare** five types of bonds that are commonly traded in the United States.
7. **Explain** how capital markets and secondary markets get their names.

SECTION 3 *(pages 334–338)*

8. **Explain** what the Efficient Market Hypothesis means to investors.
9. **Compare** the NYSE with the other organized stock exchanges.

10. **Describe** the nature of the Over-The-Counter market.
11. **Compare** the similarities and differences between the Dow-Jones Industrial Average and the Standard & Poor's 500.
12. **Explain** how options contracts are different from futures contracts.

Critical Thinking

1. **Drawing Conclusions** If you contacted several local banks to get their rates paid on various CDs, you would find that rates vary only slightly from one institution to another. Do you think the similarities are caused by collusion or by efficient markets? Explain.
2. **Identifying Alternatives** The financial assets listed in the chapter are representative of those available in the American economy but are not complete. Research to find other assets, such as commercial paper and banker's acceptances, that could be added to the list.

Applying Economic Concepts

1. **Risk-Return Relationship** List five possible investments a person could make if funds were available. Rank the investments in order of how much risk each entails (from highest to lowest). Then rank the investments according to expected returns (from highest to lowest). What is the significance of the rankings to the risk-return relationship?
2. **Financial Assets** Visit a local bank or a nonbank financial institution and ask for its free brochure that outlines the institution's investment opportunities such as savings accounts, certificates of deposit, money market accounts, and stock brokerage accounts. Write a brief report describing the financial assets the institution generates or trades.

Reinforcing Skills

HOW TO READ STOCK MARKET REPORTS

You learned how to read stock market reports in the skill lesson in this chapter. Analyze the stock market listing below, from one of the issues of The Wall Street Journal. *Then answer the questions that follow.*

52 Weeks							Vol				
Hi	**Lo**	**Stock**	**Sym**	**Div**	**Yld%**	**PE**	**100s**	**Hi**	**Lo**	**Close**	**NetChg**
90¼	44	Nike B	NKE	.80	1.5	11	4775	53⅞	51¾	52	−1½
49⅛	33¾	Penney JC	JCP	1.44	3.5	12	7107	41⅞	41¼	41⅝	+⅜
43⅝	34½	PepsiCo	PEP	.64	1.5	24	11641	41⅞	41¼	41½	−⅛
13⅛	8¼	Pier 1	PIR	.10	.9	21	2846	11	10¾	10⅞	+¼
34⅛	23	WalMart	WMT	.13	.5	29	43968	27⅞	27	27⅝	+⅝

1. What was the highest price paid for PepsiCo during the 52-week period?
2. What was the closing price for WalMart on this particular day?
3. Which stock showed the greatest loss on this particular day? What was the loss?
4. How many shares of Penney JC were traded on this particular day?
5. Which stock paid the highest dividend?
6. Which stock cost the most per share on this particular day?
7. How many shares of Nike were traded on this particular day?
8. If you had purchased 100 shares of Pier 1 at the year's lowest price, how would you be doing on this particular day?

Individual Activity

The chapter stated that successful investors tend to avoid complex investments that they do not fully understand. Explain why you might agree or disagree with this advice.

Cooperative Learning Activity

In your local newspaper, find a listing of a stock, a corporate bond, a Treasury note, and a mutual fund. Organize into four groups, and have each group interpret one of the listings. Share your results with the rest of the class.

Writing About Economics

THE PERSUASIVE STYLE

In the **Journal Writing** activity on page 319, you were asked to invest $50,000 in a stock portfolio and to track the progress of your stock(s) for one week or more. Using the persuasive style of writing discussed on page 554, write an editorial describing the results of your stock purchases and whether investing in stock is a profitable or unprofitable way to spend your money.

REPLACE WELFARE WITH WORKFARE?

After the Great Depression of the 1930s, the United States created a number of welfare programs to help reduce economic instability and insecurity. Over time, however, the cost and effectiveness of welfare programs has been questioned. A growing number of people would like to replace welfare programs with workfare—programs requiring people to exchange some of their labor for benefits. The two views here were voiced at a hearing before a congressional Subcommittee on Trade, Productivity, and Economic Growth.

Pro

Only 15% of welfare mothers work at a given time, according to government surveys, and the rate is still lower among the long-term cases. Workfare is one of the keys to solving poverty and dependency in the United States. If more of the poor worked, many fewer would need support. . . .

Allegedly, [the welfare program Aid to Families with Dependent Children] breaks up families because eligibility is usually limited to single parents with children, and it discourages work because most of what recipients earn is deducted from their welfare grants. . . .

On balance, workfare is certainly worthwhile. The long-term poor are notably unresponsive to the opportunities around them. They have not taken advantage of existing employment, as recent immigration groups have, nor have benefit-oriented social programs done much to help them. Workfare . . . [is] the most promising development in social policy since the Great Society.

—FROM LAWRENCE M. MEAD, ASSOCIATE PROFESSOR OF POLITICS AT NEW YORK UNIVERSITY

▲ *Social welfare programs were developed to aid people in need, like this family displaced by a drought in Oklahoma.*

▼ *Training classes help welfare recipients increase their skills.*

The Aid to Families with Dependent Children (AFDC) program provides aid to single parents.

▼ Workfare requires people to exchange some of their labor for benefits.

Con The assumption that the only thing that keeps welfare recipients on the rolls is a lack of motivation to work is a gross misconception. Half of recipients . . . find jobs and leave welfare in their own right after a relatively brief stay in the program. The remainder of employable recipients, who make up only approximately 7% of all those receiving welfare, remain in the program for longer than two year stints. But this is the group that is least likely to benefit from workfare, or be motivated by experience, since they face the types of more serious academic and skill deficiencies that are not affected or improved by short-term work assignments.

Another misconception about what workfare is and is not . . . is the widespread assumption that the program saves money. Recent experiences with workfare in state after state prove the contrary—that in fact the program costs substantially more than it saves through reduced welfare payments.

—MORTON H. SKLAR, LEGAL COUNSEL AND DIRECTOR OF JOBS WATCH

Analyzing the Case Study

1. What is workfare?
2. What evidence does Lawrence Mead cite to explain that workfare should replace welfare?
3. What evidence does Morton Sklar cite to explain that workfare should not replace welfare?
4. With which opinion do you agree? Why?

MACRO-
ECONOMICS:
POLICIES

A recession is when your neighbor is out of work. A depression is when you're out of work.

—Harry S Truman

Economics and You

In this unit, discover what part economics plays in the following situations:
• The sale of a used car does not add to the country's total gross domestic product.
• Your dollar bill buys less than 6 cents worth of the goods and services that it bought in 1900.

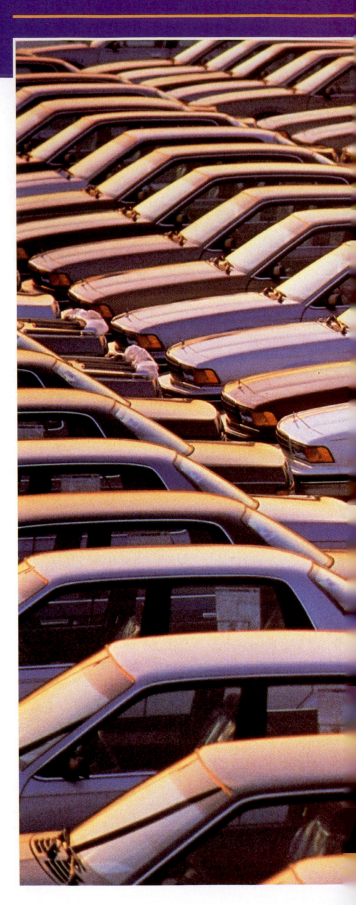

In the United States, macroeconomic policies try to stimulate the nation's overall economic growth.

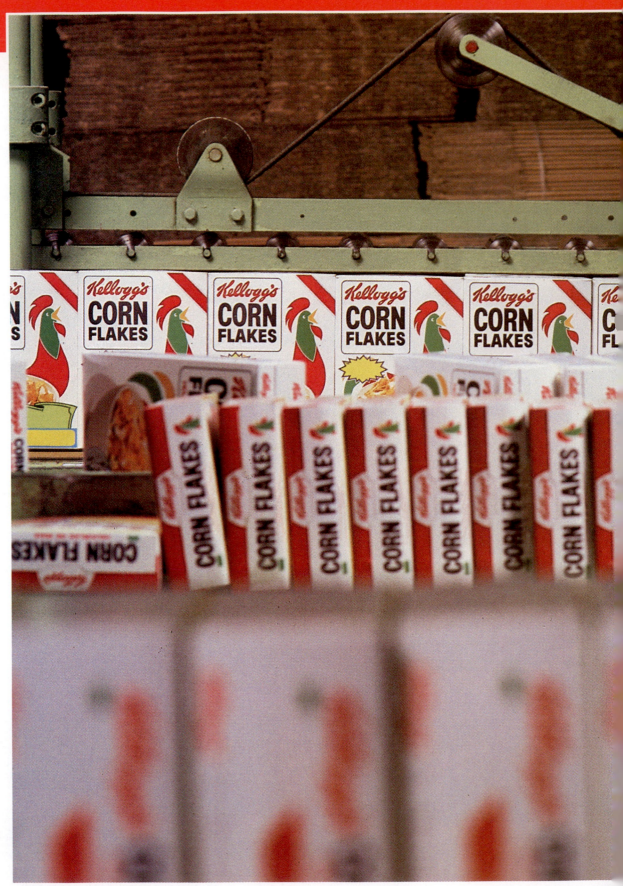

Any final product manufactured within the United States is included in the country's GDP.

CHAPTER 14

Gross Domestic Product

SECTION 1
Measuring the Nation's Output

SECTION 2
Measuring the Nation's Income

SECTION 3
GDP and Changes in the Price Level

CHAPTER PREVIEW

People to Know

- John Maynard Keynes
- Restaurant Manager

Applying Economic Concepts to Your Life

Gross Domestic Product As you grow older, you will probably want to have a decent car, a comfortable home, and more leisure time. Others want the same. The total dollar amount of all final output produced in a year's time in the United States is its *Gross Domestic Product* (GDP). GDP is important to you and to others—that is why you hear so much about it.

Journal Writing

For one week, clip articles from the newspaper that refer to one of the following: consumer expenditures, business expenditures, government expenditures, and exports or imports. In your journal, correctly log the expenditures under one of the four headings.

Section Preview

Objectives

After studying this section, you will be able to:

1. **Explain** how Gross Domestic Product is measured.
2. **Describe** the limitations of GDP.
3. **Understand** the importance of GDP.

Key Terms

national income accounting, structures, intermediate products, secondhand sales, nonmarket transactions, underground economy

Applying Economic Concepts

Nonmarket Transactions Do you contribute to the Gross Domestic Product? You do when you work at a job in the market economy. Your help around the house or mowing your own lawn does not contribute to GDP, however. *Nonmarket transactions* such as chores or lawn mowing may seem like work to you, but they do not count in government statistics.

Just as economists study the amount of goods and services that single producers bring to market, they also study the total amount of goods or services the economy as a whole produces. To study such massive amounts of output, economists use **national income accounting**—a system of statistics and accounts that keeps track of production, consumption, saving, and investment in the economy.

This data then becomes part of the National Income and Product Accounts (NIPA) kept by the United States Department of Commerce. These accounts are used to measure how the economy is doing and to trace long-term trends. The NIPA is like a statistical road map that tells Americans where they are and how they got there.

Gross Domestic Product

The single most important measure of overall economic performance is Gross Domestic Product (GDP)—the dollar amount of all final goods and services produced within a country's national borders in a year. GDP is one of the most comprehensive statistics kept concerning the economy's performance.

Measurement

From a conceptual point of view, the measurement of GDP is fairly easy to understand. Basically, all final goods and services produced in a 12-month period are multiplied by their prices to get the dollar value of production.

Figure 14.1 shows GDP computed in this way. The first column of the figure contains 3 broad categories of production used in the NIPA: goods, services, and structures. The last category, **structures,** includes residential housing, apartments, and buildings for commercial purposes. The second column lists some of the final goods and services produced in the year. The next two columns contain the quantity produced and the average price of each product. To get GDP, multiply the quantity of each good by its price and then add the results, as done in the last column of the figure.

Sampling and Survey Methods

Because a listing such as that in **Figure 14.1** would be far too long to compile for today's economy, government statisticians generally use sampling techniques and other methods to estimate both the quantity and the respective prices of the individual products. By using sampling techniques, however, the figures become less accurate.

Most of the figures used to compute GDP are based on reliable estimates. A few others are little more than educated guesses. Imagine, for example, how hard it would be to determine the exact value of all the lawns

Figure 14.1
Estimating Gross Domestic Product

Gross Domestic Product is the dollar value of all final goods, services, and structures produced within a country's borders in a year. Conceptually, GDP can be measured by multiplying the quantity of every product by its price, and then adding the results. In the hypothetical case on the right, GDP amounts to $7 trillion. **What problem arises because the GDP uses sampling techniques?**

	Product	Quantity (millions)	Price (each)	Dollar Value (millions)
Goods	Automobiles	6	$16,000	$96,000
	Replacement Tires	10	$40	$400
	Shoes	55	$40	$2,200
	...*	...*	...*	...*
Services	Haircuts	150	$8	$1,200
	Income Tax Filings	30	$150	$4,500
	Legal Advice	45	$200	$9,000
	...*	...*	...*	...*
Structures	Single Family	3	$75,000	$225,000
	Multifamily	5	$300,000	$1,500,000
	Commercial	1	$1,000,000	$1,000,000
	...*	...*	...*	...*
			Total Gross Domestic Product = $7 trillion	

Note: ...*other goods, services, and structures

students mow for neighbors. At best, only a reasonable approximation of the value could be made. GDP figures are accepted as being a reasonably complete, but not a perfect, measure of the total production that occurs in an economy in one year's time.

Intermediate Products

When the Department of Commerce analyzes the tons of data that flow into its offices, it faces several classification decisions concerning what should, and should not, be included in the figures that measure GDP. One such decision involves the exclusion of **intermediate products**—products used in making other products already counted in GDP. Replacement tires for automobiles, for example, can be counted in GDP, but tires for new cars cannot. Some newly produced tires will be placed on new cars, and the value of those tires will be built into the price of the car. If intermediate products are not eliminated from GDP, they would be counted twice, making GDP seem larger than it actually is.

The same problem occurs with other intermediate goods such as flour, sugar, and salt. If these items are bought for final use by the consumer, they should be counted as part of the final output, and therefore as part of GDP. If the products are used in the production of bread or any other bakery good bought by the consumer, they should not be counted.

Secondhand Sales

Another classification decision involves the exclusion of **secondhand sales**—the sales of used goods. When products already produced are transferred from one person or group to another, no new wealth is created. Although the sale of a used car, house, clothes, or compact disc player may give others cash that they can use on new purchases, only the original sale is included in GDP.

Production Within National Borders

The final characteristic of GDP is that it represents total production within the nation's borders, regardless of who owns the resources. Japanese automobiles produced in Kentucky, Indiana, Ohio, or Tennessee count in GDP even if the plants are owned by investors who live outside the United States. Conversely, production in United States-owned plants that are located in Mexico or Canada is not counted in GDP.

Other Considerations

Although GDP is the most comprehensive measure of output for the economy, some factors reduce its reliability. These other considerations do not make GDP any less useful as a measure of final output, but they do help keep its importance in perspective.

Reporting Delays

Because of the magnitude of the task, some unavoidable delays occur when final GDP figures are reported. The reporting process includes so much data that GDP estimates are made only quarterly, or every 3 months. The figures are revised for months after that, so it takes a while to discover how the economy actually performed. As a result, a gap exists between actual GDP and reported GDP. To know how the economy is performing today may require a wait of nearly 6 months for revised figures.

Composition of Output

Increases in GDP generally are considered desirable because they imply that people had jobs and earned an income. GDP alone, however, tells nothing about the composition of output. If GDP increases by $10 billion, for example, we know that additional output took place. While the initial increase in production might be viewed positively, people might feel differently if they discover that the extra production took the form of military nerve gas stockpiles rather than schools, libraries, and public parks.

A decline in GDP is usually interpreted to mean that the country is not doing as well as before. Would people be as upset if they knew the decline was caused by a new, inexpensive, miracle drug that reduced the need for medical services and made other drugs on the market obsolete? In the long run, the drug might make people healthier and able to produce more. **1**

Quality of Life

Aggregate figures for total production tell little about the impact of that production on the quality of life. The construction of 10,000 new homes may initially appear to be good for the economy. If the homes threaten a wildlife refuge or destroy the natural beauty of an area, however, the value of the homes may be

Secondhand Sales *The antiques sold in this store do not create new wealth and, therefore, are not counted in the GDP.* **How do secondhand sales differ from intermediate products?**

viewed differently. In practice, GDP does not factor in quality of life issues, but it is helpful to think about such matters to gain a better understanding of GDP.

Some economists have suggested using a Measure of Economic Welfare (MEW), which would be constructed by making certain adjustments to GDP. Factors such as the number of hours lost in traffic jams, the cost of air and water pollution, and the cost of crime would be deducted from GDP. Other factors such as increases in leisure time and healthier lives would be added. **2**

Exclusion of Nonmarket Activities

Another feature of GDP is the exclusion of **nonmarket transactions**—transactions that do not take place in the market. Some exclusions are caused by a problem of measurement. GDP does not take into account the value of people's services when they mow their own lawns or perform their own home maintenance. These activities are counted only when they are done for pay outside the home.

Perhaps the largest group of nonmarket transactions excluded from GDP includes the services that homemakers provide. If homemakers received pay for the cooking, cleaning, laundering, child care, and other household chores they usually perform, billions of dollars would be spent every year for these services.

Illegal Activities

Many other activities take place in the market, but they are excluded from GDP because they are illegal and are not reported. A whole range of unreported activities exists, including some gambling, smuggling, prostitution, drugs, and counterfeiting. These unreported illegal activities, plus some legal ones that are not disclosed for tax reasons, are part of the **underground economy**.

Importance of GDP Analysis

Despite the limitations of GDP, most economists agree that it is a fairly good indicator of economic health. When interpreted properly, GDP analysis becomes a useful tool in economic understanding. It is one of the few statistics generally regarded as a measure of both the economy's performance and its general health. ☑

Economic Performance

Generally, Americans want to hear that the United States has a large GDP. Production is valued because it is the primary way of supplying the additional goods and services needed to both satisfy people's wants and to improve the way people live. In

QUICK CHECK

Checking Understanding	*Applying Economic Concepts*
1. How is a decline in GDP usually interpreted? 2. How would the proposed Measure of Economic Welfare differ from GDP?	**Gross Domestic Product** A key concept of GDP is that it includes only the goods produced in a given nation. The American GDP, for example, does not include automobiles made at an American-owned plant in Canada, but does include Hondas made in Ohio with Japanese funds.

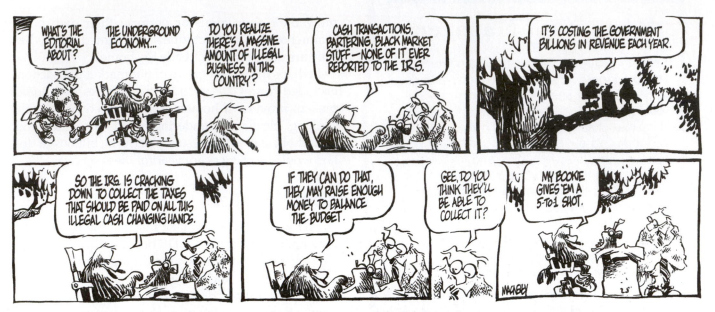

Underground Economy *Although estimates differ, economists generally agree that between 5 and 15 percent of all economic activity is part of the underground economy and is not included in GDP.* **What activities make up the underground economy?**

measuring GDP, Americans keep track of production to know how they are doing and to tell where they have been or might be going.

Economic Health

When GDP grows, people realize that the additional production will help satisfy more of their wants and needs. If GDP does not grow, people become unhappy and dissatisfied with government or its leaders. One way they express this is by voting for a different President or other elected officials. Historically, during periods of economic decline, everyone suffers—especially incumbents.

When GDP does not grow, new economic policies are often proposed and implemented in the belief that they will stimulate the economy. Their success—or lack of success—is measured in terms of how GDP reacts. For these reasons, GDP is the single most important economic statistic compiled today.

SECTION 1 REVIEW

Reviewing Terms and Facts

1. **Define** national income accounting, structures, intermediate products, secondhand sales, nonmarket transactions, underground economy.
2. **Describe** how GDP is measured.
3. **List** five factors to be aware of when considering GDP.

4. **Identify** two other uses of GDP.

Critical Thinking

5. **Making Generalizations** In what situations might society benefit from a low GDP?

Applying Economic Concepts

6. **Gross Domestic Product** Explain why GDP goes down when you quit your job to go to college.

PROFILES IN ECONOMICS

JOHN MAYNARD KEYNES
(1883–1946)

John Maynard Keynes, a British economist, is widely regarded as the most important economist of the twentieth century. He wrote numerous books and articles that focused on short-run problems instead of the long-run equilibrium solutions prevalent at the time. Keynes defended his short-run approach on the grounds that "in the long run, we are all dead."

His most famous and influential work was *The General Theory of Employment, Interest, and Money*, which appeared in 1936. The book, written during the depths of the Great Depression, offered new

theories soon took the world by storm.

EDUCATION AND BACKGROUND Keynes was a remarkable person. He first showed his interest in economics at age 5, when he became interested in the theory of interest rates. He attended Eton and Cambridge University to study mathematics, but two of the world's leading economists—A.C. Pigou and Alfred Marshall—finally encouraged him to study economics.

After graduation, Keynes took a civil service position and then returned to Cambridge as a lecturer and editor of the leading economic journal in Great Britain.

He served with distinction in a number of government positions. Keynes made a small fortune in stocks and foreign currencies, was a patron of the arts, and married the most popular and beautiful woman of his era.

OUTPUT-EXPENDITURE MODEL

Keynes's *General Theory* divided the economy into the four sectors —consumer, investment, government, and foreign— used in the output-expenditure model. Keynes hypothesized that the instability observed during the Great Depression resulted from a collapse of business spending, which could be offset by increased government spending. The theories were revolutionary, but they quickly gained the support of government and economists alike.

Soon, the label *Keynesian economics* stood for any government taxing and spending policies designed to stimulate the private sector. The national income and product accounts that are used today to track GNP, GDP, National Income, Personal Income, and Disposable Personal Income are all derived from the sector approach outlined in Keynes's *General Theory*.

Keynesian economics supported hiring artists in the 1930s to paint murals in public buildings. This mural, painted by Maxwell B. Starr, is in the Rockdale, Texas, post office.

insights on the way the economy worked. The policy recommendations derived from his

Examining the Profile

1. **Synthesizing Information** Provide an example of an expenditure that would fall under the heading *Keynesian economics*.

2. **For Further Research** Find out why Keynesian economics is also called *interventionist*.

Measuring the Nation's Income

Section Preview

Objectives

After studying this section, you will be able to:

1. **Explain** why GNP is a better measure of total income than GDP.

2. **Discuss** five measures of the nation's income.

3. **Identify** the three domestic sectors of the United States economy and the income received by each.

4. **State** the four sectors used in an output-expenditure model.

Key Terms

Gross National Product, net national product, capital consumption allowances, national income, indirect business tax, personal income, retained earnings, undistributed corporate profits, disposable personal income, household, unrelated individual, family, output-expenditure model, personal consumption expenditures, gross private domestic investment, net exports of goods and services

Applying Economic Concepts

Disposable Personal Income
Examine your payroll withholding statement carefully to see how much was taken out in the form of taxes and other deductions such as FICA. The net pay that you brought home was part of what economists call *disposable personal income*. It is one of the major measures of the nation's income—and you own a part of it!

The National Income and Product Accounts (NIPA) uses five measures of the nation's total income. This income is paid to different sectors of the economy, which use the income to purchase more output. This is similar to the circular flow concept examined in Chapter 1.

The Concept of Aggregate Income

Whenever anything is produced in the United States economy, and this includes all of the goods, services, and structures listed in **Figure 14.1**, payments are made to the four factors of production—land, capital, labor, and entrepreneurship.

If the United States economy were a closed economy, having no contact with the outside world, GDP would be similar to a two-sided coin. One side would represent the total amount of output produced, while the other side would represent the total payments to all factors of production. GDP would measure income as well as output.

In actuality, GDP includes foreign-owned goods produced in the United States. In addition, GDP excludes income earned by U.S.-owned resources that are employed outside the national borders. As a result, GDP is not a proper measure of the total income earned by American citizens. GDP can, however, be used to derive five measures of income. 1

Five Measures of Income

In order to convert total output to total income, two adjustments must be made to GDP. The new measure can then be broken down into component parts, providing five separate measures of the nation's income.

Gross National Product

The largest measure of an economy's total income, shown in **Figure 14.2**, is **Gross National Product** (GNP). GNP is the dollar value of all final goods, services, and structures produced in one year with labor and property supplied by United States residents. ☑

To go from GDP to GNP, it is necessary to add all payments that Americans receive from outside the

Figure 14.2
The National Income and Product Accounts

The National Income and Product Accounts show the relationship between GDP—the aggregate measure of the nation's output—and five measures of the nation's income.

What is the main difference between GDP and GNP?

Source: *Survey of Current Business*, 1993
(Data for first quarter)

Gross Domestic Product (GDP)	**$6,145.8**
Plus: Payments to American citizens who employ resources outside the U.S.	126.5
Less: Payments to foreign-owned resources employed inside the U.S.	117.1
Gross National Product (GNP)	**$6,155.2**
Less: Capital consumption allowances and adjustments (depreciation)	661.2
Net National Product (NNP)	**$5,494.0**
Less: Indirect business taxes and subsidies	579.8
National Income (NI)	**$4,914.2**
Plus: Government transfer payments to persons	884.8
Less: Undistributed corporate profits, corporate income taxes, and Social Security contributions	561.4
Personal Income (PI)	**$5,237.6**
Less: Individual taxes and nontax payments	655.9
Disposable Personal Income (DI)	**$4,581.7**

United States. Then one must subtract all payments made to foreign-owned resources in the United States. **2**

Figure 14.2 shows that GDP and GNP are approximately the same size. This is merely a coincidence, however, as the two measures are fundamentally different. In this case, the United States merely happened to have approximately the same amount of investment in the rest-of-the-world (ROW) as the ROW had invested in the United States. For many other countries, the difference between GNP and GDP can be much larger.

Net National Product

The second largest measure of the nation's total income is **net national product** (NNP)—GNP minus **capital consumption allowances**, the depreciation and other deterioration of the capital stock that takes place as a result of production.

When the economy produces a given amount of goods, services, and structures in a given year, some of the capital equipment is used up. According to **Figure 14.2**, GNP amounted to $6,155.2 billion. If the amount of worn-out and used-up capital goods amounts to

QUICK CHECK

Checking Understanding
1. Why is GDP not a proper measure of the total income earned by American citizens?
2. What calculations are necessary to go from GDP to GNP?

Applying Economic Concepts
☑ **Gross National Product** Until recently, the United States reported the GNP rather than the GDP as the principal measure of economic performance. Note that GNP says nothing about production taking place within national boundaries.

$661.2 billion, the net amount of production—the net national product—would be $5,494.0 billion.

National Income

Another measure of the nation's total income is **national income** (NI), net national product minus all taxes—except the corporate profits tax—that businesses must pay as a cost of doing business. Examples of these taxes, also known as **indirect business taxes**, are excise taxes, property taxes, licensing fees, customs duties, and general sales taxes.

Personal Income

Still another measure of the nation's total income is **personal income** (PI)—the total amount of income going to consumers before individual income taxes are subtracted. To go from national to personal income, four adjustments must be made.

First, income that does not go to the consumer must be subtracted from national income. One such type of income is **retained earnings**, also known as **undistributed corporate profits**. These are the profits that corporations keep to reinvest in new plants and equipment.

The second type of income that must be subtracted consists of the income taxes paid by corporations. This is a form of income to government. The third type of income that must be subtracted is Social Security contributions. After these three types of income have been subtracted from national income, transfer payments in the form of unemployment insurance, Social Security, medicaid, and several other forms of assistance must be added back in. The resulting total is personal income.

Disposable Personal Income

The smallest measure of income is **disposable personal income** (DI)—the total amount of income the consumer sector has at its disposal after individual income taxes. This is an important measure because it reflects the actual amount of money the consumer sector is able to spend. **1**

At the individual level, a person's disposable income is equal to the amount of money received from an employer after taxes and Social Security have been taken out. The $584.59 net pay on the check in **Figure 9.8** on page 225, plus the $3.20 of miscellaneous deductions, is disposable personal income.

The $3.20 is part of disposable income because the deduction was for something other than FICA or taxes. The wage earner could even choose to have more of the salary withheld to cover contributions to a credit union, to a social agency like the United Way, or to buy savings bonds. These contributions would not lower a person's disposable personal income, however. Payroll deductions are merely one way of allocating disposable income. ☑

Economic Sectors and Circular Flows

It is useful to think of the economy as being made up of several different parts, called sectors. These sectors receive various components of the national income, and they use this income to purchase the total output. Sectors, described below and illustrated in **Figure 14.3**, are critical links in the circular flow of economic activity.

Consumer Sector

One sector of the macro economy is the consumer sector. Its basic unit is the **household**, which is made up of all persons who occupy a house, apartment, or room that constitutes separate living quarters. A household includes related family members and all others—such as lodgers, foster children, and employees—who share the living quarters.

As long as the person or persons occupy a separate place of residence, a household also can consist of an **unrelated individual**. This is a person who lives alone or with nonrelatives even though he or she may have family living elsewhere. The concept of a household is somewhat broader than that of a **family**—a group of two or more persons related by blood, marriage, or adoption living together.

All three definitions have value to the United States Bureau of the Census. The definition of the household is especially useful because the demand for durable goods, such as stoves, water heaters, furnaces, and refrigerators, is more closely tied to the number of households than to the number of families. Many households, even when made up of persons not related by blood, marriage, or adoption, tend to behave as a single economic unit.

The consumer sector, shown as C in **Figure 14.3**, receives its income in the form of the disposable personal income described above and illustrated in **Figure 14.2**. In a sense, the consumer sector receives the income that is left over after all of the depreciation, taxes, and FICA payments are made, plus the income received in transfer payments that are added back in.

Investment Sector

A second sector of the macro economy is the business, or investment, sector. It is made up of proprietorships, partnerships, and corporations. It is the productive sector responsible for bringing the factors of production together to produce output.

The income to the investment sector, labeled I in **Figure 14.3**, is the depreciation, retained earnings, and personal savings borrowed from consumers through the financial system. Depreciation is considered a form of income because businesses are allowed to treat it as an expense and subtract it from their profits before they pay taxes. Because the depreciation never leaves the firm, it is a form of income to that sector.

Government Sector

A third sector in the macro economy is the government, or public, sector. It includes the local, state, and federal levels of government. When speaking of the government sector, the reference is to government in general rather than to a specific level.

The government sector, shown as G in **Figure 14.3**, receives its income from indirect business taxes, corporate income taxes, Social Security contributions, and personal income taxes from the consumer or household sector.

Foreign Sector

A fourth sector of the macro economy is the foreign sector, usually identified as F, but not shown in **Figure 14.3**. This sector includes all consumers and producers outside the United States. This sector, unlike the other sectors, does not have a source of income specific to it. Instead, the sector represents the difference between the dollar value of goods sent abroad and the dollar value of goods purchased from abroad. If the two are reasonably close, the foreign sector appears to be fairly small, even when there are a large number of goods and services being traded in both directions. **2**

QUICK CHECK

Checking Understanding

1. How is disposable personal income different from personal income?
2. What does the foreign sector include?

Applying Economic Concepts

☑ **Disposable Personal Income** Employees can choose a variety of payroll deductions. One is contributions to a 401K—a company-sponsored retirement plan. Another is a flexible spending account that sets aside money for medical emergencies. Both deductions are tax-deferred.

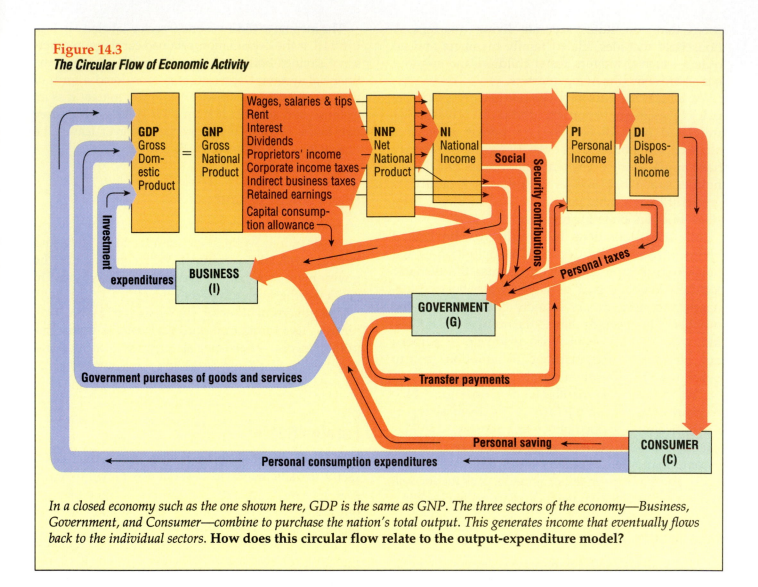

Figure 14.3
The Circular Flow of Economic Activity

In a closed economy such as the one shown here, GDP is the same as GNP. The three sectors of the economy—Business, Government, and Consumer—combine to purchase the nation's total output. This generates income that eventually flows back to the individual sectors. **How does this circular flow relate to the output-expenditure model?**

The Output-Expenditure Model

The circular flow in **Figure 14.3** is complete when the **output-expenditure model** is introduced—a macroeconomic model used to show aggregate demand by the consumer, investment, government, and foreign sectors. When this is written algebraically as

$$GDP = C + I + G + F,$$

the equation becomes the formal output-expenditure model used to explain and analyze the performance of the economy.

The consumer sector spends its income on the goods and services used by households and unrelated individuals. These **personal consumption expenditures** include groceries, rent, books, automobiles, clothes, and almost anything else people buy.

The investment, or business, sector spends its income on plant, equipment, inventories, and other investment goods. These expenditures, known as **gross private domestic investment**, represent the total value of capital goods created in the economy during the year. The term *gross* is used because purchases of all capital goods are included.

The government sector spends its income on many categories, including national defense, income security, interest on the debt, hospital care, roads, and education. The only major government expenditure

Exports *United States exports make up part of what is considered the foreign sector of the macro economy.* **In addition to exports, what else is included in the foreign sector?**

not included in total output is transfer payments, because this money is used by others to buy goods and services that are part of the total GDP.

The foreign sector also buys many goods and services—tractors, computers, airplanes, and farm products—that make up GDP. In addition, it supplies other products—British woolens, Japanese cars, Korean shirts, and Brazilian shoes—to be consumed at home. For this reason, the foreign sector's purchases are called **net exports of goods and services**, a term that refers to the difference between the United States's exports and its imports.

SECTION 2 REVIEW

Reviewing Terms and Facts

1. **Define** Gross National Product, net national product, capital consumption allowances, national income, indirect business tax, personal income, retained earnings, undistributed corporate profits, disposable personal income, household, family, unrelated individuals, output-expenditure model, personal consumption expenditures, gross private domestic investment, net exports of goods and services.

2. **Describe** the difference between GNP and GDP.
3. **List** the five aggregate measures of income.
4. **Identify** the sectors used in the output-expenditure model.

Critical Thinking

5. **Synthesizing Information** Disposable personal income shows up as part of the aggregate expenditures in the output-expenditure model. Write the equation for this model and then indicate where your net pay would fit in.

Applying Economic Concepts

6. **Disposable Personal Income** After the consumer sector gets its disposable personal income, it saves a portion and then spends the rest on goods and services. How does this compare to the way you allocate your disposable income?

Predicting Consequences

Did you ever wish you had a crystal ball so that you could see into the future? Making a decision would be much easier if you could know the results ahead of time. Predicting future events is very difficult. You can, however, develop skills that will help you identify the logical consequences of your decisions or actions. The skill of predicting consequences will help you understand how economic decisions made now may affect the future economy.

Explanation

Every decision or action produces logical results, or consequences. You can try to predict consequences by identifying and analyzing each possible outcome to see how likely it is to occur. To make accurate predictions about the consequences of economic decisions, you must use information about the present situation as well as about past economic trends.

Follow these steps to predict consequences:
- Gather information about the decision or action.
- Use your knowledge of economics and human behavior to identify what consequences could result.
- Analyze each of the consequences by asking: How likely is it that this will occur?

Practice

Read the article on this page about corporate downsizing. Then answer the questions that follow.

1. How does the author of this article view downsizing by United States corporations?
2. What are the possible consequences of downsizing?
3. How likely is it that downsizing will achieve the results that corporate leaders intended?
4. What is the basis for your prediction?

This is, indeed, an era when U.S. corporations are . . . sometimes seeing "downsizing" turn out to be "dumbsizing." That's when they discover that their efforts do not improve profits or productivity, but cause them more problems instead.

Less than half of the companies that have downsized since 1988 have improved their profits, and only one-third of the companies have seen better productivity. . . .

The fallout from poorly planned downsizing . . . is that workers' morale drops. They may fear for their own jobs. Or . . . angered by the layoffs, they may see no reason to expend more energy to help the company.

"A price will be paid one day by workers, companies, and the U.S. economy from such relentless and thoughtless downsizing," says Harvard University economist Paul Krugman. "The reductions will only lead to worse morale, less commitment among workers, and lower productivity."

—Chicago Tribune, September 12, 1993

Additional Practice

For further practice in predicting consequences, complete the Reinforcing Skills exercise in the Chapter 14 Review on page 367.

GDP and Changes in the Price Level

Section Preview

Objectives

After studying this section, you will be able to:

1. **Explain** how a price index is constructed.
2. **Describe** three price indices.
3. **Understand** the difference between real and current GDP.

Key Terms

price index, market basket, consumer price index, producer price index, wholesale price index, implicit GDP price deflator, current GDP, nominal GDP, real GDP, GDP in constant dollars

Applying Economic Concepts

Market Basket When statisticians construct the consumer price index, they use a *market basket* consisting of items most frequently purchased by consumers. The way you and others spend your income helps determine the products in the market basket.

A major problem with GDP is that it is subject to distortions because of inflation—a rise in the general price level. With inflation, output may appear to grow from one year to the next without actually doing so.

To see how this happens, compare the GDP in **Figure 14.1** with the GDP in **Figure 14.4**. Assume that the second table was compiled one year after the first, and that the inflation rate during that year was 10 percent. The second and third columns in each table show that the composition and quantity of output was the same for both years. In other words, there was no real change in the amount of goods and services produced.

The fourth column in each table, however, is not the same. Neither is the fifth. In these columns, everything costs 10 percent more in the second table than in the first one. This makes GDP rise by 10 percent, or $700 billion, revealing the effects of inflation. The major problem is that the dollar value of the final output went up without any real underlying changes in the quantity of goods and services produced.

Constructing a Price Index

To reduce the distortions of inflation, economists construct a **price index**—a statistical series that can be

Figure 14.4
Estimating Gross Domestic Product

Inflation can distort the value of Gross Domestic Product from one year to the next. The GDP is 10 percent larger in the figure on the right than it was in Figure 14.1. A comparison of the two reveals that all of the increase was caused by higher prices—there were no changes in the actual number of goods, services, and structures produced. **Why is it desirable to remove inflation from GDP?**

	Product	Quantity (millions)	Price (each)	Dollar Value (millions)
Goods	Automobiles	6	$17,600	$105,600
	Replacement Tires	10	$44	$440
	Shoes	55	$44	$2,420
	...*	...*	...*	...*
Services	Haircuts	150	$9	$1,350
	Income Tax Filings	30	$165	$4,950
	Legal Advice	45	$220	$9,900
	...*	...*	...*	...*
Structures	Single Family	3	$82,500	$247,500
	Multifamily	5	$330,000	$1,650,000
	Commercial	1	$1,100,000	$1,100,000
	...*	...*	...*	...*
			Total Gross Domestic Product = $7.7 trillion	

Note: ...*other goods, services, and structures

Figure 14.5
Constructing the Consumer Price Index

The Bureau of Labor Statistics measures items in terms of their 1982 base-year price. The total value of the items is assigned a base value of 100 percent. As time goes by, prices change, giving the new market basket a different total value. The new price index is computed by dividing the cost of the new market basket by the old basket. **Why is the market basket the same from one year to the next?**

Item	Description	Price Base Year (1982)	Price Second Period (1983)	Price October (1993)
1.	Toothpaste (7 oz.)	$1.40	$1.49	$2.25
2.	Milk (1 gal.)	1.29	1.29	1.79
3.	Peanut butter (2 lb. jar)	2.50	2.65	3.73
4.	Light bulb (60 watt)	.45	.48	.65
.....	.....	.....	.....	.....
364.	Automobile engine tune-up	40.00	42.00	64.75
Total Cost of Market Basket:		$1,792.00	$1,895.94	$ 2,610.94
Index Number:		100%	105.8%	145.7%

used to measure changes in prices over time. It can be compiled for a specific product or for a range of items.

It is not difficult to construct a price index. First, a base year—a year that serves as the basis of comparison for all other years—is chosen. The particular year chosen can vary. The base year is used only in a comparative sense and generally is updated as time goes by.

Second, a **market basket** of goods is selected. These are goods representative of the purchases that will be made over time. Although the number of items in the market basket is a matter of judgment, it must remain fixed after the selection is made. The advantage of this market basket concept is that it captures the overall trend in prices.

Finally, the price of each item in the market basket is recorded and then totaled. The total represents the prices of the market basket in the base year and is assigned a value of 100 percent.

Figure 14.5 shows how a price index can be constructed for a representative market basket with a large number of items. Because 1982 is used as the base year, the prices in the base-year column are lower than those today. The total of the market prices—$1,792.00—is assigned a value of 100 percent, which is the index number for that year.

In order to see how prices change from one year to the next, the price for each of the items must be recorded for the base year and then recorded again a year later. Because the total of the items for the second year—$1,895.94—is 5.8 percent higher than the total for the first year, the new index number is 105.8. The prices for each year that follows also must be recorded and

totaled to find the new index number. This procedure is repeated until the price index is finished.

Major Price Indices

Price indices can be constructed for a number of different purposes. Some measure changes in the price of a single item. Some measure the price changes of imported goods, while others do the same for agricultural products. Of all these measures, three are especially important. They are the consumer price index, the producer price index, and the implicit GDP price deflator.

Consumer Price Index

The **consumer price index** (CPI) reports on price changes for about 90,000 items in 364 categories. Prices for the goods and services currently sampled are taken from 85 geographically distributed areas around the country. Some of the items are surveyed in all the areas, while others are sampled in only a few.

The consumer price index is compiled monthly by the Bureau of Labor Statistics and is published for the economy as a whole. There also are separate indices for 28 selected areas around the country. **1**

Producer Price Index

The **producer price index**, formerly called the **wholesale price index**, measures price changes received by domestic producers for their output. It

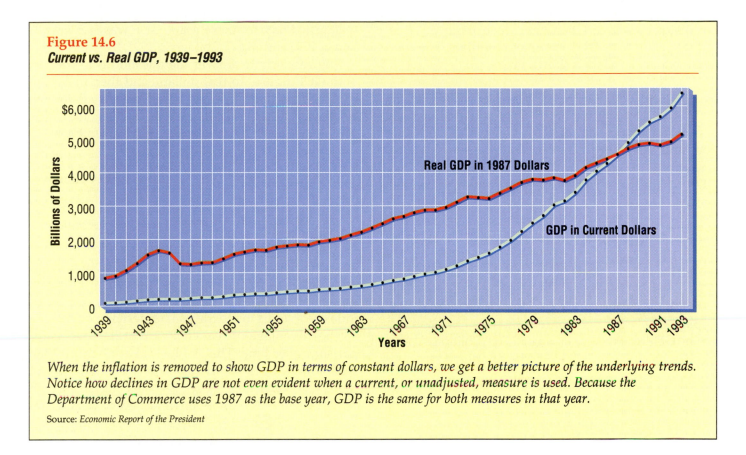

Figure 14.6
Current vs. Real GDP, 1939–1993

When the inflation is removed to show GDP in terms of constant dollars, we get a better picture of the underlying trends. Notice how declines in GDP are not even evident when a current, or unadjusted, measure is used. Because the Department of Commerce uses 1987 as the base year, GDP is the same for both measures in that year.

Source: *Economic Report of the President*

uses a sample of about 3,000 commodities and has a base year of 1982.

The producer price index also is reported monthly by the Bureau of Labor Statistics. Although it is compiled for all commodities, it also is broken down into subcategories that include farm products, fuels, chemicals, rubber, pulp and paper, and processed foods.

Implicit GDP Price Deflator

The **implicit GDP price deflator** measures price change in GDP. It has a base year of 1987 and can be used to remove the effects of inflation from GDP.

Because GDP is a measure of the final output of goods and services and covers thousands of items instead of hundreds, many economists believe it is a good, long-run indicator of the price changes that consumers face. Because the deflator is compiled quarterly, however, it is not as useful for measuring month-to-month changes in inflation. **2**

Real vs. Current GDP

When GDP is not adjusted for inflation, it is called **current GDP**, **nominal GDP**, or simply GDP. When

Checking Understanding

1. How often is the CPI compiled?
2. Why do many economists consider the GDP price deflator to be a good long-run indicator of price changes?

Applying Economic Concepts

 Inflation Some economists think that the CPI might promote further inflation because 40 million Social Security recipients receive cost-of-living raises based on inflation. In addition, about 6 million workers receive cost-of-living adjustments based on inflation.

the distortions of inflation have been removed, it is called **real GDP** or **GDP in constant dollars**. The conversion to real dollars is shown below.

Converting GDP to Real Dollars

Suppose unadjusted GDP for 1980 was $2,708.0 billion, and we want to convert it to constant dollars. The procedure is to divide the current or nominal GDP by the price index, and then multiply by 100 because the index number is really a percent. Because we are adjusting GDP for inflation, we use the implicit GDP price deflator for that year:

(1980 GDP ÷ implicit GDP price deflator) × 100
= GDP in constant dollars

According to the U.S. Department of Commerce, the implicit GDP price deflator for 1980 was 71.71 and the actual GDP for that year was $2,708.0 billion. Using these numbers, real GDP would be computed as

($2,708.0 billion ÷ 71.71) × 100 = $3,776.3 billion.

The real GDP for 1980 is $3,776.3 billion in terms of 1987 dollars. This is higher than it was before conversion because prices were higher in 1987 than in 1980.

Comparing GDP in Different Years

Now suppose we want to know if there was any real increase in GDP between 1990 and 1991. According to

unadjusted data for those years, GDP was $5,522.2 billion in 1990 and $5,677.5 billion in 1991.

The best way to answer the question is to convert both GDP figures to real dollars, and then make the comparison. If the implicit GDP price deflator for 1990 was 113.22, and if the deflator for 1991 was 117.77, the computations would appear as follows:

1990:

($5,522.2 billion ÷ 113.22) × 100 = $4,877.4 billion

1991:

($5,677.5 billion ÷ 117.77) × 100 = $4,820.8 billion

Real GDP, then, actually dropped between 1990 and 1991. The increase in nominal GDP from $5,522.2 billion to $5,677.5 billion was caused by inflation. Removing the inflation by deflating with a price index enables us to see the real, underlying trend.

The advantage of real GDP is that it allows comparisons over time. This is illustrated in **Figure 14.6**, which shows the comparison between current and real GDP. When GDP is not adjusted for inflation, it appears as if GDP simply increases every year. When we take out the inflation, however, we get a much better look at the performance of real GDP.

Today, the impact of inflation cannot be ignored. For this and other reasons, almost all modern statistics are reported in both current and real terms. To have an understanding of one without the other would be to understand only part of the picture.

SECTION 3 REVIEW

Reviewing Terms and Facts

1. **Define** price index, market basket, consumer price index, producer price index, wholesale price index, implicit GDP price deflator, current GDP, nominal GDP, real GDP, GDP in constant dollars.
2. **Explain** why a market basket is used whenever a price index is constructed.
3. **List** three major price indices.

4. **Provide** an example in which real GDP would be greater than current GDP.

Critical Thinking

5. **Making Comparisons** One difficulty with using the market basket concept of making comparisons over long periods is that the composition of the market basket changes. What do you think a typical market basket 20 years

ago might have had in it that we do not use today? What do you think a future market basket might have that we do not have today?

Applying Economic Concepts

6. **Market Basket** If you were to construct a market basket of goods and services that high school students typically consume, what would you select?

Gross Domestic Product

Vocabulary

The following terms are defined in Chapter 14:

SECTION ONE
- national income accounting (p. 348)
- structures (p. 348)
- intermediate products (p. 349)
- secondhand sales (p. 349)
- nonmarket transaction (p. 351)
- underground economy (p. 351)

SECTION TWO
- Gross National Product (p. 354)
- net national product (p. 355)
- capital consumption allowances (p. 355)
- national income (p. 356)
- indirect business tax (p. 356)
- personal income (p. 356)
- retained earnings (p. 356)
- undistributed corporate profits (p. 356)
- disposable personal income (p. 356)
- household (p. 356)
- unrelated individual (p. 357)
- family (p. 357)
- output-expenditure model (p. 358)
- personal consumption expenditures (p. 358)
- gross private domestic investment (p. 358)
- net exports of goods and services (p. 359)

SECTION THREE
- price index (p. 361)
- market basket (p. 362)
- consumer price index (p. 362)
- producer price index (p. 362)
- wholesale price index (p. 362)
- implicit GDP price deflator (p. 363)
- current GDP (p. 363)
- nominal GDP (p. 363)
- real GDP (p. 364)
- GDP in constant dollars (p. 364)

Section 1
Measuring the Nation's Output (pages 348–352)

GDP is the nation's most comprehensive measure of total output. It counts only final goods, services, and structures that are produced in the United States, regardless of who owns the resources. Because it counts only final products, **intermediate goods** and **secondhand sales** are excluded.

GDP tells us nothing about the composition of output or the quality of life. Some nonmarket activities, such as the services supplied by homemakers, are excluded from coverage. Other activities are illegal or are not reported and, therefore, belong to the **underground economy**.

Reviewing the Main Idea
How does GDP measure the total output of the economy?

Section 2
Measuring the Nation's Income (pages 354–359)

The difference between GDP and GNP is that GDP counts only production in the United States, regardless of who owns the resources. In contrast, GNP is a measure of income received by American citizens, regardless of where their productive resources are located.

There are five measures of income, including GNP. They include **net national product**, **national income**, **personal income**, and **disposable personal income**.

The economy can also be organized into the consumer or **household** sector, the business or investment sector, the government sector, and the foreign sector. The **output-expenditure model**, expressed as GDP = C + I + G + F, shows how GDP is consumed by the four sectors of the economy.

Reviewing the Main Idea
What is the difference between GDP and GNP?

Section 3
GDP and Changes in the Price Level (pages 361–364)

Economists use a **price index** to track the movement of prices over time. Price indices are based on a **market basket** of representative products selected for a given base year.

Price indices can be constructed for any product, group of products, or group of consumers. Three of the most popular include the **consumer price index**, the **producer price index**, and the **implicit GDP price deflator**.

Reviewing the Main Idea
What is the purpose of a price index?

Reviewing Key Terms

Examine the pairs of words below. Then write a sentence explaining what each of the pairs have in common.

1. base year
   market basket
2. capital consumption allowances
   undistributed corporate profits
3. Gross National Product
   Net National Product
4. household
   unrelated individuals
5. intermediate products
   secondhand sales
6. nominal GDP
   current GDP
7. personal consumption expenditures
   gross private domestic investment
8. real GDP
   GDP in constant dollars
9. retained earnings
   undistributed corporate profits
10. underground economy
    nonmarket transactions

Reviewing the Facts

SECTION 1 *(pages 348–352)*
1. **Describe** the three categories of products that make up GDP.
2. **List** five characteristics of GDP.
3. **Explain** why GDP is an important concept.

SECTION 2 *(pages 354–359)*
4. **Explain** why GDP is not the correct measure of total income.
5. **Identify** the five measures of the nation's income.

6. **Describe** the three main sectors that make up the United States economy.
7. **Describe** the output-expenditure model.

SECTION 3 *(pages 361–364)*
8. **Explain** why price indices are used to measure the economy.
9. **Identify** three of the major price indices the federal government calculates.
10. **Explain** how the government uses the implicit GDP price deflator to convert nominal GDP to real GDP.

Critical Thinking

1. **Predicting Consequences** Suppose that politicians wanted to examine the growth of real output over the last 10 years. What conclusions would they reach if they used GDP measured in current dollars? How would these conclusions be different if they examined GDP measured in real dollars?
2. **Expressing Problems Clearly** Write a paragraph defending the use of GDP to an individual who argues that life should be measured by more than GDP. Be certain to address the issue of quality of life in your paragraph.

Applying Economic Concepts

1. **Gross Domestic Product** Defend or refute the use of the Measure of Economic Welfare (MEW), rather than GDP, to measure the economy's overall well-being.
2. **Disposable Personal Income** Some economists believe that disposable personal income is almost as important a measure of economic performance as GDP. What do you think? Provide reasons for your answer.

Reinforcing Skills

PREDICTING CONSEQUENCES

Read the following article about a global work force, then answer the questions that follow.

A fundamental shift is under way in how and where the world's work gets done—with potentially ominous consequences for wealthy, industrialized nations. The key to this change: the emergence of a truly global labor force, talented and capable of accomplishing just about anything, anywhere. . . . Says [one executive], "The average American doesn't realize that there is a truly competitive work force out there that is vying for their jobs. The rest of the world is catching up."

Just what is driving U.S. companies—and some from Europe and Japan—to locate that new plant . . . in Bangalore, India, . . . or Guadalajara, Mexico. . . ? It isn't only the search for cheap labor. Corporations also want to establish sophisticated manufacturing and service operations in markets that promote the most growth, often emerging nations.

—"Your New Global Work Force," *Fortune*, December 14, 1992

1. Why have many U.S. corporations begun relocating in recent years?
2. What are the possible consequences of relocating?
3. How likely is it that relocating will achieve the results that corporate leaders intended? What is the basis for your prediction?

Individual Activity

Construct a "high school price index." Survey students to see how they spend their money, and then identify the largest categories of expenditures.

Identify several specific items in each category, and locations where the items can be purchased in your community. Price the items on a per week basis for one month. Compare your price index with those of the rest of the class.

Cooperative Learning Activity

Working in groups of four, have each member choose one of the four measures of the nation's total income besides GNP. Each person is responsible for answering the following questions about its measure: (a) What does your measure show? (b) What is added or subtracted to find the measure? (c) To whom would this measure be most valuable? (d) Why? Have each member present his or her conclusions to the group. Then have each group compare their conclusions.

Writing About Economics

THE INFORMATIVE STYLE

In the **Journal Writing** activity on page 347, you were asked to clip and log newspaper articles under one of the following headings: consumer expenditures, business expenditures, government expenditures, and exports or imports. Using the informative style of writing discussed on page 554, answer the following questions: Who or what makes up each sector? What does each sector produce?

The construction of new houses is perceived as a sign of economic growth.

CHAPTER 15

Population, Economic Growth, and Business Cycles

SECTION 1
Population

SECTION 2
Economic Growth

SECTION 3
Business Cycles and Fluctuations

CHAPTER PREVIEW

People to Know

- Walter E. Williams
- Systems Analyst

Applying Economic Concepts to Your Life

Economic Growth Do you want to get ahead in the world? Do you want a quality education, a good job, and all the so-called comforts of life? Do you think other people want the same things? The nation's *economic growth* is everyone's key to a better future. A growing economy means an expanding economy, one that continues to provide more people with what they want or need.

Journal Writing

For one week, write in your journal all the goods and services your local government provides that you use and that you observe others using.

Section Preview

Objectives

After studying this section, you will be able to:

1. **Explain** how population is estimated in the United States.
2. **Describe** the factors affecting future population growth.

Key Terms

census, urban population, rural population, center of population, demographer, fertility rate, life expectancy, net immigration, baby boom, population pyramid, dependency ratio

Applying Economic Concepts

Urban vs. Rural You have probably heard the terms *urban* and *rural* so often that you are unaware that they are economic terms. They are, and the term that fits you depends on where you live. If you live in a town with a population of more than 2,500, you are considered an urban resident. If your community's population is less than 2,500, you are a rural resident.

The size and growth of its population is important to every society. Population means people, and people provide labor. Labor, in turn, provides for people's needs and wants.

The rate at which population grows influences economic growth. If a nation's population grows too fast, per capita output may fall. The country could end up with more mouths than it can feed. Conversely, if a nation's population grows too slowly, there may not be enough workers to sustain economic growth.

The United States Population

The Constitution of the United States requires the government to periodically take a **census**, an official count of all people, including their place of residence. Because the official census occurs every 10 years, it is called the *decennial census*. The nation's founders initiated the decennial census to apportion the number of representatives each state elects to Congress. 1

Counting the Population

The federal government conducted the first census in 1790. Throughout the 1800s, temporary agencies, created each decade, conducted the counts. In 1902 Congress permanently established the Bureau of the

Census. Today, the Bureau works year-round, conducting monthly surveys relating to the size and other characteristics of the population.

When the Bureau of the Census conducts the decennial census, it uses the household as its primary survey unit. About 5 in every 6 households receives a "short form," which takes just a few minutes to fill out. The remaining households receive a "long form," which includes more questions and serves to generate a more detailed profile of the population. Bureau employees use different methods to count special groups, such as homeless persons, who do not normally conform to the household survey unit.

The Census Bureau tabulates and presents its data in a number of ways. One classification denotes the size of the **urban population**. Urban residents are generally those living in incorporated villages or towns with 2,500 or more inhabitants. The contrasting **rural population** makes up the remainder of the total population, including those persons who live in sparsely populated areas along the fringes of cities. 2

Historical Growth

The population of the United States has grown considerably since colonial times. The rate of growth, however, has steadily declined. Between 1790 and 1860, the population grew at a compound rate of 3.02

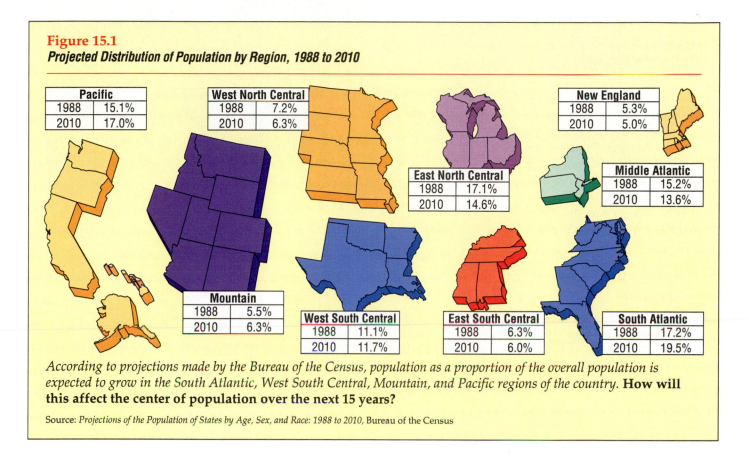

Figure 15.1
Projected Distribution of Population by Region, 1988 to 2010

Pacific	
1988	15.1%
2010	17.0%

West North Central	
1988	7.2%
2010	6.3%

New England	
1988	5.3%
2010	5.0%

East North Central	
1988	17.1%
2010	14.6%

Middle Atlantic	
1988	15.2%
2010	13.6%

Mountain	
1988	5.5%
2010	6.3%

West South Central	
1988	11.1%
2010	11.7%

East South Central	
1988	6.3%
2010	6.0%

South Atlantic	
1988	17.2%
2010	19.5%

According to projections made by the Bureau of the Census, population as a proportion of the overall population is expected to grow in the South Atlantic, West South Central, Mountain, and Pacific regions of the country. **How will this affect the center of population over the next 15 years?**

Source: *Projections of the Population of States by Age, Sex, and Race: 1988 to 2010*, Bureau of the Census

percent a year. From the beginning of the Civil War until 1900, the average fell to 2.23 percent. From 1900 to the beginning of World War II, the rate dropped to 1.38 percent, and from then until 1993, it hovered just under 1.28 percent. Experts predict that sometime after 1995, the rate will fall below 1 percent.

Historically, the census also shows a steady trend toward smaller households. During colonial times, household size averaged 5.8 people. By 1960 the average had fallen to 3.33, and by 1992 to 2.62 people. The figures reflect a worldwide trend toward smaller families in industrial countries where couples often view children as a financial liability. The figures also show that more individuals are living alone today than ever before.

Regional Change

Census reports over the years have indicated significant changes in where people live. **Figure 15.1** shows the most recent and expected shifts in population distribution. According to the map, the growth of population in the West and South will offset the loss of population in the Northeast and Central Plains regions.

Checking Understanding

1. Why does the federal government conduct a census every 10 years?
2. What is the difference between an urban population and a rural population?

Applying Economic Concepts

☑ **Population** How many siblings do you have? How many siblings do your parents have? Your grandparents? Poll adults you know to find out their reasons for limiting their number of children.

Figure 15.2
The Center of Population

The center of population is the point where the country would balance if the map were flat and every American weighed the same. The center has moved steadily to the west and south following the growth of population since the first census was conducted in 1790. **Where was the center of population for the 1990 census?**

Source: *1993 Statistical Abstract of the United States*

Another indicator of distribution shifts is the **center of population**—the point where the country would balance if it could be laid flat and all the people weighed the same. In 1790 the center was 23 miles east of Baltimore, Maryland. Since then, it has moved farther west, as **Figure 15.2** illustrates. By the year of the 1990 decennial census, the center of population had reached a point about 9.7 miles southeast of Steelville, Missouri.

Projected Population Trends

Population trends interest many groups of people. Politicians, for example, closely watch distribution shifts to see how voting patterns may change. Community leaders are interested because increases or decreases in local population impact services such as sanitation, education, crime prevention, and fire protection. Businesses use census data to help determine new plant locations, products and services, and sales territories. **1**

Factors Affecting Growth

In November 1992, the Bureau of the Census released a report called *Population Projections of the United States by Age, Sex, Race, and Hispanic Origin: 1992 to 2050*. The report offered three population growth scenarios—high, middle, and low—that could take place in the United States between 1990 and 2050.

The three scenarios are estimates only. They are based on factors developed by **demographers**—people who study growth, density, and other characteristics of population. According to demographers, the three most important factors affecting population growth are fertility, life expectancy, and net immigration levels. **2**

The first factor, the **fertility rate**, is the number of births that 1,000 women are expected to undergo in their lifetime. A fertility rate of 2,110, for example, translates to 2.11 births per woman. For its middle growth projection, the one most likely to occur, the Bureau of the Census assumed a fertility rate of 2,119 for the United States. That rate is barely above the replacement rate—the rate at which the number of births in a population just offsets the number of deaths.

The second factor, **life expectancy**, is the average remaining life span of people who reach a given age. The Bureau of the Census predicts that life expectancy at birth will go from 75.8 years to 82.1 years by 2050.

The third major factor, **net immigration**, considers the net change in population caused by people moving into and out of the country. The Bureau's report assumes a constant net immigration of about 880,000 per year (1,040,000 immigrants and 160,000 emigrants). It also takes into account changes in the immigration laws made in 1991 and certain other factors, such as undocumented immigration from Mexico and the Caribbean.

Considering the three factors above, and assuming that the Bureau's middle-growth projection holds true, the rate of population growth in the United

Population Projections
Life expectancy at birth is projected to be 82.1 years in the United States by the year 2050. **What is the projected United States population by 2050?**

States will continue to decline. The growth rate is likely to hold at .90 percent from 1995 to 2000. It will decline to .82 percent between 2000 and 2005, and then continue to decrease until it reaches .49 percent by 2050. At that time, the resident United States population should total about 380 million people.

Projections by Age and Sex

In making its projections, the Bureau of the Census assumed that the aging of the baby boom generation will drive many characteristics of the population. People born during the **baby boom**, the high birthrate years from 1946 to 1964, make up a sizeable portion of the population. As shown in **Figure 15.4** on page 375, people born during the baby boom generation create a pronounced bulge in the **population pyramid**, a type of bar graph that shows the breakdown of population by age and sex. ☑

In the population pyramid for 1990, the baby boomers fall into the age bracket beginning at 25 and ending at 44. As years pass, more births add to the bottom of the pyramid and shift earlier groups upward into higher age brackets. In the population pyramid for the year 2000 on page 391, the baby boomers have aged 10 years and have moved into the 35–54 bracket.

Eventually, the baby boomers will reach their retirement years and want to collect pensions, Social Security, medicare, and medicaid benefits. Because most of these payments are transfer payments, they will place a heavy burden on the younger and

QUICK CHECK

Checking Understanding

1. Why are people interested in population trends?
2. What are the most important factors affecting population growth, according to demographers?

Applying Economic Concepts

☑ **Baby Boom** Baby boomers fueled the economy. During the 1950s, school enrollments increased by 13 million, the sale of musical instruments reached $149 million a year, the number of Girl Scouts and Brownies doubled, and the number of Little Leagues reached nearly 6,000.

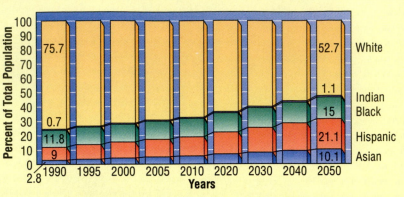

Figure 15.3
Projected Change in U.S. Population by Race and Ethnic Origin, 1990–2050

According to projections made by the United States Bureau of the Census, the distribution of population by race will change dramatically by the middle of the next century. **Which ethnic components of the population are expected to make the largest gains? The largest losses?**

Source: *Population Projections in the United States, by Age, Sex, Race and Hispanic Origin: 1992–2050,* U.S. Bureau of the Census.

relatively smaller working population. The burden becomes evident with changes in the **dependency ratio**—a ratio based on the number of children and elderly for every 100 persons in the working-age bracket of 18 through 64. The dependency ratio in 1992 stood at 62.9. According to Census Bureau projections, it will rise to 67.5 by 2020, to 77.5 in 2030, and to 78.0 by the year 2040.

Notice what the population pyramids indicate about gender. Compare the left sides of the pyramids with the right. The right sides in both pyramids are larger in the older age brackets, showing that women tend to outlive men. Separate population pyramids can also be created for any racial or ethnic group.

Projections by Race and Ethnic Origin

Figure 15.3 shows some projections that the Bureau of the Census makes according to race and ethnic origins of the population. In 1990 whites were the largest component in the total population. The numbers of African Americans, Hispanic Americans, Asian Americans, and Native Americans followed in that order.

Differences in fertility rates, life expectancies, and immigration rates will change racial statistics dramatically in the future. By 2050, the Asian component of the population will increase nearly 5 times, and the Hispanic component will almost double. The number of African Americans will also increase. Whites will retain a bare majority of 52.7 percent.

SECTION 1 REVIEW

Reviewing Terms and Facts

1. **Define** census, urban population, rural population, center of population, demographer, fertility rate, life expectancy, net immigration, baby boom, population pyramid, dependency ratio.
2. **Describe** the recent changes in population growth on a regional basis.
3. **List** the three most important factors that determine future population growth.

Critical Thinking

4. **Predicting Consequences** At some point, the baby boomers will reach their retirement years. How will this development affect your generation? How do you think the baby boomers will feel about the same development?

Applying Economic Concepts

5. **Urban vs. Rural** What could happen to your community that might cause it to be classified as rural instead of urban, or urban instead of rural?

Interpreting Population Pyramids

Demographers, economists, government officials, businesspeople, and others use population pyramids to study human populations. Population pyramids help demographers see at a glance whether the population of an area is mostly old or young, and whether it is mostly male or female. In addition, it is possible to tell if a change in the growth rate of an area's population is imminent. Such information can help businesspeople and government officials plan for the future. An increase in the percentage of very young children, for example, will probably create a need for more schools.

Explanation

A population pyramid is a type of bar graph that shows how the population of an area, such as a country or a city, is divided by age and by sex.

Look at the pyramid on this page. Note that each bar stands for a certain age group, with the youngest age group at the bottom. A line divides each bar to show the percentage of males and females in each age group. Male percentages are shown on the left side of the graph, female percentages on the right side.

Use the following steps to interpret population pyramids.

- Read the title of the population pyramid to see what area is being analyzed.
- Read the percentages along the horizontal axis.
- Examine the ages along the vertical axis.
- Compare the bars for each age group and sex.

Practice

Study the population pyramid on this page. Then answer the following questions.

1. What does the population pyramid show?
2. Which age group is largest for males? For females?
3. Which age group is smallest for males? For females?
4. Which gender has a larger percentage of people that are 70 years old and over?
5. What percentage of the population is in the 30-to-40 age groups?
6. What percentage of the population is in your age group?

Additional Practice

For further practice in interpreting population pyramids, complete the Reinforcing Skills exercise in the Chapter 15 Review on page 390.

Figure 15.4

Distribution of the U.S. Population by Age and Sex, 1990

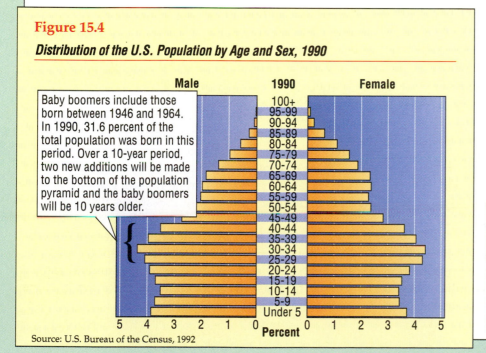

Baby boomers include those born between 1946 and 1964. In 1990, 31.6 percent of the total population was born in this period. Over a 10-year period, two new additions will be made to the bottom of the population pyramid and the baby boomers will be 10 years older.

Source: U.S. Bureau of the Census, 1992

Economic Growth

Section Preview

Objectives

After studying this section, you will be able to:

1. **Describe** how economists measure the growth of the United States economy.
2. **Explain** the importance of economic growth.
3. **Outline** the factors of economic growth.
4. **Relate** productivity to economic growth.

Key Terms

real GDP per capita, growth triangle, standard of living, tax base, renewable resources, capital-to-labor ratio, labor productivity

Applying Economic Concepts

Standard of Living Do your worldly possessions make your life easier? Would more possessions make you even more comfortable? When you think about such questions, you are thinking about your *standard of living*. The standard of living measures only the material side of your life, but it will probably always be important to you.

Economic growth, one of the seven major goals of the United States economy, has the potential for improving everyone's lot in life. *Everyone* includes not only every American, but also people living in other countries.

Economic Growth in the United States

In order to see the potential of economic growth, we need to know how to measure it. Two measures are equally important. Both relate to topics already covered in earlier chapters.

Measuring Growth

When we measure economic growth in the short term—for a period of one to five years—real GDP is a fairly satisfactory gauge. Changes in real GDP on a quarterly or annual basis are the statistics we hear about most often in the news.

When it comes to the long run, however, real GDP does not tell the whole story. Because population also grows, **real GDP per capita**—the dollar amount of real GDP produced for every person in the

economy—is a better measure. Most economists feel that it is the single most important measure of long-term growth.

Dividing the real GDP by the population yields the real GDP per capita figure. If the population grows faster than real GDP, the average amount of output produced for each person in the economy falls. If the population grows more slowly than real GDP, there will be more goods and services available for everyone.

The Historical Record

Figure 15.5 compares real GDP with real GDP per capita. In 1992, for example, real GDP in terms of constant dollars was about $4.92 trillion. Because the population in that year was 255.4 million, the total output for each man, woman, and child in the country amounted to about $19,265.

Rates of growth become evident in a **growth triangle**—a table that traces annual rates of growth for various periods of time. **Figure 15.6** shows that there was no growth in real GDP per capita between 1929 and 1940. From 1940 to 1970, the annual rate was 2.4 percent, and from 1970 to 1980, it fell to 1.7 percent. Between 1980 and 1990, however, the annual rate of growth for real GDP per capita fell to 1.6 percent, one of the lowest rates since the 1950s.

Because of low numbers like those above, economists and other experts realize that the United States could be doing better. Recent growth rates are not cause for alarm, but they are cause for concern. As a result, many federal economic policies have been proposed to stimulate long-term economic growth. Many more such policies will undoubtedly be proposed in the future.

Importance of Economic Growth

Economic growth benefits a country in many ways. It raises the standard of living, eases the burden of government, and helps solve domestic problems. It can also boost the economies of foreign trade partners.

Standard of Living

A major feature of a free enterprise economy is its ability to increase real per capita output enough to allow people to raise their standard of living. The **standard of living** means the quality of life based on the possession of necessities and luxuries that make life easier. In the end, a free enterprise system also increases people's free time, allowing them to devote more attention to families, hobbies, and recreational activities.

Government Spending

Economic growth benefits government at all levels by enlarging the **tax base**—the incomes and properties that may be taxed. Enlarged tax bases increase government revenues, which can add to the number and quality of public services.

Domestic Problems

Like most countries of the world, the United States faces varying degrees of poverty, inadequate medical care, inequality of opportunity, and economic insecurity. Most of these problems stem from economic need. Economic growth creates more jobs and income for more people, thus helping to alleviate social ills at their source.

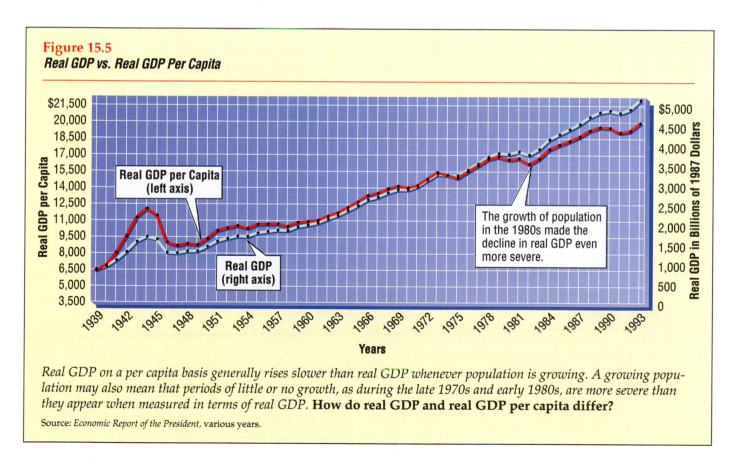

Figure 15.5
Real GDP vs. Real GDP Per Capita

Real GDP on a per capita basis generally rises slower than real GDP whenever population is growing. A growing population may also mean that periods of little or no growth, as during the late 1970s and early 1980s, are more severe than they appear when measured in terms of real GDP. **How do real GDP and real GDP per capita differ?**

Source: *Economic Report of the President,* various years.

Figure 15.6
Annual Growth Rates of Real GDP Per Capita

The most comprehensive measure of long-term economic growth is real GDP per capita. If we do not take population growth into account, changes in real GDP can be overstated. To find the annual compound rate between two dates, find the beginning year on the horizontal axis and read up to the ending year on the vertical axis. **Why is real GDP per capita considered the best measure of long-term economic growth?**

> Most of the decline during the Great Depression took place by 1933. There was no growth at all between 1929 and 1940.

> To find the annual rate of growth during the 1970s, start with 1970 on the horizontal axis and read up to the 1980 row.

> On a per capita basis, the economy grew slightly slower in the 1980s than it did in the 1970s.

Ending Year

Ending Year	1929	1940	1945	1950	1955	1960	1965	1970	1975	1980	1985	Ending Year
1929												1929
1933	-9.2%											1933
1939	-0.6%											1939
1940	0.0%											1940
1945	3.2%	10.8%										1945
1950	1.5%	3.1%	-4.0%									1950
1955	1.7%	3.0%	-0.7%	2.7%								1955
1960	1.5%	2.3%	-0.3%	1.6%	0.5%							1960
1965	1.7%	2.5%	0.5%	2.1%	1.8%	3.1%						1965
1970	1.8%	2.4%	0.8%	2.1%	1.8%	2.5%	2.0%					1970
1975	1.7%	2.2%	0.9%	1.9%	1.7%	2.1%	1.6%	1.3%				1975
1980	1.7%	2.2%	1.1%	1.9%	1.8%	2.1%	1.8%	1.7%	2.1%			1980
1985	1.7%	2.2%	1.1%	1.9%	1.8%	2.0%	1.7%	1.7%	1.9%	1.6%		1985
1990	1.7%	2.1%	1.2%	1.9%	1.7%	2.0%	1.7%	1.7%	1.8%	1.6%	1.7%	1990

Starting Year

Source: *Economic Report of the President,* various years.

Helping Other Nations

Economic growth increases American demand for foreign trade products. When the United States purchases the goods of other countries, it helps create jobs and income in those countries. New or increased income enables those people to buy goods and services from the United States, which may also create new jobs here. Consumers in the United States and the countries with which it trades benefit from an increased variety of competitively priced goods and services.

An increase in foreign trade also helps other countries allocate resources to their most efficient uses. When people in the United States purchase foreign products, productive resources in those countries are attracted to the growing export industries. The resources of many nations are put to their most productive use. In the long run, this stimulates world economic growth.

Global Role Model

A number of emerging nations have not yet formed their political and economic ideologies. These nations tend to copy the economic and political systems of established industrial nations. Many people in the United States believe that emerging nations will be best able to help themselves if they adopt a free market system.

In the past, countries of the free world and the communist world each tried to influence the economic development of emerging countries. The competition ended in recent years with the fall of communism in Europe and the breakup of the Soviet Union. Successful economic growth in the United States may help some of these nations select their economic system.

Factors Influencing Economic Growth

The ability of an economy to produce output determines its growth. A number of considerations are involved, including the quantity and quality of the factors of production—land, capital, labor, and entrepreneurship. The availability and organization of these resources determine how the economy grows.

Land

The United States abounds in most natural resources. Unlike such island nations as Great Britain and Japan, it need not depend heavily on international trade for raw materials. Although minerals such as chromium, cobalt, crude oil, and diamonds must be imported, the United States is reasonably self-sufficient in many natural resources.

Even so, the United States needs to conserve its natural resources. Many of the natural resources most Americans take for granted—clean air and water, forests, and fertile land—are dwindling rapidly. Only some of these resources are **renewable resources**, ones that can be replenished. Reseeding, for example, can restore some but not all forests for use in the foreseeable future. Trees such as California redwoods and giant firs require centuries to grow to full size. 1 ☑

Capital

An increasing supply of high-quality capital stock favors overall economic growth. In real terms, the capital stock in the United States has been growing at a rate of about $100 billion a year since 1980.

Economists sometimes speak of the **capital-to-labor ratio**, which they obtain by dividing total capital stock by the number of workers in the labor force. The ratio expresses the average amount of capital stock each worker uses in his or her job. In today's civilian workforce, the average worker uses about $20,000 worth of capital equipment and $23,500 worth of capital structures. A high capital-to-labor ratio usually encourages economic growth.

Capital goods result from production. Consequently, it is possible to influence their creation. The key is saving, and the key to saving is the consumer. When people cut back on consumption in order to save and invest, they free up factors of production to generate new capital. **2**

Reducing consumption so that more can be saved is not always possible. In some countries, people are so poor and their incomes so low that they must spend everything they earn just to exist. In these countries, there is very little saving and, therefore, low investment in capital goods. Without capital goods, overall output remains low. People are

trapped by circumstances. They are too poor to save, but their incomes can rise only if they have savings to invest in capital goods.

Labor

In order for any country's economy to grow, it must have a skilled and growing labor force. In general, the size of the labor force is related to the size of the population. If the rate of population growth in the United States continues to decline as it has in the past, the labor force growth rate could also decline. Workers from other countries, however, could make up for a labor shortage if it occurs. New additions to the labor force, such as retirees and others who traditionally have stayed at home, could also help offset a labor shortage.

QUICK CHECK

Checking Understanding

1. What are renewable resources?
2. How does saving influence economic growth?

Applying Economic Concepts

 Environment In 1990 the Environmental Protection Agency reported that nearly 150 million Americans lived in areas where the air was considered unhealthy. After much debate, Congress amended the Clean Air Act in 1990, setting standards for factories, oil refiners, and automakers.

Observers consider the American labor force more skilled today than it was in the past. Some have reached their conclusions after measuring the increasing number of school years that workers complete. In 1970, for example, the median number of school years workers had completed was 12.1. By 1991 this number had reached 12.7. Soon, it will exceed 13. At that point, one-half of the labor force will have a high school education plus one year of college or its equivalent.

A number of other factors, such as worker desire and motivation, also affect the quality of the labor force. At present, economists do not have reliable measures for such factors.

Entrepreneurs

The entrepreneur's role as agent of change qualifies him or her as a key to economic growth. A country can have all the other growth potentials, but without entrepreneurs who are willing to innovate and take risks, the economy is apt to lag.

As a group, entrepreneurs require little more than a business climate that allows them to succeed. Such a climate would probably include a minimum of government regulation and an economic system that allows them to keep much of their profits. Accordingly, a tax code with low marginal rates for upper income brackets would be more favorable for entrepreneurs than a code with high marginal rates.

DID YOU KNOW?

Length of Service The American labor force is among the most skilled in the world; it is also among the most mobile. In 1991 nearly 30 percent of American workers had been with their present employer for less than 1 year. More than one-half of American male workers have 6 or more different jobs during their first 10 years after joining the labor force. The average American worker is likely to remain with one company for 13 years. By comparison, the average Japanese worker remains with the same company for 22 years.

Productivity and Growth

Productivity refers to the efficient use of productive inputs to create goods and services. Without productivity, economic growth does not occur.

Historical Record

Productivity is measured in terms of labor inputs, even though labor is only one factor of production. Because labor is the variable input, productivity is usually defined as **labor productivity**—the rate of growth of output per unit of labor input.

Figure 15.7 shows the history of labor productivity in the United States economy since 1959. The growth of labor productivity has been somewhat uneven. Between 1959 and 1978, the productivity index increased from 64.5 to 100.4, for an annual compound growth rate of 2.36 percent per year. Between 1978 and 1993, however, the productivity rate averaged only .85 percent per year.

Productivity is still growing, but at a rate slow enough to threaten economic growth and the general standard of living. Declining productivity growth has cost the United States some of its competitive edge. In 1981, for example, Japan replaced the United States as the world's leading automobile manufacturer.

Effects

If productivity falters, the entire economy suffers. When declining labor productivity in the United States is combined with a rise in the price level, the prices of goods and services become higher than those that other countries charge. Inexpensive imports encourage people and firms to buy foreign-made products instead of American-made ones.

As productivity decreases, companies cut jobs and lay off workers. Only some of the laid-off workers will be able to find jobs in other industries. Some highly-trained workers find they must take jobs in industries that do not utilize all their skills. If workers have to take time to retrain or learn new skills, the economy suffers yet another decline in productivity.

Causes

No one completely understands the dynamics of productivity. Economists can measure it and relate it

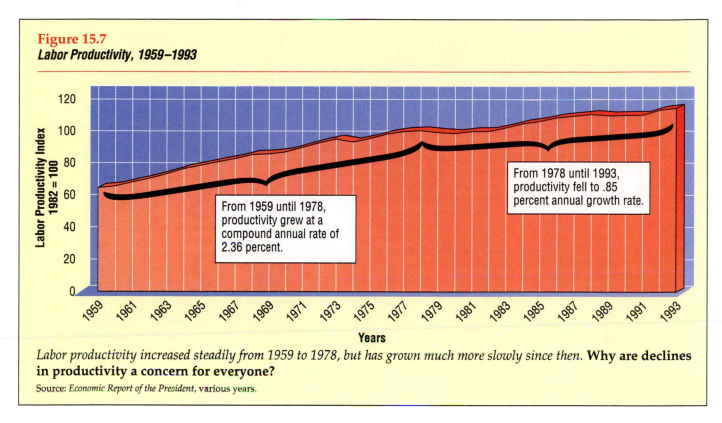

Figure 15.7
Labor Productivity, 1959–1993

From 1959 until 1978, productivity grew at a compound annual rate of 2.36 percent.

From 1978 until 1993, productivity fell to .85 percent annual growth rate.

Labor productivity increased steadily from 1959 to 1978, but has grown much more slowly since then. **Why are declines in productivity a concern for everyone?**

Source: *Economic Report of the President,* various years.

to economic growth. What remains unclear, however, is just what drives the overall economic system.

Some people feel that productivity in the United States is down because workers are too lax in their work habits and do not care enough about the companies that employ them. Others say that employers are indifferent and do not care enough about their workers. Still others charge that the tax structure discourages companies from reinvesting earnings in new capital and equipment. Others criticize the educational system.

Each of the views has some truth. The fact remains, however, that the United States has been unable to reverse its declining rate of productivity growth. How to increase productivity is one of the major questions facing the American economy today.

SECTION 2 REVIEW

Reviewing Terms and Facts

1. **Define** real GDP per capita, growth triangle, standard of living, tax base, renewable resources, capital-to-labor ratio, labor productivity.
2. **Describe** two measures of economic growth.
3. **List** five important aspects of economic growth.

4. **Identify** the factors influencing economic growth.
5. **Explain** the consequences of a declining labor productivity rate.

Critical Thinking

6. **Determining Cause and Effect** Why is productivity important to a nation's standard of living?

Applying Economic Concepts

7. **Standard of Living** Identify your most valued material possession. List the ways in which this possession enhances your standard of living.

PROFILES IN ECONOMICS

WALTER E. WILLIAMS
(1936–   )

Walter E. Williams is a contemporary American economist, author, and Professor of Economics at George Mason University. Dr. Williams's views are decidedly free market and often controversial. His many publications have opposed the minimum wage, affirmative action, and agricultural price supports.

THE MINIMUM WAGE While many people support the minimum wage as a means to prevent the exploitation of unskilled workers, Dr. Williams would rather see it abolished. His reasons are compelling:

saying there was less racism in 1948 than there is today. You can't explain it by saying that blacks had more education than whites in 1948. You have to explain it by increases in both the level and coverage of the minimum wage law.

ECONOMIC FREEDOM According to Williams, economic freedom is the key to both economic growth and the distribution of wealth. He often points to the rapid economic development of Hong Kong, Korea, Taiwan, and Singapore as evidence of economic growth without government intervention. He even opposes agricultural price supports and affirmative action for minorities on the same grounds.

AFFIRMATIVE ACTION In the case of affirmative action, Williams argues that programs designed to create a special opportunity for one group do more than exclude another group. They tarnish the achievements of the very minorities they sought to protect.

I think many government programs have harmed blacks in making achievements less credible. For example, whatever inspiration Harvard or the University of Virginia has in requiring so many articles in the law journals to be written by women or by minorities reduces the credibility of a black student or a female student having written for the law journal.

Perhaps Williams is controversial, but he likes to challenge his readers and his students with provocative views. Williams is one of the few columnists in the country whose fans have organized an official booster club, a club that many people suspect was the source of the recent campaign buttons stating "Walter Williams—Libertarian for President '92."

Williams uses South Korea's economy as an example of growth without government interference. Here, a South Korean worker tests fiber optics.

In 1948, black teen-age unemployment was less than that of whites. Compare it with today and it's the opposite. You can't explain it by

Examining the Profile

1. **Analyzing Information** Why is Williams against affirmative action programs?

2. **For Further Research** Find out why Williams believes that quotas are unconstitutional.

Business Cycles and Fluctuations

Section Preview

Objectives

After studying this section, you will be able to:

1. **Explain** the phases of the business cycle.
2. **Trace** the history of business cycles in the United States.
3. **Identify** five causes of business cycles.

Key Terms

business cycle, business fluctuation, recession, peak, trough, expansion, trend line, depression, depression scrip, econometric model, index of leading indicators

Applying Economic Concepts

Economic Security Do you have a job and a paycheck on which you and/or others depend? When the economy is slow, workers can experience job layoffs—and economic hardship. Among the seven major goals of the United States economy, *economic security* is one goal prized by Americans. To understand how economic security can sometimes suffer, we must understand business cycles.

To economists, **business cycles** are the recurring ups and downs of real GDP. The term *cycles* suggests that the ups and downs occur systematically, perhaps even predictably. Other economists prefer to talk about **business fluctuations** instead. The term *fluctuations* implies that real GDP will go up and down from time to time, but not in a regular and predictable manner.

Phases of the Business Cycle

Figure 15.8 shows the two phases of a business cycle. The first is **recession**, a period of decline in the economy as measured by changes in real GDP. In economic terms, a recession occurs when real GDP declines for two quarters, or six months, in a row. It begins when the economy reaches a **peak**—the point where real GDP stops going up. It ends when the economy reaches a **trough**—the turnaround point where real GDP stops going down.

As soon as the declining real GDP bottoms out, the economy moves into the second phase of the cycle, **expansion**—a period of recovery from a recession. Expansion continues until the economy reaches a new peak. If no periods of recession and expansion occurred, the economy would follow an even growth path

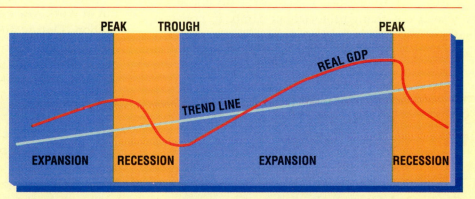

Figure 15.8
Phases of the Business Cycle

The business cycle is marked by alternating phases of recession and expansion. The economy is in recession when real GDP declines for two quarters or more in a row. The trough marks the turning point when real GDP starts to go up again, changing the recession into an expansion. **How are the recessionary periods in this graph illustrated?**

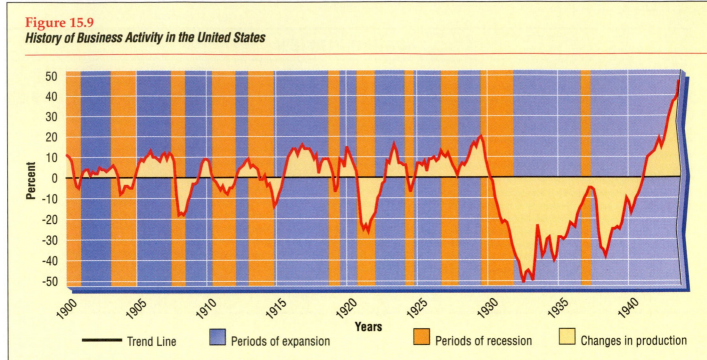

Figure 15.9
History of Business Activity in the United States

Percent

Years

——— Trend Line   Periods of expansion   Periods of recession   Changes in production

The United States has a long history of business cycles or fluctuations. **From examining this graph, how does the Great Depression compare to other recessionary periods in our history?**

called a **trend line**. As **Figure 15.8** shows, the economy departs from and then returns to its trend line as it passes through phases of recession and expansion.

If a recession becomes very severe, it may turn into a **depression**—a state of the economy with large numbers of people out of work, acute shortages, and excess capacity in manufacturing plants. Most experts agree that the Great Depression of the 1930s was the only depression the United States has ever had.

If the economy grows relatively fast during a recovery, it may surpass the trend line enough to raise real GDP to new heights. An occasional decline in real GDP will not change the overall climb. If, however, real GDP declines two quarters in a row, the economy by definition goes back into a recession.

Business Cycles in the United States

As **Figure 15.9** shows, business activity in the United States has followed an irregular course throughout the twentieth century. The worst and most prolonged downturn was the Great Depression. The years since World War II have taken on a special pattern of their own.

The Great Depression

The stock market crash on October 29, 1929, or "Black Tuesday," marks the beginning of the Great Depression. Between 1929 and 1933, GDP fell from approximately $103 to $55 billion—a decline of nearly 50 percent. At the same time, the number of people out of work rose nearly 800 percent—from 1.6 to 12.8 million. During the worst years of the Depression, one out of every four workers was jobless. Even workers who had jobs suffered. The average manufacturing wage, which had reached 55 cents an hour by 1933, plunged to 5 cents an hour in many areas.

Many banks across the country failed. The FDIC did not exist at the time, so depositors were not protected. To prevent panic withdrawals, the federal government declared a "bank holiday" in March 1933. Every bank in the country closed for several days, and many banks never reopened.

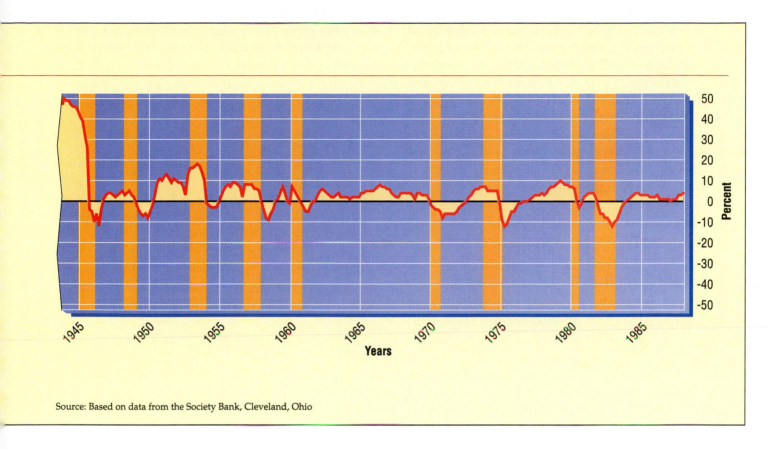

Source: Based on data from the Society Bank, Cleveland, Ohio

The money supply fell by one-third. Currency was in such short supply that towns, counties, chambers of commerce, and other civic bodies resorted to printing their own money, known as **depression scrip**. It amounted to several billion dollars and was used to pay teachers, firefighters, police officers, and other municipal employees. **1**

Causes of the Great Depression

Economists have not pinpointed an exact cause of the Great Depression, but a number of different factors seem to have contributed. One factor was the disparity in the distribution of income. A great number of very poor and very rich people lived in American society. The poor could not stimulate the economy with consumer spending because they had little or no income. The rich had the income, but often used it for such nonproductive activities as stock market speculation. **2**

Easy and plentiful credit appears to have played a role, too. Many people in the late 1920s borrowed heavily. Their debts made them vulnerable to credit contractions, high interest rates, and even minor business fluctuations. When the crunch came, heavily indebted people had nothing to fall back on. ✔

Economic conditions in other parts of the world also played a part. During the 1920s, the United States

Checking Understanding

1. What was depression scrip?
2. How did the distribution of income contribute to the Great Depression?

Applying Economic Concepts

✔ **Buying on Credit** When the automobile was mass-produced, many people had their first debt. By 1927, two out of three cars were bought on credit. In 1928, 85 percent of furniture, 80 percent of phonographs, and 75 percent of radios were also bought on credit.

made many foreign loans, which helped support a high level of international trade. Shortly before the Depression began in the United States, the government had to withdraw many of these loans. Without the loans, some foreign nations could no longer buy American goods, so American exports fell sharply.

At the same time, high American tariffs on imports kept many countries from selling goods to the United States. Some countries depended heavily on their sales to the United States, and before long, they too were faced with economic crises. As the Depression spread from country to country, world trade declined, and American exports dropped even further.

Business Cycles Since World War II

The Great Depression was over by 1940, and the United States economy had returned to its growth trend line. At the same time, massive government spending for wartime goods added an equally huge stimulant to the economy during most of the early 1940s.

Recession returned in 1945, but it did not last. As soon as the war was over, consumers went on a buying binge that stimulated expansion again. The economy has experienced several more recessions since 1945, but each downturn was short compared with the length of the recovery that followed. The average recession lasted 11 months, the average expansion 34 months.

All the recessions since 1945 have taken place in fairly regular sequence. Two striking exceptions are worth noting, however. The first occurred in the mid-1960s, during the Vietnam War. Again, massive federal spending on the war effort probably warded off a recession.

The second exception was the mid-1980s. A few economic indicators identified some weakness in 1987, but real GDP never turned down long enough for recession to occur. Many economists believe that the heavy deficit spending of the 1980s stimulated the economy to such an extent that a recession could not develop.

Causes of Business Cycles

Over the years, economists have offered a number of different reasons why business cycles occur. Each

theory has some validity, but none can claim to be the single explanation. In most cases, several factors work together to cause a cycle.

Capital Expenditures

Changes in capital expenditures are one possible cause of business cycles. When the economy is expanding, businesses expect future sales to be high, so they invest heavily in capital goods. Companies may build new plants or expand the capacity of existing ones. They may buy new equipment to replace older equipment in their plants.

After a while, businesses may decide they have expanded far enough. They begin to pull back on their capital investments, causing layoffs in the capital goods industries and, eventually, recession.

Inventory Adjustments

Inventory adjustments, or changes in the level of business inventories, are a second possible cause of business cycles. Some businesses cut back their inventories at the first sign of an economic slowdown, and then build them back up again at the first sign of an upturn. Either action causes investment expenditures—and real GDP—to fluctuate.

The influence of inventory adjustments showed up clearly in the business cycle of the late 1940s. Right after World War II, businesses in the United States invested heavily in inventories to fill shelves depleted during the war years. By 1948 consumer demand caught up with the backlog, and people stopped buying. Inventories built up on store and factory shelves, so businesses stopped investing in inventory. The resulting recession of 1949 lasted for about a year.

Innovation and Imitation

A third possible cause of business cycles is innovation. An innovation may be a new product or a new way of performing a task. When a business innovates, it often gains an edge on its competitors because its costs go down or its sales go up. In either case, profits increase, and the business grows.

If other businesses in the same industry want to keep up, they must copy what the innovator has done or come up with something even better. Generally, the imitating companies must invest heavily to do this, and an investment boom follows. After the innovation takes hold in the industry, however, the situation changes. Further investments are unnecessary, and economic activity may slow. Meanwhile, the fluctuation of investments has produced a business cycle.

Monetary Factors

A fourth possible cause of business cycles are the credit and loan policies of the commercial banking system and the Federal Reserve. When "easy money" policies are in effect, interest rates are low and loans are easy to get. Easy money encourages the private sector to borrow and invest, which stimulates the economy for a short time. Eventually the increased demand for loans causes interest rates to rise, which in turn discourages new borrowers.

As borrowing and spending slow down, the level of economic activity declines. Lenders think twice about making new loans or renewing old ones. The economy keeps declining until interest rates fall and the business cycle begins over again.

External Shocks

A final potential cause of business cycles is external shocks, such as increases in oil prices, wars, and international conflict. Some shocks drive the economy up; others drive it down.

The economy may get a boost when a new supply of natural resources is discovered. The unexpected discovery of oil in the North Sea gave Great Britain's economy a positive shock in the 1970s. World oil prices were at an all-time high, so Britain earned sizeable revenue from its oil sales. High oil prices shocked the economy of the United States, too, but in a negative way. Expensive oil reduced business activity and depressed the economy.

Predicting Business Cycles

Because of the huge costs of economic instability, much work has been done to forecast business cycles. Economists use two methods to make their forecasts. One involves macroeconomic modeling, while the other makes use of statistical predictors.

Econometric Models

An **econometric model** is a macroeconomic model that uses algebraic equations to describe how the economy behaves. Most models used today are based on some adaptation of the output-expenditure model:

$$GDP = C + I + G + F.$$

For example, an economist might use X to stand for exports and M for imports instead of the F for the foreign sector:

$$GDP = C + I + G + (X - M).$$

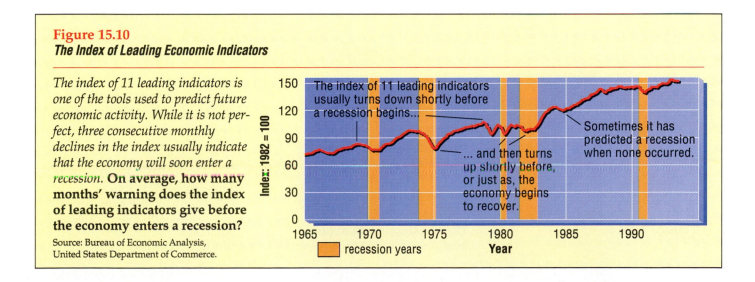

Figure 15.10
The Index of Leading Economic Indicators

The index of 11 leading indicators is one of the tools used to predict future economic activity. While it is not perfect, three consecutive monthly declines in the index usually indicate that the economy will soon enter a recession. **On average, how many months' warning does the index of leading indicators give before the economy enters a recession?**

Source: Bureau of Economic Analysis, United States Department of Commerce.

The index of 11 leading indicators usually turns down shortly before a recession begins...

... and then turns up shortly before, or just as, the economy begins to recover.

Sometimes it has predicted a recession when none occurred.

Index: 1982 = 100

recession years   Year

Other equations in the model also may be substituted for some of the variables. Suppose that households annually spend a fixed amount of money, designated as *a*, along with 95 percent of their disposable personal income. In this case, C = a + .95 (DI). If this were substituted for the C in the output-expenditure model, the equation would read:

$$GDP = a + .95 (DI) + I + G + (X - M).$$

The equation can also be broken down into smaller and smaller components. Econometric models such as this can have as few as 20 or as many as 1,000 variables. To get a prediction of GDP for the coming quarter, forecasters put in the latest figures for the money supply, interest rates, the dollar value of exports and imports, and anything else that is needed. Because most econometric models are programmed to be solved by computer, very little time is needed to obtain a solution.

As the quarter unfolds, actual changes in the economy are compared to the predictions of the model. The model is then updated, thus enhancing its accuracy. Some models give reasonably good forecasts for up to 9 months, but accuracy goes down considerably after that. Overall, short-term econometric models have proven their value and are used extensively.

Index of Leading Indicators

A second method used to predict turning points in business cycles is the **index of leading indicators**. The index is a composite of 11 statistical series that usually turns down before real GDP turns down, and turns up before real GDP turns up.

Some statistical indicators, such as the length of the average workweek—which tends to shrink just before a recession begins—are fairly good predictors of change in real GDP. Still, no single series has proven completely reliable. To resolve this problem, 11 individual series are combined into an overall index that closely patterns the behavior of real GDP, making the index of leading indicators a useful tool.

The behavior of this composite index can be seen in **Figure 15.10**. The orange areas represent recessions and the blue areas expansions. The average time between a dip in the index and the onset of recession is about 12 months. The average time between a rise in the index and expansion is about 3 months.

In general, economists think the index of leading indicators predicts a recession when it turns down 3 months in a row. Since 1965, however, the index has predicted 3 recessions that never occurred. The first was in 1966 during the heavy expenditures of the Vietnam War. The second and third were during the deficit spending of the 1980s.

The index of leading indicators is a reasonably good, but not completely reliable, indicator of future economic activity. Therefore, the information it supplies is used along with the results that other econometric models generate. Together, the results generally let the forecaster predict how real GDP will behave in the short run.

SECTION 3 REVIEW

Reviewing Terms and Facts

1. **Define** business cycle, business fluctuation, recession, peak, trough, expansion, trend line, depression, depression scrip, econometric model, index of leading indicators.
2. **Identify** the two main phases of a business cycle.

3. **Assess** the severity of the Great Depression.
4. **List** five causes of business cycles.
5. **Identify** two ways to predict business cycles.

Critical Thinking

6. **Demonstrating Reasoned Judgment** Supply evidence to support the following statement: Activities of the federal government can impact the economy.

Applying Economic Concepts

7. **Economic Security** If you were the head of a household, how would you plan your spending if you had an accurate prediction of future business cycles?

Vocabulary

The following terms are defined in Chapter 15:

SECTION ONE
- census (p. 370)
- urban population (p. 370)
- rural population (p. 370)
- center of population (p. 372)
- demographer (p. 372)

- fertility rate (p. 372)
- life expectancy (p. 372)
- net immigration (p. 372)
- baby boom (p. 373)
- population pyramid (p. 373)
- dependency ratio (p. 374)

SECTION TWO
- real GDP per capita (p. 376)
- growth triangle (p. 376)

- standard of living (p. 377)
- tax base (p. 377)
- renewable resources (p. 379)
- capital-to-labor ratio (p. 379)
- labor productivity (p. 380)

SECTION THREE
- business cycle (p. 383)
- business fluctuation (p. 383)

- recession (p. 383)
- peak (p. 383)
- trough (p. 383)
- expansion (p. 383)
- trend line (p. 384)
- depression (p. 384)
- depression scrip (p. 385)
- econometric model (p. 387)
- index of leading indicators (p. 388)

Section 1
Population (pages 370–374)

The Constitution of the United States requires a **census** of the population every 10 years. The Bureau of the Census conducts the count. It classifies the population in several ways, including a division into **urban** and **rural populations**. The annual rate of population growth was more than 3 percent until the Civil War, but has declined steadily since then.

The Bureau of the Census projects a continuation of the decline in the growth rate until the year 2050. The factors that contribute to this trend are a replacement level **fertility rate**, a slightly longer **life expectancy**, and constant **net immigration**. Projections by age and sex show the continuing influence of the **baby boom**, a large generation that will ultimately increase the **dependency ratio**. The racial and ethnic mix will also change.

Reviewing the Main Idea
Why are changes in population important to any country?

Section 2
Economic Growth (pages 376–381)

Because of changes in population, long-term economic growth is usually measured in terms of **real GDP per capita**. For shorter, year-to-year periods, real GDP unadjusted for population is used. Economic growth is important for at least five reasons. First, it raises everyone's **standard of living**. Second, it increases the **tax base** and makes it easier for government to carry out some programs. Third, it helps alleviate some domestic problems that are caused by lack of jobs. Fourth, it helps the economies of other nations. Finally, economic growth at home makes the economic and political systems of the United States models for the emerging nations of the world.

Reviewing the Main Idea
Why is economic growth one of the seven major goals of the United States economy?

Section 3
Business Cycles and Fluctuations (pages 383–388)

Economic performance in terms of real GDP fluctuates over time in a pattern called a **business cycle**. The two phases of the cycle are **recession** and **expansion**. The economy reaches a **peak** when an expansion ends, and a **trough** when a recession ends.

Business cycles result from a number of factors—including changes in capital and inventory spending by businesses, stimuli supplied by innovations and imitations, monetary factors, and external shocks.

Economists use **econometric models** to predict future economic activity. The models simulate economic activity and provide reasonably accurate short-term predictions.

Reviewing the Main Idea
What are business cycles?

Reviewing Key Terms

Write a sentence for each pair of terms below.

1. urban population; rural population
2. demographers; center of population
3. fertility rate; life expectancy
4. baby boom; dependency ratio
5. capital-to-labor ratio; labor productivity
6. business cycle; business fluctuation
7. recession; peak
8. peak; expansion
9. trough; depression
10. depression; depression scrip
11. trend line; business cycle

Reviewing the Facts

SECTION 1 *(pages 370–374)*
1. **Describe** the historical growth of population in the United States.
2. **Describe** how the population of the United States is expected to change by the year 2050.

SECTION 2 *(pages 376–381)*
3. **Trace** the record of economic growth in the United States.
4. **Explain** the importance of economic growth to the United States and other countries.
5. **Name** the factors that are essential for economic growth.
6. **Describe** the relationship between productivity and economic growth.

SECTION 3 *(pages 383–388)*
7. **Identify** the two phases through which a business cycle fluctuates.
8. **List** the factors that contributed to the Great Depression.
9. **Describe** the five probable causes of the business cycle.
10. **Explain** two methods that economists use to predict business cycles.

Critical Thinking

1. **Synthesizing Information** Review the population projections for growth and distribution shown in **Figure 15.1** on page 371. Suppose that you are planning to open a new department store. In what region of the country would you locate your store? What special lines of merchandise would you feature? Explain your answers.
2. **Formulating Questions** Assume that you could go back in time and interview Americans living in the 1930s. Prepare a list of questions that you would like to ask about living conditions during the Great Depression.

Applying Economic Concepts

1. **Economic Growth** Obtain from the library a copy of the most recent monthly report of leading economic indicators. Describe recent movements of the index. Explain what you think the movements indicate for future economic growth.
2. **Standard of Living** Under what circumstances, if any, do you think you might prefer economic security to a rise in standard of living?

Reinforcing Skills

INTERPRETING POPULATION PYRAMIDS

Use the population pyramid on page 391 to answer the following questions.
1. What does the population pyramid show?
2. Which age group is largest for males? For females?
3. Which age group is smallest for males? For females?
4. Which gender has a larger percentage of people that are 70 years old and over?
5. What percentage of the population is in the 30-to-40 age groups? How does this compare to the same age groups in **Figure 15.4** on page 375?
6. What percentage of the population is in your age group?

Individual Activity

Find the most recent real GDP per capita in **Figure 15.5** on page 377. Assume that after taxes, the amount equals your annual income. Assume also that you are living alone and must provide for all your wants and needs. Use local newspaper advertisements to get an idea of current prices for rent, food, clothing, and automobiles. Use your findings to list what you might spend for housing, food, clothing, transportation, and entertainment without exceeding your annual income. Explain why you would or would not be content with your standard of living. How do you think society and the economy in your community would change if everyone lived on a net income equal to the real GDP per capita?

Cooperative Learning Activity

Productivity is important wherever goods and services are produced. Compile a class list of suggestions for improving overall educational productivity in your school or school district. (More audiovisual equipment or computers and different class populations are a few possibilities.) Working in groups of four, have each group select a different item from the class list. In your group, make an outline of how and why you think your item would increase productivity. Compare your outline with those of the other groups. Take a class vote to reach consensus on the two suggestions you would most like to submit to the Board of Education.

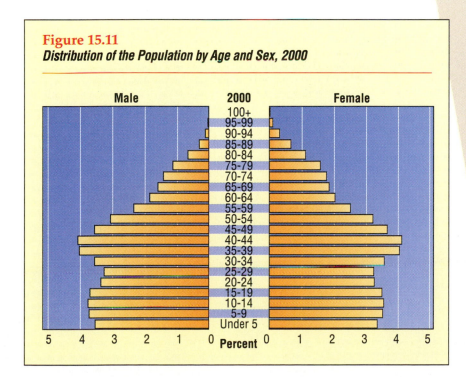

Figure 15.11
Distribution of the Population by Age and Sex, 2000

Writing About Economics

THE PERSUASIVE STYLE

In the **Journal Writing** activity on page 369, you were asked to note government goods and services that you and others in your community use. Select one item from your notes. Construct a flowchart and write brief entries to show how a growing economy might improve or expand the public good or service you selected. Then, using the persuasive style of writing discussed on page 554, write appropriate captions to highlight important aspects of your flowchart.

At any given time, millions of Americans are unemployed.

CHAPTER 16

Unemployment, Inflation, and Poverty

SECTION 1
Unemployment

SECTION 2
Inflation

SECTION 3
Poverty and the Distribution of Income

CHAPTER PREVIEW

People to Know

- Wilma Mankiller
- Sociologist

Applying Economic Concepts to Your Life

Economic Stability Do you worry about the future? If you are concerned about getting a job, earning a decent income, or keeping up with inflation, you are not alone. Many people do, which is why the concept of *economic stability* is important to everyone.

Journal Writing

For one week, summarize in your journal current trends in inflation and unemployment rates that you read about in newspapers such as *The Wall Street Journal* or your local paper.

SECTION 1
Unemployment

Section Preview

Objectives

After studying this section, you will be able to:

1. **Explain** how the Bureau of Labor Statistics determines if a person is employed.
2. **Describe** five kinds of unemployment.

Key Terms

unemployed, unemployment rate, frictional unemployment, structural unemployment, cyclical unemployment, seasonal unemployment, technological unemployment, automation, full employment

Applying Economic Concepts

Employment Did you work for at least one hour per week for pay or profit last summer? One hour may not sound like much, but it is a significant number to the United States Bureau of Labor Statistics, especially if they are trying to decide whether or not you have *employment*.

Nearly one-half of the population of the United States belongs to the civilian labor force, and at any given time, millions of these people are without jobs. Being without a job is a problem that has affected almost everyone, and it affects some people more than others. The issue is so important that full employment is one of the seven economic and social goals of the American economy.

Measuring Unemployment

To understand the severity of joblessness, we need to know how it is measured, as well as what the measure overlooks. The measure of joblessness is the unemployment rate, one of the most closely watched statistics in the economy. 1

The Unemployment Rate

During the middle of any given month, thousands of specialists from the Bureau of the Census begin their monthly survey of 55,800 households in nearly 2,000 counties in all 50 states. Census workers are looking for the **unemployed**—people available for work who made a specific effort to find a job during the past month and who, during the most recent survey week, worked less than 1 hour for pay or profit. People are also classified as unemployed if they worked in a family business without pay for less than 15 hours a week.

After the Census workers collect their data, they turn it over to the Bureau of Labor Statistics for analysis and publication. At any given time, millions of Americans are unemployed.

Unemployment also is expressed in terms of the **unemployment rate**, the number of unemployed individuals divided by the total number of persons in the civilian labor force. As **Figure 16.1** shows, the unemployment rate tends to rise dramatically during recessions and then come down slowly afterward. The unemployment rate is very sensitive to downturns in real GDP and is one of the lingering economic costs of a recession.

Limitations of the Unemployment Rate

It might seem that a measure as extensive and comprehensive as the unemployment rate would summarize the problem. If anything, however, the unemployment rate understates employment conditions for two reasons.

First, the unemployment rate does not count those who have become so frustrated or discouraged that they have stopped looking for work. These labor-force "dropouts" may include nearly 1 million people during recessionary periods. Although they are not working, these people are not classified as unemployed because they did not try to find a job within the past four weeks.

Second, people are considered employed even when they hold part-time jobs. Someone who has lost

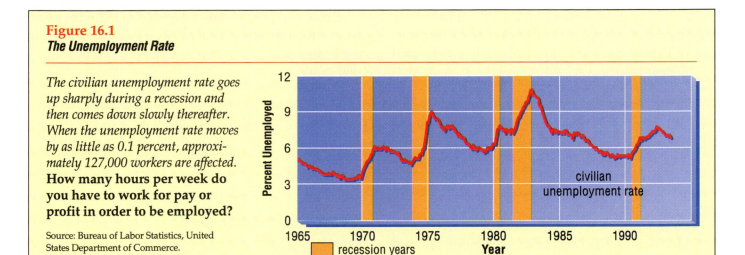

Figure 16.1
The Unemployment Rate

The civilian unemployment rate goes up sharply during a recession and then comes down slowly thereafter. When the unemployment rate moves by as little as 0.1 percent, approximately 127,000 workers are affected. **How many hours per week do you have to work for pay or profit in order to be employed?**

Source: Bureau of Labor Statistics, United States Department of Commerce.

Percent Unemployed

civilian unemployment rate

recession years

Year

a high-paying job, but is working just one hour a week at a minimum wage job, would still be considered employed. As a result, being employed is not the same as being fully employed.

Small movements in the unemployment rate have a tremendous impact on the economy. With a civilian labor force of approximately 127 million people, a 0.1 percent rise in the unemployment rate would mean that nearly 127,000 people had lost their jobs. This number is more than the population of cities such as Laredo, Texas; Evansville, Indiana; Boise, Idaho; or Tallahassee, Florida.

Kinds of Unemployment

Economists have identified several different kinds of unemployment. The nature and cause of each affect how much unemployment can be reduced in the economy.

Frictional Unemployment

One kind of unemployment is **frictional unemployment**—unemployment caused by workers who are "between jobs" for one reason or another. If these workers do not work for one week between jobs, they can be classified as unemployed.

The economy always has some workers who have left one job to look for or to take another. As long as workers change jobs, some frictional unemployment will be present. ☑

Structural Unemployment

A second—and more serious—kind of unemployment is **structural unemployment**. Structural unemployment occurs when a fundamental change in the operations of the economy reduces the demand for workers and their skills. **2**

Consumer tastes sometimes change, and certain goods and services no longer are in demand. In the

QUICK CHECK

Checking Understanding

1. What is the measure of joblessness?
2. Why does structural unemployment occur?

Applying Economic Concepts

☑ **Unemployment** Many economists believe that some frictional unemployment is a sign that the economy is healthy. The reasoning goes that many workers have left low-paying jobs for higher-paying jobs and have taken time off between the two.

early 1900s, people reduced their demand for horses, buggies, and buggy whips in favor of domestic automobiles. Later, tastes changed in favor of foreign-made automobiles, causing considerable unemployment in Michigan, Ohio, and the industrial Northeast.

Industries may change the way they operate. During the 1990-1991 recession, a series of mergers and cost reductions trimmed the white-collar labor forces in the banking and computer industries. This change was sudden and left millions of highly skilled people out of work. Many of these workers had to develop new skills before they could find employment in other industries.

Sometimes the government contributes to structural unemployment when it changes the way it does business. Congress's decision to close military bases in the 1990s is a prime example. Military bases are much larger than private companies, and the impact of the base closings is concentrated in select regions and communities. Some areas may be able to attract new industry that would employ many of the unemployed workers, but most workers will have to develop new skills or move to other regions.

Cyclical Unemployment

A third kind of unemployment is **cyclical unemployment**—unemployment directly related to swings in the business cycle. During a recession, for example, many people put off buying certain durable goods such as automobiles, refrigerators, washers, dryers, and new homes. As a result, some industries lay off workers until the economy recovers.

Cyclical unemployment may be mixed with other kinds of unemployment. In 1991 the economy underwent structural unemployment among the white-collar workforce, along with cyclical unemployment because of the recession.

Even though cyclical unemployment is serious, affected workers generally get their jobs back when the economy improves. Accordingly, many try to wait out the recession by living on savings or by taking temporary jobs.

Seasonal Unemployment

A fourth kind of unemployment is **seasonal unemployment**—unemployment resulting from changes in the weather or changes in the demand for certain products. Many carpenters and builders, for example, have less work during the winter than during the spring and summer because some tasks, such as replacing a roof or digging a foundation, are harder to do when the weather is cold. Other workers, such as cashiers and clerks in retail stores, are especially in demand during holidays when stores register about 25 percent of their annual sales.

The difference between seasonal and cyclical unemployment relates to the period of measurement. Cyclical unemployment takes place over the course of the business cycle, which may last 3 to 5 years. Seasonal unemployment takes place every year, regardless of the general health of the economy.

Technological Unemployment

A fifth kind of unemployment is **technological unemployment**—unemployment caused when workers with less skills, talent, or education are replaced by machines that do their jobs. Technological unemployment happens when workers face the threat of **automation**—production with mechanical or other processes that reduces the need for workers.

In some cases, automation results in massive unemployment. Japan, for example, pioneered the use of large mechanized factories. Entire assembly lines in industries such as automobiles and steel are staffed by one-fifth of the workers needed in similar American plants.

Because technological unemployment results partly from new methods of production, it is similar to structural unemployment. The major difference

THE WALL STREET JOURNAL

BURBANK

"Uh-oh."

Technological Unemployment *When technological unemployment occurs, many workers find they have to learn new skills.* **What causes technological unemployment?**

between the two is that other factors totally unrelated to more efficient means of production can cause structural unemployment.

The Concept of Full Employment

Economists and others have long wrestled with the concept of full employment. Full employment does not mean zero unemployment. Instead, **full employment** is the lowest possible unemployment rate with the economy growing and all factors of production being used as efficiently as possible.

Economists have also debated whether or not there is an acceptable level of unemployment. During the 1960s, it was thought that full employment meant an unemployment rate of about 4 percent or below. Most believed that efforts to reduce unemployment below this figure would not be successful.

Although President Lyndon Johnson implemented many programs to try to lower the rate, it remained in the 5 to 6 percent range for most of the early 1960s. The rate finally did drop below 4 percent during the Vietnam War when wartime spending stimulated the economy and the draft thinned the ranks of the unemployed.

The unemployment rate returned to the 5 to 6 percent range in the early 1970s. A recession in 1973 drove the rate as high as 9 percent, but for the rest of the decade it remained in the 6 to 7 percent range. By 1980 the unemployment rate rose again and hit a peak of 10.8 percent in November of that same year. It dropped in 1981, and by 1989 reached a monthly low of 5.1 percent. After that, the unemployment rate began to rise again.

As a result of this experience, most economists have given up the idea of a 4 percent unemployment rate as a measure of full employment. Today, most argue that full employment is reached when the unemployment rate drops below 5 percent.

PROFILES IN ECONOMICS

As the first female principal chief of the Cherokee Nation, Wilma Mankiller compares her job to "being president of a tiny country, a CEO, and a social worker." Mankiller, whose name comes from an eighteenth-century warrior, leads 130,000 Cherokees who make up the second-largest Native American nation after the Navajos.

CHEROKEE HERITAGE

Mankiller's ancestors once lived in the Great Smoky Mountain region. During the winter of 1838-1839, federal troops forced 13,000 to 17,000

Cherokees to move to Indian Territory, in present-day Oklahoma. Thousands died along the journey known as the "Trail of Tears."

Today, many Cherokees battle poverty, ill health, unemployment, and low self-esteem. Wilma Mankiller, who was born in Tahlequah—the Cherokee capital—experienced firsthand the problems of her people. As chief, Mankiller's goal is helping Cherokees solve their own economic problems. She says, "I always try to emphasize that we can do anything if we set our minds to it."

HANDS-ON LEADERSHIP

Mankiller began working with the Cherokee Nation in 1977. She organized the citizens of Bell, a rural Cherokee community near Stillwell, to build a 16-mile water pipeline. The Bell

Mankiller spearheaded several community projects.

project had several results. It provided water to a community that had none. It proved that community empowerment can succeed. In addition, it brought Wilma Mankiller into the public eye.

Mankiller was elected deputy chief in 1983, and she succeeded Chief Ross Swimmer when he resigned in 1985. After a hard-fought campaign in 1987, Mankiller was elected principal chief. She began her second term in 1991.

The Cherokee Nation has an annual budget of more than $50 million. It operates industries, health clinics, and cultural programs employing nearly 2,000 people. In 1990 Chief Mankiller signed the Tribal Self-Governance Agreement giving the Cherokees control of $6.1 million in federal funding.

OPTIMISTIC OUTLOOK

Chief Mankiller remains optimistic about the future. She says,

I think the most positive thing happening is that people are beginning to understand that they can live and work in a very modern, fast-moving society . . . but also celebrate who they are as Cherokees and maintain a sense of self.

Examining the Profile

1. **Recognizing Ideologies** What is Mankiller's view about solving the economic problems of the Cherokees?

2. **For Further Research** Find out how other Native American nations are using free enterprise to fight poverty. Examples include the Choctaws in Mississippi and the Yavapais in Arizona.

Inflation

Objectives

After studying this section, you will be able to:

1. **Explain** how inflation is measured.

2. **Discuss** five causes of inflation.

3. **Analyze** the destabilizing consequences of inflation.

Key Terms

price level, deflation, creeping inflation, galloping inflation, hyperinflation

Applying Economic Concepts

Inflation Have you ever rushed to a store to purchase an item because you thought its price would rise? Remember all the confusion and anxiety it caused? *Inflation* affects the economy in the same way—it causes economic instability because people change their spending habits and generally act differently when they expect prices to rise.

Inflation is a special kind of economic instability—one that deals with changes in the level of prices rather than the level of employment and output. Even so, changes in prices, employment, and output are linked.

Inflation in the United States

To better understand the concept of inflation, you must examine how it is measured. A variety of terms describe the severity of inflation.

Measuring Inflation

Two terms are often used to describe prices. One is the *price level*; the other is *inflation*. The **price level** refers to the relative magnitude of prices at one point in time and is generally used for comparative purposes. Today's price level may be higher, lower, or about the same as prices five years ago.

To measure the price level, economists select a market basket of goods and construct a price index such as the consumer price index, the producer price index, or the implicit GDP price deflator. **Figure 16.2** shows how the consumer price index looks from 1900 to the present. This index uses a base of 1982-84 = 100, and shows that the biggest increase in the price level took place after 1970.

Inflation is a rise in the general price level and is generally reported in terms of annual rates of change. If, for example, the price level at the beginning of one year is 152, and it reaches 158 by the beginning of the next, the inflation would be computed as follows (note that everything is multiplied by 100 at the end to convert the decimal to a percent):

$$\text{inflation rate} = \frac{\Delta \text{ price level}}{\text{beginning price level}} \times 100$$

Or,

$$\text{inflation rate} = \frac{(158 - 152)}{152} \times 100$$

$$= 3.95\%$$

After the change in the price level is converted to a rate, the rate is shown separately, as in **Figure 16.3**. The figure also shows that inflation tends to rise near the end of an expansion, and that the unemployment and slack economic conditions during a recession tend to reduce the effect of the inflation somewhat.

From time to time, unusual circumstances may cause **deflation**, or a decrease in the general price level. Only two significant deflations have taken place in the 1900s. One was during the post-World War I recession of the early 1920s. The other was during the Great Depression of the 1930s.

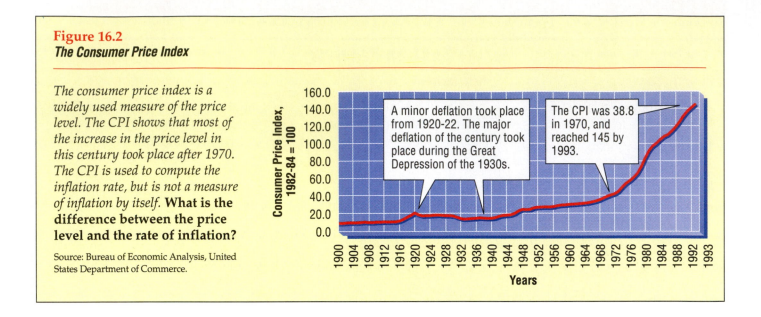

Figure 16.2
The Consumer Price Index

The consumer price index is a widely used measure of the price level. The CPI shows that most of the increase in the price level in this century took place after 1970. The CPI is used to compute the inflation rate, but is not a measure of inflation by itself. **What is the difference between the price level and the rate of inflation?**

Source: Bureau of Economic Analysis, United States Department of Commerce.

A minor deflation took place from 1920-22. The major deflation of the century took place during the Great Depression of the 1930s.

The CPI was 38.8 in 1970, and reached 145 by 1993.

Degrees of Inflation

Several terms describe the severity of inflation. One is **creeping inflation**—inflation in the range of 1 to 3 percent per year. Another is **galloping inflation**, a more intense form of inflation that can go as high as 100 to 300 percent. Many Latin American countries and many countries in the former communist bloc have experienced rates in this range in recent years. When inflation gets totally out of control—in the range of 500 percent a year and above—it turns into **hyperinflation**. Hyperinflation, however, does not happen very often and generally is the last stage before a total monetary collapse. ✅

The record for hyperinflation was set in Hungary, when huge amounts of currency were printed to pay the government's bills during World War II. By the end of the war, it was claimed that 828 octillion (828,000,000,000,000,000,000,000,000,000) *pengös* equaled one prewar *pengö*. Because all the zeros would not fit on the bills, the larger denomination notes had their amounts spelled out in words rather than numbers.

Other countries such as Argentina, Mexico, and the former Soviet Union have had brief bouts with hyperinflation. Fortunately, inflation in the United States has never reached such proportions. Rates during the 1970s and early 1980s ranged from 5 percent to more than 15 percent as measured by the consumer price index.

Causes of Inflation

Several explanations have been offered for the causes of inflation. These explanations include the demand-pull theory, the government deficit, the cost-push theory, the wage-price spiral, and excessive monetary growth. Because no simple test determines which is better than the others, each has some validity.

Demand-Pull

One explanation is the demand-pull theory. According to this theory, all sectors in the economy try to buy more than the economy can produce.

Consumers, businesses, and governments converge on stores to buy goods and services, which causes shortages. Merchants can afford to lose some customers, so some merchants raise their prices. Others do not offer discounts or run sales. In either case, the result is the same—the price level rises.

Government Deficit

Another approach involves the federal government's deficit. Basically, this explanation is a variant of the demand-pull theory. While demand-pull blames excess demand on all sectors, the government deficit approach blames inflation only on the federal deficit.

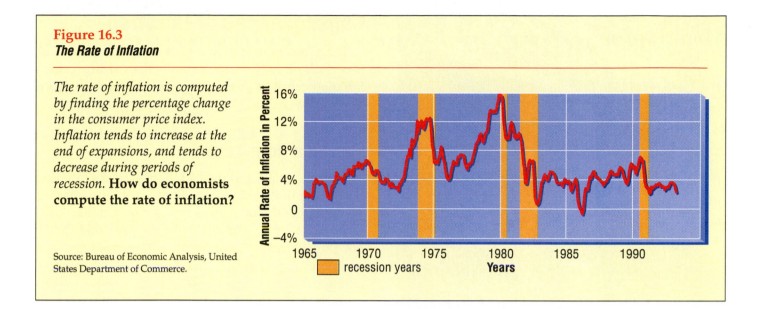

Figure 16.3
The Rate of Inflation

The rate of inflation is computed by finding the percentage change in the consumer price index. Inflation tends to increase at the end of expansions, and tends to decrease during periods of recession. **How do economists compute the rate of inflation?**

Source: Bureau of Economic Analysis, United States Department of Commerce.

The federal deficit can contribute to inflation, especially if the Federal Reserve System expands the money supply to keep the interest rate down. If the debt is not monetized, some borrowers will be crowded out as interest rates rise. In such a situation, the federal deficit may have a greater destabilizing impact on output and employment than on the price level.

Cost-Push

A third explanation economists put forth is the cost-push theory. It says that labor groups—as well as others who drive up prices of inputs for manufacturers—cause inflation.

This situation might take place when a strong national union wins a large wage contract, forcing producers to raise prices to consumers to recover the labor costs. An unexpected increase in the cost of nonlabor inputs also could cause the price level to rise. Such a price rise occurred during the 1970s when oil prices went from $5 to $35 a barrel. **1**

Wage-Price Spiral

Still another explanation says that no single group is to blame for inflation. According to this explanation, a self-perpetuating spiral of wages and prices gets started that is difficult to stop. **2**

Higher prices force workers to ask for higher wages. If they get the higher wages, producers try to recover them with higher prices. If either side tries to increase its relative position with a larger price hike than before, the rate of inflation keeps rising.

Excessive Monetary Growth

A final reason given for inflation is excessive monetary growth. The monetary growth becomes excessive when the money supply grows faster than real GDP.

Checking Understanding

1. What is the cost-push theory?
2. According to the wage-price spiral theory, what is to blame for inflation?

Applying Economic Concepts

 Hyperinflation Another example of hyperinflation occurred in Germany after World War I. Prices soared so high that people had to take wheelbarrows full of money to pay for groceries!

Consequences of Inflation

The problem of inflation is more severe than most people think and involves more than rising prices. Inflation can have a destabilizing effect on an economy for several reasons.

The Dollar Buys Less

The immediate and most obvious effect of inflation is that the dollar buys less. Because the purchasing power of the dollar falls as prices rise, a dollar loses value over time. For example, in 1993 the dollar bought less than 6 cents worth of the goods and services that it bought in 1900. **Figure 16.4** shows this falling value.

Decreased purchasing power is especially hard on retired people with fixed incomes because their money buys a little less each month. Those not on fixed incomes, such as doctors, lawyers, bankers, plumbers, and accountants, are better able to cope. They can increase their fees to have additional income.

Spending Habits Change

A second destabilizing effect is that inflation can cause consumers and investors to change their spending habits, which disrupts the economy. Prices go up during an inflationary period, and the price of money—the interest rate—is no exception. In the early 1980s, the interest rate in the United States rose so high that consumer spending on durable goods, especially housing, fell dramatically.

During the recession of 1981, the impact of the interest rate on housing was particularly severe. Suppose, for example, that a young couple wanted to borrow $60,000 for 20 years to buy a house. At a 10 percent interest rate, their monthly mortgage payment would be $579.01. At 14 percent, the payment would be $746.11. In 1981 some mortgage rates reached 18 percent, which meant a monthly payment of about $926 for the same loan. As a result, the housing industry almost collapsed.

Businesses also adjusted their spending habits. In 1981, when interest rates on business loans often exceeded 20 percent, many merchants cut back on factory orders to reduce the cost of borrowing.

Consequences of Inflation *Inflation can cause consumers to change their spending habits, which may result in business closings.* **Why are people on fixed incomes especially hard-hit during inflationary periods?**

According to this theory, which may be the most popular of all, any extra money that is created will increase some group's purchasing power. When this money is spent, it causes a demand-pull effect that drives up prices.

Those who prefer the excess money theory to demand-pull point out that credit alone cannot keep inflation going. At some point, they say, borrowers will have gotten all the credit they can handle and the effects of demand-pull will taper off. Therefore, for inflation to continue, the money supply must grow faster than the increase in real output.

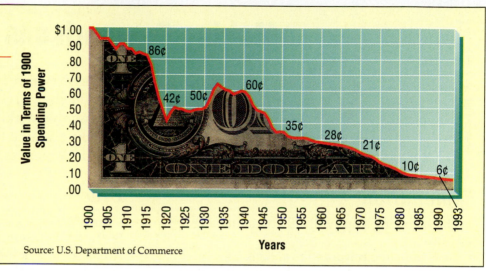

Figure 16.4
The Declining Value of the Dollar

When the price level goes up, the purchasing power of the dollar goes down. When the price level goes down, as it did during the Great Depression, the purchasing power of the dollar goes up. Today, the dollar buys less than 6 percent of the goods and services it purchased in 1900. **If inflation continues, what will happen to the purchasing power of the dollar?**

Source: U.S. Department of Commerce

Eventually the factories had to lay off workers because of the decline in orders.

Speculation Increases

A third destabilizing effect of inflation is that it tempts some people to speculate heavily in an attempt to take advantage of a higher price level. People who ordinarily put their money in reasonably safe investments begin buying condominiums, diamonds and gemstones, works of art, and other exotic items that usually increase in price. Because such purchases divert spending from normal channels, some structural unemployment may take place.

The Distribution of Income Is Altered

Finally, inflation alters the distribution of income. During long inflationary periods, lenders are generally hurt more than borrowers. Loans made earlier are repaid later in inflated dollars—or dollars with less purchasing power because they buy less.

Suppose, for example, that a person borrows money to buy bread selling at 50 cents a loaf. If the amount borrowed was $100, it would buy 200 loaves of bread. If inflation sets in, and if the price doubles by the time the loan is paid back, the lender will be able to buy only 100 loaves of bread when the money is returned. Inflation in the long run, then, favors debtors over creditors.

SECTION 2
REVIEW

Reviewing Terms and Facts

1. **Define** price level, deflation, creeping inflation, galloping inflation, hyperinflation.
2. **Describe** how the CPI is used to compute the inflation rate.
3. **List** the five causes of inflation.
4. **Identify** four ways inflation destabilizes the economy.

Critical Thinking

5. **Understanding Cause and Effect** Explain the effect that inflation has on the financial positions of borrowers and lenders. If you managed a bank, what interest rate would you charge to overcome the disadvantage of long-term inflation?

Applying Economic Concepts

6. **Inflation** What does an inflation rate of 4 percent mean?

CRITICAL THINKING SKILL

Making Comparisons

Which brand of hair spray costs less? Which football team has the best record? Which teacher gives the most homework? These questions involve making comparisons. When you make a comparison, you examine two or more examples to identify their similarities and differences.

Explanation

The following steps will aid you in making comparisons:
- Determine the purpose for making the comparison.
- Read or study each item to be compared.
- Identify similarities and differences among the items you are comparing.
- Draw conclusions based on the comparisons you made.

Practice

In 1990 *Fortune* magazine conducted a survey to find out how 25-year-olds feel about their careers. All those interviewed were college graduates who work for major corporations or professional firms. Read the excerpts below, then answer the questions that follow.

1. What is the purpose for this comparison?
2. What are the similarities among Angela, Linda, and Rick?
3. What are the differences among Angela, Linda, and Rick?
4. According to these three people, how did the attitudes of the previous generation differ from their own?
5. What conclusion can you draw from this comparison?

Angela, a corporate communicator who turned down two promotions:

> *Job satisfaction is the most important thing to me. . . . In those other jobs, I would have had less responsibility, less of a challenge. The only benefit was more money. . . . I asked the advice of managers who had been around awhile. They said that ten or 20 years ago it would have been a black mark to turn down those jobs. . . . But in this environment, I feel that I can afford to be selective.*

Linda, an engineer at the same corporation where her father has worked for 30 years:

> *I feel guilty for saying this, but I don't feel the same kind of loyalty his [her father's] generation felt. They stayed through thick and thin. I wouldn't feel bad about going [elsewhere] if that's what was needed to develop my career. . . . Maybe a career isn't all it's cracked up to be. It's still important to me, but it's not the No. 1 thing in my life.*

Rick, an investment broker who left a major bank to work for a smaller firm:

> *I want to be happy and fulfilled—socially and culturally— and to progress in the work world to the point where I'm happy with myself. I'm not shooting for a title. . . . Our generation is much less political in the workplace than the ones that preceded us. . . . I want to earn my place with grace and style, not to lick someone else's heels for it.*

—"What 25-Year-Olds Want," *Fortune,* August 27, 1990

Additional Practice

For further practice in making comparisons, complete the Reinforcing Skills exercise in the Chapter 16 Review on page 415.

Poverty and the Distribution of Income

Section Preview

Objectives

After studying this section, you will be able to:

1. **Explain** how economists measure the distribution of income.
2. **Discuss** the reasons for the inequality of income.
3. **Describe** how poverty levels are defined and measured.
4. **Discuss** six antipoverty programs.

Key Terms

Lorenz curve, blue-collar worker, white-collar worker, poverty threshold, income-to-poverty ratio, welfare, food stamps, negative income tax, enterprise zone, workfare

Applying Economic Concepts

Distribution of Income Do you compare what you make to the earnings of others? The Department of Commerce does, too. It measures and ranks incomes to examine the *distribution of income.*

In the United States, as elsewhere, people do not have the same income. Economists use the term *distribution of income* to describe the way income is distributed among individuals, families, households, and other groups.

The Distribution of Income

Economists analyze the distribution of income in several ways. It can be analyzed by looking at households, families, single individuals, geographic regions, race and ethnic origin, sex, or educational attainment.

A more common method is to use the family as the basic income unit and then rank all families from lowest to highest. After the incomes are ranked, the ranking is divided into quintiles, or fifths, and then examined.

Table **A** in **Figure 16.5** shows quintile data for two different years. This data is then shown as a **Lorenz curve**—a curve that shows how much the actual distribution of income varies from an equal distribution. In Graph **B,** 4.4 percent of the total income is the amount that the lowest quintile receives. This amount is combined with the income the next quintile earns, and then plotted as point **a.** This number is then added to the income that the middle quintile earns and is plotted as point **b**—showing that the poorest 60

percent of the families earned 31.5 percent of the total income. This process continues until the cumulative values of all quintiles are plotted.

If all families received exactly the same income, the Lorenz curve would appear as a diagonal line running from one corner of the graph to the other. Therefore, 20 percent of the families would earn 20 percent of the income, and 80 percent of the families would earn 80 percent of the income. Because all families do not receive the same income, however, the curve showing the actual income distribution is not a diagonal. The area on the graph between the diagonal and the Lorenz curve shows the degree of income inequality. The larger this area, the more unequal the distribution of income.

Reasons for Income Inequality

A number of reasons explain why the incomes of various groups may be different. They include education, wealth, discrimination, ability, and monopoly power.

Education

Some people have higher incomes than others because they have more education. Education puts them in a better position to get higher-paying jobs

Figure 16.5
The Distribution of Income by Families

(A) Family Income Ranked by Quintiles

	1980	1992	
	Quintile	Quintile	Cumulative
Lowest Fifth	5.2%	4.4%	4.4%
Second Fifth	11.5%	10.6%	15.0%
Third Fifth	17.5%	16.5%	31.5%
Fourth Fifth	24.3%	24.0%	55.5%
Highest Fifth	41.5%	44.5%	100.0%
Top 5 percent	15.3%	17.6%	

(B) The Lorenz Curve

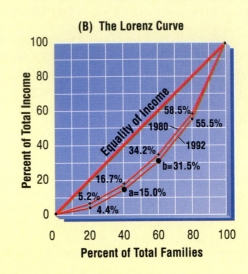

Source: *Money Income of Households, Families, and Persons in the United States: 1992.* U.S. Department of Commerce, Bureau of the Census.

The Lorenz curve is often used to show the distribution of income in the United States. Between 1980 and 1992, the distribution of income became more unequal, with each lower quintile earning slightly less than it did in the earlier period. **What five factors help explain why some groups have more income than others?**

---

that require a higher level of skills. Although exceptions exist, there generally is a strong relationship between median income and level of education.

Wealth

Income also tends to vary because some people in the United States hold more wealth than others, and the distribution of wealth is even more unequal than the distribution of income. When wealth holders are ranked from highest to lowest, the top fifth has 75 percent of all the wealth in the country. The bottom two-fifths, which is 40 percent of the people in the country, have less than 2 percent of the total wealth.

This inequality clearly has an impact on people's ability to earn income. Wealthy families can send their children to expensive colleges and universities. The wealthy can also afford to set their children up in business so they can earn a better income. Even if the wealthy choose not to work, they can make investments that will bring them tax-free income.

Discrimination

Discrimination is another factor that influences the distribution of income. Women may not be promoted to executive positions in some companies because male executives believe that women cannot handle the pressures of such jobs. Certain unions may deny immigrants or ethnic minorities membership on the grounds that certain ethnic groups "don't belong" in certain professions.

Although discrimination is against the law, it still takes place. When it does occur, discrimination causes women and minority groups to be crowded into other labor markets where oversupply drives down wages.

Ability

Some people earn more income because they have certain natural abilities, such as a professional athlete who earns millions of dollars every year. Such athletes as Barry Bonds, Larry Johnson, Shaquille O'Neal, and Steffi Graf earn high incomes because they have unique abilities or talents. The same is true of popular performers such as Oprah Winfrey, Harrison Ford, or David Letterman.

Monopoly Power

Another important reason for differences in the distribution of income is the degree of monopoly power that certain groups hold. Unions, for example, have considerable power and have been able to obtain higher wages for their members. Union carpenters, electricians, truck drivers, auto workers, and other **blue-collar workers**—industrial or factory workers who receive wages—generally are paid higher wages than those workers who are not in unions. Some **white-collar workers**—clerical, business, or professional workers who generally are salaried—also hold a degree of monopoly power. The American Medical Association, for example, has been successful in limiting the number of people in its profession by limiting enrollments in medical schools.

Poverty

Poverty is a relative measure that depends on prices, the standard of living, and the incomes that others earn. What may seem like poverty to one person may seem like riches to another. Even so, government figures show that more than 14.5 percent of all Americans lived in poverty in 1992. To understand how this happens, the definition of poverty as well as poverty-related issues must be examined.

Defining Poverty

Families and individuals are defined as living in poverty if their incomes fall below a certain level, or threshold. The **poverty threshold** is the annual dollar benchmark used to evaluate the money income that families and unrelated individuals receive. If families and unrelated individuals have an annual income below the threshold, they are in poverty. Additional supplements such as food stamps, subsidized housing, and medicaid do not count in the computation. **Figure 16.6** outlines the poverty thresholds for 1992 and 1993.

In 1964 the Social Security Administration developed poverty thresholds using two studies the United States Department of Agriculture did in the 1950s. The first study developed four alternative, but

nutritionally adequate, food plans for individuals and families of different sizes. The least expensive food plan was then selected as the food budget that would keep people out of poverty.

The second study found that families typically spend one-third of their total income on food. To obtain the threshold, the Social Security Administration simply multiplied the least expensive food budget by three. Today, the thresholds are indexed to the inflation rate so they go up just enough every year to offset the increase in the price level.

Income-to-Poverty Ratios

The Lorenz curve ranked family incomes but did not tell anything about the number of people in poverty. The United States Department of Commerce uses a different method to make this comparison.

Figure 16.6
Poverty Thresholds

Size of Family Unit	1992	1993
1 person	$6,810	$6,970
2 persons	9,190	9,430
3 persons	11,570	11,890
4 persons	13,950	14,350
5 persons	16,330	16,810
6 persons	18,710	19,270
7 persons	21,090	21,730
8 persons	23,470	24,190
9 persons	25,850	26,650

Thresholds for Alaska and Hawaii are slightly higher.

Families and unrelated individuals who have incomes below the official poverty thresholds listed above are defined as being in poverty. Only money income is counted. Other aid such as food stamps, medicaid, and subsidized housing, while helpful, is not counted. These thresholds are indexed annually to the rate of inflation. **How were the poverty guidelines first established?**

Source: *The Federal Register*, various editions.

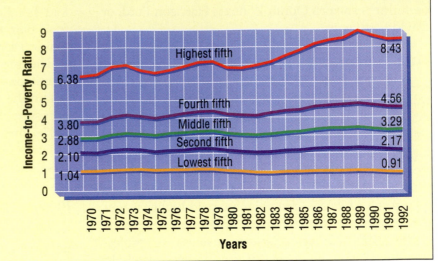

Figure 16.7
Average Income-to-Poverty Ratios

Income-to-poverty ratios are used to adjust for the differences in family sizes. When ranked by quintiles, all groups except for the lowest made some progress between 1970 and 1992. The .91 ratio for the lowest fifth means that the average family income for that group is only 91 percent of the poverty threshold. **What has happened to the lowest and the highest fifths over time?**

Source: *Money Income of Households, Families, and Persons in the United States: 1992.* U.S. Department of Commerce.

The measure is the **income-to-poverty ratio**, which divides family income by the poverty level. This measure, according to the Department of Commerce, has the advantage of compensating for family size:

. . . a four-person family containing two related children under 18 with an income in 1991 of $25,000 would have an income-to-poverty level of 1.81 (i.e. $25,000/$13,812). A two-person family . . . with an income of $25,000 in 1991 would have a much higher ratio of 2.72 ($25,000/$9,120). A ratio under 1.00 indicates that the family was below the poverty level during the calendar year. Income-to-poverty ratios . . . adjust for family size and economies of scale, enabling more reasonable comparisons of economic well-being between families.

—U.S. Department of Commerce, *Money Income of Households, Families, and Persons in the United States: 1991*

These ratios, like family incomes, can be ranked and divided into quintiles. For 1992, **Figure 16.7** shows that, on average, the entire lowest quintile—or 20 percent of American families—have incomes that place them below the poverty threshold.

To see how the distribution of poverty changes over time, one can examine the average income-to-poverty ratio for each quintile to see if it is going up or down. For incomes to become more equal over time, the ratios for the upper quintiles would have to fall and the ratios for the lower quintiles would have to rise. **Figure 16.7** shows exactly the opposite.

What Caused the Gap to Grow?

According to the Bureau of the Census, the growing spread in the distribution of income that took place in the 1980s occurred for several reasons. The first involved a structural change in the economy as industry changed from goods production to service production. Because wages are typically lower in the service industries such as fast-food chains, movie theaters, and entertainment parks, weekly paychecks tend to be lower. ☑

The second reason for the spread in income distribution was the growing gap between well-educated and poorly educated workers. During the 1980s, wages for the highly skilled soared, while wages for the less skilled tended to remain about the same. The addition of many low-skilled immigrants during this period helped widen the disparity.

A third reason, declining unionism—especially among low-skilled workers—added to the growing differential. Unions have successfully kept the wages of their workers well above the wages paid to nonunion workers. The decline of unions meant that many of the low-skilled workers had to work elsewhere for less pay. **1**

The fourth reason for the income gap concerns the changing structure of the American family. The shift from married-couple families to single-parent families and other nonfamily household living arrangements tends to lower average family income.

Distribution of Income
One reason for the spread in income distribution is the increasing number of workers in low-paying service jobs, such as fast-food servers. **How has the changing structure of the family contributed to the income distribution disparity?**

Antipoverty Programs

Over the years, the federal government has instituted a number of programs to help the needy. Most come under the general heading of **welfare**—economic and social programs that provide regular assistance from the government or private agencies because of need. These welfare programs provide three basic kinds of help—income assistance, general assistance, and assistance in the form of social service programs. Other antipoverty programs include proposals for a negative income tax, enterprise zones, and workfare.

Income Assistance

Programs that provide direct cash assistance to those in need fall into the category of income assistance. One such program is Aid to Families with Dependent Children (AFDC). Under it, a family in need because of the death, continuous absence, or permanent disability of a parent can receive cash payments.

Although the program is subject to broad federal guidelines, individual states can determine whether a family is eligible for benefits and how large the benefits should be. For this reason, benefits vary widely from state to state. **2**

Another income assistance program is the Supplemental Security Income (SSI), which makes cash payments to blind or disabled persons age 65 and older. Originally, the states administered the program because benefits varied so much from state to state. The federal government took it over in 1979.

General Assistance

Programs that assist poor people but do not provide direct cash assistance fall into the category of

Checking Understanding	Applying Economic Concepts
1. How did the decline of unionism affect the general level of wages? 2. Who determines which families are eligible for AFDC?	**Income** While the wages of many workers dropped in the 1980s, the richest Americans accrued even more wealth—until the richest 1 percent owned 36 percent of the country's total wealth.

Figure 16.8
Per Capita Personal Income by State

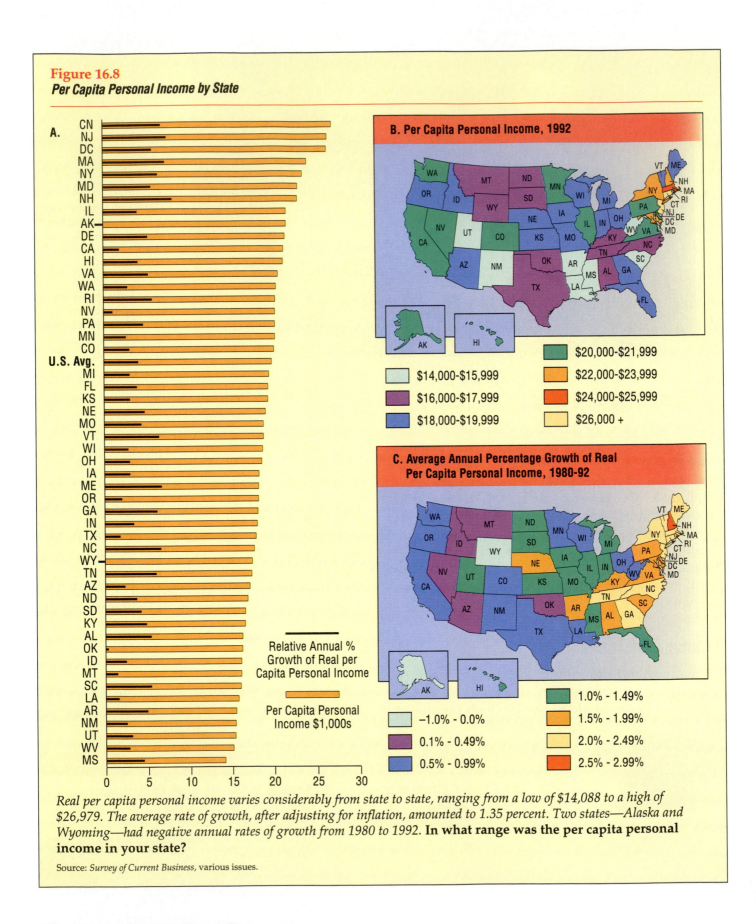

A.

States (top to bottom): CN, NJ, DC, MA, NY, MD, NH, IL, AK, DE, CA, HI, VA, WA, RI, NV, PA, MN, CO, **U.S. Avg.**, MI, FL, KS, NE, MO, VT, WI, OH, IA, ME, OR, GA, IN, TX, NC, WY, TN, AZ, ND, SD, KY, AL, OK, ID, MT, SC, LA, AR, NM, UT, WV, MS

X-axis: 0, 5, 10, 15, 20, 25, 30

Relative Annual % Growth of Real per Capita Personal Income

Per Capita Personal Income $1,000s

B. Per Capita Personal Income, 1992

Legend:
- $14,000-$15,999
- $16,000-$17,999
- $18,000-$19,999
- $20,000-$21,999
- $22,000-$23,999
- $24,000-$25,999
- $26,000 +

C. Average Annual Percentage Growth of Real Per Capita Personal Income, 1980-92

Legend:
- −1.0% - 0.0%
- 0.1% - 0.49%
- 0.5% - 0.99%
- 1.0% - 1.49%
- 1.5% - 1.99%
- 2.0% - 2.49%
- 2.5% - 2.99%

Real per capita personal income varies considerably from state to state, ranging from a low of $14,088 to a high of $26,979. The average rate of growth, after adjusting for inflation, amounted to 1.35 percent. Two states—Alaska and Wyoming—had negative annual rates of growth from 1980 to 1992. **In what range was the per capita personal income in your state?**

Source: *Survey of Current Business*, various issues.

HELP WANTED

Sociologist

▼

Government agency seeks sociologist to evaluate welfare programs in midwestern urban community. Your duties will include gathering firsthand information from people receiving welfare. You will prepare reports to be used in a comparative study of similar programs in other communities. Your conclusions about the effectiveness of urban welfare programs will help formulate government policy. We are seeking an individual who is skilled in research and analysis and who can communicate ideas clearly.

▼

Education: Master's degree in Sociology
Salary range: $25,500–$31,000

general assistance. One example is the food stamp program that serves millions of Americans. **Food stamps** are government-issued coupons that can be redeemed for food. They may be given or sold to eligible low-income persons. If, for example, a person pays 40 cents for a $1 food coupon, that person is getting a dollar's worth of food for a fraction of its cost. The program, which began in 1961 and became law in 1964, is different from other programs because it is based solely on income. Age, race, and physical condition play no part in determining eligibility. **1**

Another general assistance program is medicaid—a joint federal-state medical insurance program. Under the program, the federal government pays a majority of health-care costs, and the state governments pay the rest. Medicaid serves millions of Americans, including children, the visually impaired, and the disabled. ☑

Social Service Programs

Over the years, the individual states have developed a wide variety of social service programs to help the needy. These include such areas as child abuse prevention, foster care, family planning, job training, child welfare, and day care.

Although the states control the kinds of services the programs provide, the federal government matches part of the cost. To be eligible for matching funds, a state must file an annual service plan. If the plan is approved, the state is free to select the social issues it wishes to address, set the eligibility requirements, and decide how the program is to be carried out.

Negative Income Tax

The **negative income tax** is a proposed type of tax that would make cash payments to certain groups below the poverty line. Called a negative income tax, it is different from the antipoverty programs listed above because it is a market-based program designed to encourage people to work. **2**

Under the negative income tax, the federal government would set an income level below which people do not have to pay taxes. Then, the government would pay a certain amount of money to any person who earned less than that level. A person who earned no income during a year might receive $3,000, making that person's total income for the year $3,000. Someone else who actually earned $3,000 might receive $1,500 from the government, bringing that person's annual income to $4,500. A third person who made $6,000 would receive nothing from the government, but would also not make enough to pay taxes.

Anyone who earned more than $6,000, however, would have to pay some taxes. In addition, as income got higher, so would the taxes. A person with an

Checking Understanding

1. How do food stamps lower recipients' grocery bills?
2. How does the negative income tax differ from other antipoverty programs?

Applying Economic Concepts

 Income Distribution Large-scale social welfare programs began during the Great Depression. Economic conditions were so bad that private charities could not help everyone who needed financial assistance. Today, charities and the government share the costs of public assistance.

income of $10,000 might pay a tax of $1,500, while a person with an income of $15,000 might pay $3,000.

The negative income tax could be cost-effective because it would eliminate costly welfare programs, yet still allow people to have money to spend as they saw fit. Government would also save because it would have fewer administrative costs. Although the tax is not used, many people believe it would be a reasonable alternative to the existing welfare programs.

Enterprise Zones

Special **enterprise zones** are areas where companies can locate free of certain local, state, and federal tax laws and operating restrictions. The zones benefit businesses and area residents because people can find work without worrying about transportation, and run-down areas can begin to grow.

Nearly everyone agrees that one of the best weapons in the fight against poverty is a healthy and growing economy. The enterprise zone concept is an attempt to focus some of that growth directly in the areas that need it most, making more employment opportunities available.

Workfare Programs

Because of rising welfare costs, many state and local governments require those who receive welfare to provide labor in exchange for benefits. **Workfare** is a program that requires welfare recipients to

Enterprise Zones *Quincy Market in Boston, Massachusetts, has been revitalized with shops, boutiques, and restaurants.* **How do enterprise zones help businesses and area residents?**

exchange some of their labor for benefits. People on workfare often assist law enforcement officials or sanitation and highway crews, or perform other types of community service work.

The work is required of almost everyone except those with very young children, the disabled, and the elderly. Supporters of the program argue that the recipients learn skills on the job.

SECTION 3 REVIEW

Reviewing Terms and Facts

1. **Define** Lorenz curve, blue-collar worker, white-collar worker, poverty threshold, income-to-poverty ratio, welfare, food stamps, negative income tax, enterprise zone, workfare.
2. **Describe** how the distribution of income is measured.
3. **List** the five main reasons for inequality of income.
4. **Explain** how income-to-poverty ratios are used to measure the growing inequality of income.
5. **Identify** the major programs and proposals designed to alleviate the problem of poverty.

Critical Thinking

6. **Analyzing Information** Some people have said that the "rich got richer" in the 1980s. What factors can you cite to explain that what actually happened was more complex than this simple statement?

Applying Economic Concepts

7. **Distribution of Income** What would happen to the Lorenz curve if there were no social welfare programs?

Vocabulary

The following terms are defined in Chapter 16:

SECTION ONE
- unemployed (p. 394)
- unemployment rate (p. 394)
- frictional unemployment (p. 395)
- structural unemployment (p. 395)

- cyclical unemployment (p. 396)
- seasonal unemployment (p. 396)
- technological unemployment (p. 396)
- automation (p. 396)
- full employment (p. 397)

SECTION TWO
- price level (p. 399)
- deflation (p. 399)

- creeping inflation (p. 400)
- galloping inflation (p. 400)
- hyperinflation (p. 400)

SECTION THREE
- Lorenz curve (p. 405)
- blue-collar worker (p. 407)
- white-collar worker (p. 407)

- poverty threshold (p. 407)
- income-to-poverty ratio (p. 408)
- welfare (p. 409)
- food stamps (p. 411)
- negative income tax (p. 411)
- enterprise zone (p. 412)
- workfare (p. 412)

Section 1
Unemployment (pages 394–397)

The Bureau of the Census identifies **unemployed** persons in monthly samples of approximately 55,800 households across the country. The number of unemployed is then divided by the civilian labor force to express unemployment as a rate. The **unemployment rate** is comprehensive but does not count the dropouts, nor does it distinguish between full- and part-time employment.

The kinds of unemployment include **frictional unemployment, structural unemployment, cyclical unemployment, seasonal unemployment,** and **technological unemployment.**

Reviewing the Main Idea
What is unemployment, and how is it measured?

Section 2
Inflation (pages 399–403)

Economists measure the **price level** with the CPI, the GDP implicit price deflator, and the producer price index. The change in the price level is the **inflation rate**, which is usually expressed in terms of percentage changes. **Creeping inflation, galloping inflation,** and **hyperinflation** are terms used to describe the severity of inflation.

Generous credit conditions and excessive growth of the money supply are underlying causes of inflation. When these conditions are present, various kinds of inflation—including demand-pull, deficit spending, cost-push, and wage-price spiral—can take place. Inflation erodes the value of the dollar and forces consumers and businesses to change their spending habits.

Reviewing the Main Idea
What causes inflation, and how does it destabilize the economy?

Section 3
Poverty and the Distribution of Income (pages 405–412)

A number of factors account for the unequal distribution of income, including educational levels, wealth, discrimination, ability, and monopoly power. Poverty is a relative measure determined by comparing the amount of money income families earn to the **poverty threshold**. **Income-to-poverty ratios** are also used to compensate for differences in family sizes, and all measures show a growing gap between incomes.

Various antipoverty programs have been introduced to help those in need. Government assistance programs include Aid to Families with Dependent Children, Supplemental Security Income, **food stamps**, and other programs. Economists have proposed a **negative income tax**, while others have proposed **enterprise zones** and **workfare**.

Reviewing the Main Idea
What is poverty, and what programs can be used to alleviate it?

CHAPTER 16 REVIEW

Reviewing Key Terms

Write the letter of the key term that best matches each definition below.

a. blue-collar workers
b. cyclical unemployment
c. unemployed
d. food stamps
e. frictional unemployment
f. full employment
g. income-to-poverty ratio
h. inflation
i. Lorenz curve
j. poverty threshold
k. price level
l. seasonal unemployment
m. structural unemployment
n. technological unemployment
o. white-collar workers
p. workfare

1. an unemployment rate below 5 percent
2. an example of a welfare program
3. annual benchmark the Social Security Administration determines
4. caused by a shift in demand or a change in the way the economy operates
5. caused by annual changes in weather, holiday seasons
6. caused by periodic swings in business activity
7. caused by workers who are "between jobs" for short periods
8. describes the requirement that welfare recipients exchange labor for benefits
9. happens when workers face the threat of automation
10. industrial workers who receive wages
11. measured by changes in the CPI
12. measure of income that compensates for family size
13. measured by the CPI
14. shows how much the actual distribution of income differs from an equal distribution
15. workers who receive salaries
16. works less than one hour per week for pay or profit

Reviewing the Facts

SECTION 1 *(pages 394–397)*
1. **Describe** how the unemployment rate is computed.
2. **Identify** the major types of unemployment.
3. **Explain** what is meant by full employment.

SECTION 2 *(pages 399–403)*
4. **Compare** the difference between the price level and inflation.
5. **Identify** the five types of inflation.
6. **List** four destabilizing effects of inflation.

SECTION 3 *(pages 405–412)*
7. **Explain** what is meant by the distribution of income.
8. **Identify** five major reasons for inequality in the distribution of income.
9. **Explain** how the Lorenz curve is used to show the inequality of income distribution.
10. **Name** six antipoverty programs.

Critical Thinking

1. **Analyzing Information** Of the reasons for income inequality listed in the chapter, which reason would be most difficult for government to influence or control? Explain.
2. **Synthesizing Information** Explain how the government calculates the rate of inflation.

Applying Economic Concepts

1. **Employment** Explain why full employment does not mean that everyone has a job.
2. **Inflation** List two causes of inflation for which the government may be responsible.

414 UNIT 4: *Macroeconomics: Policies*

Reinforcing Skills

MAKING COMPARISONS

Read the excerpts below, then answer the questions that follow.

(1) An 84-mpg car is an example of the good that could come from government-industry cooperation. . . .

President Clinton last week announced that the federal technological candy store would be opened to the Big Three. Energy-, space-, and defense-based federal researchers will work with auto researchers to spur technological advances. The goal: to create a prototype that triples the mileage of existing cars by 2003.

The nation clearly would benefit from such a dream machine. It would cut pollution that fouls our air and reduce our dangerous dependence on foreign oil. Government and business might achieve similar benefits in other industries.

(2) Industry should be driven by the marketplace, not by government aid. Last Wednesday, in what the White House called a "model for the new partnership between government and industry," President Clinton made two disturbing announcements.

First, the federal government will assist the Big Three automakers in developing an affordable, fuel-efficient, low-pollution passenger car. . . . If there's a demand for these cars, manufacturers will do what's necessary to satisfy the demand. But taxpayers shouldn't be forced to buy a product they never asked for. . . .

Our nation was founded on the principle that government should be strictly limited. . . .

—*USA Today*, October 4, 1993

1. What is the purpose for this comparison?
2. How does the second view differ from the first?
3. What conclusion can you draw from this comparison?

Individual Activity

Unemployment is an experience most people would like to avoid. Review the five kinds of unemployment identified in this chapter. Write a paragraph explaining how you could prepare in order to avoid each kind. Consider such factors as education, type of job, and location you might choose.

Cooperative Learning Activity

Organize into a number of groups corresponding to the categories of job listings in the Help Wanted ads of your local newspaper. Group A, for example, could be assigned the sales ads; Group B, the medical ads; and so on. Each group should count the total number of jobs listed, find the average wage from among those that list salaries, and list the general qualifications for different jobs in each set of ads. After all facts are compiled, compare job categories. Where are the best opportunities?

Writing About Economics

THE EXPRESSIVE STYLE

In the **Journal Writing** activity on page 393, you were asked to summarize current trends in inflation and unemployment that you read about in newspapers. Now, write a two-page story on one of the following topics using the expressive writing style discussed on page 554.

A. Unemployment in Your City

B. Hyperinflation During World War II

C. Poverty in the United States

The mental and social health of society is an important concern for economists.

CHAPTER 17

Achieving Economic Stability

SECTION 1
The Cost of Economic Instability

SECTION 2
Macroeconomic Equilibrium

SECTION 3
Stabilization Policies

SECTION 4
Economics and Politics

CHAPTER PREVIEW

People to Know

- Laura D'Andrea Tyson
- Urban and Regional Planner

Applying Economic Concepts to Your Life

Monetary Policy Do you have a savings account that pays interest? Has the interest rate ever gone up? If so, your bank might have increased rates because the Fed had raised interest rates to combat inflation and encourage people to save. The Fed's control over interest rates is an example of *monetary policy*.

Journal Writing

For one week, keep a journal of newspaper articles detailing inflation rates and unemployment statistics. Both figures are measures of economic instability.

Section Preview

Objectives

After studying this section, you will be able to:

1. **Explain** the economic costs of instability.

2. **Describe** the social costs of instability.

Key Terms

stagflation, GDP gap, misery index, discomfort index

Applying Economic Concepts

Misery Index Do you know someone who has suffered from unemployment and inflation at the same time? If so, you probably understand the frustration and feelings of helplessness that accompany that situation. Millions of others do, too, which is why economists have invented a measure called a *misery index*.

Unemployment and inflation are forms of economic instability closely tied to long-term economic growth. The instability carries an enormous cost—one that can be measured in economic as well as human terms.

The Economic Costs

On one level, unemployment and inflation are simply numbers that are collected, reported in the press, or plotted on a graph. At another level, they represent enormous economic failures that waste the resources of the nation and its people.

Stagflation

In the past, recessions brought inflation under control. Although no one really wanted a recession, it did work to resolve this problem. **1**

By the 1970s, however, inflation was becoming more persistent. Recessions still reduced inflation

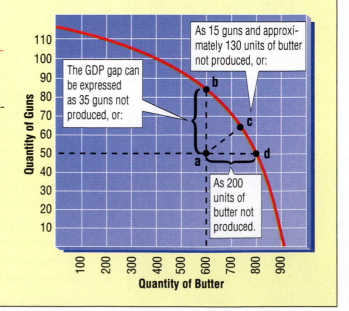

Figure 17.1
The GDP Gap and the Production Possibilities Frontier

When all resources are fully employed, a country can produce anywhere along its production possibilities frontier. When some resources are idle, or are not employed efficiently, production falls short of its potential. The GDP gap is the difference between the actual production at point a and the potential production as indicated by points b, c, or d. **What happens to employment if GDP declines even a fraction of a percentage?**

The GDP gap can be expressed as 35 guns not produced, or:

As 15 guns and approximately 130 units of butter not produced, or:

As 200 units of butter not produced.

Quantity of Guns

Quantity of Butter

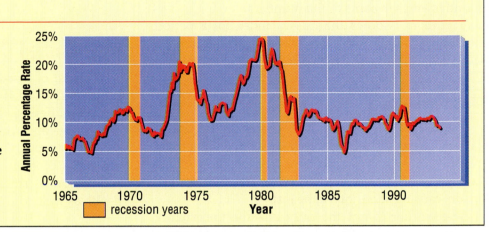

Figure 17.2
The Misery Index

The misery index is the sum of the monthly inflation and unemployment rates. It is not an official government statistic, but it is often used as a measure of consumer distress during periods of high unemployment and inflation. **Why is the misery index also called the discomfort index?**

Source: Bureau of Economic Analysis, United States Department of Commerce.

somewhat, but the economy began to encounter **stagflation**—a period of stagnant growth and inflation. Many periods of stagflation have plagued the nation since the beginning of the 1970s, and the problem is likely to recur.

The GDP Gap

The **GDP gap** is the difference between the actual GDP and the potential GDP that could be produced if all resources were fully employed. The gap is a measure of the cost of unemployed resources in terms of output not produced.

The GDP gap, illustrated in **Figure 17.1**, shows the production possibilities curve in the classic guns versus butter example. Note that the output not produced because of resources that lay idle can be measured in either guns, butter, or a combination of the two items.

In a more dynamic sense, business cycles or fluctuations make the size of this gap vary over time. The scale of GDP is also such that if GDP declines even a

fraction of a percentage point, the amount of lost production and income can be enormous.

In 1993, for example, the GDP of the United States economy exceeded $6 trillion. If a $6 trillion economy declines just one-fourth of 1 percentage point, $15 billion of production would be lost. This amount is more than the federal government spent on agriculture or the administration of justice during the entire 1992 fiscal budget year. Described in other terms, this amount would be equal to 750,000 workers losing jobs that paid $20,000 each for an entire year. In practice, the effects of a decline in GDP generally are spread out over a large area rather than being concentrated in just one spot, but they are no less severe.

The Misery Index

The **misery index**, sometimes called the **discomfort index**, is the sum of the monthly inflation and unemployment rates. Although it is not an official government statistic, it is a more comprehensive measure of consumer suffering during periods of high

Checking Understanding

1. In the past, what problem did recessions bring under control?

Applying Economic Concepts

Stagflation By 1989 the stagflation of the early 1970s and 1980s had completely disappeared. Inflation was under control, and unemployment stood near 5 percent.

inflation and unemployment. The index is relevant only over long periods because of the wide month-to-month swings in some of the numbers.

Figure 17.2 shows the misery index for a period beginning in 1965. The index was at its worst from the mid-1970s through the early 1980s.

Uncertainty

When real GDP declines, a great deal of uncertainty exists. A worker may not buy something because of concern over his or her job. This uncertainty usually translates into purchases that are not made, causing some jobs to be lost.

The worker is not the only one the uncertainty affects. The owner of a business producing at capacity may decide against an expansion although new orders are arriving daily. Instead, the producer—aware that the demand for products is greater than the supply—may try to raise prices, which increases inflation. The producer may also try to decrease overtime or even lay off workers in anticipation of a downturn.

The Social Costs

The cost of instability can be measured in dollars rather easily, but it is harder to measure in terms of human suffering. In human terms, the costs are almost beyond comprehension. Because of these social costs, everyone agrees that stability must be achieved. Economists are interested not only in the production of society, but in its mental and social health as well.

Wasted Resources

Human suffering during periods of instability goes beyond not having more goods and services that raise the standard of living. The labor resource is wasted, with people wanting work but not being able

Family Values *A healthy economy means that people will be more certain of their ability to provide for themselves and their families.* **What are some benefits of a healthy economy?**

to find it. The economy has failed to satisfy the basic human need to be a useful and productive member of society. This labor situation is particularly acute in inner cities where unemployment rates run high among minority groups.

Wasted resources are not limited to just human resources. Factories with idle capacity are waiting to be utilized. Natural resources may also lie unused or go to waste.

Political Instability

Politicians also suffer from the consequences of economic instability. When times are hard, voters are dissatisfied, and incumbents are often thrown out of office. If too much economic instability exists, as during the Great Depression of the 1930s, voters are often willing to vote for radical change. As a result, economic stability adds to the political stability of our nation.

Crime and Family Values

High crime rates, too few economic and social opportunities for minorities, the loss of individual freedoms, and the lack of stability for many Americans are all grounds for concern. Many people believe that some of these social ills cannot be cured without the help of a strong and stable economy.

When the economy is healthy, society can more easily deal with its social problems. Communities have higher tax collections, which can increase police protection and municipal services. Companies are more willing to hire disadvantaged persons and provide on-the-job training.

A healthy economy means that people will be more certain of their ability to provide for themselves and their families. When people can do this, they are more positive about the future in general.

Economic instability affects other parts of society, too. When the economy is healthy, families make numerous purchases, many of them on credit. If the economy declines, some debtors may lose income and have to declare bankruptcy to end their debts.

SECTION 1 REVIEW

Reviewing Terms and Facts

1. **Define** stagflation, GDP gap, misery index, discomfort index.
2. **Explain** how economists measure the economic cost of instability.
3. **Describe** the social cost of instability.

Critical Thinking

4. **Making Generalizations** If the GDP gap in a given year rises dramatically, what types of unemployment and inflation data would be present?

Applying Economic Concepts

5. **Misery Index** How might the psychological strains that many people feel in difficult economic times help prolong the economic downturn?

Macroeconomic Equilibrium

Section Preview

Objectives

After studying this section, you will be able to:

1. **Explain** the concept of aggregate supply.
2. **Describe** the importance of aggregate demand.
3. **Examine** the nature of macroeconomic equilibrium.

Key Terms

aggregate supply curve, aggregate demand curve, macroeconomic equilibrium

Applying Economic Concepts

Equilibrium Have you ever experienced one of those rare moments when you feel completely satisfied and do not want to change anything that you are doing? The economy behaves like that sometimes. The situation is called *equilibrium*, and variables such as price and quantity will remain unchanged unless something happens to disturb the system.

When we study markets, we often use the tools of supply and demand to show how the equilibrium price and quantity of output are determined. When we study the economy as a whole, we can use the concepts of supply and demand in much the same way.

Aggregate Supply

Individual firms try to maximize their profits by finding the quantity of output at which the marginal cost of producing the next unit of output is equal to the marginal revenue from the sale of that output. If the price that consumers are willing to pay increases, producers would increase their production.

The Aggregate Supply Curve

If, at any given price level, the annual production of all final goods and services within a country's borders were added together, we would have a measure of GDP. At a different level of prices, firms would adjust their profit-maximizing quantities of output, producing a slightly different level of GDP. If it were somehow possible to keep adjusting the price level to see how total output changed, we could then construct an **aggregate supply curve**, which shows the real level of GDP that could be produced at various price levels.

Figure 17.3 shows how an aggregate supply curve for the whole economy might look. It is shown as upward sloping, but with a horizontal as well as vertical range. The horizontal range represents various levels of output that coexist with large amounts of unemployed resources. If the economy is producing at point **a**, output can be expanded to point **b** by putting some of the resources to work without causing any change in the general price level.

Any expansion of real GDP beyond point **b**, which has an output of Q_1, is not possible without some increase in the price level, however. By the time the economy has reached point **c**, the price level has risen to P_1 because firms have been competing for increasingly scarce resources. Point **c** is also the location where all resources are fully employed. When firms try to expand production beyond Q_2, they merely drive up prices.

Increase in Aggregate Supply

The aggregate supply curve, like the supply curve of the individual firm, can increase. Most of the increases in aggregate supply are tied to the cost of production for the individual firm. If the cost goes down for all firms, aggregate supply increases, which shows as a shift to the right.

Factors that might lower the costs of production for all individual firms include the discovery of less

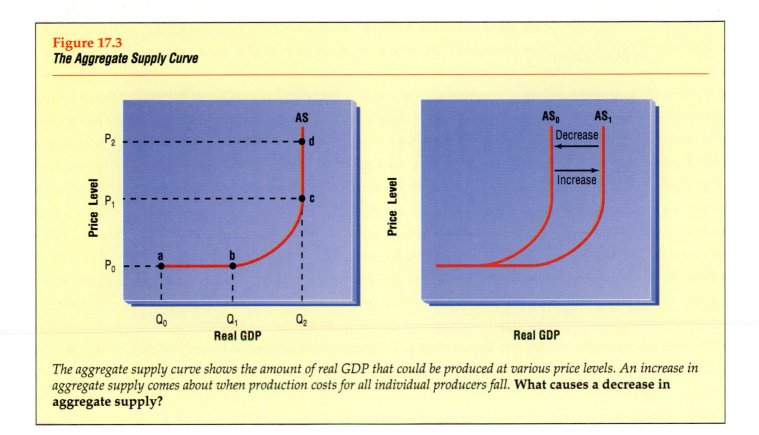

Figure 17.3
The Aggregate Supply Curve

The aggregate supply curve shows the amount of real GDP that could be produced at various price levels. An increase in aggregate supply comes about when production costs for all individual producers fall. **What causes a decrease in aggregate supply?**

expensive natural resources, lower prices for imported oil, and lower interest rates. Increases in labor productivity, new technologies, a liberalization of immigration laws, and lower taxes would also shift the aggregate supply curve to the right. **1** ☑

Decrease in Aggregate Supply

Factors that tend to increase the cost of production for an individual firm tend to decrease aggregate supply. These factors include higher prices for foreign oil, higher interest rates, and lower labor productivity.

Other factors decreasing aggregate supply include higher government taxes and the tightening of immigration laws, which would deny some firms a source of cheap labor. Any increase in cost that causes firms to offer fewer goods and services for sale at each and every price would shift the aggregate supply curve to the left. **2**

Aggregate Demand

Aggregate demand is like aggregate supply in several respects. First, it is an aggregate, or summary,

Checking Understanding

1. What factors might lower production costs for all firms?
2. How do higher taxes affect aggregate supply?

Applying Economic Concepts

☑ **Aggregate Supply** During the 1970s the price of imported oil skyrocketed—from about $5 a barrel to about $35. The increase affected many industries because petroleum is used in products as diverse as aspirin, carpets, compact discs, and toothpaste.

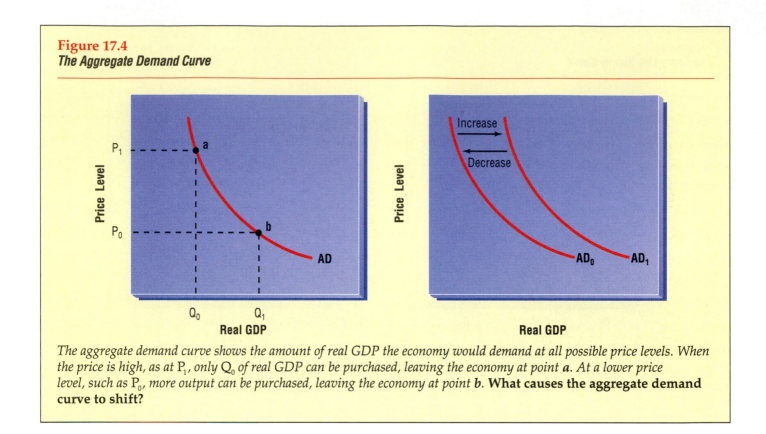

Figure 17.4
The Aggregate Demand Curve

*The aggregate demand curve shows the amount of real GDP the economy would demand at all possible price levels. When the price is high, as at P_1, only Q_0 of real GDP can be purchased, leaving the economy at point **a**. At a lower price level, such as P_0, more output can be purchased, leaving the economy at point **b**.* **What causes the aggregate demand curve to shift?**

measure of the demand of all economic units in the economy. Second, it can be represented in the form of a graph. Third, aggregate demand can either increase or decrease over time.

The Aggregate Demand Curve

Figure 17.4 illustrates the **aggregate demand curve,** a graph showing the quantity of real GDP that would be purchased at each possible price level in the economy. This curve represents the sum of consumer, business, and government demands at various price levels. It slopes downward and to the right like the demand curve for individuals, but for an entirely different reason.

The reason is based on the underlying assumption that the economy can have only one money supply at a time. The size of this supply is fixed and has a different purchasing power at every possible price level. When prices are very high, a given money supply will purchase a limited amount of output, such as that represented by point **a.** When prices are much lower, everyone will be able to buy relatively more GDP, leaving everyone at point **b.** If the price level

dropped further, even more GDP could be purchased, which is why the curve tends to slope downward and to the right.

Increase in Aggregate Demand

The aggregate demand curve, like the aggregate supply curve, can increase or decrease depending on certain conditions. An important factor is a change in the amount of money that people save. If consumers collectively save less and spend more, the increase in consumer spending would increase aggregate demand, shifting the aggregate demand curve to the right.

Expectations about future economic conditions often affect consumer, business, and government spending. If better economic conditions are forecast, all sectors may spend more, shifting aggregate demand to the right.

Finally, an increase in transfer payments—financed through deficit spending—or a general reduction in taxes could increase the spending of the consumer sector. The effect might be short-lived, but some increased spending would take place.

Decrease in Aggregate Demand

Expectations can also play a major role in decreasing aggregate demand. If any of the sectors anticipate a bleak economic or political climate, they will cut back on spending, which will have the collective impact of purchasing less GDP at every price level.

Higher taxes and lower transfer payments could also reduce aggregate spending. Such decisions shift the aggregate demand curve to the left because all sectors collectively buy less GDP at all levels of prices.

Equilibrium

Figure 17.5 shows the aggregate demand and supply curves put together, indicating macroeconomic equilibrium. **Macroeconomic equilibrium** is determined by the intersection of the aggregate supply and aggregate demand curves and is the level of real GDP consistent with a given price level.

In the figure, **Q** is the level of real GDP that is consistent with the price level **P**. If the economy is growing, with newer levels of output larger than previous ones, the price level may or may not change.

Figure 17.5 points out a dilemma facing economic policymakers. The economy must be allowed to grow to new levels of real GDP, but it must do so without unduly increasing the price level, which causes inflation. A number of economic policies are available, and each affects the aggregate supply and aggregate demand curves in different ways.

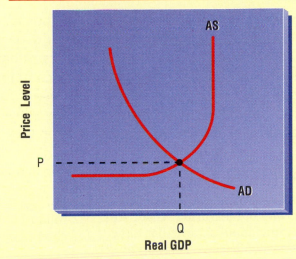

Figure 17.5
Macroeconomic Equilibrium

The economy is at equilibrium when the quantity of real GDP demanded is equal to the real GDP supplied at a given price level. The question facing economic policymakers is how to increase real GDP without increasing the price level. **Why is it important to not increase the price level?**

Aggregate supply and demand curves are useful concepts, providing a framework for analyzing a problem. They can be used to give an idea of the way and direction that things will change, but they do not yield exact predictions. Even so, they are becoming increasingly important in analyzing the issue of macroeconomic equilibrium.

SECTION 2
REVIEW

Reviewing Terms and Facts

1. **Define** aggregate supply curve, aggregate demand curve, macroeconomic equilibrium.
2. **Describe** the factors that would cause aggregate supply to increase.
3. **List** the factors that would cause aggregate demand to decrease.

4. **Describe** the policy objectives economic policymakers face.

Critical Thinking

5. **Making Comparisons** How do aggregate supply and demand differ from simple supply and demand?

Applying Economic Concepts

6. **Equilibrium** How would a decrease in business investments affect the macroeconomic equilibrium?

ECONOMIC SKILL

Understanding a Public Opinion Poll

Do you prefer peppermint or chocolate chip ice cream? Do you think schools should be in session year-round? Which presidential candidate did you favor in the last election? Manufacturers, community leaders, and politicians use questions such as these to find out what people think about certain issues. They often rely on a public opinion poll to collect the information they need.

Explanation

A *public opinion poll* is a scientific way of measuring what people think about a particular topic at a particular time. A group of people, known as a *sample*, are asked the same set of questions. The sample consists of people who are typical of the general population. The opinions of those in the sample, therefore, will be representative of the opinions held by the population as a whole.

The accuracy of a public opinion poll depends upon the following factors:

1. **Choosing a sample that resembles the general public as closely as possible.** Most pollsters use a **random sample,** or one in which each person within the entire group being polled has an equal chance of being selected.
2. **Wording questions carefully.** Responsible pollsters avoid using wording that tends to influence answers.
3. **Controlling the way the poll is taken.** Some polls are conducted face-to-face because many people hesitate to respond to telephone or mail polls. The interviewer's manner should not affect the answers people give.
4. **Drawing accurate conclusions.** Professional pollsters collect and analyze huge amounts of data. They must keep in mind that some answers may not be reliable and that public opinion changes rapidly.

Practice

Study the excerpts below from a public opinion poll on the American school system. Then answer the questions that follow.

Even if it might mean higher taxes, would you favor spending more money on your community's public schools, or would you favor spending less or about the same amount of money?
   More 47%
   About the same 43%
   Less 8%
   Not sure 2%

Tell me whether you agree or disagree with each statement:

School districts that decide to raise more money to pay for better schools should be allowed to do so.
   Agree 86%
   Disagree 13%
   Not sure 1%

To ensure more equal spending among districts, financing of the public school system should be taken out of the hands of local government and moved toward federal or state governments.
   Agree 43%
   Disagree 52%
   Not sure 5%

Most of the money for schools should continue to come from local taxes, not state or federal taxes.
   Agree 41%
   Disagree 56%
   Not sure 3%

Keeping in mind that they are paid out of taxes, do you think public school teachers are paid enough, too little, or too much?
   Enough 35%
   Too much 6%
   Too little 55%
   Not sure 4%

—Survey of 1,250 adults conducted Aug. 26-31, 1992, for *Business Week* by Louis Harris & Associates, Inc.

1. Based on the results of this poll, what conclusions can you draw about the public's view of teachers' paychecks?
2. Do most people feel that financing of the public school system should be handled by local, state, or federal government?
3. Do most people favor local taxes or state and federal taxes as the source of money for schools?

Additional Practice

For further practice in understanding public opinion polls, complete the Reinforcing Skills exercise in the Chapter 17 Review on page 441.

Section Preview

Objectives

After studying this section, you will be able to:

1. **Explain** the operations and impact of fiscal policy.
2. **Distinguish** between supply-side economics and fiscal policy.
3. **State** the basic assumptions of monetary policy.

Key Terms

fiscal policy, Keynesian economics, consumption function, multiplier, accelerator, automatic stabilizer, unemployment insurance, supply-side economics, Laffer curve, monetarism, wage-price controls

Applying Economic Concepts

Fiscal Policy You may know someone who collects unemployment insurance, Social Security, or medicare. These programs stabilize a person's income in the event of a layoff, a retirement, or a medical emergency. They are called automatic stabilizers—one of the tools of *fiscal policy*.

Economic growth, full employment, and price stability are three of the seven major economic goals of the American people. In order to reach these goals, sound economic policies must be designed and implemented.

Economic stability can be achieved in several ways. Some people favor policies that stimulate aggregate demand, while others favor ones that stimulate aggregate supply. Still others prefer policies that promote the growth of the money supply. Sometimes these policies are consistent with each other. At other times, they are not.

Demand-Side Policies

Demand-side policies are federal policies designed to increase or decrease total demand in the economy by shifting the aggregate demand curve to the right or to the left. One approach is known as **fiscal policy**—the use of government spending and taxing to influence economic activity—and is perhaps the most popular way to influence the economy.

Fiscal policies are derived from **Keynesian economics**, a set of actions designed to lower unemployment by stimulating aggregate demand. John Maynard Keynes put forth these theories in 1936, and they dominated the thinking of economists until the 1970s.

The Keynesian Framework

Keynes provided the basic framework with the output-expenditure model, GDP = C + I + G + F. According to this model, any change in GDP on the left side of the equation could be traced to changes on the right side of the equation. The question was, which of the four components caused the instability?

According to Keynes, the net impact of the foreign sector (F) was so small that it could be ignored. The government sector (G) was not the problem either, because its expenditures were normally stable over time. Spending by the consumer sector (C), stated Keynes, was the most stable of all. It was so stable that it could even be specified in terms of a **consumption function**, a schedule showing relatively constant and predictable levels of spending associated with different levels of disposable income. Ruling out F, G, and C, it then appeared that the business or investment sector (I) was to blame for the instability.

In Keynes's theory, investment sector spending was not only unstable, but had a magnified effect on other spending. If investment spending declined by $50 billion, for example, many workers would lose their jobs. These workers in turn would spend less and pay fewer taxes. Soon, the amount of spending by all sectors in the economy would be down by more than the initial decline in investment. This effect is called the **multiplier**, and says that a change in investment spending will have a magnified effect on total spending.

Keynesian Economics
Keynesian economics states that economic activity will be stimulated if the federal government invests in projects such as hydroelectric plants. **What role do government deficits have according to this theory?**

The multiplier is believed to be about 2 in today's economy. Therefore, if investment spending goes down by $50 billion, the decline in overall spending could reach $100 billion.

Conditions are likely to be made even worse by the **accelerator**—the change in investment spending caused by a change in total spending. After a decline in overall spending gets started, it causes investment spending to be reduced even further. Before long, the economy is trapped in a downward spiral. The combined multiplier-accelerator effect is important because it adds to the instability of GDP.

The Role of Government

Keynes argued that only the government was able to step in and offset changes in investment sector spending. This action would take the form of fiscal policy in which the government implements spending and/or taxation policies to influence economic activity. **1**

The government could take a direct role and set up its own spending to offset the decline in spending by businesses. It could also play an indirect role by lowering taxes and enacting other measures to encourage businesses and consumers to spend more.

Suppose the government wanted to take direct steps right away to offset a $50 billion decline in business spending. To do this, it could spend $10 billion to build a dam in a rural area, give $20 billion in grants to cities to fix up poor neighborhoods, and spend another $20 billion in several other ways. In this way, the $50 billion that business did not spend would be replaced by the $50 billion the government spends. Thus, the overall sum of C + I + G + F would remain unchanged.

Instead of spending the $50 billion, perhaps the government could reduce tax rates by that amount and give investors and consumers more purchasing power. If the $50 billion not collected in taxes were spent, the initial decline in investment spending would be offset, and the sum for C + I + G + F again would remain the same.

Either way, the government would likely run the risk of a growing federal deficit. In Keynes's view, the deficit was unfortunate, but needed to stop further declines in economic activity. When the economy recovered, tax collections would rise, the government would run a surplus, and the debt could be paid back.

The Keynesian model gave short-term government deficits legitimacy. The justification for temporary federal deficits was one of the lasting contributions of

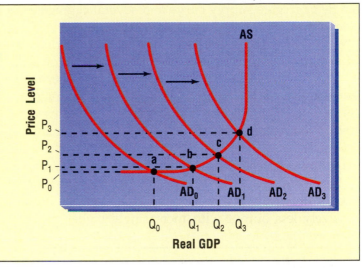

Figure 17.6
Fiscal Policy and the Aggregate Demand Curve

*Fiscal policies are designed to increase aggregate demand. Successive increases in aggregate demand—or moving the economy from **a** to **d**—put increasing pressure on the price level as the unemployed resources in the economy find employment.* **What are two limitations of fiscal policy?**

Keynesian economics and a major departure from the economic thinking of the time. ☑

Automatic Stabilizers

Another key component of fiscal policy is the role of **automatic stabilizers**, programs that automatically trigger benefits if changes in the economy threaten people's incomes. Two important stabilizers are unemployment insurance and federal entitlement programs. **2**

Unemployment insurance is insurance that employers pay for through payroll taxes. Nearly all American workers who lose their jobs through no fault of their own can collect this insurance. Workers who are fired because of misconduct or who quit without good reason generally cannot collect it.

Although workers generally have to wait several weeks to collect benefits, most end up getting payments of about one-third to one-half of their weekly pay. The benefits vary from state to state. Under normal conditions, most states allow workers to collect the insurance for up to 26 weeks. When unemployment is high, however, they may be allowed to collect longer.

Federal entitlement programs, also known as entitlements, are social welfare programs designed to provide minimum health, nutritional, and income levels for selected groups of people. They include such federal programs as welfare, government pensions, medicare, medicaid, and Social Security.

Congress provides guidelines that determine who qualifies for—or is entitled to—these benefits. The availability of these programs is a guarantee that economic instability or some other factor will not cause aggregate demand to fall below a certain level for selected groups of people.

Fiscal Policy and Aggregate Demand

The impact of fiscal policies can be illustrated with the aggregate demand curve. **Figure 17.6** shows a

---

Checking Understanding

1. What did Keynes believe to be the only way to offset changes in investment sector spending?
2. What are two examples of automatic stabilizers?

Applying Economic Concepts

 Federal Deficit Keynes probably did not foresee the massive federal deficits of the American economy today. He thought that the deficits caused by government spending during downturns would end after prosperity was restored.

single aggregate supply curve and several aggregate demand curves. When aggregate demand is very low, as during the Great Depression or other periods of severe economic downturns, the economy would be at point **a,** where AD_0 intersects AS. Increases in government spending—public works projects, transfer payments, or even tax reductions—could be used to increase aggregate demand to AD_1. Because many resources are unemployed, the movement of the economy from **a** to **b** causes very little price inflation.

Further attempts to increase aggregate demand, shown in **Figure 17.6** as AD_2 and AD_3, produce successively less output with increasingly higher price

levels. Eventually, all attempts the government sector makes to increase aggregate demand would only increase the price level, without increasing the production of real GDP.

Limitations of Fiscal Policy

Keynes envisioned the role of government spending as a counterbalance to changes in investment spending. The ideal situation would be for government to increase spending to offset declines in business spending, and to decrease spending whenever business spending recovered. In practice, however,

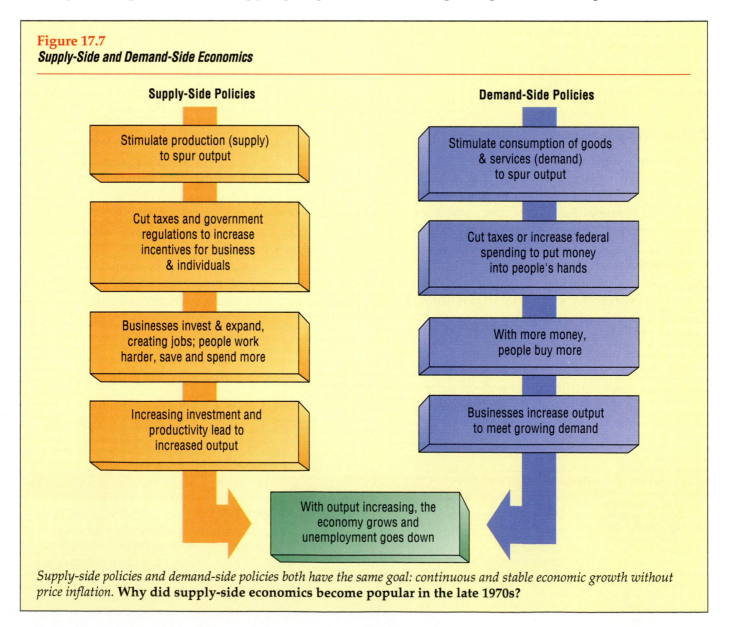

Figure 17.7
Supply-Side and Demand-Side Economics

Supply-Side Policies

Stimulate production (supply) to spur output

Cut taxes and government regulations to increase incentives for business & individuals

Businesses invest & expand, creating jobs; people work harder, save and spend more

Increasing investment and productivity lead to increased output

Demand-Side Policies

Stimulate consumption of goods & services (demand) to spur output

Cut taxes or increase federal spending to put money into people's hands

With more money, people buy more

Businesses increase output to meet growing demand

With output increasing, the economy grows and unemployment goes down

Supply-side policies and demand-side policies both have the same goal: continuous and stable economic growth without price inflation. **Why did supply-side economics become popular in the late 1970s?**

the federal government seems unable to bring its spending under control, especially when it comes to reducing expenditures or balancing its budget. **1**

In addition, planning federal expenditures to offset changes in investment spending seems almost impossible. Even if Congress knew that investment spending would be down next year, it is highly unlikely that offsetting federal expenditures could be approved in time. Any expenditure bill introduced in Congress would be debated, taken apart, rewritten, and possibly loaded with a host of unrelated amendments before it was ever passed. Even if the bill was passed in record time, the money might not actually be spent for years, especially if the bill authorized the construction of new roads, bridges, or buildings.

As a result, the most effective counter-cyclical fiscal policies used today are the automatic stabilizers. The advantage of the stabilizers is that spending approval is not needed whenever the economy enters a recession, or whenever people lose jobs and need unemployment insurance coverage. **2**

Supply-Side Policies

Economic policies designed to stimulate output and lower unemployment by increasing production in the economy are known as **supply-side economics**. The supply-side views began to interest people in the late 1970s because demand-side policies did not seem to be controlling the country's growing unemployment and inflation. In the 1980s, supply-side policies became the hallmark of President Reagan's administration.

Comparison with Demand-Side Policies

The differences between supply-side economics and demand-side economics are smaller than most people realize. Both policies, which are summarized in **Figure 17.7**, use national income accounts to measure the economy's performance. Both policies accept the multiplier and the accelerator. Both policies have the same goal in mind—increasing production and decreasing unemployment without increasing inflation.

Supply-side economists believe, however, that the role of government has increased to the point at which individual incentives to work, save, and invest are being destroyed. They want the government to take a smaller role in economic affairs, while letting the free market play a larger role. This approach contrasts with that of the demand-siders, who want to stimulate output by generating demand with increased levels of government spending.

Smaller Role for Government

A key issue for supply-siders is government's role in the economy, which they believe must be reduced. One way to do this is to reduce the number of federal agencies. Another way to make government's role smaller is through deregulation—removing established regulations with which industries must comply. Deregulation is a major objective of supply-siders and is favored by some demand-siders as well.

Under the administration of President Jimmy Carter, major steps were taken to deregulate the energy, airline, and trucking industries to encourage competition. The Reagan administration continued deregulation efforts in the savings and loan industry, hoping to bring about more competition.

Federal Tax Structure

Another target of supply-siders is the federal tax burden on individuals and businesses. They believe that if taxes are too high, people will not want to work, and businesses will not produce as much as

Checking Understanding

1. According to Keynesian theory, how should declines in business spending be offset?
2. What are the most effective counter-cyclical fiscal policies used today?

Applying Economic Concepts

Deregulation Many people believe that certain industries should be subject to more government regulation. These people want the government to reregulate the banking and airline industries, among others.

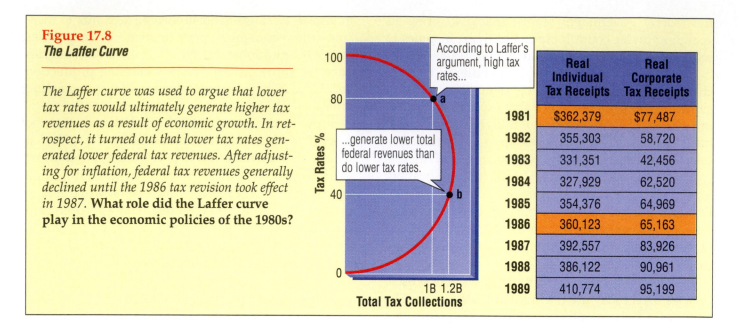

Figure 17.8
The Laffer Curve

The Laffer curve was used to argue that lower tax rates would ultimately generate higher tax revenues as a result of economic growth. In retrospect, it turned out that lower tax rates generated lower federal tax revenues. After adjusting for inflation, federal tax revenues generally declined until the 1986 tax revision took effect in 1987. **What role did the Laffer curve play in the economic policies of the 1980s?**

According to Laffer's argument, high tax rates...

...generate lower total federal revenues than do lower tax rates.

	Real Individual Tax Receipts	Real Corporate Tax Receipts
1981	$362,379	$77,487
1982	355,303	58,720
1983	331,351	42,456
1984	327,929	62,520
1985	354,376	64,969
1986	360,123	65,163
1987	392,557	83,926
1988	386,122	90,961
1989	410,774	95,199

they could. Lower tax rates, they argue, allow individuals and businesses to keep more of the money they earn, which encourages them to work harder. This would give workers more money to spend in the long run. Government would also gain as total tax collections go up because of the extra activity.

The **Laffer curve**—a hypothetical relationship between federal tax rates and tax revenues—illustrates the supply-siders' belief. It was the basis for President Reagan's tax cut of 1981, which reduced income taxes 25 percent over a 3-year period. The Laffer curve, along with the inflation-adjusted individual and corporate tax revenues collected between 1981 and 1986, are shown in **Figure 17.8**. **1**

Today, economists feel that either the assumptions or the interpretation of the Laffer curve are invalid. The increased revenue collections as a result of the deep tax cuts simply never materialized. After adjusting for inflation, both individual income tax receipts and corporate tax receipts were lower in 1986 than they were in 1981. Because tax collections never went up, the federal budget showed a deficit instead. Real tax collections did not surpass their 1981 levels until after the 1986 tax revisions took effect in 1987.

Supply-Side Policies and Aggregate Supply

Supply-side policies can be illustrated in terms of the aggregate supply curve. **Figure 17.9** shows a single aggregate demand curve and several aggregate supply curves.

When aggregate supply is very low, the economy would be at point **a**, where AS_0 intersects AD. If supply-side policies were successfully instituted, the aggregate supply curve would shift to AS_1, moving the point of macroeconomic equilibrium to **b**. Without any corresponding change in aggregate demand, real output would grow, and the price level would come down.

Further attempts to increase aggregate supply to move the economy to **c** has even less impact on the price level. If the aggregate supply curve does have a horizontal range—a matter of conjecture—then the price level could never be reduced below P_0.

Limitations of Supply-Side Policies

Perhaps the main limitation of supply-side policies is a lack of enough experience with them to know how they affect the economy. Even the concepts of aggregate supply and aggregate demand are largely conceptual, making it difficult to predict the exact consequence of any particular supply-side policy based on the shapes of the two curves.

In the case of the Laffer curve, total tax collections, when adjusted for inflation, actually declined after the 1981 tax reductions were implemented. The result is that one of the main foundations of the supply-side school was found to be weak.

Nevertheless, policies that promote productivity, reduce unnecessary paperwork, or otherwise allow the economy to grow to its maximum potential are certainly worthwhile. Everyone, including demand-siders, favors policies such as these.

Finally, supply-side economic policies are designed more to restore economic growth rather than to remedy economic instability. No matter how fast or slow the economy grows, it seems to have a tendency to fluctuate around its trend line. Supply-side policies during the Reagan presidency tended to weaken the automatic stabilizers by making the federal tax structure less progressive and by reducing many of the "safety net" programs.

Monetary Policies

Both demand-side economics and supply-side economics are concerned about stimulating production and employment. Neither policy assigns much importance to the money supply. A doctrine called **monetarism**, however, places primary importance on the role of money and its growth.

Monetarists believe that fluctuations in the money supply can be a destabilizing element that leads to unemployment and inflation. They favor policies that lead to stable, long-term monetary growth at levels low enough to control inflation. **2**

Reviewing the Tools of Monetary Policy

When the Federal Reserve System conducts monetary policy, it generally tries to affect the cost and the availability of credit by expanding and contracting the money supply. The Fed's main tools in this regard are open market operations, the discount rate, and a change in the reserve requirement. ✔

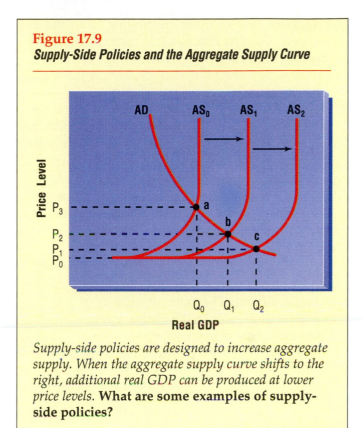

Figure 17.9
Supply-Side Policies and the Aggregate Supply Curve

Supply-side policies are designed to increase aggregate supply. When the aggregate supply curve shifts to the right, additional real GDP can be produced at lower price levels. **What are some examples of supply-side policies?**

If the Fed wants to expand the money supply through open market operations, it will buy government securities. This increases the excess reserves in the banking system and makes loan expansion possible. The Fed may also lower the discount rate in an effort to lower the cost of credit for borrowers. Lowering the reserve requirement is a third possibility, but is unlikely to be used as long as the other monetary policy tools work.

If the Fed wants to contract the money supply, it would sell securities in the open market to drain reserves from the banking system. It could also raise

Checking Understanding

1. What graphic illustrates supply-side economics?
2. According to monetarists, how do fluctuations in the money supply affect the economy?

Applying Economic Concepts

 Monetary Policy Although monetary policy and fiscal policy both are designed to stabilize the economy, a different part of the government is responsible for each. The Fed conducts monetary policy. Congress and the President conduct fiscal policy.

the discount rate to make borrowing from the Fed more costly. Finally, and as a last resort, it could raise the reserve requirement.

Interest Rates and Inflation

In the short run, expansionist monetary policy can be used to lower interest rates. This action would reduce the cost of consumer and business borrowing and shift the aggregate supply curve to the right. Real GDP would tend to increase, but so would the possibility of future inflation. The money supply can grow over time, but how fast should the money supply be allowed to grow?

Most monetarists believe that if the money supply is allowed to grow at a slow but steady rate, inflation will be controlled. The rates of growth of real GDP and productivity would determine the rate at which the money supply grows.

If the rate of growth of real GDP were 3 percent, and that of productivity 1 percent, the money supply would grow at about 4 percent without causing inflation. At this rate, there would be just enough extra money each year to buy the additional goods and services the economy produces. With less money in circulation, inflation would slowly be reduced and, in time, would fade altogether.

This approach to inflation control is in sharp contrast to others tried earlier. In the early 1970s, for example, President Richard Nixon tried to stop inflation by imposing **wage-price controls**—regulations that make it illegal for businesses to give workers raises or to raise prices without the explicit permission of the government. Most monetarists at the time said the controls would not work. The economy ultimately proved the economists correct; the controls did little to stop inflation.

Monetary Policy and Unemployment

Monetarists argue that attempts to cut unemployment by expanding the money supply provide only temporary relief. They argue that excessive rates of monetary growth eventually drive up prices and interest rates.

Higher interest rates raise the cost of borrowing for businesses, which shifts the aggregate supply curve to the left. The increased cost of borrowing also shifts the aggregate demand curve to the left. The result is that real GDP could fall back to its original level—but at a different and much higher price level. The result would appear almost as if the aggregate supply and demand curves shifted up together, rather than to the left.

An overly expansionist monetary policy, then, will cause long-term inflation. Monetary policy is not a long-term cure for unemployment.

SECTION 3 REVIEW

Reviewing Terms and Facts

1. **Define** fiscal policy, Keynesian economics, consumption function, multiplier, accelerator, automatic stabilizer, unemployment insurance, supply-side economics, Laffer curve, monetarism, wage-price controls.
2. **Describe** the objectives of demand-side policies.

3. **Identify** the main assumptions of supply-side policies.
4. **Name** the tools of monetary policy.

Critical Thinking

5. **Making Comparisons** How do demand-side policies and supply-side policies differ?

Applying Economic Concepts

6. **Fiscal Policy** Fiscal policy is one of the tools designed to stabilize the economy. How does it shift the aggregate demand curve?

PROFILES IN ECONOMICS

LAURA D'ANDREA TYSON

(1947–   )

Laura Tyson has one of the most difficult, yet most interesting, jobs in Washington, D.C. Dr. Tyson is Chair of the President's Council of Economic Advisers. Her job is to explain economics to everyone, from the President on down.

Tyson received her Ph.D. in Economics from the Massachusetts Institute of Technology, which has one of the most prestigious graduate programs in economics in the country. She spent 10 years teaching economics at the University of California at Berkeley. In addition to being an accomplished economist, she is the first woman to chair the Council of

Tyson announces the 1993 federal budget.

Economic Advisers, and the second woman to be a member of the Council.

Tyson follows a pragmatic, no-nonsense approach to solving economic problems. While many other economists tend to rely on abstract and highly theoretical models, Tyson often prefers to recommend proactive government intervention. As Chair of the Council, one of her responsibilities is to offer advice on a wide range of issues.

TRADE POLICY In her latest book, *Who's Bashing Whom? Trade Conflict in High-Technology Industries*, Tyson advocates a hard-line approach in foreign trade negotiations, especially with Japan. In one widely quoted passage, she is openly skeptical of the efficiency of the market, maintaining that

We must not be hoodwinked by the soothing notion that, in the absence of U.S. intervention, the fate of America's high-technology industries will be determined by market forces.

HEALTH CARE Tyson offers an opinion on the issue of financing health care. She notes:

Sin taxes are also interesting, because they would help finance access to health care while at the same time reduce the need for it. Usually we talk about cigarette taxes, where clearly the correlation between use and adverse health effects is very high. There is also compelling evidence that higher beer taxes save the lives of young adult males because they get into fewer car wrecks.

Tyson is described by acquaintances as being open, approachable, and cheerful, yet determined and polite—characteristics that serve her well in her grueling job of chairing the President's Council of Economic Advisers.

Examining the Profile

1. **Making Inferences** What is Tyson's view toward free market operations in foreign trade?

2. **For Further Research** Find out more about Tyson's view toward the trade imbalance between Japan and the United States.

SECTION 4
Economics and Politics

Section Preview

Objectives

After studying this section, you will be able to:

1. **Explain** why monetary policy sometimes conflicts with other economic policies.
2. **Recognize** that economists have differing views.
3. **Understand** the way that politics and economics interact.

Key Terms

Council of Economic Advisers

Applying Economic Concepts

Diversity of Opinion Friends often disagree over how something should be done. Economists behave the same way. They often see the economic problems of the world differently and offer different solutions. Much *diversity of opinion* exists among economists.

Someone looking at the economic history of the United States might decide that economists have not had much success coping with the problems of economic instability and growth. Inflation is sometimes a problem; unemployment goes up and down; recessions come and go. Despite all of this, more progress has been made than most people realize.

A major difficulty with the pursuit of stabilization and growth policies is that the problem goes beyond a simple analysis of aggregate supply and demand curves. Many dynamics are involved.

An Independent Monetary Authority

An interesting feature of the American economy is that fiscal policy is in the hands of elected officials, but monetary policy is not. Monetary policy is the responsibility of the Federal Reserve System (the Fed).

Monetary and fiscal policy can—and often do—operate at cross-purposes. During an election year, for example, a President may want to stimulate GDP and take credit for a growing economy. Politicians can lower taxes, increase Social Security payments, and approve federal spending projects.

The Fed, however, might have different ideas. If inflation is a problem at the time, the Fed might want to follow a tight monetary policy to slow the growth of money and reduce inflation. High interest rates

generally go along with tight money, and they will work against the expansion the President hopes for.

This situation occurred during the presidential campaign of 1992. Because of the threat of inflation, the Fed was pursuing a tighter monetary policy than President Bush wanted. The economy had entered a recession in 1990. The slow economic growth may have convinced many people to vote for other candidates instead. The election was fairly close, leading many people to conclude that the state of the economy was indeed a factor that influenced the election's outcome. **1**

Congress so far has not been willing to make the Fed less independent. Most members of Congress believe that the power to create money should be in the hands of an independent agency rather than in those of elected officials.

Why Economists Differ

Because economists have different backgrounds and experience, their advice can often seem contradictory. One reason for the differences is that most economic explanations and theories are a product of the problems of the times. Demand-side economics, for example, came about during the 1930s when the unemployment rate was at record highs. Because the government sector was so small at the time, supply-side policies designed to make government's role even smaller probably would not have helped much.

The monetarist point of view emerged in the 1960s and 1970s when inflation soared. Because demand-side economics were not designed to deal with inflation, new solutions were needed. The problem with the monetarist view, however, was that it offered long-term solutions but little short-term relief. **2**

The supply-side explanations eventually grew out of frustration with the economic health of the country and the solutions that the demand-siders and monetarists offered. Again, something new and different seemed to be needed.

For the most part, economists generally do not define their position as purely demand-side, supply-side, or monetarist. Many demand-siders are monetarists when it comes to controlling inflation. Many monetarists are supply-siders when it comes to agreeing on the potential burden of the tax structure. Supply-siders and demand-siders even agree on multiplier-accelerator interactions. Economists often take a middle road that incorporates many points of view.

Change has become a fact of life in the United States. As long as society keeps changing, new problems will continue to arise. From each new set of problems, new theories are bound to emerge.

Economic Politics

In the 1800s, the science of economics was known as "political economics." After a while, however, the economists broke away from the political theorists and tried to establish economics as a science in its own right.

In recent years, the two fields have merged again. This time, however, they have done so in a way best described as "economic politics." Today, politicians are concerned with the economic consequences of what they do.

Economic Awareness *Staying informed about the workings of the economy will help in such activities as job searches or tax preparation.* **What is the Council of Economic Advisers?**

The Council of Economic Advisers

Generally, economists and politicians work together fairly closely. The President of the United States, for example, has a three-member **Council of Economic Advisers** to report on economic developments and to propose strategies. The economists basically are the advisers, while the politicians direct or implement the policies.

This system has two weaknesses. The first is that the politicians are not always willing—or able—to

	Checking Understanding	**Applying Economic Concepts**
QUICK CHECK	1. Why might monetary and fiscal policy be at odds during an election year? 2. When did the monetarist point of view emerge?	☑ **Role of Government** Congress established the Council of Economic Advisers in 1946 to promote growth and stability. The President, with Senate approval, appoints the advisers.

follow the economists' advice. A President may want a balanced budget, but to achieve this, the economic advisers may recommend raising taxes. If one of the President's campaign pledges was to not raise taxes, the economists' advice may be ignored.

Another problem is that the political system does not always react quickly enough to deal with current economic problems. In 1974, for example, the American economy entered a severe recession. At the time, it was considered the worst recession since the 1930s. Nearly everyone felt that something should be done to stimulate the economy.

After the recession was well underway, Congress approved a $100 refund on income taxes to stimulate the economy. The refunds were mailed during the second quarter of 1975, shortly after the recession ended and too late to stimulate the economy in the way originally intended.

When the 1990 recession began, politicians simply waited for it to go away. Monetary policy was used to give the economy a "soft landing," but the recession was deeper than expected and the subsequent recovery was anemic.

Increased Understanding and Awareness

Despite everything, economists have had some success in the description, analysis, and explanation of economic activity. They have managed to develop many statistical measures of the economy's performance, as well as models that are well suited to economic analysis and explanation. In the process, they have helped the American people become more aware of the workings of the economy. This awareness has benefited everyone, from the student just starting out to the politician who must answer to the voters.

Today, economists know enough about the economy to prevent a depression like the one in the 1930s. It is doubtful that economists know enough—or can convince others that they know enough—to avoid minor recessions. They can, however, devise policies to stimulate growth and to help certain groups when unemployment rises or inflation strikes.

SECTION 4 REVIEW

Reviewing Terms and Facts

1. **Define** Council of Economic Advisers.
2. **Explain** why Congress wants to continue having an independent monetary authority.
3. **List** several reasons economists differ.
4. **Explain** what *economic politics* means.

Critical Thinking

5. **Making Inferences** Suppose that, in an election year, Congress passes a massive tax cut although inflation is at 9 percent. What actions might the Fed take during such economic times?

Applying Economic Concepts

6. **Diversity of Opinion** Why do monetary and fiscal policies often operate at cross-purposes? What impact does this conflict have on the economy?

Vocabulary

The following terms are defined in Chapter 17:

SECTION ONE
- stagflation (p. 419)
- GDP gap (p. 419)
- misery index (p. 419)
- discomfort index (p. 419)

SECTION TWO
- aggregate supply curve (p. 422)
- aggregate demand curve (p. 424)
- macroeconomic equilibrium (p. 425)

SECTION THREE
- fiscal policy (p. 427)
- Keynesian economics (p. 427)

- consumption function (p. 427)
- multiplier (p. 427)
- accelerator (p. 428)
- automatic stabilizer (p. 429)
- unemployment insurance (p. 429)
- supply-side economics (p. 431)
- Laffer curve (p. 432)
- monetarism (p. 433)

- wage-price controls (p. 434)

SECTION FOUR
- Council of Economic Advisers (p. 437)

Section 1

The Cost of Economic Instability (pages 418–421)

Low economic growth and economic instability have both economic and social costs. The economic costs can be measured as **stagflation** or the **GDP gap**. The social costs include the frustration of being unemployed, potential political instability, increased crime, and damage to family values. Strong economic growth is more than an economic ideal. It is one of the foundations of a healthy society.

Reviewing the Main Idea

What are the economic and social costs of economic instability?

Section 2

Macroeconomic Equilibrium (pages 422–425)

Macroeconomic equilibrium can be analyzed with the help of **aggregate supply** and **aggregate demand curves**. The aggregate supply curve represents the sum of all production that would take place at every possible price level. Aggregate demand represents the total demand by all sectors of the economy at all possible price levels. When aggregate supply and demand are combined, their intersection defines **macroeconomic equilibrium**.

Reviewing the Main Idea

How is macroeconomic equilibrium similar to the equilibrium in individual markets?

Section 3

Stabilization Policies (pages 427–434)

Demand-side policies, also known as **fiscal policies**, are designed to affect the aggregate demand curve through federal spending and taxation. Supply-side policies affect the aggregate supply curve. They include a smaller role for government, a lower federal tax structure, and other measures to reduce paperwork and regulation in the business sector. Monetary policies include open market operations, changes in the discount rate, and in extreme circumstances, changes in the reserve requirement.

Reviewing the Main Idea

What are the three main approaches to stabilization and growth?

Section 4

Economics and Politics (pages 436–438)

The United States has an independent monetary authority—the Federal Reserve System. As long as the Fed has responsibility for monetary policy and elected officials have responsibility for fiscal policy, the two may not agree. While economics is a social science in its own right, the fields of economics and politics are closely intertwined. The President has a **Council of Economic Advisers** but may not always be able to follow their advice for political reasons.

Reviewing the Main Idea

What does the historical record reveal about the conduct of economic policy?

Reviewing Key Terms

Classify each of the terms below into one of the following categories:

A. supply-side policies
B. demand-side policies
C. monetarist policies

1. aggregate demand curve
2. aggregate supply curve
3. automatic stabilizer
4. consumption function
5. deregulation
6. entitlements
7. fiscal policy
8. Keynesian economics
9. Laffer curve
10. open market operations

Reviewing the Facts

SECTION 1 *(pages 418–421)*
1. **List** two statistics used to identify the problems of growth and economic instability.
2. **Name** some of the social costs of instability.

SECTION 2 *(pages 422–425)*
3. **Describe** the difference between the supply curve of a firm and the aggregate supply curve.
4. **Identify** the factors that would cause the aggregate demand curve to increase.
5. **Discuss** what is meant by macroeconomic equilibrium.

SECTION 3 *(pages 427–434)*
6. **Identify** the major tools of fiscal policy.
7. **List** the main assumptions of the supply-siders.
8. **Describe** the short-term and long-term impacts of monetary policy.

SECTION 4 *(pages 436–438)*
9. **Explain** why the monetary policies of the Fed are not always consistent with the objectives of fiscal policy.

10. **Explain** why new problems will arise in the economy, even as old ones are solved.
11. **State** an example of how politics sometimes overrides sound economic policies.

Critical Thinking

1. **Drawing Conclusions** Why is the misery index a more personal measure of the social costs of instability than other concepts such as the GDP gap?
2. **Making Predictions** What would happen to the aggregate demand curve—as shown below— if there was a sudden growth in consumer spending fueled by a massive tax cut? How would such a shift affect macroeconomic equilibrium and the general price level?

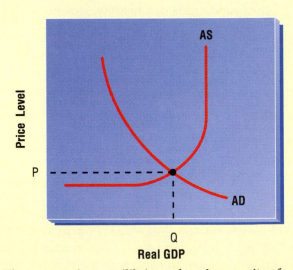

Macroeconomic Equilibrium

The economy is at equilibrium when the quantity of real GDP demanded is equal to the real GDP supplied at a given price level. The question facing economic policymakers is how to increase real GDP without increasing the price level.

Applying Economic Concepts

1. **Monetary Policy** At one time or another, most Presidents have complained about the independence of the Fed. Do you think this independence should be maintained, or that elected officials should have more control over monetary policy? Support your answer.

2. **Diversity of Opinion** Some economists favor policies that stimulate demand, while others favor those that stimulate the supply of goods and services. Still others prefer policies based on the growth of the money supply. With which group do you agree? Support your choice.

Cooperative Learning Activity

Organize into two groups. One group will represent members of Congress. The other group will represent officials of the Federal Reserve System. You have just been notified of the following economic statistics: Two months ago inflation was at 5 percent; last month it shot up to 8 percent. Meet with the members of your group to determine what fiscal and monetary policies should be followed, bearing in mind that the national elections are four months away.

Reinforcing Skills

UNDERSTANDING A PUBLIC OPINION POLL

To understand the effectiveness of public opinion polls, conduct your own poll. Follow the guidelines below.

1. Word your questions carefully.
2. Choose a sample that resembles the general public as closely as possible.
3. Conduct face-to-face polling, and do not allow your manner to affect people's answers.
4. Draw accurate conclusions, keeping in mind that some answers may not be reliable and that public opinion changes rapidly.

Individual Activity

Both demand-side and supply-side policies are designed to ensure stable economic growth. The approaches differ, however, on what should be done to achieve this goal. Assume that real GDP growth was negative during the last quarter. Make a two-column chart. In the left column, list the policies that demand-side economists would follow to help the economy. Place the supply-side solutions in the right column. How do the two approaches differ?

Writing About Economics

THE INFORMATIVE STYLE

In the **Journal Writing** activity on page 417, you kept track of unemployment and inflation statistics. Using the informative style of writing discussed on page 554, explain what these statistics are and how they reflect the overall health of the economy.

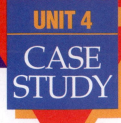
MANAGED COMPETITION OF HEALTH CARE

An intensive debate over health care reform began with the presidential election of 1992. After the election, the Clinton administration proposed a system of managed health care as a way to contain costs and to provide everyone with medical coverage.

The debate over managed competition—which is not unique to health care—revolves around a single issue: Are consumers better off when they individually shop for health care coverage, or are they better off pooling their buying power and then choosing from one of many federally approved health care packages?

▲ *Hillary Rodham Clinton headed the task force that studied health care reform in the United States.*

Pro

Managed competition solves the problems of access and cost containment through a powerful restructuring of the entire health marketplace, designed to empower consumers. Providers and consumers are given strong incentives to choose high-quality, affordable health care through provider-insurer partnerships, which are required to cover anyone who chooses the plan regardless of their health. . . .

Under this complex proposal, private providers and insurers form Accountable Health Partnerships (AHPs) that will compete with each other based on the quality and cost of care provided . . . Each AHP will be required to periodically provide information about the cost and quality of their services, giving consumers a basis for comparing the effectiveness and efficiency of competing plans. . . .

Managed competition . . . will keep the good parts of our current system intact while providing access to affordable health care for all Americans, controlling the costs, and allowing for any necessary refinements over time.

—CONGRESSMAN PETE PETERSON, APRIL 1993.

▼ *Physician assistants perform gall-bladder surgery.*

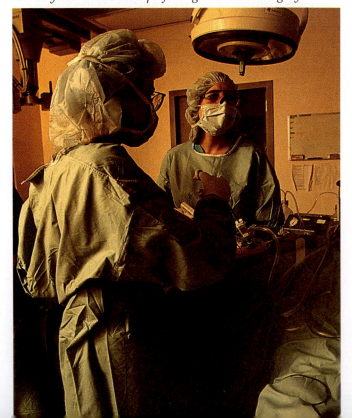

◄ Opponents of managed care claim that benefits such as vision checkups will not be covered.

▼ Many Americans are trying to avoid health care costs by being more health conscious.

Con Managed competition envisions a health care system in which the ability to enroll in any plan other than the least-cost plan is based on a consumer's ability to pay additional premiums. . . . Under a system of managed competition, many middle-class families will be unable to afford additional premiums, as well as deductibles, copayments and balance billing if allowed. Because subsidies may be provided only for low-income Americans, the middle-class may be forced into the lowest cost plan.

Many managed care . . . systems do not include such needed services as vision, dental, mental health care, alcohol and substance abuse treatment, rehabilitative therapies, assistive technology and long-term care. And they also make patients wait for care. . . .

[A]dministrative costs are not minimized because the system maintains multiple insurers, each with their own payrolls, marketing programs, insurance forms and other overhead costs. . . .

Competition has been shown to drive up, not reduce, health care costs as competing plans purchase duplicative equipment and technology in order to attract medical specialists and consumers.

—EDWIN S. ROTHSCHILD, PUBLIC AFFAIRS DIRECTOR, CITIZEN ACTION, APRIL 1993.

Analyzing the Case Study

1. What is managed competition?
2. What evidence does Peterson cite to explain that managed competition would benefit the health care system?
3. What evidence does Rothschild cite to explain that managed competition would hinder the health care system?
4. With which opinion do you agree? Why?

UNIT 5

INTERNATIONAL AND GLOBAL ECONOMICS

Our interest will be to throw open the doors of commerce, and to knock off its shackles, giving freedom to all persons for the vent of whatever they may choose to bring into our ports, and asking the same in theirs.

—Thomas Jefferson

 Economics and You

In this unit, discover what part economics plays in the following situations:

• Imported goods sometimes cost more than domestically produced ones.

• Capitalism has triumphed over communism.

• Population growth rates on the other side of the world affect you.

The many ships filling Hong Kong's harbor symbolize the interdependency among nations in the global economy.

At this international trade show, various countries display their consumer electronics products.

CHAPTER 18

International Trade

SECTION 1
Absolute and Comparative Advantage

SECTION 2
Barriers to International Trade

SECTION 3
Financing and Trade Deficits

CHAPTER PREVIEW

People to Know

- Bill Gates
- Customs Inspector

Applying Economic Concepts to Your Life

International Trade Is *international trade* important to you? On average, Americans spend more than $2,300 per year on imported goods and services. Look at the labels on your clothes, in your shoes, on food products you buy, or even on the car you drive—and you see why international trade is important to everyone.

Journal Writing

For one week, be aware of every manufactured item you handle—from the clothes you put on in the morning to the cafeteria trays used in your school. Analyze each item for its producer. In your journal, log the items you use daily and note whether each is domestically produced or foreign-made.

Absolute and Comparative Advantage

Section Preview

Objectives

After studying this section, you will be able to:

1. **Explain** the importance of international trade in today's economy.
2. **Describe** the meaning of absolute advantage.
3. **Relate** the importance of comparative advantage to international trade policies.

Key Terms

absolute advantage, comparative advantage

Applying Economic Concepts

Comparative Advantage When you and a friend team up to do something, how do you divide the work? If you want to get the job done quickly, you probably specialize and perform the task that you do best. If this is the way you work, you already know about *comparative advantage*.

The key to trade—whether among people, states, or countries—is specialization. Some people specialize in cutting hair. Others specialize in fixing television sets. These people exchange their services for money, which they then use to buy the specialized talents and services of others.

Different regions of the United States specialize in certain economic activities in much the same way. Pittsburgh, for example, is a center of the steel industry, and Detroit specializes in automobiles. The Midwest and High Plains areas are known for wheat farming. Texas is recognized for oil and cattle, while Florida and California are famous for citrus fruit. All of these states trade with one another so that people in one area can consume the goods and services that workers in other areas offer.

What is true of specialization in the United States is also true in other regions of the world. Each region or country generally produces what it is best suited to do. As a result, international trade allows all countries the opportunity to take advantage of local production efficiencies. ✓

Absolute Advantage *Colombia produces 90 percent of the world's emeralds. This gives the country an absolute advantage over most nations in regard to emerald production.* **What is the key to trade?**

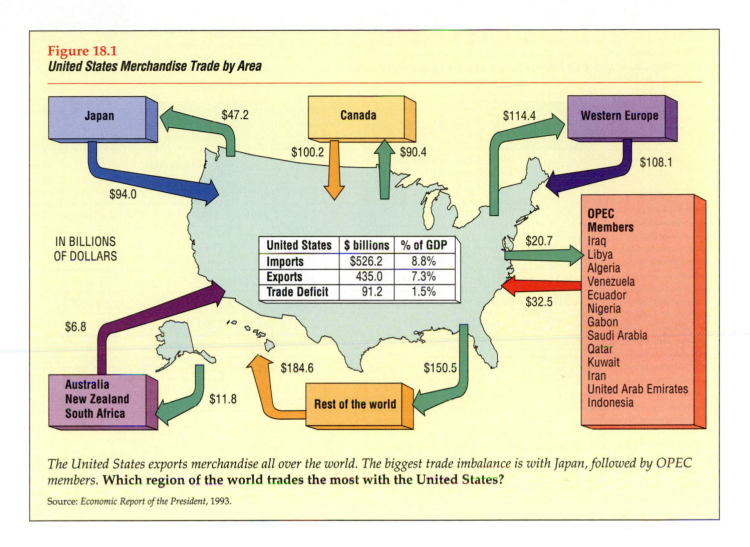

Figure 18.1
United States Merchandise Trade by Area

Japan

$47.2

Canada

Western Europe

$114.4

$100.2 $90.4

$108.1

$94.0

IN BILLIONS
OF DOLLARS

$20.7

United States	$ billions	% of GDP
Imports	$526.2	8.8%
Exports	435.0	7.3%
Trade Deficit	91.2	1.5%

$32.5

OPEC
Members
Iraq
Libya
Algeria
Venezuela
Ecuador
Nigeria
Gabon
Saudi Arabia
Qatar
Kuwait
Iran
United Arab Emirates
Indonesia

$6.8

$184.6 $150.5

Australia
New Zealand
South Africa

$11.8

Rest of the world

The United States exports merchandise all over the world. The biggest trade imbalance is with Japan, followed by OPEC members. **Which region of the world trades the most with the United States?**

Source: *Economic Report of the President*, 1993.

The United States and International Trade

In recent years, international trade has become increasingly important to all nations. Most of the products exchanged are goods, although a growing number of services—such as insurance and banking—are also bought and sold.

The Extent of Trade

The United States relies extensively on international trade. In 1992 alone, imports of goods and services amounted to about $650 billion. This number corresponds to approximately $2,300 for every person in the country, and has grown steadily over the years. **1**

Figure 18.1 shows the trade patterns for merchandise between the United States and the rest of the

QUICK CHECK

Checking Understanding

1. In 1992, what was the value of United States imports per person?

Applying Economic Concepts

☑ **International Trade** International trade is similar to trade between cities, states, or regions within a country. The main difference is that international trade involves different currencies, tariffs, and greater distances.

Figure 18.2
American Dependency on Trade: Imports as a Percent of Consumption

Raw Material	Imports as a Percent of Consumption	Primary Foreign Sources	Use of Raw Material
Industrial Diamonds	100	South Africa, Australia, Zaire, Botswana	Industrial cutting tools, oil well drills
Columbium	100	Brazil, Canada, Thailand	Atomic energy reactors, hardened steel
Mica (sheet)	100	India, Belgium, France	Electrical insulation, ceramics
Strontium	100	Mexico, Spain	Flares, fireworks
Manganese	100	South Africa, Gabon, France	Stainless steel, dry cell batteries, industrial dies
Bauxite	100	Australia, Guinea, Jamaica	Anything made of aluminum
Platinum	88	South Africa, United Kingdom, Russia	Electrical components, jewelry, dentistry, electroplating
Tantalum	85	Thailand, Germany, Brazil	Surgical instruments and missile parts
Cobalt	82	Zaire, Zambia, Canada	High-temperature jet fighter engines
Chromium	80	South Africa, Zimbabwe, Turkey	Chrome, ball bearings, trim on appliances and cars
Tungsten	75	China, Bolivia, Canada	High-temperature materials, lamp filaments, instruments

International trade is the primary means by which nations, including the United States, obtain many essential yet scarce materials. **How does the lack of certain raw materials force nations to become interdependent?**

Source: *Statistical Abstract of the United States, 1992*

world. The sheer volume of this trade between nations of such different geographic, political, and religious characteristics is proof that trade is beneficial. Nations trade for the same reasons individuals do—because they are free to do so, and they believe they are better off with trade than without it.

The Necessity of Trade

Without international trade, many products would not be available on the world market. Bananas, for example, would not leave Honduras, nor would coffee beans leave Brazil. Some people think of international trade as a way to obtain exotic products and fancy consumer goods, but the issue is more complex than that.

Many imports, for example, are necessities such as oil, clothing, and shoes. We also import minerals, metals, and raw materials that are not available in the United States. **Figure 18.2** lists some essential raw materials that would not be available without trade.

Absolute Advantage

In some cases, it may be cheaper for a country to import a product than to manufacture it. The differences in production costs from one country to another form a basis for international trade. The production costs vary because of differences in natural resources, climate, labor force, and capital. When a country is able to produce more of a given product than another, it has an **absolute advantage**.

Consider, for example, the case of two countries—Alpha and Beta—which are the same size in terms of area, population, and capital stock. Only their climate and soil fertilities differ. In each country, only two crops can be grown—coffee and cashew nuts.

If both countries devote all of their efforts to producing coffee, Alpha can produce 40 million pounds and Beta 6 million. Alpha has an absolute advantage in the production of coffee. If both countries devote all their efforts to the production of cashew nuts, Alpha can produce 8 million pounds and Beta 6 million. Alpha also has an absolute advantage in the production of cashew nuts.

For years, people thought that absolute advantage was the basis for trade because it enabled a country to produce enough of a good to consume domestically as well as to export. The theory of absolute advantage did not explain how a large country could trade with a small country to the benefit of both.

Comparative Advantage

Even when one country enjoys an absolute advantage in the production of all goods, trade between it and another country is still beneficial if one country can produce a product relatively more efficiently. The more efficient country has a **comparative advantage** in the production of a good if it can produce that good at a relatively lower opportunity cost.

Alpha, for example, has a comparative advantage in the production of coffee. Given a fixed amount of resources, it can produce relatively more coffee than

nuts. If Alpha were to specialize in the production of one good, it would choose coffee beans.

Beta, however, does a relatively better job of producing cashew nuts. Its comparative advantage in cashew nuts would lead Beta to specialize in their production.

The concept of comparative advantage is based on the assumption that everyone will be better off producing the products they produce relatively best. This concept applies to individuals, companies, states, and regions as well as to nations.

When nations specialize in the goods they are most efficient at producing, the total world output is greater. Take, for example, the case of the United States and Brazil. The United States has excellent supplies of iron and coal. It also has the capital and the labor that are needed to produce tractors and farm machinery efficiently. Brazil, in contrast, does not have as much capital or skilled labor. It does have the amount and kind of land, labor, and climate to produce coffee efficiently.

The United States, therefore, has a comparative advantage in the production of tractors and farm machinery. Brazil has a comparative advantage in the production of coffee. Trade between the two countries would be valuable to both. Each country could produce its specialty at a lower cost and enjoy larger total consumption.

SECTION 1 REVIEW

Reviewing Terms and Facts

1. **Define** absolute advantage, comparative advantage.
2. **Explain** why international trade is crucial to the United States today.
3. **Explain** why world output is larger when international trade is based on comparative advantage.

Critical Thinking

4. **Making Generalizations** Are the products that your state produces and sells to others based on absolute advantage or on comparative advantage? Explain your answer.

Applying Economic Concepts

5. **Comparative Advantage** If you were to open a business with two of your best friends, how would you divide the work to be done? Do your decisions regarding who does what reflect comparative advantage? Explain.

BILL GATES
(1955–   )

"Our success," says Bill Gates, "is based on only one thing: good products. It's not very complicated." The success of Microsoft Corporation's products has made Gates—cofounder and CEO—possibly the richest person in the United States.

TEENAGE WIZARDRY While in high school, Gates designed a class scheduling program so that he could take courses with the prettiest girls in his school. He also started Traf-O-Data, a computer traffic analysis company.

At age 19, Gates dropped out of pre-law at Harvard University to pursue his

interest in computer technology. Gates and his friend Paul Allen wrote a condensed operating-system language, which they licensed to a computer manufacturer. From this success, Gates

The development of Windows® has brought Bill Gates phenomenal wealth.

and Allen established Microsoft Corporation in 1975.

INTO THE BIG LEAGUES In 1980 IBM—the computer industry leader—asked Gates to develop an operating system for its new personal computer. Gates bought a system from a small company for $50,000. He revamped it and licensed it to IBM for $125,000. The system was called MS-DOS, for Microsoft Disk Operating System. Because Gates retained ownership of MS-DOS, he was in a position to market the system to other companies. In 1981 IBM

unveiled its PC, setting off the personal computer boom. MS-DOS became the dominant operating system in the market.

Microsoft went public in 1986, and the stock did better than expected. Gates, who owned 45 percent of the company, became a millionaire several hundred times over. Smaller investors gained also. A hundred shares bought for $2,100 in March 1986 were worth $77,850 in February 1993.

CONTINUING SUCCESS At age 38, Bill Gates had an estimated net worth of $7 billion. Much of Gates's success came from his unique combination of technological expertise and an understanding of the computer needs of the average user. Windows®, an operating program featuring simplified commands and eye-catching graphics, swept the market. By 1993 Windows® was selling 1 million copies a month, and Microsoft operating systems ran nearly 90 percent of the world's PCs. Entrepreneurs such as Bill Gates are the driving force for much of the change in a free enterprise economy.

Examining the Profile

1. **Predicting Consequences** How might the Microsoft story have been different if Gates had sold MS-DOS to IBM rather than retaining ownership?

2. **For Further Research** Find out how the Apple-IBM alliance called "Taligent" poses a challenge to Microsoft. Write a summary of your findings.

Section Preview

Objectives

After studying this section, you will be able to:

1. **Explain** how international trade can be restricted to protect special interests.
2. **Cite** the main argument for protection.
3. **Relate** the history of the free trade movement.

Key Terms

tariff, quota, protective tariff, revenue tariff, protectionist, infant industries argument, balance of payments, trade deficit, most favored nation clause, General Agreement on Tariffs and Trade (GATT), North American Free Trade Agreement (NAFTA)

Applying Economic Concepts

Quotas Do you think the prices of some goods are too high? If you do, you are like many other people. Over the years, *quotas* have limited the import of some foreign goods to protect some industries in the United States. The high-priced imports do protect some American workers, but they also affect your pocketbook.

Although international trade can bring many benefits, some people object to it because it can displace selected industries and groups of workers in the United States. It is not unusual to hear workers say they have lost their jobs because of unfair foreign competition. Therefore, while many people support international trade, some strongly oppose it.

Restricting International Trade

Historically, trade has been restricted in two major ways. One is through **tariffs**—taxes placed on imports to increase their price in the domestic market. The other is through **quotas**—limits placed on the quantities of a product that can be imported.

Tariffs

Governments levy two kinds of tariffs—protective and revenue. A **protective tariff** is a tariff high enough to protect less efficient domestic industries. Suppose, for example, that it costs $1 to produce each gadget in the United States. Each gadget made in another country, however, can be imported for 35 cents, including transportation costs. If a tariff of 95 cents is placed on each imported gadget, the cost climbs to $1.30—more than the cost of the American-made gadget. The

domestic industry is protected from being undersold by a foreign industry.

The **revenue tariff** is designed to raise money. It must be high enough to generate funds when imported goods enter the country, yet not so high as to prohibit imports. If the tariff on imported gadgets was 40 cents, the price of the imports would be 75 cents, or 25 cents less than the price of the American-made ones. The tariff would be raising revenue rather than protecting domestic producers from foreign competition.

In practice, all tariffs raise some revenue and offer some protection. Before the Civil War, tariffs were the chief source of revenue for the federal government. From the Civil War to 1913, tariffs provided about one-half of the government's total revenue. In 1913 the federal income tax was passed, which gave the government a new and more lucrative source of revenue.

Quotas

Foreign goods sometimes cost so little that even a high tariff on them may not protect the domestic market. In such cases, the government generally uses a quota to keep foreign goods out of the country.

Quotas can be more powerful than tariffs, and may have more of an impact on international trade. A quota can be set as low as zero to keep a product from entering the country at all. If the total supply of a

Protectionism *These workers believe that foreign imports cost American workers their jobs. Thus, they want imports restricted.* **What arguments do protectionists use in support of trade restrictions?**

product is restricted, domestic consumers will not be able to consume as much of it and domestic producers can charge higher prices for it.

By 1981, for example, domestic automobile producers faced intense competition from lower-priced Japanese automobiles. Rather than lower their own prices, domestic manufacturers wanted President Reagan to establish automobile import quotas on Japanese cars. The Reagan administration told the Japanese to voluntarily restrict auto exports, and they reluctantly agreed. As a result, Americans had fewer cars from which to choose, and the prices of all cars were higher than they would otherwise have been.

During the Bush administration, "voluntary" import quotas were imposed on steel. The quotas protected jobs in the domestic steel industry, but at the cost of higher steel prices for the rest of the country.

Other Barriers

Tariffs and quotas are not the only barriers to trade. Many imported foods, for example, are subject to health inspections far more rigorous than those given to domestic foods. Another tactic is to require a

license to import. If the government is slow to grant the license, or if the license fees are too high, international trade is restricted. 1

Arguments For Protection

International trade has been a subject of debate for many years. Some people, known as **protectionists**, favor tariffs, quotas, and other trade barriers. Others, known as free traders, favor fewer trade restrictions.

National Defense

One of the most important arguments for trade barriers centers on national defense. Protectionists argue that without trade barriers, a country could become too specialized and end up too dependent on other countries.

During wartime, a country might not be able to get such critical supplies as food, oil, and weapons. The governments of such countries as Israel and South Africa have developed large armaments industries for such crises. They want to be sure they will have a which industries are critical to national defense must also be considered. The steel, auto, ceramic, and electronic industries all have argued at one time or another that they are critical to national defense.

Infant Industries

The **infant industries argument**—the belief that new or emerging industries should be protected from foreign competition—is also used to justify trade barriers. Protectionists claim that these industries need to gain strength and experience before they can compete against developed industries in other countries. Trade barriers would give them the time they need to develop. If infant industries compete against foreign industries too soon, they might fail. **2**

Many people are willing to accept the infant industries argument only if protection will eventually be removed, allowing the industry to compete on its own. Some Latin American countries have tried using tariffs to protect their infant automobile industries, with tariffs as high as several hundred percent. In some cases, the tariff raised the price of used American-made cars to more than double the cost of new ones in the United States.

Protecting Domestic Jobs

A third argument—the one used most often—is that tariffs and quotas protect domestic jobs from cheap foreign labor. Workers in the shoe industry, for example, have protested the import of lower-cost Italian, Spanish, and Brazilian shoes. Garment workers have opposed the import of lower-cost Korean, Chinese, and Indian clothing. Steelworkers have blocked foreign-made cars from company parking lots to

"You like protectionism as a 'working man.' How about as a consumer?"

Protectionism *Arguments exist both for and against protectionism.* **How might the issue of protectionism differ for a worker and a consumer?**

domestic supply source if hostilities break out or other countries impose economic boycotts.

Free traders admit that national security is a compelling argument for trade barriers. They believe, however, that having a reliable source of domestic supply must be weighed against the reality that the supply will be smaller and possibly less efficient than it would be with free trade. The problem of deciding

Checking Understanding

1. How can import licenses restrict international trade?
2. What is the infant industries argument?

Applying Economic Concepts

✓ **National Defense** Despite the end of the cold war, the 1993 defense budget was close to $280 billion. Some suggest that the United States support weapons research but put off producing the weapons until a need for them becomes clear, and cost controls are assured.

International Trade *KFC and other food franchises have expanded worldwide.* **How does the protection of inefficient industries hurt the economy?**

show their displeasure with the foreign-made steel used in producing the cars.

Whether limiting foreign trade preserves American jobs is hard to prove. In the long run, those industries that find it hard to compete are generally inefficient. Many people believe these industries should be allowed to die out to free their resources for use elsewhere. The problem, however, lies in the short run, when unemployment and hardship are likely to occur. Workers want to keep their jobs or live in the communities in which they grew up.

When inefficient industries are protected, the economy produces less and the standard of living goes down. Because of unnecessarily high prices, people buy less of everything, including those goods produced by protected industries. If prices get too high, substitute products will be found.

Free traders argue that the profit-and-loss system is one of the major features of the American economy. Profits reward the efficient and hard-working, while losses eliminate the inefficient and weak.

Keep the Money at Home

Another argument for trade barriers claims that limiting imports will keep American money in the United States instead of allowing it to go abroad.

Free traders, however, point out that the American dollars that go abroad generally come back again. The Japanese, for example, use the dollars they receive for their automobiles to buy American cotton, soybeans, and airplanes. These purchases benefit American workers in those industries.

The same is true of the dollars used to buy oil from the Middle East. The money comes back to the United States when oil-wealthy foreigners buy American-made oil technology, Kentucky horse farms, and Hollywood mansions. Keeping the money home hurts those American industries that depend on exports for their jobs. 1

Helping the Balance of Payments

Another argument involves the **balance of payments**—the difference between the money paid to and received from other nations. Protectionists argue that restrictions on imports help the balance of payments. When the economy runs a **trade deficit**—a deficit in the "goods" component of the balance of payments—it is spending more on imports than it earns on exports. As a result, money leaves the country, some jobs are lost, and the dollar is threatened. ✔️

What protectionists overlook, however, is that the dollars return to the United States to stimulate

Free Trade *Free traders argue that limiting tariffs and quotas allows consumers to choose from a wide variety of both domestic and foreign products.* **What is the purpose of the GATT?**

employment in other industries. In the United States economy, the balance of payments adjusts automatically to deficits and surpluses. Most economists do not believe that interfering with free trade can be justified on the grounds of helping the balance of payments.

The Free Trade Movement

Using trade barriers to protect domestic industries and jobs works only if other countries do not use trade barriers. If they do, all countries suffer because

they have neither the benefits of efficient production nor access to less costly inputs from other nations.

Tariffs During the Great Depression

In 1930 the United States passed the Smoot-Hawley Tariff, one of the highest in history. It set import duties so high that the price of many imported goods rose nearly 70 percent. When other countries did the same, international trade nearly came to a halt. **2**

Before long, most countries realized that high tariffs hurt more than they helped. As a result, in 1934 the United States passed the Reciprocal Trade

---

QUICK CHECK

Checking Understanding

1. Who is hurt when American dollars are kept in the United States?
2. What effect did the Smoot-Hawley Tariff have on international trade?

Applying Economic Concepts

 Trade Deficit Two measures of the trade deficit are often confused. The most comprehensive includes both goods and services, and is simply called the trade deficit, or the deficit on current account. If services are excluded, it is called the merchandise trade deficit.

Figure 18.3
The North American Free Trade Agreement

The North American Free Trade Agreement (NAFTA) makes up the largest single free-trade area in the world, larger than that of the European Union. **How does NAFTA affect the market for goods and services in North America?**

Source: United States Commerce Department, Mexican Commerce Secretariat

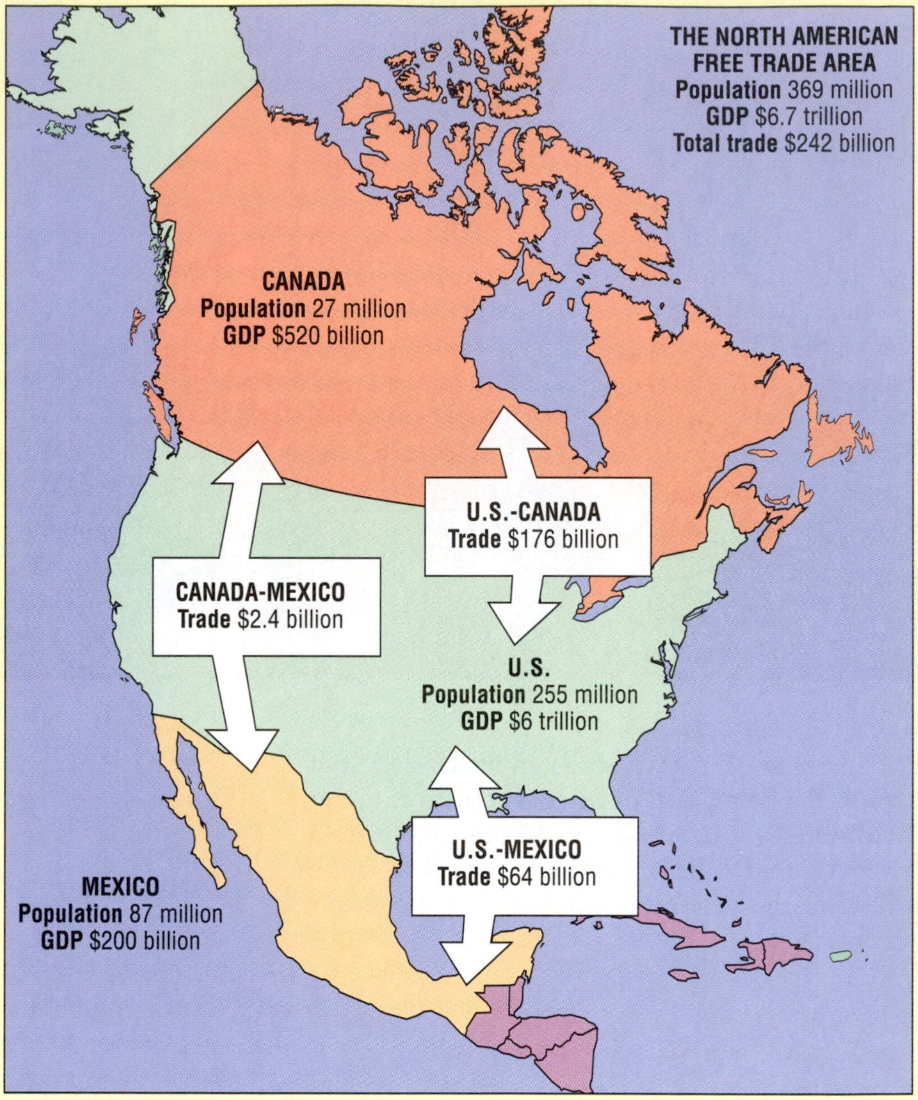

THE NORTH AMERICAN FREE TRADE AREA
Population 369 million
GDP $6.7 trillion
Total trade $242 billion

CANADA
Population 27 million
GDP $520 billion

U.S.-CANADA
Trade $176 billion

CANADA-MEXICO
Trade $2.4 billion

U.S.
Population 255 million
GDP $6 trillion

U.S.-MEXICO
Trade $64 billion

MEXICO
Population 87 million
GDP $200 billion

Agreements Act, which allowed it to reduce tariffs up to 50 percent if the other countries agreed. The act also contained the **most favored nation clause**—a provision allowing a country with such an agreement to receive the same tariff reduction that the United States negotiates with another country.

Suppose, for example, that the United States and China have a trade agreement with a most favored nation clause. If the United States then negotiates a tariff reduction with another country, the reduction would also apply to China. This clause is very important to a foreign country, because its goods will then sell at a lower price in the American market.

Tariffs After World War II

In 1947, 23 countries signed the **General Agreement on Tariffs and Trade** (GATT). The GATT extended tariff concessions and worked to do away with import quotas. Later, the Trade Expansion Act of

1962 gave the President of the United States the power to negotiate further tariff reductions. As a result of this legislation, tariffs were significantly reduced in 1967 and 1979, with more than 100 countries agreeing to reduce the average level of tariffs. Other barriers to trade, such as quotas, unnecessary inspections, and licensing requirements, were also reduced.

Most recently, many nations have worked on the Uruguay Round—trade negotiations that began in 1987 and were concluded in December 1993. The goal of these negotiations was to reduce many of the nontariff barriers that still exist in world trade.

Because so many countries have been willing to reduce tariffs and quotas under GATT, international trade is flourishing. Tariffs that once nearly doubled the price of many goods now increase the average cost only a small percentage. Tariffs have been dropped altogether on some categories of goods. As a result, stores are able to offer a wide variety of industrial and consumer goods.

NAFTA

The **North American Free Trade Agreement** (NAFTA), which the Bush administration proposed and the Clinton administration concluded, is another attempt to liberalize free trade. Before NAFTA, United States goods entering Mexico faced an average tariff of 10 percent. At the same time, half the goods entering the United States from Mexico were duty-free, while the other half faced an average tax of only 4 percent.

Exceptions did exist, however. A 32 percent tariff on brooms imported from Mexico protected broom makers in southern Illinois. The high tariff barriers protected the jobs of up to 3,000 workers who hand-wired sheaves of broomcorn to wooden handles. NAFTA will reduce the tariff on Mexican brooms to zero over a 15-year period, which will threaten these American jobs.

Free trade is good in general, but it is not painless. Some workers will be displaced when nations agree on trade pacts that lower barriers to trade. As a result, NAFTA is a topic of intense debate.

SECTION 2 REVIEW

Reviewing Terms and Facts

1. **Define** tariff, quota, protective tariff, revenue tariff, protectionist, infant industries argument, balance of payments, trade deficit, most favored nation clause, General Agreement on Tariffs and Trade (GATT), North American Free Trade Agreement (NAFTA).
2. **Describe** three barriers to international trade.
3. **List** five arguments for protection.
4. **Identify** three legislative acts since 1933 that have helped liberalize international trade.

Critical Thinking

5. **Demonstrating Reasoned Judgment** If you were a member of Congress approached by a delegation of autoworkers seeking additional tariff or quota protection, how would you respond? Defend your response.

Applying Economic Concepts

6. **Quotas** Explain how a quota on a good or service produced in your community can protect the jobs in a particular industry. Then explain how the same quota might be harmful to others.

Recognizing Bias

Two of your friends have just seen a horror movie. You meet them as they are coming out of the theater. One friend says, "That was the scariest movie I've ever seen in my life! I'll never get to sleep tonight." The other friend says, "Are you kidding? That movie was so boring, I almost fell asleep in it." Who is right? How could two people have such different ideas about the same movie?

Explanation

Most people have preconceived feelings and attitudes that affect their point of view. This viewpoint, or *bias*, influences the way they interpret events. A person's writing often reflects his or her bias. Therefore, an idea that is stated as a fact may be only an opinion. Recognizing bias will help you judge the accuracy of what you hear or read.

To recognize bias, follow these steps:

- Identify the author and examine his or her views and reasons for writing the material.
- Look for language that reflects emotion or generalizations.

- Examine the writing for imbalanced presentation—leaning to one viewpoint and failing to provide equal coverage of other viewpoints.
- Identify statements of fact.
- Determine how the author's bias is reflected in the work.

Practice

Read the two excerpts on this page about the North American Free Trade Agreement (NAFTA). Then answer the questions that follow.

1. Based on the excerpt, why did Lloyd Bentsen favor NAFTA?
2. What evidence of bias do you find in Bentsen's argument?
3. What language in *The Nation* editorial reflects emotion or generalizations?
4. What conclusions might you draw about NAFTA from these excerpts?

A country doesn't stay competitive by running away from its problems, by closing its borders and erecting a protectionist wall. You stay competitive by facing economic challenges head on, responding to change and training workers to aggressively take on the competition. . . .

The United States has an ambitious program to restore growth to the economy. We must not underestimate the importance of NAFTA in executing our strategy and in keeping the U.S. competitive in world markets. Virtually every sector of our economy . . . will benefit from NAFTA. It is a good agreement—good for business and good for consumers.

NAFTA will mean jobs. NAFTA will mean better wages. NAFTA will mean growth. And NAFTA will mean prosperity.

—Lloyd Bentsen, Secretary of the Treasury, *The New York Times*, July 21, 1993

The North American Free Trade Agreement . . . sounded dandy when President Bush proposed it in preparation for his 1992 campaign. . . . But when its various elements are analyzed, it looks unnervingly like a cost-inefficient, socially regressive and ultimately self-destructive [hoax].

. . . NAFTA is no simple exercise in good-neighborliness. . . . To ratify the treaty is to condemn U.S. workers to more hard times, to confine Mexican workers in an economic ghetto . . . , to reduce the power of labor against ownership, to ravage the American industrial landscape and to transform forever the dream of America as a just and prosperous place of hope.

—Editorial in *The Nation*, June 14, 1993

Additional Practice

For further practice in recognizing bias, complete the Reinforcing Skills exercise in the Chapter 18 Review on page 469.

Financing and Trade Deficits

Section Preview

Objectives

After studying this section, you will be able to:

1. **Explain** how foreign currency is used in trade.

2. **Describe** the problem of a trade deficit and the main solution to the problem.

Key Terms

foreign exchange, foreign exchange market, foreign exchange rate, fixed exchange rate, devaluation, floating exchange rate, flexible exchange rate, foreign exchange futures, trade-weighted value of the dollar

Applying Economic Concepts

Foreign Exchange Do you have souvenir foreign currency—Canadian dollars, Mexican pesos, British pounds, French francs, or perhaps some other currency? If so, you own *foreign exchange*, just as some big investors around the world do.

Trade between nations is similar to exchange between individuals. The major difference is that each country has its own monetary system. Because of the different currencies used, financing world trade is complicated.

Financing International Trade

Scenarios like the following occur every day across the globe. A clothing firm in the United States wants to import business suits from a company in Great Britain. Because the British firm pays its bills in a currency called *pound sterling*, it likewise wants to receive payment in sterling. Therefore, the American firm must exchange its dollars for British pounds.

Foreign Exchange

In the field of international finance, foreign currencies are known as **foreign exchange** and are bought and sold in the **foreign exchange market**. Included in this market are banks that help secure foreign currencies for importers, as well as banks that accept foreign currencies from exporters.

Suppose that one pound sterling, £1, is equal to $1.55. If the business suits are valued at £1,000 in London, the American importer can go to an American bank and buy a £1,000 check for $1,550 plus a small service charge. The American firm then pays the British merchant, and the suits are imported.

American exporters sometimes accept foreign currency or checks written on foreign banks for their goods. They deposit the payments in their own banks, which helps the American banking system build a supply of foreign currency. This currency then can be sold to American firms that want to import goods from other countries. As a result, the importer and the exporter end up with the currency of their own countries.

When the price of one country's currency is described in terms of another country's currency, it is known as the **foreign exchange rate**. The rate can be quoted in terms of the United States dollar equivalent, as in $1.55 = £1, or in terms of foreign currency per United States dollar, £.6437 = $1. Most often, however, the rate is reported in both, as shown in the foreign currency listings in **Figure 18.4**.

Fixed Exchange Rates

In the past, two major kinds of exchange rates existed—fixed and flexible. For most of the 1900s, the world depended on **fixed exchange rates**—a system under which the price of one currency is fixed in terms of another so that the rate does not change.

When the world was on a gold standard, each country defined its currency in terms of a given amount of gold. Before 1971, for example, the United States dollar was worth 1/35 ounce of gold, and the British pound, 1/12.5 ounce of gold. After the gold content was specified, the value of one country's

HELP WANTED

Customs Inspector

Do you like detailed work? Are you able to accept responsibility and deal with people in a firm but friendly manner? Consider a career with the Treasury Department, working as a customs inspector. Your duties will include examining baggage at airports or seaports to ensure that all merchandise is declared and that duties are paid. You will also inspect commercial and noncommercial cargoes to determine admissibility and the amount of tax due. We will train you in laws governing imports and exports and in inspection procedures.

Education: College degree preferred, civil service exam required
Median salary: $31,500

currency could be measured in terms of the value of another country's currency. The British pound was backed by 2.8 times as much gold as the American dollar. Therefore, the British pound was worth $2.80.

Gold served as the common denominator that allowed comparisons of currencies, and it also kept exchange rates in line. Suppose that a country allowed its money supply to grow too fast and then spent some of the money on imports. Under a gold standard, the other countries holding the currency had the right to demand that it be converted into gold. Because no country wanted to lose its gold, each worked to keep its money supply under control.

This practice did not work in the 1950s and 1960s, however, when the United States developed a huge appetite for imports. During that time, it bought large quantities of foreign goods with dollars. At first, foreign countries willingly held dollars because they were acceptable as an international currency. Year after year, dollars went to other countries to buy imports, but only a small amount of these dollars came back as other countries bought American exports.

As dollars began to pile up in the rest of the world, many countries wondered if the United States could honor its promise that the dollar was "as good as gold." France and several other countries sent their dollars back to the United States, demanding gold in return at the rate of $35 an ounce.

The United States faced a problem if all countries tried to redeem their dollars for gold. Several solutions to the problem existed. The United States could have limited imported goods. Other countries might have retaliated, however, and limited American products. The United States could have restricted the growth of the money supply, but this action might have led to a recession. The country could have decided on **devaluation**—making currency worth less in terms of gold. Other countries might have followed suit and reduced their gold content by as much or more. Because many American politicians

Figure 18.4
A Typical Foreign Exchange Rate Listing

EXCHANGE RATES
Friday September 10, 1993
The New York foreign exchange selling rates below apply to trading among banks in amounts of $1 million and more, as quoted at 3 p.m. Eastern time by Bankers Trust Co., Telerate and other sources. Retail transactions provide fewer units of foreign currency per dollar.

Country	U.S. $ equiv. Fri.	Currency per U.S. $ Fri.
Argentina (Peso)	1.01	.99
Australia (Dollar)	.6503	1.5378
Britain (Pound)	1.5536	.6437
Canada (Dollar)	.7609	1.3143
Czech. Rep. (Koruna)		
Commercial rate	.0354988	28.1700
Chile (Peso)	.002531	395.06
China (Renminbi)	.174856	5.7190
Finland (Markka)	.17640	5.6690
France (Franc)	.17867	5.5970
Germany (Mark)	.6266	1.5960
Israel (Shekel)	.3586	2.7888
Japan (Yen)	.009409	106.28
Mexico (Peso)		
Floating rate	.3213368	3.1120
South Korea (Won)	.0012387	807.30
Taiwan (Dollar)	.037495	26.67

In the first column of the listing, one British pound costs 1.5536 American dollars. The second column shows that one United States dollar is worth .6437 British pounds. **Why do many local and financial papers carry daily exchange rate listings such as the one above?**

Source: Adapted from the *Wall Street Journal*, September 10, 1993

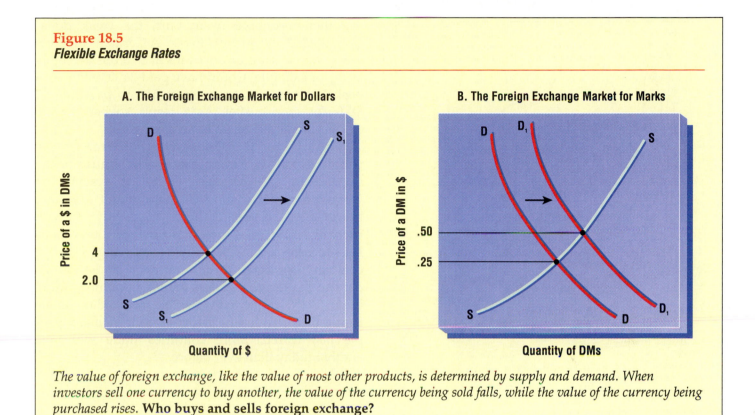

Figure 18.5
Flexible Exchange Rates

A. The Foreign Exchange Market for Dollars

Price of a $ in DMs

Quantity of $

B. The Foreign Exchange Market for Marks

Price of a DM in $

Quantity of DMs

The value of foreign exchange, like the value of most other products, is determined by supply and demand. When investors sell one currency to buy another, the value of the currency being sold falls, while the value of the currency being purchased rises. **Who buys and sells foreign exchange?**

viewed devaluation as an admission of failure, they opposed such a move.

Instead, President Richard Nixon solved the problem in August 1971, by announcing that the United States no longer would redeem dollars for gold. This action saved the gold stock for other purposes. At the same time, however, it angered many foreign holders of American dollars who were planning to cash them in for gold. **1** ☑

Flexible Exchange Rates

When the United States went off the gold standard, the world monetary system went to a **floating** or **flexible exchange rate**. Under this system, the forces of supply and demand establish the value of one country's currency in terms of the value of another country's currency.

The supply and demand graphs in **Figure 18.5** show flexible exchange rates. Before 1971, for example, the price of the German mark (DM) in the United States was 25 cents, and the price of the dollar in Germany was 4 DMs. In the years that followed, however, the United States imported more from Germany than it exported.

As importers in the United States sold dollars for DMs, the supply of dollars in the foreign currency

Checking Understanding

1. Why did President Nixon break the link between gold and the dollar in 1971?

Applying Economic Concepts

☑ **Gold Bullion** Fort Knox, a 109,000-acre complex near Louisville, Kentucky, is the site of the United States Bullion Depository. It holds more than $6 billion in gold bars. The nearly pure gold bars are each slightly smaller than a building brick, yet each weighs 27.5 pounds.

"Then it's agreed. Until the dollar firms up,
we let the clamshell float."

Copyright by: Ed Fisher, ©1971, The New Yorker Magazine, Inc.

Flexible Exchange Rates *Under a system of flexible exchange rates, the value of a currency is determined by supply and demand.* **What is the term given to the currency of other nations that is used in trade?**

market increased. The increased supply drove the value of the dollar down. At the same time, the growing demand for DMs drove up the value of the DM.

In the early 1970s, for example, it cost 12,000 DMs to make a Volkswagen. At 4 DMs per $1, an American importer paid $3,000 to buy the Volkswagen. Even after adding shipping charges and other expenses, the importer still could sell the automobile at a competitive price. As more cars were imported, however, the supply of dollars in the foreign exchange market increased. At the same time, the demand for DMs rose and caused the value of the dollar to drop.

When the dollar reached 2 DMs, the new exchange rate cost the importer more dollars. The importer now had to pay $6,000 for 12,000 DMs. At the higher price, the car no longer was as competitive as before. Excessive imports thus caused the deficit in the balance of payments. The value of the dollar declined, making imports cost more.

Although imports were hurt, the weak dollar caused American exports to rise. A German company that bought American soybeans at $6 a bushel before 1971, for example, would have paid 24 DMs for each bushel. After 1971, however, it had to pay only 12 DMs for each bushel. As a result, soybeans were cheaper, and more could be sold abroad.

When the world first adopted flexible rates, some people feared they might not work because of the fluctuations in exchange rates. The system has worked better than most people thought it would, however. A company can even buy **foreign exchange futures**—currencies on the futures market—to protect against changing exchange rates. A company can agree to buy currency 30, 90, or 180 days in the future at prices agreed upon now. More importantly, the switch to flexible rates did not interrupt the growth in international trade as many people had feared. More countries trade with one another today than ever before.

The Trade Deficit

The United States has a trade deficit. What do these numbers really mean, and how does the deficit affect the economy?

The Problem of a Trade Deficit

A large, long-lasting trade imbalance reduces the value of a country's currency on the foreign exchange markets. Devalued currency causes a chain reaction that affects output and employment in that country's industries. The large deficit in the United States balance of payments in the mid-1980s, for example, flooded the foreign exchange markets with dollars. An increase in the supply of dollars, as illustrated in **Figure 18.5**, causes the dollar to lose some of its value on the foreign currency markets.

When the dollar gets weaker, Americans have to pay more for imports, and foreigners pay less for American exports. As imports fall and exports rise, unemployment in the import industries results. In time, however, the dollar will get strong again and the process reverses. The economy may adjust slowly to changes in the value of the dollar, but the adjustments do take place. ✓

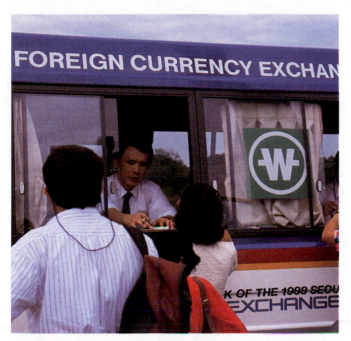

Foreign Exchange *At the 1988 Summer Olympics, foreign tourists exchange their currency for South Korean* won.
What is a foreign exchange rate?

The resulting shift in employment between export and import industries is one of the biggest problems with a trade deficit. In the automobile industry, for example, Japanese cars once undercut the price of cars being produced in Detroit, causing severe unemployment for both domestic autoworkers and domestic car dealerships. As the Japanese yen rose against the dollar in the early 1990s, however, the price of Japanese cars increased, making domestic automobiles more attractive and restoring some of the employment in that industry. As consumers began to demand more American-made cars relative to foreign-made ones, employment generated by foreign-car imports fell. **1**

International Value of the Dollar

Since floating rates became the standard in 1971, the Federal Reserve System has kept a statistic called the **trade-weighted value of the dollar**. This index shows the strength of the dollar against a group of foreign currencies. When the index falls, the dollar is weak in relation to other currencies. When the index rises, the dollar is strong.

Figure 18.6 shows how the trade-weighted value of the dollar has changed from 1973 to 1993. When the dollar reached its strongest level in 1985, foreign goods became less expensive, and American exports became more costly for the rest of the world. As a result, imports rose, exports fell, and the United States suffered a record trade deficit of $163 billion in 1986.

As the deficits persisted, the value of the dollar fell, making imports more expensive and exports more attractive to the rest of the world. By 1991, the overall deficit in the balance of payments had fallen to just under $4 billion. The trade deficit will continue to rise and fall as the value of the dollar continues to change.

Correcting Trade Deficits

Under flexible exchange rates, trade deficits automatically correct themselves through the price system. A strong currency, for example, will probably lead to a deficit in the balance of payments. The bigger the deficit, and the longer it lasts, the more likely the value of the currency will fall. Because the time span for the whole process varies, improvement in trade balances cannot be predicted very accurately. **2**

Trade imbalances can sometimes be improved with quotas, tariffs, or other means. Most economists believe that when legislators use these methods, however, threatened industries receive only temporary relief. Past attempts to legislate trade have largely

---

QUICK CHECK

Checking Understanding

1. What is one of the biggest problems with a trade deficit?
2. How do trade deficits correct themselves under flexible exchange rates?

Applying Economic Concepts

 Trade Deficit In recent years, the trade deficit has attracted almost as much attention as the federal budget deficit. Unlike the latter, however, the trade deficit has the potential to be self-correcting.

Figure 18.6
The Trade-Weighted Average Value of the Dollar

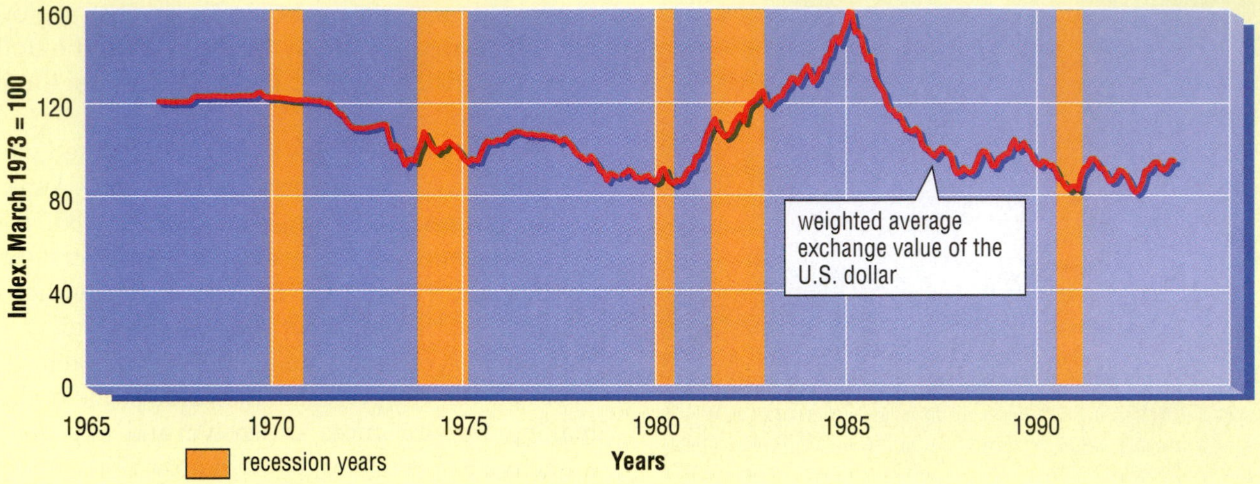

When the value of the dollar goes up, American exports go down and imports rise, which causes problems for the balance of payments. When the value of the dollar goes down, imports become more expensive, and the balance of payments tends to improve. **What causes the value of the dollar to fluctuate?**

Source: *The Economic Bulletin Board*, Bureau of Economic Analysis.

failed. As a result, many people believe a country should adjust slowly to change, rather than all at once.

Deficits and surpluses in a country's balance of payments generally tend to be temporary. When the dollar became strong in 1985, people worried about unemployment in export industries. When the dollar weakened in 1991, people worried about unemployment in import industries. As long as deficits and surpluses in a country's balance of payments generally correct themselves, the United States and many other countries no longer need to design economic policies just to improve their balance of payments.

SECTION 3
REVIEW

Reviewing Terms and Facts

1. **Define** foreign exchange, foreign exchange market, foreign exchange rate, fixed exchange rate, devaluation, floating exchange rate, flexible exchange rate, foreign exchange futures, trade-weighted value of the dollar.

2. **Describe** how the value of foreign exchange is determined.
3. **Explain** how trade deficits are corrected.

Critical Thinking

4. **Making Generalizations** How do exchange rates influence international trade?

Applying Economic Concepts

5. **Foreign Exchange** How does a weak American dollar affect you as a consumer? How does a strong dollar affect you?

Vocabulary

The following terms are defined in Chapter 18:

SECTION ONE
- absolute advantage (p. 450)
- comparative advantage (p. 451)

SECTION TWO
- tariff (p. 453)
- quota (p. 453)
- protective tariff (p. 453)
- revenue tariff (p. 453)
- protectionist (p. 454)
- infant industries argument (p. 455)
- balance of payments (p. 456)
- trade deficit (p. 456)

- most favored nation clause (p. 458)
- GATT (p. 458)
- NAFTA (p. 459)

SECTION THREE
- foreign exchange (p. 461)
- foreign exchange market (p. 461)
- foreign exchange rate (p. 461)

- fixed exchange rate (p. 461)
- devaluation (p. 462)
- floating exchange rate (p. 463)
- flexible exchange rate (p. 463)
- foreign exchange futures (p. 464)
- trade-weighted value of the dollar (p. 465)

Section 1

Absolute and Comparative Advantage (pages 448–451)

The United States is heavily involved in international trade. In 1993 the average American spent more than $2,300 for imported goods and services. **Absolute advantage** means that a country can produce more of a good than another country can. The basis for trade today is **comparative advantage**. If people and countries specialize in the things they do relatively more efficiently, and if they engage in trade to secure the things they do not produce, then total world output will increase.

Reviewing the Main Idea

What economic concept explains the mutual gains from trade?

Section 2

Barriers to International Trade (pages 453–459)

In the past, barriers to trade included **tariffs** and **quotas**. More recently, other nontariff barriers—including licensing, health certifications, and voluntary quotas—have been used to restrict the free flow of products.

Those who support trade barriers often do so on the grounds of national defense, **infant industries**, protecting domestic jobs, keeping the money home, and helping the **balance of payments**. Free traders believe all of these arguments are flawed, with the exception of the infant industries argument. For the infant industries argument to be valid, the protection eventually must be removed so that the industry can compete on its own.

Trade barriers helped make the conditions of the Great Depression even worse. Since 1934 the world has moved toward freer trade. The **GATT** contributed to much progress worldwide, and proponents of **NAFTA** would like to remove all trade barriers in North America.

Reviewing the Main Idea

How have the barriers to trade been removed over the years?

Section 3

Financing and Trade Deficits (pages 461–466)

Foreign exchange is the basis of international transactions. The value of foreign exchange is determined in markets where foreign currencies are bought and sold. The current system of **flexible exchange rates** means that the value of foreign currencies fluctuates along with the supply and demand for them.

The large **trade deficits** in the mid-1980s resulted partly from a strong dollar. When the **trade-weighted value of the dollar** declined, the trade deficit improved. Because deficits tend to be self-correcting, most nations no longer design economic policies just to improve the balance of payments.

Reviewing the Main Idea

In a world of flexible exchange rates, how do nations deal with trade imbalances?

Reviewing Key Terms

For each of the pairs of terms below, write a sentence or short paragraph showing how the two are related.

1. absolute advantage
   comparative advantage
2. balance of payments
   trade deficit
3. balance of payments
   flexible exchange rates
4. devaluation
   fixed exchange rate
5. foreign exchange
   flexible exchange rates
6. protectionist
   infant industries
7. protective tariff
   revenue tariff
8. tariff
   quota
9. trade deficit
   trade-weighted value of the dollar

Reviewing the Facts

SECTION 1 *(pages 448–451)*
1. **Describe** the extent of United States involvement in world trade.
2. **Describe** a case in which the United States might have an absolute advantage over another country in the production of a good.
3. **Explain** how comparative advantage can make trade between countries of different sizes possible.

SECTION 2 *(pages 453–459)*
4. **Name** three barriers to international trade.
5. **Describe** five protectionist arguments.

6. **Describe** the role of GATT in the free trade movement.

SECTION 3 *(pages 461–466)*
7. **Differentiate** between fixed and flexible exchange rates.
8. **Explain** how deficits can be self-correcting when currency values are allowed to be flexible.

Critical Thinking

1. **Determining Relevance** Many industries claim they are vital to the country's defense. Which industries do you think qualify? Explain your choices.
2. **Demonstrating Reasoned Judgment** Do you favor protection as a national trade policy? Why or why not?
3. **Demonstrating Reasoned Judgment** It has been announced that the government has to generate additional revenue. To do this, it can raise taxes or increase tariff rates. Which do you as a consumer prefer? Give reasons to support your choice.
4. **Analyzing Information** Some people feel the United States should return to a system of fixed exchange rates. Defend or oppose this view.

Applying Economic Concepts

1. **Comparative Advantage** Think of a project you recently completed with a friend. How could you have completed the project more efficiently, applying the principle of comparative advantage? Explain.
2. **Quotas** You have just started a business manufacturing toothbrushes. Would you favor a quota on imported toothbrushes? Why or why not?

Reinforcing Skills

RECOGNIZING BIAS

Read the following excerpt, then answer the questions that follow.

Leisure is the new watchword in Japan. The world's champion exporter of cars and VCRs is setting its sights on becoming a "lifestyle superpower." The pathway to this new world leadership was set out in 1992 by the Japanese government's Economic Planning Agency, which called on Japanese workers to work fewer hours and take longer vacations as part of an overall plan to achieve "a better quality of life." The objective is to reduce the standard work week to 40 hours from 44, eliminate Saturday work, and get employees to take the vacations to which they are entitled. This would cut average annual working hours to 1,800 from 2,000, making Japan's hours more comparable to those of the U.S. and Canada.

For Westerners, whose governments are obsessed with improving productivity and competitiveness, getting people to work less and enjoy life more does not seem to be much of a challenge. But in Japan, it involves a sea of change in attitudes. . . .

—From "The Harried Quest for a Leisure Class: Can the Japanese Learn to Enjoy Life?" by Alan Freeman, *World Press Review*, September 1993.

1. What evidence of bias do you find in this argument?
2. What language in the excerpt reflects emotion or generalizations?
3. What conclusions might you draw about Japanese workers and their work ethic from these excerpts?

Individual Activity

The North American Free Trade Agreement (NAFTA) has been highly controversial. Keeping in mind what you know about tariffs and international trade, where do you stand on this issue? Outline three arguments in support of your position.

Cooperative Learning Activity

Working in groups of four, have each group choose one familiar item that is imported in the United States. Collect information about that item, including where it comes from and how much it costs. Learn why the country produces this item and what it imports from the United States. Compare your information with the rest of the class's.

Writing About Economics

THE PERSUASIVE STYLE

In the **Journal Writing** activity on page 447, you were asked to log items you use daily and note whether each is domestically produced or foreign-made. Using the persuasive writing style discussed on page 554, write an editorial giving your opinion on international trade. Present evidence supporting your position.

The communist economy of China has recently begun to experiment with capitalism.

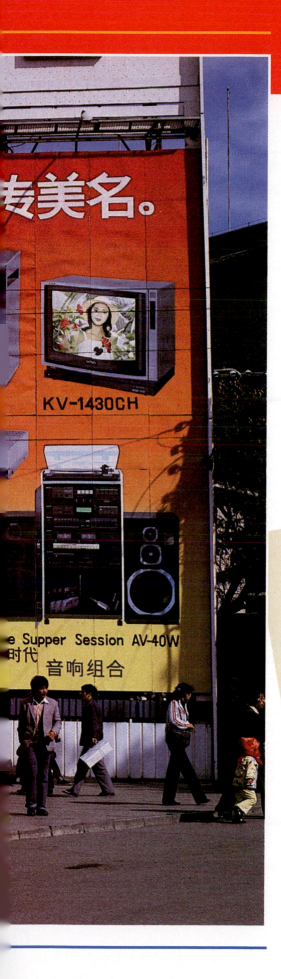

CHAPTER 19

Comparative Economic Systems

SECTION 1
The Spectrum of Economic Systems

SECTION 2
The Rise and Fall of Communism

SECTION 3
The Transition to Capitalism

SECTION 4
The Various Faces of Capitalism

CHAPTER PREVIEW

People to Know

- Karl Marx
- Statistician

Applying Economic Concepts to Your Life

Capitalism Have you ever used your lawn mower to cut someone else's yard, watched the neighbor's child, or organized a group for a car wash? The freedom to use your own tools and labor in pursuit of profits is one of the main features of capitalism. Capitalism is more than an ideology. It is the way we live and the way the world is headed.

Journal Writing

For one week, summarize in your journal news articles you read about events in eastern Europe and the Commonwealth of Independent States, and other former Soviet bloc nations. Focus on articles that relate to those regions working to convert from a command economy to a market economy.

Section Preview

Objectives

After studying this section, you will be able to:

1. **Explain** the advantages and disadvantages of capitalism.
2. **Describe** the differences between socialism, capitalism, and communism.
3. **Compare** the features of communism to other types of economic systems.

Key Terms

socialism, communism

Applying Economic Concepts

Surplus Value Have you ever felt exploited because you thought you were paid less than the value of your labor? If so, you have something in common with Karl Marx, who founded communism and introduced the concept of *surplus value* that is extracted from labor.

To deal with the fundamental problem of scarcity, three types of economic systems exist—traditional, market, and command. Command economies often have a communist form of government. Countries with market economies are called capitalist nations, and socialist countries often have a combination of both command and market economies.

The three forms of organization—communism, socialism, and capitalism—are shown in **Figure 19.1**. At the far left is communism, in which a strong central government influences almost every economic decision. At the far right is capitalism, in which government has a limited role. As one moves from left to right along the spectrum, both the ownership of resources and the degree of government involvement in the operation of the economy change. No fine line separates communism, socialism, and capitalism. They appear on the spectrum as having a greater or lesser degree of government involvement and private ownership of resources.

Capitalism

Under capitalism, the means of production are privately owned. Supply and demand determines prices, and businesses are free to direct resources into activities that promise the greatest profits.

Advantages of Capitalism

The main advantage of capitalism is efficiency. If there are many buyers and sellers, if resources are reasonably mobile, and if buyers and sellers are reasonably well-informed, then resources will be directed to their most profitable and efficient use. **1**

This efficiency is a result of individual freedom and the operation of the price system. Individuals have the freedom to purchase the goods and services that best satisfy their preferences. Producers have the freedom to direct productive resources into activities that consumers demand most. Prices serve as signals to both consumers and producers.

Capitalism has the flexibility to accommodate change. When consumer preferences change, or when the price of resources changes, signals are sent through the price system and everyone adjusts accordingly. Capitalism has evolved and adapted into a system capable of answering the basic WHAT, HOW, and FOR WHOM questions in a decentralized manner.

Disadvantages of Capitalism

Capitalism has a few weaknesses. Although it is efficient in satisfying the demands of consumers, it does not always satisfy everyone's needs.

Figure 19.1
The Spectrum of Economic Systems

The spectrum of economic systems runs from communism on the left to capitalism on the right. The distinguishing feature is the ownership of the factors of production and the role of government in deciding WHAT, HOW, and FOR WHOM to produce. Since the collapse of the Soviet Union, many countries have shifted more toward capitalism. **What reasons are given for the collapse of the Soviet Union?**

	COMMUNISM	SOCIALISM	CAPITALISM
	Directed by Command		Directed by the Free Market
Ownership of Resources	All productive resources are government owned and operated.	Basic productive resources are government owned and operated; the rest are privately owned and operated.	Productive resources are privately owned and operated.
Allocation of Resources	Centralized planning directs all resources.	Government plans ways to allocate resources in key industries.	Capital for production is obtained through the lure of profits in the market.
Role of Government	Government makes all economic decisions.	Government directs the completion of its economic plans in key industries.	Government may promote competition and provide public goods.

At a collective level, capitalism ignores the production of many public goods such as roads, public schools, a system of justice, and national defense. The market produces private goods and services—items that can be withheld if people refuse to pay for them. At an individual level, capitalism produces only for those who have demand, which means the ability and willingness to pay. A system of pure capitalism would ignore poor people, the unemployed, and less productive members of society. **2**

Pure capitalism can also be unstable, as illustrated by the Great Depression. Life under capitalism can be harsh for some people unless the system has been modified by adding safety nets in the form of unemployment insurance, Social Security, and other entitlement programs. ☑

Socialism

Under **socialism**, many of the basic productive resources are government owned and operated, with prices playing a major role in the allocation of resources. Most socialist societies are democracies in which elected officials and, ultimately, the people direct the allocation of resources in key industries.

QUICK CHECK

Checking Understanding

1. What is the main advantage of capitalism?
2. What people does pure capitalism tend to ignore?

Applying Economic Concepts

☑ **Capitalism** Pure capitalism does not exist in the world today. Most countries that are essentially capitalist have some government regulation, making them mixed or modified free enterprise economies.

Advantages of Socialism

Socialism addresses the FOR WHOM question directly. Those who are not fortunate or productive enough to earn a competitive income still share in the benefits of society. These benefits may include free education, health care, welfare, access to the arts and cultural events, and even guaranteed jobs in government-owned industries.

Although the government owns the majority of productive resources in a socialist society, people use their electoral power to influence many of the HOW, WHAT, and FOR WHOM questions. Those who might have been left on the fringes of a capitalist society—the unemployed and the homeless—can benefit more fully from the activities of a socialist society.

Disadvantages of Socialism

Socialism is normally less efficient than capitalism. If workers receive government guarantees of jobs, more workers will be hired than are really necessary, driving up the cost of production.

The price system still plays a vital role, but its efficiency is reduced when the government substitutes its judgment for the discipline of the market. Finally, special interests often become entrenched and have a political influence far in excess of their numbers. When this happens, decisions over WHAT, HOW, and FOR WHOM to produce tend to be waged at the ballot box rather than in the marketplace.

Communism

Under pure **communism**, which is both a political and an economic framework, all property is collectively owned, and labor is organized for the common advantage of the community. Because private property does not exist, the state owns all economic goods, including factories and other means of production.

Theoretically, communism is a selfless society where everyone works to the best of their abilities and consumes according to their needs. Goods and services have no prices, eliminating the need for wages, rents, interest rates, or profits. Theoretical communism has no social classes and no need for a central government authority.

To date, no modern country has achieved the ideal of pure communism. Countries such as China and the former Soviet Union instead developed rigid command-type economies where the state—usually represented by a single authoritarian party—claimed the ideal of pure communism as its eventual goal. The advantages and disadvantages listed below relate to the realities of communism as found in these countries, not to the theoretical ideal.

Advantages of Communism

One of the main advantages of communism, from the worker's point of view, is security. The state directs workers into their jobs, and workers are not fired or dismissed as they could be in other societies.

The state also provides a broad range of public goods such as health care, education, and a military defense system. Because of the guarantee of a steady job, workers seldom face job uncertainty.

Disadvantages of Communism

The disadvantages of communism are numerous. First, individual freedom is lost. People have little or no say in their jobs and are not free to move elsewhere if they are dissatisfied. The bureaucracy determines

DID YOU KNOW?

How Many Statisticians Does It Take?

Predicting the economy is not only more difficult than predicting the weather but sometimes less reliable. Official statistics often are inaccurate. Governments struggle to improve the situation, but hiring more statisticians does not seem to be the solution. A 1993 survey indicated that Germany and France employed the most government statisticians. Canada and Australia ranked highest regarding the accuracy and integrity of their reports, however.

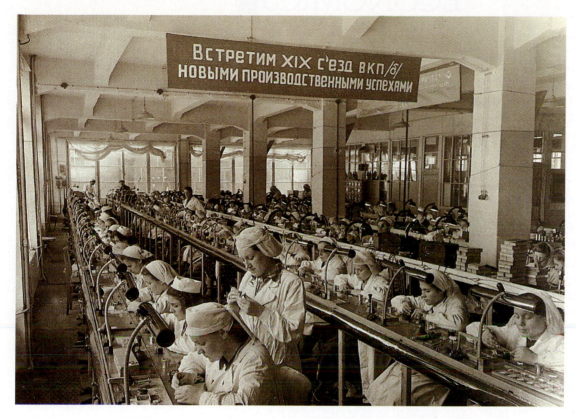

Command Economy
Women workers assemble pocket watches at the 2nd State Watch Factory in Moscow in 1952. **How does a lack of incentives affect job performance?**

pay, and most people receive the same pay regardless of how hard they work.

The lack of incentives can cause frustration on the job, low productivity, and shoddy products. Most communist states place a high priority on military preparedness, resulting in the neglect of consumer goods that are highly prized in other parts of the world.

One of the biggest drawbacks to communism is the inefficiency of centralized planning. The resources needed to execute the planning and the overwhelming obstacles to effective execution are serious problems that communist countries encounter after reaching a certain size. The virtual collapse of the Soviet economy is evidence of these inefficiencies.

SECTION 1 REVIEW

Reviewing Terms and Facts

1. **Define** socialism, communism.
2. **Describe** the main advantages of capitalism.
3. **Describe** one advantage of socialism.
4. **Describe** three disadvantages of communism.

Critical Thinking

5. **Making Comparisons** How does the role of the individual differ under capitalism, socialism, and communism?

Applying Economic Concepts

6. **Surplus Value** According to Karl Marx, employers take advantage of their employees by paying them less than they are worth in order to make a larger profit. Do you think Marx's opinion is valid in the United States today? Why or why not?

KARL MARX

(1818–1883)

Karl Marx was an economic historian, social scientist, and revolutionary. He earned his doctorate in philosophy and history from the University of Berlin, but because of his radical views, he could not get a teaching position.

Throughout the 1840s, he wandered from Cologne to Paris to Brussels. He joined with socialist and radical groups and edited radical newspapers. Persecuted by Prussian and Parisian authorities, Marx fled to London in 1849 where he began a life of exile and, eventually, died in poverty.

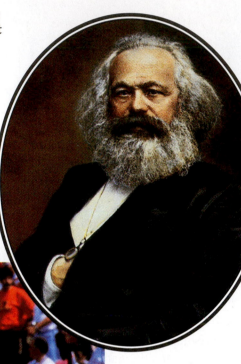

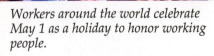

Workers around the world celebrate May 1 as a holiday to honor working people.

THE COMMUNIST MANIFESTO Marx is best known for *The Communist Manifesto*, published in 1848, and *Das Kapital*, the first volume of which was published in 1867. In these works, he argues that all history has been a class struggle. In each era, one class was pitted against another: master against slave, lord against serf, capitalist against worker—the haves against the have-nots.

Marx divided the society of his day into the *proletariat*—people who must work for a living because they have no means of production of their own—and capitalists or *bourgeoisie*—people who own land and capital and hire labor.

LABOR EXPLOITATION Marx argued that labor was exploited in a capitalist society. Marx gave the name *surplus value* to the difference between the wage paid and the market value of the worker's output. He believed this difference became the capitalist's profit.

In Marx's view, the recurring cycles of prosperity and depression were capitalism's greatest defect. With each recurring cycle, workers would suffer more than before, while money and power would fall into the hands of the capitalists. Hostilities would build between the working class and the capitalists until the oppressed workers would rise up in a violent revolution. During the transition, the proletariat would have to depend on its political power through a strong government.

THEORETICAL COMMUNISM After everyone became equal, however, no single class would have power over another. Government no longer would be needed and could be eliminated. In this ideal state of communism, everyone would produce to the best of their abilities, and everyone would consume to the extent of their needs.

Examining the Profile

1. **Analyzing Information** According to Marx, through what stages must society go before it can reach the ideal state of communism?

2. **For Further Research** Find out how the former Soviet Union adapted Marx's philosophies to the Soviet economy.

The Rise and Fall of Communism

Section Preview

Objectives

After studying this section, you will be able to:

1. **Explain** the rise of the Soviet economy under Lenin and Stalin.
2. **Describe** the complexities of a centrally planned economy.
3. **Understand** the forces that brought about the collapse of communism as an economic system.

Key Terms

Five-Year Plan, collectivization, Gosplan, state farm, collective farm, piecework, storming, perestroika

Applying Economic Concepts

Perestroika Have you ever thought that some aspects of the economy should be changed from top to bottom? Perhaps health care or welfare comes to mind. If so, then you believe in *perestroika*, which is the Russian term for "restructuring."

In the absence of pure communism, the former Soviet Union is the most frequently cited example of a communist economic system. The early Soviet economy showed the main advantage of a command system—that it can mobilize resources and change direction in a short period of time. The sudden disintegration of the Soviet economy in the late 1980s, however, demonstrates the weaknesses of communism.

The Economy Under Lenin and Stalin

In 1917 a revolutionary named Vladimir Ilyich Ulyanov, or Lenin, overthrew the government of Russia. In its place, he set up a communist government. Lenin was a strong believer in theoretical communism, and he quickly took steps to develop a communist society. Large estates were taken from the rich, and the land was divided up and given to the peasants. Lenin also outlawed private property and turned the country's few factories over to the workers.

Forced Industrialization

The workers, however, could not manage the factories. Before long, production fell and the economy began to disintegrate. People lost faith in the money supply, and a system of barter emerged. The government sent armed forces to the farms to confiscate surplus food for the hungry city dwellers and industrial workers. The angry farmers retaliated by reducing their production so there would be no surplus crops.

The government then tried to increase production by assigning workers to the jobs it wanted done. Those who did not obey were sent to prison. Agricultural and industrial production fell even further, and internal strife spread throughout the country.

By 1921, when the situation was at its worst, Lenin introduced his New Economic Policy (NEP) to reintroduce some capitalist methods. Peasants now could lease land and hire labor, and small, privately owned businesses could operate. Many of the *kulaks*, or most prosperous peasants, fared well under the NEP.

Central Planning Under Stalin

By 1927, many changes had taken place. Russia had become the Soviet Union, and the country was under Communist party control. Lenin had died, and Joseph Stalin was the new leader. Stalin feared war with the western democracies and wanted to transform the Soviet economy from an agricultural to an industrial one.

Lenin *In November 1917, Bolshevik party leader Lenin seized control of the Russian government.* **What did Lenin's NEP reintroduce?**

To accomplish this goal, he canceled the NEP and, in 1928, introduced the government's first **Five-Year Plan**—a comprehensive, centralized economic plan designed to achieve rapid industrialization. The plan announced quotas for all industries to fulfill. By 1933, industry was to increase its output 250 percent and agriculture its output 150 percent. 1

Collective Agriculture

Under Stalin's leadership, the process of **collectivization**—the forced common ownership of all agricultural, industrial, and trading enterprises—began. Not surprisingly, many people who prospered under the NEP opposed the reforms. Peasants even destroyed their livestock and sabotaged their equipment rather than turn their property over to the collective farms.

Stalin's retaliation was brutal. Millions of people were killed or imprisoned. Ukrainian grain stores were seized in the winter of 1932, causing the starvation

of more than 5 million peasants. The suffering in the cities was nearly as harsh. Workers were forced into employment in heavy industry, strikes were forbidden, and the standard of living deteriorated drastically.

Transformation to Industry

Industry fared better than agriculture. Industry grew so fast that many new factories stood idle. New workers could not be trained quickly enough, and unskilled labor ruined much of the usable factory equipment.

Although the first Five-Year Plan did not achieve all of its goals, the government continued with more planning. The second plan proved more successful than the first. World War II interrupted the third plan, and the fourth was devoted largely to rebuilding those industries destroyed during the war. The plans that followed concentrated heavily on defense industries, space exploration, and some consumer goods.

The Soviet Economy After Stalin

Stalin's brutal regime ended in 1953. By then the Soviet economy had successfully completed its transition from a backward agrarian economy to a major industrial power. The Soviet government and its comprehensive system of planning dominated the Soviet economy, but the real force was the ruling Communist party. It decided on economic policy, did the actual planning, and put the plans into effect.

Complexities of Central Planning

In the Soviet economy, the central planning authority, or **Gosplan**, devised the Five-Year Plans and broke them down into one-year periods for implementation. As the Soviet economy grew, this process became increasingly complex.

Consider the difficulties in a single industry such as shoes. First, the planners have to decide how many shoes should be produced in any given year. This amount would depend on the population and the number of pairs that each person, on average, would need. The planners would then have to decide how many pairs to make of each style, including colors, sizes, and widths.

Next, the various sizes, grades, and amounts of leather, dye, metal eyelets, thread, glue, and other materials needed to produce the shoes must be estimated. After the central planners developed this data, individual factories were given monthly and annual quotas. A factory that produced thread would be told how much thread of every diameter and color to produce for use in other industries.

Similar decisions had to be made for all industries, including clothing, farm implements, stationery, and military goods. The planners detailed everything that would be needed in the economy right down to nails and paper clips. Even these minor items required the planners to make estimates of iron ore, coal, coke, blast furnaces, mining equipment, and even trains and ore cars.

To ensure the growth of the economy from one year to the next, all the planners had to do—or so they thought—was to increase the quotas given to the factories. In short, the central planners determined almost everything beforehand. Plant managers and workers had almost no say in how things were to be done. 2

Agriculture

The situation was similar in agriculture, where food was raised on state, collective, and peasant farms. The state owned and operated the **state farms**. Workers on the state farms were paid for the number of items they produced. All output was turned over to the government at set prices.

Peasant families worked **collective farms**, or small farms collected into a single unit for joint operation. The land, buildings, tools, livestock, and machines belonged to the government, which bought a certain amount of produce per acre. Peasant families were allowed to keep their homes and household goods, a few cattle, and a small plot of land for themselves.

The agricultural sector was one of the major problems for the Soviet economy. One reason was that many of the planners were political appointees who did not understand the industry they supervised. Alexander Solzhenitsyn, Soviet dissident and author of *The Gulag Archipelago*, recounted the story of one bureaucrat who ordered that the crops be planted by broadcasting the seed on top of the late spring snows. The theory was that the snow would melt and nourish the seed at the same time. Instead, birds ate some of the grain. The rest mildewed. When the snows melted, the provinces were out of seed and the ensuing crop was a disaster.

Despite its efforts, the government was not able to make agriculture as efficient as that of many capitalist countries. In the mid-1980s, before the collapse of the Soviet Union, nearly 25 percent of the workforce was in agriculture. In the United States at the time, only 3 percent of the workforce was in agriculture.

The Collapse of the Soviet Economy

The Soviet Union made considerable progress with industrialization, but it never caught up to the United States. Despite its larger population and land area, the Soviet Union's GNP never exceeded two-thirds of that of the United States. The Soviet Union lagged much further behind when measuring such items as automobiles, telephones, televisions, and other consumer goods. A number of factors that could not be overcome eventually led to the collapse of the Soviet economy.

Lack of Effective Incentives

To offset low morale in the factories, a number of incentive programs were attempted. One involved

Checking Understanding

1. What was the purpose of the Five-Year Plan?
2. What did planners think they had to do to ensure economic growth?

Applying Economic Concepts

 Communism Stalin established one of the most brutal dictatorships in history. He demanded complete obedience and used terror to achieve it. People accused of disloyalty were either shot or sent to labor camps in Siberia.

the use of **piecework**, meaning that workers are paid for each piece of output they produce rather than for the number of hours they work.

Although this system may seem like a good idea, piecework quotas often were set at unrealistically high levels. This led to **storming**, where workers kept a slow pace until the last week of the month, and then sped up just enough to fill the quota. The rush at the end often affected the quality of the products. Because of storming, knowledgeable Soviet shoppers often avoided buying goods made at the end of the month.

Other incentives included patriotic and emotional appeals. Workers who had outstanding records or did something special were awarded hero medals, such as the Order of Lenin and the Hero of Social Labor. Some of these medals brought rewards such as free public housing or vacations.

Yet another approach to incentives was a wage system based on job performance, with skilled and more productive workers receiving higher pay. While this incentive is used extensively in capitalist societies, however, it was never used widely in the former Soviet economy.

Production Quotas

As with incentives, quotas also failed at the factory level. During the 1950s, the Soviet economy had a reputation for producing some of the world's poorest consumer and industrial goods. Shoe factories, for example, were given quotas in terms of millions of pairs of shoes. Because small shoes could be made fastest, more were made than were needed. When the quotas were changed to measure production in the amount of shoe leather consumed, the result was shoes with some of the thickest soles in the world.

Production of Consumer Goods

Another major problem was the inadequate supply of consumer goods. After World War II, the Soviet people were asked to make sacrifices so their children might have a better life. Many willingly did so.

In the 1970s and 1980s, those children were adults. When they were asked to make sacrifices so their children could have a better life, they were not as willing as their parents had been. The new generation had not suffered from the ravages of war. In addition, they

were more aware of the standards of living in other parts of the world. As a result, they were impatient for more consumer goods.

Perestroika

When Mikhail Gorbachev assumed power in 1985, the Soviet economy was weaker than anyone imagined. The main cause was the burden imposed by centralized planning. The economy had become too complex and too large to be managed in the traditional manner.

Plant managers were under increasing pressure to meet or exceed quotas. Glitches in planning, however, were creating shortages and other problems that made life difficult for the plant managers. To facilitate the process, "fixers" called *tolkachi* were employed to resolve shortages or dispose of excess inventories. The tolkachi soon became indispensable to producers who wanted to fulfill their quotas. At the same time, they also caused problems for other plants whenever they rerouted a shipment or otherwise interrupted the master plan of the central planners.

Accordingly, Gorbachev introduced a policy of **perestroika**, the fundamental restructuring of the

Perestroika *Mikhail Gorbachev did more than any other person to end the cold war and lift the iron curtain from Europe. He was unsuccessful, however, in saving the former Soviet Union's faltering economy. Here, Gorbachev is shown at the New York Stock Exchange.* **What was perestroika?**

economy and government. Under the restructuring, Five-Year Plans were retained, but the various ministries of production were to be converted to efficient, state-owned enterprises that would compete in a market economy. Plant managers were given more freedom to buy and sell in pursuit of profits, and small business was encouraged.

Perestroika represented a halfway point between a market economy and centralized planning. Gorbachev, however, did not remain in power long enough to see his plans realized. Whether perestroika would have worked is a matter of conjecture. Those in industry who opposed Gorbachev's reforms allowed shortages and other problems to persist, and then used these problems as proof that the reforms were failing. Gorbachev's successor, Boris Yeltsin, faced similar opposition. Ultimately, the collapse of the economy, the collapse of the political leadership, and the stresses of ethnic diversity and unrest combined to cause the downfall of the Soviet Union.

SECTION 2
REVIEW

Reviewing Terms and Facts

1. **Define** Five-Year Plan, collectivization, Gosplan, state farm, collective farm, piecework, storming, perestroika.
2. **Explain** why Stalin wanted forced industrialization.
3. **Identify** several complexities of central planning.
4. **Describe** how central planning contributed to the breakdown of the Soviet economy.

Critical Thinking

5. **Making Predictions** Based upon recent changes, is the former Soviet Union moving toward capitalism or away from capitalism? Give evidence to support your conclusions.

Applying Economic Concepts

6. **Perestroika** Since the mid-1980s, the former Soviet Union has undergone tremendous changes, some of which led to hyperinflation. Why would this hyperinflation hinder the movement toward capitalism?

Identifying Assumptions

A familiar television commercial claims that you will become more popular if you use breath mints. The message is based on two assumptions: 1) that most people want to become more popular; 2) that popularity is linked to fresh breath.

Explanation

An *assumption* is an idea believed to be true but not necessarily supported by facts. You need to be able to identify assumptions to determine the validity of statements or arguments.

To identify assumptions in written material, use the following steps:
- Read the information carefully.
- Identify the writer's point of view.
- Identify the stated and unstated assumptions underlying the writer's views.
- Determine whether the writer's conclusions or claims are based on assumptions that are supported by facts.

Today it is inconceivable, unless war intervenes, that any western democratic government would abandon capitalism as an act of policy. . . . The past 150 years of material advance in the West has shown beyond doubt that social change is tightly linked to economic growth. . . . Yet throughout the period, people have feared change as much as they have wanted growth.

. . . governments . . . ought to keep two broad choices in mind. One, in effect, is to give way to the pressures that will tend to impede the market system—[i.e.], to [favor] more trade protection, help for declining industries, an ever-expanding welfare state. . . .

The alternative is to continue the work of the 1980s . . . to extend the scope of the market. This means, among other things, freer trade; policies to protect workers unlucky enough to be in declining industries, rather than policies to save their jobs; and a welfare state that helps the poor, not the middle class. This may be politically impossible: capitalism is held in low esteem in the countries it made rich. It is, nonetheless, the pro-change, pro-growth, choice.

—Clive Crook, "The Future of Capitalism" from *The Economist*, Sept. 11, 1993.

Practice

Read the excerpts on this page from an article about the future of capitalism. Then answer the questions that follow.
1. What assumption does the author make about the future of capitalism?
2. According to the author, what kind of change is linked to economic growth?
3. What government policies does the author assume will promote the growth of capitalism?
4. What is the basis for the author's assumption that extending capitalism may be politically impossible?
5. Do you think the author's assumptions are supported by fact? Why or why not?

Additional Practice

For further practice in identifying assumptions, complete the Reinforcing Skills in the Chapter 19 Review on page 495.

The Transition to Capitalism

Section Preview

Objectives

After studying this section, you will be able to:

1. **List** four problems encountered when an economy makes the transition to capitalism.

2. **Recognize** the major countries and regions that are making the transition to capitalism.

Key Terms

privatization, Solidarity, black market, Great Leap Forward

Applying Economic Concepts

Inflation Have you ever noticed that the prices of goods and services keep rising? Under capitalism, supply and demand interact to set prices, and moderate *inflation* is to be expected. In eastern Europe and the former Soviet Union, however, the move from a command economy to a market economy has resulted in hyper-inflation.

Historically, communism and capitalism have been viewed as two opposing political and economic structures. The collapse of communism, however, does not mean that the transition to capitalism will be smooth, or that it will be made at all. An examination of the problems will show why.

Problems of Transition

An economy will face several major problems when and if it makes the transition to capitalism. These problems are discussed below.

Privatization

The primary feature of capitalism is private property—especially capital, which is sometimes referred to as the means of production. Because most communist governments owned the means of production, a way had to be found to convert state-owned factories to private ownership, a process known as **privatization.**

In Poland, Hungary, and the Czech Republic, this transition was accomplished using vouchers. Vouchers were certificates either given to people or sold at very low prices, depending on the country. As the vouchers were distributed, the government drew up a list of companies to be privatized and then orga-

nized as a corporation. The corporate shares were auctioned, and people would bid for the shares using their vouchers for payment. As people exchanged their vouchers for shares, ownership of the previously state-owned enterprises transferred to private hands.

In other cases, the transition governments simply sold state-owned companies to foreign corporations. The government then used the funds to pay other bills or make other purchases. These transactions bypassed the citizens and transferred ownership to foreign investors.

Loss of Political Power

Under communism, the Communist party was the ruling class. The transition to capitalism stripped this group of its political power and transferred this power to the new class of entrepreneurs and capitalists.

In countries where the Communists were literally thrown out—as in Poland, Czechoslovakia, and Hungary—the Communist leaders lost their power before industry was privatized. In these countries, the voucher system worked reasonably well.

In other countries, former Communist leaders grabbed a large share of vouchers, and thus a large portion of ownership in many privatized companies. In the most blatant cases, some of which occurred in

At midnight on November 9, 1989, East German officials opened the infamous Berlin Wall that divided East and West Berlin for 28 years. **What problems face former communist countries as they make the transition to capitalism?**

Russia following the collapse of the Soviet Union, the ownership of companies was simply transferred to politicians who were influential during the transition period. Former political leaders converted their political power to economic power in the form of resource ownership.

The Discipline of Capitalism

Many countries that desire a capitalist structure have focused on the benefits to be obtained, but not the costs. The costs can hinder or even discourage a country from making the transition.

The disadvantages of capitalism, made apparent during the Great Depression, included instability, unemployment, and social unrest. At that time, the United States did not have the fiscal policies, the automatic stabilizers, and the social welfare nets needed to lessen the devastation of the Depression. Now that such assistance exists, most economists agree that another Great Depression will never occur in the United States. 1

The same cannot be said for the nations in transition. They have not yet developed the automatic stabilizers and the social welfare nets that cushion the instabilities of capitalism. During the transition phase, nations will most likely experience the instabilities of early capitalism—the unemployment, the inflation, and the lost production—long before they experience the benefits. ✅

Responding to New Incentives

Finally, countries that make the transition to capitalism have to learn to live with a whole new set of incentives. The government in the former Soviet Union, for example, told its people what to do for decades. Now people must learn how to make decisions on their own. They must learn how to take the initiative, how to interpret prices, and how to fend for themselves because the government no longer guarantees their jobs nor keeps prices artificially low.

These adjustments will be enormous, perhaps even prohibitive, for some people. Many will even long for the past when life was simpler. These people may not want to go through the discipline of capitalism. Attitudes like these will be a major obstacle to the transition.

Countries and Regions in Transition

Despite the transitional problems, the rise of capitalism is one of the most remarkable phenomena of the late twentieth century. Today, nations and regions all over the globe are making the transition.

Russia

Privatization in Russia is well underway, despite the sometimes uncertain nature of the political leadership. In July 1992, President Boris Yeltsin signed a decree stating that state enterprises had to be reorganized as stock corporations by the end of the year. By the end of 1993, Russia planned to privatize more than 300 state enterprises.

Smaller businesses were being privatized at a rapid rate. By 1993 nearly one-half of the shops and one-third of the restaurants in St. Petersburg were in private hands. The percentages were slightly lower in Moscow. In some of the outlying regions, however, privatization proceeded at an even faster rate.

Several voucher plans have been used to privatize, with some of the plans giving the state the majority of shares. Even so, private ownership of the means of production is becoming a reality in the country that for so long preached the evils of private ownership.

Eastern Europe

The nations of eastern Europe, especially those that were unwilling members of the Soviet bloc, are the newest nations to embrace capitalism. The struggle for freedom began in Poland with **Solidarity**, the independent and sometimes illegal union that Lech Walesa established in 1980. Solidarity was influential in securing a number of political freedoms in Poland.

Figure 19.2
New and Emerging Stock Markets

Country	Number of Listed Companies (As of 6/93)	Country	Number of Listed Companies (As of 6/93)
Argentina	176	Morocco	62[1]
Brazil	559	Nigeria	163
Chile	258	Pakistan	652
China	53[1]	Peru	231
Colombia	80	Philippines	173
Egypt	656[1]	Poland	18
Greece	130	Portugal	175
Hong Kong	390	Russia	N.A.
Hungary	25	South Korea	692
India	2,950	Sri Lanka	196
Indonesia	159	Taiwan	271
Israel	477	Thailand	331
Jamaica	50	Turkey	142
Malaysia	390	Venezuela	149
Mexico	188	Zimbabwe	62

[1]As of December 1992

New and emerging stock markets are now found all over the world, and more are still to come. **Why is the corporate form of organization a necessary component of capitalism?**

Source: *The Wall Street Journal*, September 24, 1993.

QUICK CHECK

Checking Understanding

1. What safeguards ensure that the United States will never again face an economic downturn as severe as the Great Depression?

Applying Economic Concepts

☑ **Market Failures** Russia has gone through tough economic times since the collapse of communism. Soaring unemployment and inflation have led some Russians to wish for a return to Soviet rule. Most Russians, however, accept that the transition to capitalism will be difficult.

Communes *Although China has recently begun to experiment with capitalism, many communes still harvest crops, such as this one in Shaanxi Province.* **How has capitalism affected business in China?**

Eventually, the Communist party lost power, and interest in capitalism grew. Political reform slowed privatization plans at first, but capitalism finally appeared to be under way again in the wake of progress by Poland's neighbors. Nearly 8,000 companies were marked for privatization by the mid-1990s.

Hungary is another country well on the way to capitalism. Hungary was often regarded as the most Western of the Eastern bloc countries, and it often had a flourishing **black market**—a market in which entrepreneurs and merchants sold goods illegally. Hungary's experience with markets helped ease the transition to capitalism. By the beginning of 1993, the private sector produced nearly one-half of the country's GNP. (For international comparisons, economists often prefer to use GNP—a measure of income—rather than GDP—a measure of output.)

The Czech Republic is yet another country in transition. By early 1993, more than 40 percent of the economy was in private hands. Progress accelerated after the separation of the Czech and Slovak Republics, a separation based in part on the Slovakian concern about adopting the capitalist ways of the West. The Czechs, who were strongly influenced by the economic success of the former West Germany, are now more able to pursue reforms.

The Baltic states of Estonia, Latvia, and Lithuania show some indications of moving toward capitalism. Some are still developing their political independence, but many people expect the Baltic states to make the transition to capitalism. When that happens, these countries will organize their own stock exchanges and join the list of new and emerging markets that appear in **Figure 19.2**.

Latin America

In the past, many Latin American countries followed a path of economic development that combined socialism and isolationism based on the infant industries argument. Mexico accelerated the move to capitalism and open markets in 1989, as it made plans to restructure its economy for the North American Free Trade Agreement (NAFTA). Under President Salinas de Gortari, the government sold thousands of state-owned companies and cut back on the government bureaucracy.

Chile has also taken major steps to foster the growth of capitalism. It has privatized airlines, telephone services, and utilities. Chile even used the billions deposited in its pension funds to supply capital for new entrepreneurs. As a result, the country exports copper, lumber, fruit, and even software to the rest of the world. Chile's markets include the United States, which imports millions of Popsicle sticks, and Japan, which imports chopsticks.

Argentina has similarly embarked on a crash program to remove government from the everyday business of running the economy. The country has sold oil fields, petrochemical plants, and a number of other formerly state-owned businesses. The Argentinian army was even moved out of barracks in Buenos Aires so that the real estate could be sold to private interests.

China

The People's Republic of China has had a communist economy since 1949. That year, the Chinese Communists, under the leadership of Mao Zedong, gained control of the country. Over the years, China modeled itself after the Soviet Union, adopting a series of Five-Year Plans to manage its growth.

In 1958 the **Great Leap Forward**—the second Five-Year Plan—tried to institute a system of pure communism and an industrial and agricultural revolution almost overnight. Industrialization was pushed and, at the same time, collectivization of agriculture was intensified. Farmers were forced off their land and made to live and work on large, state-owned farms. The Great Leap Forward turned out to be a disaster, however. The agricultural experiment failed, and the economy never came close to achieving the planned degree of industrialization. Even the gains made during the first Five-Year Plan were lost.

Other plans followed, but by the late 1970s, the government decided that the country no longer could follow the growth models of either the Soviet Union or other command-type economies. China and its population were too large, and communication not developed enough for large-scale centralized planning. Industrializing the cities enough to provide jobs for nearly one-fourth of the world's population would be nearly impossible.

More recently, the Chinese have begun to experiment with capitalism. Some private business is allowed, and managers of state-owned enterprises have more authority to make decisions. Although the central planners still set overall production goals, managers can sell their products at competitive prices and hire and fire workers. In addition, small incentives are offered to promote productivity among workers and managers.

China was influenced by the success of other capitalist economies in Asia, including Taiwan, South Korea, Hong Kong, and Singapore. One of China's provinces, the Guangdong Province just north of Hong Kong, copied many of the free-market practices of the region. At one time, Guangdong's capitalism was almost an embarrassment to China, but now it is touted as a free-market success story and a role model for the rest of China.

SECTION 3 REVIEW

Reviewing Terms and Facts

1. **Define** privatization, Solidarity, black market, Great Leap Forward.
2. **List** four problems a country is likely to encounter when converting to capitalism.
3. **Identify** two major countries that are making the transition to capitalism.

Critical Thinking

4. **Formulating Questions** Suppose you are visiting one nation in eastern Europe adopting a market economy. What questions would you ask local officials to determine whether they are successfully moving toward capitalism?

Applying Economic Concepts

5. **Inflation** Assume that your salary is 300 rubles per month. The government-controlled price of bread is 5 rubles, and you buy 5 loaves each month. What percentage of your income do you spend on bread? After the government deregulates prices, bread costs 15 rubles. What percentage of your income goes to buy bread? How does the inflation affect your standard of living?

The Various Faces of Capitalism

Section Preview

Objectives

After studying this section, you will be able to:

1. **Explain** the factors that encouraged economic growth in Japan.
2. **Rank** the "Asian Tigers" according to per capita GNP.
3. **Describe** Sweden's retreat from socialism.

Key Terms

capital-intensive, *keiretsu*

Applying Economic Concepts

Economic Growth Have you ever looked at the labels inside your clothes? If so, you may have noticed that many of them were made in Korea, Taiwan, China, or Hong Kong. Asian economies have experienced explosive *economic growth* recently. They now compete directly with American enterprises.

Capitalism is a force that is sweeping the world. It is also a force that has many different faces. The common element of capitalism is that the factors of production are privately owned and controlled, but there are many variations on this theme.

Japan

Japan, like the United States, has a capitalist economy. Unlike the United States, however, Japan's government is very involved in the day-to-day activities of the private sector.

At the end of World War II, Japan was a devastated country. Today, it is the second largest industrial nation in the world, with a GNP about 60 percent of that of the United States. Between 1980 and 1991, Japan's real growth of output averaged 3.1 percent annually, one of the highest growth rates in the world.

Worker Attitudes

One of the reasons for Japan's success is the workers' intense loyalty to their employers. Many workers join large companies for life. In return, the company supplies such benefits as wedding halls where marriages can be performed, schools, and vacation resorts.

Japanese workers take great pride in the quality of their work. A company's entire workforce often arrives early to take part in group calisthenics and meditation exercises. Workers often sing company songs to boost their spirits. If a worker is behind in a task, others who can help do so. Those who cannot help stay at their stations and clean their work areas, arrange their tools, and prepare for the next day. No one leaves the work floor or goes home until every worker's tasks have been completed. ☑

Capital Investment

Another reason for Japan's success is the ability and willingness of the Japanese to develop new technology. Because of their relatively small population, they have worked to boost productivity by developing industries that are **capital-intensive**. In such industries, a large amount of capital is used for every person employed in manufacturing. Today, the Japanese are recognized as the world leader in the area of industrial robots. As a result, most factories require only a fraction of the workers that similar factories in other countries need. **1**

Most large Japanese firms also belong to a *keiretsu* (ky • reht • soo)—a tightly knit group of firms governed by an external board of directors. The *keiretsu* are often made up of firms that compete with one another. The role of the governing board is to ensure that competition does not get so fierce that individual firms are threatened. A similar agreement in the United States among competing firms would be illegal under our antitrust laws.

Worker Attitudes *Japan's economic success is a result in part of its workers' loyalty and pride in their products.* **What other factors have contributed to Japan's success?**

The Role of Government

Japan has a relatively small public sector. The government has only a modest military capability and is not burdened with welfare spending. As a result, taxes are low, which allows individuals to save their money or spend it on consumer goods.

The Japanese government works closely with businesses to limit foreign competition in the domestic market. The government provides fewer public goods than do most other capitalist societies, but the government is also more closely allied with businesses than in other countries.

A Closed Economy?

Although the Japanese have been successful, their economy is generally closed to the products of foreign producers. When foreign companies tried to sell their goods in Japan, many encountered numerous obstacles ranging from delayed government permission to huge amounts of paperwork.

Delays in getting permission to sell are so common that many businesses have been completely discouraged from exporting to Japan. Some companies found that, while they were waiting for permission, Japanese companies introduced and sold products similar to theirs. Actions such as these have led to accusations that Japan uses discriminatory policies toward foreign-made products.

Until recently, Japan was even reluctant to import rice, a food staple, in order to protect domestic rice producers. As a result, the cost of rice to the Japanese consumer is several times higher than it would be if Japan imported rice from the world markets.

A High Cost of Living

Protectionism in Japan may help certain segments of the economy such as the rice farmers, but it does not help the consumer. Because foreign competitors supply so few goods, products generally are high-priced. Citrus fruits cost about six times more in Japan than they do in the United States. Clothing costs two to three times as much, and even cameras and electronics cost more in Japan than elsewhere. **2**

For years, the Japanese have been making electronic consumer goods and selling them abroad. Recently, Japanese citizens discovered they can purchase their own goods cheaper in Hawaii than they can in their own country. As a result, Japanese cameras, radios, and other electronic equipment are

QUICK CHECK

Checking Understanding

1. What is a capital-intensive industry?
2. How has protectionism harmed Japanese consumers?

Applying Economic Concepts

 Worker Attitudes Some Japanese employers are making efforts to reduce their employees' work hours. Some firms have to halt elevators or shut off the air-conditioning to make sure that employees stick to their official hours.

among the most popular souvenirs Japanese vacationers bring back from their trips abroad.

The current Japanese economy benefits the capitalists. The benefits of economic growth have not trickled down to the Japanese consumer the way they have in other countries.

Reliance on Trade

If Japan wants its growth to continue, it must actively engage in international trade. As an island nation with few natural resources, it must import most of its oil as well as a number of other critical materials. The Japanese are expected to aggressively develop their export markets so they can buy more imports.

Japan's huge trade imbalances with the rest of the world, however, have driven up the value of Japanese currency, the yen. When the value goes too high, the Japanese economy will export fewer cars, cameras, and other consumer products. At the same time, current Japanese policies are keeping low-cost rice, clothing, and other imports out of the country and away from Japanese consumers.

DID YOU KNOW?

China in Charge On July 1, 1997, China will take charge of Hong Kong, thereby ending 150 years of British rule. The countdown for the transfer of Hong Kong began in 1984 when British Prime Minister Margaret Thatcher and Chinese Premier Zhao Ziyang signed the Sino-British Joint Declaration. The document established the principle of "one country, two systems" for Hong Kong, allowing Hong Kong to keep its capitalist economy within the socialist system of China for 50 years. At first, the pending reunification caused hundreds of thousands of people to leave Hong Kong for Canada, Australia, and the United States. Many have returned, however, with the belief that Hong Kong will change China more than China will change Hong Kong.

The Asian Tigers

Three other Asian countries—Singapore, Taiwan, and South Korea—have made striking economic progress during the last 20 years. The British colony of Hong Kong has also experienced explosive growth. Collectively, the four are called the "Asian Tigers." Each has based its growth on capitalism, but each has taken a slightly different path.

Hong Kong

The British colony of Hong Kong is the most progressive and successful of the four. Hong Kong has a population of about 6 million and is recognized as perhaps the freest market economy in the world, with virtually no government interference.

Entrepreneurs in Hong Kong have developed a manufacturing-based economy that uses technology other countries have already developed. Their major industrial products include textiles, clothing, electronic games, telephones, radios, watches, electronic components, and toys.

Producers in Hong Kong are exceptionally efficient, and their manufacturing plants are among the most flexible in the world. Companies that want to bring products to the market as quickly as possible often turn to Hong Kong because producers there can turn a prototype into a finished assembly-line product faster than any other producer.

Hong Kong's embrace of capitalism has resulted in considerable economic growth. Its per capita GNP is nearly 60 percent that of the United States, and more than 35 times greater than that of China. Hong Kong faces an uncertain future, however, because control of the colony will return to China in 1997. China has promised not to interfere with Hong Kong's economic development, but the impact of the transition is difficult to predict.

Singapore

The second Asian Tiger is Singapore, with a per capita GNP almost as large as Hong Kong's. The population in Singapore is slightly more than 3 million, and the approach to economic growth is markedly different from the other Asian Tigers.

More than 1,000 multinationals have been attracted to Singapore with the help of generous tax breaks, government subsidies, and government-sponsored training of employees. Unlike Hong Kong, Singapore has made a determined effort to develop its own technologies through extensive spending on research and development.

The government of Singapore is trying to develop a few select industries, including telecommunications services, software, and biotechnology. The government has spent millions on laboratories, attracting top scientists from all over the world. The biotechnology industry has scored some original successes, one of which includes the transfer of firefly genes—which glow in the dark—to orchids.

Taiwan

The Republic of China, also known as Taiwan, is an island about the size of West Virginia located off the coast of the People's Republic of China. Taiwan's population is about 21 million, and the per capita GNP is approximately one-third that of the United States.

Taiwan's economic development called for the Taiwanese government to intervene in various markets to direct the flow of resources. For example, the government would set artificially high rates on savings accounts to attract deposits from consumers. The savings would then be lent to targeted industries at artificially low rates to stimulate growth. The subsidies to both the savers and the borrowers were expensive,

but they also helped direct an enormous amount of funds into capital formation.

Planning continues to be a feature of the Taiwanese economy in the 1990s. The most recent plan identified 10 industries—including telecommunications, consumer electronics, semiconductors, precision machinery, aerospace, pharmaceuticals, and others—for government-assisted intervention.

Taiwan was one of the early economic powers in Asia, but some people wonder if the centralized planning process will hamper future economic growth. Despite its early start, the per capita GNP in Taiwan has fallen far behind those of Hong Kong and Singapore.

South Korea

South Korea has the smallest per capita GNP of the Asian Tigers at 28 percent of that of the United States. South Korea was devastated by civil war in the early 1950s, however, so it had much more to overcome than did the others.

In the past, a group of technocrats governed Korea with the help of the military. The factors of production were privately owned, but a small number of powerful business families dominated the private economy.

These business families were the main source of campaign funds to politicians. Therefore, politicians often granted them favors, allowing them to develop

Figure 19.3
Capitalism in Asia—The Asian Tigers

Because of the dynamic growth and economic progress made by South Korea, Hong Kong, Singapore, and Taiwan since the end of World War II, they are sometimes called the "Asian Tigers." Some observers have even suggested that the Guangdong Province of mainland China could be added to this list. **How have the Asian Tigers relied on capitalism to spur their economic growth?**

and dominate consumer goods, shipbuilding, steel, and automotive industries. At first, the close-knit relationship between the politicians and the families contributed dramatically to economic growth. Growth slowed somewhat in the 1990s, however, as the political structure became more democratic and feuds arose between the top families and the new politicians. South Korea's further economic growth will depend on whether the private economy adapts to competition and relies less on its relationship with the political sector.

Sweden

Sweden is a mature industrial nation once regarded as the "socialist state that works." The reputation was apt because Sweden provided a broader range of social welfare programs for its citizens than did any other free-world country.

Some of the basic industries were nationalized, but Sweden also had a considerable amount of private enterprise. The country, therefore, was not a model of pure socialism in the traditional sense.

The Welfare State

Many worker benefits were instituted during the 44-year rule of the Socialist party. During this time, wages were high, jobs were easy to find, and unemployment was in the 1 to 3 percent range. The Swedish economy—with its generous maternity, education, disability, and old-age benefits—was thought to be the model of European socialism.

Because government owned some but not all basic industry, it relied on steep taxes to pay for the benefits. In the mid-1980s, tax receipts were about 50 percent of GNP. In some cases, additional income that Swedish citizens earned was taxed at an 80 percent rate, meaning that a person who earned an additional $100 would keep only $20. Some individuals left the country to avoid high taxes. When tennis star Bjorn Borg was at the peak of his career, he resided outside of Sweden to avoid paying high taxes.

Many others devised ways to avoid paying taxes. Some craft workers resorted to barter. A carpenter who built some cabinets for an auto mechanic, for example, might be paid with repair work on the family car.

Restructuring

Eventually, the heavy tax burden and the additional costs of the welfare state began to cut into Sweden's economic growth. Growing inflation added to the problems, as did a massive government deficit. Growing discontent with conditions finally led to the defeat of the Socialist party in 1976.

A free-market government was elected in 1991, and by 1993, the public sector had been reduced to one-third of the jobs in the economy. Taxes on individuals and corporations had likewise been cut to where they were among the lowest in Europe. Many government-owned businesses had been privatized, and more are scheduled to be converted.

SECTION 4 REVIEW

Reviewing Terms and Facts

1. **Define** capital-intensive, *keiretsu*.
2. **Describe** how worker attitudes in Japan contribute to economic growth.
3. **State** which "Asian Tiger" faces the most uncertain future. Give reasons for your choice.

4. **Explain** how Sweden's retreat from socialism affected the nation's tax rates.

Critical Thinking

5. **Making Predictions** How might continued economic growth in Asia affect industries in the United States?

Applying Economic Concepts

6. **Economic Growth** How has Sweden's transition from socialism to capitalism helped promote economic growth?

Comparative Economic Systems

Vocabulary

The following terms are defined in Chapter 19:

SECTION ONE
- socialism (p. 473)
- communism (p. 474)

SECTION TWO
- Five-Year Plan (p. 478)
- collectivization (p. 478)
- Gosplan (p. 478)
- state farm (p. 479)
- collective farm (p. 479)
- piecework (p. 480)
- storming (p. 480)

- perestroika (p. 480)

SECTION THREE
- privatization (p. 483)
- Solidarity (p. 485)
- black market (p. 486)
- Great Leap Forward (p. 487)

SECTION FOUR
- capital-intensive (p. 488)
- keiretsu (p. 488)

Section 1

The Spectrum of Economic Systems (pages 472–475)

The world's economic systems can be shown on a spectrum ranging from those systems with almost total government control to those that include very little government regulation. Under capitalism, individuals own the means of production, and the interaction of supply and demand determines prices. Under **socialism,** the government owns many of the means of production, and elected officials allocate and manage these resources. In contrast, the government owns all means of production under pure **communism.**

Reviewing the Main Idea

How does the ownership of resources differ under capitalism, socialism, and communism?

Section 2

The Rise and Fall of Communism (pages 477–481)

In 1917 a revolution overthrew the government of Russia and instituted a communist system. By 1927, the country was under Communist party control and had changed its name to the Soviet Union. Under a series of **Five-Year Plans,** Communist leaders tried to achieve rapid industrialization. The plans included the **collectivization** of agriculture and the transformation of industry—both of which were under complete government control. **Gosplan,** the central planning authority, determined every aspect of industrial and agricultural production. Despite efforts to increase production, including **piecework** and quotas, the command economy proved a miserable failure. By the early 1990s, the Soviet economic system had collapsed.

Reviewing the Main Idea

How did the Communists try to boost agricultural and industrial development?

Section 3

The Transition to Capitalism (pages 483–487)

The former communist systems face several challenges as they try to move toward capitalism. These challenges include **privatization** of capital resources, the shift in political power from Communists to elected officials, and the new incentives of a capitalist economy. Russia and eastern Europe have had varying amounts of success in this shift toward capitalism. At the same time, other economic systems throughout the world have been experimenting with the move toward a capitalist economy.

Reviewing the Main Idea

What challenges face nations as they try to institute a capitalist system?

Section 4

The Various Faces of Capitalism (pages 488–492)

Since World War II, many nations have moved toward capitalism, although its exact form varies from country to country. Japan, long a capitalist system, achieved phenomenal economic growth with a combination of worker loyalty and new technology. The economies of the "Asian Tigers"—Singapore, Taiwan, Hong Kong, and South Korea—also grew. At the same time, Sweden moved away from socialism.

Reviewing the Main Idea

What factors helped Japan's economy to grow?

Reviewing Key Terms

Write the key term that best completes the following sentences.

a. state farm
b. socialism
c. black market
d. capital-intensive
e. privatization
f. Five-Year Plan
g. collective farm
h. communism
i. perestroika
j. storming

1. In most former communist countries, state-owned enterprises are being converted to private ownership, a process known as —— .
2. To direct production, Soviet planners adopted a —— .
3. Under —— the government owns all the means of production.
4. In the Soviet agricultural system, the state owned and operated each —— .
5. Soviet leader Mikhail Gorbachev introduced a policy of —— , the fundamental restructuring of the economy and government.
6. In the Soviet Union, groups of peasant families, each of which was allowed to keep its home and household goods, a few cattle, and a small plot of land, worked each —— .
7. Most nations of Eastern Europe had a flourishing —— where entrepreneurs and merchants sold goods illegally.
8. Under —— , the government owns many, but not all, the basic productive resources.
9. In —— industries, a large amount of capital is used for every person employed in manufacturing.
10. Piecework quotas often led to —— , in which workers worked slowly until the last week of the month and then sped up just enough to get the quota filled.

Reviewing the Facts

SECTION 1 *(pages 472–475)*
1. **Explain** the role of the government in a capitalist economic system.
2. **Describe** how the people in a socialist economy help allocate the use of resources.
3. **Describe** who answers the basic economic questions in a communist system.

SECTION 2 *(pages 477–481)*
4. **State** what practices the New Economic Policy instituted.
5. **Describe** the problems that central planning caused in the Soviet economy.
6. **Explain** the impact that perestroika had on the Soviet economy.

SECTION 3 *(pages 483–487)*
7. **List** the problems that nations may face as they try to make the transition from communism to capitalism.
8. **Name** the nations that are currently trying to adapt to a market economy and describe the specific problems they are facing in their transition.

SECTION 4 *(pages 488–492)*
9. **Explain** the role the government plays in Japan's economy.
10. **Describe** how the approaches to economic growth differ in the regions of Hong Kong and Singapore.
11. **Trace** Sweden's transition from socialism to capitalism.

Critical Thinking

1. **Evaluating Information** Do you think five-year plans could work in the United States? Why or why not?

2. **Drawing Conclusions** The Communists promised people that their system would lead to workers' paradises throughout the world. By the early 1990s, however, communist systems and their command economies in most countries had collapsed. Why do you think communism was such a failure?

Applying Economic Concepts

1. **Capitalism** Many nations are attempting to switch from communism or socialism to capitalism. Often, the transition has been quite difficult. What suggestions would you make to the leaders of these nations to help ease the transition to capitalism?
2. **Economic Growth** The "Asian Tigers" have experienced rapid economic growth and development. Do you think they can sustain this growth rate? Why or why not?

Reinforcing Skills

IDENTIFYING ASSUMPTIONS

Read the excerpt below, then answer the questions that follow.

America's factories are making more than American people can use; American soil is producing more than they can consume. Fate has written our policy for us; we must get an ever-increasing portion of foreign trade.
— from a speech by Albert Beveridge, U.S. Senator, 1898

1. What assumption does the speaker make about the future of American trade?
2. According to the speaker, what kind of change is linked to economic growth?
3. What is the basis for the speaker's assumption that extending trade may be possible?
4. Do you think the speaker's assumptions are supported by fact? Why or why not?

Individual Activity

Choose one of the nations profiled in this chapter. Go to the library to find information on recent events in the nation's move toward capitalism. Construct a collage of headlines about these developments. Include with the collage a brief assessment of how the nation is working through the transition.

Cooperative Learning Activity

Organize into two groups. One group will represent former communist governments attempting to change to a capitalist system. The other group will represent officials from the United States trying to aid the transition. Each group should meet separately to devise a plan of action. The groups should then meet together to come up with a plan that will ensure a peaceful transition.

Writing About Economics

THE EXPRESSIVE STYLE

In the **Journal Writing** activity on page 471, you were asked to keep track of events in eastern Europe and the former Soviet Union. Using the expressive style of writing discussed on page 554, write a summary paragraph of current developments in either of those regions of the world.

Buyers and sellers engage in voluntary exchange at a market in Peru.

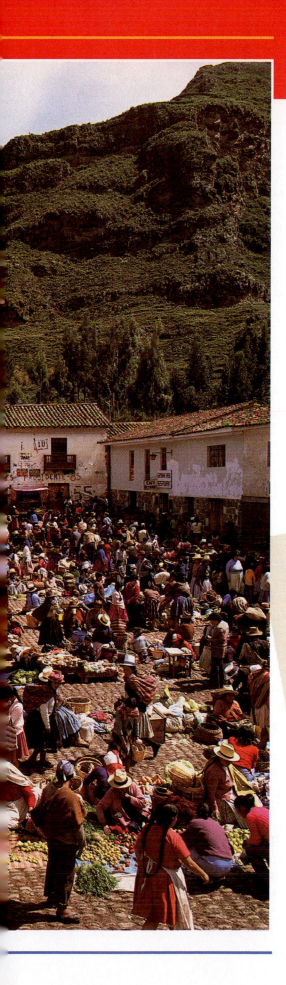

Developing Countries

CHAPTER PREVIEW

People to Know

- Sir Arthur Lewis
- Peace Corps Volunteer

Applying Economic Concepts to Your Life

Per Capita GNP How long would it take you to earn $500? Is that a large sum of money? You may be surprised to learn what percentage of the world population has an annual *per capita GNP* of less than $500.

Journal Writing

For one week, keep a journal of all the economic problems of developing nations that you hear reported in the news. List the countries in one column and their problems in a second column.

Economic Development

Section Preview

Objectives

After studying this section, you will be able to:

1. **State** the concern for the plight of the developing countries.

2. **Identify** the obstacles to economic development.

Key Terms

developing country, crude birthrate, zero population growth, external debt, capital flight

Applying Economic Concepts

Life Expectancy Think about what you want to do in life. How long will it take you to do all you want? If you lived in a developing country, your *life expectancy* would be much shorter than it is right now. Your life might even be half over before you reached the age of 25.

Many people are concerned about the economic condition of **developing countries**—countries whose average per capita GNP is a fraction of that in more industrialized countries. Most developing countries are located in Africa, Asia, and Latin America.

Interest in Economic Development

The international community's concern for the developing countries is humanitarian as well as economic and political. In many ways, developing economies are similar to other economies of the world. The major difference is that their problems are much greater.

Concern for Developing Countries

The first concern is humanitarian. Industrialized countries of the world often believe it is their moral responsibility to help those who have less than they do. Many people in developing countries starve to death or die from diseases related to inadequate diets. Under such conditions, countries enjoying abundance find it difficult not to offer help.

The second concern is economic. Assistance to developing countries helps assure the industrial nations of a stable supply of certain raw materials. Developing countries also provide markets for the products of industrial nations. Developing countries buy about one-third of United States exports. This amount is more than the combined purchases of the Common Market, Japan, and Australia. In the long run, helping developing countries increases international trade.

The third concern is political. Despite the increasing failure of communism, various political ideologies wage a continuing struggle for the allegiance of developing countries. These ideological groups, in turn, struggle against industrial nations to gain more allies and greater political strength.

A gap between industrialized and developing countries has long existed, but never has it been so obvious or important as it is today. The growing difference in incomes has led to greater unrest and social disorder in different parts of the world. Many people in developing countries want some of the abundance enjoyed in industrialized countries. When these people do not achieve what they want as quickly as they would like, the result can be revolution, social upheaval, and even war.

Per Capita GNP

In 1991, 43 countries had per capita GNPs of less than $500. According to **Figure 20.1**, the majority of these countries are in Africa and Asia. The map contrasts the wealth of the industrialized nations and the developing nations, scaling each country to show the size of its GNP relative to other countries. Thus, the United States, which has the largest GNP in the world, is the largest area on the map. Countries with smaller GNPs are scaled accordingly.

The map is also color coded to show countries with similar per capita GNPs. When viewed this way, the contrast is clearly shown between the industrialized economies of North America, western Europe, and Japan, and the developing countries of South America, the Caribbean, Africa, and Asia. The gap between industrialized and developing countries is enormous. In the past few years, it has become even wider because many developing countries have experienced negative rates of growth.

Another reason for the growing gap between industrialized and developing countries is the small size of the output for many countries. Gambia's economic growth of almost 6 percent between 1990 and 1991 added the equivalent of only $20 to its per capita GNP. In comparison, a 1 percent economic growth in the United States for the same year would have added more than $218 to its per capita GNP.

Obstacles to Economic Development

Before examining some of the possible solutions to the plight of developing countries, we need to take a closer look at some common problems.

Population

One major obstacle to economic development is population growth. The populations of most developing countries grow at a rate much faster than those of industrialized countries. One reason for this growth is the high **crude birthrate**—the number of live births per 1,000 people. **Figure 20.2** shows that the countries with the highest birthrates in the world are developing countries, while the lowest birthrates are found in industrialized countries.

In some developing countries, the population is so large that there is barely enough fertile land and other resources to support it. Many less developed countries depend extensively on agriculture, adding to the problem. In these countries, an incentive to have many children exists. Most farms are worked by families, and children can work in the fields at an early age. More children means more workers. In addition, having many children ensures the parents that someone will look after them in their old age.

Another problem for developing countries is increasing life expectancy—the average remaining lifetime in years for persons who reach a certain age. Better education, international aid, and emphasis on health-care facilities help people live longer. A high life expectancy coupled with a high crude birthrate makes it difficult to increase per capita GNP.

Finally, people have different views on what is the proper rate of population growth. Some feel that the earth is too crowded already and that societies should work for **zero population growth** (ZPG)—the condition in which the average number of births and deaths balance so that a population stops growing. Others feel that population growth is a natural event and that efforts to disrupt it are morally and religiously wrong.

Natural Resources

Another obstacle to economic growth is limited natural resources. No country can develop beyond its resource potential. Unproductive land or a harsh climate can limit economic growth. A shortage or lack of natural resources or energy sources needed for industry also hinders growth. Some countries may be fortunate enough to discover a valuable mineral to finance development, but most focus on agriculture.

International agencies, such as the World Bank, fund agricultural projects. Recently, the World Bank has undertaken projects to control the desert locust in East Africa. It also has funded projects to develop cotton, clove, cashew, tobacco, and tea crops in Tanzania and Ghana, as well as to increase the production of millet and sorghum in northern Nigeria.

Education and Technology

Still another obstacle to economic development is a lack of appropriate education and technology. Many developing countries do not have a highly literate population or the high level of technical skills needed to build an industrial society. In addition, most do not have money to train engineers and scientists.

Many developing countries cannot even afford to provide free public education for school-age children. In those that can, not everyone is able to take advantage of it. In many cases, children must work to help feed their families. As a result, much of the population may not have the basic skills needed to continue with higher education when it is offered.

Foreign Debt

A major problem facing nations today is the size of their **external debt**—money borrowed from foreign banks and governments. Some nations have borrowed so much they may never be able to repay loans.

According to most estimates, the total external debt for all developing countries was more than $1 trillion in 1992. Two countries—Mexico and Brazil—each owe $100 billion to investors in other countries, mainly the United States. For Mexico, this figure equals about two-thirds of the country's GNP. For Brazil, the debt owed to others is closer to 40 percent of its total GNP.

When debts get this large, countries have trouble even paying interest on the loans. As a result, some developing nations talk about defaulting, or not repaying borrowed money. Most people do not expect this to happen, however, because developing countries fear that lending nations may retaliate. In addition, a country that defaults on its loans may never be able to borrow again.

When countries approach default, borrowers and lenders often try to revise the repayment schedule. Some lenders have found creative ways to resolve the debt crisis. Recently, for example, the Philippines was unable to repay a major loan to the Bank of America. The Bank of America accepted an offer of 40 percent stock ownership in the Bank of the Philippines instead of the repayment.

Capital Flight

Another problem for developing nations is **capital flight**—the legal or illegal export of a nation's currency and foreign exchange. Capital flight may cause countries to face a cash shortage, which prevents them from paying interest on their foreign debt. At a minimum, it limits the funds available for capital investment.

For the most part, capital flight takes place when corrupt officials smuggle money out of the country and deposit it abroad. A Nigerian investigation found that corrupt officials were depositing $25 million abroad daily at the peak of the oil boom in the 1970s. This may be one reason why Nigeria experienced a negative per capita rate of growth from 1973 to 1983, although it was an OPEC nation with rich oil reserves.

At other times, capital flight occurs because people living in the borrowing countries have no faith in their government or the future of the country's economy.

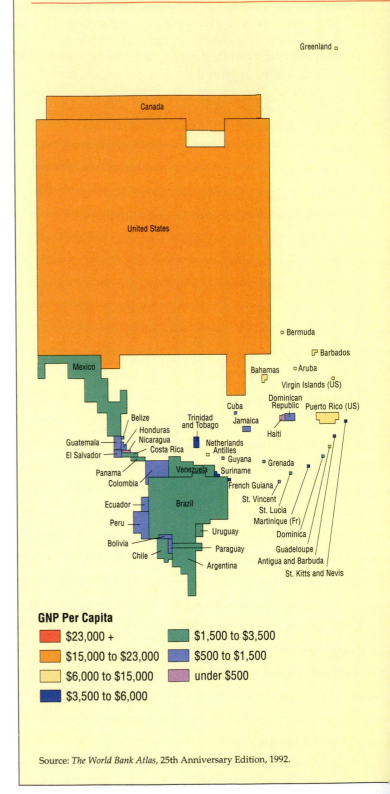

Figure 20.1
Gross National Product and Gross National Product Per Capita

GNP Per Capita

- $23,000 +
- $15,000 to $23,000
- $6,000 to $15,000
- $3,500 to $6,000
- $1,500 to $3,500
- $500 to $1,500
- under $500

Source: *The World Bank Atlas*, 25th Anniversary Edition, 1992.

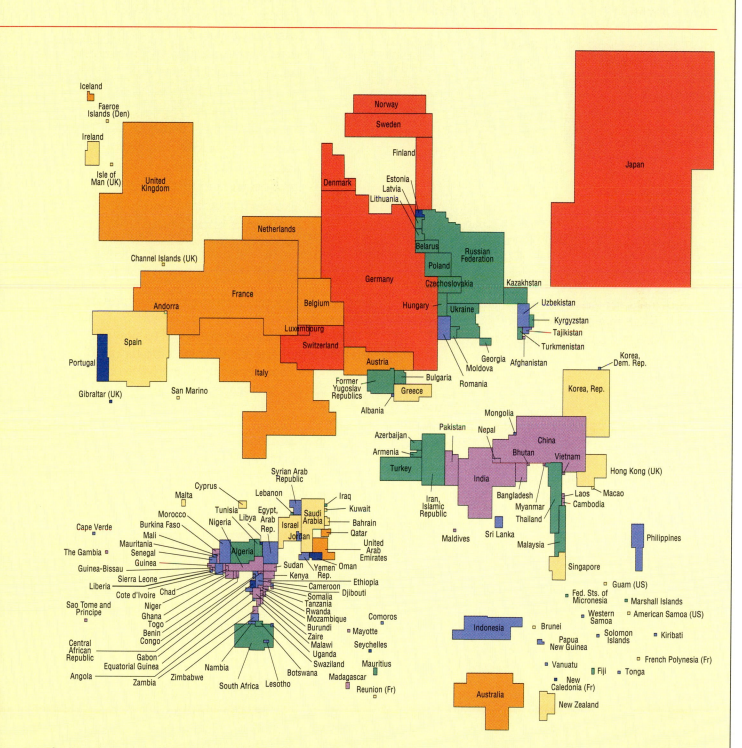

If every country's land area was proportional to its Gross National Product, the world would look like the map in this figure. When GNP is computed on a per capita basis, we get another view of a country's productivity. **Which countries have a per capita GNP larger than the United States's?**

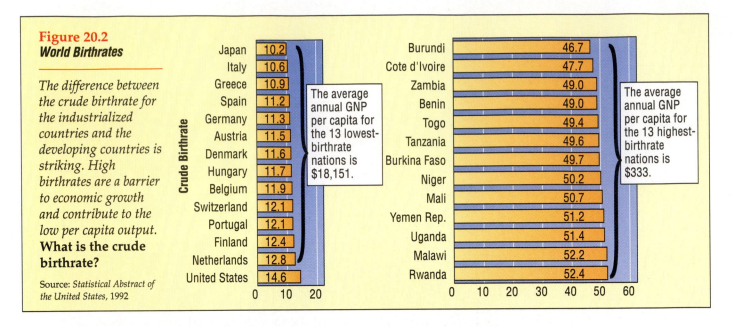

Figure 20.2
World Birthrates

The difference between the crude birthrate for the industrialized countries and the developing countries is striking. High birthrates are a barrier to economic growth and contribute to the low per capita output.
What is the crude birthrate?

Source: *Statistical Abstract of the United States, 1992*

Country	Crude Birthrate
Japan	10.2
Italy	10.6
Greece	10.9
Spain	11.2
Germany	11.3
Austria	11.5
Denmark	11.6
Hungary	11.7
Belgium	11.9
Switzerland	12.1
Portugal	12.1
Finland	12.4
Netherlands	12.8
United States	14.6

The average annual GNP per capita for the 13 lowest-birthrate nations is $18,151.

Country	Crude Birthrate
Burundi	46.7
Cote d'Ivoire	47.7
Zambia	49.0
Benin	49.0
Togo	49.4
Tanzania	49.6
Burkina Faso	49.7
Niger	50.2
Mali	50.7
Yemen Rep.	51.2
Uganda	51.4
Malawi	52.2
Rwanda	52.4

The average annual GNP per capita for the 13 highest-birthrate nations is $333.

Business owners, for example, may deposit their profits abroad. When they want to expand or invest, they try to borrow from industrialized nations.

Government

Government also can be an obstacle to economic development. A country whose government often changes will have a hard time developing economically. Such constant changes impede long-term planning. Economic development is made even more difficult if the political changes occur through violent revolution where industrial facilities may be destroyed.

Economic development also will be slowed if a government is not honest. Corrupt officials can damage the economy in several ways. One way is by depositing the nation's savings in a personal account in a foreign bank. Another way is by spending huge sums meant for the economy on lavish personal living.

In either case, the people see the results of their labor being spent recklessly or enriching someone else while their lives remain the same. This discourages them and reduces their incentive to save or invest.

SECTION 1 REVIEW

Reviewing Terms and Facts

1. **Define** developing country, crude birthrate, zero population growth, external debt, capital flight.
2. **List** three reasons people are concerned about developing countries.
3. **List** six factors that may be obstacles to economic development.

4. **Explain** why it is difficult for some developing countries to slow the rate of population growth.

Critical Thinking

5. **Identifying Alternatives** Suppose you are an official in charge of economic development in a developing country. Choose the first two obstacles to economic development that you would address and tell why you would tackle them first.

Applying Economic Concepts

6. **Life Expectancy** Explain why an official of a developing nation would have both positive and negative views of increasing life expectancy.

PROFILES IN ECONOMICS

W. ARTHUR LEWIS

(1915–1991)

Economist Sir W. Arthur Lewis achieved many firsts. He attended school in his native St. Lucia, and he earned a scholarship to attend the London School of Economics. In 1937 he graduated first in his class. Soon after, while working on a Ph.D. in Economics, he was the first black to receive an assistant lectureship at the same institution. In 1979 he was the first black to win the Nobel Prize in Economics (jointly with Theodore Schultz) for his work on the economic problems of developing nations.

Workers in Sri Lanka pick tea.

DEVELOPING NATIONS In particular, Lewis challenged the prevailing view that the supply of labor in developing nations was upward sloping, so that an increase in the demand for labor resulted in an increase in wages.

Real wages, noted Lewis, tended to stay at low levels for many developing nations regardless of the increases in demand for labor. The only solution, he reasoned, was that the supply curve for labor had to be perfectly elastic— or horizontal rather than upward sloping—so that an increase in demand would leave wages unchanged. His theory explained why countries such as Sri Lanka are still underdeveloped, although they have been developing for nearly 100 years.

Lewis did not claim to have solved the problems of the developing countries. His contributions, however, have made existing economic models and theory more applicable to realistic conditions.

TRANSITION Lewis explained how he felt about his illustrious career:

I had never meant to be an economist. . . . What was this economics? I had never heard of it before, and nobody in St. Lucia knew what it was. . . . Looking backward . . . I have lived through a period of transition. . . . I have been subject to all the usual disabilities—refusal of accommodations, denial of jobs for which I had been recommended, generalized discourtesy, and the rest of it. All the same, some doors that were supposed to be closed opened as I approached them. I have got used to being the first black to do this or that, which gets to be more difficult as the transition opens up new opportunities. Having to be a role model is a bit of a strain, but I try to remember that others are coming after me, and that whether the door will be shut in their faces as they approach will depend to some small extent on how I conduct myself.

—from *Lives of the Laureates*, by Spencer and Breit, 1990

Examining the Profile

1. **Demonstrating Reasoned Judgment** Why would an increase in demand for labor not increase the wage rate in developing countries?

2. **For Further Research** Find out more about the economy of Sri Lanka.

A Framework for Development

Section Preview

Objectives

After studying this section, you will be able to:

1. **Explain** the stages of economic development.
2. **Describe** the steps industrialized countries need to take to help developing countries.
3. **Describe** the steps developing countries need to follow to help themselves.

Key Terms

primitive equilibrium, takeoff, World Bank

Applying Economic Concepts

Primitive Equilibrium *Primitive equilibrium* is the first stage on the road to a nation's economic development. It is called *primitive* because no formal economic organization exists. It is called *equilibrium* because nothing is changing.

Economic development is a formidable task. Many approaches have been suggested and implemented with various levels of success. The steps below outline how a country might develop from a primitive economy to an industrialized one.

Stages of Economic Development

Some economists have suggested that developing countries normally pass through several stages on their way to economic development. Others have argued that the process is not uniform for all countries. A country, for example, may not go from one stage to the next in a logical manner. It may skip one stage altogether, or it may be in more than one stage at the same time. It is helpful to think of economic development as occurring in stages, and the boundaries between these stages are not always clear-cut.

Primitive Equilibrium

The first stage toward economic development is **primitive equilibrium**. It is primitive in the sense that the society has no formal economic organization. An example might be the Inuit of the past century who shared the spoils of the hunt with other families in the village.

A people—or country—in primitive equilibrium often have no monetary system and may not be economically motivated. No real capital investment exists. The society is in equilibrium, in which nothing changes. Rules are handed down from one generation to the next, and culture and tradition direct economic decision making.

Breaking With Primitive Equilibrium

The second stage of economic development is one of transition. It consists of a break with primitive equilibrium and a move toward economic and cultural changes. The break may be brief and sudden, or it may take many years.

Generally, the break results from outside forces showing a different, more attractive way of life. Missionaries and tourists, as well as war, travel, and business ventures with other countries, reveal to the people different ways of living. **1**

A country does not grow economically in this transition stage, but old customs begin to crumble. People begin to question their traditions, and they observe new patterns of living. Social unrest often accompanies this stage.

Takeoff

The third stage of development—**takeoff**—is not reached until the barriers of primitive equilibrium are overcome. A country in the takeoff stage begins to grow more rapidly than before. Still, that nation is far from reaching maturity or developing its greatest economic potential.

Several reasons explain the economic growth that occurs during this stage. One reason is that customs have been put aside, and people have begun to seek new and better ways of doing things. Another reason is that the people have begun to imitate the new or different techniques that outsiders have brought into the country. Still another reason is that outside help from an industrial nation may be providing financial, educational, or military aid.

During the takeoff stage, a country starts to save and invest more of its national income. New industries grow rapidly, and profits are reinvested in them. Industry uses new production techniques, and agricultural productivity greatly improves. Although the country still is not developed, it is moving away from economic stagnation.

Semidevelopment

The fourth stage is semidevelopment. In it, the makeup of the country's economy changes. National income grows faster than population, which leads to higher per capita income. At the same time, the core of the country's industry is built. The nation spends heavily on capital investment, and technological advances are made.

As industry grows, so does transportation, communications, medicine, law, and other services. The country begins to find its place in the international economy. It starts to make the goods it once bought from other countries. Before long, the semideveloped country starts to sell finished products to other nations.

High Development

The final stage of development is that of being highly developed. In this stage, efforts to obtain food, shelter, and clothing are more than successful. Most people have their basic needs and wants met. They turn their attention to services and such consumer goods as washing machines, refrigerators, and televisions.

The nation no longer emphasizes industrial production. Instead, it increases services and provides more public goods. Mature service and manufacturing sectors are signs of a highly developed economy.

Priorities for Industrialized Nations

The International Bank for Reconstruction and Development, also known as the **World Bank,** is an agency designed to channel funds from industrialized nations to developing ones. As a result of its considerable experience with developing nations, the World Bank has a list of recommendations for industrialized countries. 2

Reduce Trade Barriers

Trade barriers, especially nontariff barriers, need to be reduced or eliminated. In the United States, reducing barriers would result in such actions as importing more beef from Argentina. The World Bank has estimated that eliminating trade barriers would generate as much as $50 billion annually in export earnings for the developing countries.

Checking Understanding

1. What generally causes the break with primitive equilibrium?
2. What is the function of the World Bank?

Applying Economic Concepts

✓ **World Bank** After World War II, with aid from the United States and the World Bank, Japan emerged as the dominant economy of Asia. From 1953 to 1966, Japan was an active borrower from the World Bank. By 1970 Japan had become a major lender.

Reform Macroeconomic Policy

Macroeconomic policies in the industrialized countries that reduce deficits, stabilize inflation, lower interest rates, and stabilize foreign currency fluctuations would greatly improve world economic development. If the industrialized economies grow, their increased international trade often includes and benefits the developing economies.

Increase Financial Support

The industrialized nations need to provide more external financing to the developing countries. This financing could be direct aid, or it could be indirect aid to international agencies such as the World Bank or the International Monetary Fund (IMF), which also works with developing nations.

Traditionally, the majority of United States foreign aid has been granted to achieve political aims. Between one-half and two-thirds of all United States foreign aid has been paid for military supplies and training, either directly or indirectly. More than 50 percent of all indirect military aid is paid to Israel and Egypt.

Support Policy Reform

The industrialized countries are encouraged to support the internal policy reforms of the developing countries, especially when the countries are trying to develop freer and more efficient market economies. Transactions on common economic grounds lead to a more favorable business climate between the industrialized and developing countries.

Priorities for the Developing Countries

The World Bank also has a list of recommendations for the developing countries. The developing countries face the responsibility for directing their own economic development and future.

Invest in People

Governments in developing countries need to invest more in education, family planning, nutrition, and basic health care. The wealth of any nation resides in the strength and vitality of its people.

Improve the Climate for Free Enterprise

Many of the price controls, subsidies, and other regulations that restrict the free development of markets should be removed. The World Bank suggests that competitive markets—not politicians—make the allocation decisions.

Open Economies to International Trade

Many developing economies have quotas, tariffs, and other barriers to trade. These barriers are used to

Investment in People *The World Bank encourages developing nations to invest in their people by providing basic health care.* **What is the reasoning for investing in people?**

protect domestic jobs and to protect infant industries. At the same time, however, the trade barriers protect inefficient industries and hold down a country's standard of living. Countries that open their markets to the world will benefit from comparative advantage and will ultimately develop competitive specialties of their own.

Revise Macroeconomic Policies

Developing countries, like the industrialized ones, need to follow policies curbing inflation, reducing borrowing, and decreasing deficits. Their policies also must allow market incentives such as profits, so that the economies can begin to sustain their own growth.

SECTION 2 REVIEW

Reviewing Terms and Facts

1. **Define** primitive equilibrium, takeoff, World Bank.
2. **List** the stages of economic development.
3. **Describe** four recommendations that the World Bank has for developed countries.
4. **Describe** four recommendations that the World Bank has for developing countries.

Critical Thinking

5. **Making Inferences** The International Bank for Reconstruction and Development was organized near the end of World War II. Why do you think it was originally founded?

Applying Economic Concepts

6. **Primitive Equilibrium** Imagine that a society is in primitive equilibrium—nothing is changing internally to begin economic development. Describe an event that could be a potential source of change.

ECONOMIC SKILL

Comparing Statistics

Suppose you turn on the television during a professional football game. The announcer gives the statistics for one of the teams—number of completed passes, yards gained by rushing, number of first downs, number of times the quarterback was sacked. Can you tell whether that team is winning or losing the game?

Explanation

To have meaning, statistics must be compared. In the example of the football game, you must compare both teams' statistics to determine which team is playing better. To understand economic statistical data, you might compare differences over a period of time, or you might compare statistics for two or more groups.

Comparisons of economic information often are made by interpreting a statistical table. To interpret statistics in a table, use the following steps.
- Read the title of the table to find out what information is presented.
- Read the headings of the columns and rows to find out how the information is presented.

Practice

The table below shows aid provided to developing nations by donor countries. Study the table, then answer the questions that follow.

1. What information about foreign aid does the table present?
2. In 1991, how much foreign aid did France provide?
3. Which country provided more total aid—Japan or Denmark?
4. Which of the countries listed in the table provided the most total aid in 1991? What was the amount?
5. What percentage of GNP did United States foreign aid represent in 1991?
6. Based on percentage of GNP, which country listed in the table provided the most foreign aid? What was the percentage?
7. Based on a comparison of these statistics, what conclusion can you draw about the amount of foreign aid provided by industrialized nations?

Figure 20.3
Net Official Development Assistance (ODA) from Major Sources

Donor group or country	ODA as percentage of GNP 1991	Total ODA (billions of dollars) 1991	Donor group or country	ODA as percentage of GNP 1991	Total ODA (billions of dollars) 1991
France	0.62	7.5	Australia	0.38	1.0
Germany	0.41	6.9	Austria	0.34	0.5
Italy	0.30	3.3	Canada	0.45	2.6
United Kingdom	0.32	3.2	Finland	0.76	0.9
Netherlands	0.88	2.5	Japan	0.32	10.9
Denmark	0.96	1.2	New Zealand	0.25	0.1
Spain	0.23	1.2	Norway	1.14	1.2
Belgium	0.42	0.8	Sweden	0.92	2.1
Portugal	0.31	0.2	Switzerland	0.36	0.9
Ireland	0.19	0.1	United States	0.20	11.3

Source: World Economy Survey, 1993.

Additional Practice

For further practice in comparing statistics, complete the Reinforcing Skills exercise in the Chapter 20 Review on page 517.

Financing Economic Development

Section Preview

Objectives

After studying this section, you will be able to:

1. **Describe** one internal and two external sources of funds for economic development.

2. **Explain** the role of international lending and developing agencies.

3. **Explain** how regional cooperation can assist economic growth.

Key Terms

expropriation, free-trade area, customs union, European Union, European Community, ECU, cartel, population density

Applying Economic Concepts

Growth and Development Sound economic development depends on more than the infusion of large amounts of capital into developing countries. These nations must also address such issues as saving, investing, and providing incentives for their people.

For a developing country to foster industries in which it has a comparative advantage, it needs capital. Funds may be needed, for example, to provide irrigation for farms or heavy equipment for mining. Without capital, a developing country may not be able to build roads and highways needed for bringing products to ports for shipment to the rest of the world.

This financial capital generally can come from three different sources. It can be generated internally, lent or supplied by outside agencies, or obtained as a result of regional cooperation.

Development With Internal Funds

Internal funds are a source of capital. In many cases, they may be the only source of capital for a developing country. To generate these internal funds or savings, an economy must produce more than it consumes.

Savings in a Market Economy

If a developing country is modeled after a market economy, the incentive to save stems from the profit motive. Entrepreneurs are free to pursue the most profitable activities. Banks, for example, pay varying interest rates that are set by the forces of supply and demand. If the demand for money is high, the rate

Internal Funds *Generating internal funds has made Hong Kong an economic power.* **What must an economy do to generate internal funds?**

will rise, and more saving will be encouraged. Saving, in turn, produces financial capital.

One economy that developed in this way is that of Hong Kong, which has been called one of the freest market economies in the world. Government interferes very little, and people are free to pursue almost any economic activity they desire. Although its per capita GNP is about 60 percent of that of the United States, in 1991 it was more than 35 times greater than China's GNP.

Many developing countries are so poor that there is barely enough production to fulfill basic consumption. It takes longer for savings to be obtained, but some countries have developed in this manner.

Savings in a Command Economy

Other developing countries, such as Cuba, the Dominican Republic, El Salvador, and Uganda, have had command economies at one time or another. In each case, a dictator tried to force saving on the economy. The governments of these countries argued that individual citizens were so poor that they did not have the incentive to save on their own. As a result, the governments felt they had to mobilize resources themselves.

Many people were forced to work on farms, roads, or other projects the government thought were needed for economic development. To boost agricultural output, China's government at one time forced people out of the cities and factories to work on farms.

History shows that although command economies can mobilize resources, they do not always use them to promote economic growth. Resources often are mobilized for political reasons. In addition, nearly all forced mobilizations fail to instill long-term incentives in the people. When resources are mobilized for the wrong reasons, the cost in personal, economic, and political freedoms is higher than most people want to pay. 1

Development With External Funds

No matter what system of government a less developed country has, it is never easy for it to develop economically with internal funds. Therefore, some developing countries try to obtain external funds. There are three ways they can do this.

Attracting Private Investment

One way a country can obtain external funds is to attract private funds from foreign investors who might be interested in the country's natural resources. This happened in the Middle East with its abundance of oil, in Chile with its abundance of copper, and in Asia with its abundance of mahogany and teakwood.

A country rich in mineral resources might grant exclusive mining rights or favorable tax rates to foreign companies or investors willing to build factories on its soil. The country also might be able to provide low-cost labor, which would make investment even more attractive.

Foreign investments should be beneficial to both the investor and the host country. The developing country wants projects that will foster development, not exploit scarce resources. Investors want a reasonable return on their investment. Many corporations have not forgotten the billions of dollars lost during the takeover of American oil facilities in Iran, copper mines in Chile, and agricultural plantations in Cuba. Many investors no longer are willing to take major risks unless they are sure that the developing country is politically stable. ✓

Developing countries that follow a policy of **expropriation**—the taking over of foreign property without some sort of payment in return—make it harder for all developing nations to attract foreign capital from industrialized countries.

Assistance From Industrialized Countries

Another way a country can obtain external funds is through grants or borrowing from foreign governments. The United States and other industrialized countries, including Canada and those in western Europe, grant aid to developing countries.

The former Soviet bloc also gave economic assistance to developing countries. More than 50 percent of its aid, however, went to Cuba, Ethiopia, Afghanistan, and Iraq. Like much of the foreign aid other nations grant, it was given mostly to promote political, rather than economic, ends.

Some economic aid also is provided by the OPEC nations—members of the Organization of Petroleum Exporting Countries. These nations generally limit aid to only a few countries and organizations. The OPEC nation of Saudi Arabia, for example, sends most of its foreign aid to Syria and the Palestine Liberation Organization.

Borrowing From International Agencies

A third way a country can get external financial assistance is by obtaining a loan from an international agency. Two such agencies are important to global economic development.

The International Bank for Reconstruction and Development—the World Bank—was mentioned earlier. The World Bank helps developing countries with loans and guarantees of loans from private sources. It is a corporation owned by the member nations of the International Monetary Fund, and it lends nearly $23 billion annually to developing countries. One of the owners is the United States, which contributes more than $1 billion annually.

In the past, many of the loans have been for projects such as dams, roads, and factories. More recently, loans have been made to developing nations in an effort to get them to change their economic policies. Rather than lend money for a particular project, the World Bank may grant a general loan that the borrowing country can use any number of ways. In return, the World Bank may ask the country to lower a tariff barrier, end a budget deficit, or reduce the level of inflation.

The World Bank has several affiliates. One is the International Finance Corporation (IFC)—an agency that invests in private businesses and other enterprises. The International Development Association (IDA) makes soft loans—loans that may never be paid back—to the neediest countries. The rates on IDA loans are interest-free and may be for periods of 35 or 40 years. The IDA is the lender of last resort for countries that cannot get external financing elsewhere.

The International Monetary Fund (IMF) was formed in 1944 by countries wanting to set up an international system of fixed exchange rates. Each country agreed to contribute a pool of currency and gold for use in fixing exchange rates at agreed-upon levels.

When the world went to a system of flexible rates in 1971, the IMF adjusted its role. Today it offers advice to all nations on monetary and fiscal policies. It also helps support the currency of some developing nations with loans so that the countries can compete in an open market. **2**

After the Berlin Wall came down and the Soviet Union collapsed, a number of former Soviet bloc countries wanted to trade their currencies on global exchanges. The IMF provided loans to help with the conversion. Today, the Hungarian *forint*, the Polish

QUICK CHECK

Checking Understanding

1. What may result if resources are mobilized for the wrong reasons?
2. What is the function of the IMF?

Applying Economic Concepts

☑ **Foreign Investment** By the early 1950s, U.S. corporations virtually controlled Cuba. Nearly 90 percent of its mines, ranches, and oil; half of its sugar crop; and 3 million acres of its land belonged to Americans. At the same time, most Cubans suffered tremendous poverty.

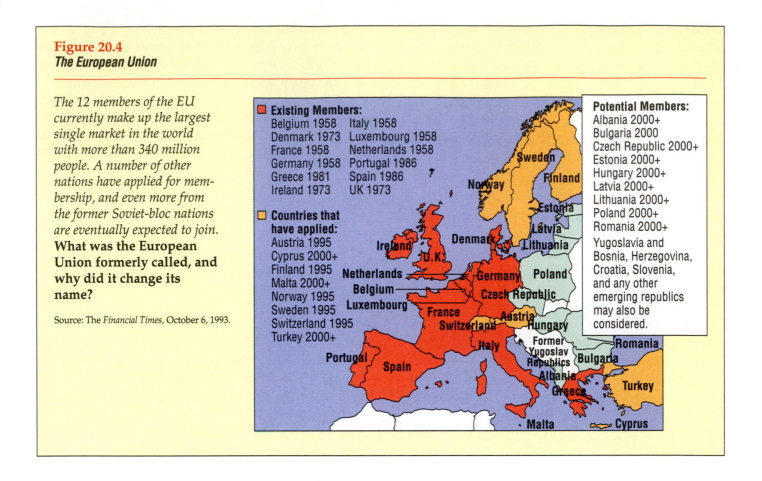

Figure 20.4
The European Union

The 12 members of the EU currently make up the largest single market in the world with more than 340 million people. A number of other nations have applied for membership, and even more from the former Soviet-bloc nations are eventually expected to join. **What was the European Union formerly called, and why did it change its name?**

Source: The *Financial Times*, October 6, 1993.

Existing Members:
Belgium 1958   Italy 1958
Denmark 1973   Luxembourg 1958
France 1958   Netherlands 1958
Germany 1958   Portugal 1986
Greece 1981   Spain 1986
Ireland 1973   UK 1973

Countries that have applied:
Austria 1995
Cyprus 2000+
Finland 1995
Malta 2000+
Norway 1995
Sweden 1995
Switzerland 1995
Turkey 2000+

Potential Members:
Albania 2000+
Bulgaria 2000
Czech Republic 2000+
Estonia 2000+
Hungary 2000+
Latvia 2000+
Lithuania 2000+
Poland 2000+
Romania 2000+
Yugoslavia and Bosnia, Herzegovina, Croatia, Slovenia, and any other emerging republics may also be considered.

zloty, and the Czech Republic's *koruna* are all listed on world markets. This is important because investors must be able to purchase the currencies of these countries to conduct international trade with them.

Regional Cooperation

Some developing countries have joined together to form a **free-trade area**—an agreement in which two or more countries reduce trade barriers and tariffs among themselves. The free-trade area does not try to set uniform tariffs for nonmembers. Other countries have formed a **customs union**—an agreement in which two or more countries abolish tariffs and trade restrictions among themselves and adopt uniform tariffs for nonmember countries. **1**

The European Union

One of the most successful examples of regional cooperation in the world today is the **European Union** (EU). The EU, formerly known as the **European Community** (EC), consists of the 12 member nations shown in **Figure 20.4.**

In January 1993, the EC became the single largest unified market—in terms of population and GDP—in the world, even larger than the United States. It is a single market because no internal barriers regulate the flow of workers, financial capital, or goods and services. On November 1, 1993, as a result of the Maastricht Treaty, the EC became the European Union. Citizens of the EU hold common passports and can vote in European elections, and can travel anywhere in the EU to work, shop, save, and invest.

The EU has its own monetary unit called the ECU. **ECU** stands for European Currency Unit and is a measure of value rather than a form of paper currency. The final step in European integration is the adoption of a single currency, planned for 1998.

The EU collects revenues in the form of a VAT (Value Added Tax) and then distributes the funds to its members on the basis of need. Hundreds of billions

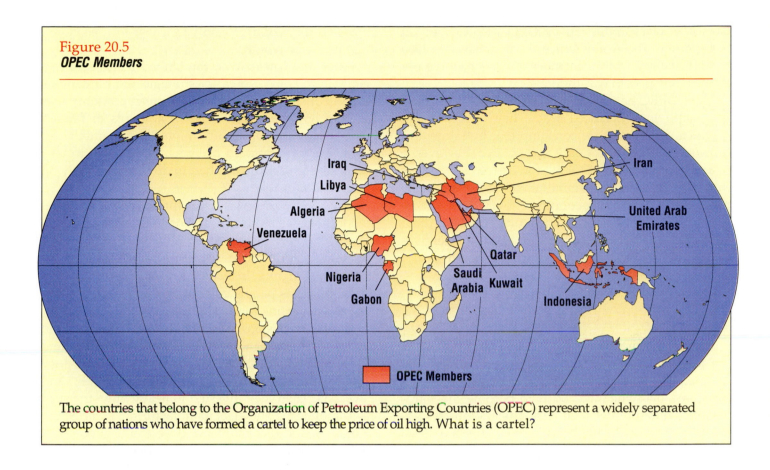

Figure 20.5
OPEC Members

Iraq
Libya
Algeria
Venezuela
Nigeria
Gabon
Qatar
Saudi Arabia
Kuwait
Iran
United Arab Emirates
Indonesia

■ OPEC Members

The countries that belong to the Organization of Petroleum Exporting Countries (OPEC) represent a widely separated group of nations who have formed a cartel to keep the price of oil high. What is a cartel?

of dollars have been redistributed in this manner and have been used to build highways, rail systems, and other public goods that will benefit the EU.

Because of the success of the EU, and because of the collapse of communism in eastern Europe, a number of countries have applied for membership. These countries are listed in Figure 20.4

OPEC

A number of oil-producing nations have joined to form a cartel—a group of producers or sellers who agree to limit the production or sale of a product to control prices. Shown in Figure 20.5, OPEC's members were able to take advantage of a natural monopoly and push up world oil prices. Since it was organized in 1960, OPEC has successfully transferred trillions of dollars from the industrialized nations to the OPEC members as a result of higher prices.

Even with all this financial capital, however, the growth rates of most OPEC nations were low by most standards. In Iran, revolution interrupted the development of the domestic economy. Kuwait was overrun by Iraq, and Iraq suffered huge losses during the Persian

QUICK CHECK

Checking Understanding

1. How does a free-trade area differ from a customs union?

Applying Economic Concepts

☑ **European Union** The European Union is built on the largest customs union in the world. NAFTA, discussed on pages 458-459, makes up the largest free-trade area in the world.

Gulf War. Overproduction by OPEC also pushed oil prices down. The World Bank estimated that from 1980 to 1991, the only OPEC member to have positive per capita GNP growth was Indonesia.

Most OPEC nations were not able to absorb their oil wealth in a balanced way. They bought many products for immediate consumption. Investment in other sectors of the economy was ignored, however.

The growth rates of OPEC for 1980 to 1991 show that huge amounts of capital alone do not solve the problems of developing countries. To have sound economic development, countries must also address such issues as saving, investment, and the incentives that cause people to work and improve their lives.

The South Korean Success Story

One of the most successful developing nations is the Republic of Korea, also known as South Korea. Despite its bleak prospects nearly 40 years ago, it overcame overwhelming odds to become the third-largest economic power in Asia and the nineteenth-largest economy in the world. From the late 1950s until the mid-1980s, South Korean exports grew at a rate of 25 percent per year. In addition, its real per capita GNP growth was in the 5 to 10 percent range.

In the early 1950s, South Korea was one of the poorest nations in Asia. It had the highest **population density**—number of people per square mile of land area—in the world. It also had a war-torn economy that had to be rebuilt.

After the Korean War, the United States sent foreign aid to South Korea for strategic and humanitarian reasons. Because the South Korean economy was ruined, however, even massive amounts of foreign aid would have done little more than maintain the country's low standard of living. For growth to take place, the South Koreans had to do more than rely on foreign aid.

The South Korean government decided to focus on labor-intensive industries and open its markets to free trade. It gave businesses incentives to follow this strategy. In addition, the government did not try to do everything at once. Instead, it focused on a few industries so that its people could gain experience producing and exporting for world markets.

Taking these steps, businesses in the South Korean economy first began to produce inexpensive toys and consumer goods for the world market. Next, they moved into textiles such as shirts, dresses, and sweaters. Then they invested in heavy industry, such as shipbuilding and steel manufacturing. Later, South Korea produced consumer and electronic goods such as radios, televisions, microwave ovens, and home computers. Most recently, the country has been making a strong bid as a leading producer of automobiles. The South Korean experience shows that a country can change a war-damaged economy to a well-developed, highly industrial one.

SECTION 3 REVIEW

Reviewing Terms and Facts

1. **Define** expropriation, free-trade area, customs union, European Union, European Community, ECU, cartel, population density.

2. **Describe** two external sources of funds for economic development.

3. **List** two important international lending and development agencies.

4. **Identify** an example of regional cooperation for economic growth.

Critical Thinking

5. **Drawing Conclusions** Developing nations often need capital from foreign investors. What economic and political conditions serve to encourage this kind of investment?

Applying Economic Concepts

6. **Growth and Development** Provide an example to support the following statement: Economic growth in developing nations is often slowed by internal political problems and external political goals of industrialized nations.

Vocabulary

The following terms are defined in Chapter 20:

- zero population growth (p. 499)
- external debt (p. 500)
- capital flight (p. 500)
- World Bank (p. 505)
- ECU (p. 512)
- cartel (p. 513)
- population density (p. 514)

SECTION ONE
- developing country (p. 498)
- crude birthrate (p. 499)

SECTION TWO
- primitive equilibrium (p. 504)
- takeoff (p. 504)

SECTION THREE
- expropriation (p. 511)
- free-trade area (p. 512)
- customs union (p. 512)
- European Union (p. 512)
- European Community (p. 512)

Section 1

Economic Development (pages 498–502)

Developing countries have the same problems that industrialized countries have—the major difference being that their problems are much larger. Concern for developing countries is humanitarian as well as political. In 1991, 43 countries representing more than one-half of the world's population each had a per capita GNP of less than $500.

Developing countries face numerous challenges, including high **crude birthrates** and increasing life expectancies. A shortage of natural resources, limited education and technology, a heavy burden of **external debt, capital flight,** and corrupt and inefficient governments add to their problems.

Reviewing the Main Idea

How are the problems of developing countries different from the problems of most industrialized countries?

Section 2

A Framework for Development (pages 504–507)

It helps to think of economic development as proceeding in stages, although every nation does not follow the same stages. The stages include **primitive equilibrium**, breaking with primitive equilibrium, **takeoff**, semidevelopment, and high development.

The **World Bank** recommends that industrialized nations reduce trade barriers, reform macroeconomic policies, increase financial support, and support the policy reforms of the developing countries.

The World Bank also recommends that the developing nations themselves invest in their people, improve the climate for enterprise, open their economies to international trade, and revise their economic policies.

Reviewing the Main Idea

What can the industrialized nations do to help the developing countries, and what can the developing countries do to help themselves?

Section 3

Financing Economic Development (pages 509–514)

Developing countries need to encourage saving to provide a domestic source of investment funds. Command economies often try to force saving by mobilizing resources in a manner that ignores individual freedoms. Attempts to secure capital through **expropriation** often backfire, because foreign investors become fearful of investing.

External funds are sometimes available from foreign governments and banks. Other institutions, like the World Bank and the International Monetary Fund, also provide assistance.

Some countries have been able to help themselves through regional cooperation. This sometimes takes the form of a **free-trade area** or a **customs union** such as the **European Community,** now the **European Union.** The oil-producing nations organized the OPEC **cartel** to increase the price of oil.

Reviewing the Main Idea

How can a developing country secure the funds necessary for economic development?

Reviewing Key Terms

Write the key term that best completes the following sentences.

a. population density
b. customs union
c. primitive equilibrium
d. external debt
e. capital flight

f. expropriation
g. free-trade area
h. cartel
i. crude birthrate
j. takeoff

1. A _____ is the formal arrangement to limit the production of a product.
2. A cooperative trade arrangement among nations that does not set uniform tariffs for nonmembers is called a _____.
3. A _____ is a cooperative trade arrangement among nations that sets uniform tariffs for nonmembers.
4. A developing country may have a very high _____ , contributing to rapid population growth.
5. When _____ becomes too large, countries have difficulty paying the interest.
6. The least developed stage in economic development is called _____.
7. The third stage of economic development is the _____.
8. The problem of _____ occurs when corrupt officials take money out of the country and deposit it abroad.
9. When _____ takes place, it is harder for developing nations to attract foreign capital from industrialized countries.
10. The number of people per square mile of land is a measure of _____.

Reviewing the Facts

SECTION 1 *(pages 498–502)*
1. **Identify** three reasons why industrialized countries are concerned about the problems of developing nations.
2. **Explain** why government can be an obstacle to economic development.

3. **Name** the condition in which the average number of births and deaths are approximately equal.
4. **Identify** two reasons for the occurrence of capital flight.

SECTION 2 *(pages 504–507)*
5. **Describe** what happens in a developing country in the stage of breaking with primitive equilibrium.
6. **Identify** four changes that take place in the take-off stage of economic development.
7. **List** the four World Bank recommendations for developing nations.

SECTION 3 *(pages 509–514)*
8. **Name** three sources of financial capital for development.
9. **Explain** how a developing country can attract foreign capital.
10. **List** three international agencies that provide funds for economic development.

Critical Thinking

1. **Predicting Consequences** What do you think would happen if industrialized nations and international agencies chose to withdraw support for developing nations?
2. **Demonstrating Reasoned Judgment** Would it be effective policy for the United States to increase financial aid to developing nations, regardless of their internal political conditions or economic policies? Explain the reasoning behind your answer.

Applying Economic Concepts

1. **Primitive Equilibrium** Why is it increasingly unlikely that countries in the world today may remain in the primitive equilibrium stage of economic development?
2. **Growth and Development** How will the economic growth and development of developing countries affect you in the future?

Reinforcing Skills

COMPARING STATISTICS

1. What information about languages does the table present?
2. What language—besides English—is the most widely spoken in the United States?
3. What languages listed in the table are spoken by more than 1 million Americans?
4. With a total United States population of about 255 million, what percentage of Americans speak Spanish?
5. Based on a comparison of these statistics, what conclusions can you draw about languages spoken in the United States?

Individual Activity

Economic growth is only one measure of progress. For you as an individual, growth and progress can be measured in terms of physical size and skills, mental achievement, economic gains, and social skills. Write a paragraph comparing your present self with yourself two years ago. What "stages" have you gone through to become the person you are? What are your future goals?

Cooperative Learning Activity

Organize into three groups, each choosing one of the following regions: Latin America, Africa, and Asia. Each student in the group should research a different nation in his or her region. Determine the relative progress of the country based on per capita GNP, life expectancy, literacy rate, and rate of economic growth. Compare your findings.

Figure 20.6
Languages in the United States

Language	Number of Speakers	State with Highest %
1. Spanish	17,339,172	New Mexico
2. French	1,702,176	Maine
3. German	1,547,099	North Dakota
4. Italian	1,308,648	New York
5. Chinese	1,249,213	Hawaii
6. Tagalog	843,251	Hawaii
7. Polish	723,483	Illinois
8. Korean	626,478	Hawaii
9. Vietnamese	507,069	California
10. Portuguese	429,860	Rhode Island
11. Japanese	427,657	Hawaii
12. Greek	388,260	Massachusetts
13. Arabic	355,150	Michigan
14. Hindi	331,484	New Jersey
15. Russian	241,798	New York
16. Yiddish	213,064	New York
17. Thai/Lao	206,266	California
18. Persian	201,865	California
19. French Creole	187,658	Florida
20. Armenian	149,694	California

Source: Bureau of the Census, April 1993

Writing About Economics

THE CLASSIFICATORY STYLE

In the **Journal Writing** activity on page 497, you tracked economic problems of foreign nations that you heard reported in the news. Imagine that you are the chairperson for a United Nations committee studying the possibility of regional cooperation to resolve problems. Using the classificatory style of writing described on page 554, write an agenda for this week's meeting. Include all topics to be discussed and guest speakers to be present.

Power generated by windmills is considered an alternative energy source.

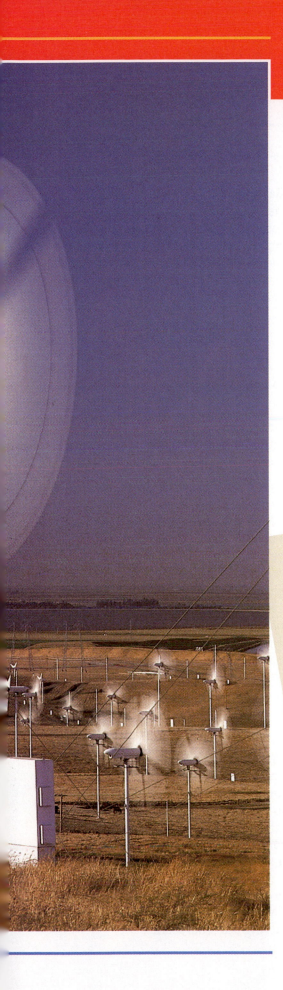

CHAPTER 21

Global Economic Challenges

SECTION 1
The Global Demand for Resources

SECTION 2
Economic Incentives and Resources

SECTION 3
Applying the Economic Way of Thinking

CHAPTER PREVIEW

People to Know

- Thomas Malthus
- Economic Geographer

Applying Economic Concepts to Your Life

Trade-Offs An empty lot is scheduled to be sold. The school board wants to buy the spot to build a new athletic facility. Local businesses want the land to add parking spaces for their customers. The city wants to build a park. Clearly, a limited resource—land—has more than one alternative use. *Trade-offs* are involved, and a choice has to be made. That's why we study economics—to become better decision makers.

Journal Writing

For one week, keep a journal of all the natural resources you use. Classify each as a renewable or nonrenewable resource.

The Global Demand for Resources

Objectives

After studying this section, you will be able to:

1. **Explain** Malthus's views on population growth.

2. **Explain** the importance of conserving nonrenewable resources.

3. **List** ways that people are using renewable energy resources to conserve scarce resources.

Key Terms

subsistence, embargo, gasohol, aquifer

Applying Economic Concepts

Scarcity Do you live in an area that has a water shortage? Has your local government ever passed temporary laws restricting lawn watering and washing cars? If so, you have experienced the economic principle of *scarcity* firsthand.

Scarcity has been defined as the fundamental economic problem. You experience scarcity at the personal level. Scarcity is also a problem at the national level, even for relatively prosperous nations such as the United States. At the global level, scarcity reveals itself through food and energy shortages, which are compounded as world population grows.

In many respects, the earth is a very small planet. A global perspective helps us to use our economic knowledge to make the world a better place in which to live.

The Population Issue

The issue of population growth has fascinated the world since Thomas Malthus published his *Essay on the Principles of Population* in 1798. His views, published nearly 200 years ago, are still relevant because of the earth's growing population and its demand for resources.

Malthus's Views on Population

Thomas Malthus argued that population would grow faster than its ability to feed itself. The problem, he stated, was that population tended to grow geometrically, or at a rapidly increasing rate, as in the numbers 1, 2, 4, 8, 16, 32, 64, and so on. The ability of the earth to feed people, however, would grow at a

slower constant rate, such as 1, 2, 3, 4, 5. . . . He feared that if population growth were not checked, the future would be bleak:

Famine seems to be the last, the most dreadful resource of nature. The power of population is so superior to the power of the earth to provide subsistence . . . that premature death must in some shape or other visit the human race. The vices of mankind are active and able ministers of depopulation. . . . But should they fail in this war of extermination, sickly seasons, epidemics, pestilence, and plague advance in terrific array and sweep off thousands and tens of thousands. Should success still be incomplete, gigantic inevitable famine stalks in the rear, and with one mighty blow, levels the population with the food of the world.

—Thomas Malthus, *Essay on Population*, 1798

Eventually, the masses of the world would be reduced to a condition of **subsistence**—the state in which a population produces barely enough to support itself.

In many countries—especially in the larger cities—poverty is widespread. The Indian city of Calcutta, for example, has about 12 million people, and its population is expected to reach 14 million by the year 2000. Calcutta is one of the most crowded and poorest cities in the world. Hundreds of thousands of street dwellers beg and search for food in the city dumps and refuse piles. At night they sleep in the streets. Similar conditions exist in other parts of the world. In these places, the Malthusian prediction of a subsistence standard of living is a cruel reality.

Was Malthus Wrong?

In many other parts of the world, conditions are much better. Malthus did not foresee the enormous advances in productivity, which have allowed an increasing standard of living to accompany a growing population. He also did not foresee that families might choose to have fewer children.

Malthus's predictions may not have been entirely accurate for the industrialized countries, but they still have long-run consequences for all nations. Today, for example, population pressures in other parts of the world are causing problems for many industrialized countries, including the United States, which is besieged by many illegal immigrants from China and Haiti. As a result, many experts argue that it is in everyone's interest to control global population growth.

World Population Trends

Figure 21.1 shows the rate of population growth for various nations during the 1980s. The world

---

Figure 21.1
World Population Growth Rates

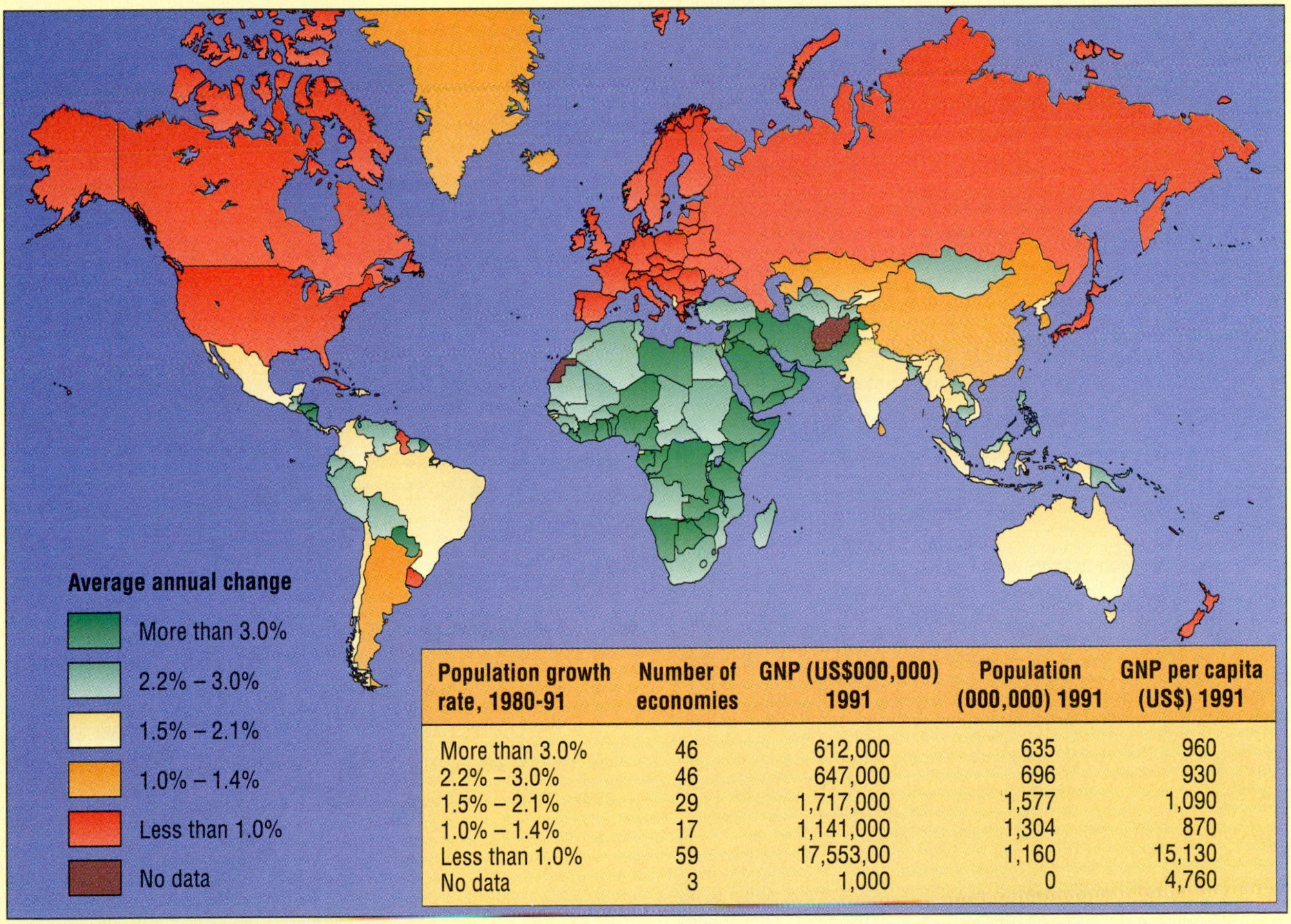

Average annual change

- More than 3.0%
- 2.2% – 3.0%
- 1.5% – 2.1%
- 1.0% – 1.4%
- Less than 1.0%
- No data

Population growth rate, 1980-91	Number of economies	GNP (US$000,000) 1991	Population (000,000) 1991	GNP per capita (US$) 1991
More than 3.0%	46	612,000	635	960
2.2% – 3.0%	46	647,000	696	930
1.5% – 2.1%	29	1,717,000	1,577	1,090
1.0% – 1.4%	17	1,141,000	1,304	870
Less than 1.0%	59	17,553,00	1,160	15,130
No data	3	1,000	0	4,760

Source: *The World Bank Atlas*, 25th Anniversary Edition, 1992

Population growth is highest in many of the countries that have the lowest standards of living. Conversely, population growth is lowest in countries with high standards of living. **What was Malthus's view on population?**

population is growing at about 1.7 percent a year. Although this amount may not seem very large, the consequences can be enormous over time. Every year, the population increase is equivalent to adding another Mexico to the world. If the population keeps growing at this rate, it will be about 6.3 billion by the end of the century, more than 8 billion by 2020, and nearly 15 billion by 2050. At this rate, the population of the world will more than double from the time you graduate from high school until you retire at age 65.

Nonrenewable Energy Sources

The depletion of many important resources compounds population pressures. Energy is one of these resources. As a factor of production, energy belongs to the category called *land* and is necessary for production to take place. Energy also makes life more comfortable. In the form of gasoline, it powers cars. In the form of electricity, it heats and cools homes. 1

Nonrenewable resources occur in several forms—including oil, natural gas, and coal. Historically, low prices encouraged the consumption of each.

Oil

Between 1900 and 1970, energy consumption in the United States doubled almost every 14 years. Oil was refined into gasoline, and because prices were relatively low, automobiles were large, heavy, and got poor gas mileage.

The low cost of oil even affected living habits. People tended to live some distance from where they worked, and many spent hours traveling to and from their jobs. Heating oil was inexpensive, so houses tended to be large, spacious, and poorly insulated.

In 1973, however, the oil-producing countries of the Middle East placed an **embargo**—a restriction on the export or import of a commodity in trade—on oil sales to the West. The embargo caused energy shortages in many parts of the world, which drove up prices. During the embargo, the price of oil went from less than $5 to more than $35 a barrel. Oil prices have decreased since then, but the oil that was consumed when prices were low will never be recovered.

Natural Gas

To protect consumers, the federal government followed a policy of controls that kept the price of natural gas low for many years. Policies were eventually changed in the late 1960s, but the artificially low prices had significant side effects.

When natural gas was inexpensive, people found many ways to use it. They heated their homes and swimming pools with it and built their factories and technology around it. Because natural gas was so inexpensive, it was even burned off at the wellhead to allow drillers to get to the more valuable oil. Over the years, trillions of cubic feet of natural gas were wasted because it was so inexpensive.

Coal

Another nonrenewable resource is coal. Today, nearly two-thirds of the world's known coal reserves are in the United States, Russia, and China. Although coal is plentiful, it too will eventually run out. Estimates based on the present rate of consumption indicate that the reserves will last about 200 years.

Renewable Energy Sources

Before 1973, little incentive to develop renewable energy sources such as solar, hydroelectric, or wind power existed. The oil embargo and soaring oil prices, however, provided this incentive. Americans became

Natural Resources *The demand for scarce resources is one of the most pressing problems facing all nations. As cities expand in the United States, suburbs encroach upon farmland.* **What alternative energy sources are Americans considering?**

concerned about the cost of energy and their dependence on foreign countries. As a result, they began to look for alternatives.

Solar Power

One alternative is solar power, which for many years interested mostly inventors and scientists. After the embargo, however, the federal government began issuing grants to researchers to find ways to reduce solar energy costs. Congress passed laws giving taxpayers credits for installing energy-saving devices in

their homes. This legislation encouraged many homeowners to insulate, install storm windows, and equip their homes with solar-powered water heaters. **2**

Hydroelectric Power

Another alternative is hydroelectric power, which historically had been used to power the mills and factories of the Northeast. The power was reliable, and its source—water—was free at the time. The drawback was that most dams were small and could not distribute power very efficiently to other locations.

QUICK CHECK

Checking Understanding

1. Energy is considered part of which factor of production?
2. How did federal legislation encourage the development of solar power?

Applying Economic Concepts

Population Growth You can use the "rule of 70" to find out how long it takes anything to double. Divide 70 by the rate of growth to find the number of years. For example, population would double in 70 ÷ 1.7, or 41.2 years.

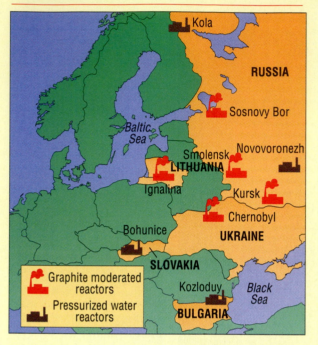

Figure 21.2
The Most Dangerous Nuclear Reactors

Graphite moderated reactors

Pressurized water reactors

Western governments have identified 9 nuclear power plants in the former Soviet Union and Eastern Europe, with a total of 24 reactors, that must be permanently closed. **What are the pros and cons of nuclear energy?**

Source: *Business Week*, June 8, 1993

Nuclear Energy

Interest also grew in nuclear energy, which generates about 10 percent of the commercial electricity used in the United States. The future of nuclear power, however, is uncertain for several reasons. Nuclear energy produces highly hazardous by-products, the safe disposal of which poses a major problem. In addition, construction costs of nuclear reactors are staggering. Lastly, many people are convinced that nuclear power presents a danger to health and the environment. The 1986 meltdown of the reactor in Chernobyl, Ukraine, reminded the world of the hazards of nuclear power.

Other Fuels

Other alternative energy sources include wood and **gasohol**—a fuel that is a mixture of 90 percent unleaded gasoline and 10 percent grain alcohol. Although gasohol has not been accepted as quickly as supporters first hoped, it still has a small share of the market in some areas. Wood stoves, in contrast, have grown rapidly in popularity, especially in high-cost energy areas such as the industrial Northeast.

Private industry has developed other lesser-known alternatives. Major food firms have made progress in converting chicken waste to fuel in the form of methane gas. This gas can then be recycled for industrial and commercial use.

When oil was obtained cheaply from the Middle East, waterpower became less important. By the late 1950s, most of the commercial power dams in the United States had been abandoned. When oil became more expensive, however, steps were taken to bring some of the dams back into use. Today, it is estimated that hydroelectric power could reduce imported oil usage by about 20 percent.

Wind Power

A third alternative is wind-generated electricity. In the early 1980s, sales of wind-driven equipment for generating electricity amounted to hundreds of millions of dollars. Many wind farms were built, producing enough electricity to power a medium-sized city.

Other Resources

Resources other than those used to generate energy also may be in danger. These include water and land.

Water

In the past, American concern with water focused mainly on the pollution of the country's waterways. Today, however, the focus is on the availability of water and the realization that water is in critical supply in many parts of the country.

More than 80 percent of the water consumed in the United States is used in agriculture. Most of this water is used in surface irrigation, which has a high evaporation rate. As a result, much water is lost into the atmosphere.

Farmers have been able to tap large sources of water from rivers, streams, ponds, and **aquifers**—underground water-bearing rock formations. Aquifers supply nearly 40 percent of the water that farmers use and are the source of fresh water for many communities.

One of the largest aquifers in the country is the Ogallala Aquifer, which supplies water to the High Plains states from Texas to Nebraska. So much water has been pumped out, however, that the aquifer's water table has been dropping about 3 feet a year. Some experts even predict that it will run out of water within the next 40 or 50 years.

The shortage of water is also a problem in Southern California. Over the years, some plans have been proposed and projects have been undertaken to bring in water from areas hundreds of miles away.

When water was plentiful at very low prices, farmers used a great deal of it in areas not otherwise suitable for farming. Consumers also used it freely. They watered their lawns, washed cars, used large-capacity washing machines, filled bathtubs, and ran showers for long periods of time. When water became scarce and its price went up, however, consumers began to conserve by washing their cars less often, installing water-saving devices in the bathroom, and reducing other usage of water around the home.

Land

Another valuable natural resource subject to the demands of a growing world population is land. Land, however, is different from other resources because there is a fixed supply of land that cannot be moved from one place to another.

A growing population often occupies the best farmland, which reduces the amount of land to be farmed. Many early settlers, for example, located in river valleys because the land was fertile and the rivers provided transportation. As the population grew, towns and cities replaced the early river settlements. As communities grew, factories, roads, and houses were built on the fertile land near the rivers. The development of this land forced the farmers to move to the outskirts.

This growth pattern repeated itself many times, and some of the finest farmland eventually ended up beneath expressways, shopping centers, and housing developments. Because many farmers willingly sold their land to industrial and housing interests, this trend would be nearly impossible to reverse today.

When the farmers sold their land, they often relocated to areas where the land was less fertile but also inexpensive. Since then, the development and availability of fertilizers, pesticides, herbicides, and other technological advances have kept the farmers' productivity very high.

SECTION 1 REVIEW

Reviewing Terms and Facts

1. **Define** subsistence, embargo, gasohol, aquifer.
2. **Describe** how Malthus believed population growth would affect the future of the planet.
3. **Explain** how the oil embargo affected gasoline consumption.
4. **List** the renewable sources of energy that are providing alternatives to nonrenewable resources.

5. **Describe** the effects that a growing population has on scarce resources such as aquifers.

Critical Thinking

6. **Making Comparisons** How do renewable resources differ from nonrenewable resources?

Applying Economic Concepts

7. **Scarcity** During the oil embargo, many people openly advocated nonprice gasoline rationing. Some favored allowing each automobile owner to use 10 gallons per week. What are the pros and cons of such a mandatory rationing program?

PROFILES IN ECONOMICS

THOMAS MALTHUS
(1766–1834)

Thomas Malthus was an English economist, sociologist, and member of the clergy who pioneered modern population study. He was a kind, gentle person dedicated to his father and his church. He was also the economist who is credited with giving economics the title of "the dismal science."

EDUCATION Thomas Malthus was born to wealthy parents and was educated at home by his father and by private tutors. At age 18 he enrolled at Jesus College, Cambridge, to study mathematics and the classics.

While he was away from home, Thomas and his father

The government of China took strong steps to encourage smaller families.

often exchanged letters debating the popular issues of the day. At one point, the elder Malthus

became fascinated with a popular utopian vision that promised eventual peace, prosperity, and equality for all. Thomas attacked the argument in a 50,000-word letter to his father. The elder Malthus was so impressed that he encouraged Thomas to publish the treatise for others to read. The result was *An Essay on the Principle of Population as It Affects the Future Improvement of Society*, published in 1798.

POPULATION THEORY The book was an instant success that was to forever change the way people viewed population. In it, Malthus argued that poverty and distress would be the eventual fate of people, not the popular utopian vision. He reasoned that population would increase at a geometric rate (1, 2, 4, 8, 16, . . .), while food supplies would increase at an arithmetic rate (1, 2, 3, 4, 5, . . .).

SUBSISTENCE STANDARD OF LIVING According to this progression, population growth would eventually outstrip the available food supply, resulting in famine, misery, and a subsistence standard of living for the masses.

At first, Malthus thought only three factors could check the growth of population: war, famine, and disease. Several years later, he added a fourth check: moral restraint. Separately or together, these factors could raise the death rate and/or lower the birthrate. In Malthus's view, however, these restraints on population growth would not be enough to prevent most of the world from forever remaining at the subsistence level. Despite his considerable accomplishments in other aspects of economics, Malthus is best remembered for his pessimistic views on population.

Examining the Profile

1. **Evaluating Information** Do you agree or disagree with Malthus's predictions about population? Why or why not?

2. **For Further Research** Find out what Malthus's other contributions to economics were.

Economic Incentives and Resources

Section Preview

Objectives

After studying this section, you will be able to:

1. **Explain** how the price system helps conserve water, natural gas, and oil.

2. **Describe** government efforts to limit pollution.

3. **State** the importance of using resources wisely.

Key Terms

deep gas, glut, pollution, acid rain, pollution permit

Applying Economic Concepts

Markets and Prices Have you ever planned a trip? Did you budget how much you would have to spend on gasoline? Did you pay attention to where you could get the cheapest price per gallon? Shopping for the best price is an example of how *markets and prices* operate in the free enterprise system.

Most economic systems require incentives to make them work smoothly. In a market economy, incentives such as the profit motive and prices can be used to preserve scarce resources.

The Price System

Before the oil embargo of the 1970s, energy prices were low, a situation that encouraged consumption. When prices jumped after the oil crisis, people became much more energy conscious. Cars became more fuel efficient, houses became more energy efficient, and entire industries began to think about ways to save energy. These actions helped prolong the existing supplies of nonrenewable resources and encouraged the development of new energy sources. The examples below show how the price system helps promote the conservation of scarce resources.

Irrigation

When farmers pump water out of the ground to water their crops, they use pumps driven by electricity or natural gas. When water tables fall because of pumping, it costs more to pump the water. As long as farmers continue to make a profit on their crops, they will pay the higher price for the water.

Initially, the higher cost of water will make everyone use it more efficiently, thus saving a scarce resource. In time, the falling water table will make some of the shallow wells useless. Deeper, more costly wells will be drilled instead. At this point, the price system will become relevant again. Deeper wells will be dug for profitable crops, while unprofitable crops will be abandoned.

Ultimately, the price system works to establish an equilibrium between the rising cost of recovering water and the depleted water tables. Although some crops and fields will be abandoned, they are likely to be the ones that were the least productive in the first place. As a result, the actual amount of agricultural output will not be much less than it is at present.

Deregulating Natural Gas

When the price of natural gas was low in the 1960s, the quantity demanded was high. Because government regulated the price, however, producers had little incentive to increase its production. Congress tried to stimulate gas discovery and production by lifting the price controls on **deep gas**—pockets of natural gas 15,000 feet or more below the earth's surface. This incentive increased its price to 3 or 4 times that of gas found above 15,000 feet. As a result, exploration for gas increased. Later, all gas price controls were removed, which encouraged even more production.

The lack of interest on the part of oil and gas producers in drilling for shallow gas was consistent with the law of supply, which maintains that the lower the price

Irrigation *Surface irrigation systems are fairly common in the United States.* **How can the price system be used to preserve water?**

paid to producers, the less will be brought to market. Also consistent with the law of supply was the effort by producers to produce the deregulated deep gas.

Post-Embargo Oil Production

The higher price for oil after 1973 dramatically affected the production of oil. When oil was priced below $5 a barrel, few countries were willing to devote large resources to retrieve it. When the price increased to $35 and more, many countries increased their production almost overnight. **1**

By 1981, prices began to fall because of a worldwide **glut**—a substantial oversupply—of oil. A decline in demand caused by a recession contributed to the worldwide oversupply of oil. People had also learned to conserve energy, which further reduced the demand for oil. The collective impact of the increase in world supply and the decline in demand caused OPEC to lose some of its ability to control the supply of oil. This control slipped even further after the Persian Gulf War, when some OPEC members increased oil production to replenish their financial reserves depleted during the war.

Pollution and Economic Incentives

Pollution is the contamination of air, water, or soil by the discharge of poisonous or noxious substances.

Pollution is a problem that most countries today must face.

The Incentive to Pollute

For years, factories have located along the banks of rivers so they could dump their refuse into the moving waters. Some factories, which generated smoke and other air pollutants, located farther from the water, but their tall smokestacks still blew the pollutants long distances. Others tried to avoid the problem by digging refuse pits on their property and burying their toxic wastes.

In all three situations, factory owners were trying to lower production costs by using the environment as a giant waste-disposal system. From an economic point of view, the reasoning was sound. Firms get ahead when they lower production costs. Those who produce the most at the least cost make the most profits.

The costs of pollution to society as a whole, however, are huge. For example, **acid rain**—a mixture of water and sulfur dioxide that makes a mild form of sulfuric acid—falls over much of North America, damaging countless rivers and streams. Ecosystems in other areas may be poisoned by fertilizer buildup and raw sewage runoff.

The damage caused by pollution is extensive, but it can be controlled. One way to control pollution is through legislated standards. Another way is through economic incentives.

Legislated Standards

Legislated standards include laws that specify the minimum standards of purity for air, water, and auto emissions. Congress, for example, has declared that all automobiles sold in the United States must meet certain pollution standards. If they do not meet the standards, the Environmental Protection Agency will not certify them, and they cannot be sold domestically.

Although affected industries have objected to them, some legislated standards have worked quite well. The auto industry complained loudly for years that it could not meet the tougher clean air standards. When pressed to do so, however, most auto manufacturers managed to meet them. Some other companies did not fare as well. They decided to close down rather than to spend the money needed to upgrade their aging capital stock.

A Pollution Tax

Besides legislation, another method of controlling pollution is to have companies pay taxes on the amount of pollutants they release. The size of the tax would depend on the severity of the pollution and the quantity of toxic substances being released. **2**

Suppose a community wants to reduce air pollution caused by 4 factories, each of which releases large quantities of coal dust. A tax of $50 for every ton of coal dust released into the air would be applied to each factory. The total tax paid over the course of the year depends on the number of tons discharged. Devices attached to the top of the factory's smokestacks would measure the amount during a one-week period. After the average rate of discharge is established, the factory would be billed accordingly.

Each company would have the choice of paying the tax or removing the pollutants themselves. Suppose

Pollution *Chemicals used in this paper mill have killed the surrounding forest as well as polluted the adjoining river.* **What is acid rain?**

two factories find that if they install scrubbers, they can remove the coal dust for $40 a ton—$10 a ton less than the tax would cost. More than likely, they would choose to install the scrubbers rather than pay the tax. The community would then be left with only two factories still polluting its air. If the quality of the air meets the standard, nothing further needs to be done.

If, however, air quality still is below the desired level, the tax can be raised to $60 or $70 a ton. Eventually, this tax hike might cause a third factory to install its own pollution equipment. If the air still is not clean

Checking Understanding

1. How did the oil embargo affect the production of oil?
2. What is a pollution tax?

Applying Economic Concepts

☑ **Role of Government** The Environmental Protection Agency enforces the Clean Air Act, originally passed in 1963 and amended since then. The law sets standards for clean air and penalizes industries that pollute air and water.

enough, the community then could raise the tax again until the fourth factory decides to install scrubbers.

This tax approach, suggested by many economists, does not try to remove all pollution. It does, however, allow individual companies freedom of choice. It also provides flexibility that legislated standards lack and may prevent some plants from closing entirely.

Some firms would rather pay the tax than clean up their own pollution. These firms, however, help fund the pollution clean-up campaign. Consumers will not have to fund the effort out of their income, sales, or property taxes.

Pollution Permits

The Environmental Protection Agency (EPA) uses a similar system to reduce sulfur dioxide emissions, a key component of acid rain. The EPA's target is to ultimately reduce sulfur dioxide emissions to a level of 9 million tons per year.

The EPA started its program by issuing sulfur dioxide permits to utilities in 1993. The **pollution permits** allowed the utilities to release emissions into the air, and the utilities are not allowed to operate without the permits. If a utility has more permits than it needs, it can sell them in 1-ton increments. Thus, utilities that want to spend money on emissions cleanup could sell their permits, and use the cash to clean up their production. Those who prefer to purchase and use the permits are also allowed to do so.

The first set of pollution permits went on sale in March 1993 at the Chicago Board of Trade. The 1-ton permits brought prices ranging from $122 to $450 each. Several environmental groups also purchased the pollution permits. They planned to retire the permits to make them scarcer, and therefore more expensive, for the utilities.

The EPA will issue additional permits in successive years, but fewer permits will be issued as time goes on. Ultimately, the utilities will either have to pay very high prices for the permits, or they will have to buy antipollution devices.

Using Resources Wisely

The resource challenge is vital to the study of economics. Resources become scarce when the quantity demanded for them is greater than the quantity supplied. In a market economy, the price system plays a major role in the allocation of resources. It tells consumers when resources are scarce. It also helps decision makers allocate resources more wisely. For this reason, economists who believe in a market economy are optimistic about the future, especially if the price system is allowed to function and fulfill its role in the economy.

Even the amount of energy reserves is a function of price. Not long ago, it was thought that the United States natural gas reserves would last only another 30 years. That prediction, however, was made when the price of natural gas was low. When the price increased, less natural gas was bought, and the given reserves stretched further. At the same time, the higher price encouraged more exploration, and more reserves were found. As a result, supplies will last longer.

SECTION 2
REVIEW

Reviewing Terms and Facts

1. **Define** deep gas, glut, pollution, acid rain, pollution permit.
2. **Describe** how deregulation has affected the natural gas industry.
3. **Explain** how a pollution tax encourages industries to stop polluting.

Critical Thinking

4. **Making Comparisons** How do legislated standards and economic incentives differ in regard to pollution control?

Applying Economic Concepts

5. **Markets and Prices** Suppose that the demand for natural gas increases sharply because of a series of extremely harsh winters. How would a price increase affect gas usage as well as research efforts by natural gas companies?

Analyzing Trends

The business section of a newspaper reports a trend toward lower interest rates. An automobile dealer advertises a trend in smaller cars. In some cases, a trend is a short-lived fad. In other cases, a trend is general changes in patterns that indicate progress.

Explanation

Trends in economic development can be determined by studying statistical information over a period of time. To analyze a trend, you should ask the following questions:

1. What definite patterns or directions can be seen on the graph?
2. Does the information extend over a significant period of time so that trends can be clearly determined?
3. What could be some underlying causes of the trends shown on the graph?
4. What additional information would make the graph more helpful in analyzing trends?

Practice

The examples that follow show changes for three groups of countries in gross national product per capita and energy consumption per capita over a 20-year period. The following three groups of countries are compared:

A. *Industrialized countries,* or members of the Organization for Economic Cooperation and Development (OECD).
B. *Rapidly industrializing countries* (RICs); examples include Thailand, Indonesia, Malaysia, Mexico, Brazil, and Chile.
C. *Developing countries;* examples include 40 low-income countries in Africa, Asia, and Latin America.

Study the trends indicated on the graphs below, then answer the questions that follow.

1. What trend in GNP per capita is indicated for all three groups of countries?
2. Which group of countries experienced the most significant growth in GNP per capita?
3. What trend does Graph A indicate regarding the gap between rich and poor countries?
4. Based on Graph B, how are industrialization and energy consumption related?
5. Describe the trend in energy use indicated on Graph B.

Figure 21.3

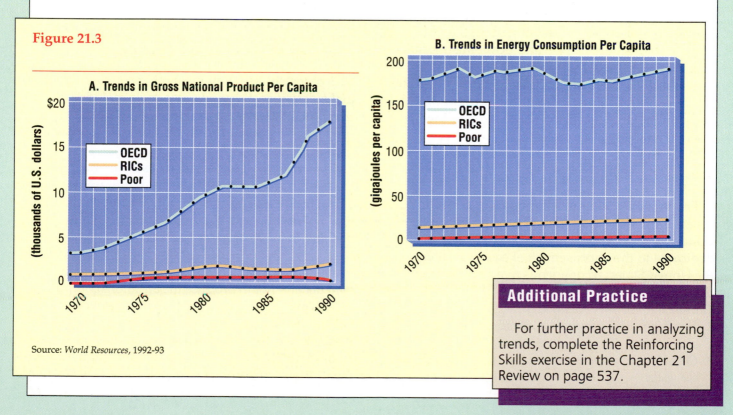

A. Trends in Gross National Product Per Capita

B. Trends in Energy Consumption Per Capita

Source: *World Resources,* 1992-93

Additional Practice

For further practice in analyzing trends, complete the Reinforcing Skills exercise in the Chapter 21 Review on page 537.

Applying the Economic Way of Thinking

Section Preview

Objectives

After studying this section, you will be able to:

1. **Explain** why economics has become a generalized theory of choice.
2. **Understand** how our market economy will be able to cope with the future.

Key Terms

cost-benefit analysis, modified free enterprise economy

Applying Economic Concepts

Cost-Benefit Analysis Have you ever decided not to do something because the cost of doing it was greater than the benefits that would be received? Economists call this *cost-benefit analysis*—and they use this analysis often. Perhaps you are starting to think like an economist.

As a science, economics is concerned with the way in which people cope with scarcity. Because scarcity is a universal problem, the study of economics is important to everyone.

A Framework for Decision Making

Through the study of economics, you learn that choices must be made. You begin to discover different ways to analyze a problem and that alternatives must be considered. The late economist Kenneth Boulding observed that economics has evolved to the point that it has now become a generalized theory of choice. Economics provides a framework for decision making and helps people to become better decision makers.

A Reasoned Approach

Economic decision making requires a careful, reasoned approach to problem solving. The National Council on Economic Education, an organization dedicated to the improvement of economic literacy in the United States, recommends five steps to economic decision making:

1. *State the problem or issue.*
2. *Determine the personal or broad social goals to be attained.*
3. *Consider the principal alternative means of achieving the goals.*
4. *Select the economic concepts needed to understand the problem and use them to appraise the merits of each alternative.*
5. *Decide which alternative best leads to the attainment of the most goals or the most important goals.*
   —*A Framework for Teaching the Basic Concepts,* 1993

These steps provide useful guidelines to decision making. Life is full of trade-offs, and you will be better equipped to deal with the future if you know how to analyze the problems you will encounter.

Decision Making at the Margin

Economists use a number of tools to help them make decisions. Some of these tools include production possibilities curves, supply and demand curves, production functions, and the National Income and Product Accounts.

One of the most important decision-making tools is the concept of marginal analysis. For example, when a firm makes a decision to produce additional output, it compares the extra cost of production with the extra benefits to be gained. If the benefits outweigh the costs, the firm decides to continue with the additional production. If the costs outweigh the benefits, the firm decides not to produce the additional output. [1]

This process—**cost-benefit analysis**—involves comparing the costs of a course of action to its benefits. Firms use cost-benefit analysis when they make decisions to produce or purchase additional capital equipment. Many government agencies use it when they evaluate programs. Individuals also use it when they make decisions. Cost-benefit analysis is even used to make choices among economic goals. Some choices will work against one goal while favoring another, but evaluating the costs and benefits of each choice helps in making decisions.

Coping With the Future

Everyone wants to know what will happen to the economy in the future. How will it adjust, and what course will it take in the future? Part of the answer can be found by examining the past.

The Triumph of Capitalism

During the 1930s, the forces of socialism and communism were sweeping the world, while capitalist countries were in economic depression. Communism in the Soviet Union had considerable impact upon the world, and socialist parties were on the rise in the European colonies in Africa.

Since then, communism in the former Soviet Union has collapsed under the weight of its own inefficiencies. Many socialist countries have embraced capitalism and the discipline of the market system. In addition, many developing countries have chosen capitalism as their economic system. Many emerging economic powers—including Hong Kong, Singapore, South Korea, and Taiwan—owe much of their remarkable growth to capitalism.

Capitalism is now the dominant economic force in the world, but it is not the laissez-faire capitalism of the past. Capitalism has changed because people have addressed some of the weaknesses that Karl Marx and others discovered many years ago.

The capitalism of the 1930s was ruthlessly efficient in that it provided only for those who produced or

earned enough to buy the necessities of life. Early capitalism had little room for the elderly, the ill, or the incapacitated. Many economies today, including that of the United States, have a **modified free enterprise economy,** or modified private enterprise system. This is a free-market economy based on capitalism, yet modified by its people to satisfy the economic goals of freedom, efficiency, equity, security, full employment, price stability, and economic growth. **2**

Markets and Prices

A modified free enterprise economy allows buyers and sellers to freely make the decisions that satisfy their wants and needs. The forces of supply and demand interact to establish prices in a market.

Checking Understanding

1. What is marginal analysis?
2. How was American capitalism of the past different from American capitalism today?

Applying Economic Concepts

☑ **Comparative Systems** The intense rivalry between capitalism in the United States and communism in the former Soviet Union dominated global politics from 1945 to the early 1990s. Known as the cold war, the rivalry ended with the collapse of the Soviet Union.

Alternatives *As the twenty-first century approaches, solar power will become a priority. As in the past, the capitalist system will allow producers and consumers to reallocate resources.* **How does change occur in a market economy?**

Prices, in turn, act as signals, causing producers and consumers to alter their spending decisions.

Prices also influence the allocation of resources across markets. The high price of oil in the 1970s made other energy sources competitive. In the 1980s, the high prices of personal computers attracted producers. Competition soon lowered prices and made the same computers affordable to mass markets.

A market economy has many advantages, including the ability to adjust to change gradually, without the need for government intervention. As long as the forces of supply and demand are allowed to function, they will send producers and consumers the signals needed to reallocate resources. Although no one knows what the future will bring, to date capitalism has demonstrated its ability to adapt.

SECTION 3 REVIEW

Reviewing Terms and Facts

1. **Define** cost-benefit analysis, modified free enterprise economy.
2. **Describe** the reasoned approach to decision making.
3. **Explain** how a market economy adapts to change.

Critical Thinking

4. **Synthesizing Information** Provide an example of how prices act as a signal to you as a buyer and/or seller.

Applying Economic Concepts

5. **Cost-Benefit Analysis** Think of a decision you must make in the next few days. How will you use your estimates of the costs and benefits to make your decision?

Vocabulary

The following terms are defined in Chapter 21:

SECTION ONE
- subsistence *(p. 520)*
- embargo *(p. 522)*
- gasohol *(p. 524)*
- aquifer *(p. 525)*

SECTION TWO
- deep gas *(p. 527)*
- glut *(p. 528)*
- pollution *(p. 528)*
- acid rain *(p. 528)*
- pollution permit *(p. 530)*

SECTION THREE
- cost-benefit analysis *(p. 532)*
- modified free enterprise economy *(p. 533)*

Section 1

The Global Demand for Resources (pages 520–525)

Despite the predictions of Thomas Malthus nearly 200 years ago, many regions have experienced steadily rising standards of living, largely because of technology. Developing nations with high birthrates, however, face the threat of subsistence standards of living.

As the world population has increased over the years, people have become increasingly concerned about the rapid depletion of nonrenewable energy sources such as oil, natural gas, and coal. Many Americans became acutely aware of this depletion in the 1970s after the countries of the Middle East started an oil **embargo.** The embargo encouraged Americans to seek alternative energy sources. These renewable resources include solar power, hydroelectric power, wind power, nuclear energy, and **gasohol**—a combination of unleaded gasoline and grain alcohol. Americans are also looking for ways to conserve water and ensure the wise use of land resources.

Reviewing the Main Idea

What renewable energy sources are Americans investigating as alternatives to nonrenewable resources?

Section 2

Economic Incentives and Resources (pages 527–530)

Since the oil embargo of the 1970s, rising gasoline prices have provided a great incentive to preserve resources. The price system of our market economy encourages the conservation of other resources as well. The deregulation of natural gas, for example, encouraged producers to drill for **deep gas.** As the American population has grown and used more energy resources, people have become concerned about **pollution,** or the contamination of air, water, or soil by the discharge of poisonous or noxious substances. In response to this concern, the government has passed legislation and economic incentives—including **pollution permits**—to clean up the environment. All of this legislation is aimed at encouraging people to use resources wisely.

Reviewing the Main Idea

How does the price system encourage the preservation of resources in a market economy?

Section 3

Applying the Economic Way of Thinking (pages 532–534)

Economics has become a generalized theory of choice and a framework for decision making. The National Council on Economic Education has recommended a five-point approach to decision making. The final decision involves **cost-benefit analysis,** which compares the cost of a decision to the benefits gained.

Capitalism is the dominant type of economic organization in the world today. Supply and demand establish prices, and prices serve as signals to both producers and consumers. Markets are flexible in that future changes affect prices and, therefore, the allocation of resources. This flexibility enables our **modified free enterprise economy** to adjust to future events.

Reviewing the Main Idea

How does the economic way of thinking help people to become better decision makers?

Reviewing Key Terms

Write the term that best completes the following sentences.

a. pollution permits
b. deep gas
c. modified free enterprise economy
d. glut
e. acid rain
f. pollution
g. aquifer
h. embargo
i. gasohol
j. subsistence

1. The state in which the population produces barely enough to support itself is _____ .
2. The United States has a _____, a system that has been altered by its people to satisfy economic goals.
3. A restriction on the export or import of a commodity in trade is a(n) _____.
4. _____ is a mixture of 90 percent unleaded gasoline and 10 percent grain alcohol.
5. An underground water-bearing rock formation is a(n) _____.
6. Natural gas found in pockets 15,000 feet or more beneath the earth's surface is _____ .
7. By 1981, oil prices began to fall because of a worldwide _____ , or a substantial oversupply.
8. _____ is the contamination of air, water, or soil by the discharge of poisonous or noxious substances.
9. A mixture of water and sulfur dioxide that makes a form of sulfuric acid is _____ .

Reviewing the Facts

SECTION 1 *(pages 520–525)*

1. **Describe** why, despite Malthus's predictions, certain parts of the world have enjoyed steadily increasing standards of living.
2. **Explain** where the most rapid rates of population growth are found.
3. **List** the three major nonrenewable energy resources.
4. **Describe** the major drawback of nuclear energy.

SECTION 2 *(pages 527–530)*

5. **Explain** how American consumers and the automobile industry reacted to the oil price increases of the 1970s.
6. **Explain** how the reluctance of oil and gas producers to drill for shallow gas was consistent with the law of supply.
7. **Describe** what the Environmental Protection Agency hopes to accomplish by issuing pollution permits.
8. **State** how the price system in a market economy helps ensure that resources are used wisely.

SECTION 3 *(pages 532–534)*

9. **List** the steps involved in economic decision making.
10. **State** the importance of cost-benefit analysis.
11. **State** why adapting to change is important for an economic system.

Critical Thinking

1. **Making Predictions** In what ways can Americans ensure the wise use of resources? How might the world be different in 50 years if we do not use resources wisely today?
2. **Analyzing Information** How do the laws of supply and demand apply to the resource challenge?

Applying Economic Concepts

1. **Modified Free Enterprise Economy** The United States has a modified free enterprise economy in which the government regulates some industries. Do you think the government should play a smaller or larger role in regulating the American economy? Give reasons to support your answer.
2. **Scarcity** Scarce natural resources are a problem that concerns citizens throughout the world. What can you personally do to help conserve resources?

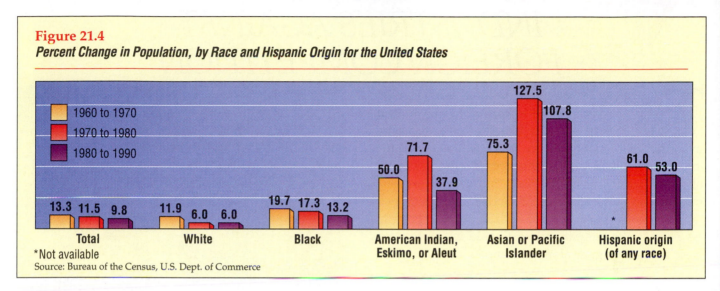

Figure 21.4
Percent Change in Population, by Race and Hispanic Origin for the United States

Legend:
- 1960 to 1970
- 1970 to 1980
- 1980 to 1990

Total: 13.3, 11.5, 9.8
White: 11.9, 6.0, 6.0
Black: 19.7, 17.3, 13.2
American Indian, Eskimo, or Aleut: 50.0, 71.7, 37.9
Asian or Pacific Islander: 75.3, 127.5, 107.8
Hispanic origin (of any race): *, 61.0, 53.0

*Not available
Source: Bureau of the Census, U.S. Dept. of Commerce

Reinforcing Skills

ANALYZING TRENDS

Analyze the graph above, then answer the following questions.

1. What patterns can be seen on the graph?
2. Does the information extend over a significant period of time so that trends can be clearly determined? Explain.
3. What could be some underlying causes of the trends shown on the graph?
4. What additional information would make the graph more helpful in analyzing trends?

Individual Activity

Research the process of using radiation for preserving and growing food. List the types of food products that are affected and the government agencies regulating the process. What are the benefits and possible side-effects of the radiation? You might contact a local environmental protection group to find more information. Report your findings to the class.

Cooperative Learning Activity

Organize into two groups. One group will represent environmentalists opposing the extension of a large chemical plant that uses nuclear energy. The other group will represent the plant owners who say that the expansion will add 500 jobs to the local economy. The environmentalists fear that an expanded facility will be unsafe. Meet together to come up with a plan that is safe, yet still helps the economy.

Writing About Economics

THE PERSUASIVE STYLE

In the **Journal Writing** activity on page 519, you were asked to make a list of all the natural resources you used in a week and classify them as renewable or nonrenewable. Using the persuasive style of writing discussed on page 554, write a paragraph explaining how the resources can be preserved and what everyone should do to preserve them.

PROTECTING DOMESTIC INDUSTRIES AGAINST FOREIGN COMPETITION

The winners in free trade are the consumers who get a wider variety of lower-priced goods from which to choose. The losers are the domestic industries that cannot produce as efficiently as the same industries in other nations. The recent economic success of Japan, which thrives on trade but goes to extreme measures to protect its domestic industries, has created the impression that protectionism can promote growth. As a result, the question arises: Should we protect our basic industries against foreign competition?

Pro

The classical theory of free trade . . . doesn't deal with the fact that much "comparative advantage" today is created not by markets but by government action. If Boeing got a head start on the 707 from multibillion-dollar military contracts, is that a sin against free trade? Well, sort of. . . . If Japan uses public capital, research subsidies, and market-sharing cartels to launch a highly competitive semiconductor industry, is *that* protection? Maybe so, maybe not.

. . . [I]n a world where technology is highly mobile and interchangeable, there is a real risk that comparative advantage comes to be defined as whose work force will work for the lowest wage.

. . . Our competitors, increasingly, are not free marketeers in our own mold. It is absurd to let foreign mercantilist enterprise overrun U.S. industry in the name of free trade. . . .

[S]urely it is reasonable to fashion plans for [protecting] particular key sectors like steel, autos, machine tools, and semiconductors. The idea is not to close U.S. markets, but to limit the rate of import growth in key industries.

—FROM ROBERT KUTTNER'S "THE FREE TRADE FALLACY," *THE NEW REPUBLIC*

▲ *Caterpillar tractors are exported to Japan.*

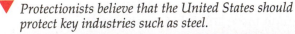

▼ *Protectionists believe that the United States should protect key industries such as steel.*

A customs official inspects Mexican-made Dodge trucks as they enter the United States.

▼ Chiquita bananas are unloaded in Gulfport, Mississippi.

Con Protectionism is, in effect, a "make work" jobs program—but a ridiculously expensive one, both directly and indirectly.

. . . [S]teelworkers (when they are working) make more than the median American income. Protectionism to preserve wage levels is just a redistribution of national wealth; it creates no new wealth. Nothing is wrong with redistribution, but . . . it's hard to see why the government should intervene to protect steelworker's wages at the expense of general national prosperity. This is especially true when millions are unemployed who would happily work for much less, and there is no jobs program for them.

. . . After you add the few hopeless loser industries where we must allegedly create barriers to save American wages, you've got the whole economy locked up, and whether this will actually encourage efficiency or the opposite is, at the very least, an open question. And if every major country protects every major industry, there will be no world market for any of them to conquer.

—FROM MICHAEL KINSLEY'S "KEEP FREE TRADE FREE," *THE NEW REPUBLIC*

Analyzing the Case Study

1. Who benefits most from international trade?
2. What evidence does Robert Kuttner cite to explain that protectionism is needed to protect basic industries from foreign competition?
3. What evidence does Michael Kinsley cite to explain that protectionism will negatively affect the United States economy?
4. With which opinion do you agree? Why?

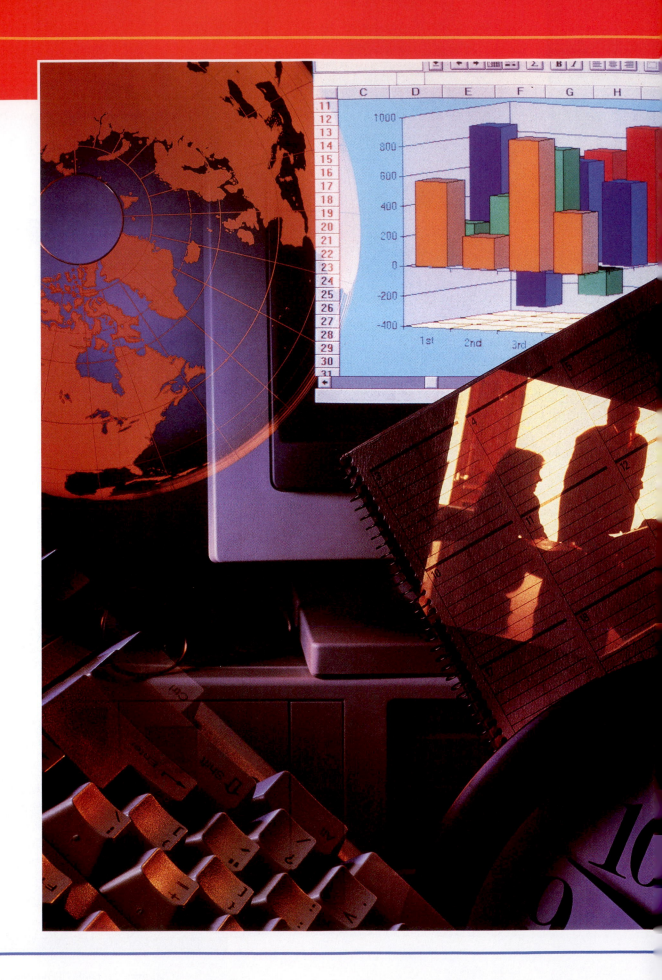

APPENDIX

Contents

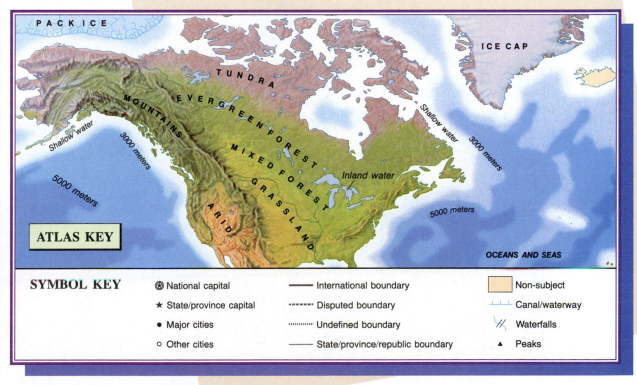

ATLAS KEY

SYMBOL KEY

◉ National capital	——— International boundary	Non-subject
★ State/province capital	------- Disputed boundary	┴┴ Canal/waterway
● Major cities	·········· Undefined boundary	⫻ Waterfalls
○ Other cities	——— State/province/republic boundary	▲ Peaks

OCEANS AND SEAS

ATLAS

ARCTIC OCEAN

BEAUFORT SEA

Point Barrow

ALASKA (U.S.)

Bering Strait

Mackenzie R.

Great Bear Lake

Great Slave Lake

HUDSON BAY

BAFFIN BAY

Davis Strait

Cape Farvel

LABRADOR SEA

BERING SEA

Denali (Mt. McKinley) 20,320 ft. (6,393 m.)

NORTH AMERICA

ROCKY MOUNTAINS

Lake Winnipeg

CANADA

GULF OF ALASKA

Cape Mendocino

Yukon R.

GREAT PLAINS

Missouri R.

Great Lakes

Chicago

New York

ATLANTIC OCEAN

International Date Line (Sunday)

UNITED STATES

Los Angeles

MEXICO

Mississippi R.

APPALACHIAN Mts.

Cape Hatteras

Tropic of Cancer

HAWAIIAN IS. (U.S.)

See inset below
GULF OF MEXICO

PACIFIC OCEAN

Mexico City

CARIBBEAN SEA

VENEZUELA

GUYANA

SURINAME

FRENCH GUIANA (FRANCE)

COLOMBIA

Equator

GALÁPAGOS IS. (ECUADOR)

ECUADOR

AMAZON BASIN

Amazon R.

Cape São Roque

PERU

Pariñas Point

SOUTH AMERICA

BRAZIL

WESTERN SAMOA

MATO GROSSO PLATEAU

BOLIVIA

TONGA

PARAGUAY

GRAN CHACO

Paraná R.

Rio de Janeiro

São Paulo

Tropic of Capricorn

ANDES MOUNTAINS

Mt. Aconcagua 22,834 ft. (6,960 m.)

URUGUAY

Buenos Aires

West Longitude

CHILE

ARGENTINA

FALKLAND IS. (U.K.)

Strait of Magellan

Cape Horn

Drake Passage

SOUTH GEORGIA I. (U.K.)

Antarctic Circle

GULF OF MEXICO

BAHAMAS

CUBA

Tropic of Cancer

TURKS AND CAICOS IS. (U.K.)

ATLANTIC OCEAN

MEXICO

BELIZE

HAITI

DOMINICAN REPUBLIC

VIRGIN ISLANDS (U.S. AND U.K.)

ANTIGUA AND BARBUDA

JAMAICA

PUERTO RICO (U.S.)

ST. KITTS AND NEVIS

GUADELOUPE (FRANCE)

GUATEMALA

DOMINICA

HONDURAS

CARIBBEAN SEA

MARTINIQUE (FRANCE)

ST. LUCIA

EL SALVADOR

N

ST. VINCENT AND THE GRENADINES

PACIFIC OCEAN

NICARAGUA

ARUBA (NETHERLANDS)

NETHERLANDS ANTILLES (NETHERLANDS)

BARBADOS

GRENADA

TRINIDAD AND TOBAGO

COSTA RICA

0   250   500 Miles
0   250   500 Kilometers

PANAMA

COLOMBIA

VENEZUELA

GUYANA

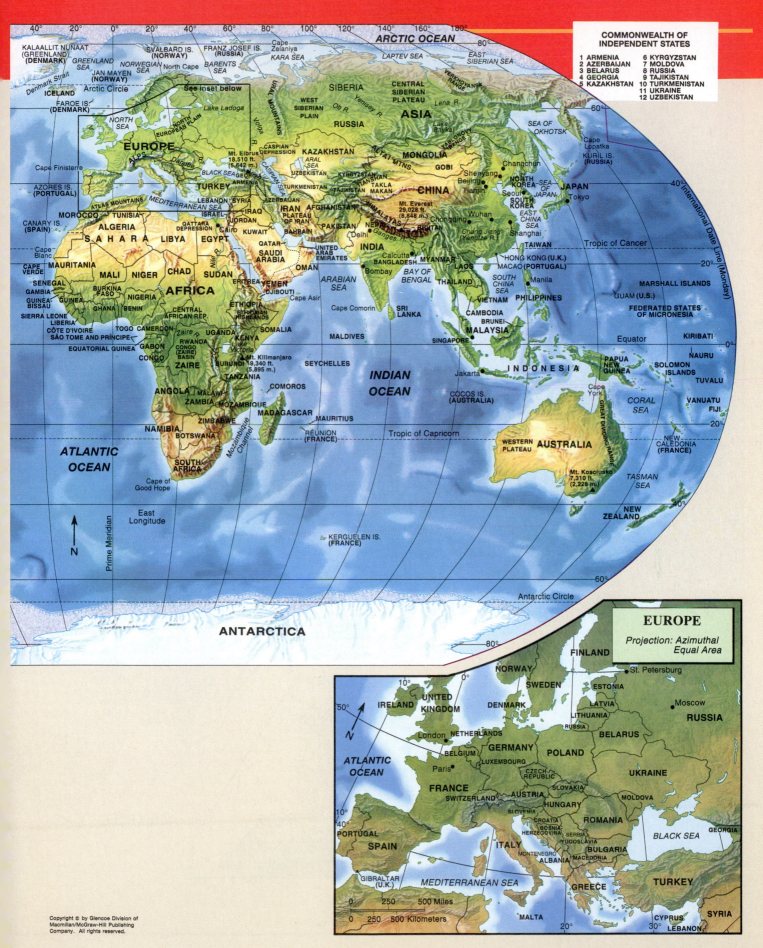

ARCTIC OCEAN

KALAALLIT NUNAAT
(GREENLAND)
(DENMARK)

SVALBARD IS.
(NORWAY)

FRANZ JOSEF IS.
(RUSSIA)

Cape
Zelaniya

LAPTEV SEA

EAST
SIBERIAN SEA

ICELAND

FAROE IS.
(DENMARK)

GREENLAND
SEA

NORWEGIAN
SEA

JAN MAYEN
(NORWAY)

North Cape

BARENTS
SEA

KARA SEA

VERKHOYANSK RANGE

Denmark Strait

Arctic Circle

See Inset below

NORTH
SEA

NORTH
EUROPEAN PLAIN

Lake Ladoga

SIBERIA

CENTRAL
SIBERIAN
PLATEAU

Lena R.

60°

SEA
OF
OKHOTSK

Cape
Lopatka

KURIL IS.
(RUSSIA)

Cape Finisterre

EUROPE

ALPS

Danube

WEST
SIBERIAN
PLAIN

Ob R.

Yenisey R.

RUSSIA

ASIA

AZORES IS.
(PORTUGAL)

BLACK SEA

Mt. Elbrus
18,510 ft.
(5,642 m.)

CASPIAN
DEPRESSION

Volga

ARAL
SEA

KAZAKHSTAN

ALTAI MTNS.

MONGOLIA

GOBI

Changchun

SEA OF
JAPAN

JAPAN

Tokyo

40°

MOROCCO

TUNISIA

TURKEY

GEORGIA
ARMENIA

CASPIAN SEA

AZERBAIJAN

UZBEKISTAN

TURKMENISTAN

TAJIKISTAN

TIAN SHAN

TAKLA
MAKAN

CHINA

Beijing
Shenyang

Tianjin

Seoul

NORTH
KOREA

SOUTH
KOREA

EAST
CHINA
SEA

CANARY IS.
(SPAIN)

ATLAS MOUNTAINS

ALGERIA

LIBYA

MEDITERRANEAN SEA

LEBANON
ISRAEL

SYRIA

IRAQ

JORDAN

IRAN

PLATEAU
OF IRAN

AFGHANISTAN

PAKISTAN

HIMALAYAS

Mt. Everest
29,028 ft.
(8,848 m.)

NEPAL

BHUTAN

Chongqing

Wuhan

Chang Jiang
(Yangtze R.)

Shanghai

TAIWAN

Tropic of Cancer

20°

Cape
Blanc

SAHARA

EGYPT

QATTARA
DEPRESSION

Cairo

Nile R.

KUWAIT

BAHRAIN

QATAR

UNITED
ARAB
EMIRATES

SAUDI
ARABIA

Delhi

Gangs R.

INDIA

Calcutta

BANGLADESH

MYANMAR

HONG KONG (U.K.)

MACAO (PORTUGAL)

SOUTH
CHINA
SEA

Manila

MARSHALL ISLANDS

CAPE
VERDE

MAURITANIA

MALI

NIGER

CHAD

SUDAN

ERITREA

YEMEN

OMAN

ARABIAN
SEA

Bombay

BAY OF
BENGAL

LAOS

THAILAND

VIETNAM

CAMBODIA

PHILIPPINES

GUAM (U.S.)

SENEGAL

GAMBIA

GUINEA-
BISSAU

GUINEA

BURKINA
FASO

NIGERIA

BENIN

GHANA

TOGO

AFRICA

DJIBOUTI

ETHIOPIA

ETHIOPIAN
HIGHLANDS

Cape Asir

Cape Comorin

SRI
LANKA

MALDIVES

BRUNEI

MALAYSIA

FEDERATED STATES
OF MICRONESIA

SIERRA LEONE

LIBERIA

CÔTE D'IVOIRE

CAMEROON

CENTRAL
AFRICAN REP.

UGANDA

KENYA

SOMALIA

SINGAPORE

Equator

KIRIBATI

NAURU

0°

EQUATORIAL GUINEA

SÃO TOME AND PRÍNCIPE

GABON

CONGO

ZAIRE

CONGO
(ZAIRE)
BASIN

RWANDA

BURUNDI

Lake
Victoria

Mt. Kilimanjaro
19,340 ft.
(5,895 m.)

TANZANIA

SEYCHELLES

INDIAN
OCEAN

Jakarta

I N D O N E S I A

Cape
York

PAPUA
NEW
GUINEA

SOLOMON
ISLANDS

TUVALU

ANGOLA

MALAWI

ZAMBIA

MOZAMBIQUE

COMOROS

MADAGASCAR

MAURITIUS

COCOS IS.
(AUSTRALIA)

CORAL
SEA

VANUATU

FIJI

ATLANTIC
OCEAN

ZIMBABWE

NAMIBIA

BOTSWANA

Mozambique Channel

RÉUNION
(FRANCE)

Tropic of Capricorn

WESTERN
PLATEAU

AUSTRALIA

GREAT DIVIDING RANGE

NEW
CALEDONIA
(FRANCE)

20°

SOUTH
AFRICA

Cape of
Good Hope

East
Longitude

Prime Meridian

N

KERGUELEN IS.
(FRANCE)

Mt. Kosciusko
7,310 ft.
(2,228 m.)

TASMAN
SEA

NEW
ZEALAND

40°

60°

Antarctic Circle

80°

ANTARCTICA

International Date Line (Monday)

Copyright © by Glencoe Division of
Macmillan/McGraw-Hill Publishing
Company. All rights reserved.

COMMONWEALTH OF
INDEPENDENT STATES

1 ARMENIA
2 AZERBAIJAN
3 BELARUS
4 GEORGIA
5 KAZAKHSTAN
6 KYRGYZSTAN
7 MOLDOVA
8 RUSSIA
9 TAJIKISTAN
10 TURKMENISTAN
11 UKRAINE
12 UZBEKISTAN

EUROPE

Projection: Azimuthal
Equal Area

FINLAND

NORWAY

St. Petersburg

SWEDEN

ESTONIA

LATVIA

Moscow

IRELAND

UNITED
KINGDOM

DENMARK

LITHUANIA

RUSSIA

RUSSIA

BELARUS

N

London

NETHERLANDS

BELGIUM

GERMANY

POLAND

ATLANTIC
OCEAN

Paris

LUXEMBOURG

CZECH
REPUBLIC

SLOVAKIA

UKRAINE

FRANCE

SWITZERLAND

AUSTRIA

HUNGARY

MOLDOVA

SLOVENIA

ROMANIA

GEORGIA

PORTUGAL

SPAIN

ITALY

CROATIA

BOSNIA
HERZEGOVINA

SERBIA

YUGOSLAVIA

MONTENEGRO

ALBANIA

MACEDONIA

BULGARIA

BLACK SEA

TURKEY

GIBRALTAR
(U.K.)

MEDITERRANEAN SEA

GREECE

CYPRUS

SYRIA

LEBANON

MALTA

0   250   500 Miles

0   250   500 Kilometers

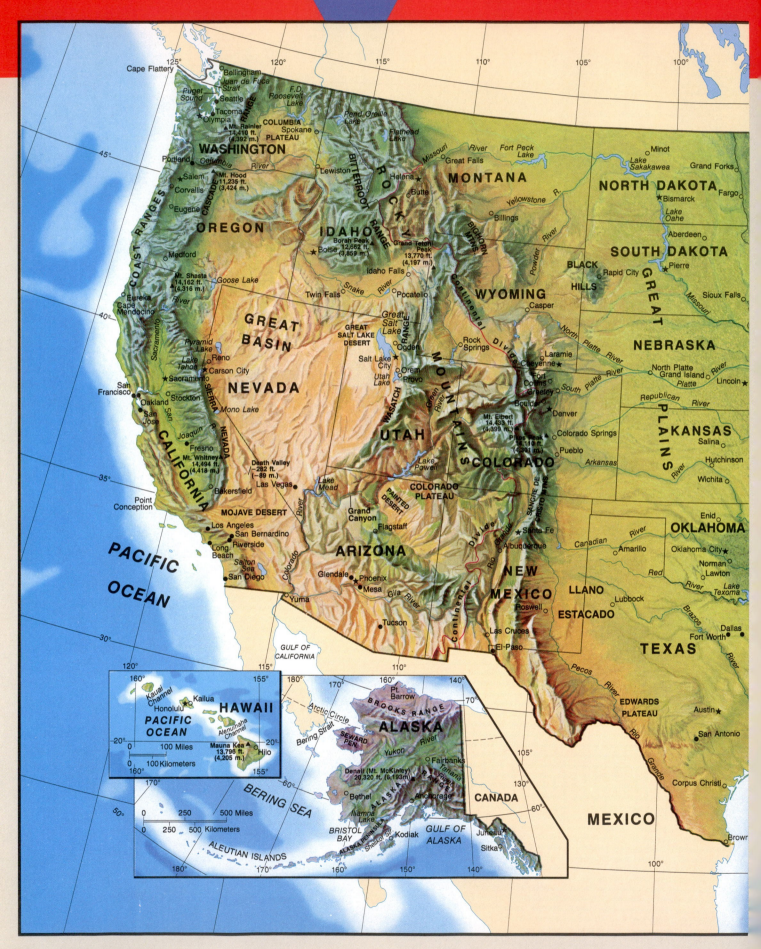

CANADA

MINNESOTA

WISCONSIN

Lake of the Woods

Red Lake

Duluth

Minneapolis ★ St. Paul

Rochester

Sioux City

IOWA

Mississippi River

Cedar Rapids

Dubuque

Davenport

Omaha
Council Bluffs ★ Des Moines

CENTRAL

Topeka ★ Kansas City

Lawrence

Kansas City

Independence

Jefferson City ★

MISSOURI

Springfield

Tulsa

OZARK PLATEAU

Harry S. Truman Res.

R.S. Res.

ARKANSAS

Fort Smith

North Little Rock

Little Rock ★

Hot Springs

Pine Bluff

Lake Eufaula

Sam Rayburn Reservoir

Toledo Bend Res.

Shreveport

LOUISIANA

Houston

Lake Charles

Lafayette

Lake Pontchartrain

Baton Rouge ★

New Orleans

Biloxi

Hattiesburg

MISSISSIPPI

Jackson ★

Meridian

Mobile

Pensacola

ALABAMA

Montgomery ★

Birmingham

Tuscaloosa

Columbus

GEORGIA

Albany

Macon

Augusta

Columbia

SOUTH CAROLINA

Charleston

Savannah

MICHIGAN

Lake Superior

Lake Michigan

Lake Huron

Green Bay

Appleton

Milwaukee

Racine

Madison ★

Rockford

Chicago

Aurora

Joliet

Gary

Hammond

South Bend

ILLINOIS

Peoria

Springfield ★

Decatur

INDIANA

Muncie

Indianapolis ★

Wabash R.

Evansville

East St. Louis

St. Louis

Ohio River

Owensboro

KENTUCKY

Frankfort ★

Louisville

Lexington

Nashville ★

TENNESSEE

Chattanooga

Memphis

Knoxville

Cumberland River

Tennessee River

Huntsville

Greenville

CUMBERLAND

APPALACHIAN PLATEAU

Grand Rapids

Flint

Lansing

Detroit

Ann Arbor

Toledo

Fort Wayne

Dayton

OHIO

Columbus

Cincinnati

Akron

Canton

Youngstown

Cleveland

Erie

Lake Erie

PENNSYLVANIA

Pittsburgh

Wheeling

WEST VIRGINIA

Parkersburg

Charleston

Huntington

Roanoke

VIRGINIA

Richmond

Mt. Mitchell 6,684 ft. (2,037 m.)

Winston-Salem

Greensboro

Durham

Raleigh ★

NORTH CAROLINA

Charlotte

Spartanburg

Greenville

LOWLAND

Niagara Falls

Lake-Ontario

Rochester

Buffalo

Binghamton

NEW YORK

Syracuse

Utica

Albany ★

St. Lawrence River

MAINE

Moosehead Lake

Bangor

Augusta ★

Lewiston

Portland

Mt. Washington 6,288 ft. (1,905 m.)

Lake Champlain

Burlington

Montpelier ★

N.H.

VT.

Concord ★

Manchester

MASS.

Boston ★

Worcester

Springfield

Providence ★

R.I.

CONN.

Hartford ★

New Haven

Yonkers

New York

Newark

N.J.

Trenton ★

Allentown

Philadelphia

Camden

Harrisburg ★

Wilmington

Dover ★

DEL.

DELAWARE BAY

MD.

Baltimore

Annapolis ★

Arlington

Washington D.C.

Newport News

Norfolk

CHESAPEAKE BAY

ATLANTIC OCEAN

Cape Cod

Cape Hatteras

Charleston

FLORIDA

COASTAL PLAIN

Jacksonville

Tallahassee ★

Orlando

Cape Canaveral

Tampa

St. Petersburg

Lake Okeechobee

Palm Beach

Miami Beach

Miami

Cape Sable

Key West

Strait of Florida

GULF OF MEXICO

N

Copyright © by Glencoe Division of Macmillan/McGraw-Hill Publishing Company. All rights reserved.

THE BAHAMAS

CUBA

45°

40°

70°

35°

30°

25°

75°

95°

90°

85°

80°

75°

70°

UNITED STATES

⊛ National capital

★ State capital

● Major city

○ Other city

— International boundary

— State boundary

| 0 | 100 | 200 Miles |

| 0 | 100 | 200 Kilometers |

Projection: Albers Equal Area

UNITED STATES MAP   **545**

Budgeting

To increase your wealth, financial planners recommend that you control your expenditures to live within your means. You can accomplish this by making a **budget**—a plan that matches expenditures with income. Budgeting can help you manage your money better and prevent you from buying goods and services you do not really need or cannot afford.

The first step in setting up a budget is to obtain a **spreadsheet**—a large sheet of paper with columns for weeks and months, and rows for different categories of expenditures. You can buy spreadsheets in an office supply store, make one of your own, or use a computer software program designed for this purpose.

Next, decide whether you want to set up your budget on a weekly, monthly, or yearly basis. If you get paid every two weeks, you might want to set up an annual budget with 26 biweekly columns. If you get paid monthly, you might prefer to set up an annual budget with 12 monthly columns, like the one illustrated below.

The first row of your budget should consist of the income you expect to have for each period. Be sure to record your **net income**—the income received after taxes have been taken out. The remainder of the rows should be used to list your expenditures.

List your monthly expenditures, such as rent and utility bills. Then list miscellaneous expenditures, such as clothing or gifts. Because you do not know how many unexpected expenditures you will have, allow 5 to 10 percent of your net income for this category. Set up an additional category for repairs or maintenance of items you may own, such as a car. These items likely are too large to be included in the miscellaneous category.

Keep in mind that it is more efficient and sometimes easier to spread larger expenditures across time. Your car insurance, for example, may be due every six months. Rather than try to budget the entire payment in one or two periods, set aside enough money each period so that you have the entire amount on hand when the bill arrives.

Monitor your budget to make sure that the amounts you have allotted for each expenditure are reasonable. If you find that a category does not reflect your actual spending, adjust it. A benefit of a budget is that it can show you where you need to increase or decrease your spending.

Applying Life Skills

1. Why is making a budget important?
2. What are the steps involved in making a budget?
3. What does it mean to monitor a budget?

	Jan	Feb	March	April	May	June	July	Aug	Sep	Oct	Nov	Dec
Net Income												
Rent												
Auto												
Telephone												
Utilities												
Cable												
Food												
Clothing												
Entertainment												
Miscellaneous												

Maintaining a Checking Account

Properly maintaining a checking account takes time and effort. Checking accounts generally are not free unless you are able to deposit—and not use—a minimum sum of money, which generally varies from $500 to $1,000. If you do not maintain the required minimum, you may pay a monthly fee.

Contact several banks to compare the terms of their checking accounts. Then order checks printed with your full name, current address, and telephone number. When you write checks, make all figures and amounts legible. Write the amount in the box on the extreme right and on the line on the left, using all the space available so that no one can change the amount. Be sure to date the checks correctly and sign them clearly and accurately. Immediately record in your checkbook the date the check was written, to whom it was written, and the amount for which it was written.

You should balance your checkbook every month after receiving a statement from the bank. The statement will tell you which checks the bank has received and which deposits it has recorded. It will also tell you what the balance of your account is at the time the statement was issued. It is your responsibility to **reconcile** your account—make sure your balance agrees with the bank's balance. To reconcile your account, follow these steps:

1. In your checkbook, mark each check entry listed on your bank statement with an *X* to show that the check has been processed. As you do this, make sure the amount of each check recorded in your checkbook matches the amount on the statement.
2. List the checks you wrote but that were not processed. Total the amounts of these checks, then add the total to the balance you have written in your checkbook.
3. Subtract any fees or charges indicated on the bank statement, such as a monthly service charge or a charge for new checks.
4. Subtract any cash withdrawals you made from automatic teller machines (ATMs).
5. Compare this balance with the balance on your bank statement. If no mistakes were made, your balance should match the bank's.

If the two balances do not match, look for mistakes. If you do not clear up the error immediately,

---

Tom Smith
1427 Blackwood Drive
Copper Canyon, TX 75067
(817) 555-1140

001

Feb. 2   19XX   1-32 / 280

Pay to the Order of: Jack Jones   54.00

Fifty-Four and No/100s   Dollars

FIRST STATE BANK
DALLAS, TEXAS

Tom Smith

⑆011000044⑆ 183506844 ⑈

---

call the bank. The error may carry over to the next month and make balancing your checkbook even more difficult. If the balance gets too far out of line, a check may **bounce**, or be returned for insufficient funds, which will cost you a fee of $10 or $20. If a number of checks bounce, it could give you a bad credit rating.

Applying Life Skills

1. Why is having a checking account convenient for many consumers?
2. How do you balance a checkbook?
3. What does it mean when a check bounces?

LIFE SKILL

Filing an Income Tax Return

If you work, you probably have to file income tax forms with the federal government and, in some cases, with the state and/or city in which you live or work. The first step in filing income tax forms is to fill out a withholding statement with your employer. The federal withholding form, known as a W-4, asks for such information as your name and address, social security number, marital status, and any special allowances for disabilities or dependents. This form is shown below. The purpose of the W-4 is to help your employer determine how much money to withhold from each of your paychecks. If you do not complete the form properly, your employer may not withhold enough money, and you will have to pay additional taxes.

as union dues or uniforms, and uninsured losses from theft or natural disasters.

At the beginning of each year, the Internal Revenue Service sends out tax forms with detailed instructions on how to complete them. You can find the same forms at most post offices, public libraries, or banks. You may complete the forms yourself or have them completed by a professional tax preparer. The fee for

Form **W-4** Department of the Treasury Internal Revenue Service	**Employee's Withholding Allowance Certificate** ▶ For Privacy Act and Paperwork Reduction Act Notice, see reverse.	OMB No. 1545-0010 19**93**

| 1 | Type or print your name and middle initial | Last name | 2 | Your social security number |

| Home address (number and street or rural route) | 3 ☐ Single ☐ Married ☐ Married, but withhold at higher Single rate Note: *If married, but legally separated, or spouse is a nonresident alien, check the Single box.* |
| City or town, state, and ZIP code | 4 If your last name differs from that on your social security card, check here and call 1-800-772-1213 for more information . . . . ▶ ☐ |

5	Total number of allowances you are claiming (from line G above or from the worksheets on page 2 if they apply)	**5**	
6	Additional amount, if any, you want withheld from each paycheck	**6** $
7	I claim exemption from withholding for 1993 and I certify that I meet ALL of the following conditions for exemption:

- Last year I had a right to a refund of **ALL** Federal income tax withheld because I had **NO** tax liability; **AND**
- This year I expect a refund of **ALL** Federal income tax withheld because I expect to have **NO** tax liability; **AND**
- This year if my income exceeds $600 and includes nonwage income, another person cannot claim me as a dependent.

If you meet all of the above conditions, enter "EXEMPT" here . . . . ▶ **7**

Under penalties of perjury, I certify that I am entitled to the number of withholding allowances claimed on this certificate or entitled to claim exempt status.

Employee's signature ▶   Date ▶   , 19

| 8 | Employer's name and address (Employer: Complete 8 and 10 only if sending to the IRS) | 9 Office code optional | 10 Employer identification number |

Cat. No. 10220Q

Keep your pay stubs and the receipts for your expenditures together in a safe place. By law, every January your employer must provide you with a W-2 form, which summarizes your earnings for the year. You should check the information on your pay stubs against the information on the W-2. Some expenditures are tax deductible and will save you money by lowering your taxes. You must be able to prove, however, that you actually made the expenditures. Your proof is the receipts that you have saved.

Depending on the current tax laws, deductible expenses may include mortgage interest, medical bills and pharmaceutical expenses, child-care expenses, charitable contributions, such work-related expenses

this service varies according to the complexity of your tax return and the amount of time it takes to prepare it. You generally must file the completed forms by midnight, April 15.

Applying Life Skills

1. What is a W-4 form? What is its purpose?
2. In preparing to file an income tax form, why are receipts important?
3. What are some examples of tax deductible expenses?

Renting an Apartment

If you decide to rent an apartment, take time to choose wisely. Determine the best location in terms of getting back and forth from work or school and convenience for shopping. Decide if you want a furnished or unfurnished apartment. Consider how much space you need to have adequate storage and be comfortable. Most importantly, determine how much rent you can afford to pay. Monthly rent plus related expenses should not be more than one week's take-home pay.

To find an apartment, consult the classified section of newspapers, ask friends for recommendations, or hire a rental agent. Never agree to rent an apartment until you have personally seen it. The best time to do this is during an evening or on a weekend, which will reveal the surrounding noise level and what the neighbors are like. If possible, talk to some of the people in the apartment complex to learn the advantages and disadvantages of moving into the area.

Inspect the apartment and the surrounding area carefully for the following:

1. Is the building well-built, well-maintained, and well-lit?
2. Is the apartment the right size? Does it have a convenient floor plan, enough wall space for your furniture, and adequate lighting and electrical outlets?
3. How many windows are there? Do they open and close easily? Are there screens and storm windows?
4. Is the apartment air-conditioned? Does it have its own heating and cooling controls?
5. Are major appliances, such as a stove and refrigerator, in good working condition?
6. Is the apartment carpeted? Are there drapes, blinds, or shades for the windows?
7. Does the building have fire walls? Smoke alarms?
8. Are laundry equipment and storage facilities available?
9. Is there trash collection or disposal? Where? How often? By whom? Who pays for it?
10. What kind of burglary protection is there?
11. What are the parking facilities?

After you have selected the apartment you want, you probably will have to sign a **lease,** a written agreement between you and the landlord that states the major terms of your occupancy. It generally includes a description of the rental property; the amount of rent to be paid and when it is due; how much deposit is required, what it covers, and under what conditions it may be forfeited; and how long the lease is in force and under what conditions it may be renewed. The lease also should include the terms for rent increases; who pays for specific utilities and repairs; what alterations you can make on the property; how much notice you must give before moving; whether you can rent the apartment to someone else; and whether children, pets, or roommates are allowed.

Before signing a lease, inspect the apartment with the landlord. Point out and write down all the damage to walls, floors, appliances, and fixtures. Attach a copy of this list to the lease so that you cannot be held responsible for damage done before you moved into the apartment. Check to see if a security deposit is required in addition to the rental deposit. If it is, determine the amount and under what conditions it will be returned. Insist that this information be included in the lease. Find out who pays for personal injury or loss of personal property due to the landlord's negligence. Make sure all the blanks in the lease are filled in or crossed out and all verbal contracts you made with the landlord are included.

Applying Life Skills

1. What are some things to consider if you decide to rent an apartment?
2. When is the best time to look for an apartment?
3. What is a lease? What does it include?

Borrowing Money

When borrowing money, you assume some risks. Being in debt is dangerous and can lead to personal bankruptcy. Before you decide to borrow money, keep the following factors in mind:

1. Do not borrow so much that if you become ill or lose your job, you no longer will be financially stable.
2. Stagger your debts. Spread out your payments so they are not all due at the same time.

If you have a legitimate need to borrow money, you might consider asking a family member or a friend for a loan. Life insurance companies, savings institutions, credit unions, commercial banks, retail organizations, and finance companies also lend money. The many types of loans that are available to consumers include the following:

- **Installment sales credit,** the most common type of loan available, is generally taken out to buy such merchandise as household furniture or appliances. The consumer makes an initial deposit on the goods and agrees to pay the balance, plus interest and service charges, in equal installments over a period of time.
- **Installment cash credit** is a direct cash loan often used for vacations, home improvements, or other personal expenses. No down payment is required, but the loan, plus interest and other charges, must be repaid in equal installments over a specified period of time.
- **Single lump sum credit** is a direct cash loan requiring that the amount borrowed plus interest be repaid on a specified day.
- **Open-ended or revolving credit** allows consumers to purchase goods and services from merchants on credit, often without a down payment. In some cases, the consumer may repay the entire balance within 30 days without any interest charges. Monthly payments are required thereafter, with interest being computed on the outstanding balance.
- **Credit card loans** are loans made through the use of a bank credit card. The payment plans for this type of loan vary widely. In some cases, the consumer pays an annual fee for the use of the card. In other cases, the consumer may have to pay the balance in full at the end of the month, or make monthly installment payments.

Regardless of the type of loan you obtain, you are entitled by law to information about the cost of credit. First, you are entitled to know the **finance charge**—the total dollar amount the credit will cost, including interest charged plus any carrying or service charge. Second, you are entitled to know the **annual percentage rate (APR)**—the interest cost of the loan on a yearly basis. Because repayment schedules differ, the APR is your guide to the true cost of the loan.

To obtain a loan, you must be a good credit risk. The lender checks on your character, your ability to repay the loan, and your capital assets. To determine your creditability, lenders often check with a **credit bureau**—an agency that collects credit information on consumers. If your **credit rating**—a record of debt and payment history—is not good or is in doubt, you probably will be denied credit. Thus, to maintain a good credit rating, you should pay debts on time.

If your request for a loan is granted, you should check to make sure that the contract for the loan does not include any of the following:

1. An **add-on clause,** which allows the seller to keep title to an entire list of items until all payments on the loan have been completed.
2. A **balloon clause,** which makes the final payment larger than the other monthly payments.
3. An **acceleration clause**, which allows the lender to demand an immediate payment in full if one payment is not made.

Applying Life Skills

1. What are some wrong reasons for borrowing?
2. What kinds of loans are available for consumers?
3. What is a credit rating? Why is it important to maintain a good one?

Buying Insurance

Almost everyone needs some kind of insurance. Your parents, for example, may have several types of insurance—homeowners insurance in case of theft, fire, or natural disaster; automobile insurance in case of accident or disability; and health insurance to cover them if they are hospitalized or ill for a long time.

You need insurance to protect yourself. How much and what kind of insurance you need depends on your lifestyle, your job, your age, and many other factors. You need enough insurance to protect your belongings and potential income, but not so much that paying for it strains your budget.

There are six major types of insurance that you should consider:

- **Whole life insurance**, sometimes called ordinary life insurance, pays money to your survivors in the event of your death. It also carries a provision for savings against which you can borrow. You may collect the savings in one lump sum when you retire. Although this type of insurance can be expensive, it offers a combination of coverage to those who cannot buy individual coverage.

- **Term insurance** offers one type of coverage only—payment to your survivors in the event of your death.

- **Health insurance** covers medical and hospital bills if you become ill. Some health insurance policies also cover medication. A good policy covers approximately 80 percent of medical expenses.

- **Automobile insurance** can provide several different kinds of coverage: **Liability** coverage protects you from claims and lawsuits if you cause an accident. **Collision** covers damage to your automobile if another vehicle hits it.

- **Homeowners insurance** covers a homeowner when his or her home or property has been damaged. Mortgage lenders generally insist that a homeowner carry this type of insurance until his or her mortgage has been paid in full.

- **Property liability** protects renters and homeowners against claims of negligence filed by others when an accident occurs on the renter's or homeowner's property.

Deciding exactly what insurance to buy can be confusing. Different insurance companies often offer the same type of insurance under different names, which makes it difficult to know if separate insurance companies are talking about the same kind of policy. In addition, the product—coverage—is invisible. The consumer cannot tell how much the policy will pay until something happens for which he or she wants to collect payment.

When you are buying insurance, keep the following factors in mind:

1. Group policies—policies offered to a group of people, generally by an employer or organization—tend to be less expensive than individual policies purchased from an insurance agent.
2. Always consult more than one agent before buying a policy. Describe your needs carefully to each agent, and ask each to recommend a policy and provide a written list of benefits and estimates of costs. Inform each agent that you are consulting other agents and intend to compare costs and benefits before making any decision. Base your decision to buy a policy on the results of your comparison.

Applying Life Skills

1. Why do consumers need insurance?
2. What are six major types of insurance?
3. What factors should you consider when buying insurance?

LIFE SKILL

Paying for College

College costs have risen steadily in recent years. If you need financial aid, regardless of the reason, start researching for aid in your junior year or early in your senior year of high school. Check with your guidance counselor about federal aids and state, military, ethnic, and fraternal grants.

Generally, students from low-income families are eligible for some aid even if their grades are low. Students from middle-income families generally are eligible for less aid and then only if they have good grades. These students will have to rely more on subsidized student loans and special scholarships. Students from high-income families generally are not eligible for aid.

Financial aid comes in three basic forms—loans, which must be repaid; scholarships and grants, which need not be repaid; and jobs. Most financial-aid sponsors distribute their money through colleges. Therefore, contact the financial aid office of the college(s) of your choice. Because most colleges send out financial aid applications only upon request, you should obtain these forms early and then file them with your application for admission. Missing the appointed deadline will reduce your chances for aid.

LOANS There are four major types of student loans. The *National Direct Student Loan* is granted only to needy students. The funds come from the federal government, but individual colleges choose the students who receive them. The loan is interest-free while you are in school. After graduating, you have 10 years to

repay the loan at low interest. To apply for this type of loan, contact the financial aid office at the college(s) of your choice.

The *Government Guaranteed Student Loan* is made by financial institutions, which are guaranteed repayment by the federal government. While you are in school, the government pays the interest, which is generally 9 percent. After you graduate, you have 10 years to repay the loan. Like the National Direct

Student Loan, this loan is granted to you rather than to your parents. To apply, contact financial institutions.

A *bank loan* requires you or your parents to begin repayment while you are still in college. Although interest rates vary on this type of loan, they generally are higher than those on government loans.

A *special student loan* is one offered by colleges, civic and professional groups, and other organizations. The interest rates vary on these loans.

SCHOLARSHIPS AND GRANTS Scholarships provide another source of financial aid. In most cases, income plays no part in eligibility. Some available scholarships include:

- *national, state, and college merit scholarships* awarded on the basis of academic excellence.
- *athletic scholarships* awarded to students who excel in a sport or sports.
- *talent scholarships* awarded to students gifted in the arts.
- *Reserve Officers' Training Corps scholarships* awarded to students willing to spend four years in the armed forces after graduation.

Grants also are available, but they generally are for the needy only. For those who qualify, *Pell Grants* can be used at any accredited college, vocational school, technical institute, nursing school, and the like. Grades play no role in eligibility.

WORK AND STUDY The third basic kind of financial aid is in the form of a job. Several different programs fall into this category. One is the *College Work-Study Program* sponsored by the federal government. To be eligible, you must be a full-time student who would not be able to attend school without the job. Another program is *cooperative education*. Under this program, you work six months and go to school six months each year. What you earn on the job will pay your tuition.

If you are seeking financial aid for college, keep the following in mind:

- Start your investigation early.
- Apply for every scholarship or grant for which you may qualify.
- You can borrow from more than one program.

Applying Life Skills

1. If you need financial aid for college, when should you begin your search?
2. What are three forms of financial aid?
3. What kinds of scholarships are available?

Preparing a Resume

One of the most critical parts of finding a job is preparing a resume. A good resume provides a brief history of your strengths, abilities, and accomplishments. A prospective employer's decision to interview you often depends on his or her reaction to your resume.

Before writing your resume, conduct an inventory of your strengths and weaknesses by asking yourself questions such as: What kinds of skills and talents do I have? What is my work history? How much formal education have I had? What were my grades and class standings? In what activities have I participated? What are my goals? What kind of work do I want? What salary would I be willing to accept?

When you have answered these questions, organize the entries on your resume. Begin with your name, address, and telephone number. Indicate the position or kind of position you are seeking. List all your relevant work experience, beginning with your most recent job. Include the dates of your employment, the names of the companies for which you worked, and the positions you held.

List the schools you have attended. Include any special honors or awards you have received and any activities in which you have been or are involved.

Provide at least three references, all of whom know you well enough to vouch for your abilities or strengths. Do not use relatives as references, and do not use more than two teachers. Keep in mind that you may adjust the format of your resume.

Applying Life Skills

1. Why is a resume an important step in finding a job?
2. What kinds of questions should you ask yourself when preparing a resume?
3. What kinds of items should you list on a resume?

Writing for Various Purposes

THE INFORMATIVE STYLE The informative writing style is used to tell a story that flows smoothly, with events often appearing in the order in which they happen. To tell the story in this style, use a story plan made up of four elements—time, place, people, and events.

Discuss what happened, when it happened, why it happened, how it happened, and who was involved. When writing in the informative style, it is important to not show approval or disapproval. Simply present the facts in an objective way without displaying emotion or injecting your opinion.

THE EXPRESSIVE STYLE The expressive writing style generally is used if the main purpose is to describe an event or scene in a way that will make the reader feel he or she is actually sharing in the experience. In this style, use as many aspects of the five senses—sight, sound, taste, smell, and touch—as possible. In this way, you create vivid images in the mind of the reader. Try to use strong, active verbs that command the reader to see what you have seen, hear what you have heard, and smell, taste, and feel as you have.

THE PERSUASIVE STYLE The persuasive writing style is used to present a specific opinion or to try to persuade the reader to agree with a certain opinion. In this style, facts and other information may be given. These facts, however, are added to support your point of view and to persuade the reader to agree with you.

In writing a persuasive argument, it is important to state the problem clearly and give your position on the issue. Then present the evidence you have gathered to support your position and to refute any opposing position. Conclude your argument by restating your position and summing up the evidence.

THE CLASSIFICATORY STYLE Writers often use the classificatory writing style to organize information about a topic or subject into smaller and simpler categories. There are several different ways that writers classify information. One way is to compare how two things or events are alike or different. Another is by listing advantages and disadvantages. Writers using the classificatory style often need to define their categories or ideas to help readers understand unfamiliar terms.

Bobby Little
4144 Valley Court
Cranston, Illinois 60505
(708) 555-2242

Position Desired   Seeking part-time employment during the school year: Prefer to work one afternoon or evening per week plus one day of the weekend; willing to work full-time during the summer.

Work Experience   June 1992–Present: Part-time Cook, McDonald's, Inc., Cranston, Illinois

January 1992–May 1992: Part-time Stock Clerk, Brown's Hardware Store, Cranston, Illinois

Education   Senior at Scott High School, Class of 1994, currently an honors student

Honors and Awards   First Place medal (computer division), State of Illinois Science Fair, for project entitled "NYSE: The Stock Market Simulation," April 1994

Air Force Best Overall Project Award, State of Illinois Science Fair, April 1994

First Place, Computer Division, Blake County Science Fair, May 1994

Outstanding Physical Education/Health Student Award, Scott High School, Spring 1992

Special Interests   Computers, strategy games, playing the guitar

Member of Scott High School Chess Club (September 1992-May 1994)

Member of Scott High School Spanish Club (September 1991-May 1994)

References   Ms. Alice Williamson, Department of Science, Scott High School, Cranston, Illinois 60505 (708) 555-3414

Mr. John Brown, Owner, Brown's Hardware Store, Cranston, Illinois 60505 (708) 555-3633

Mr. Richard Adams, McDonald's, Inc., Cranston, Illinois 60505 (708) 555-8970

GLOSSARY

A

ability-to-pay principle of taxation belief that taxes should be paid according to level of income regardless of benefits received (p. 214)

absolute advantage country's ability to produce more of a given product than can another country (p. 450)

accelerated depreciation schedule that spreads depreciation over fewer years than normal to generate larger tax reductions (p. 231)

accelerator change in investment spending caused by a change in overall spending (p. 428)

acid rain pollution in form of rainwater mixed with sulfur dioxide, a mild form of sulfuric acid (p. 528)

agency shop arrangement under which non-union members must pay union dues (p. 190)

aggregate demand curve hypothetical curve showing different levels of real GDP that could be purchased at various price levels (p. 424)

aggregate supply curve hypothetical curve showing different levels of real GDP that could be produced at various price levels (p. 422)

agricultural bank commercial bank with more than 25 percent of its loans in agriculture (p. 313)

alternative minimum tax personal income tax rate that applies to cases where taxes would otherwise fall below a certain level (p. 231)

appropriations bill legislation earmarking funds for certain purposes (p. 243)

aquifer underground water-bearing rock formation (p. 525)

articles of partnership formal legal papers specifying the arrangements between partners, including the way profits and losses are divided (p. 57)

assets properties, possessions and claims on others; usually listed as entries on a balance sheet (p. 302)

automatic stabilizer program that automatically provides benefits to offset a change in people's incomes; unemployment insurance, entitlement programs (p. 429)

automation production with mechanical or other processes that reduces the need for workers (p. 396)

average tax rate total taxes paid divided by the total taxable income (p. 215)

B

baby boom historically high birthrate years in the United States from 1946 to 1964 (p. 373)

balance of payments difference between money paid to, and received from, other nations in trade; *balance on current account* includes goods and services, *merchandise trade balance* counts only goods (p. 456)

balance sheet condensed statement showing assets, liabilities, and net worth of an economic unit (p. 302)

balanced budget annual budget in which expenditures equal revenues (p. 258)

balanced budget amendment state or federal constitutional amendment requiring government to spend no more than it collects in taxes and other revenues, excluding borrowing (p. 249)

bank holding company corporation that owns one or more banks (p. 296)

bank holiday brief period during which all banks or depository institutions are closed to prevent bank runs (p. 281)

bankruptcy court-granted permission to an individual or business to cease or delay payment on some or all debts for a limited amount of time (p. 61)

barter economy moneyless economy that relies on trade or barter (p. 266)

base year year serving as point of comparison for other years in a price index or other statistical measure (p. 204)

benefit principle of taxation belief that taxes should be paid according to benefits received regardless of level of income (p. 213)

Better Business Bureau business-sponsored nonprofit organization providing information on local companies to consumers (p. 71)

bill consolidation loan popular type of consumer loan used to pay off multiple existing loans (p. 322)

black market market in which economic products are sold illegally (p. 486)

blue-collar worker industrial or factory worker who receives a wage rather than a salary (p. 407)

board of directors representatives of common shareholders elected to set policies and goals, hire professional managers for a corporation (p. 60)

bond formal contract to repay borrowed money and interest on the borrowed money at regular future intervals (p. 61)

boycott protest in the form of a refusal to buy, including attempts to convince others to join (p. 184)

break-even point production needed if the firm is to recover its costs; production level where total cost equals total revenue (p. 122)

bullion ingots or bars of precious metals, usually gold or silver (p. 268)

business cycle systematic changes in real GDP marked by alternating periods of expansion and contraction (p. 383)

business fluctuation changes in real GDP marked by alternating periods of expansion and contraction that occur on a less than systematic basis (p. 383)

business organization profit-seeking enterprise that produces goods and/or services; includes sole proprietorships, partnerships, corporations (p. 54)

C

call option contract giving investors the option to buy commodities, equities, or financial assets at a specific future date using a price agreed upon today (p. 338)

capital tools, equipment, and factories used in the production of goods and services; one of four factors of production (p. 9)

capital consumption allowances wear and tear on capital equipment that is subtracted from GNP to get NNP (p. 355)

capital flight legal or illegal export of a nation's currency and foreign exchange (p. 500)

capital good tool, equipment, or other manufactured good used to produce other goods and services; a factor of production (p. 20)

capital-intensive production method requiring relatively large amounts of capital relative to labor (p. 488)

capital market market in which financial capital is loaned and/or borrowed for more than one year (p. 332)

capitalism market economy in which the factors of production are privately owned (p. 43)

capital-to-labor ratio measure obtained by dividing the total capital stock by the labor force (p. 379)

cartel group of sellers or producers acting together to raise prices by restricting availability of a product; OPEC (p. 513)

cease and desist order ruling requiring a company to stop an unfair business practice that reduces or limits competition (p. 169)

census complete count of population, including place of residence (p. 370)

center of population point where the country would balance if it were flat and everyone weighed the same (p. 372)

central bank bank that can lend to other banks in times of need, a "bankers' bank" (p. 280)

certificate of deposit receipt showing that an investor has made an interest-bearing loan to a financial institution (p. 304)

chamber of commerce nonprofit organization of local businesses whose purpose is to promote their common interests (p. 71)

change in demand consumers demand different amounts at every price, causing the demand curve to shift to the left or the right (p. 88)

change in quantity demanded movement along the demand curve showing that a different quantity is purchased in response to a change in price (p. 86)

change in quantity supplied change in amount offered for sale in response to a price change; movement along the supply curve (p. 106)

change in supply different amounts offered for sale at each and every possible price in the market; shift of the supply curve (p. 106)

charter written government approval to establish a corporation; includes company name, address, purpose of business, number of shares of stock, and other features of the business (p. 59)

civilian labor force non-institutionalized part of the population, aged 16 to 65, either working or looking for a job (p. 182)

closed shop illegal arrangement under which workers must join a union before they are hired (p. 190)

coins metallic forms of money such as pennies, nickels, dimes, and quarters (p. 300)

collateral property or other security used to guarantee repayment of a loan (p. 308)

collective bargaining process of negotiation between union and management representatives over pay, benefits, and job-related matters (p. 70)

collective farm small farms in the former Soviet Union owned by the state, but operated by families who shared in some of the profits (p. 479)

collectivization forced common ownership of factors of production; used in the former Soviet Union in agriculture and manufacturing under Stalin (p. 478)

collusion agreements, usually illegal, among producers to fix prices, limit output, or divide markets (p. 157)

command economy economic system characterized by a central authority that makes most of the major economic decisions (p. 33)

commercial bank depository institution that, until the mid-1970s, had the exclusive right to offer checking accounts (p. 281)

commodity money money that has an alternative use as a commodity; gunpowder, flour, corn (p. 267)

common stock certificate of ownership in a corporation entitling owner to vote for board of directors, but has last claim on dividends and assets (p. 60)

communism economic and political system in which factors of production are collectively owned and directed by the state; theoretically classless society in which everyone works for the common good (p. 474)

company union union organized, supported, and even financed by an employer (p. 184)

comparable worth doctrine stating that equal pay should be given for jobs of comparable difficulty (p. 200)

comparative advantage country's ability to produce a given product relatively more efficiently than another country; production at a lower opportunity cost (p. 451)

complements products that increase the usefulness or value of other products; products related in such a way that an increase in the price of one reduces the demand for both (p. 89)

compulsory arbitration situation forcing labor and management to use a mediator to reach a binding settlement (p. 191)

conglomerate firm with four or more businesses making unrelated products, with no single business responsible for a majority of its sales (p. 65)

conspicuous consumption use of an expensive good or service to impress others (p. 21)

constant dollars dollar amounts or prices that have been adjusted for inflation; same as real dollars (p. 204)

consumer person who uses goods and services to satisfy wants and needs (p. 21)

consumer cooperative nonprofit association that buys bulk amounts of consumer goods so that its members can purchase at prices below those charged by regular businesses;

same as co-op (p. 69)

consumer good good intended for final use by consumers rather than businesses (p. 20)

consumer price index index used to measure price changes for a market basket of frequently used consumer items (p. 362)

consumer sovereignty role of consumer as ruler of the market when determining the types of goods and services produced (p. 47)

consumption process of using up goods and services to satisfy wants and needs (p. 21)

consumption function schedule showing relatively constant and stable spending patterns by the consumer sector at different levels of income (p. 427)

co-op see **cooperative** (p. 69)

cooperative nonprofit association performing some kind of economic activity for the benefit of its members; includes consumer, service, and producer cooperatives (p. 69)

copyright exclusive right given to an author or artist to sell, publish, or reproduce his or her work for their lifetime plus 50 years (p. 160)

corporate income tax tax on corporate profits paid by corporations (p. 219)

corporation form of business organization recognized by law as a separate legal entity with all the rights and responsibilities of an individual, including the right to buy and sell property, enter into legal contracts, sue and be sued (p. 59)

cost-benefit analysis way of thinking that compares the cost of an action to its benefits (p. 532)

Council of Economic Advisers three-member group that devises strategies and advises the President of the United States on economic matters (p. 437)

coupon stated interest on a corporate, municipal or government bond (p. 326)

craft union labor union whose workers perform the same kind of work; same as trade union (p. 184)

credit union nonprofit service cooperative that accepts deposits, makes loans, and provides other financial services (p. 70)

creditor person or institution to whom money is owed (p. 312)

creeping inflation relatively low rate of inflation, usually 1 to 3 percent annually (p. 400)

crowding-out effect higher than normal interest rates and diminished access to financial capital faced by private investors when government increases its borrowing in financial markets (p. 258)

crude birthrate number of live births per 1,000 people (p. 499)

currency paper component of the money supply, today consisting of Federal Reserve notes (p. 300)

current dollars dollar amounts or prices that are not adjusted for inflation (p. 202)

current GDP Gross Domestic Product measured in current prices, unadjusted for inflation (p. 363)

current yield bond's annual coupon interest divided by purchase price; measure of a bond's return (p. 327)

customs duty tax on imported products (p. 220)

customs union group of countries that have agreed to reduce

trade barriers among themselves and adopt uniform trade barriers for nonmembers (p. 512)

cyclical unemployment unemployment directly related to swings in the business cycle (p. 396)

D

deep gas natural gas located 15,000 feet or more below the earth's surface (p. 527)

deficiency payment cash payment making up the difference between the market price and the target price of an agricultural crop (p. 146)

deficit spending annual government spending in excess of taxes and other revenues (p. 253)

deflation decrease in the general level of prices (p. 399)

demand combination of desire, ability, and willingness to buy a product (p. 82)

demand curve graph showing the quantity demanded at each and every possible price that might prevail in the market at a given time (p. 84)

demand deposit account (DDA) account whose funds can be removed by writing a check and without having to gain prior approval from the depository institution (p. 281)

demand elasticity measure of responsiveness relating change in quantity demanded (dependent variable) to a change in price (independent variable) (p. 92)

demand schedule listing showing the quantity demanded at all possible prices that might prevail in the market at a given time (p. 84)

demographer person who studies growth, density, and other characteristics of the population (p. 372)

dependency ratio ratio of children and elderly per 100 persons in the 18-64 working age bracket (p. 374)

depreciation gradual wear on capital goods during production (p. 118)

depression state of the economy with large numbers of unemployed, declining real incomes, overcapacity in manufacturing plants, general economic hardship (p. 384)

depression scrip currency issued by towns, chambers of commerce, and other civic bodies during the Great Depression of the 1930s (p. 385)

deregulation relaxation or removal of government regulations on business activities (p. 284)

devaluation action taken by a country to make its currency worth less in terms of gold or another currency (p. 462)

developing country country whose average per capita income is only a fraction of that in more industrialized countries (p. 498)

diminishing marginal utility decreasing satisfaction or usefulness as additional units of a product are acquired (p. 90)

diminishing returns stage of production where output increases at a decreasing rate as more units of variable input are added (p. 115)

discomfort index unofficial statistic that is the sum of monthly inflation and the unemployment rate; same as **misery index** (p. 419)

discount rate interest rate the Federal Reserve System charges on loans to financial institutions (p. 307)

discount window physical location at the Federal Reserve System where loans are made to depository institutions (p. 308)

disposable personal income personal income less individual income taxes; total income available to the consumer sector after income taxes (p. 356)

distribution of income way in which the nation's income is divided among families, individuals, or other designated groups (p. 240)

dividend check paid to stockholders, usually quarterly, representing portion of corporate profits (p. 59)

division of labor division of work into a number of separate tasks to be performed by different workers; same as **specialization** (p. 23)

DJIA see **Dow-Jones Industrial Average** (p. 336)

Dow-Jones Industrial Average (DJIA) statistical series of 30 representative stocks used to monitor price changes on the New York Stock Exchange (p. 336)

dual banking system situation from 1863 to the present that allows banks to choose federal or state charters (p. 279)

durable good good that lasts more than three years when used regularly; can include a capital or a consumer good (p. 20)

E

easy money policy monetary policy resulting in lower interest rates and greater access to credit; associated with an expansion of the money supply (p. 306)

econometric model macroeconomic model using algebraic equations to describe how the economy behaves and is expected to perform in the future (p. 387)

economic institution organization or group of persons that use, and sometimes represent, the factors of production (p. 54)

economic interdependence economic activities in one part of the country or world affect what happens elsewhere (p. 23)

economic model set of assumptions in a table, graph, or equations used to describe or explain economic behavior (p. 134)

economic product good or service that is useful, relatively scarce, and transferable to others (p. 20)

economic system organized way a society provides for the wants and needs of its people (p. 32)

economics social science dealing with the study of how people satisfy seemingly unlimited and competing wants with the careful use of scarce resources (p. 11)

economies of scale increasingly efficient use of personnel, plant, and equipment as a firm becomes larger (p. 159)

ECU European Currency Unit; monetary unit used by the European Union (p. 512)

Efficient Market Hypothesis (EMH) argument that stocks are always priced about right, and that bargains are hard to find because they are closely watched by so many investors (p. 334)

elastic type of elasticity where the percentage change in the independent variable (usually price) causes a more than

proportionate change in the dependent variable (usually quantity demanded or supplied) (p. 92)

embargo prohibition on the export or import of a product (p. 522)

energy bank commercial bank with more than 25 percent of its loans in energy (p. 313)

enterprise zone economically depressed areas where government regulations have been suspended in an effort to attract business (p. 412)

entitlement program or benefit using established eligibility requirements to provide health, nutritional, or income supplements to individuals (p. 260)

entrepreneur risk-taking individual in search of profits; one of four factors of production (p. 10)

equilibrium price price where quantity supplied equals quantity demanded; price that clears the market (p. 138)

equilibrium wage rate wage rate leaving neither a surplus nor a shortage in the market (p. 195)

equities stocks that represent ownership shares in corporations (p. 334)

estate tax tax on the transfer of property when a person dies (p. 220)

European Community former customs union made up of 12 European nations; became the European Union in November of 1993 (p. 512)

European Union successor of the European Community established in November of 1993 by the Maastricht Treaty (p. 512)

excess reserves financial institution's cash, currency, and reserves not needed to back existing loans; potential source of new loans (p. 303)

excise tax general revenue tax levied on the manufacture or sale of selected items (p. 219)

expansion period of growth of real GDP; recovery from recession (p. 383)

expropriation government confiscation of private- or foreign-owned goods without compensation (p. 511)

external debt borrowed money that a country owes to foreign countries and banks (p. 500)

externality economic side effect that affects an uninvolved third party (p. 166)

F

fact-finding agreement between union and management to have a neutral third party collect facts about a dispute and present non-binding recommendations (p. 191)

factor market market where productive resources are bought and sold (p. 24)

factors of production productive resources that make up the four categories of land, capital, labor, and entrepreneurship (p. 9)

family two or more persons living together that are related by blood, marriage, or adoption (p. 357)

federal budget annual plan outlining proposed expenditures and anticipated revenues (p. 243)

federal budget deficit excess of federal expenditures over tax and revenue collections (p. 243)

federal debt total amount of money the federal government has borrowed from others (p. 254)

Federal Reserve note currency issued by the Fed that eventually replaced all other types of federal currency (p. 280)

Federal Reserve System privately owned, publicly controlled, central bank of the United States (p. 280)

fertility rate number of births that 1,000 women are expected to undergo in their lifetime (p. 372)

fiat money money by government decree; has no alternative value or use as a commodity (p. 267)

FICA Federal Insurance Contributions Act; tax levied on employers and employees to support Social Security and medicare (p. 218)

finance company firm that makes loans directly to consumers and specializes in buying installment contracts from merchants who sell on credit (p. 322)

financial asset document that represents a claim on the income and property of the borrower; CDs, bonds, Treasury bills, mortgages (p. 321)

financial capital money used to buy the tools and equipment used in production (p. 9)

financial intermediary institution that channels savings to investors; banks, insurance companies, savings and loan associations, credit unions (p. 321)

financial system network of savers, investors, and financial institutions that work together to transfer savings to investment uses (p. 320)

fiscal policy use of government spending and revenue collection measures to influence the economy (p. 427)

fiscal year 12-month financial planning period that may not coincide with the calendar year; October 1 to September 30 for the federal government (p. 243)

Five-Year Plan comprehensive centralized economic plan used by the Soviet Union and China to coordinate development of agriculture and industry (p. 478)

fixed cost cost of production that does not change when output changes (p. 118)

fixed exchange rate system under which the value of currencies were fixed in relation to one another; the exchange rate system in effect until 1971 (p. 461)

fixed income income that does not increase even though prices go up (p. 40)

flexible exchange rate system that relies on supply and demand to determine the value of one currency in terms of another; exchange rate system in effect since 1971, same as **floating exchange rate** (p. 463)

floating exchange rate see **flexible exchange rate** (p. 463)

floor price see **price floor** (p. 142)

food stamps government-issued coupons that can be exchanged for food (p. 411)

foreign exchange foreign currencies used by countries to conduct international trade (p. 461)

foreign exchange futures contracts allowing individuals to buy foreign currencies at some future date, at a price agreed upon today (p. 464)

foreign exchange market market where foreign currencies

used in trade are bought and sold (p. 461)

foreign exchange rate price of one country's currency in terms of another currency (p. 461)

fractional reserve system system requiring financial institutions to set aside a fraction of their deposits in the form of reserves (p. 302)

franchise exclusive right to produce or sell a certain product in an area or region (p. 159)

free enterprise economy market economy in which privately owned businesses have the freedom to operate for a profit with limited government intervention; same as **private enterprise economy** (p. 24)

free product relatively plentiful and abundant product not scarce enough to be a major concern in the study of economics; includes sunshine, rainfall (p. 20)

free-trade area group of countries that have agreed to reduce trade barriers among themselves, but lack a common tariff barrier for nonmembers (p. 512)

frictional unemployment unemployment caused by workers changing jobs or waiting to go to new ones (p. 395)

fringe benefit benefit received by employees in addition to wages and salaries; includes paid vacations, sick leave, retirement, insurance (p. 57)

full employment lowest sustainable unemployment rate thought possible in the economy (p. 397)

futures contracts to buy or sell commodities or financial assets at a specific future date, using a price agreed upon today (p. 338)

futures market market where futures contracts are bought and sold (p. 338)

G

galloping inflation relatively intense inflation, usually ranging from 100 to 300 percent annually (p. 400)

gasohol mixture of 90 percent unleaded gasoline and 10 percent grain alcohol (p. 524)

GATT see **General Agreement on Tariffs and Trade** (p. 458)

GDP gap difference between what the economy can and does produce; annual opportunity cost of unemployed resources (p. 419)

GDP in constant dollars Gross Domestic Product after adjustments for inflation; same as **real GDP** (p. 364)

General Agreement on Tariffs and Trade (GATT) agreement signed in 1947 between 23 countries that extended tariffs concessions and worked to do away with import quotas (p. 458)

general partnership see **partnership** (p. 57)

geographic monopoly market situation where a firm has a monopoly because of its location or the small size of the market (p. 159)

gift tax tax on donations of money or wealth that is paid by the donor (p. 220)

giveback wage, fringe benefit, or work rule given up when renegotiating a contract (p. 199)

glass ceiling seemingly invisible barrier hindering advancement of women and minorities in a male-dominated organization (p. 200)

glut substantial oversupply of a product (p. 528)

gold certificate paper currency backed by gold; issued in 1863 and popular until recalled in 1934 (p. 275)

gold standard monetary standard under which a country's currency is equivalent to, and can be exchanged for, a specified amount of gold (p. 275)

good tangible economic product that is useful, relatively scarce, transferable to others; used to satisfy wants and needs (p. 20)

Gosplan central planning authority in former Soviet Union that devised and directed Five-Year plans (p. 478)

government monopoly monopoly created and/or owned by the government (p. 160)

grant-in-aid transfer payment from one level of government to another not involving compensation (p. 240)

Great Depression greatest period of economic decline in United States history, lasting from approximately 1929 to 1939 (p. 185)

Great Leap Forward China's disastrous second five-year plan begun in 1958 that forced collectivization of agriculture and rapid industrialization (p. 487)

greenback paper currency not backed by gold that was printed by the United States government in 1861; notes were printed front and back in green ink (p. 274)

grievance procedure contractual provision outlining the way future disputes and grievance issues will be resolved (p. 191)

Gross Domestic Product (GDP) dollar value of all final goods, services, and structures produced within a country's national borders during a one-year period (p. 256)

Gross National Product (GNP) total dollar value of all final goods, services, and structures produced in one year with labor and property supplied by a country's residents, regardless of where the production takes place; largest measure of a nation's income (p. 354)

gross private domestic investment total expenditures by the investment sector in the output-expenditure model (p. 358)

growth triangle table showing the rates of growth of a statistical series between any two dates (p. 376)

H

horizontal merger combination of two or more firms producing the same kind of product (p. 64)

household basic unit of consumer sector consisting of all persons who occupy a house, apartment, or separate living quarters (p. 356)

human capital sum of peoples' skills, abilities, health, and motivation (p. 23)

hyperinflation abnormal inflation in excess of 500 percent per year; last stage of a monetary collapse (p. 400)

imperfect competition market structure where all conditions of pure competition are not met; monopolistic competition, oligopoly, and monopoly (p. 155)

implicit GDP price deflator index used to measure price changes in Gross Domestic Product (p. 363)

incidence of a tax final burden of a tax (p. 228)

income effect that portion of a change in quantity demanded caused by a change in a consumer's real income when the price of a product changes (p. 87)

income-to-poverty ratio ratio of family income divided by poverty level; measure used to compensate for differences in family sizes (p. 408)

inconvertible fiat money standard fiat money that cannot be exchanged for gold or silver; Federal Reserve notes today (p. 276)

incorporate process required to form a corporation, involves permission from federal government or state where the business will have its headquarters (p. 59)

independent pricing pricing policy by an imperfect competitor that ignores other producers and some market conditions (p. 157)

independent union labor union not affiliated with the AFL-CIO (p. 187)

index of leading indicators composite index of 11 economic series that move up and down in advance of changes in the overall economy; statistical series used to predict business cycle turning points (p. 388)

indexing adjustment of tax brackets to offset the effects of inflation (p. 217)

indirect business tax tax paid as a cost of doing business; license fees, property taxes, customs duties (p. 356)

individual income tax tax levied on the wages, salaries, and other income of individuals (p. 216)

Individual Retirement Account (IRA) retirement account in the form of a long-term time deposit, with annual contributions of up to $2,000 per year not taxed until withdrawn during retirement (p. 331)

industrial union labor union whose workers perform different kinds of work (p. 184)

industry collectively, all firms producing in a market; the supply side of the market (p. 152)

inelastic type of elasticity where the percentage change in the independent variable (usually price) causes a less than proportionate change in the dependent variable (usually quantity demanded or supplied) (p. 92)

infant industries argument argument that new and emerging industries should be protected from foreign competition until they are strong enough to compete (p. 455)

inflation rise in the general level of prices (p. 40)

injunction court order issued to prevent a company or union from taking action during a labor dispute (p. 192)

intangible personal property ownership rights to property as opposed to the property itself; includes stocks, bank accounts (p. 224)

interest payment made for the use of borrowed money; usually paid at periodic intervals for long-term bonds or loans (p. 61)

intergovernmental revenue funds one level of government receives from another level of government (p. 222)

intermediate products products directly excluded from GDP computations because they are components of other final products included in GDP; new tires and radios for use on new cars (p. 349)

Internal Revenue Service (IRS) branch of Treasury Department that collects taxes (p. 216)

International Bank for Reconstruction and Development see **World Bank** (p. 505)

inventory stock of goods held in reserve; includes finished goods waiting to be sold and raw materials to be used in production (p. 56)

investment tax credit tax credit given for purchase of equipment (p. 231)

J

jumbo CD certificate of deposit of $100,000 or more (p. 328)

junk bond corporate bond, generally rated as lower than medium or speculative grade, that pays high returns to compensate for the high risk of default (p. 328)

jurisdictional dispute disagreement, usually between unions, as to which has authority to perform certain kinds of work (p. 187)

K

keiretsu independently owned group of Japanese firms joined and governed by an external board of directors in order to regulate competition (p. 488)

Keynesian economics government spending and taxation policies suggested by John Maynard Keynes to stimulate the economy; synonymous with fiscal policies or demand-side economics (p. 427)

L

labor people with all their abilities and efforts; one of four factors of production, does not include the entrepreneur (p. 10)

labor mobility ability and willingness of labor to relocate, usually for higher wages (p. 196)

labor productivity growth rate of total output per unit of labor input; measure of productive efficiency (p. 380)

labor union organization that works for its members' interests concerning pay, working hours, health coverage, fringe benefits, other job related matters (p. 70)

Laffer curve graph showing that lower tax rates will supposedly stimulate higher tax revenues (p. 432)

laissez-faire philosophy that government should not interfere with business activity (p. 152)

land natural resources or "gifts of nature" not created by human effort; one of four factors of production (p. 9)

Law of Demand rule stating that more will be demanded at lower prices and less at higher prices; inverse relationship between price and quantity demanded (p. 86)

Law of Supply rule stating that more will be offered for sale at high prices than at lower prices (p. 106)

Law of Variable Proportions rule stating that short-run output will change as one input is varied while others are held constant (p. 111)

legal reserves currency and deposits used to meet the reserve requirement (p. 302)

legal tender fiat currency that must be accepted for payment by decree of government (p. 274)

liabilities debts and obligations owed to others; usually listed as entries on a balance sheet (p. 302)

life expectancy average remaining life span in years for persons who attain a given age (p. 372)

limited liability situation in which an owner's responsibility for a company's debts are limited to the size of the owner's investment in the firm; applies to common shareholders and limited partners in a limited partnership (p. 59)

limited life situation in which a firm legally ceases to exist when an owner dies, quits, or a new owner is added; applies to sole proprietorships and partnerships (p. 57)

limited partnership form of partnership where one or more partners are not active in the daily running of the business, and whose liability for the partnership's debt is restricted to the amount invested in the business (p. 57)

liquidity potential for being readily convertible into cash or other financial assets (p. 304)

lockout management refusal to let employees work until company demands are met (p. 184)

long run production period long enough to change amount of variable and fixed inputs used in production (p. 111)

Lorenz curve curve showing how much the actual distribution of income differs from an equal distribution (p. 405)

loss leader item intentionally sold below cost to attract customers (p. 138)

luxury good good for which demand increases faster than income when income rises (p. 220)

M

M1 money supply components conforming to money's role as medium of exchange; coins, currency, checks, other demand deposits, traveler's checks (p. 311)

M2 money supply components conforming to money's role as a store of value; M1, savings deposits, time deposits (p. 311)

macroeconomic equilibrium level of real GDP consistent with a given price level; intersection of aggregate supply and aggregate demand (p. 425)

macroeconomics that part of economic theory dealing with the economy as a whole and decision making by large units such as governments and unions (p. 182)

margin requirement minimum deposits left with a stockbroker to be used as partial payment on other securities (p. 300)

marginal analysis decision making that compares the extra cost of doing something to the extra benefits gained (p. 121)

marginal cost extra cost of producing one additional unit of production (p. 119)

marginal product extra output due to the addition of one more unit of input (p. 114)

marginal revenue extra revenue from the sale of one additional unit of output (p. 121)

marginal tax rate tax rate that applies to the next dollar of taxable income (p. 215)

marginal utility satisfaction or usefulness obtained from acquiring one more unit of a product (p. 89)

market meeting place or mechanism allowing buyers and sellers of an economic product to come together; may be local, regional, national, or global (p. 23)

market basket representative collection of goods and services used to compile a price index (p. 362)

market economy economic system in which supply, demand, and the price system help people make decisions and allocate resources; same as **free enterprise economy** (p. 34)

market equilibrium condition of price stability where the quantity demanded equals the quantity supplied (p. 134)

market failure market where any of the requirements for a competitive market—adequate competition, knowledge of prices and opportunities, mobility of resources, and competitive profits—are lacking (p. 163)

market structure market classification according to number and size of firms, type of product, and type of competition (p. 152)

maturity life of a bond or length of time funds are borrowed (p. 326)

measure of value one of the three functions of money that allows it to serve as a common denominator to measure value (p. 266)

mediation process of resolving a dispute by bringing in a neutral third party (p. 191)

medicaid joint federal-state medical insurance program for low-income people (p. 246)

medicare federal health-care program for senior citizens, regardless of income (p. 218)

medium of exchange money or other substance generally accepted in exchange; one of the three functions of money (p. 266)

member bank bank belonging to the Federal Reserve System (p. 294)

member bank reserves reserves kept by member banks at the Fed to satisfy reserve requirements (p. 302)

merger combination of two or more business enterprises to form a single firm (p. 64)

microeconomics branch of economic theory that deals with behavior and decision making by small units such as individuals and firms (p. 82)

minimum wage lowest legal wage that can be paid to most workers (p. 142)

misery index unofficial statistic that is the sum of monthly inflation and the unemployment rate; same as **discomfort index** (p. 419)

mixed economy see **modified private enterprise economy** (p. 48)

modified free enterprise economy free enterprise system with some government involvement; same as **modified private enterprise economy** (p. 533)

modified private enterprise economy free enterprise market economy where people carry on their economic affairs freely, but are subject to some government intervention and regulation (p. 48)

modified union shop arrangement under which workers have the option to join a union after being hired (p. 190)

monetarism school of thought stressing the importance of stable monetary growth to control inflation and stimulate long-term economic growth (p. 433)

monetary policy actions by the Federal Reserve System to expand or contract the money supply in order to affect the cost and availability of credit (p. 302)

monetary standard mechanism that keeps a money supply durable, portable, divisible, and stable in value; gold standard, silver standard, fiat money standard (p. 272)

monetary unit standard unit of currency in a country's money supply; American dollar, British pound (p. 269)

monetizing the debt process of creating enough additional money to offset federal borrowing so that interest rates remain unchanged (p. 310)

money anything that serves as a medium of exchange, a measure of value, and a store of value (p. 266)

money market market in which financial capital is loaned and/or borrowed for one year or less (p. 332)

money market mutual fund firm that pools funds collected from small savers to make larger loans to investors willing to pay high rates of return (p. 330)

monopolistic competition market structure having all conditions of pure competition except for identical products; form of imperfect competition (p. 155)

monopoly market structure characterized by a single producer; form of imperfect competition (p. 158)

moral suasion Federal Reserve System's use of persuasion to accomplish monetary policy; Congressional testimony, press releases (p. 308)

most favored nation clause trade law allowing a third country to enjoy the same tariff reductions the United States negotiates with another country (p. 458)

multinational corporation producing and selling without regard to national boundaries and whose business activities are located in several different countries (p. 66)

multiplier change in overall spending caused by a change in investment spending (p. 427)

municipal bond bond, often tax exempt, issued by state and local governments; known as *munis* (p. 329)

mutual fund company that sells stock in itself and uses the proceeds to buy stocks and bonds issued by other companies (p. 323)

mutual savings bank depositor-owned savings institution operated for the benefit of depositors (p. 281)

N

NAFTA see **North American Free Trade Agreement** (p. 459)

national bank commercial bank chartered by the National Banking System; member of the Fed (p. 274)

National Bank note currency backed by government bonds, issued by national banks starting in 1863 and generally disappearing from circulation in the 1930s (p. 274)

National Banking System system of federally chartered, inspected, and regulated banks established in 1863, now members of the Fed (p. 274)

national currency see **National Bank note** (p. 274)

national income net national product less indirect business taxes; measure of a nation's income (p. 356)

national income accounting system of accounts used to track the nation's production, consumption, savings, and income statistics (p. 348)

natural monopoly market where average costs are lowest when all output is produced by a single firm (p. 158)

need basic requirement for survival; includes food, clothing, and/or shelter (p. 20)

negative externality harmful side effect that affects an uninvolved third party; external cost (p. 166)

negative income tax tax system that would make cash payments in the form of tax refunds to individuals when their income falls below certain levels (p. 411)

Negotiable Order of Withdrawal (NOW) type of checking account that pays interest (p. 282)

net exports of goods and services net expenditures by the output-expenditure model's foreign sector (p. 359)

net immigration net population change after accounting for those who leave as well as enter a country (p. 372)

net national product (NNP) Gross National Product minus depreciation charges for wear and tear on capital equipment; measure of net annual production generated with labor and property supplied by a country's citizens (p. 355)

net worth excess of assets over liabilities, usually listed as a separate summary on a balance sheet; measure of the value of a business (p. 302)

nominal GDP see **current GDP** (p. 363)

nonbank financial institution nondepository institution that channels savings to investors; finance companies, insurance companies, pension funds (p. 322)

noncompeting labor grades broad groups of unskilled, semiskilled, skilled, and professional workers who do not compete with one another (p. 194)

nondurable good item that lasts for less than three years when used regularly; can be a capital or a consumer good (p. 20)

nonmarket transaction economic activity not taking place in the market and, therefore, not included in GDP; services of homemakers, work around the home (p. 351)

nonprice competition competition involving the advertising of a product's appearance, quality, or design, rather than its price (p. 156)

nonprofit organization economic institution that operates like a business but does not seek financial gain; schools, churches, community service organizations (p. 69)

non-recourse loan agricultural loan that carries neither a penalty nor further obligation to repay if not paid back (p. 144)

North American Free Trade Agreement (NAFTA) agreement signed in 1993 to reduce tariffs between the United States, Canada, and Mexico (p. 459)

NOW Account see **Negotiable Order of Withdrawal** (p. 282)

O

oligopoly market structure in which a few large sellers dominate and have the ability to affect prices in the industry; form of imperfect competition (p. 156)

open market operations monetary policy in the form of bond sales or purchases in bond markets (p. 307)

opportunity cost cost of the next best alternative use of money, time, or resources when one choice is made rather than another (p. 15)

options contracts giving investors an option to buy or sell commodities, equities, or financial assets at a specific future date using a price agreed upon today (p. 338)

options markets markets where options, including put options and call options, are traded (p. 338)

organizational chart visual representation of a company's structure showing how different parts of the organization are related (p. 61)

output-expenditure model macroeconomic model describing aggregate demand by the consumer, investment, government, and foreign sectors; GDP = C + I + G + F (p. 358)

overhead broad category of fixed costs that includes interest, rent, taxes, and executive salaries (p. 118)

Over-The-Counter market (OTC) electronic marketplace for securities not listed on organized exchanges such as the New York Stock Exchange (p. 336)

P

par value principal of a bond or total amount borrowed (p. 326)

paradox of value apparent contradiction between the high value of nonessentials and low value of essentials (p. 22)

partnership unincorporated business owned and operated by two or more people who share the profits and have unlimited liability for the debts and obligations of the firm; same as **general partnership** (p. 57)

patent exclusive government-granted right to sell or use any new art, machine, item of manufacture, or composition (p. 160)

payroll withholding statement document attached to a paycheck summarizing pay and deductions (p. 225)

payroll withholding system system that automatically deducts income taxes from paychecks on a regular basis (p. 216)

peak point in time when real GDP stops expanding and begins to decline (p. 383)

pension regular allowance for someone who has worked a certain number of years, reached a certain age, or who has suffered from an injury (p. 323)

pension fund fund that collects and invests income until payments are made to eligible recipients (p. 323)

per capita per person basis; total divided by population (p. 238)

perestroika fundamental restructuring of the Soviet economy; policy introduced by Gorbachev (p. 480)

personal consumption expenditures total consumer sector expenditures that consist of households and unrelated individuals (p. 358)

personal income total amount of income going to the consumer sector before individual income taxes are paid (p. 356)

picket demonstration before a place of business to protest a company's actions (p. 184)

piecework compensation system that pays workers for units produced, rather than hours worked (p. 480)

pollution contamination of air, water, or soil by the discharge of a poisonous or noxious substance (p. 528)

pollution permit federal permit allowing a public utility to release pollutants into the air; a form of pollution control (p. 530)

population density number of people per square mile of land area (p. 514)

population pyramid diagram showing the breakdown of population by age and sex (p. 373)

portfolio diversification strategy of holding several investments to protect against risk (p. 334)

positive externality beneficial side effect that affects an uninvolved third party (p. 167)

poverty threshold annual dollar benchmark used to evaluate the money income received by families and unrelated individuals (p. 407)

preferred stock nonvoting ownership stock whose claim on the income and assets of the corporation come ahead of the common shareholder (p. 60)

premium monthly, quarterly, semiannual, or annual price paid for an insurance policy (p. 323)

price ceiling maximum legal price that can be charged for a product (p. 141)

price discrimination illegal practice of charging customers different prices for the same product (p. 169)

price-fixing agreement, usually illegal, by firms to charge a uniform price for a product (p. 157)

price floor lowest legal price that can be charged for a product (p. 142)

price index statistical series used to measure changes in the price level over time (p. 361)

price leadership independent pricing decisions made by a dominate firm on a regular basis that results in generally uniform industry-wide prices (p. 157)

price level relative magnitude of prices at a given point in time as measured by a price index (p. 399)

price war fierce price competition between sellers, sometimes to the point where price is below the cost of the product (p. 157)

primary market market in which only the original issuer will repurchase a financial asset; government savings bonds, IRAs, small CDs (p. 332)

prime rate best or lowest interest rate commercial banks charge their customers (p. 309)

primitive equilibrium first stage of economic development during which the economy is static (p. 504)

principal amount borrowed when getting a loan or issuing a bond (p. 61)

private enterprise economy see **free enterprise economy** (p. 24)

private property concept giving people the right to control their possessions as they wish; characteristic of capitalism and free enterprise (p. 45)

private sector that part of the economy made up of private individuals and businesses (p. 239)

privatization conversion of state-owned factories and other property to private ownership (p. 483)

problem bank list banking regulator's confidential list of weak and potentially unsound banks (p. 312)

producer cooperative nonprofit association of producers helping members sell or market products; found mostly in agriculture (p. 70)

producer price index index used to measure prices received by domestic producers; formerly called the **wholesale price index** (p. 362)

product differentiation real or imagined differences between competing products in the same industry (p. 155)

product market market where goods and services are offered for sale (p. 24)

production process of creating goods and services with the combined use of land, capital, labor, and entrepreneurship (p. 22)

production function graphic portrayal showing how a change in the amount of a single variable input affects total output (p. 112)

production possibilities frontier diagram representing maximum combinations of goods and/or services an economy can produce when all productive resources are fully employed (p. 16)

productivity degree to which productive resources are used efficiently; normally refers to labor, but can apply to all factors of production (p. 22)

professional association nonprofit organization of professional or specialized workers seeking to improve working conditions, skill levels, and public perceptions of its profession (p. 71)

professional labor workers with a high level of professional and managerial skills (p. 194)

profit extent to which persons or organizations are better off at the end of a period than they were at the beginning; usually measured in dollars (p. 46)

profit-maximizing quantity of output level of production where marginal cost is equal to marginal revenue (p. 122)

profit motive driving force that encourages people and organizations to improve their material well-being; characteristic of capitalism and free enterprise (p. 46)

progressive tax tax where percentage of income paid in tax rises as level of income rises (p. 215)

property tax tax on tangible and intangible possessions such as real estate, buildings, furniture, stocks, bonds, and bank accounts (p. 224)

proportional tax tax in which percentage of income paid in tax is the same regardless of the level of income (p. 215)

proprietorship see **sole proprietorship** (p. 54)

protectionist person who would protect domestic producers with tariffs, quotas, and other trade barriers (p. 454)

protective tariff tax on an imported product designed to protect less efficient domestic producers (p. 453)

proxy ballot allowing a shareholder's representative to vote on corporate matters (p. 60)

public disclosure requirement forcing a business to reveal information about its products or its operations to the public (p. 170)

public good economic product that is consumed collectively; highways, national defense, police and fire protection (p. 167)

public sector that part of the economy made up of the local, state, and federal governments (p. 239)

public utility company providing essential services such as water and electricity to consumers, usually subject to some government regulations (p. 72)

pure competition market structure characterized by a large number of independent and well-informed buyers and sellers of an identical product—none of which are large enough to influence the price—along with relative ease of entry and exit in the industry (p. 152)

put option contract giving investors the option to sell commodities, equities, or financial assets at a specific future date using a price agreed upon today (p. 338)

Q

quantity supplied amount offered for sale at a given price; point on the supply curve (p. 106)

quantity theory of money hypothesis that the supply of money directly affects the price level over the long run (p. 309)

quota limit on the amount of a good that can be allowed into a country (p. 453)

R

ration coupon certificate allowing holder to receive a given amount of a rationed product (p. 131)

rationing system of allocating goods and services without prices (p. 131)

raw materials unprocessed natural resources used in production (p. 112)

real dollars see **constant dollars** (p. 204)

real estate investment trust (REIT) company organized to make loans to home builders (p. 323)

real GDP Gross Domestic Product after adjustments for inflation; same as **GDP in constant dollars** (p. 364)

real GDP per capita Gross Domestic Product adjusted for inflation and divided by the total population; total dollar amount of all final output produced for every person in the country after compensating for inflation (p. 376)

real property wealth in the form of real estate, buildings, and permanent attachments (p. 224)

rebate partial refund of the original price of a product (p. 140)

recession decline in real GDP lasting at least two quarters or more (p. 383)

regressive tax tax where percentage of income paid in tax goes down as income rises (p. 215)

Regulation Q federal regulation that once set maximum interest rates that could be paid on demand deposits (p. 285)

Regulation Z provision extending truth-in-lending disclosures to consumers (p. 299)

renewable resources natural resources that can be replenished for future use (p. 379)

reserve requirement formula used to compute the amount of a depository institution's required reserves (p. 302)

retained earnings corporate earnings kept by a corporation rather than being paid out to shareholders; same as **undistributed corporate profits** (p. 356)

revenue firm's receipts from the sale or rental of its product, also includes money from other sources such as dividends and interest (p. 62)

revenue tariff tax placed on imported goods to raise revenue (p. 453)

right-to-work law state law making it illegal to require a worker to join a union (p. 186)

risk situation in which the outcome is not certain, but the probabilities can be estimated (p. 325)

run on the bank sudden rush by depositors to withdraw all deposited funds, generally in anticipation of bank failure or closure (p. 281)

rural population those persons not living in urban areas (p. 370)

S

S&P 500 see **Standard & Poor's 500** (p. 337)

sales tax general state or city tax levied on a product at the time of sale (p. 222)

saving absence of spending that frees resources for use in other activities or investments (p. 320)

savings the dollars that become available for investors to use when others save (p. 320)

savings account interest-bearing deposit not requiring prior notice before making a withdrawal (p. 304)

savings and loan association (S&L) depository institution that historically invested the majority of its funds in home mortgages (p. 282)

savings bank savings institution owned by stockholders rather than by depositors (p. 282)

savings bond low-denomination, non-transferable bond issued by the federal government, usually through payroll-savings plans (p. 329)

scarcity fundamental economic problem facing all societies that results from a combination of scarce resources and people's virtually unlimited wants (p. 8)

seasonal unemployment unemployment caused by annual changes in the weather or other conditions that prevail at certain times of the year (p. 396)

seat membership in a stock exchange such as the New York Stock Exchange (p. 335)

secondary market market in which all financial assets can be sold to someone other than the original issuer; corporate bonds, government bonds (p. 332)

secondhand sales sales of used goods; category of activity not included in GDP computation (p. 349)

securities exchange physical place where buyers and sellers meet to exchange securities (p. 335)

seizure temporary government takeover of a company to keep it running during a labor-management dispute (p. 192)

selective credit controls rules pertaining to loans for specific commodities or purchases such as margin requirements for common stock (p. 308)

semiskilled labor workers who can operate machines requiring a minimum amount of training (p. 194)

seniority length of time a person has been on a job (p. 196)

service work or labor performed for someone; economic product that includes haircuts, home repairs, forms of entertainment (p. 20)

service cooperative nonprofit association of consumers dealing with services rather than goods; includes credit unions, some insurance and credit agencies (p. 70)

set-aside contract guaranteed contract or portion thereof reserved for a targeted, usually minority, group (p. 201)

share draft checking account offered by a credit union (p. 283)

shareholder see **stockholder** (p. 59)

short run production period so short that only variable inputs can be changed (p. 111)

shortage situation where quantity supplied is less than quantity demanded at a given price (p. 136)

silver certificate paper currency backed by, and redeemable for, silver from 1886 to 1968 (p. 275)

sin tax relatively high tax designed to raise revenue and discourage consumption of a socially undesirable product (p. 210)

skilled labor workers who can operate complex equipment and require little supervision (p. 194)

Social Security federal program of disability and retirement benefits that covers most working people (p. 40)

socialism economic system in which government owns some factors of production and has a role in determining what and how goods are produced (p. 473)

sole proprietorship unincorporated business owned and run by a single person who has rights to all profits and unlimited liability for all debts of the firm; most common form of business organization in the United States (p. 54)

Solidarity independent Polish labor union founded in 1980 by Lech Walesa (p. 485)

specialization assignment of tasks so that each worker performs fewer functions more frequently; same as division of labor (p. 22)

specie money in the form of gold or silver coins (p. 268)

spot market market in which a transaction is made immediately at the prevailing price (p. 338)

stages of production phases of production—increasing, decreasing, and negative returns (p. 114)

stagflation combination of stagnant economic growth and inflation (p. 419)

Standard & Poor's 500 (S&P 500) statistical series of 500 stocks used to monitor prices on the NYSE, American Stock Exchange, and OTC market (p. 337)

standard of living quality of life based on ownership of necessities and luxuries that make life easier (p. 377)

state bank bank that receives its charter from the state in which it operates (p. 272)

state farm large farms owned and operated by the state in the former Soviet Union (p. 479)

stock certificate of ownership in a corporation; common or preferred stock (p. 59)

stock certificate see **stock** (p. 59)

stockbroker person who buys or sells securities for investors (p. 335)

stockholder person who owns a share or shares of stock in a corporation; same as shareholders (p. 59)

store of value one of the three functions of money allowing people to preserve value for future use (p. 266)

storming Soviet practice of rushing production at month's end to fulfill quotas, often resulting in production of shoddy goods (p. 480)

strike union organized work stoppage designed to gain concessions from an employer (p. 184)

structural unemployment unemployment caused by a fundamental change in the economy that reduces the demand for some workers (p. 395)

structures category in the national income and product accounts that includes residential structures, apartments, and commercial buildings (p. 348)

subsidy government payment to encourage or protect a certain economic activity (p. 108)

subsistence state in which a society produces barely enough to support itself (p. 520)

substitutes competing products that can be used in place of one another; products related in such a way that an increase in the price of one increases the demand for the other (p. 88)

substitution effect that portion of a change in quantity demanded due to a change in the relative price of the product (p. 87)

supply schedule of quantities offered for sale at all possible prices in a market (p. 104)

supply curve graphical representation of the quantities produced at each and every possible price in the market (p. 105)

supply elasticity responsiveness of quantity supplied to a change in price (p. 109)

supply schedule tabular listing showing the quantities produced or offered for sale at each and every possible price in the market (p. 105)

supply-side economics economic policies designed to increase aggregate supply or shift the aggregate supply curve to the right (p. 431)

surcharge additional tax or charge added to other charges already in place (p. 231)

surplus situation where quantity supplied is greater than quantity demanded at a given price (p. 135)

 T

takeoff third stage of economic development during which barriers of primitive equilibrium are overcome (p. 504)

tangible personal property all tangible items of wealth not permanently attached to land or buildings (p. 224)

target price agricultural floor price set by the government to stabilize farm incomes (p. 144)

tariff tax placed on an imported product (p. 453)

tax assessor person who examines and values property for tax purposes (p. 224)

tax base incomes and properties that are potentially subject to tax by local, state, or federal governments (p. 377)

tax-exempt income from a bond or other investment not subject to tax by federal or state governments (p. 329)

tax loophole exception or oversight in the tax law allowing taxpayer to avoid taxes (p. 212)

tax return annual report filed with local, state, or federal government detailing income earned and taxes owed (p. 216)

technological monopoly market situation where a firm has a monopoly because it owns or controls a manufacturing method, process, or other scientific advance (p. 159)

technological unemployment unemployment caused by technological developments or automation that make some worker's skills obsolete (p. 396)

theory of negotiated wages explanation of wage rates based on the bargaining strength of organized labor (p. 196)

theory of production theory dealing with the relationship between the factors of production and the output of goods and services (p. 111)

thrift institution savings & loan associations, mutual savings banks, and other depository institutions historically catering to savers (p. 281)

tight money policy monetary policy resulting in higher interest rates and restricted access to credit; associated with a contraction of the money supply (p. 306)

time deposit interest-bearing deposit requiring prior notice before a withdrawal can be made, even though the requirement may not always be enforced (p. 304)

total cost variable plus fixed cost; all costs associated with production (p. 119)

total product total output or production by a firm (p. 113)

total revenue total receipts; price of goods sold times quantity sold (p. 121)

trade deficit balance of payments outcome when spending on imports exceeds revenues received from exports (p. 456)

trade-offs alternatives that must be given up when one is chosen rather than another (p. 14)

trade union see **craft union** (p. 184)

trade-weighted value of the dollar index showing strength of the United States dollar against a market basket of other foreign currencies (p. 465)

trading desk physical location at the New York Federal Reserve district bank where the purchase and sale of government bonds is managed (p. 307)

traditional economy economic system in which the allocation of scarce resources and other economic activity is the result of ritual, habit, or custom (p. 32)

traditional theory of wage determination explanation of wage rates relying on theory of supply and demand (p. 195)

transfer payment payment for which the government receives neither goods nor services in return (p. 239)

Treasury bill short-term United States government obligation with a maturity of one year or under in denominations of $10,000 (p. 331)

Treasury bond United States government bond with maturity of 10 to 30 years (p. 330)

Treasury coin note paper currency printed from 1890 to 1893, redeemable in both gold and silver (p. 275)

Treasury note United States government obligation with a maturity of 2 to 10 years (p. 330)

trend line growth path the economy would follow if it were not interrupted by alternating periods of recession and recovery (p. 384)

trough point in time when real GDP stops declining and begins to expand (p. 383)

trust illegal combination of corporations or companies organized to hinder competition (p. 169)

trust fund special account used to hold revenues designated for a specific expenditure such as Social Security, medicare, or highways (p. 256)

truth-in-lending laws federal laws requiring that complete and accurate loan disclosures be made to consumers (p. 299)

two-tier wage system wage scale paying newer workers a lower wage than others already on the job (p. 199)

U

underground economy unreported legal and illegal activities that do not show up in GDP statistics (p. 351)

undistributed corporate profits see **retained earnings** (p. 356)

unemployed state of working for less than one hour per week for pay or profit in a non-family owned business, while being available and having made an effort to find a job during the past month (p. 394)

unemployment insurance government program providing payments to the unemployed; an automatic stabilizer (p. 429)

unemployment rate ratio of unemployed individuals divided by total number of persons in the civilian labor force, expressed as a percentage (p. 394)

union shop arrangement under which workers must join a union after being hired (p. 190)

unit elastic elasticity where a change in the independent variable (usually price) generates a proportional change of the dependent variable (quantity demanded or supplied) (p. 94)

United States note paper currency with no backing, first printed by the United States government in 1862 to finance the Civil War (p. 274)

unlimited liability requirement that an owner is personally and fully responsible for all losses and debts of a business; applies to proprietorships, general partnerships (p. 56)

unlimited life condition of continued legal existence of a corporation when an owner dies, sells, or transfers ownership (p. 62)

unrelated individual person living alone or with nonrelatives even though that person may have relatives living elsewhere (p. 357)

unskilled labor workers not trained to operate specialized machines and equipment (p. 194)

urban population those persons living in incorporated cities, towns, and villages with 2,500 or more inhabitants (p. 370)

user fee fee paid for the use of good or service; form of a benefit tax (p. 220)

utility ability or capacity of a good or service to be useful and give satisfaction to someone (p. 22)

V

value worth of a good or service as determined by the market (p. 21)

value added tax tax on the value added at every stage of the production process (p. 229)

variable cost production cost that varies as output changes; labor, energy, raw materials (p. 118)

vertical merger combination of firms involved in different steps of manufacturing or marketing (p. 64)

voluntary arbitration agreement by labor and management to place a dispute before a third party for a binding settlement (p. 191)

voluntary exchange act of buyers and sellers freely and willingly engaging in market transactions; characteristic of capitalism and free enterprise (p. 44)

W

wage-price controls policies and regulations making it illegal for firms to give raises or raise prices (p. 434)

wage rate prevailing pay scale for work performed in a given area or region (p. 195)

wampum form of money made from shells and devised by Native Americans, used widely in early colonial America (p. 267)

want way of expressing or communicating a need; a broader classification than needs (p. 20)

wealth sum of tangible economic goods that are scarce, useful, and transferable from one person to another; excludes services (p. 22)

welfare government or private agency programs that provide general economic and social assistance to needy individuals (p. 409)

white-collar worker clerical, business, or professional worker receiving a salary rather than a wage (p. 407)

wholesale price index see **producer price index** (p. 362)

wildcat bank generally fraudulent bank that operated in remote areas in the early 1800s (p. 273)

workfare program requiring welfare recipients to provide labor in exchange for benefits (p. 412)

World Bank international agency that makes loans to developing countries; formally the International Bank for Reconstruction and Development (p. 505)

Z

zero population growth condition in which the average number of births and deaths balance so that population size is unchanged (p. 499)

A

ability-to-pay principle of taxation/principio de tributación sobre la solvencia creencia que los impuestos se deben pagar de acuerdo al nivel de ingresos sin considerar los beneficios recibidos (p. 214)

absolute advantage/ventaja absoluta habilidad de un país para producir más de un producto en particular que los otros países (p. 450)

accelerated depreciation/depreciación acelerada programa que extiende la depreciación a lo largo de menos años de lo normal para generar mayores reducciones de impuestos (p. 231)

accelerator/acelerador cambio en el gasto causado por un cambio en el gasto global (p. 428)

acid rain/lluvia ácida contaminación en la forma de agualluvia mezclada con dióxido de sulfuro, forma leve de ácido sulfúrico (p. 528)

agency shop/taller gremial arreglo bajo el cual miembros que no son de la unión tienen que pagar cuotas de unión (p. 190)

aggregate demand curve/curva de demanda global curva hipotética que muestra distintos niveles del PIB real que se podrían producir a distintos niveles de precio (p. 422)

aggregate supply curve/curva de oferta global curva hipotética que muestra distintos niveles del PIB real que se podrían producir a distintos niveles de precio (p. 422)

agricultural bank/banco de crédito agrícola banco comercial con más de 25 por ciento de sus préstamos para la agricultura (p. 313)

alternative minimum tax/impuesto mínimo alternativo índice de impuesto sobre la renta que se aplica a casos en que los impuestos de otro modo caerían por debajo de cierto nivel (p. 231)

appropriations bill/proyecto de ley para asignación de fondos legislación para asignar fondos para ciertos propósitos (p. 243)

aquifer/acuífero formación subterránea rocosa que contiene agua (p. 525)

articles of partnership/contrato de asociación documento legal que especifica formalmente los acuerdos entre socios, incluyendo la forma en que se han de dividir las ganancias y las pérdidas (p. 57)

assets/haberes propiedades, posesiones y demandas a otras personas; generalmente, aparecen anotadas como asiento en el estado de cuentas (p. 302)

automatic stabilizer/estabilizador automático programa que automáticamente provee beneficios para compensar por un cambio en los ingresos de la gente; seguro de desempleo, programas de derecho a gratificación (p. 429)

automation/automatización producción, tanto mecánica como de otros procesos, que reduce la necesidad de trabajadores (p. 396)

average tax rate/tasa impositiva media total de impuestos pagados dividido por el total de renta imponible (p. 215)

B

baby boom/auge de bebés años en Estados Unidos, entre 1946 y 1964, en que hubo una alta tasa de natalidad (p. 373)

balance of payments/balanza de pagos diferencia entre dinero que se paga o que se recibe de otras naciones en actividad comercial; *balance de cuenta corriente* incluye bienes y servicios, *balanza comercial de mercancía* toma en cuenta sólo los bienes (p. 456)

balance sheet/estado de cuentas extracto de cuenta que muestra el activo y el pasivo y el valor neto de una unidad económica (p. 302)

balanced budget/presupuesto balanceado presupuesto anual en el que los gastos están a la par con los ingresos (p. 258)

balanced budget amendment/enmienda al presupuesto balanceado enmienda constitucional estatal o federal que requiere que el gobierno no gaste más de lo que recauda en impuestos y otros ingresos, a exclusión de préstamos (p. 249)

bank holding company/sociedad inversionista bancaria corporación que posee uno o más bancos (p. 296)

bank holiday/cierre bancario breve período durante el cual todos los bancos o instituciones de depósitos cierran para evitar los pánicos bancarios (p. 281)

bankruptcy/quiebra permiso que concede la corte a una persona o a un negocio para cesar o aplazar pago de algunas o todas las deudas durante un tiempo limitado (p. 61)

barter economy/economía de trueque economía sin dinero que depende del comercio o trueque (p. 266)

base year/año base año que sirve como punto de comparación para otros años en un índice de precios u otra estadística (p. 204)

benefit principle of taxation/principio de tributación acerca de beneficios creencia de que los impuestos se deben pagar de acuerdo con los beneficios que se reciban independiente del nivel de ingreso (p. 213)

Better Business Bureau organización sin fines de lucro patronizada por el comercio la cual provee al consumidor información acerca de las compañías locales (p. 71)

bill consolidation loan/préstamo para la consolidación de cuenta tipo popular de préstamo al consumidor que se usa para saldar múltiples préstamos en existencia (p. 322)

black market/mercado negro mercado en que se venden productos económicos ilegalmente (p. 486)

blue-collar worker/obrero trabajadores industriales o de factoria quienes reciben jornal en vez de salarios (p. 407)

board of directors/junta de directores representantes de accionistas ordinarios elegidos para instituir políticas y metas, alquilar gerentes profesionales para una corporación (p. 60)

bond/fianza contrato formal para devolver el dinero y los intereses sobre dinero prestado durante intervalos sistemáticos en el futuro (p. 61)

boycott/boicot protesta en la forma de rehusar a comprar, que incluye el esfuerzo para convencer a otras personas a tampoco comprar (p. 184)

break-even point/punto muerto producción necesaria si la firma ha de recuperar sus costos; nivel de producción en que el costo total equivale al ingreso total (p. 122)

bullion/lingote barras de metales nobles sin acuñar, por lo general oro o plata (p. 268)

business cycle/ciclo comercial cambios sistemáticos en el PIB real acentuados por periodos alternantes de expansión y contracción (p. 383)

business fluctuation/fluctuación comercial cambios en el PIB acentuados por períodos alternantes de expansión y contracción que ocurren en una base menos que sistemática (p. 383)

business organization/organización comercial empresa en pos de ganancias que produce bienes y/o servicios; incluye propietarios exclusivos, sociedades, corporaciones (p. 54)

C

call option/opción de compra contrato que da a los inversionistas la opción de comprar productos, acciones o bienes financieros en una fecha específica en el futuro y usando el precio que se acordó hoy (p. 338)

capital/capital implementos, equipo y fábricas que se usan en la producción de bienes y servicios; uno de cuatro factores de producción (p. 9)

capital consumption allowances/reservas para depreciación uso y desgaste de bienes de capital que se resta del PNB para obtener el PNN (p. 355)

capital flight/fuga de capitales exportación legal o ilegal de la moneda y las divisas de una nación (p. 500)

capital good/bienes de capital implemento, equipo u otros bienes fabricados que se emplean para producir otros bienes y servicios; un factor de producción (p. 20)

capital-intensive/con gran intensidad de capital método de producción que requiere relativamente grandes cantidades de capital con relación a la mano de obra (p. 488)

capital market/mercado de capital mercado en el que el capital financiero se presta por más de un año (p. 332)

capitalism/capitalismo economía mercantil en la cual los factores de producción son de propiedad privada (p. 43)

capital-to-labor ratio/relación capital-trabajo medida obtenida al dividir el total de las acciones de capital por la fuerza de trabajo (p. 379)

cartel/cartel grupo de vendedores o productores que obran conjuntamente para subir los precios al restringir la disponibilidad de un producto; OPEC (p. 513)

cease and desist order/orden de cesar y desistir fallo que ordena que una compañía pare una práctica comercial injusta que reduce o limita la competencia (p. 169)

census/censo cuenta completa de la población, incluyendo el lugar de residencia (p. 370)

center of population/centro de población punto donde el país se equilibraría si fuera plano y todo el mundo pesara lo mismo (p. 372)

central bank/banco central banco que le presta a otros bancos en momentos de necesidad, el "banco de los banqueros" (p. 280)

certificate of deposit/certificado de depósito recibo que indica que un inversionista ha hecho un préstamo con

intereses a una institución financiera (p. 304)

chamber of commerce/cámara de comercio organización sin fines de lucro cuyo propósito es promover los intereses comunes de los negocios locales (p. 71)

change in demand/cambio en demanda los consumidores demandan distintas cantidades en cada precio, haciendo que la curva de demanda cambie hacia la izquierda o la derecha (p. 88)

change in quantity demanded/cambio en cantidad demandada un movimiento en la curva de relación entre demanda y precio que demuestra que se está comprando una cantidad distinta debido a un cambio de precio (p. 86)

change in quantity supplied/cambio en la cantidad suplida cambio en la cantidad que se ofrece a la venta en respuesta a un cambio de precio; movimiento a lo largo de la curva de abastecimiento (p. 106)

change in supply/cambio en abastecimiento distintas cantidades ofrecidas a la venta a todos los precios posibles del mercado; cambio en la curva de abastecimiento (p. 106)

charter/carta constitucional aprobación escrita del gobierno para establecer una corporación; incluye el nombre de la compañía, la dirección, propósito del negocio, número de acciones y otros aspectos del negocio (p. 59)

civilian labor force/fuerza de trabajo civil parte de la población no institucionalizada, entre los 16 y 65 años, que está trabajando o buscando trabajo (p. 182)

closed shop/taller cerrado arreglo ilegal bajo el cual los trabajadores tienen que ser miembros de una unión antes de que los emplee (p. 190)

coins/monedas formas metálicas de dinero tal como el centavo, las monedas de cinco, diez y de 25 centavos (p. 300)

collateral/fianza propiedad u otra seguridad que se usa para garantizar el pago de un préstamo (p. 308)

collective bargaining/negociación colectiva proceso de negociación entre la unión y los representantes administrativos acerca de pago, beneficios y asuntos relacionados al trabajo (p. 70)

collective farm/granja colectiva en la antigua Unión Soviética, pequeñas granjas de propiedad del estado, pero operadas por familias que participaban en algunas de las ganancias (p. 479)

collectivization/colectivización propiedad común forzada de los factores de producción; se usó en la antigua Unión Soviética en la agricultura y en la industria manufacturera bajo Stalin (p. 478)

collusion/colusión acuerdos, por lo general ilegales, entre los productores para fijar los precios, limitar la producción o dividir los mercados (p. 157)

command economy/economía de mando sistema económico que se caracteriza por una autoridad central que hace la mayoría de las decisiones económicas (p. 33)

commercial bank/banco comercial institución depositoria que, hasta mediados de los años 70, tenía el derecho exclusivo de ofrecer cuentas de cheques (p. 281)

commodity money/dinero como producto dinero que tiene un uso alternativo como producto; pólvora, harina, maíz (p. 267)

common stock/acciones ordinarias certificado de propiedad en una corporación que autoriza al dueño a votar por la junta de directores, pero que tiene la última reclamación acerca de los dividendos y el capital (p. 60)

communism/comunismo sistema económico y político en el que los factores de producción son de propiedad colectiva y dirigidos por el estado; teoréticamente, una sociedad sin clases en que todos trabajan para el bien común (p. 474)

company union/sindicato de empresa unión organizada, sostenida y hasta financiada por el patrón (p. 184)

comparable worth/valor comparable doctrina que declara que se debe pagar lo mismo por trabajos de comparable dificultad (p. 200)

comparative advantage/ventaja comparativa habilidad del país de producir un cierto producto con relativamente más eficiencia que otro país; la oportunidad de producción al costo más bajo (p. 451)

complements/complementos productos que aumentan la utilidad o valor de otros productos; productos relacionados de tal modo que el aumento del precio de uno reduce la demanda de ambos (p. 89)

compulsory arbitration/arbitraje obligatorio situación que fuerza a los trabajadores y a la administración a usar un mediador para alcanzar un arreglo obligatorio (p. 191)

conglomerate/conglomerado de empresas firma con cuatro o más negocios que hacen productos no relacionados, sin ningún negocio en particular que sea responsable de la mayoría de sus ventas (p. 65)

conspicuous consumption/consumo suntuario uso de bienes y servicios caros para impresionar a las otras personas (p. 21)

constant dollars/dólares constantes las cantidades o precios al que se ajusta el dólar debido a la inflación; igual que **dólares reales** (p. 204)

consumer/consumidor persona que usa bienes y servicios para satisfacer sus necesidades y deseos (p. 21)

consumer cooperative/cooperativa de consumidor asociación sin fines de lucro que compra bienes de consumidor en grandes cantidades para que así sus miembros puedan comprar a precios por debajo de los que cobran los negocios regulares (p. 69)

consumer good/bienes del consumidor bienes cuyo fin está dirigido a los consumidores en vez del comercio (p. 20)

consumer price index/índice de precios de consumidor índice que se usa para medir los cambios de precio de la cesta de compra de los productos que el consumidor usa con más frecuencia (p. 362)

consumer sovereignty/soberanía del consumidor papel del consumidor como soverano del mercado a la hora de determinar los tipos de bienes y servicios que se producen (p. 47)

consumption/consumo proceso de consumir bienes y servicios para satisfacer las necesidades y deseos (p. 21)

consumption function/función del consumo gráfica que indica que para los distintos niveles económicos del sector del consumidor, los patrones de gasto son relativamente constantes y estables (p. 427)

co-op ver **cooperativa** (p. 69)

cooperative/cooperativa asociación sin fines de lucro que lleva a cabo algún tipo de actividad económica para el beneficio de sus miembros; incluye las cooperativas de consumidor, de servicios y de productores (p. 69)

copyright/derecho de autor derecho exclusivo que se con-

cede a un autor o artista para vender, publicar o reproducir su trabajo durante su vida más 50 años (p. 160)

corporate income tax/impuesto sobre la renta de corporación impuesto que pagan las corporaciones sobre sus ganancias de corporación (p. 219)

corporation/corporación una forma de organización comercial reconocida por la ley como una entidad legal independiente con todos los derechos y responsabilidades de individuo, inclusive el derecho de comprar y vender propiedad, entrar en contratos legales, demandar y ser demandada (p. 59)

cost-benefit analysis/análisis de costo-ventajas forma de pensar que compara el costo de una acción con sus ventajas (p. 532)

Council of Economic Advisers/Consejo de Asesores Económicos grupo de tres miembros que idea estrategias y aconseja al Presidente de los Estados Unidos acerca de asuntos económicos (p. 437)

coupon/cupón interés declarado de un bono de una corporación, de un municipio o del gobierno (p. 326)

craft union/sindicato de artesanos gremio laboral cuyos trabajadores llevan a cabo el mismo tipo de trabajo; igual que un **sindicato gremial** (p. 184)

credit union/cooperativa de crédito cooperativa de servicios sin fines de lucro que acepta depósitos, hace préstamos y provee otros servicios financieros (p. 70)

creditor/acreedor persona o institución a quien se le debe dinero (p. 312)

creeping inflation/inflación reptante índice de inflación bajo, generalmente de 1 a 3 por ciento anualmente (p. 400)

crowding-out effect/efecto de exclusión tasas de interés más altas de lo normal y disminución del acceso al capital financiero a que se enfrentan los inversionistas privados cuando el gobierno aumenta sus préstamos en los mercados financieros (p. 258)

crude birth rate/tasa de natalidad bruta número de nacimientos por 1,000 personas (p. 499)

currency/efectivo componente de papel del abastecimiento de dinero, hoy consiste en billetes de la Reserva Federal (p. 300)

current dollars/dólares corrientes cantidades o precios del dólar que no han sido ajustados para reflejar la inflación (p. 202)

current GDP/PIB imperante Producto Interno Bruto que se mide por los precios imperantes, sin ajustarlos para reflejar la inflación (p. 363)

current yield/rendimiento imperante el interés anual del cupón de un bono dividido por el precio de compra; medida de las ganancias de un bono (p. 327)

customs duty/derechos aduaneros impuestos sobre productos importados (p. 220)

customs union/unión aduanera grupo de países que han acordado reducir las barreras de intercambio comercial entre sí y han adoptado barreras comerciales uniformes para los países que no son miembros (p. 512)

cyclical unemployment/desempleo cíclico desempleo directamente relacionado a oscilaciones en el ciclo económico (p. 396)

D

deep gas/gas profundo gas natural situado a 15,000 pies o más debajo de la superficie de la tierra (p. 527)

deficiency payment/aportación para enjugar un déficit aportación en efectivo para alcanzar la diferencia entre el precio del mercado y el precio indicativo de una cosecha agrícola (p. 146)

deficit spending/gastos deficitarios gastos anuales del gobierno en exceso de los impuestos y otros ingresos (p. 253)

deflation/deflación disminución en el nivel general de los precios (p. 399)

demand/demanda combinación de deseo, habilidad y voluntad de comprar un producto (p. 82)

demand curve/curva de demanda gráfica que ilustra la cantidad que se demanda a cada precio que puede prevalecer en el mercado en cualquier momento dado (p. 84)

demand deposit account/cuentas de depósito a la vista (CDV) cuentas cuyos fondos pueden retirarse al escribirse un cheque y sin la previa aprobación de la institución depositoria (p. 281)

demand elasticity/elasticidad de demanda medida de responsividad que relaciona el cambio en la cantidad demandada (variable dependiente) a un cambio en precio (variable independiente) (p. 92)

demand schedule/programa de demanda lista que indica la cantidad demandada a todos los precios posibles que pueden prevalecer en el mercado en cualquier momento dado (p. 84)

demographer/demógrafo persona que estudia el crecimiento, la densidad y otras características de la población (p. 372)

dependency ratio/relación de dependencia relación de niños a envejecientes por 100 personas dentro de la categoría de trabajo de las edades entre los 18-64 años (p. 374)

depreciation/depreciación desgaste gradual de los bienes de capital durante la producción (p. 118)

depression/depresión estado de la economía con grandes números de desempleados, disminución de ingresos reales, exceso de capacidad en las plantas manufactureras, dificultades económicas generales (p. 384)

depression scrip/vale de depresión moneda emitida por los pueblos, las cámaras de comercio y otras entidades cívicas durante la Gran Depresión de los años 30 (p. 385)

deregulation/eliminación de restricciones relajamiento o eliminación de los reglamentos del gobierno sobre las actividades comerciales (p. 284)

devaluation/devaluación acción que toma un país para que su moneda valga menos en relación al oro u otra moneda (p. 462)

developing country/país en desarrollo país cuyo promedio de ingresos per cápita es tan sólo una fracción del de los países más industrializados (p. 498)

diminishing marginal utility/utilidad marginal decreciente satisfacción o utilidad decreciente a medida que se van adquiriendo unidades adicionales de un producto (p. 90)

diminishing returns/rendimientos decrecientes etapa de producción en la que el rendimiento aumenta a un ritmo disminuyente a medida que se añaden más unidades de insumo variable (p. 115)

discomfort index/índice de incomodidad estadística no oficial de la suma de la inflación mensual y el índice de desempleo; igual al **índice de miseria** (p. 419)

discount rate/tasa de descuento tasa de interés que el Sistema de Reserva Federal cobra a las instituciones financieras por los préstamos (p. 307)

discount window/ventana de descuento local físico en el Sistema de Reserva Federal donde se hacen los préstamos a las instituciones depositorias (p. 308)

disposable personal income/ingreso personal disponible el ingreso personal menos los impuestos personales; todo el ingreso disponible al sector consumidor después de los impuestos (p. 356)

distribution of income/distribución de ingresos modo por el cual los ingresos de la nación se dividen entre familias, individuos u otros grupos designados (p. 240)

dividend/dividendo cheque que se paga a los accionistas, por lo general trimestralmente, representa una porción de las ganancias de la corporación (p. 59)

division of labor/división de trabajo división de trabajo en un número de tareas separadas para llevarse a cabo por distintos trabajadores; igual que **especialización** (p. 23)

DJIA ver **Dow-Jones Industrial Average** (p. 336)

Dow-Jones Industrial Average (DJIA) serie de estadísticas representativas de 30 acciones que se usan para seguir los cambios de precio en la New York Stock Exchange (p. 336)

dual banking system/sistema bancario doble situación desde 1863 hasta el presente que permite que los bancos elijan cartas constitucionales federales o del estado (p. 279)

durable goods/bienes durables bienes que duran más de tres años con uso regular; puede incluir capital o un objeto de consumidor (p. 20)

E

easy money policy/política de dinero abundante política monetaria que resulta en tasas de interés más bajas y mayor acceso a crédito; se asocia con la expansión del abastecimiento de dinero (p. 306)

econometric model/modelo econométrico modelo macroeconómico que usa ecuaciones algebraicas para describir cómo la economía se conduce y cómo se espera que se conduzca en el futuro (p. 387)

economic institution/institución económica organización o grupo de personas que usan y a veces representan los factores de producción (p. 54)

economic interdependence/interdependencia económica las actividades económicas en una parte del país o del mundo afectan lo que sucede en otro lugar (p. 23)

economic model/modelo económico conjunto de suposiciones en una tabla, gráfica o ecuaciones que se usan para describir o explicar la conducta económica (p. 134)

economic product/producto económico bienes o servicios útiles, relativamente escasos y transferibles a otras personas (p. 20)

economic system/sistema económico manera organizada de una sociedad proveer las necesidades de sus integrantes (p. 32)

economics/economía ciencia social que trata acerca del

estudio de cómo la gente satisface los aparentemente ilimitados y competitivos deseos mediante el uso cuidadoso de escasos recursos (p. 11)

economies of scale/economías de escala aumento de la eficacia del uso del personal, la planta y el equipo a medida que la empresa aumenta de tamaño (p. 159)

ECU Unidad monetaria europea; unidad monetaria que usa la Unión Europea (p. 512)

Efficient Market Hypothesis/Hipótesis de Mercado Eficiente (HME) argumento acerca de que las acciones siempre tienen el precio adecuado, y que las rebajas son difíciles de hallar porque muchísimos inversionistas siempre las están vigilando (p. 334)

elastic/elástico tipo de elasticidad en que el cambio de porcentaje en la variable independiente (generalmente el precio) causa un cambio más que proporcionado en la variable dependiente (generalmente la cantidad demandada u ofrecida) (p. 92)

embargo/embargo prohibición de la exportación o importación de un producto (p. 522)

energy bank/banco de energía banco comercial con más del 25 por ciento de sus préstamos en energía (p. 313)

enterprise zone/zona de iniciativa áreas económicamente deprimidas donde se han suspendido las reglamentaciones del gobierno para poder atraer el comercio (p. 412)

entitlement/titularidad programa o beneficio que usa los requerimientos de la eligibilidad establecida para proveer suplementos de salud, de alimentación o de ingresos a individuos (p. 260)

entrepreneur/empresario individuo arriesgado en busca de ganancias; uno de cuatro factores de producción (p. 10)

equilibrium price/precio de equilibrio precio en que la cantidad ofrecida equivale a la cantidad demandada; precio que aprueba el mercado (p. 138)

equilibrium wage rate/índice del equilibrio salarial índice salarial que no deja ni exceso ni escacez en el mercado (p. 195)

equities/capital accionario acciones que representan acciones de propiedad en las corporaciones (p. 334)

estate tax/impuesto sucesorio impuesto por el traspaso de propiedad cuando una persona muere (p. 220)

European Community/Comunidad Europea antigua unión aduanera compuesta de 12 naciones europeas; se convirtió en la Unión Europea en noviembre del 1993 (p. 512)

European Union/Unión Europea la sucesora de la Comunidad Europea que estableció el Tratado de Maastricht en noviembre del 1993 (p. 512)

excess reserves/reservas excesivas dinero efectivo, divisas y reservas de una institución financiera que no se necesitan para respaldar préstamos en existencia; fuente potencial de nuevos préstamos (p. 303)

excise tax/impuesto sobre el consumo impuesto sobre ingresos generales recaudado sobre la manufactura o venta de objetos selectos (p. 219)

expansion/expansión periodo de crecimiento del PIB real; recuperación de la recesión (p. 383)

expropriation/expropiación cuando el gobierno confisca bienes de propiedad privada o extranjera sin compensación (p. 511)

external debt/deuda externa dinero prestado que un país debe a países y bancos extranjeros (p. 500)

externality/factores externos efecto secundario de la economía que afecta a un tercero que no está envuelto (p. 166)

F

fact-finding/indagación de los hechos acuerdo entre la unión y la empresa de pedirle a un tercero recoja los hechos acerca de una disputa y presente recomendaciones sin obligaciones (p. 191)

factor market/mercado de factor mercado en que se venden y se compran recursos productivos (p. 24)

factors of production/factores de producción recursos productivos que componen las cuatro categorías de tierra, capital, trabajo y espíritu empresarial (p. 9)

family/familia dos o más personas que viven juntas y que están vinculadas por sangre, matrimonio o adopción (p. 357)

federal budget/presupuesto federal plan anual que traza los gastos propuestos y las ganancias que se anticipan (p. 243)

federal budget deficit/déficit del presupuesto federal exceso de gastos federales sobre la recaudación de impuestos e ingresos (p. 243)

federal debt/deuda federal cantidad total de dinero que el gobierno federal ha pedido prestado de los demás (p. 254)

Federal Reserve Note/vale de la Reserva Federal moneda emitida por la Reserva Federal que con el tiempo sustituyó a todos los otros tipos de moneda federal (p. 280)

Federal Reserve System/Sistema de Reserva Federal banco central de los Estados Unidos, de propiedad privada y cuyo control es público (p. 280)

fertility rate/tasa de fecundidad número de alumbramientos que se espera que 1,000 mujeres experimenten en sus vidas (p. 372)

fiat money/moneda fiduciaria dinero por decreto del gobierno; no tiene valor alternativo ni uso como producto básico (p. 267)

FICA Acta de Contribuciones del Seguro Federal; gravamen impuesto sobre los patrones y empleados para sostener al Seguro Social y al Medicare (p. 218)

finance company/compañía financiera firma que hace préstamos directamente a los consumidores y que se especializa en la compra de contratos a plazos de los comerciantes que venden a crédito (p. 322)

financial asset/haber financiero documento que representa un derecho a los ingresos y la propiedad del prestatario; CDs, bonos, letras del Tesoro, hipotecas (p. 321)

financial capital/capital financiero dinero que se usa para comprar implementos y equipo que se usa en la producción (p. 9)

financial intermediary/intermediario financiero institución que canaliza los ahorros a los inversionistas; bancos, compañías de seguro, sociedades de ahorro y préstamo, cooperativas de crédito (p. 321)

financial system/sistema financiero red de personas que ahorran, inversionistas e instituciones financieras que colaboran para transferir los ahorros a usos de inversión (p. 320)

fiscal policy/política fiscal el uso de las medidas que usa el gobierno para gastos y recaudación de ingresos para influenciar la economía (p. 427)

fiscal year/año fiscal periodo de 12 meses para la planificación financiera que no necesariamente coincide con el año civil; del 1 de octubre al 30 de septiembre para el gobierno federal (p. 243)

Five-Year Plan/Plan de Cinco Años plan económico centralizado y abarcante que usó la Unión Soviética y la China para coordinar el desarrollo de la agricultura y la industria (p. 478)

fixed cost/costo fijo costo de producción que no cambia cuando cambia la producción (p. 118)

fixed exchange rate/cotización de divisa fija sistema bajo el cual el valor de una divisa se fijó en relación al de las otras; sistema de cotización que estuvo en efecto hasta el 1971 (p. 461)

fixed income/renta fija renta que no aumenta aunque los precios suban (p. 40)

flexible exchange rate/cotización de divisa flexible sistema que depende de oferta y demanda para determinar el valor de una moneda en términos de otra; sistema de cotización en efecto desde el 1971, igual a la **cotización flotante** (p. 463)

floating exchange rate/cotización flotante ver **cotización de divisa flexible** (p. 463)

floor price/precio mínimo precio legal más bajo que se puede cobrar por un producto (p. 142)

food stamps/sellos para la compra de alimentos cupones que emite el gobierno y que se canjean por alimentos (p. 411)

foreign exchange/divisas divisas que usan los países para conducir comercio internacional (p. 461)

foreign exchange futures/letras para entrega futura contratos que permiten que una persona compre divisas para una fecha futura, al precio que se fija hoy (p. 464)

foreign exchange market/mercado de divisas mercado en que se compran y venden las divisas que se usan para el intercambio comercial (p. 461)

foreign exchange rate/cotización de divisas precio de la moneda de un país en relación a la moneda de otro país (p. 461)

fractional reserve system/sistema de reserva fraccionada sistema que dicta que las instituciones financieras aparten una fracción de sus depósitos en la forma de reservas (p. 302)

franchise/franquicia derecho exclusivo para producir o vender cierto producto en un área o región (p. 159)

free enterprise economy/economía de libre empresa economía de mercado en la que los comercios privados tienen la libertad de operar para obtener ganancias con intervención limitada del gobierno; lo mismo que **economía de empresa privada** (p. 24)

free product/producto liberal producto relativamente abundante no lo suficientemente escaso para causar una gran preocupación en el estudio de economía; incluye el sol y la lluvia (p. 20)

free-trade area/zona de comercio libre grupo de países que han acordado reducir las barreras comerciales entre sí, pero que carecen de una barrera arancelaria para los países no miembros (p. 512)

frictional unemployment/desempleo friccional desempleo causado por trabajadores cuando cambian de trabajo o al

esperar ir a nuevos empleos (p. 395)

fringe benefit/beneficio complementario beneficio que recibe el empleado además de sueldos y salarios; incluye vacaciones pagas, licencia por enfermedad, retiro y seguro (p. 57)

full employment/empleo total la constante del índice de desempleo más bajo que se pueda pensar posible en la economía (p. 397)

futures/futuros contratos para comprar o vender mercancías o bienes financieros a una fecha específica en el futuro, usando un precio que se acordó hoy (p. 338)

futures market/mercado de futuros mercado donde se compran y se venden los contratos de futuros (p. 338)

G

galloping inflation/inflación galopante inflación relativamente intensa, generalmente alcanza desde 100 a 300 por ciento anualmente (p. 400)

gasohol mezcla de 90 por ciento gasolina sin plomo y 10 por ciento alcohol de grano (p. 524)

GATT/AGTC ver **Acuerdo General para Tarifas y Comercio** (p. 458)

GDP gap/laguna del PIB diferencia entre lo que la economía puede producir y lo que, de hecho, produce; costo de oportunidad anual de los recursos desempleados (p. 419)

GDP in constant dollars/PIB en dólares constantes el Producto Interno Bruto considerando la inflación; es igual al PIB (p. 364)

General Agreement on Tariffs and Trade/Acuerdo General para Tarifas y Comercio (AGTC) acuerdo firmado por 23 países en 1947 que extendía las conseciones de tarifas y que obró para eliminar las cuotas de importación (p. 458)

general partnership/asociación general ver **asociación** (p. 57)

geographic monopoly/monopolio geográfico situación del mercado en la que una firma tiene un monopolio debido al sitio en que está situada o a la pequeñez del mercado (p. 159)

gift tax/impuesto sobre donaciones y legados impuesto sobre donaciones de dinero o riquezas que tiene que pagar el donante (p. 220)

giveback/devolución de beneficios en la renegociación de un contrato, sueldo, beneficio complementario o regla de trabajo que se pierde (p. 199)

glass ceiling/techo de cristal barrera aparentemente invisible que impide que las mujeres y las minorías avancen en una organización dominada por los hombres (p. 200)

glut/abarrotamiento superabundancia de un producto (p. 528)

gold certificate/certificado de oro billete de banco respaldado por oro; emitido en 1863 y popular hasta que fue retirado en 1934 (p. 275)

gold standard/patrón de oro patrón monetario bajo el cual la moneda de un país equivale a, y se puede cambiar por, una cantidad específica de oro (p. 275)

good/bien producto económico tangible y útil, relativamente escaso, transferible a otras personas; se usa para satisfacer necesidades y deseos (p. 20)

Gosplan autoridad central de planificación en la antigua Unión Soviética que ideó y dirigió los planes de Cinco Años (p. 478)

government monopoly/monopolio fiscal monopolio creado por o/ de la propiedad del gobierno (p. 160)

grant-in-aid/donativo del gobierno transferencia de pago desde un nivel del gobierno a otro y que no incumbe compensación (p. 240)

Great Depression/Gran Depresión el periodo de mayor disminución económica en la historia de los Estados Unidos, duró aproximadamente desde 1929 hasta 1939 (p. 185)

Great Leap Forward/Gran Salto Adelante el segundo desastroso plan de cinco años de la China iniciado en 1958, forzó la colectivización de la agricultura y la rápida industrialización (p. 487)

greenback billete de banco no respaldado por oro que el gobierno de los Estados Unidos emitió en 1861; el frente y el dorso de los billetes estaban imprimidos con tinta verde (p. 274)

grievance procedure/procedimiento para la presentación de reclamaciones provisión contractual que delínea la forma en que se resolverán futuras disputas y asuntos de quejas (p. 191)

Gross Domestic Product/Producto Interno Bruto (PIB) valor en dólar de todos los productos, servicios y estructuras finales dentro de las fronteras nacionales de un país durante el periodo de un año (p. 256)

Gross National Product/Producto Nacional Bruto (PNB) valor total en dólar de todos los productos, estructuras y servicios finales producidos en un año con la mano de obra y la propiedad suplidas por los residentes de un país, sin importar donde toma lugar la producción; la mayor medida de los ingresos de una nación (p. 354)

gross private domestic investment/inversión interna privada bruta en el modelo producción-gastos, gasto total de parte del sector inversionista (p. 358)

growth triangle/triángulo de crecimiento tabla que muestra los índices de crecimiento de una serie estadística entre dos fechas cualquiera (p. 376)

H

horizontal merger/fusión horizontal combinación de dos o más empresas que producen el mismo producto (p. 64)

household/unidad familiar unidad básica del sector del consumidor que consiste de todas las personas que ocupan una casa, apartamento o vivienda separada (p. 356)

human capital/capital humano suma de las destrezas, habilidades, salud y motivación (p. 23)

hyperinflation/hiperinflación inflación anormal en exceso de 500 por ciento por año; última etapa de un colapso monetario (p. 400)

I

imperfect competition/competencia imperfecta estructura mercantil en la que no se satisfacen todas las condiciones de competencia pura; competencia monopolística, olipolio y monopolio (p. 155)

implicit GDP price deflator/deflactor implícito del precio PIB índice que se usa para medir los cambios de precio del Producto Interno Bruto (p. 363)

incidence of a tax/incidencia de un impuesto carga final de un impuesto (p. 228)

income effect/efecto de ingreso aquella porción de un cambio en cantidad demandada causada por un cambio en el ingreso real de un consumidor cuando el precio de un producto cambia (p. 87)

income-to-poverty ratio/relación ingreso-pobreza relación del ingreso familiar dividido por el nivel de pobreza; medida que se usa para compensar por las diferencias en los tamaños de familia (p. 408)

inconvertible fiat money standard/estándar inconvertible de la moneda fiduciaria moneda fiduciaria que no se puede cambiar por oro o plata; los vales de la Reserva Federal de hoy en día (p. 276)

incorporate/incorporar proceso requerido para formar una corporación, involucra permiso del gobierno federal o el estado donde el negocio tendrá su sede (p. 59)

independent pricing/fijación independiente de precios política de fijación de precios por parte de un competidor imperfecto que ignora a los otros productores y ciertas condiciones del mercado (p. 157)

independent union/unión independiente gremio no afiliado con la AFL-CIO (p. 187)

index of leading indicators/índice de indicadores anticipados índice compuesto de 11 series económicas que suben y bajan en anticipo a cambios en la economía global; series estadísticas que se usan para predecir los puntos críticos del ciclo comercial (p. 388)

indexing/indización ajuste de las escalas de impuestos para contrarrestar los efectos de la inflación (p. 217)

indirect business tax/impuesto comercial indirecto impuesto que se paga como un gasto por hacer negocios; gastos de licencia, impuestos de propiedad, derechos de aduana (p. 356)

individual income tax/impuesto sobre la renta personal impuesto sobre jornales, salarios y otros ingresos de las personas (p. 216)

Individual Retirement Account (IRA) cuenta de retiro personal, cuenta de retiro en la forma de depósito a largo plazo, con contribuciones anuales de hasta $2,000 exemptas de impuestos hasta que se saquen durante el retiro (p. 331)

industrial union/unión industrial gremio cuyos trabajadores llevan a cabo distintos tipos de trabajo (p. 184)

industry/industria colectivamente, todas las firmas que producen en un mercado; en el mercado, el lado que hace la oferta (p. 152)

inelastic/no elástica tipo de elasticidad en el cual el porcentaje de cambio en la variable independiente (usualmente el precio) causa un cambio menos que proporcionado en la variable dependiente (usualmente la cantidad demandada u ofrecida) (p. 92)

infant industries argument/argumento de las industrias nacientes argumento de que a las industrias nuevas que están surgiendo se las debe proteger de la competencia extranjera hasta que estén lo suficiente fuertes para competir (p. 455)

inflation/inflación aumento en el nivel general de los precios (p. 40)

injunction/mandato judicial orden de la corte dictada para evitar que una compañía o unión tome acción durante una disputa laboral (p. 192)

intangible personal property/propiedad personal intangible derechos de propiedad de bienes en contraste con la propiedad en sí; incluye acciones, cuentas bancarias (p. 224)

interest/interés pago que se hace por el uso de dinero prestado; usualmente se paga a intervalos periódicos para bonos o préstamos de largo plazo (p. 61)

intergovermental revenue/ingresos intergubernamentales fondos, que en el gobierno, se reciben de un nivel a otro (p. 222)

intermediate products/productos intermediarios productos directamente excluidos de las computaciones del PIB ya que son componentes de otros productos finales incluidos en el PIB; llantas y radios nuevos para usarse en autos nuevos (p. 349)

Internal Revenue Service (IRS)/Servicio de Rentas Internas rama del Departamento de Tesorería que recauda impuestos (p. 216)

International Bank for Reconstruction and Development/ Banco Internacional para Reconstrucción y Desarrollo ver **World Bank** (p. 505)

inventory/inventario abastecimiento de bienes en reserva; incluye bienes terminados esperando venderse y materias primas que se usan en producción (p. 56)

investment tax credit/crédito impositivo de inversión crédito impositivo que se da para la compra de equipo (p. 231)

J

jumbo CD/CD jumbo certificado de depósito de $1,000,000 o más (p. 328)

junk bond/bono especulativo bono de corporación, generalmente considerado por debajo del grado mediano o especulativo, que paga grandes ganancias para compensar los grandes riesgos de incumplimiento (p. 328)

jurisdictional dispute/controversia sobre jurisdicción desacuerdo, por lo general entre uniones, en cuanto a quién tiene la autoridad para efectuar ciertos tipos de trabajo (p. 187)

K

keiretsu grupo de firmas japonesas de propiedad privada unidas y gobernadas por una junta directiva exterior para poder regular la competencia (p. 488)

Keynesian economics/economía keynesiana políticas del gobierno para gastos e impuestos sugeridas por John Maynard Keynes para estimular la economía; sinónimo de las políticas fiscales o de la economía del lado de la demanda (p. 427)

L

labor/trabajo la gente con todas sus habilidades y esfuerzos; uno de los cuatro factores de producción, no incluye al empresario (p. 10)

labor mobility/mobilidad laboral habilidad y voluntad laboral de reubicarse, por lo general por sueldos más altos (p. 196)

labor productivity/productividad laboral índice de crecimiento del rendimiento total por unidad de insumo; medida de la eficiencia de productividad (p. 380)

labor union/sindicato obrero organización que obra en beneficio de los intereses de sus miembros respecto a pago, horas de trabajo, seguro médico, beneficios complementarios y otros asuntos relacionados al trabajo (p. 70)

Laffer curve/curva Laffer gráfica que muestra que las tasas impositivas más bajas supuestamente estimulan mayores recaudaciones impositivas (p. 432)

laissez-faire/liberalismo filosofía de que el gobierno no debe interferir con las actividades comerciales (p. 152)

land/tierra recursos naturales o "dones de la naturaleza" no creados por el esfuerzo humano; uno de cuatro factores de producción (p. 9)

Law of Demand/Ley de Demanda regla que dicta que se demanda más a precios bajos y menos a precios altos; relación inversa entre precio y cantidad demandada (p. 86)

Law of Supply/Ley de Oferta regla que dicta que se ofrece más a la venta a precios altos que a precios bajos (p. 106)

Law of Variable Proportions/Ley de Proporciones Variables regla que dicta que la producción a corto plazo cambia a medida que un insumo es variado mientras otros se mantienen constante (p. 111)

legal reserves/reservas legales moneda y depósitos que se usan para cumplir con los requisitos de reserva (p. 302)

legal tender/moneda legal moneda fiduciaria que por decreto del gobierno hay que aceptar por pago (p. 274)

liabilities/compromisos deudas y obligaciones que se le deben a otras personas; usualmente anotadas como partidas en el estado de cuentas (p. 302)

life expectancy/expectativa de vida promedio de la duración de vida restante en años para personas que logran una cierta edad (p. 372)

limited liability/responsabilidad limitada situación en la cual la responsabilidad de un dueño por las deudas de una compañía están limitadas al tamaño de su inversión en la firma; se aplica a accionistas ordinarios y socios limitados en una sociedad en comandita simple (p. 59)

limited life/vida limitada situación en la cual una firma deja de existir legalmente al morir o renunciar un dueño o al agregarse uno nuevo; se aplica a propietarios únicos y a sociedades (p. 57)

limited partnership/sociedad limitada forma de sociedad en la que uno o más socios no participan activamente en el funcionamiento diario del negocio y cuyas responsabilidad por la deuda de la sociedad se limita a la cantidad invertida en el negocio (p. 57)

liquidity/liquidez potencial para conversión rápida a efectivo u otros bienes financieros (p. 304)

lockout/cierre patronal rehuso patronal de dejar que los empleados trabajen hasta que se cumplan las demandas de la compañía (p. 184)

long run/largo plazo periodo de producción lo bastante largo para cambiar la cantidad de insumos variables y fijos que se usan en la producción (p. 111)

Lorenz curve/curva de Lorenz curva que muestra cuánto la distribución en sí de los ingresos varía de una distribución igual (p. 405)

loss leader/artículo de promoción artículo que se vende intencionalmente por debajo de costo para atraer a los clientes (p. 138)

luxury good/bienes de lujo bienes cuya demanda aumenta mucho más rápido de lo que aumentan los ingresos (p. 220)

M

M1 componentes del abastecimiento de dinero que se conforman al papel del dinero como medio de intercambio; monedas, divisas, cheques, otros depósitos a la vista, cheques de viajeros (p. 311)

M2 componentes del abastecimiento de dinero que se conforman al papel del dinero como fuente de valor; M1, depósitos de ahorros, depósitos a plazo (p. 311)

macroeconomic equilibrium/equilibrio macroeconómico nivel de PIB consistente con un nivel de precio dado; intersección de oferta y demanda globales (p. 425)

macroeconomics/macroeconomía esa parte de la teoría económica que trata con la economía como un total y con la adopción de decisiones por grandes unidades como los gobiernos y las uniones (p. 182)

margin requirement/requerimiento marginal depósitos mínimos que se quedan con el corredor para usarlos como pago parcial de otros valores (p. 300)

marginal analysis/análisis marginal adopción de decisión que compara el costo extra de hacer algo con los beneficios extras que se obtienen (p. 121)

marginal cost/costo marginal costo extra de producir una unidad de producción adicional (p. 119)

marginal product/producto marginal producción extra debida a adición de una unidad más de insumo (p. 114)

marginal revenue/ingreso marginal ingreso extra de la venta de una unidad de producto adicional (p. 121)

marginal tax rate/tasa impositiva marginal tasa impositiva que se aplica al próximo dólar de ingreso sujeto a impuesto (p. 215)

marginal utility/utilidad marginal satisfacción o utilidad que se obtiene de adquirir una unidad más de un producto (p. 89)

market/mercado lugar de encuentro o mecanismo que permite que los compradores y vendedores de un producto económico se reunan; puede ser local, regional, nacional o global (p. 23)

market basket/cesta de mercado colección representativa de los bienes y servicios que se usan para compilar un índice de precios (p. 362)

market economy/economía de mercado sistema económico en el cual la oferta y la demanda y el sistema de precios ayudan a la gente a tomar decisiones y a asignar los recursos; lo mismo que **economía de libre comercio** (p. 34)

market equilibrium/equilibrio del mercado condición de la estabilidad del precio en que la cantidad demandada es igual a la cantidad ofrecida (p. 134)

market failure/fallo del mercado mercado que carece de cualquiera de los requisitos de un mercado competidor, como competencia adecuada, conocimiento de precios y oportunidades, mobilidad de recursos y ganancias competitivas (p. 163)

market structure/estructura del mercado clasificación del mercado de acuerdo al número y tamaño de las firmas, tipo de producto y tipo de competición (p. 152)

maturity/madurez vida de un bono o longitud del tiempo que los fondos están prestados (p. 326)

measure of value/medida de valor una de las tres funciones del dinero que le permite servir como denominador común para medir el valor (p. 266)

mediation/mediación proceso de resolver un conflicto al incluir a un tercero neutral (p. 191)

medicaid programa de seguro médico del gobierno federal y el estado para personas de ingresos bajos (p. 246)

medicare programa federal de cuidados de salud para envejecientes, que no toma en cuenta sus ingresos (p. 218)

medium of exchange/medio de cambio dinero u otra sustancia generalmente aceptada en intercambio; una de las tres funciones del dinero (p. 266)

member bank/banco miembro banco que pertenece al Sistema de Reserva Federal (p. 294)

member bank reserves/reservas de banco miembro reservas que mantienen los bancos miembros en la Reserva Federal para satisfacer los requisitos de reserva (p. 302)

merger/fusión combinación de dos o más empresas comerciales para formar una sóla firma (p. 64)

microeconomics/microeconomía rama de la teoría de la economía que trata con la conducta y las decisiones que adoptan las pequeñas unidades tales como los individuos y las firmas (p. 82)

minimum wage/sueldo mínimo sueldo legal más bajo que se le puede pagar a la mayoría de trabajadores (p. 142)

misery index/índice de miseria estadística no oficial que es la suma de la inflación mensual y la tasa de desempleo; igual al **índice de incomodidad** (p. 419)

mixed economy/economía mixta ver **economía de empresa privada modificada** (p. 48)

modified free enterprise economy/economía de libre empresa modificada sistema de libre empresa con un poco de participación del gobierno; igual que **economía de empresa privada modificada** (p. 533)

modified private enterprise economy/economía de empresa privada modificada economía de mercado de libre empresa donde la gente lleva a cabo sus asuntos económicos libremente, pero están sujetos a algunas intervenciones y regulaciones del gobierno (p. 48)

modified union shop/empresa de exclusividad gremial modificada arreglo bajo el cual los trabajadores tienen la opción de unirse a una unión luego de habérseles empleado (p. 190)

monetarism/monetarismo escuela de pensamiento que enfatiza la importancia del crecimiento monetario estable para controlar la inflación y estimular el crecimiento económico de largo plazo (p. 433)

monetary policy/política monetaria acciones que toma el Sistema de Reserva Federal para ampliar o reducir el abastecimiento de dinero para afectar el costo y disponibilidad de crédito (p. 302)

monetary standard/estándar monetario mecanismo que mantiene un abastecimiento de dinero, durable, portátil, divisible y estable en valor; el estándar del oro, el estándar de la plata, el estándar de la moneda fiduciaria (p. 272)

monetary unit/unidad monetaria unidad monetaria estándar del abastecimiento monetario de un país; el dólar americano, la libra británica (p. 269)

monetizing the debt/monetización de la deuda proceso de crear suficiente dinero adicional para contrarrestar los préstamos del gobierno de modo que las tasas de interés permanezcan sin cambiar (p. 310)

money/dinero cualquier cosa que sirva como medio de intercambio, una medida de valor y un abastecimiento de valor (p. 266)

money market/mercado monetario mercado en el cual el capital financiero se ha prestado por un año o menos (p. 332)

money market mutual fund/fondo común de inversiones firma que une los fondos que recoge de los pequeños ahorradores para hacerle préstamos grandes a inversionistas dispuestos a pagar altas tasas de rendimiento (p. 330)

monopolistic competition/competición monopolística estructura mercantil que posee todas las condiciones de competición pura a excepción de tener productos idénticos; una forma de competición imperfecta (p. 155)

monopoly/monopolio estructura mercantil caracterizada por un solo productor; una forma de competición imperfecta (p. 158)

moral suasion/persuasión moral el uso que el Sistema de Reserva Federal hace de la persuasión para lograr política monetaria; testimonio congresional, comunicados de prensa (p. 308)

most favored nation clause/cláusula de la nación más favorecida derecho mercantil que permite a un país tercero disfrutar las mismas rebajas de tarifas que los Estados Unidos negocia con otro país (p. 458)

multinational/multinacional corporación que produce y vende sin importarle las fronteras nacionales y cuyas actividades comerciales están situadas en varios países diferentes (p. 66)

multiplier/multiplicador cambio en el gasto global causado por un cambio en el gasto de inversión (p. 427)

municipal bond/bono municipal bono, a menudo exempto de impuestos, emitido por el gobierno estatal o local; conocido como *munis* (p. 329)

mutual fund/fondo mutuo compañía que vende acciones de sí misma y usa las ganancias para comprar acciones y bonos emitidos por otras compañías (p. 323)

mutual savings bank/banco mutualista de ahorro institución de ahorro de propiedad de los depositantes que opera para beneficio de ellos (p. 281)

NAFTA ver **Acuerdo Norteamericano de Comercio Libre** (p. 459)

national bank/banco nacional un banco comercial establecido por el Sistema Bancario Nacional; miembro del Fed (p. 274)

National Bank Note/billete del Banco Nacional moneda respaldada por bonos del gobierno, emitida por bancos nacionales comenzando en 1863 y que por lo general desapareció de circulación alrededor de los años 30 (p. 274)

National Banking System/Sistema Bancario Nacional sistema de bancos constituidos, inspeccionados y regulados federalmente que se estableció en 1863, ahora son miembros del Sistema Federal (p. 274)

national currency/moneda nacional ver **billete del Banco Nacional** (p. 274)

national income/ingresos nacionales producto nacional neto

menos los impuestos comerciales indirectos; medida de los ingresos de una nación (p. 356)

national income accounting/contabilidad de los ingresos nacionales sistema de cuentas que se usa para seguir la producción, el consumo, los ahorros, las estadísticas de los ingresos de la nación (p. 348)

natural monopoly/monopolio natural mercado en que los costos promedios son más bajos cuando toda la producción la produce una sola firma (p. 158)

need/necesidad requisito básico para supervivencia; incluye comida, ropa y/o albergue (p. 20)

negative externality/factores externos negativos efectos secundarios negativos que afectan a un tercero no partícipe; costo externo (p. 166)

negative income tax/impuesto negativo sobre la renta sistema de impuestos que hace pagos efectivos en la forma de reembolsos de impuestos cuando los ingresos de las personas caen por debajo de ciertos niveles (p. 411)

Negotiable Order of Withdrawal (NOW) orden negativa de retiro, tipo de cuenta de cheques que paga intereses (p. 282)

net exports of goods and services/exportaciones netas de bienes y servicios gastos netos según el modelo de producción-gastos del sector extranjero (p. 359)

net immigration/inmigración neta carga de población neta después de tomar en cuenta las personas que salen o entran del país (p. 372)

net national product/producto interno neto (PIN) Producto Interno Bruto menos los cargos de depreciación por uso y desgaste del equipo capital; medida de la producción anual neta generada con la mano de obra y la propiedad suplida por los ciudadanos de un país (p. 355)

net worth/valor neto exceso de bienes por encima de las responsabilidades, usualmente anotados como un resumen separado en el estado de cuentas; medida del valor de un negocio (p. 302)

nominal GDP ver **PIB imperante** (p. 363)

nonbank financial institution/institución financiera no bancaria institución no depositoria que canaliza los ahorros a los inversionistas; compañías financieras, compañías de seguro, fondos de pensiones (p. 322)

noncompeting labor grades/grados de mano de obra no competitivos amplios grupos de trabajadores no calificados, semicalificados, calificados y profesionales que no compiten entre sí (p. 194)

nondurable good/bienes perecederos objetos que duran menos de tres años con uso regular; pueden ser bienes capitales o del consumidor (p. 20)

nonmarket transaction/transacción fuera del mercado actividad económica que no toma lugar en el mercado y, por lo tanto, no está incluída en el PIB; los servicios de las amas de casa, trabajo del hogar (p. 351)

nonprice competition/competición sin precio competición que implica la publicidad de la apariencia de un producto, su calidad o diseño en vez de su precio (p. 156)

nonprofit organization/organización sin fines de lucro institución económica que opera como un negocio pero que no busca ganancias; escuelas, iglesias, organizaciones de servicios para la comunidad (p. 69)

non-recourse loan/préstamo sin recurso préstamo de agricultura que no lleva ni penalidad ni demás obligaciones de pago (p. 144)

North American Free Trade Agreement/Tratado Norte-americano de Libre Comercio (NAFTA) tratado firmado en 1993 para reducir las tarifas entre los Estados Unidos, Canadá y México (p. 459)

NOW ACCOUNT ver **Negotiable Order of Withdrawal** (p. 282)

O

oligopoly/oligarquía estructura mercantil en la que unos cuantos vendedores grandes dominan la industria y tienen la habilidad de afectar los precios; forma de competición imperfecta (p. 156)

open market operations/operaciones de mercado abierto política monetaria en la forma de compra y venta de bonos en el mercado de bonos (p. 307)

opportunity cost/costo de oportunidad cuando se hace una elección en lugar de otra, el costo de la mejor alternativa que sigue para el uso del dinero, tiempo o recursos (p. 15)

options/opciones contratos que dan al inversionista una opción de comprar o vender bienes, capitales o bienes financieros a una fecha específica en el futuro usando el precio acordado hoy (p. 338)

options market/mercado de opciones mercados donde las opciones, incluso las opciones de venta y de compra, se intercambian (p. 338)

organizational chart/gráfica organizacional representación visual de la estructura de una compañía que muestra cómo las distintas partes de la organización se relacionan (p. 61)

output-expenditure model/modelo de producción-gastos modelo macroeconómico que describe la demanda total del consumidor, la inversión, gobierno y los sectores extranjeros; PIB = C + I + G + SE (p. 358)

overhead/gastos generales categoría amplia de gastos fijos que incluyen intereses, alquiler, impuestos y salarios de ejecutivos (p. 118)

Over-The-Counter market (OTC) mercado electrónico extra-bursátil para valores no anotados en casas de cambio organizadas como la New York Stock Exchange (p. 336)

P

par value/valor a la par capital de un bono o la cantidad total pedida en préstamo (p. 326)

paradox of value/paradoja de valores contradicción aparente entre el alto valor de objetos no esenciales y el bajo valor de los esenciales (p. 22)

partnership/sociedad negocio no incorporado operado por dos o más dueños quienes comparten las ganancias y que tienen responsabilidad ilimitada por las deudas y obligaciones de la firma; igual que **sociedad colectiva** (p. 57)

patent/patente derecho exclusivo concedido por el gobierno para vender o usar cualquier arte nuevo, máquina, objeto de manufactura o composición (p. 160)

payroll withholding statement/estado de cuenta de retención de nómina documento adherido al cheque de pago que resume el pago y las deducciones (p. 225)

payroll withholding system/sistema de retención de

nómina sistema periódico que automáticamente deduce del cheque de pago los impuestos sobre la renta (p. 216)

peak/apogeo punto en el tiempo cuando el PIB cesa de aumentar y comienza a declinar (p. 383)

pension/pensión pago regular para alguien que ha trabajado cierto número de años, ha alcanzado cierta edad o ha sufrido algún daño (p. 323)

pension fund/fondo de pensiones fondo que recauda e invierte ingresos hasta que se hacen pagos a los titulares que tienen derecho (p. 323)

per capita/per cápita en base a persona; el total dividido por la población (p. 238)

perestroika reestructuramiento fundamental de la economía soviética; política introducida por Gorbachev (p. 480)

personal consumption expenditures/gastos de consumo personal gastos globales del sector del consumidor que consisten de las unidades familiares y personas no relacionadas (p. 358)

personal income/ingresos personales cantidad total de ingresos que van al sector del consumidor antes de que se paguen los impuestos sobre la renta (p. 356)

picket/piqueteo demostración ante un establecimiento comercial para protestar las acciones de una compañía (p. 184)

piecework/trabajo por pieza sistema de compensación que paga a los trabajadores por las unidades producidas, en vez de las horas trabajadas (p. 480)

pollution/polución contaminación del aire, agua o tierra por la descarga de una sustancia venenosa o nociva (p. 528)

pollution permit/permiso de polución permiso federal que permite que las empresas de servicios públicos liberen polutantes en el aire; una forma de controlar la contaminación (p. 530)

population density/densidad demográfica número de personas por milla cuadrada de área de terreno (p. 514)

population pyramid/pirámide demográfica diagrama que muestra la distribución de la población por edad y sexo (p. 373)

portfolio diversification/diversificación de cartera estrategia de retener varias inversiones para protección contra riesgos (p. 334)

positive externality/factores externos positivos efectos secundarios beneficiosos que afectan a un tercero no involucrado (p. 167)

poverty threshold/umbral de pobreza cota de referencia anual del dólar usada para evaluar el ingreso monetario recibido por familias e individuos no relacionados (p. 407)

preferred stock/acciones preferidas acciones de dueños que no votan y cuyo reclamo a los ingresos y a los bienes de la corporación viene por encima de los accionistas ordinarios (p. 60)

premium/prima precio que se paga mensualmente, trimestralmente, semianual o anual por una póliza de seguro (p. 323)

price ceiling/precio máximo máximo precio legal que se puede cobrar por un producto (p. 141)

price discrimination/descriminación de precio práctica ilegal de cobrarle a los clientes distintos precios por el mismo producto (p. 169)

price-fixing/fijación de precios acuerdo, usualmente ilegal, que hacen las compañías para cobrar un precio uniforme por un producto (p. 157)

price floor/precio mínimo precio legal más bajo que se puede cobrar por un producto (p. 142)

price index/índice de precios serie estadística que se usa para medir cambios en el nivel de los precios a lo largo del tiempo (p. 361)

price leadership/liderazgo de precios decisiones que una firma dominante toma periódicamente sobre la fijación de precios y que resulta en precios que por lo general son uniformes por toda la industria (p. 157)

price level/nivel de precios magnitud relativa de los precios en un momento determinado según los mide un índice de precios (p. 399)

price war/guerra de precio competencia de precio encarnizada entre vendedores, hasta el punto que el precio baja por debajo del costo del producto (p. 157)

primary market/mercado primario mercado en que sólo el emisor original volverá a comprar un haber financiero; bonos de ahorros del gobierno, los IRA, pequeños CD (p. 332)

prime rate/tasa preferencial tasa de interés mejor o más baja que los bancos comerciales cobran a sus clientes (p. 309)

primitive equilibrium/equilibrio primitivo primera etapa del desarrollo económico durante la cual la economía está estática (p. 504)

principal/capital cantidad que se pide prestada cuando se obtiene un préstamo o se emite un bono (p. 61)

private enterprise economy/economía de empresa privada ver **economía de empresa libre** (p. 24)

private property/propiedad privada concepto que les da a las personas el derecho de controlar sus posesiones como deseen; característica del capitalismo y el libre comercio (p. 45)

private sector/sector privado aquella parte de la economía compuesta por personas privadas y negocios (p. 239)

privatization/privatización conversión de factorías y otras propiedades del gobierno a propiedad privada (p. 483)

problem bank list/lista de bancos problemas de los reguladores bancarios, lista confidencial de bancos débiles y posiblemente poco firmes (p. 312)

producer cooperative/cooperativa de productores asociación sin fines de lucro de productores que ayuda a sus miembros a vender o mercadear sus productos; mayormente se halla en la agricultura (p. 70)

producer price index/índice de precios de productor índice que se usa para medir los precios recibidos de los productores domésticos; anteriormente denominado **índice de precios al por mayor** (p. 362)

product differentiation/diferenciación de precios diferencias reales o imaginadas entre productos que compiten en la misma industria (p. 155)

product market/mercado de productos mercado donde se ponen a la venta los bienes y servicios (p. 24)

production/producción proceso de crear bienes y servicios con el uso combinado de tierra, capital, mano de obra y espíritu empresarial (p. 22)

production function/función de producción rendimiento gráfico que muestra cómo un cambio en la cantidad de una sola variable de insumo afecta la producción total (p. 112)

production possibilities frontier/frontera de posibilidades de producción diagrama que representa el máximo de combinaciones de bienes y/o servicios que una economía puede producir cuando se emplean a plenitud todos los recursos (p. 16)

productivity/productividad grado hasta cual los recursos productivos se usan eficientemente; normalmente se refiere a mano de obra, pero puede aplicarse a todos los factores de producción (p. 22)

professional association/asociación profesional organización sin fines de lucro de trabajadores profesionales o especializados que buscan mejorar las condiciones de trabajo, los niveles de habilidades y la percepción pública de su profesión (p. 71)

professional labor/trabajo profesional trabajadores con un alto nivel de habilidades profesionales y gerenciales (p. 194)

profit/ganancias nivel al que personas y organizaciones mejoran al cabo de un periodo de lo que estaban al principio; usualmente se mide en dólares (p. 46)

profit-maximizing quantity of output/cantidad de producto para el máximo de ganancias nivel de producción en que el costo marginal equivale al ingreso marginal (p. 122)

profit motive/motivo de ganancia fuerza motriz que anima a la gente y organizaciones a mejorar su bienestar material; característica del capitalismo y el libre comercio (p. 46)

progressive tax/tributación progresiva tributación en que un porcentaje del ingreso que se paga en impuestos sube al subir el nivel de ingreso (p. 215)

property tax/impuesto sobre los bienes impuesto sobre posesiones tangibles e intangibles como bienes raíces, edificios, muebles, acciones, bonos y cuentas bancarias (p. 224)

proportional tax/impuesto proporcional tributación en que un porcentaje de los ingresos que se paga en impuestos es igual sin importar el nivel de ingreso (p. 215)

proprietorship/patrimonio ver **patrimonio personal** (p. 54)

protectionist/proteccionista persona que proteje a los productores domésticos con tarifas, cuotas y otras barreras comerciales (p. 454)

protective tariff/arancel proteccionista impuesto sobre un producto importado diseñado para proteger a los productores domésticos menos eficientes (p. 453)

proxy/poderes papeleta de poder que permite que el representante de un accionista vote en asuntos de empresas (p. 60)

public disclosure/revelación pública requisito que fuerza a un negocio a que revele al público información acerca de sus productos u operaciones (p. 170)

public good/bien público producto económico que se consume colectivamente; autopistas, defensa nacional, protección de la policía y de los bomberos (p. 167)

public sector/sector público esa parte de la economía compuesta de los gobiernos locales, estatales y federales (p. 239)

public utility/empresa de servicios públicos compañía que provee servicios esenciales como el agua y la electricidad a los consumidores, usualmente sujeta a algunas regulaciones del gobierno (p. 72)

pure competition/competencia pura estructura mercantil caracterizada por un gran número de independientes y bien informados compradores y vendedores de un producto idéntico—ninguno de los cuales es lo suficientemente grande para influenciar el precio—asímismo con relativa facilidad de entrada y salida de la industria (p. 152)

put option/opción de venta contrato que da a los inversionistas la opción de vender productos, valores o bienes finacieros a una fecha específica en el futuro usando el precio que se acordó hoy (p. 338)

Q

quantity supplied/cantidad ofrecida cantidad ofrecida en venta a un precio dado; punto en la curva de oferta (p. 106)

quantity theory of money/teoría de la cantidad del dinero hipótesis de que a largo plazo el abastecimiento de dinero afecta directamente el nivel del precio (p. 309)

quota/cuota límite de cantidad de bienes que se pueden permitir en un país (p. 453)

R

ration coupon/cupón de raciones certificado que permite al portador recibir una cantidad específica de un producto racionado (p. 131)

rationing/racionamiento sistema de distribución de bienes y servicios sin precios (p. 131)

raw materials/materias brutas recursos naturales sin procesar que se usan en la producción (p. 112)

real dollars/dólares reales ver **dólares constantes** (p. 204)

real estate investment trust/compañía fiduciaria de inversiones en bienes raíces compañía organizada para hacer préstamos a los constructores de casas (p. 323)

real GDP/PIB real Producto Interior Bruto después de ajustes para la inflación; igual que **PIB en dólares constantes** (p. 364)

real GDP per capita/PIB real per cápita Producto Interior Bruto ajustado para la inflación y dividido por la población total; cantidad total de dólar de todo producto final producido para cada persona en el país después de compensar por la inflación (p. 376)

real property/propiedad real riquezas en la forma de bienes raíces, edificios y accesorios permanentes (p. 224)

rebate/descuento devolución parcial del precio original de un producto (p. 140)

recession/recesión reducción en el PIB real que dura al menos dos trimestres o más (p. 383)

regressive tax/impuesto regresivo impuesto en que un porcentaje del ingreso que se paga en imposiciones baja cuando los ingresos suben (p. 215)

Regulation Q/Regulación Q regulación federal que una vez fijó tasas de interés máximo que se podían pagar sobre depósitos a la vista (p. 285)

Regulation Z/Regulación Z provisión que extiende a los consumidores revelaciones de veracidad de préstamos (p. 299)

renewable resources/recursos renovables recursos naturales que se pueden reabastecer para uso futuro (p. 379)

reserve requirement/requisito de reserva fórmula que se usa para calcular la cantidad de reservas que requiere una institución depositoria (p. 302)

retained earnings/utilidades no distribuidas ganancias de sociedad que una corporación retiene en vez de pagárselas a los accionistas; igual que **ganancias de corporación no**

distribuidas (p. 356)

revenue/ingresos los recibos de venta o alquiler de los productos de una compañía, también incluye dinero de otras fuentes como dividendos e intereses (p. 62)

revenue tariff/tarifa de ingresos impuesto sobre bienes importados para recaudar fondos (p. 453)

right-to-work law/ley de derecho al trabajo ley estatal que hace ilegal el requerir que un trabajador sea miembro de una unión (p. 186)

risk/riesgo situación en la cual el resultado no es cierto, pero las probabilidades se pueden estimar (p. 325)

run on the bank/pánico bancario prisa repentina de los depositantes por sacar todos sus fondos, generalmente en anticipación al fallo o cierre del banco (p. 281)

rural population/población rural aquellas personas que no viven en áreas urbanas (p. 370)

S

S&P 500 ver **Standard & Poor 500** (p. 337)

saving/ahorrar ausencia de gastos que libera los recursos para usarlos en otras actividades o inversiones (p. 320)

savings/ahorros los dólares que se hacen disponibles para que los inversionistas los usen cuando otras personas ahorran (p. 320)

savings account/cuenta de ahorros depósito que paga interés y que no requiere aviso previo antes de retirarse (p. 304)

savings and loan association/sociedad de ahorro y préstamo institución depositoria que históricamente invierte la mayoría de sus fondos en hipotecas de casas (p. 282)

savings bank/banco de ahorros institución de ahorros propiedad de los accionistas en vez de los depositantes (p. 282)

savings bond/bono de ahorros bono, no transferible, de baja denominación emitido por el gobierno federal, usualmente a través de planes de ahorros de nómina (p. 329)

scarcity/escasez problema económico fundamental que enfrentan todas las sociedades como resultado de una combinación de escasos recursos y las necesidades ilimitadas de la gente (p. 8)

seasonal unemployment/desempleo estacional desempleo causado por cambios anuales en el clima y otras condiciones que prevalecen durante ciertas épocas del año (p. 396)

seat/asiento afiliación en una bolsa de valores como la New York Stock Exchange (p. 335)

secondary market/mercado secundario mercado en el que todos los bienes finacieros se pueden vender a alguien excepto al emisor original; bonos de empresa privada, bonos del gobierno (p. 332)

secondhand sales/ventas de segunda mano venta de bienes usados; categoría de actividad no incluida en la computación del PIB (p. 349)

securities exchange/bolsa de valores lugar físico donde los compradores y los vendedores se reunen para intercambiar valores (p. 335)

seizure/incautación cuando el gobierno toma temporáneamente una compañía para mantenerla operando durante un conflicto obrero-patronal (p. 192)

selective credit controls/controles de crédito selectivo reglas que atañen a préstamos para productos específicos o compras como requisitos marginales para acciones ordinarias (p. 308)

semiskilled labor/mano de obra semientrenada trabajadores que pueden operar máquinas que requieren la mínima cantidad de entrenamiento (p. 194)

seniority/antigüedad cantidad de tiempo que una persona ha estado en un puesto de trabajo (p. 196)

service/servicio obra o trabajo efectuado por alguien; producto económico que incluye cortes de pelo, reparaciones del hogar, formas de entretenimiento (p. 20)

service cooperative/cooperativa de servicio sociedad de consumidores sin fines de lucro que trata con servicios en vez de con bienes; incluye las cooperativas de crédito y algunas agencias de seguro y de crédito (p. 70)

set-aside contract/contrato de destinación especial contrato o parte de un contrato garantizado reservado para un grupo señalado, usualmente un grupo minoritario (p. 201)

share draft/giro de acción cuenta de cheques ofrecida por una cooperativa de crédito (p. 283)

shareholder/accionista persona que es dueña de acciones en una corporación (p. 59)

short run/corto plazo periodo de producción tan corto que sólo se pueden cambiar los insumos variables (p. 111)

shortage/escasez situación donde la cantidad ofrecida es menor que la cantidad demandada a un precio dado (p. 136)

silver certificate/certificado de plata papel moneda respaldado y redimible con plata desde 1886 hasta 1968 (p. 275)

sin tax/impuesto de pecado impuesto relativamente alto diseñado para recaudar ingresos y desanimar el consumo de productos socialmente indeseables (p. 210)

skilled labor/mano de obra adiestrada trabajadores que pueden operar equipo complejo y que requieren poca supervisión (p. 194)

Social Security/Seguro Social programa federal de beneficios de invalidez y retiro que cubre a la mayoría de las personas que trabajan (p. 40)

socialism/socialismo sistema económico en el cual el gobierno es dueño de algunos factores de producción y tiene un papel en la determinación de qué bienes se producirán y cómo (p. 473)

sole proprietorship/propietario contable único de empresa negocio no incorporado de la propiedad y operación de una sóla persona quien tiene el derecho a todas las ganancias y responsabilidades sin límite por todas las deudas de la firma; la forma más común de organización comercial en los Estados Unidos (p. 54)

Solidarity/Solidaridad gremio obrero independiente de Polonia fundado en 1980 por Lech Walesa (p. 485)

specialization/especialización asignación de tareas para que cada trabajador haga menos funciones más frecuentemente; igual que **división de trabajo** (p. 22)

specie/especie dinero en la forma de monedas de oro o plata (p. 268)

spot market/mercado de entrega immediata mercado en el cual se hace una operación inmediatamente al precio imperante (p. 338)

stages of production/etapas de producción fases de producción—aumento, disminución y rendimiento negativo (p. 114)

stagflation combinación de estancamiento del crecimiento económico y la inflación (p. 419)

Standard & Poor's 500/Las 500 de Standard & Poor (S&L 500)

serie estadística de las 500 acciones que se usan para observar los precios en la bolsa de valores de la NYSE, American Stock Exchange y el mercado extrabursátil (p. 337)

standard of living/estándar de vida calidad de vida basada en la propiedad de necesidades y lujos que hacen la vida más fácil (p. 377)

state bank/banco del estado banco que recibe su escritura de constitución del estado en que opera (p. 272)

state farm/granja del estado granjas enormes de la propiedad y operación del estado en la antigua Unión Soviética (p. 479)

stock/acción certificado de propiedad en una corporación; acciones preferidas y ordinarias (p. 59)

stockbroker/agente de bolsa persona que compra y vende valores para los inversionistas (p. 335)

stockholder/accionista La persona dueña de acciones de una corporación (p. 59)

store of value/fuente de valor una de las tres funciones del dinero que permite a las personas que preserven el valor para uso futuro (p. 266)

storming/tempestear práctica soviética de apresurar la producción al final del mes para cumplir las cuotas, con frecuencia resultando en la producción de chapucería (p. 480)

strike/huelga paro del trabajo organizado por la unión diseñado para obtener concesiones del patrón (p. 184)

structural unemployment/desempleo estructural desempleo causado por un cambio fundamental en la economía que reduce la demanda de algunos trabajadores (p. 395)

structures/estructuras categoría en los ingresos y cuentas de productos de la nación que incluye las estructuras residenciales, apartamentos y edificios comerciales (p. 348)

subsidy/subsidio pago del gobierno para animar o proteger cierta actividad económica (p. 108)

subsistence/subsistencia estado en que una sociedad escasamente produce lo suficiente para sostenerse (p. 520)

substitutes/sustitutos productos de competición que se pueden intercambiar; productos relacionados de tal forma que un aumento en el precio de uno aumenta la demanda por los otros (p. 88)

substitution effect/efecto de sustitución esa porción de un cambio en la cantidad de la demanda debido a un cambio en el precio relativo del producto (p. 87)

supply/oferta curva de cantidades que se ofrecen a la venta a todos los precios posibles del mercado (p. 104)

supply curve/curva de oferta gráfica de las cantidades producidas en cada uno de los precios del mercado (p. 105)

supply elasticity/elasticidad de oferta sensibilidad de la cantidad ofrecida al cambio de precio (p. 109)

supply schedule/tabla de oferta tabla que muestra las cantidades producidas u ofrecidas a la venta a cada precio del mercado (p. 105)

supply-side economics/economía de oferta política económica diseñada para aumentar la oferta global o para desplazar la curva de oferta global hacia la derecha (p. 431)

surcharge/sobretasa impuesto adicional o carga que se añade a otros cargos ya establecidos (p. 231)

surplus/superávit situación en que la cantidad ofrecida es mayor que la cantidad demandada a un precio dado (p. 135)

T

takeoff/despegue tercer etapa de desarrollo económico durante el cual las barreras de equilibrio primitivo se han vencido (p. 504)

tangible personal property/bienes personales tangibles todos los objetos tangibles de riquezas no empotradas en la tierra o los edificios (p. 224)

target price/precio indicativo precio más bajo de agricultura fijado por el gobierno para estabilizar los ingresos agrarios (p. 144)

tariff/tarifa impuesto sobre productos importados (p. 453)

tax assessor/tasador de impuestos persona que examina y evalúa propiedades para propósitos de impuestos (p. 224)

tax base/base impositiva ingresos y propiedades que están potencialmente sujetas a impuestos locales, estatales y del gobierno federal (p. 377)

tax-exempt/exento de impuestos ingresos de bonos u otras inversiones no sujetas a impuestos por el gobierno del estado y el federal (p. 329)

tax loophole/laguna tributaria excepción o descuido en la ley de impuestos que permite que los contribuyentes eviten impuestos (p. 212)

tax return/declaración de impuestos reporte anual que se registra con el gobierno local, el estatal o el federal y que detalla los ingresos que se ganaron y los impuestos que se deben (p. 216)

technological monopoly/monopolio tecnológico situación mercantil en que una firma tiene el monopolio porque es propietaria de/o controla un método o un proceso de manufactura u otro adelanto científico (p. 159)

technological unemployment/desempleo tecnológico desempleo causado por desarrollos tecnológicos o automatización que hace que las destrezas de algunos trabajadores sean obsoletas (p. 396)

theory of negotiated wages/teoría de salarios negociados explicación de las escalas de salarios basada en la fuerza de negociación del movimiento sindical (p. 196)

theory of production/teoría de producción teoría que trata con la relación entre los factores de producción y la producción de bienes y servicios (p. 111)

thrift institution/institución de pequeños ahorros sociedades de ahorros y préstamo, bancos mutualista de ahorro y otras instituciones depositorias que históricamente han provisto a los ahorradores (p. 281)

tight money policy/política de dinero escaso política monetaria que resulta en tasas de interés más altas y acceso restringido al crédito; se asocia con la contracción del abastecimiento de dinero (p. 306)

time deposit/depósito a plazo depósito que paga intereses y que requiere previo aviso antes de poder sustraerlo, aunque no siempre se cumple el requisito (p. 304)

total cost/costo total costo variable y costo fijo; todos los gastos asociados a la producción (p. 119)

total product/producto total rendimiento o producción total de una firma (p. 113)

total revenue/ingreso total total de recibos; precio de los bienes vendidos por la cantidad vendida (p. 121)

trade deficit/déficit comercial resultados de la balanza de pagos cuando los gastos de las importaciones exceden los ingresos recibidos de las exportaciones (p. 456)

trade-offs/compensación alternativas a las que hay que renunciar cuando se escoge una en lugar de otra (p. 14)

trade union/sindicato gremial ver **sindicato de artesanos** (p. 184)

trade-weighted value of the dollar/valor del dólar ponderado según el comercio exterior índice que indica la fuerza del dólar americano contra la cesta de mercado de otras divisas (p. 465)

trading desk/oficina de cambio sitio actual en el banco del distrito de la Reserva Federal de Nueva York donde se efectúa la compra y venta de bonos del gobierno (p. 307)

traditional economy/economía tradicional sistema económico en el que la distribución de escasos recursos y otra actividad económica es el resultado de rito, hábito o costumbre (p. 32)

traditional theory of wage determination/teoría tradicional de determinación de salario explicación del índice salarial basado en la teoría de oferta y demanda (p. 195)

transfer payment/transferencia de pago pago por el cual el gobierno no recibe ni bienes ni servicios de vuelta (p. 239)

Treasury bill/letra del Tesoro bono de corto plazo del gobierno de los Estados Unidos que madura al año o menos, en denominaciones de $10,000 (p. 331)

Treasury bond/bono del Tesoro bono del gobierno de los Estados Unidos que madura entre 10 y 30 años (p. 330)

Treasury coin note/pagaré del Tesoro en moneda papel moneda emitido desde 1890 hasta 1893, redimible tanto en oro o plata (p. 275)

Treasury note/pagaré del Tesoro obligación del gobierno de los Estados Unidos que madura entre 2 a 10 años (p. 330)

trend line/tendencia rumbo de crecimiento que seguiría la economía si no se interrumpiera por periodos alternantes de recesión y recuperación (p. 384)

trough/sima punto en el tiempo cuando el PIB real deja de declinar y comienza a ensanchar (p. 383)

trust/sociedad fiduciaria combinación ilegal de corporaciones o compañías que se organizan para impedir la competición (p. 169)

trust fund/fondo fiduciario cuenta especial que se usa para retener ingresos designados para un gasto específico como el Seguro Social, medicare o las autopistas (p. 256)

truth-in-lending laws/leyes de veracidad para préstamos leyes federales que requieren que a los consumidores se les haga una divulgación completa y precisa de la información acerca de los préstamos (p. 299)

two-tier wage system/sistema de salario de dos niveles escala de salario que paga a los nuevos trabajadores un sueldo más bajo que a los que ya estaban trabajando (p. 199)

U

underground economy/economía subterránea actividades ilegales sin reportar que no aparecen en las estadísticas del PIB (p. 351)

undistributed corporate profits/ganancias de corporación no distribuidas ver **utilidades no distribuidas** (p. 356)

unemployed/desempleado condición de trabajar por menos de una hora por semana por paga o provecho en un negocio que no es de la familia, en tanto que se está disponible y se ha hecho el esfuerzo de hallar trabajo durante el mes pasado (p. 394)

unemployment insurance/seguro de desempleo programa de gobierno que provee pagos a los desempleados; un estabilizador automático (p. 429)

unemployment rate/índice de desempleo relación de personas desempleadas dividida por el número total de personas en la fuerza de trabajo civil, expresado como un porcentaje (p. 394)

union shop/empresa de exclusividad gremial arreglo bajo el cual los trabajadores tienen que unirse a una unión tras ser empleados (p. 190)

unit elastic/elasticidad de la unidad elasticidad en que un cambio en la variable independiente (usualmente el precio) genera un cambio proporcional de la variable dependiente (cantidad demandada u ofrecida) (p. 94)

United States note/pagaré de los Estados Unidos papel moneda sin respaldo, emitida por el gobierno de los Estados Unidos inicialmente en 1862 para financiar la Guerra Civil (p. 274)

unlimited liability/responsabilidad sin límite requisito de que un propietario es personal y plenamente responsable por todas las pérdidas y deudas de un negocio; se aplica a propietarios, sociedades generales (p. 56)

unlimited life/vida sin límite condición de la existencia legal continuada de una corporación cuando el dueño muere, vende o transfiere la propiedad (p. 62)

unrelated individual/individuo no relacionado persona que vive sola o con personas que no son sus parientes aunque esa persona tenga parientes que vivan en otro lugar (p. 357)

unskilled labor/mano de obra no adiestrada trabajadores no entrenados para operar máquinas y equipo especializados (p. 194)

urban population/población urbana aquellas personas que viven en ciudades incorporadas, pueblos y aldeas con 2,500 ó más habitantes (p. 370)

user fee/tarifas para el usuario tarifa que se paga por usar unos bienes o servicios; forma de un impuesto de beneficio (p. 220)

utility/utilidad habilidad o capacidad de un bien o de un servicio para ser útil y darle satisfacción a alguien (p. 22)

value/valor valor de un bien o servicio según lo determina el mercado (p. 21)

value added tax/impuesto de valor agregado impuesto sobre el valor agregado a cada etapa del proceso de producción (p. 229)

variable cost/costo variable costo de producción que varía según cambia la producción; la mano de obra, la energía, la materia prima (p. 118)

vertical merger/fusión vertical combinación de firmas envueltas en distintos pasos de la manufactura o el mercadeo (p. 64)

voluntary arbitration/arbitraje voluntario acuerdo por parte de los sindicatos laborales y la administración de colocar una disputa delante de un tercero para llegar a un arreglo en firme (p. 191)

voluntary exchange/intercambio voluntario hecho en el cual los compradores y los vendedores participan libre y voluntariamente en operaciones mercantiles; característica del capitalismo y el libre comercio (p. 44)

wage-price controls/controles de salario-precio políticas y regulaciones que hacen ilegal el que las firmas den aumento o suban los precios (p. 434)

wage rate/escala de salarios escala de pago prevalente para trabajo efectuado en una cierta área o región (p. 195)

wampum forma de dinero hecho de conchas e ideado por los indios americanos, se usó ampliamente en los tiempos coloniales en los Estados Unidos (p. 267)

want/carencia modo de expresar o comunicar una necesidad; una clasificación más amplia que necesidades (p. 20)

wealth/riquezas suma de los bienes económicos tangibles que son escasos, útiles y transferibles de una persona a otra; excluye servicios (p. 22)

welfare/asistencia social programas del gobierno o de las agencias privadas que proveen asistencia económica y social a personas necesitadas (p. 409)

white-collar worker/empleado de corbata trabajador de oficina, comercial o profesional que percibe un salario y no un jornal (p. 407)

wholesale price index/índice de precios al por mayor ver **índice de precio de productor** (p. 362)

wildcat bank/banco especulador generalmente, banco fraudulento que operaba en áreas remotas a principios de los 1800 (p. 273)

workfare programa que requiere que los beneficiarios de asistencia social provean trabajo en cambio por los beneficios (p. 412)

World Bank/Banco Mundial agencia internacional que hace préstamos a países en vías de desarrollo; antiguamente el Banco Internacional para Reconstrucción y Desarrollo (p. 505)

zero population growth/crecimiento demográfico nulo condición en la que el número promedio de nacimientos y muertes se equilibran de modo que el tamaño de la población no cambia (p. 499)

Vocabulario

Los siguientes términos se definen en el Capítulo 1:

SECCIÓN UNO
- escasez *(p. 8)*
- factores de producción *(p. 9)*
- tierra *(p. 9)*
- capital *(p. 9)*
- capital financiero *(p. 9)*
- trabajo *(p. 10)*
- empresario *(p. 10)*
- economía *(p. 11)*

SECCIÓN DOS
- compensaciones *(p. 14)*
- costo de oportunidad *(p. 15)*
- límites de posibilidades de producción *(p. 16)*

SECCIÓN TRES
- necesidad *(p. 20)*
- deseo *(p. 20)*
- producto gratis *(p. 20)*
- producto económico *(p. 20)*
- bienes *(p. 20)*
- bienes de consumidor *(p. 20)*
- bienes capital *(p. 20)*
- bienes durables *(p. 20)*
- bienes no durables *(p. 20)*
- servicio *(p. 20)*
- consumidor *(p. 21)*
- consumo *(p. 21)*
- consumo suntuario *(p. 21)*
- valor *(p. 21)*
- paradoja de valores *(p. 22)*
- utilidad *(p. 22)*
- riqueza *(p. 22)*
- producción *(p. 22)*
- productividad *(p. 22)*
- especialización *(p. 22)*
- división del trabajo *(p. 23)*
- capital humano *(p. 23)*
- interdependencia económica *(p. 23)*
- mercado *(p. 23)*
- mercado de factor *(p. 24)*
- mercado de producto *(p. 24)*
- economía de libre empresa *(p. 24)*

Sección uno

La escasez y la ciencia de la economía (páginas 8-12)

La mayoría de las cosas en la vida no son gratis. Los maestros de economía usan el término "no hay nada gratis" *(TINSTAAFL—There is No Such Thing As A Free Lunch)*— para describir este concepto.

El problema económico fundamental es la **escasez,** el resultado de recursos limitados en un mundo de deseos sin límite. Estos recursos o **factores de producción** son **la tierra, el capital, el trabajo** y **la empresaría.** Estos proveen los medios con los que una sociedad puede producir y distribuir sus bienes y servicios. Es debido a la escasez que todas las sociedades deben enfrentar las tres preguntas básicas de QUÉ, CÓMO y PARA QUIÉN producir.

Repasar la idea principal

¿Cómo se relaciona el término "no hay nada gratis" *(TINSTAAFL)* a la escasez?

Sección dos

Compensaciones y costo de oportunidad (páginas 14-17)

Las personas hallan **compensaciones** entre las alternativas. El **costo de oportunidad** de una decisión económica es la alternativa que se pierde cuando se escoge una acción sobre otra. Los países tienen que aceptar compensaciones al decidir producir ciertos bienes en vez de otros. Los economistas usan los **límites de posibilidades de producción** para ilustrar el concepto del costo de oportunidad.

Repasar la idea principal

¿Cómo se mide el costo? ¿Cómo puede ser ilustrado?

Sección tres

Conceptos económicos básicos (páginas 19-26)

Todas las personas tienen **necesidades** básicas, tales como el deseo de sobrevivir y necesidades de un nivel más alto, tales como el éxito y el amor. El **deseo** es una forma de expresar una necesidad, pero su concepto abarca mucho más que una necesidad.

El estudio de la economía trata acerca de aquellos **bienes** y **servicios** que son útiles, relativamente escasos y transferibles a otros. La **riqueza** tiene valor monetario e incluye recursos naturales, **bienes del consumidor** y **bienes de capital.**

Los **consumidores** ayudan a determinar cuales bienes y servicios serán producidos. Los factores de producción deben ser usados para que la **producción** pueda ocurrir. La **productividad** trata del uso eficiente de los recursos. La productividad tiende a aumentar cuando los trabajadores se especializan en lo que pueden hacer mejor y cuando se hacen inversiones en el **capital humano.**

El estudio de la economía ayuda a las personas a hacer decisiones de consumidor y de negocios con más conocimiento. También los ayuda a comprender cómo una **economía de libre empresa**—en la cual los consumidores y los negocios privados, no el gobierno—juntos hacen las decisiones del QUÉ, CÓMO y PARA QUIÉN.

Repasar la idea principal

¿Cuáles son los cinco conceptos económicos clave?

Sistemas económicos y adopción de decisiones

Vocabulario

Los siguientes términos se definen en el Capítulo 2:

- economía autoritaria (p. 33)
- economía de mercado (p. 34)

SECCIÓN UNO
- sistema económico (p. 32)
- economía tradicional (p. 32)

SECCIÓN DOS
- Seguro Social (p. 40)
- inflación (p. 40)
- renta fija (p. 40)

SECCIÓN TRES
- capitalismo (p. 43)
- intercambio voluntario (p. 44)
- propiedad privada (p. 45)
- provecho (p. 46)
- afán de lucro (p. 46)
- soveranía del consumidor (p. 47)
- economía mixta (p. 48)
- economía de empresa privada modificada (p. 48)

Sección uno

Sistemas económicos (páginas 32-36)

Los **sistemas económicos** ayudan a las sociedades a realizar sus deseos y a satisfacer las necesidades de su población. Los tres sistemas de economía que han evolucionado con el tiempo son la tradicional, la autoritaria y la de mercado.

En una **economía tradicional,** las preguntas de QUÉ, CÓMO y PARA QUIÉN se contestan por medio de las tradiciones y costumbres pasadas de generación a generación. Todos tienen un papel específico, pero esto puede resultar en una economía que permanece estancada.

En una **economía autoritaria,** una autoridad central decide las tres preguntas básicas. El individuo tiene un papel mínimo, o ninguno, en el planeamiento económico. Sin embargo, las economías autoritarias tienen una ventaja grande—la habilidad de cambiar los planes de producción rápidamente.

La **economía de mercado** se caracteriza por la libertad y la descentralización en hacer decisiones. Las economías de mercado tienen varias ventajas. Entre éstas se encuentra la habilidad de ajustarse a los cambios gradualmente, la libertad personal, una gran falta de intervención del gobierno y una gran variedad de bienes y servicios disponibles al consumidor.

Repasar la idea principal
¿Por qué es necesaria la decisión económica?

Sección dos

Evaluar el rendimiento económico (páginas 38-41)

Una sociedad puede usar sus metas para evaluar su sistema económico. En Estados Unidos, estas metas incluyen la libertad económica, la eficiencia económica, la igualdad económica, la seguridad económica, el empleo para todos, la estabilidad de precios y el crecimiento económico.

Aunque casi todos los americanos están de acuerdo con estas metas, no es siempre posible satisfacer a todos al mismo tiempo. Las metas de las personas también van a cambiar en el futuro mientras nuestra economía evoluciona.

Repasar la idea principal
¿Qué diferencias hay entre las decisiones económicas hechas en las economías tradicionales, autoritarias y de mercado?

Sección tres

El capitalismo y la libre empresa (páginas 43-48)

El sistema económico de Estados Unidos se basa en **el capitalismo** y la libre empresa. Las características del capitalismo incluyen cuatro partes principales: libertad económica, el **intercambio voluntario,** la **propiedad privada** y el **afán de lucro.**

La fuerza movilizadora de la economía es el empresario en busca de provecho propio. Los consumidores también desempeñan un papel primordial en ayudar a determinar QUÉ producir. El gobierno desempeña el papel de protector, proveedor y consumidor de bienes y servicios, regulador y promovedor de metas. La economía de los Estados Unidos hoy en día es una **economía mixta** o **economía de empresa privada modificada,** en la cual las personas proceden con sus asuntos económicos libremente pero con ciertas regulaciones gubernamentales.

Repasar la idea principal
¿Qué papel desempeña el empresario en la economía de Estados Unidos? ¿El papel del consumidor? ¿El papel del gobierno?

Organizaciones comerciales e instituciones económicas

Vocabulario

Los siguientes términos se definen en el Capítulo 3:

SECCIÓN UNO

- institución económica (p. 54)
- organización comercial (p. 54)
- propiedad exclusiva (p. 54)
- responsabilidad general (p. 56)
- inventario (p. 56)
- beneficios complementarios (p. 57)
- vida limitada (p. 57)
- sociedad (p. 57)
- sociedad general (p. 57)
- sociedad en comandita simple (p. 57)
- contrato de asociación (p. 57)
- responsabilidad limitada (p. 59)
- corporación (p. 59)
- incorporar (p. 59)
- carta constitucional (p. 59)
- acciones (p. 59)
- accionista (p. 59)
- dividendo (p. 59)
- acciones ordinarias (p. 60)
- junta directiva (p. 60)
- acciones preferidas (p. 60)
- sustituto (p. 60)
- bono (p. 61)
- capital (p. 61)
- interés (p. 61)
- gráfica institucional (p. 61)
- quiebra (p. 61)
- vida sin límite (p. 62)
- ingreso (p. 62)

SECCIÓN DOS

- fusión (p. 64)
- fusión horizontal (p. 64)
- fusión vertical (p. 64)
- conglomerado (p. 65)
- multinacional (p. 66)

SECCIÓN TRES

- organización sin fines de lucro (p. 69)
- cooperativa (p. 69)
- cooperativa de consumidores (p. 69)
- cooperativa de servicios (p. 70)
- cooperativa de crédito (p. 70)
- cooperativa de productores (p. 70)
- gremio (p. 70)
- negociación colectiva (p. 70)
- asociación profesional (p. 71)
- cámara de comercio (p. 71)
- Better Business Bureau (p. 71)
- servicios públicos (p. 72)

Sección uno

Organizaciones comerciales (páginas 54-62)

Una **organización comercial** se puede establecer como una **propiedad exclusiva**, una **sociedad** o una **corporación.** Las propiedades exclusivas son empresas pequeñas y fáciles de administrar, donde sólo una persona es el dueño. Las sociedades tienen dos o más dueños y son, en su mayoría, un poco más grandes en tamaño que las propiedades exclusivas. Los inversionistas individuales, llamados **accionistas,** son los dueños de las corporaciones. Los dueños de **acciones ordinarias** votan para elegir a la **junta directiva,** quien, a su vez, selecciona a un equipo profesional de administración para efectuar las normas de la corporación.

Repasar la idea principal

¿Cuáles son las tres formas de organización comercial?

Sección dos

Crecimiento y expansión comercial (páginas 64-67)

Los comercios pueden expandirse a través de uniones llamadas **fusiones.** Las fusiones se llevan a cabo debido a que las compañías desean ser más grandes y eficientes. Una **fusión horizontal** ocurre cuando dos compañías similares se unen. Una **fusión vertical** es la que envuelve a dos o más compañías que están en diferentes etapas de la fabricación del producto.

Varias fusiones a veces pueden resultar en un **conglomerado**, una compañía muy grande que contiene por lo menos cuatro negocios diferentes, ninguno de los cuales es responsable por la mayoría de las ventas. Una **multinacional** puede ser una corporación corriente o un conglomerado, pero debe tener operaciones de manufactura o de servicio en un número de países diferentes.

Repasar la idea principal

¿Por qué y cómo puede expandir un comercio sus operaciones?

Sección tres

Otras organizaciones e instituciones (páginas 69-72)

Las **organizaciones sin fines de lucro** operan como un comercio, pero sin fines lucrativos. Más bien, su propósito es el contribuir al beneficio de una buena causa o el beneficiar a sus miembros. Las organizaciones sin fines de lucro incluyen a iglesias, hospitales, escuelas y **cooperativas.** También incluyen a las **negociaciones colectivas, asociaciones profesionales,** asociaciones comerciales y el gobierno.

Repasar la idea principal

¿Cuáles son las características de las organizaciones sin fines de lucro?

La demanda

Vocabulario

Los siguientes términos se definen en el Capítulo 4:

SECCIÓN UNO
- demanda *(p. 82)*
- microeconomía *(p. 82)*

- lista de demanda *(p. 84)*
- curva de relación entre demanda y precio *(p. 84)*

SECCIÓN DOS
- Ley de demanda *(p. 86)*
- cambio en cantidad demandada *(p. 86)*
- efecto de ingreso *(p. 87)*

- efecto de sustitución *(p. 87)*
- cambio de demanda *(p. 88)*
- sustitutos *(p. 88)*
- complementos *(p. 89)*
- utilidad marginal *(p. 89)*
- disminución de la utilidad marginal *(p. 90)*

SECCIÓN TRES
- elasticidad de demanda *(p. 92)*
- elástica *(p. 92)*
- inelástica *(p. 92)*
- elástica por unidad *(p. 94)*

Sección uno
¿Qué es la demanda? (páginas 82-84)

La **demanda** se mide en el mercado cuando el deseo por un producto se une a la habilidad y la intención de pagar por él. Esta doctrina económica puede ser ilustrada con una **lista de demanda** que muestra la cantidad de un producto que las personas desean comprar a diferentes precios, y con una **curva de relación entre demanda y precio,** la cual ilustra gráficamente la misma relación.

Repasar la idea principal
Represente el concepto de la demanda usando una lista y una ilustración.

Sección dos
La Ley de Demanda (páginas 86-90)

La **ley de demanda** afirma que las personas comprarán más de un producto a un precio bajo que a un precio más alto. El **cambio en cantidad demandada** significa que las personas compran diferentes cantidades de un producto si su precio cambia. Esta norma se demuestra en la ilustración con un movimiento en la curva de relación entre demanda y precio.

Cada vez que el precio de un producto cambia, ocasiona tanto un **efecto de ingreso** como un **efecto de sustitución.** Ambos ayudan a explicar por qué la curva de relación entre demanda y precio se mueve hacia abajo.

Un **cambio de demanda** significa que las personas han cambiado su decisión sobre la cantidad del producto que comprarán a cada precio diferente. Un aumento en la demanda es ilustrado con el movimiento de toda la curva hacia la derecha, una disminución se muestra con un movimiento hacia la izquierda. Los cambios de demanda ocurren debido a cambios en los ingresos de los consumidores, los gustos o los precios de bienes similares, tales como los **sustitutos** y los **complementos.**

La **utilidad marginal** tiende a disminuir con cada compra consecutiva. La norma de **disminución de la utilidad marginal** ayuda a explicar por qué la curva de relación entre demanda y precio tiene un movimiento hacia abajo. Esta afirma que los consumidores normalmente siguen comprando un producto hasta llegar a un punto en el cual el último producto comprado les da suficiente satisfacción como para justificar el precio.

Repasar la idea principal
¿Cuál es la diferencia entre un cambio de demanda y un cambio en la cantidad demandada?

Sección tres
La elasticidad de demanda (páginas 92-98)

La **elasticidad de demanda** es un concepto que relaciona los cambios en la cantidad demandada a los cambios en el precio de un producto. Si el cambio en precio produce un cambio relativamente mayor en la cantidad demandada, la demanda es **elástica.** Si el cambio en precio produce un cambio relativamente menor en la cantidad demandada, la demanda es **inelástica.** La demanda es **elástica por unidad** si un cambio en el precio no afecta los ingresos de la venta de un producto.

Es importante saber acerca de la elasticidad de demanda porque ésta les dice a los comercios cómo un cambio de precio afectará sus ingresos finales. También ayuda a predecir los cambios futuros de precio. La elasticidad de demanda es influenciada por la habilidad de posponer una compra, los productos sustitutos disponibles y el porcentaje de ingreso que la compra requiere.

Repasar la idea principal
¿Cómo los tres determinantes de la elasticidad de demanda ayudan a clasificar la naturaleza elástica o inelástica de la demanda por un producto?

Vocabulario

Los siguientes términos se definen en el Capítulo 5:

SECCIÓN UNO
- oferta *(p. 104)*
- lista de oferta *(p. 105)*
- curva de oferta *(p. 105)*
- Ley de oferta *(p. 106)*
- cantidad suplida *(p. 106)*
- cambio de cantidad suplida *(p. 106)*
- cambio de oferta *(p. 106)*
- subsidio *(p. 108)*
- elasticidad de oferta *(p. 109)*

SECCIÓN DOS
- teoría de producción *(p. 111)*
- a corto plazo *(p. 111)*
- a largo plazo *(p. 111)*
- Ley de proporciones variables *(p. 111)*
- función de producción *(p. 112)*
- materias primas *(p. 112)*
- producto total *(p. 113)*
- producto marginal *(p. 114)*
- etapas de producción *(p. 114)*
- rendimientos decrecientes *(p. 115)*

SECCIÓN TRES
- costo fijo *(p. 118)*
- gastos generales *(p. 118)*
- depreciación *(p. 118)*
- costo variable *(p. 118)*
- costo total *(p. 119)*
- costo marginal *(p. 119)*
- ingreso total *(p. 121)*
- ingreso marginal *(p. 121)*
- análisis marginal *(p. 121)*
- punto de equilibrio *(p. 122)*
- cantidad de producción para ganancia máxima *(p. 122)*

Sección uno

¿Qué es la oferta? (páginas 104-109)

La **oferta** es la cantidad de productos que los fabricantes llevarán al mercado a cada precio sin excepción. La oferta puede ser representada por una **lista de oferta** o una **curva de oferta.** La **ley de oferta** afirma que la cantidad de un producto económico ofrecido a la venta varía directamente con su precio. Si los precios están altos, los suplidores ofrecerán mayores cantidades a la venta. Si los precios están bajos, ellos ofrecerán menores cantidades a la venta.

Un **cambio de la cantidad suplida** es representado por un movimiento en la curva de oferta. Un **cambio de oferta** es un cambio en la cantidad que será ofrecida a cada precio sin excepción.

Un aumento en la oferta es ilustrado con el movimiento de la curva de oferta hacia la derecha. Una disminución en la oferta aparece como un movimiento de la curva hacia la izquierda.

Repasar la idea principal
¿Qué se entiende por oferta?

Sección dos

La teoría de producción (páginas 111-115)

La **ley de proporciones variables** afirma que la cantidad del producto final varía a la vez que se añaden más unidades provenientes de una sola fuente. Esta ley se encuentra ilustrada en la **función de producción.**

Las dos medidas más importantes del producto final son el **producto total** y el **producto marginal.** Las tres etapas de producción—rendimientos crecientes, **rendimientos decrecientes** y rendimientos negativos—muestran la manera en que el producto marginal cambia a la vez que se le añaden los ingredientes variables. La gran parte de la producción se lleva a cabo en la Etapa II bajo las condiciones de rendimientos decrecientes.

Repasar la idea principal
¿Cuáles son las tres etapas de producción?

Sección tres

La oferta y el papel que desempeña el costo (páginas 117-122)

Existen varias formas importantes de medir el costo. La primera es el **costo total,** la cual consiste del **costo fijo** y el **costo variable.** El **costo marginal** es el aumento en costos variables que proceden del producir una unidad adicional de producto final.

La combinación de costos variables y fijos a la que un comercio se enfrenta afecta la manera en la que éste opera. Cuando los costos marginales son bajos, los comercios tienden a permanecer abiertos por más tiempo. Lo opuesto tiende a pasar cuando los costos marginales son altos.

Los comercios usan dos formas de medir los ingresos para decidir qué cantidad de producto final les traerá las mayores ganancias. Estas dos medidas son el **ingreso total** y el **ingreso marginal,** el cual es el cambio en el ingreso total cuando se vende una unidad más de producto final. Un comercio aumenta al máximo sus ganancias cuando el costo marginal es exactamente igual al ingreso marginal. Puede que otras cantidades del producto final produzcan la misma ganancia, pero ningunas darán más.

Repasar la idea principal
¿Cuáles son las cuatro medidas principales del costo?

Los precios y las decisiones

Vocabulario

Los siguientes términos se definen en el Capítulo 6:

SECCIÓN UNO
- racionamiento *(p. 131)*
- cupón de racionamiento *(p. 131)*

SECCIÓN DOS
- modelo económico *(p. 134)*
- equilibrio del mercado *(p. 134)*

- superávit *(p. 135)*
- escasez *(p. 136)*
- precio equilibrado *(p. 138)*
- artículos de promoción *(p. 138)*

SECCIÓN TRES
- descuento *(p. 140)*
- precio tope *(p. 141)*
- salario mínimo *(p. 142)*

- precio mínimo *(p. 142)*
- precio meta *(p. 144)*
- préstamo sin recursos *(p. 144)*
- aportación para déficit *(p. 146)*

Sección uno

Los precios como señales (páginas 128-132)

Los precios sirven como señales tanto para los productores como para los consumidores. Los precios altos son una señal para que se produzca más y se compre menos. Los precios bajos son una señal para que se produzca menos y se compre más.

Los precios tienen varias ventajas, incluyendo la neutralidad, la flexibilidad, la libertad de selección, la ausencia de gastos administrativos y la eficiencia. Los precios también tienen la ventaja de que todos los comprenden fácilmente.

Se pueden usar otros métodos de repartición que no están relacionados con los precios, incluyendo el **racionamiento.** Estas reparticiones que no están relacionadas con precios, sin embargo, causan problemas con respecto al ser justas, a los costos altos de administración y a los incentivos aminorados para trabajar y producir.

Repasar la idea principal

¿Cómo sirven los precios de señales tanto para los consumidores como para los productores?

Sección dos

Cómo se determinan los precios (páginas 134-138)

En un mercado competitivo, las fuerzas de la oferta y la demanda establecen los precios. Si el precio es demasiado alto, un **superávit** temporal aparece hasta que el precio baje. Si el precio es demasiado bajo, una **escasez** temporal aparece hasta que el precio suba. Eventualmente, el mercado alcanza un **precio equilibrado,** el cual no causa ni escasez ni superávit.

La teoría de poner precios competitivos representa en teoría un ideal que casi nunca se puede alcanzar. Aún así, una competencia absolutamente pura no es necesaria para que la teoría sea práctica.

Repasar la idea principal

¿Cómo funciona el proceso de ajuste en un mercado cuando se está determinando un precio equilibrado?

Sección tres

El sistema de precios en acción (páginas 140-146)

Una economía de mercado está compuesta de muchos mercados diferentes y hay diferentes precios que prevalecen en cada uno. El cambio en un precio afecta a más de la repartición de recursos en ese mercado. Un cambio de precio afecta la repartición de recursos entre los mercados.

Los gobiernos a veces fijan los precios a niveles sobre o bajo el precio equilibrado. Si un precio fijo es un **precio tope,** así como con los controles de rentas, la escasez normalmente aparecerá mientras que el precio permanezca fijo. Si el precio legal es un **precio mínimo,** como en el caso del **salario mínimo,** el resultado es normalmente un superávit.

Un cambio en la oferta o la demanda puede cambiar los precios. La elasticidad de la curva de relación entre demanda y precio afecta cuán grande será el cambio de precio. Mientras más elástica sea la curva, más pequeño el cambio de precio. Mientras menos elástica sea la curva, más grande el cambio de precio.

Los respaldos de precios agriculturales crecieron dramáticamente durante los años 1930 para contribuir a los ingresos agrícolas. Los programas de apoyo de la CCC permitieron que los agricultores pidieran préstamos repaldados por sus cosechas, retuvieran el préstamo y perdieran la cosecha si los precios del mercado estaban bajos. La **aportación para déficit** se usa con más frecuencia, proveyendo al granjero con un cheque que proporciona la diferencia entre el **precio meta** y el precio actual recibido por el producto.

Repasar la idea principal

¿Cómo funcionan los precios en forma colectiva para repartir los recursos entre los mercados?

Competencia, estructuras del mercado y el gobierno

Vocabulario

Los siguientes términos se definen en el Capítulo 7:

SECCIÓN UNO
- liberalismo (p. 152)
- industria (p. 152)
- estructura del mercado (p. 152)
- competencia pura (p. 152)
- competencia imperfecta (p. 155)
- competencia monopolista (p. 155)

- diferenciación del producto (p. 155)
- competencia sin precio (p. 156)
- oligopolio (p. 156)
- colusión (p. 157)
- fijación de precios (p. 157)
- guerra de precios (p. 157)
- fijación de precios independiente (p. 157)
- liderazgo de precio (p. 157)
- monopolio (p. 158)
- monopolio natural (p. 158)
- franquicia (p. 159)

- economías de escala (p. 159)
- monopolio geográfico (p. 159)
- monopolio tecnológico (p. 159)
- patente (p. 160)
- derecho de autor (p. 160)
- monopolio fiscal (p. 160)

SECCIÓN DOS
- fallo del mercado (p. 163)
- factor externo (p. 166)
- factor externo negativo (p. 166)

- factor externo positivo (p. 167)
- bienes públicos (p. 167)

SECCIÓN TRES
- fideicomiso (p. 169)
- discriminación de precio (p. 169)
- orden de cesar y desistir (p. 169)
- divulgación pública (p. 170)

Sección uno

Competencia y estructuras del mercado (páginas 152-161)

La **competencia pura** es una **estructura del mercado** con muchos compradores y vendedores, productos económicos idénticos, acción independiente por los compradores y vendedores, participantes que están bien informados y libertad para que las compañías entren o dejen el mercado. La **competencia monopolista** tiene todas las características de la competencia pura menos la **diferenciación del producto.** El **oligopolio** es una estructura de mercado dominada por unas cuantas compañías muy grandes. El **monopolista** es un solo productor que posee el mayor control sobre la oferta y el precio. Todas las compañías, sin tener en cuenta la estructura del mercado, aumentan al máximo sus ganancias produciendo la cantidad de producto final donde el costo marginal sea igual al ingreso marginal.

Repasar la idea principal

¿Cuáles son los cuatro tipos de estructuras de mercado?

Sección dos

Fallos del mercado (páginas 163-167)

Los **fallos del mercado** ocurren cuando hay grandes desviaciones de una o más de las condiciones requeridas para la competencia pura. La competencia inadecuada es una de las características de los fallos del mercado y puede llevar al oligopolio o a los monopolios. La existencia de información inadecuada representa otro fallo del mercado. La inmovilidad de los recursos, representada por factores de producción que no pueden o quieren ser movidos a otros mercados, también presenta un obstáculo a la distribución eficiente de los recursos.

Algunas de las actividades ocasionan factores externos, o efectos económicos secundarios a terceros partidos. Los factores externos no están reflejados en los precios de las actividades que causaron los efectos secundarios en primer lugar, y por lo tanto representan una característica del fallo del mercado. Los **bienes públicos,** otro tipo de fallo del mercado, son suplidos por el gobierno porque el mercado no puede reusarle provisiones a aquellos que se niegan a pagar.

Repasar la idea principal

¿Cuáles son los cinco tipos principales de fallos del mercado?

Sección tres

El papel del gobierno (páginas 169-172)

El gobierno toma parte en los asuntos económicos que promueven y estimulan la competencia. Su actividad por medio de legislatura antimonopolista, otras clases de regulaciones y **divulgación pública** ha modificado la economía de libre empresa. Como resultado, la economía moderna es una combinación de diferentes estructuras de mercado, diferentes tipos de organizaciones comerciales y cierto grado de regulación gubernamental.

Repasar la idea principal

¿Cómo promueve el gobierno la competencia?

Empleo, trabajo y sueldo

Vocabulario

Los siguientes términos se definen en el Capítulo 8:

SECCIÓN UNO
- macroeconomía *(p. 182)*
- fuerza de trabajo civil *(p. 182)*
- sindicato de artesanos o gremial *(p. 184)*
- sindicato industrial *(p. 184)*
- huelga *(p. 184)*
- piqueteo *(p. 184)*
- boicot *(p. 184)*
- cierre patronal *(p. 184)*
- sindicato de empresa *(p. 184)*
- la Gran Depresión *(p. 185)*
- ley de derecho de trabajo *(p. 186)*

- controversia sobre jurisdicción *(p. 187)*
- sindicato independiente *(p. 187)*

SECCIÓN DOS
- empresa de exclusividad gremial *(p. 190)*
- empresa sin exclusividad gremial inicial *(p. 190)*
- empresa gremial modificada *(p. 190)*
- empresa de agencia *(p. 190)*
- procedimiento de reclamación *(p. 191)*
- mediación *(p. 191)*
- arbitraje voluntario *(p. 191)*
- arbitraje obligatorio *(p. 191)*
- investigación *(p. 191)*

- mandato *(p. 192)*
- incautación *(p. 192)*

SECCIÓN TRES
- mano de obra no calificada *(p. 194)*
- mano de obra semicalificada *(p. 194)*
- mano de obra calificada *(p. 194)*
- mano de obra profesional *(p. 194)*
- grados de mano de obra no competitiva *(p. 194)*
- escala de salarios *(p. 195)*
- teoría tradicional de determinación de salarios *(p. 195)*
- escala de salarios equilibrada *(p. 195)*

- teoría de salarios negociados *(p. 196)*
- antigüedad *(p. 196)*
- movilidad de la mano de obra *(p. 196)*

SECCIÓN CUATRO
- devolución de beneficios gremiales *(p. 199)*
- sistema salarial de dos niveles *(p. 199)*
- barrera de vidrio *(p. 200)*
- valor comparable *(p. 200)*
- contrato de destinación especial *(p. 201)*
- dólares de valor corriente *(p. 202)*
- dólares de valor real o constante *(p. 204)*
- año base *(p. 204)*

Sección uno   El Movimiento Laboral (páginas 182-187)

El crecimiento de los sindicatos fue lento en un principio porque la nación estaba compuesta en su mayoría de granjeros y dueños de negocios pequeños. El **sindicato de artesanos o gremial** fue el primero en surgir, seguido por los **sindicatos industriales.**

Las actitudes del público hacia los obreros cambiaron mucho después de **la Gran Depresión.** Durante los años 1930, el Acta Norris-LaGuardia, el Acta Wagner y el Acta de Estándares Justos de Trabajo cambieron la opiñion pública a favor de los obreros. El pasaje del Acta Taft-Hartley después de la Segunda Guerra Mundial limitó las actividades de los sindicatos.

Repasar la idea principal   ¿Cuáles actas afectaron a los obreros después de la Depresión?

Sección dos   Cómo resolver las diferencias entre los sindicatos y la administración (páginas 189-192)

Hay cuatro tipos de sindicatos: la **empresa de exclusividad gremial,** la **empresa sin exclusividad gremial inicial,** la **empresa gremial modificada** y la **empresa de agencia.** Hay varios métodos disponibles para resolver las polémicas entre los obreros y la administración si la negociación colectiva fracasa: la **mediación,** el **arbitraje,** la **investigación,** el **mandato** y la **incautación.**

Repasar la idea principal   ¿Cómo pueden ser resueltas las polémicas entre los obreros y la administración?

Sección tres   Trabajo y sueldo (páginas 194-197)

Los economistas dividen el trabajo entre cuatro **grados de mano de obra no competitiva—mano de obra no calificada, mano de obra semicalificada, mano de obra calificada** y **mano de obra profesional.** La **teoría tradicional de determinación de salarios** usa la influencia de la oferta y la demanda en el mercado para explicar la tasa de salarios. La **teoría de salarios negociados** asegura que la fortaleza de los sindicatos sea también un factor en la determinación de los salarios.

Repasar la idea principal   ¿Cómo se diferencian las teorías de determinación de salarios?

Sección cuatro   Tendencias y tópicos sobre el empleo (páginas 198-204)

Los sindicatos han decaído por tres razones: los dueños de empresas han tomado pasos muy agresivos para evitar los sindicatos, los que han entrado recientemente a la fuerza laboral tienen poca lealtad a los sindicatos de obreros y los sindicatos han cobrado demasiado en algunas industrias.

La mujer encuentra que hay una gran diferencia entre el salario que ella recibe y el que recibe el hombre. El **valor comparable** y los **contratos de destinación especial** son medidas para corregir esta diferencia.

Repasar la idea principal   ¿Cuáles son los dos tópicos de empleo?

Vocabulario

Los siguientes términos se definen en el Capítulo 9:

SECCIÓN UNO
- impuesto de pecado (p. 210)
- laguna tributaria (p. 212)
- principio del beneficio de tributación (p. 213)
- principio de tributación y solvencia (p. 214)
- tributación proporcional (p. 215)
- tasa impositiva media (p. 215)
- tributación progresiva (p. 215)
- tasa impositiva marginal (p. 215)
- tributación regresiva (p. 215)

SECCIÓN DOS
- impuestos sobre la renta (p. 216)
- sistema de retención sobre nóminas (p. 216)
- Servicio de Rentas Internas (SRI) (p. 216)
- declaración de renta (p. 216)
- indización (p. 217)
- FICA (p. 218)
- medicare (p. 218)
- impuestos sobre las utilidades (p. 219)
- impuestos sobre el consumo (p. 219)
- artículo de lujo (p. 220)
- impuesto sucesorio (p. 220)
- impuestos sobre donaciones y legados (p. 220)
- derechos aduaneros (p. 220)
- tarifas a los usuarios (p. 220)

SECCIÓN TRES
- rentas intergubernamentales (p. 222)
- impuesto sobre las ventas (p. 222)
- impuesto sobre los bienes (p. 224)
- bienes inmuebles (p. 224)
- bienes personales tangibles (p. 224)
- bienes personales intangibles (p. 224)
- tasador de impuestos (p. 224)
- declaración de retención sobre nómina (p. 225)

SECCIÓN CUATRO
- frecuencia de un impuesto (p. 228)
- impuesto al valor agregado (p. 229)
- depreciación acelerada (p. 231)
- crédito tributario para inversión (p. 231)
- sobrecargo (p. 231)
- impuesto mínimo alternativo (p. 231)

Sección uno   La economía de tributación (páginas 210-215)

El gobierno recauda miles de millones de dólares a través de tributaciones, cuotas por licencias, cuotas por la instrucción y derechos aduaneros. Los economistas usan tres criterios — la imparcialidad, la simplicidad y la eficiencia—para juzgar la efectividad de una tributación. **El principio del beneficio de tributación** y el **principio de tributación y** la **solvencia** ayudan a decidir el grupo o grupos que deberán recibir la tributación. Las tasas pueden ser divididas en tres grupos—**proporcional**, **progresiva** y **regresiva.**

Repasar la idea principal

¿Cuáles son los tres criterios de las tributaciones y los dos principios de tasación?

Sección dos   El sistema federal de tributación (páginas 216-220)

La fuente principal de ingresos para el gobierno federal es el **impuesto sobre la renta,** una tributación progresiva la cual es administrada a través del **sistema de retención sobre nóminas.** El segundo componente más grande de los ingresos federales es el FICA, el cual se recauda para cubrir el seguro social y el **medicare.** El **impuesto sobre las utilidades** es la tercera fuente principal de ingreso federal.

Repasar la idea principal

¿Cuáles son las fuentes principales de ingreso del gobierno federal?

Sección tres   Sistemas de tributación a nivel del estado y local (páginas 222-226)

Los gobiernos estatales reciben la mayoría de sus ingresos en forma de **impuestos sobre las ventas, rentas intergubernamentales,** impuestos sobre las rentas y contribuciones al retiro de sus empleados. Los gobiernos locales reciben ingresos de los **impuestos sobre los bienes,** los servicios públicos, tiendas de licores, impuestos sobre las ventas y de los gobiernos estatales y federales.

Repasar la idea principal

¿Cuáles son las fuentes principales de ingreso de los gobiernos estatales y locales?

Sección cuatro   Tópicos de impuestos de actualidad (páginas 228-232)

Ha habido tres grandes modificaciones a las leyes de impuestos, las cuales han estado vigentes desde el año 1980. El Acta de Impuestos para la Recuperación Económica de 1981 ocasionó una gran reducción en la tasa de tributaciones del individuo y de corporaciones. La ley de reforma de impuestos del 1986 cerró unos escapes a la ley que habían sido abiertos en el 1981 e hizo el código de impuesto individual más proporcional. El Acta de Reconciliación de Presupuesto Omnibus del 1993 añadió varias categorías de impuestos marginales al código de impuestos del individuo.

Repasar la idea principal

¿Cómo ha sido cambiada la reforma de impuestos desde el año 1980?

Gastos del gobierno

Vocabulario

Los siguientes términos se definen en el Capítulo 10:

SECCIÓN UNO
- per cápita *(p. 238)*
- sector público *(p. 239)*
- sector privado *(p. 239)*
- pago de traslado *(p. 239)*
- donativo del gobierno *(p. 240)*
- distribución de ingresos *(p. 240)*

SECCIÓN DOS
- presupuesto federal *(p. 243)*
- año fiscal *(p. 243)*
- déficit presupuestario federal *(p. 243)*
- proyecto de ley para asignación de fondos *(p. 243)*
- medicaid *(p. 246)*

SECCIÓN TRES
- enmienda para equilibrar el presupuesto *(p. 249)*

SECCIÓN CUATRO
- gastos deficitarios *(p. 253)*
- deuda federal *(p. 254)*
- fondo fiduciario *(p. 256)*
- Producto Interno Bruto *(p. 256)*
- efecto de exclusión *(p. 258)*
- presupuesto equilibrado *(p. 258)*
- derecho de titularidad *(p. 260)*

Sección uno

La economía de gastos del gobierno (páginas 238-241)

Los gastos en todos los niveles del gobierno a mediados del año 1993 excedían $2.18 billones, o $8,488 per cápita. La gran mayoría del aumento tuvo lugar después de los años 1930, pero hoy en día muchas personas creen que los gastos del gobierno han crecido demasiado. El gobierno paga por los bienes y servicios, algunos de los cuales pertenecen al **sector público** y por los **pagos de traslado,** tales como los **donativos del gobierno,** por los cuales el gobierno no recibe nada en cambio.

Repasar la idea principal

¿Cómo ha afectado el aumento de los gastos del gobierno a la economía en general?

Sección dos

Los gastos del gobierno federal (páginas 243-247)

El Presidente es el responsable de desarrollar el **presupuesto federal** para el **año fiscal,** el cual comienza cada 1º de octubre. Los tres componentes más grandes del presupuesto federal, que representa a más de la mitad de todos los gastos federales, son la defensa nacional, el Seguro Social y el interés de la **deuda federal.** La seguridad de ingresos, medicare y la salud son las categorías que le siguen.

Repasar la idea principal

¿Cuáles son las principales categorías de gastos del gobierno federal, desde las más importantes hasta las menos importantes?

Sección tres

Los gastos del gobierno a nivel estatal y local (páginas 249-252)

Los presupuestos estatales pasan por un proceso de aceptación el cual varía de estado a estado. Los gastos estatales más grandes incluyen el bienestar público, los estudios universitarios y las contribuciones de seguros. Otros programas incluyen las carreteras, los hospitales y el interés de la deuda estatal.

La categoría principal de gastos para los gobiernos locales es la educación elemental y secundaria. Los servicios públicos, los hospitales, el interés de la deuda estatal, el departamento de la policía, el bienestar público y otros gastos siguen a la educación.

Repasar la idea principal

¿Cuáles son las principales categorías de gastos estatales, desde las más importantes hasta las menos importantes?

Sección cuatro

Déficit federales y la deuda nacional (páginas 253-260)

La deuda federal afecta la economía de varias maneras. Los impuestos que se necesitan para pagar el interés de la deuda afecta la distribución de ingresos y también transfieren el poder de adquisición del sector privado al sector gubernamental. Los incentivos del individuo para trabajar, ahorrar e invertir también pueden afectarse. Finalmente, cuando el gobierno compite con el sector privado por fondos, es posible que la tasa de interés suba.

Repasar la idea principal

¿Cómo afectan los impuestos a la distribución de recursos?

Vocabulario

Los siguientes términos se definen en el Capítulo 11:

SECCIÓN UNO
- economía de trueque (p. 266)
- dinero (p. 266)
- medio de cambio (p. 266)
- medida de valor (p. 266)
- almacenaje de valor (p. 266)
- moneda como producto básico (p. 267)
- moneda fiduciaria (p. 267)
- wampum (p. 267)
- efectivo (p. 268)
- lingotes (p. 268)

- unidad monetaria (p. 269)

SECCIÓN DOS
- estándar monetario (p. 272)
- banco estatal (p. 272)
- banca arriesgada (p. 273)
- moneda legal (p. 274)
- greenbacks (p. 274)
- billete de los EE.UU. (p. 274)
- Sistema Bancario Nacional (p. 274)
- banco nacional (p. 274)
- billete del Banco Nacional (p. 274)
- moneda nacional (p. 274)
- certificado de oro (p. 275)
- certificado de plata (p. 275)
- billetes de la divisa de

tesorería (p. 275)
- estándar de oro (p. 275)
- estándar inconvertible de la moneda fiduciaria (p. 276)

SECCIÓN TRES
- sistema bancario dual (p. 279)
- Sistema de Reserva Federal (p. 280)
- banco central (p. 280)
- billete de la Reserva Federal (p. 280)
- pánico bancario (p. 281)
- cierre bancario (p. 281)
- banco comercial (p. 281)
- cuenta de depósito a la

vista (p. 281)
- institución de pequeño ahorro (p. 281)
- banco mutualista de ahorro (p. 281)
- banco de ahorro (p. 282)
- Orden Negociable de Retiro (p. 282)
- sociedad de ahorro y préstamo (p. 282)
- giro de acción (p. 283)

SECCIÓN CUATRO
- eliminación de restricciones (p. 284)
- Regulación Q (p. 285)

Sección uno

La evolución del dinero (páginas 266-270)

El **dinero** es cualquier materia que sirva como medio de trueque, una medida de valor y un almacén de valor. Todos los dineros útiles tienen 4 características: portabilidad, durabilidad, divisibilidad y estabilidad de valor.

Repasar la idea principal
¿Cuáles son las características y funciones del dinero?

Sección dos

La banca de ayer y los estándares monetarios (páginas 272-277)

Los países usan un **estándar monetario** para mantener el valor de su moneda. Desde la Revolución hasta la Guerra Civil, los bancos fundados por el estado con dueños privados, emitían papel monetario. En el año 1861 el gobierno nacional vendió bonos e imprimió **greenbacks** para financiar la Guerra Civil. Más tarde, otras monedas federales fueron populares, incluyendo los **certificados de oro, certificados de plata, billetes de la divisa de tesorería** y la **moneda nacional.**

El **estándar de oro** se adoptó en el año 1900. En 1934, sin embargo, la nación adoptó un **estándar inconvertible de la moneda fiduciaria,** lo que significaba que los **billetes de la Reserva Federal** y los *greenbacks* no se podrían convertir en oro.

Repasar la idea principal
¿Por qué usa un país un estándar monetario?

Sección tres

El desarrollo de la banca moderna (páginas 279-283)

El establecimiento del Sistema Nacional de la Banca (National Banking System) en 1863 trajo uniformidad al sistema bancario. El jefe de contaduría monetaria inspeccionó a los bancos miembros. La nación también tenía un **sistema bancario dual** porque muchos de los bancos fundados por los estados no se unieron al NBS. Además de los **bancos comerciales,** otras instituciones de depósito incluyeron a los **bancos mutualistas de ahorro, sindicatos de crédito** y **sociedades de ahorro y préstamo.**

Repasar la idea principal
¿Dónde se podía depositar dinero después del año 1863?

Sección cuatro

Crisis, reforma y evolución en los años 1980s (páginas 284-288)

La **eliminación de restricciones,** la tasa de intereses altos, reservas financieras inadecuadas y el fraude en los 1980 afectaron a las sociedades de ahorro y préstamo. El Congreso eliminó el estado independiente de la industria en 1989. La autoridad supervisora fue transferida a la Oficina de Supervisión de Economía.

Repasar la idea principal
¿Cómo afectó la eliminación de restricciones a las instituciones financieras?

El Sistema de la Reserva Federal y la política monetaria

Vocabulario

Los siguientes términos se definen en el Capítulo 12:

SECCIÓN UNO

- banco afiliado (p. 294)
- sociedad inversionista bancaria (p. 296)
- ley de veracidad sobre préstamo (p. 299)
- Regulación Z (p. 299)
- dinero (p. 300)
- monedas (p. 300)
- requisito marginal (p. 300)

SECCIÓN DOS

- política monetaria (p. 302)
- sistema de reserva fraccional (p. 302)
- reserva obligatoria (p. 302)
- reservas legales (p. 302)
- reservas de banco afiliado (p. 302)
- responsabilidades (p. 302)
- haberes (p. 302)
- estado de cuentas (p. 302)
- capital líquido (p. 302)
- reservas excesivas (p. 303)
- liquidez (p. 304)
- certificado de depósito (p. 304)
- cuenta de ahorros (p. 304)
- depósito a plazo (p. 304)
- política de dinero abundante (p. 306)
- política de dinero caro (p. 306)
- operaciones de mercado abierto (p. 307)
- despacho mercantil (p. 307)
- tasa de descuento (p. 307)
- ventanilla de descuento (p. 308)
- garantía (p. 308)
- persuasión moral (p. 308)
- controles selectivos de crédito (p. 308)

SECCIÓN TRES

- tasa preferencial (p. 309)
- teoría sobre la cantidad de dinero (p. 309)
- monetización de la deuda (p. 310)
- M1 (p. 311)
- M2 (p. 311)
- lista de banco problemático (p. 312)
- acreedor (p. 312)
- banco de crédito agrícola (p. 313)
- banco de energía (p. 313)

Sección uno

El Sistema de la Reserva Federal (páginas 294-300)

El Sistema de la Reserva Federal (*Fed*) es el banco central de la nación, cuyas acciones son propiedad de sus bancos miembros. Su estructura consiste de una **Junta de Directores;** un **Comité Federal de mercado abierto** que consiste de 7 miembros de la Junta y 5 presidentes de distrito; y la **Consultoría Federal** con 12 miembros.

Además de supervisar a los bancos miembros de cada estado, el *Fed* tiene gran autoridad sobre las **sociedades inversionistas bancarias,** las operaciones internacionales de todos los bancos comerciales, algunas fusiones, la autorización de cheques, la legislación del consumidor concerniente a las **leyes de veracidad sobre préstamo,** el mantenimiento de la moneda nacional y los **requisitos marginales.**

Repasar la idea principal

¿Cómo está organizado el *Fed*?

Sección dos

La política monetaria (páginas 302-308)

La **política monetaria** y la banca comercial moderna operan con un **sistema de reserva fraccional.** Las **reservas legales** que un banco mantiene determina la cantidad de préstamos que éste puede hacer. El **capital líquido** de un banco es igual a la diferencia entre su **haberes** y sus **responsabilidades.** Cuando un banco recibe un depósito, se separa cierta cantidad del depósito a un lado como una reserva contra el depósito. Si existen algunas **reservas excesivas,** el banco puede hacer préstamos nuevos.

La política monetaria afecta el tamaño de la oferta monetaria y así el nivel de la tasa de intereses, usando el sistema de reserva fraccional. El primer recurso de la política monetaria es el cambio en la **reserva obligatoria,** el cual casi nunca se usa. El segundo recurso y el más popular es las **operaciones de mercado abierto.** Un cambio en la **tasa de descuento** es el tercer recurso importante. Dos de los recursos menos usados incluyen la **persuasión moral** y los **controles selectivos de crédito** tales como los **requisitos marginales.**

Repasar la idea principal

¿Cómo le permite el sistema de reserva fraccional al *Fed* manejar la política monetaria?

Sección tres

La política monetaria, la banca y la economía (páginas 309-313)

A corto plazo, los cambios en la oferta monetaria trabajan en combinación con la demanda de dinero para impactar la tasa de intereses. A largo plazo, el impacto de la política monetaria es en la inflación.

Debido a que las personas guardan su dinero en tantas formas diferentes y en tantos tipos distintos de cuentas, el Fed ha instituido dos definiciones adicionales para el dinero. La primera es el **M1,** el cual representa el componente de transacciones monetarias. El segundo es el **M2,** el cual representa el papel que desempeña el dinero como reserva de valor.

Repasar la idea principal

¿Cuáles son los efectos a corto y largo plazo de los cambios en la oferta monetaria?

Vocabulario

Los siguientes términos se definen en el Capítulo 13:

SECCIÓN UNO
- ahorrar *(p. 320)*
- ahorros *(p. 320)*
- sistema financiero *(p. 320)*
- activo financiero *(p. 321)*
- intermediario financiero *(p. 321)*
- institución financiera no bancaria *(p. 322)*
- compañía financiera *(p. 322)*
- préstamo de consolidación de cuenta *(p. 322)*
- prima *(p. 323)*

- fondo mutuo *(p. 323)*
- pensión *(p. 323)*
- fondo de pensiones *(p. 323)*
- fondo de inversión de bienes raíces *(p. 323)*

SECCIÓN DOS
- riesgo *(p. 325)*
- cupón *(p. 326)*
- vencimiento *(p. 326)*
- paridad *(p. 326)*
- rendimiento vigente *(p. 327)*
- CD gigante *(p. 328)*
- bono arriesgado *(p. 328)*
- bono municipal *(p. 329)*
- exento de impuestos *(p. 329)*
- bono de ahorros *(p. 329)*

- fondo común de inversiones *(p. 330)*
- pagaré del Tesoro *(p. 330)*
- bono del Tesoro a largo plazo *(p. 330)*
- bono del Tesoro a corto plazo *(p. 331)*
- Cuenta de retiro individual *(p. 331)*
- mercado de capital *(p. 332)*
- mercado monetario *(p. 332)*
- mercado primario *(p. 332)*
- mercado secundario *(p. 332)*

SECCIÓN TRES
- capitales *(p. 334)*
- Hipótesis de Mercado

Eficiente *(p. 334)*
- diversificación de cartera *(p. 334)*
- agente de bolsa *(p. 335)*
- bolsa de valores *(p. 335)*
- asiento *(p. 335)*
- mercado extrabursátil *(p. 336)*
- DJIA *(p. 336)*
- 500 de S&P *(p. 337)*
- mercado al contado *(p. 338)*
- futuros *(p. 338)*
- mercado de futuros *(p. 338)*
- opciones *(p. 338)*
- opción de compra *(p. 338)*
- optición de venta *(p. 338)*
- mercados de opciones *(p. 338)*

Sección uno

Los ahorros y el sistema financiero (páginas 320-323)

El **ahorrar** es un proceso que hace posible el que haya ahorros disponibles para otros que quieran invertir. La economía tiene un **sistema financiero** que transfiere los ahorros a los inversionistas. Los **activos financieros** que se generan en el proceso son instituidos por comercios, gobiernos e **intermediarios financieros** para facilitar la transferencia de fondos de los que ahorran a los que invierten. Los intermediarios financieros incluyen **compañías financieras,** compañías de seguro de vida, **fondos mutuos, fondos de pensiones** y **fondos de inversión de bienes raíces.**

Repasar la idea principal
¿Qué intermediarios financieros existen para transferir fondos de los que ahorran a los que invierten?

Sección dos

Invertir en los activos financieros (páginas 325-332)

Hay un gran número de activos financieros disponible a los inversionistas. Los bonos instituidos por corporaciones, gobiernos estatales y locales, el gobierno de Estados Unidos y otros gobiernos forman una gran parte de los activos financieros. Los certificados de depósitos, el **mercado monetario de fondos mutuos,** y las **cuentas de retiro individual** son otros activos financieros instituidos por varias agencias privadas.

Repasar la idea principal
¿Qué activos financieros hay disponibles para los inversionistas?

Sección tres

Invertir en capitales, futuros y opciones (páginas 334-338)

Los **capitales,** o acciones, difieren de los activos financieros en que los capitales representan posesión de una corporación en vez de un préstamo. Muchos valores se intercambian en **bolsas de valores** organizadas, donde los miembros se reúnen para comprar y vender acciones.

Los inversionistas leen el **DJIA** para seguir el rendimiento de las acciones en el NYSE. El índice de **500 de Standard & Poor** muestra un grupo de 500 acciones ejemplares, las cuales están alistadas en varias bolsas de valores y también incluyen al **mercado al contado.**

Históricamente, los granjeros y compradores de productos agrícolas ingeniaron la manera de extender los contratos por más tiempo. Hoy en día, los contratos **futuros** se usan mucho. Si un inversionista desea tener la opción de salirse de la obligación de una entrega futura especificada en un contrato escrito hoy, puede que él o ella esté más interesado en un contrato de **opción.**

Repasar la idea principal
¿En qué se diferencian los capitales de los activos financieros y dónde se intercambian los capitales?

Producto interno bruto

Vocabulario

Los siguientes términos se definen en el Capítulo 14:

Sección uno

La medida de la producción nacional (página 348-352)

El **PIB** es la medida más abarcadora de la producción total de la nación. Esta sólo cuenta los productos finales, servicios y las estructuras que son producidas en Estados Unidos, sin importar quién es el dueño de los recursos. Como ésta cuenta sólo los productos finales, los **productos intermediarios** y las **ventas de segunda mano** están excluidas.

El **PIB** no nos deja saber nada respecto a la composición de la producción o el estándar de vida. Algunas actividades no relacionadas con el mercado, tales como los servicios que ejecutan las amas de casa, se excluyen de la cantidad. Otras actividades son ilegales o no son declaradas, y por lo tanto, pertenecen a la **economía oculta.**

Repasar la idea principal
¿Cómo mide el PIB la producción total de la economía?

Sección dos

La medida del ingreso nacional (páginas 354-359)

La diferencia entre el PIB y el PNB es que el PIB cuenta sólo la producción en Estados Unidos, sin importar quién posee los recursos. Por contraste, el PNB es la medida del ingreso que reciben los ciudadanos americanos, sin importar dónde están localizados sus recursos.

Hay cinco formas de medir el ingreso, incluyendo el PIB. Éstas incluyen el **producto nacional neto,** el **ingreso nacional,** el **ingreso personal** y el **ingreso personal disponible.**

La economía también se puede organizar como el **sector casero** o del consumidor, el sector comercial o de inversionistas, el sector gubernamental y el sector extranjero. El **modelo de producción-gastos,** que se expresa como PIB = C + I + G + E, demuestra como el PIB es consumido por los cuatro segmentos de la economía.

Repasar la idea principal
¿Cuál es la diferencia entre el PIB y el PNB?

Sección tres

El PIB y los cambios en el nivel del precio (páginas 361-364)

Los economistas usan un **índice de precios** para seguir el movimiento de los precios al pasar del tiempo. Los índices de precios están basados en una **cesta de mercado** con productos representantes que se seleccionan en cierto año usado como base.

Los índices de precios pueden ser preparados para cualquier producto, grupo de productos o grupos de consumidores. Tres de los más populares incluyen el **índice de precios del consumidor,** el **índice de precios del productor** y el **deflactor implícito de precios del PIB.**

Repasar la idea principal
¿Cuál es el propósito del índice de precios?

Población, crecimiento económico y ciclos económicos

Vocabulario

Los siguientes términos se definen en el Capítulo 15:

SECCIÓN UNO
- censo *(p. 370)*
- población urbana *(p. 370)*
- población rural *(p. 370)*
- centro de población *(p. 372)*
- demógrafo *(p. 372)*
- índice de fertilidad *(p. 372)*

- expectativa de vida *(p. 372)*
- inmigración neta *(p. 372)*
- *baby boom (p. 373)*
- pirámide demográfica *(p. 373)*
- relación de dependencia *(p. 374)*

SECCIÓN DOS
- PIB real per cápita *(p. 376)*
- triángulo de crecimiento *(p. 376)*

- estándar de vida *(p. 377)*
- base impositiva *(p. 377)*
- recursos renovables *(p. 379)*
- relación capital-trabajo *(p. 379)*
- productividad de la mano de obra *(p. 380)*

SECCIÓN TRES
- ciclo económico *(p. 383)*
- fluctuación económica *(p. 383)*

- recesión *(p. 383)*
- máximo *(p. 383)*
- sima *(p. 383)*
- expansión *(p. 383)*
- tendencia *(p. 384)*
- depresión *(p. 384)*
- vale de depresión *(p. 385)*
- modelo econométrico *(p. 387)*
- índice de indicadores anticipados *(p. 388)*

Sección uno

Población (páginas 370-374)

La constitución de Estados Unidos requiere un **censo** de la población cada 10 años. El Departamento del Censo hace la cuenta. Éste clasifica la población de diferentes maneras; incluyendo la división en **poblaciones urbanas** y **rurales.** El porcentaje anual de crecimiento de la población era más de 3 por ciento hasta la Guerra Civil, pero ha bajado constantemente desde entonces.

El Departamento del Censo ha proyectado la continuación de la bajada en el porcentaje de crecimiento de la población hasta el año 2050. Los factores que contribuyen a esta tendencia son un **índice de fertilidad** con nivel de reemplazo, una **expectativa de vida** un poco más larga y una **inmigración neta.** Las proyecciones de edad y sexo demuestran la continua influencia del *baby boom,* una generación muy abundante que al final aumentará la **relación de dependencia.** La mezcla racial y étnica también cambiará.

Repasar la idea principal

¿Por qué son los cambios en la población importantes para cualquier país?

Sección dos

Desarrollo económico (páginas 376-381)

Debido a los cambios en la población, el desarrollo económico a largo plazo es normalmente medido en términos del **PIB real per cápita.** Para períodos más cortos, de año a año, se usa el PIB real no-ajustado para tomar en cuenta la población. El desarrollo económico es importante por cinco razones. Primero, aumenta el **estándar de vida** de todos. Segundo, aumenta la **base impositiva** y le facilita al gobierno a desarrollar varios programas. Tercero, ayuda a aliviar algunos problemas domésticos que son causados por la falta de trabajos. Cuarto, ayuda a las economías de otras naciones. Finalmente, el desarrollo económico en casa hace del sistema económico y político de Estados Unidos un modelo para los países en desarrollo del mundo.

Repasar la idea principal

¿Por qué es el desarrollo económico una de las siete mayores metas de la economía de Estados Unidos?

Sección tres

Ciclos económicos y Fluctuaciones (páginas 383-388)

El rendimiento económico en términos del PIB real varía al pasar del tiempo en un patrón llamado **ciclo económico.** Las dos fases del ciclo son la **recesión** y la **expansión.** La economía alcanza lo **máximo** cuando una expansión termina y una **sima** cuando una recesión termina.

Los ciclos económicos son resultado de un número de factores—incluyendo los cambios en el capital y los gastos de inventario por comercios, el estímulo suplido por las innovaciones e imitaciones, factores monetarios y acontecimientos externos inesperados.

Los economistas usan **modelos econométricos** para predecir la actividad económica futura. Los modelos simulan la actividad económica y proveen predicciones a corto plazo bastante precisas.

Repasar la idea principal

¿Qué son los ciclos económicos?

Desempleo, inflación y pobreza

Vocabulario

Los siguientes términos se definen en el Capítulo 16:

SECCIÓN UNO
- desempleo (p. 394)
- índice de desempleo (p. 394)
- desempleo friccional (p. 395)
- desempleo estructural (p. 395)
- desempleo cíclico (p. 396)
- desempleo estacional (p. 396)
- desempleo tecnológico (p. 396)
- automatización (p. 396)
- empleo total (p. 397)

SECCIÓN DOS
- nivel de precios (p. 399)
- deflación (p. 399)
- inflación reptante (p. 400)
- inflación galopante (p. 400)
- hiperinflación (p. 400)

SECCIÓN TRES
- Curva de Lorenz (p. 405)
- obrero (p. 407)
- oficinista (p. 407)
- umbral de pobreza (p. 407)
- relación ingresos-pobreza (p. 408)
- asistencia social (p. 409)
- sellos para la compra de alimentos (p. 411)
- impuesto sobre la renta negativo (p. 411)
- zona de iniciativa (p. 412)
- *workfare* (p. 412)

Sección uno

El desempleo (páginas 394-397)

El Departamento del Censo identifica a las personas desempleadas en muestras mensuales que toman de aproximadamente 55,800 hogares en toda la nación. El número de desempleados es dividido entre la fuerza trabajadora civil para expresar el desempleo por medio de un porcentaje. El **índice de desempleo** es abarcador, pero no cuenta a los que desisten en buscar empleo ni distingue entre el empleo de tiempo completo y el empleo por horas.

Los tipos de desempleo incluyen el **desempleo friccional, desempleo estructural, desempleo cíclico, desempleo estacional** y el **desempleo tecnológico.**

Repasar la idea principal
¿Qué es el desempleo y cómo es tabulado?

Sección dos

La inflación (páginas 399-403)

Los economistas miden el **nivel de precios** con el CPI, el deflactor implícito de precios del PIB y el índice de precios del productor. El cambio en el nivel de precios es la tasa de inflación, la cual se expresa normalmente en términos de porcentajes de cambio. La **inflación reptante, inflación galopante** e **hiperinflación** son términos usados para describir el grado de severidad de la inflación.

Condiciones de crédito muy favorables y el aumento excesivo de la oferta monetaria son las causas bajo la inflación. Cuando estas condiciones están presentes, varios tipos de inflación—incluyendo la demanda-tirante, gastos del déficit, costo-empuje y el espiral de salario y precio—pueden ocurrir. La inflación errode el valor del dinero y obliga a los consumidores y comercios a cambiar sus hábitos de compras.

Repasar la idea principal
¿Qué causa la inflación y cómo desestabiliza a la economía?

Sección tres

La pobreza y la distribución de ingresos (páginas 405-412)

Una serie de factores causan la desigualdad en la distribución de ingresos, estos incluyen los niveles educacionales, la riqueza, la discriminación, la habilidad y el poder del monopolio. La pobreza es una medida relativa la cual se determina comparando la cantidad de dinero por ingresos que ganan las familias con el **umbral de pobreza.** La **relación ingresos-pobreza** también se usa para compensar por las diferencias en el tamaño de las familias y todas las medidas muestran una diferencia creciente entre los ingresos.

Varios programas para combatir la pobreza han sido introducidos para ayudar a los necesitados. Los programas de ayuda del gobierno incluyen la Ayuda a Familias con Niños Pequeños, Ingreso de Seguridad Suplemental, los **sellos para la compra de alimentos** y otros programas. Los economistas han propuesto un **impuesto negativo sobre la renta,** mientras que otros han propuesto **zonas de iniciativa** y *workfare.*

Repasar la idea principal
¿Qué es la pobreza y qué programas pueden usarse para aliviarla?

Vocabulario

Los siguientes términos se definen en el Capítulo 17:

SECCIÓN UNO
- estancamiento e inflación (*p. 419*)
- laguna del PIB (*p. 419*)
- índice de miseria (*p. 419*)
- índice de incomodidad (*p. 419*)

SECCIÓN DOS
- curva de abastecimiento global (*p. 422*)
- curva de demanda global (*p. 424*)
- equilibrio de macroeconomía (*p. 425*)

SECCIÓN TRES
- política fiscal (*p. 427*)
- economía keynesiana (*p. 427*)

- función del consumo (*p. 427*)
- multiplicador (*p. 427*)
- acelerador (*p. 428*)
- estabilizador automático (*p. 429*)
- seguro de desempleo (*p. 429*)
- economía de oferta (*p. 431*)
- curva de Laffer (*p. 432*)
- monetarismo (*p. 433*)

- controles de los salarios con los precios (*p. 434*)

SECCIÓN CUATRO
- Consejo de Asesores Económicos (*p. 437*)

Sección uno

El costo de la instabilidad económica (páginas 418-421)

La falta de desarrollo e instabilidad económica tiene costos tanto económicos como sociales. Los costos económicos pueden ser medidos como **estancamiento e inflación** o **laguna del PIB**. Los costos sociales incluyen la frustración por estar desempleados, la posible instabilidad política, el aumento en el crimen y el daño a los valores familiares. Un gran desarrollo económico es más que un ideal económico. Es uno de los pilares fundadores de una sociedad vibrante.

Repasar la idea principal

¿Cuáles son los costos económicos y sociales de la instabilidad económica?

Sección dos

Equilibrio de macroeconomía (páginas 422-425)

El equilibrio de macroeconomía puede ser analizado con la ayuda de la **curva de abastecimiento global** y la **curva de demanda global.** La curva de abastecimiento global representa la suma de toda la producción que podría llevarse a cabo a cada nivel de precio. La demanda global representa la demanda total de todos los sectores de la economía a todos los niveles de precio posibles. Cuando la oferta y la demanda global son combinadas, su intersección se define como el **equilibrio de macroeconomía.**

Repasar la idea principal

¿Cómo se parece el equilibrio de macroeconomía al equilibrio en los mercados individuales?

Sección tres

Políticas de estabilización (páginas 427-434)

Las políticas de la demanda, también conocidas como **políticas fiscales,** están diseñadas para que afecten la curva de demanda global a través del gasto federal y los impuestos. Las políticas de la oferta afectan la curva de abastecimiento global. Éstas incluyen un papel menos importante para el gobierno, una estructura de impuestos federales más baja y otras medidas para reducir el papeleo y la regulación en el sector comercial. Las políticas monetarias incluyen operaciones en el mercado abierto, cambios en la tasa de descuentos y en circunstancias extremas, cambios en la reserva obligatoria.

Repasar la idea principal

¿Cuáles son los tres procedimientos principales para la estabilización y el desarrollo?

Sección cuatro

La economía y la política (páginas 436-438)

Los Estados Unidos tienen una autoridad monetaria independiente—el Sistema de Reserva Federal. Mientras el *Fed* tenga la responsabilidad de establecer la política monetaria y los funcionarios tengan la responsabilidad de la política fiscal, puede que los dos no estén de acuerdo. Aunque la economía por sí misma es una ciencia social, los campos de la economía y política están muy relacionados. El Presidente tiene un **Consejo de Asesores Económicos,** pero en ocasiones él no puede seguir sus consejos por razones políticas.

Repasar la idea principal

¿Qué revela el registro histórico acerca de la conducta de la política económica?

Comercio internacional

Vocabulario

Los siguientes términos se definen en el Capítulo 18:

SECCIÓN UNO
- ventaja absoluta *(p. 450)*
- ventaja comparativa *(p. 451)*

SECCIÓN DOS
- tarifa *(p. 453)*
- cuota *(p. 453)*
- arancel proteccionista *(p. 453)*
- tarifa de ingreso *(p. 453)*
- proteccionista *(p. 454)*
- argumento de las industrias nacientes *(p. 455)*
- balanza de pagos *(p. 456)*
- déficit comercial *(p. 456)*
- cláusula de la nación más favorecida *(p. 458)*
- GATT *(p. 458)*
- TLC *(p. 459)*

SECCIÓN TRES
- divisas *(p. 461)*
- mercado de divisas *(p. 461)*
- cotización de la divisa *(p. 461)*
- cotización de la divisa fija *(p. 461)*
- devaluación *(p. 462)*
- cotización de la divisa flotante *(p. 463)*
- cotización de la divisa flexible *(p. 463)*
- letras para entrega futura *(p. 464)*
- valor ponderado del dólar según el comercio exterior *(p. 465)*

Sección uno

Ventaja absoluta y comparativa (páginas 448-451)

Los Estados Unidos están muy envueltos en el mercado internacional. En 1993 el americano promedio gastó más de $2,300 en bienes y servicios importados. **Ventaja absoluta** significa que un país puede producir más cantidad de un producto que otro país. La base para el mercado de hoy es la **ventaja comparativa.** Si las personas y los países se especializan en las cosas que ellos saben hacer con más eficiencia y usan el trueque para conseguir aquellas cosas que no pueden producir, entonces la producción global aumentará.

Repasar la idea principal

¿Qué concepto económico explica las ganancias mutuas del comercio?

Sección dos

Barreras del comercio internacional (páginas 453-459)

En el pasado, las barreras del comercio incluían las **tarifas** y las **cuotas.** En años recientes, otras barreras sin tarifas—que incluyen las licencias, certificaciones de salud y cuotas voluntarias—se han usado para restringir el paso libre de los productos.

Los que están de acuerdo con las barreras de comercio lo hacen a menudo pensando en la defensa nacional, el argumento de las industrias nacientes, la protección de trabajos domésticos, el mantener la moneda localmente y el ayudar a la **balanza de pagos.** Las personas a favor del mercado libre creen que todos estos argumentos son erróneos, con la excepción del argumento de las industrias nacientes. Para que el argumento de las industrias nacientes sea válido, la protección debe ser eliminada eventualmente para que la industria pueda competir por sí misma.

Las barreras de comercio contribuyeron a que las condiciones durante la Gran Depresión fueran aún peor. Desde 1934 el mundo se ha acercado más al comercio libre. El **GATT** contribuyó mucho al progreso mundial, y los que proponen el **TLC** desearían eliminar todas las barreras de comercio en Norteamérica.

Repasar la idea principal

¿Cómo han sido eliminadas las barreras de comercio a través de los años?

Sección tres

El financiamiento y el déficit comercial (páginas 461-466)

Las **divisas** son la base de las transacciones internacionales. El valor de las divisas se determina en los mercados donde las monedas extranjeras se compran y se venden. El sistema actual de **cotización de la divisa flexible** significa que el valor de las monedas extranjeras fluctúa con su oferta y demanda.

Los **déficits comerciales** a mediados de los años 1980 resultó en parte por un dólar poderoso. Cuando el **valor ponderado del dólar según el comercio exterior** disminuyó, el déficit comercial mejoró. Debido a que los déficits tienden a corregirse por sí mismos, la mayoría de las naciones ya no diseñan políticas económicas sólo para mejorar la balanza de pagos.

Repasar la idea principal

En un mundo de cotizaciones de la divisa flexible, ¿cómo reaccionan las naciones a la falta de equilibrio comercial?

Sistemas económicos comparativos

Vocabulario

Los siguientes términos se definen en el Capítulo 19:

SECCIÓN UNO
- socialismo (p. 473)
- comunismo (p. 474)

SECCIÓN DOS
- Plan de Cinco Años (p. 478)
- colectivización (p. 478)
- Gosplan (p. 478)
- granja estatal (p. 479)
- granja colectiva (p. 479)
- trabajo por pieza (p. 480)
- tempestear (p. 480)

- perestroika (p. 480)

SECCIÓN TRES
- privatización (p. 483)
- Solidaridad (p. 485)
- mercado negro (p. 486)
- Gran Salto Adelante (p. 487)

SECCIÓN CUATRO
- con uso intensivo de capital (p. 488)
- keiretsu (p. 488)

Sección uno

El espectro de sistemas económicos (páginas 472-475)

El sistema económico global puede mostrarse en un espectro que se extiende desde los sistemas con un control gubernamental casi total, a aquellos que incluyen muy poca regulación de gobierno. Bajo el capitalismo, los individuos poseen los medios de producción, y la interacción de la oferta y la demanda determina los precios. Bajo el **socialismo,** el gobierno posee muchos de los medios de producción y los funcionarios públicos reparten y administran estos recursos. Por otra parte, el gobierno posee todos los medios de producción bajo el **comunismo** puro.

Repasar la idea principal

¿Cómo se diferencia la posesión de recursos bajo el capitalismo, el socialismo y el comunismo?

Sección dos

El ascenso y la caída del comunismo (páginas 477-481)

En 1917 una revolución derrocó al gobierno de Rusia e instituyó un sistema comunista. Ya para 1927, el país estaba bajo el control del partido comunista y había cambiado su nombre al de la Unión Soviética. En una serie de **Planes de Cinco Años,** los líderes comunistas trataron de alcanzar rápidamente la industrialización. Los planes incluían la **colectivización** de la agricultura y la trasformación de la industria—las cuales estaban bajo el control total del gobierno. **Gosplan,** la autoridad planificadora central, determinaba todos los aspectos de la producción industrial y agrícola. A pesar de los esfuerzos para incrementar la producción, que incluían el **trabajo por pieza** y las cuotas, la economía autoritaria resultó ser un fracaso miserable. Al principio de los 1990, el sistema económico Soviético se había ya desplomado.

Repasar la idea principal

¿Cómo trataron los comunistas de incrementar el desarrollo agrícola e industrial?

Sección tres

La transición hacia el capitalismo (páginas 483-487)

Los sistemas que eran comunistas se deberán enfrentar a varios retos a la vez que tratan de mobilizarse hacia el capitalismo. Estos retos incluyen la **privatización** de los recursos de capitales, el cambio en el poder político de los comunistas al de funcionarios elegidos por voto y a los nuevos incentivos de una economía capitalista. Rusia y Europa del este han tenido cierta cantidad de éxito en este cambio hacia el capitalismo. Al mismo tiempo, otros sistemas económicos a través del mundo han estado experimentando con la movida hacia la economía capitalista.

Repasar la idea principal

¿A qué retos se enfrentan las naciones a la vez que tratan de instituir el sistema capitalista?

Sección cuatro

Las diferentes caras del capitalismo (páginas 488-492)

Desde la Segunda Guerra Mundial, muchas naciones se han movido hacia el capitalismo, aunque su forma exacta varíe de país en país. Japón, que ha sido un sistema capitalista por largo tiempo, alcanzó un desarrollo económico fenomenal con la combinación de lealtad a las corporaciones, tecnología nueva e impuestos bajos. Las economías de los "tigres asiáticos"—Singapur, Taiwan, Hong Kong y Corea del Sur—también crecieron. Al mismo tiempo, Suecia se alejó del socialismo.

Repasar la idea principal

¿Qué factores ayudaron a que la economía del Japón creciera?

Vocabulario

Los siguientes términos se definen en el Capítulo 20:

SECCIÓN UNO
- países en desarrollo (p. 498)
- tasa bruta de natalidad (p. 499)

- crecimiento demográfico nulo (p. 499)
- deuda externa (p. 500)
- fuga de capitales (p. 500)

SECCIÓN DOS
- equilibrio primitivo (p. 504)
- despegue (p. 504)
- Banco Mundial (p. 505)

SECCIÓN TRES
- expropiación (p. 511)
- zona de comercio libre (p. 512)
- unión aduanera (p. 512)
- Unión Europea (p. 512)
- Comunidad Europea (p. 512)
- ECU (p. 512)
- cartel (p. 513)

- densidad demográfica (p. 514)

Sección uno

El desarrollo económico (páginas 498-502)

Los **países en desarrollo** tienen los mismos problemas que tienen los países industrializados—la mayor diferencia está en que sus problemas son mucho peor. La preocupación sobre el bienestar de los países en desarrollo es humanitario tanto como político. En 1991, eran 43 países representando a más de la mitad de la población mundial, cada uno con un PIB per cápita de menos de $500.

Los países en desarrollo se enfrentan a varios retos, que incluyen las **tasas brutas de natalidad** y el aumento en la expectativa de vida. La escasez de recursos naturales, la educación y la tecnología limitada, la carga enorme de la **deuda externa**, la **fuga de capitales** y los gobiernos corruptos y poco eficientes aumentan sus problemas.

Repasar la idea principal

¿En qué se diferencian los problemas de los países en desarrollo a los problemas de los países más industrializados?

Sección dos

Estructura para el desarrollo (páginas 504-507)

Ayuda el pensar que el desarrollo económico ocurre en etapas, aunque cada nación no sigue las mismas etapas. Las etapas incluyen el **equilibrio primitivo,** apartándose del equilibrio primitivo, **despegue,** desarrollo medio y desarrollo alto.

El Banco Mundial recomienda que las naciones industrializadas reduzcan sus barreras de comercio, reformen sus políticas macroeconómicas, aumenten su ayuda financiera y apoyen las políticas de reforma de los países en desarrollo.

El Banco Mundial también recomienda que los países en desarrollo inviertan sus propios recursos en educar a su gente, mejoren el clima para la empresa, abran sus economías al comercio internacional y cambien sus políticas económicas.

Repasar la idea principal

¿Qué pueden hacer las naciones industrializadas para ayudar a los países en desarrollo y qué pueden hacer los países en desarrollo para ayudarse a sí mismos?

Sección tres

El financiamiento del desarrollo económico (páginas 509-514)

Los países en desarrollo necesitan estimular el ahorro para poder proveer su propia fuente de fondos para inversiones. Las economías autoritarias tratan a menudo de forzar el ahorro mobilizando los recursos de una manera que ignora las libertades del individuo. Los intentos por asegurar el capital a través de la **expropiación** a menudo resultan mal, porque los inversionistas extranjeros comienzan a tenerle miedo a la inversión.

Los gobiernos y bancos extranjeros a veces proveen fondos externos de dinero. Otras instituciones, como el Banco Mundial y el Fondo de Moneda Internacional, también ofrecen ayuda.

Algunos países han podido ayudarse entre sí a través de la cooperación a nivel regional. Esta ayuda a veces toma la forma de unas **zonas de comercio libre** o una **unión aduanera,** tal como la de la **Comunidad Europea,** ahora llamada la **Unión Europea.** Las naciones productoras de petróleo organizaron el **cartel** de la OPEC para aumentar el precio del petróleo.

Repasar la idea principal

¿Cómo puede un país en desarrollo asegurar los fondos necesarios para alcanzar prosperidad económica?

Vocabulario

Los siguientes términos se definen en el Capítulo 21:

SECCIÓN UNO
- subsistencia *(p. 520)*
- embargo *(p. 522)*

- gasohol *(p. 524)*
- acuífero *(p. 525)*

SECCIÓN DOS
- gas profundo *(p. 527)*
- saturación *(p. 528)*
- contaminación *(p. 528)*

- lluvia ácida *(p. 528)*
- permiso de contaminación *(p. 530)*

SECCIÓN TRES
- análisis costo-beneficio *(p. 532)*

- economía de libre empresa modificada *(p. 533)*

Sección uno

La demanda global de recursos (páginas 520-525)

A pesar de las predicciones de Thomas Malthus hace casi 200 años, muchas regiones han logrado que su estándar de vida haya crecido constantemente, principalmente debido a la tecnología. Las naciones en desarrollo, con sus altos por cientos de nacimientos, sin embargo, se enfrentan a la amenaza de un estándar de vida inferior.

A la vez que la población mundial ha aumentado a través de los años, las personas se han preocupado cada vez más acerca de la reducción de las fuentes no renovables de energía como el petróleo, el gas natural y el carbón. Muchos americanos se percataron agudamente de esta reducción en los años 1970 después que los países del Medio Oriente comenzaron el **embargo** de petróleo. El embargo motivó a los americanos a buscar otras fuentes de energía. Estas fuentes renovables incluyen la energía solar, energía hidroeléctrica, energía de viento, energía nuclear y **gasohol**—una combinación de gasolina sin plomo y alcohol de grano. Los americanos también están buscando diferentes formas de conservar agua y asegurar el uso prudente de las riquezas de la tierra.

Repasar la idea principal

¿Qué fuentes de energía renovables están investigando los americanos como alternativas a las fuentes no renovables?

Sección dos

Incentivos y recursos económicos (páginas 527-530)

Desde el embargo de petróleo de los 1970, los precios crecientes de gasolina han servido de gran motivación para preservar los recursos naturales. El sistema de precios de nuestra economía de mercado también es un incentivo para conservar otros recursos. La eliminación de restricciones del gas natural, por ejemplo, ha motivado a los productores a buscar **gas profundo.** A la vez que la población americana ha crecido y usado más formas de energía, las personas se han empezado a preocupar acerca de la **contaminación,** ya sea del aire, agua o de la tierra por el derrame de substancias tóxicas o nocivas. Como respuesta a esta preocupación, el gobierno ha pasado legislación e incentivos económicos—que incluyen los **permisos de contaminación**—para limpiar el ambiente. Toda esta legislación fue hecha con el propósito de motivar a las personas a usar los recursos naturales con prudencia.

Repasar la idea principal

¿Cómo motiva el sistema de precios a la preservación de recursos naturales en una economía de mercado?

Sección tres

La aplicación de la forma económica de pensar (páginas 532-534)

La economía se ha convertido en una teoría generalizada predilecta y en una estructura para tomar decisiones. El Consejo Nacional de Educación Económica ha recomendado un sistema de cinco puntos para tomar decisiones. La decisión final está relacionada con el **análisis costo-beneficio,** el cual compara el costo de una decisión a los beneficios ganados.

El capitalismo es el tipo de organización económica dominante en el mundo de hoy. La oferta y la demanda establecen los precios y los precios sirven de señal a los productores y a los consumidores. Los mercados son flexibles porque los cambios futuros afectan los precios y, así, la distribución de recursos. Esta flexibilidad hace posible que nuestra **economía de libre empresa modificada** se ajuste a los eventos en el futuro.

Repasar la idea principal

¿Cómo ayuda la forma económica de pensar a que las personas tomen mejores decisiones?

INDEX

sonal income, *fig410*; state sales tax in, *m224*; using tobacco as money in colonial times, 267

voluntary arbitration; defined, 191

voluntary exchange, 44-45, 48, 49; defined, 44; *fig44*; who benefits from, 43

voluntary import quotas; and President Bush, 454; and President Reagan, 454

vouchers; and privatization in Poland, Hungary and the Czech Republic, 483-484; and privatization in Russia, 485

W

wage-price controls; and President Nixon, 434; defined, 434; effectiveness of, 434

wage rate; defined, 195

wages; and noncompeting labor grades, 194-95; and regional wage differentials, 196-97; difference between males and females, 199-201, *fig200*; during Great Depression, 185; theories of determination, 195-96, *fig196*

wages, salaries and tips; and the circular flow of economic activity, *fig358*

Wagner Act, see **National Labor Relations Act**

Wall Street; *p319*

Walstad, William B.; on economic education, *q4*

wampum; and Narraganset Native Americans, 268; as money in colonial America, 267-68; defined, 267; stability in value, 270

Wang, Charles; and Computer Associates, 162; and Queens College, 162; as entrepreneur, 162; *p162*; profile of, 162; Shanghai, China, 162

Wanniski, Jude; on supply and demand, *q78*

wants, 19-20, 27; and advertising, 21; and scarcity, 9-10; defined, 20; in a command economy, 34; in command, traditional and market economies, *fig35*; *p19*; seemingly unlimited, *fig9*

war bond, see **government bonds**

Washington; and comparable worth, 201; and savings banks, *m282*; per capita personal income, *fig410*; state sales tax in, *m224*

Washington, George; and the origin of the dollar, 268; and the federal budget, 259

water; and Ogallala Aquifer, 525; and surface irrigation, 524-25,

p528; as a scarce resource, 524-25; relationship between use and price of, 525

wealth, 21-22, 27; Adam Smith on, 18; and Gross Domestic Product, *p350*; as reason for income inequality, 406; defined, 22; of industrialized nations vs. developing countries, 498; owned by richest 1 percent, 409

Wealth of Nations, see *Inquiry into the Nature and Causes of the Wealth of Nations, An*

weekly earnings; by occupation and union affiliation, *fig197*

welfare; defined, 409; replacing with workfare, *q342*, *q343*; training classes, *p342*

welfare programs; as automatic stabilizers, 429

West Virginia; per capita personal income, *fig410*; state sales tax in, *m224*

White population; change in U.S., 1960-90, *fig537*; projections through year 2050, *fig374*

white-collar worker; defined, 407

wholesale and retail trade; partnerships in, 61

wholesale price index, 365; defined, 362

wildcat bank; as abuse in banking, 273; defined, 273

Will, George; on airline deregulation, *q76*

Williams, Walter E.; and affirmative action, 382; and agricultural price supports, 382; and economic freedom, 382; and George Mason University, 382; and special programs for minorities, 382; and the minimum wage, 382; *p382*; profile of, 382

wind power; as renewable resource, 524

Winfrey, Oprah; and community work, 278; and Harpo Productions, 278; and personal wealth, 278; and the Phil Donahue Show, 278; as example of ability and income, 407; as talk-show host, 278; *p278*; profile, 278

Wisconsin; and savings banks, *m282*; per capita personal income, *fig410*; state sales tax in, *m224*

withholding statement; illustrated, *fig225*

women; and Civil Rights Act of 1964, 200; and comparable worth, 200-01; and discrimination, 200; and Equal Employment Opportunity Commission (EEOC), 200; and glass ceiling, 200; and

occupations, 200-01; and set-aside contracts, 201-02; cultural influences on, 199; income as percent of male, *fig200*; lower pay for, 198-201; starting own businesses, 204

women entrepreneurs, see **female entrepreneurs**

women of color; and *Essence-By-Mail*, 324

women's issues; and Anita Roddick, 42; also see **women**

workers; at the IRS, *p208*; celebrating worldwide, *p476*; median salaries and union representation, *fig197*; nonunion as percent of total employed, *fig183*; union membership by industry, *fig184*; unionized as percent of total employed, *fig183*

workfare, 413; defined, 412; as antipoverty program, 412; examples of, 412; exchanging labor for benefits, 343; replacing welfare, *q342*, *q343*

World Bank, 505, 515; and priorities for economic development, 505-07; and the Czech *koruna*, 512; and the Hungarian *forint*, 511-12; and the International Development Association, 511; and the International Finance Corporation, 511; and the Polish *zloty*, 511-12; as informational source, *fig531*; described, 505; investing in people, *p507*

World War I; and federal government spending, 239; and post war deflation, 399

World War II; and federal deficits, *fig254*; and federal government spending, 239; and Hungarian hyperinflation, 400; and rationing, 131, *p132*; and selective credit controls, 308; inventory adjustments following, 386

Wyoming; as right-to-work-law state, *fig190*; per capita personal income, *fig410*; state sales tax in, *m224*

Y

Yap Islands; and stone money, 270, *p268*

Yeltsin, Boris; and decline of Soviet economy, 481; succeeding Gorbachev, 481

yield; Treasury bonds and notes, *fig330*; also see **current yield**

Yosemite National Park; and economic role of government, *p72*

Z

Zedong, Mao; and transition to capitalism, 487

zero population growth; defined, 499

Ziyang, Chinese Premier Zhao; and transfer of Hong Kong to China, 490

ACKNOWLEDGMENTS

Cover, KS Studios; iv, Ed Bock/The Stock Market; vi, (top, l to r) The Granger Collection New York, David Levenson/Black Star, (center, l to r) courtesy The Philadelphia Coca-Cola Bottling Co., Houston Chronicle, Phil Huber/Black Star, courtesy The University of Chicago, (bottom, l to r) George Lange/Onyx, UPI/Bettmann, AP/Wide World Photos; vii, (top, l to r) Darryl Estrine/Onyx, Kevin Horan/Picture Group, Bill Nation/Sygma, Robert Milazzo, (center, l to r) UPI/Bettmann, courtesy George Mason University, Steve Jennings/Picture Group, Wally McNamee/Sygma, (bottom, l to r) Peter Sibbald/Sygma, The Granger Collection New York, courtesy Princeton University, The Granger Collection New York; viii, (l) Lester Lefkowitz/Tony Stone Images, (r) Diana Walker/Gamma-Liaison Network; ix, (l) Greg Stott/Masterfile, (r) Thomas Braise/The Stock Market; xi, (t) Matthew McVay/Stock Boston, (b) Armen Kachaturian/Gamma-Liaison Network; 4-5, Uniphoto/Pictor; 6-7, Henry Horenstein/Stock Boston; 10, (l) Tom McHugh/Photo Researchers, (lc) Wolfgang Volz/Bilderberg/The Stock Market, (rc) Doug Martin, (r) Matt Meadows; 14, Bob Daemmrich/Tony Stone Images; 17, by permission of Johnny Hart and Creators Syndicate, Inc.; 18, (t) The Granger Collection New York, (b) The Bettmann Archive; 19, Doug Martin; 21, David R. Frazier; 24, (l) Erik Svenson/Tony Stone Images, (r) Jeff Bates; 26, Brad Markel/Gamma-Liaison Network; 30-31, J. Messerschmidt/FPG International; 33, Renee Lynn/Photo Researchers; 37, Clark James Mishler/Alaska Stock Images; 38, Gabe Palmer/The Stock Market; 39, Alan Weiner/Gamma-Liaison Network; 40, King Features Syndicate; 41, George Herben/Alaska Stock Images; 42, (t) David Levenson/Black Star, (b) courtesy The Body Shop; 43, Doug Martin; 46, courtesy Johnson Publishing Company, Inc.; 47, Tim Courlas; 52-53, Matt Meadows; 54, Randy Schieber; 55, Robert Mullenix; 56, Doug Martin; 57, Matt Meadows; 58, file photo; 61, Bruce Ayres/Tony Stone Images; 68, (t) courtesy The Philadelphia Coca-Cola Bottling Company, (b) Toby Rankin/The Image Bank; 72, Michael Howell/Profiles West; 76, (t) Paul Merideth/Tony Stone Images, (b) Paul Chesley/Tony Stone Images; 77, (l) Mark Wagner/Tony Stone Images, (r) Jordan Coonrad/Airborne; 78-79, Jose L. Pelaez/The Stock Market; 80-81, Yvonne Hemsey/Gamma-Liaison Network; 82, Matt Meadows; 85, Robin Smith/Tony Stone Images; 86, Doug Martin; 88, courtesy Pepsi-Cola Co.; 90, Doug Martin; 91, (t) Houston Chronicle, (b) Dan Ford Connolly; 96, Dean Abramson/Stock Boston; 98, Hodgins in New York Daily News; 102-103, Lester Lefkowitz/Tony Stone Images; 104, Jeff Spielman/The Image Bank; 111, Robert Weber; 113, Matt Meadows; 114, Tom Tracy/FPG International; 116, (t) Phil Huber/Black Star, (b) Dennis Brack/Black Star; 118, Doug Martin; 126-127, Matthew McVay/Stock Boston; 129, (l) courtesy Apple Computer, Inc., (r) John Greenleigh/courtesy Apple Computer, Inc.; 130, (t) From The Wall Street Journal/Permission by Cartoon Feature Syndicate, (b) Reuters/Bettmann; 132, AP/World Wide Photos; 133, Danziger in The Christian Science Monitor ©1992 TCSPS; 136, Matt Meadows; 139, (t) courtesy The University of Chicago, (b) Jon Feingersh/The Stock Market; 140, Alvis Upitis/The Image Bank; 149, Reprinted by permission of Gill Fox/Connecticut Post; 150-151, Brent Turner/BLT Productions; 153, Julie Houck/Stock Boston; 155, Aaron Haupt Photography; 156, Reprinted with permission of NIKE, Inc. (Photo by Walter Iooss); 158, Chris Arend/Alaska Stock Images; 162, (t) George Lange/Onyx, (b) Claudio Edinger/Gamma-Liaison Network; 164, courtesy Lockheed Corp.; 165, David Butow/Black Star; 166, John Coletti/Stock Boston; 176, (t) Andrew Holbrooke/Gamma-Liaison Network, (b) Simon Jauncey/Tony Stone Images; 177, (l) Terry Farmer/Tony Stone Images, (r) Grant Heilman Photography; 178-179, Frank Saragnese/FPG International; 180-181, Mark Reinstein/Gamma-Liaison Network; 186, Keystone/FPG International; 188, UPI/Bettmann; 189, Archives of Labor and Urban Affairs, Wayne State University; 195, Jeff Bates; 202, (l) Wynn Miller/Tony Stone Images, (r) Billy E. Barnes/Stock Boston; 208-209, Bob Daemmrich/Stock Boston; 213, (l) George Anderson, (r) Doug Martin; 220, Greg Smith/Gamma-Liaison Network; 221, (t) AP/Wide World Photos, (b) Walter Hodges/Westlight; 226, Jeff Greenberg/Photo Researchers; 232, BORN LOSER reprinted by permission of NEA, Inc.; 236-237, J. Richardson/Westlight; 240, FRANK & ERNEST reprinted by permission of NEA, Inc.; 241, Jeff Bates; 242, (t) Darryl Estrine/Onyx, (b) Blake Little/Sygma; 247, Frank Rossotto/The Stock Market; 252, file photo; 253, Reprinted by permission Tribune Media Services; 264-265, Ed Bock/The Stock Market; 267, Reprinted by permission News America Syndicate; 268, Wolfgang Kaehler; 273, 274, file photo; 276, Jeff Bates; 278, (t) Kevin Horan/Picture Group, (b) Scott McKiernan/Gamma-Liaison Network; 284, Matt Meadows; 285, Ed Zirkle; 287, Bob Daemmrich/Uniphoto; 292-293, Mike Mazzaschi/Stock Boston; 301, (t) Bill Nation/Sygma, (b) Don Smetzer/Tony Stone Images; 318-319, Greg Stott/Masterfile; 324, (t) Robert Milazzo, (b) file photo; 342, (t) UPI/Bettmann, (b) Ed Lallo/Gamma-Liaison Network; 343, (l) Kurgan-Lisnet/Gamma-Liaison Network, (r) Aaron Haupt Photography; 344-345, Jean Miele/The Stock Market; 346-347, Gabe Palmer/The Stock Market; 350, Mark Burnett/Stock Boston; 352, Reprinted by permission Tribune Media Services; 353, (t) UPI/Bettmann, (b) Mural by Maxwell B. Starr, courtesy Rockdale Post Office, photo by Bob Daemmrich; 359, Dave Davidson/The Stock Market; 368-369, Jordan Coonrad/Airborne; 373, Doug Martin; 382, (t) courtesy George Mason University, (b) Robin Moyer/Gamma-Liaison Network; 392-393, Eugene Richards/Magnum Photos; 397, From The Wall Street Journal/Permission by Cartoon Features Syndicate; 398, (t) Steve Jennings/Picture Group, (b) James Schnepf/Gamma-Liaison Network; 402, Jon Levy/Gamma-Liaison Network; 409, Richard Hutchings/Photo Researchers; 412, Greig Cranna/Stock Boston; 416-417, Armen Kachaturian/Gamma-Liaison Network; 420, Doug Martin; 428, Bob Daemmrich/Uniphoto; 435, (t) Wally McNamee/Sygma, (b) Dennis Brack/Black Star; 437, Doug Martin; 442, (t) Diana Walker/Gamma-Liaison Network, (b) Alon Reininger/Contact Press Images; 443, (l) Bob Daemmrich/Uniphoto, (r) Paul Barton/The Stock Market; 444-445, Ron McMillan/Gamma-Liaison Network; 446-447, Cathlyn Melloan/Tony Stone Images; 448, Fred Ward/Black Star; 452, (t) Peter Sibbald/Sygma, (b) file photo; 454, Cynthia Johnson/Gamma-Liaison Network; 455, BERRY'S WORLD reprinted by permission of NEA, Inc.; 456, Greg Davis/The Stock Market; 457, Joseph Nettis/Photo Researchers; 464, Fisher, ©1992/The New Yorker Magazine; 465, Bob Daemmrich/Uniphoto; 470-471, Dallas & John Heaton/Uniphoto; 475, Sovfoto; 476, (t) The Granger Collection New York, (b) Pablo Ibarra/Gamma-Liaison Network; 478, Sovfoto; 481, Lisa Quinones/Black Star; 484, Eric Bouvet/Gamma-Liaison Network; 486, Dilip Menta/The Stock Market; 489, Martin Rogers/Uniphoto; 496-497, David Ball/The Stock Market; 503, (t) courtesy Princeton University, (b) Travelpix/FPG International; 507, Martin Rogers/Uniphoto; 509, Adina Tovy/Robert Harding Picture Library; 518-519, Thomas Braise/The Stock Market; 523, Henley & Savage/Uniphoto; 526, (t) The Granger Collection New York, (b) M.E. Warren/Uniphoto; 528, Jeff Lepore/Photo Researchers; 529, Harry M. Walker/Alaska Stock; 534, Thomas Braise/The Stock Market; 538, (t) Robert Harding Picture Library, (b) Jim Pickerell/Gamma-Liaison Network; 539, (l) Zigy Kaluzny, (r) Chris Jones/The Stock Market; 540, Ed Honowitz/Tony Stone Images; 552, Doug Martin.